Interplay

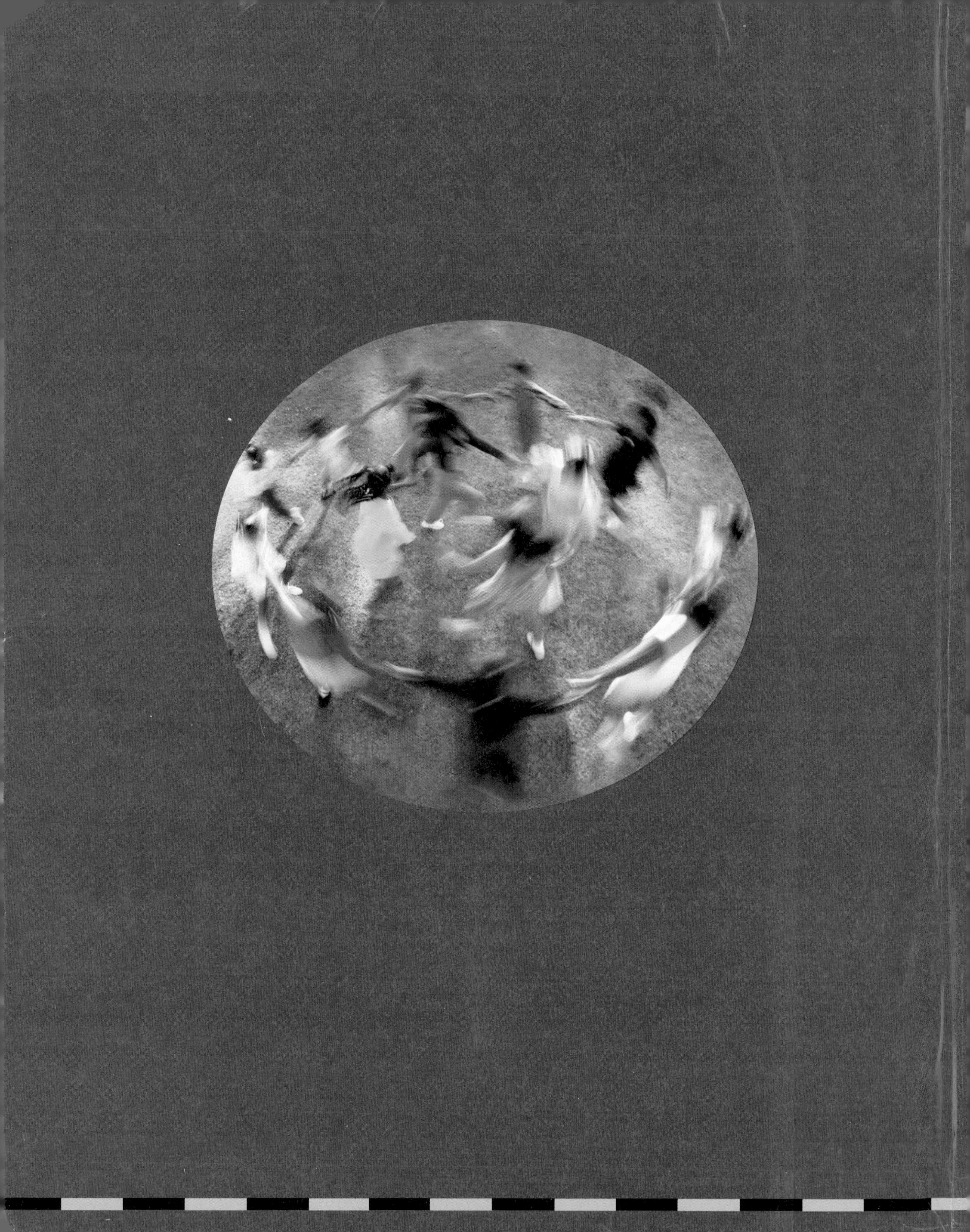

ELEVENTH EDITION

Interplay

The Process of Interpersonal Communication

Ronald B. Adler
Santa Barbara City College

Lawrence B. Rosenfeld
University of North Carolina at Chapel Hill

Russell F. Proctor II
Northern Kentucky University

New York Oxford
OXFORD UNIVERSITY PRESS
2010

Oxford University Press, Inc., publishes works that further Oxford University's objective of excellence in research, scholarship, and education.

Oxford New York
Auckland Cape Town Dar es Salaam Hong Kong Karachi
Kuala Lumpur Madrid Melbourne Mexico City Nairobi
New Delhi Shanghai Taipei Toronto

With offices in
Argentina Austria Brazil Chile Czech Republic France Greece
Guatemala Hungary Italy Japan Poland Portugal Singapore
South Korea Switzerland Thailand Turkey Ukraine Vietnam

Published by Oxford University Press, Inc.
198 Madison Avenue, New York, New York 10016
http://www.oup.com

Library of Congress Cataloging-in-Publication data
Adler, Ronald B. (Ronald Brian), 1946–
Interplay : the process of interpersonal communication / Ronald B. Adler, Lawrence B. Rosenfeld, Russell F. Proctor II. — 11th ed.
p. cm.
Includes bibliographical references and index.
ISBN 978-0-19-537959-4 (alk paper)
ISBN 978-0-19-538491-8 (instructor's edition, alk paper)
1. Interpersonal communication. I. Rosenfeld, Lawrence B. II. Proctor, Russell F. III. Title.
BF637.C45A33 2009
302.2—dc22
2008038532

Printing number: 9 8 7 6 5 4 3 2

Printed in the United States of America
on acid-free paper.

Brief Contents

Contents

Part Two: Creating and Responding to Messages

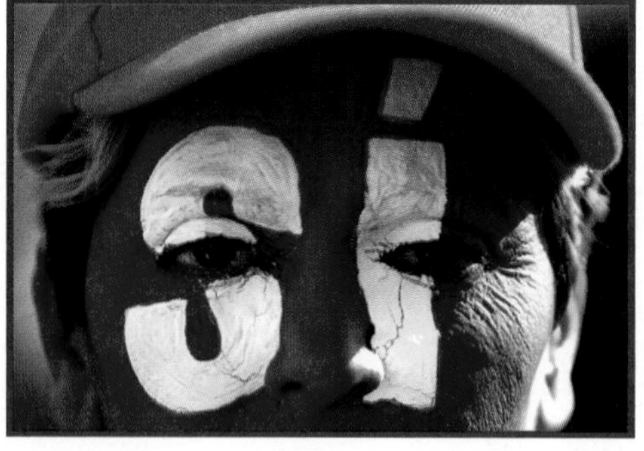

Part Three: Dimensions of Interpersonal Relationships

Preface

Much has changed over the decades since interpersonal communication became a recognized field of academic inquiry. But the rationale for its importance remains the same: The quality of communication in everyday relationships is a fundamental element of personal satisfaction, as well as a cornerstone of civil society. *Interplay* introduces readers to what scholars have learned about how communication creates and shapes personal relationships, and how these insights can help make relationships more successful and satisfying.

Basic Approach

This 11th edition of *Interplay* retains the approach that has served almost a million students and professors well. The accessible writing style is based on the belief that even complicated ideas can be presented in a straightforward way. A variety of thought-provoking photos, sidebars, and cartoons make the subject more interesting and compelling than text alone. Communication principles discussed in the book are grounded in scholarship: This edition cites more than 1,300 sources, a quarter of which are new to this edition. Research and theory aren't presented for their own sake, but rather to offer insights about how the process of interpersonal communication operates in everyday life.

New in this Edition

While the overall structure of the book will be familiar to long-time users, several changes have been made to enhance its usability and keep the content up to date. Perhaps the most noticeable change is the addition of a new chapter, "Communication in Families and at Work." These subjects were relegated to appendices in the previous edition, but users told us they wanted these important topics to have a chapter of their own, complete with sidebars and activities.

Users told us it was important that the book remain only 12 chapters long. To accomplish this goal, we carefully reworked material to trim length in ways that we'll wager even long-time users won't find noticeable. We also distributed material from the 10th edition chapter titled "Intimacy and Distance in Relationships" into other portions of the book. The material on self-disclosure is now in Chapter 3 ("Communication and the Self"), while coverage of intimacy can be found in Chapter 9 ("Dynamics of Interpersonal Relationships").

A new sidebar, **Dark Side of Communication**, has been added to each chapter. This reflects the notion that interpersonal communication sometimes involves difficult, challenging, and even unpleasant issues that can't and shouldn't be ignored. These Dark Side boxes cover topics such as cyberbullying, compulsive talkers, verbal abuse, the "silent treatment," and discrimination based on people's accents.

Other sidebars in the book have been significantly updated. Twenty of the **Focus on Research** boxes are new to this edition, covering timely subjects such as the impact of TV makeover shows on viewers' self-images; impression management in online dating; the phenomenon known as "gaydar"; gender differences in instant messaging habits; and "friends with benefits" relationships.

Eighteen of the **Film Clip** sidebars are new to this edition, including *Spanglish* (culture and communication), *Shark Tale* (identity management), *Lars and the Real Girl* (narratives), *The Devil Wears Prada* (poor listening habits), *The Break-Up* (relational stages), and *Juno* (conflict management).

Several important topics are covered more thoroughly and clearly in this new edition. These include the challenges of mediated communication (Chapter 1), cultural differences as generalizations (Chapter 2), neurobehavioral challenges in perception (Chapter 4), new information on linguistic convergence/divergence (Chapter 5), the impact of new media on interpersonal listening (Chapter 7), new sections on intimacy in computer-mediated communication, commitment in relationships, and repairing damaged relationships (all in Chapter 9), and a new section on offering constructive criticism (Chapter 10).

Ancillaries

In addition to the text, a variety of ancillaries provide resources for both students and instructors.

FOR STUDENTS

- A **Student Success Manual**, written by Leah Bryant of DePaul University, is packed with information that will help students master the course material. It includes a primer on effective study habits as well as chapter-specific material such as outlines, summaries, key terms, review questions (and answers), and critical thinking exercises.
- ***Now Playing: Learning Communication Through Film***, available as an optional printed product, looks at more than 60 contemporary and classic feature films through the lens of communication principles. Developed by Russell F. Proctor II and revised by Darin Garard of Santa Barbara City College, *Now Playing* illustrates a variety of both individual scenes and full-length films, highlighting concepts and offering discussion questions for a mass medium that is interactive, familiar, and easily accessible.

- The **companion website** at **www.oup.com/us/interplay11** offers a wealth of resources including exercises, flashcards for key terms in the book, interactive self-tests, and links to a variety of communication-related websites, including *Now Playing* online.

FOR INSTRUCTORS

- An enhanced **Instructor's Manual and Test Bank**, revised by Marcee Andersen of Johnson County Community College, provides teaching tips, exercises, and test questions that will prove useful to both new and veteran instructors. The Instructor's Manual includes teaching strategies, course outlines, chapter exercises, discussion questions, and unit wind-ups. The comprehensive Test Bank offers approximately 100 class-tested exam questions per chapter in multiple-choice, true/false, essay, and matching formats.
- An **Instructor Resource CD with Computerized Test Bank**, available to adopters, includes the full Instructor's Manual and Test Bank, as well as computerized testing software and newly revised PowerPoint® lecture presentations by Ellen Bremen of Highline Community College.
- **Instructor's Companion Website** at **www.oup.com/us/interplay11** is a password-protected site that features the Instructor's Manual, PowerPoint® lecture slides, and links to supplemental materials and films.
- ***Now Playing: Instructor's Edition***, an instructor-only print supplement, includes an introduction on how to incorporate film examples in class, more sample responses to the numerous discussion questions in the student edition of *Now Playing*, viewing guides, additional films, and references.
- Course cartridges for a variety of e-learning environments allow instructors to create their own course websites with the interactive material from the instructor and student companion websites. Contact your Oxford University Press representative for access.

Acknowledgments

Creating a book like *Interplay* simply isn't possible without the help of many talented people. We are grateful to the many colleagues whose suggestions have helped make this book a far better one: Kathleen Czech, Point Loma Nazarene University; Darlene J. Geiger, Portland State University; Em Griffin, Wheaton College; Shaorong Huang, Raymond Walters College-University of Cincinnati; Andrea Lambert, Northern Kentucky University; Beverly Merrill Kelley, California Lutheran University; Anastasia Kurylo, Marymount Manhattan

College; Kelly Morrison, Michigan State University; Jennifer A. Samp, University of Georgia; and Debbie Sonandre, Tacoma Community College; as well as the reviewers of the 10th edition: Lisa C. Hebert, Louisiana State University; Narissra Maria Punyanunt-Carter, Texas Tech University; Johance F. Murray, Hostos Community College/CUNY; Kristin K. Froemling, Radford University; Debra Gonsher, Bronx Community College; Marcanne Andersen, Anoka Ramsey Community College; Gregory W. Rickert, Lexington Community College; Gretchen R. Norling, University of West Florida; Michael Wittig, Waukesha County Technical College; and Phil Martin, North Central State College.

We salute the talented, hard-working, and cheerful team of professionals at Oxford University Press: Peter Labella, Executive Editor; Angela Kao and Frederick Speers, Development Editors; Josh Hawkins, Associate Editor; Lisa Grzan, Senior Production Editor; Paula Schlosser, Art Director; and Chelsea Gilmore and Courtney Roy, Editorial Assistants. Our thanks also go to Elliot Simon for his copyediting talents and Susan Monahan for crafting the useful indexes. Sherri Adler deserves credit for selecting the array of compelling photos that help make *Interplay* unique.

Finally, we thank our families for their love and support as we've worked on this book. These relationships remind us that the challenges and rewards of interpersonal communication are, indeed, vitally important in the "real world."

About the Authors

Ronald B. Adler is Professor Emeritus of Communication at Santa Barbara City College. He is coauthor of *Understanding Human Communication*, Tenth Edition (OUP, 2009), *Looking Out, Looking In* (2008), and *Communicating at Work: Principles and Practices for Business and the Professions* (2008). In addition to his academic pursuits, Ron works with businesses and nonprofit agencies to improve communication among coworkers as well as with clients and the public.

Lawrence B. Rosenfeld is Professor of Communication Studies and Co-Chair of the Social-Behavioral Institutional Review Board, University of North Carolina at Chapel Hill. He is the author of articles appearing in journals in communication, education, social work, sport psychology, and psychology, and of books on small group, interpersonal, and nonverbal communication. His most recent book is *When Their World Falls Apart: Helping Families and Children Manage the Effects of Disasters* (NASW Press, 2005). In 2006, Lawrence received the Gerald M. Phillips Award for Applied Communication Research from the National Communication Association.

Russell F. Proctor II is Professor of Communication Studies at Northern Kentucky University. He has taught communication courses for more than 25 years and won NKU's Outstanding Professor Award in 1997. In addition to his work on *Interplay*, he is also coauthor of *Looking Out, Looking In* (2008). Russ has written and presented extensively on the use of feature films as instructional tools in communication courses (including *Now Playing* for OUP).

Interplay

CHAPTER 1

Interpersonal Process

CHAPTER OUTLINE

After studying the material in this chapter . . .

YOU SHOULD UNDERSTAND:

1. The needs that effective communication can satisfy.
2. Four insights from the communication model.
3. Five key principles of communication.
4. Four misconceptions about communication.
5. Quantitative and qualitative definitions of interpersonal communication.
6. The similarities and differences between face-to-face and mediated communication.
7. The characteristics of competent communication.

YOU SHOULD BE ABLE TO:

1. Identify examples of the physical, identity, social, and practical needs you attempt to satisfy by communicating.
2. Demonstrate how the communication model applies to your interpersonal communication.
3. Describe the degrees to which your communication is qualitatively impersonal and interpersonal, and describe the consequences of this combination.
4. Choose the communication channel that has the best chance of accomplishing your communication goals.
5. Identify situations in which you communicate competently and those in which your competence is less than satisfactory.

KEY TERMS

- Channel (11)
- Cognitive complexity (30)
- Communication competence (25)
- Computer-mediated communication (CMC) (21)
- Content dimension (of a message) (13)
- Disinhibition (24)
- Dyad (17)
- Environment (11)
- Feedback (9)
- Noise (external, physiological, and psychological) (11)
- Qualitative interpersonal communication (17)
- Quantitative interpersonal communication (16)
- Relational dimension (of a message) (13)
- Richness (of communication media) (23)
- Self-monitoring (30)
- Transactional communication model (9)

Everyone communicates. Students and professors, parents and children, employers and employees, friends, strangers, and enemies—all communicate. We have been communicating with others from earliest childhood and will almost certainly keep doing so until we die.

Why study an activity you've done your entire life? There are at least three reasons (Morreale & Pearson, 2008). First, studying interpersonal communication will give you a new look at a familiar topic. For instance, in a few pages you will find that some people can go years—even a lifetime—without communicating in a truly interpersonal manner. In this sense, exploring human communication is rather like studying anatomy or botany—everyday objects and processes take on new meaning.

A second reason for studying the subject has to do with the staggering amount of time we spend communicating. For example, a study of over 1,000 employees at Fortune 1000 companies revealed that workers send and receive an average of 178 messages every working day (Ginsburg, 1999). Another survey (Nellermoe et al., 1999) revealed that business professionals spend 80 percent of their business day communicating with colleagues and clients. Online communication is just as pervasive as the face-to-face variety: One study showed that the majority of Internet users rely on e-mail (IT Facts, 2008), with most communicating online daily. Among teens, almost two-thirds have posted content online: creating personal websites, writing blogs, and posting online videos (Lenhart et al., 2007).

There is a third, more compelling reason for studying interpersonal communication. To put it bluntly, all of us could learn to communicate more effectively. In a nationwide survey, "lack of effective communication" was identified as the cause of relational breakups—including marriages—more often than any other reason, including money, relatives or in-laws, sexual problems, previous relationships, or children (National Communication Association, 1999). Ineffective communication is also a problem in the workplace. A group of senior executives cited lack of interpersonal skills as one of the top three skill deficits in today's workforce (Marchant, 1999). Poor communication can be physically dangerous: One study found that communication errors caused twice as many hospital admissions problems as practitioners' inadequate skills (Strachan, 2004), and another found that poor professional-patient communication was the primary problem in helping patients manage their own health care (Moffat et al., 2007).

If you pause now and make a mental list of communication problems you have encountered, you'll probably see that, no matter how successful your relationships are at home, with friends, at school, and at work, there is plenty of room for improvement in your everyday life. The information that follows will help you improve the way you communicate with some of the people who matter most to you.

Why We Communicate

Research demonstrating the importance of communication has been around longer than you might think. Frederick II, emperor of the Holy Roman Empire from 1220 to 1250, was called *stupor mundi*—"wonder of the world"—by his admiring subjects. Along with his administrative and military talents, Frederick was a leading scientist of his time. A medieval historian described one of his dramatic, if inhumane, experiments:

> He bade foster mothers and nurses to suckle the children, to bathe and wash them, but in no way to prattle with them, for he wanted to learn whether they would speak the Hebrew language, which was the oldest, or Greek, or Latin, or Arabic, or perhaps the language of their parents, of whom they had been born. But he labored in vain because all the children died. For they could not live without the petting and joyful faces and loving words of their foster mothers. (Ross & McLaughlin, 1949, p. 366)

Fortunately, contemporary researchers have found less dramatic ways to illustrate the importance of communication. In one study of isolation, five participants were paid to remain alone in a locked room. One lasted for 8 days. Three held out for 2 days, one commenting "Never again." The fifth participant lasted only 2 hours (Schachter, 1959).

The need for contact and companionship is just as strong outside the laboratory, as individuals who have led solitary lives by choice or necessity have discovered. W. Carl Jackson, an adventurer who sailed across the Atlantic Ocean alone in 51 days, summarized the feelings common to most loners in a post-voyage interview:

> I found the loneliness of the second month almost excruciating. I always thought of myself as self-sufficient, but I found life without people had no meaning. I had a definite need for somebody to talk to, someone real, alive, and breathing. (Jackson, 1978)

You might claim that solitude would be a welcome relief from the irritations of everyday life. It's true that all of us need time by ourselves, often more than we get. On the other hand, each of us has a point beyond which we do not *want* to be alone. Beyond this point, solitude changes from a pleasurable to a painful condition. In other words, we all need people. We all need to communicate.

PHYSICAL NEEDS

Communication is so important that its presence or absence affects physical health. Recent studies confirm that people who process a negative experience by talking about it report improved life satisfaction, as well as enhanced mental and physical health, relative to those who think privately about it (Francis, 2003; Sousa, 2002). A study conducted with police officers found that being able to talk easily with colleagues and supervisors about work-related trauma was related to greater physical and mental health (Stephens & Long, 2000). A study of over 3,500 people ages 24–96 revealed that the more social contact we have, the higher the level of mental function (Ybarra et al., 2008). As little as 10 minutes of talking, face to face or by phone, improves memory and boosts intellectual function.

In extreme cases, communication can even become a matter of life or death. When he was a Navy pilot, U.S. Senator John McCain was shot down over North Vietnam and held as a prisoner of war for 6 years, often in solitary confinement. He describes how POWs set up clandestine codes in which they sent messages by tapping on walls to laboriously spell out words. McCain describes the importance of keeping contact and the risks that inmates would take to maintain contact with one another:

> The punishment for communicating could be severe, and a few POWs, having been caught and beaten for their efforts, had their spirits broken as their bodies were battered. Terrified of a return trip to the punishment room, they would lie still in their cells when their comrades tried to tap them up on the wall. Very few would remain uncommunicative for long. To suffer all this alone was less tolerable than torture. Withdrawing in silence from the fellowship of other Americans . . . was to us the approach of death. (McCain, 1999, p. 12)

Communication isn't just a necessity for prisoners of war. Evidence gathered by medical researchers and social scientists (e.g., Cole et al., 2007; Duck, 1998; Fitzpatrick & Vangelisti, 2001; Mendes de-Leon, 2005; Uchino, 2004) shows that satisfying relationships can literally be a matter of life and death for people who lead normal lives. For example:

- The white blood cells of chronically lonely people display abnormal patterns of gene activation.
- People who lack strong relationships have two to three times the risk of early death, regardless of whether they smoke, drink alcoholic beverages, or exercise regularly.
- Divorced, separated, and widowed people are five to ten times more likely to need mental hospitalization than their married counterparts.
- Pregnant women under stress and without supportive relationships have three times more complications than pregnant women who suffer from the same stress but have strong social support.
- Social isolation is a major risk factor contributing to coronary disease, comparable to physiological factors such as diet, cigarette smoking, obesity, and lack of physical activity.
- Socially isolated people are four times more susceptible to the common cold than those who have active social networks.

Research like this demonstrates the importance of meaningful personal relationships, and it explains the conclusion of social scientists that communication is essential (Baumeister & Leary, 1995). Not everyone needs the same amount of contact, and the quality of communication is almost certainly as important as the quantity. Nonetheless, the point remains: Personal communication is essential for our well-being. To paraphrase a popular song, "People who need people" aren't "the luckiest people in the world": They're the *only* people!

IDENTITY NEEDS

Communication does more than enable us to survive. It is the way—indeed, the *major* way—we learn who we are (Fogel et al., 2002; Harwood, 2005). As you'll read in Chapter 3, our sense of identity comes from the way we interact with other people. Are we smart or stupid, attractive or ugly, skillful or inept? The answers to these questions don't come from looking in the mirror. We decide who we are based on how others react to us.

Deprived of communication with others, we would have no sense of identity. Consider the case of the famous "Wild Boy of Aveyron," who spent his early childhood without any apparent human contact. The boy was discovered in January 1800 while digging for vegetables in a French village garden. He could not speak, and he showed no behaviors one would expect in a social human. More significant than this absence of social skills was his lack of any identity as a human being. As author Roger Shattuck (1980, p. 37) put it, "The boy had no human sense of being in the world. He had no sense of himself as a person related to other persons." Only after the influence of a loving "mother" did the boy begin to behave—and, we can imagine, think of himself—as a human.

Contemporary stories support the essential role communication plays in shaping identity. In 1970, authorities discovered a 12-year-old girl (whom they called "Genie") who had spent virtually all her life in an otherwise empty, darkened bedroom with almost no human contact. The child could not speak and had no sense of herself as a person until she was removed from her family and "nourished" by a team of caregivers (Rymer, 1993).

Like Genie and the boy of Aveyron, each of us enters the world with little or no sense of identity. We gain an idea of who we are from the way others define us. As Chapter 3 explains, the messages we receive in early childhood are the strongest identity shapers, but the influence of others continues throughout life.

SOCIAL NEEDS

Besides helping define who we are, some social scientists have argued that communication is the principal way relationships are created (Duck & Pittman, 1994). For example, Julie Yingling (1994) asserts that children "talk friendships into existence." The same can be said for adult relationships: It's impossible to imagine how they could exist without communication, which satisfies a variety

of needs such as giving and receiving affection, having fun, helping others and being helped, and giving us a sense of self-worth (Rubin et al., 1988). Because relationships with others are so vital, some theorists have gone so far as to argue that communication is the primary goal of human existence. Anthropologist Walter Goldschmidt (1990) calls the drive for meeting social needs "the human career."

There's a strong link between the quality of communication and the success of relationships. For example, children who grow up in strong conversation-oriented families report having more satisfying same-sex friendships and romantic relationships when they become adults (Koesten, 2004). Women in one study reported that "socializing" contributed more to a satisfying life than virtually any other activity, including relaxing, shopping, eating, exercise, television, or prayer (Kahneman et al., 2004).

PRACTICAL NEEDS

We shouldn't overlook the everyday, important functions communication serves. Communication is the tool that lets us tell the hairstylist to take just a little off the sides, direct the doctor to where it hurts, and inform the plumber that the broken pipe needs attention *now!*

Beyond these obvious needs, a wealth of research demonstrates that communication is an essential part of effectiveness in a variety of everyday settings. The abilities to speak and listen effectively have been identified as the most important factors in helping graduating college students gain employment and advance in their careers: more important than technical competence, work experience, and academic background (Winsor et al., 1997). The National Association of Colleges and Employers identified "communication skills" and "interpersonal skills" among the top characteristics employers seek in job candidates (*Job Outlook 2007,* 2006). These were rated as more important than academic background, computer skills, or organizational skills. Many other studies confirm that communication skills are vital for success in the work world (e.g., Peterson, 1997; Public Forum Institute, 2002).

Communication is just as important outside of work. For example, married couples who are effective communicators report happier relationships than less skillful husbands and wives (Kirchler, 1988; Ridley et al., 2001)—a finding that has been supported across cultures (Rehman & Holtzworth-Munroe, 2007). In school, grade-point averages of college students are related positively to their communication competence (Hawken et al. 1991; Rubin & Graham, 1988); and school adjustment, dropout rate, and overall school achievement are highly related to students' having strong, supportive relationships (Heard, 2007; Rosenfeld & Richman, 1999; Rosenfeld et al., 1998). And in medical settings, the outcomes of our interactions with a physician depend on the ability of both the doctor and patient to communicate effectively (Street, 2003).

Psychologist Abraham Maslow (1968) suggests that human needs fall into five categories, each of which must be satisfied before we concern ourselves with the next one. As you read about each need, think about the ways in which communication is often necessary to satisfy it. The most basic needs are *physical:* sufficient air, water, food, and rest, and the ability to reproduce as a species. The second category of Maslow's needs involves *safety:* protection from threats to our well-being. Beyond physical and safety concerns are the *social* needs we have already mentioned. Next, Maslow suggests that each of us has the need for *self-esteem:* the desire to believe that we are worthwhile, valuable people. The final category of needs involves *self-actualization:* the desire to develop our potential to the maximum, to become the best person we can be.

The Communication Process

So far, we have talked about communication as if its meaning were perfectly clear. In fact, scholars have debated the definition of communication for years with no simple conclusions (Littlejohn, 2008). One thing *is* clear: Human communication is a complex process with many components. In this section, we will discuss some features and principles of communication.

A MODEL OF COMMUNICATION

As the old saying goes, "A picture is worth a thousand words." That's what scientists had in mind when they began creating models of the communication process in the 1950s. These early models were simplistic and usually better suited for explaining mass communication than the interpersonal variety. They characterized communication as a one-way event—something that a sender "does" by encoding a message and delivering it to a passive receiver who decodes it. This one-way process resembles an archer (the sender) shooting an arrow (the message) at a target (the receiver). Even in interpersonal settings, this linear approach sometimes makes sense. If you labor over a letter or e-mail to get the tone just right before sending it, your message is primarily a one-way effort.

Later models represented communication more like a tennis game, with people sending messages to receivers who responded with verbal or nonverbal **feedback** that indicates a response to the previous message. A back-and-forth chain of text messages seems to fit this description pretty well.

Over time, though, communication theorists have developed increasingly sophisticated **transactional communication models** in an attempt to depict all the factors that affect human interaction. No model can completely represent the process of communication, any more than a map can capture everything about the neighborhood where you live. Still, the model in Figure 1.1 provides a starting point for explaining the insights and principles discussed in the next section.

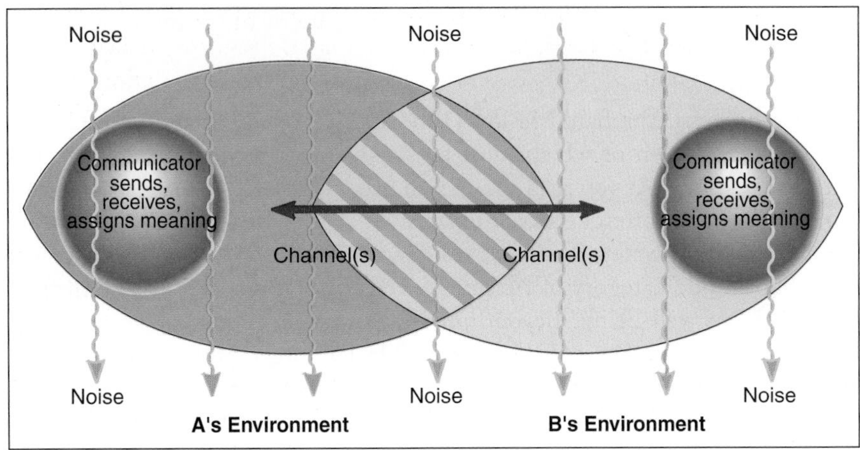

FIGURE 1.1 Communication Model

INSIGHTS FROM THE TRANSACTIONAL COMMUNICATION MODEL

The model in Figure 1.1 reflects a number of important characteristics of transactional communication. As you read on, note how the following insights help explain the richness of this process.

Sending and Receiving Are Usually Simultaneous In the following scenarios, ask yourself who is sending a message and who is receiving one.

- A teacher explaining a difficult concept to a student after class
- A parent lecturing a teenager about the family's curfew rules
- A salesperson giving a customer information about a product

The natural impulse is to identify the teacher, parent, and salesperson as senders, while the student, teenager, and customer are receivers. Now imagine a confused look on the student's face; the teenager interrupting defensively; the customer blankly staring into the distance. It's easy to see that these verbal and nonverbal responses are messages being "sent," even while the other person is talking. Because it's often impossible to distinguish sender from receiver, our communication model replaces these roles with the more accurate term *communicator* . This term reflects the fact that—at least in face-to-face situations—people are simultaneously senders and receivers who exchange multiple messages.

Meanings Exist in and among People Messages, whether they are verbal or nonverbal, don't have meanings in themselves. Rather, meanings reside in the people who express and interpret them. Imagine that a friend says, "I'm sorry," after showing up several hours late to a date. There are several possible "meanings" that this expression might have: a genuine apology, an insincere statement designed to defuse your anger, or even a sarcastic jibe. It's easy to imagine that your friend might mean one thing and you might have a different interpretation of it. The possibility of multiple interpretations means that it is often necessary to negotiate a shared meaning in order for satisfying communication to occur.

Environment and Noise Affect Communication Problems often arise because communicators occupy different **environments** (sometimes called *contexts*): fields of experience that help them make sense of others' behavior. In communication terminology, environment refers not only to a physical location, but also to the personal experiences and cultural background that participants bring to a conversation. You can appreciate the influence of environments by thinking about your beliefs about an important topic like work, marriage, or government policies. Then imagine how your beliefs might be quite different if your personal history was different.

Notice how the model in Figure 1.1 shows that the environments of A and B overlap. This intersecting area represents the background that the communicators have in common. If this overlap didn't exist, communication would be difficult, if not impossible.

While similar environments often facilitate communication, different backgrounds can make effective communication more challenging. Consider just some of the factors that might contribute to different environments, and to challenges:

- A might belong to one ethnic group and B to another;
- A might be rich and B poor;
- A might be rushed and B have nowhere to go;
- A might have lived a long, eventful life, and B is young and inexperienced;
- A might be passionately concerned with the subject and B indifferent to it.

Another factor in the environment that makes communication difficult is what scientists call **noise:** anything that interferes with the transmission and reception of a message. Three types of noise can disrupt communication. *External noise* includes those factors outside the receiver that make it difficult to hear, as well as many other kinds of distractions. For instance, too much cigarette smoke in a crowded room might make it hard for you to pay attention to another person. *Physiological noise* involves biological factors in the receiver that interfere with accurate reception: hearing loss, illness, and so on. *Psychological noise* refers to cognitive factors that make communication less effective. For instance, a woman who hears the word *gal* may become so irritated that she has trouble listening objectively to the rest of a speaker's message.

Channels Make a Difference Communication scholars use the term **channel** to describe the medium through which messages are exchanged. Along with face-to-face interaction, we have the option of using mediated channels such as phones, e-mail, and instant messages. The communication channel being used can affect the way a receiver responds to a message. For example, a typewritten love letter probably won't have the same effect as a handwritten expression of affection, and being fired from a job in person would feel different than getting the bad news in an e-mail.

Most people intuitively recognize that the selection of a channel depends in part on the kind of message they're sending. In one survey, Patrick O'Sullivan (2000) asked students to identify which channel they would find best for delivering a variety of messages. Most respondents said they would have little trouble sending positive messages face to face, but mediated channels had more appeal for sending negative messages. In particular, the students identified confessions as one type of message for which they would most likely use a mediated channel. You'll read more about computer-mediated communication later in this chapter.

COMMUNICATION PRINCIPLES

In addition to the insights offered by the communication model, there are other principles that guide our understanding of communication.

Communication Is Transactional By **transactional**, we mean that communication is a dynamic process that the participants create through their interaction with one another.

Perhaps the most important consequence of communication's transactional nature is *the mutual influence that occurs when we interact.* To put it simply, communication isn't something we do *to* others; rather, it is an activity we do *with* them. In this sense, communication is rather like dancing—at least the kind of dancing we do with partners.

Like dancing, communication *depends on the behavior of a partner.* A great dancer who doesn't consider and adapt to the skill level of his or her partner can make both of them look bad. In communication and dancing, even two talented partners don't guarantee success. When two skilled dancers perform without coordinating their movements, the results feel bad to the dancers and look foolish to an audience.

Finally, relational communication—like dancing—is a unique creation that arises out of the way in which the partners interact. The way you dance probably varies from one partner to another because of its cooperative, transactional nature. Likewise, the way you communicate almost certainly varies with different partners.

Psychologist Kenneth Gergen (1991) captures the transactional nature of communication well when he points out how our

REFLECTION

Different Relationships Illustrate Transactional Communication

I'm lucky to have two best friends, Chris and Mik. The communication in my relationships with each of them couldn't be more different. Between Chris and me, a big theme is competition. We're always trying to outsmart, outbrag, or outdo each other. If he remembers some bit of music trivia, I feel obliged to think of one that's even more obscure. When I tell a joke, he tries to come up with a funnier one. It's so bad that if one of us talks about having a bad day, the other will say that his was even worse.

My friendship with Mik is completely different. He doesn't try to outdo me. And because of that, I don't try to outdo him—in fact, I don't do much bragging around him at all. The whole feeling of my friendship with Mik is much more accepting and less competitive.

The different kinds of communication in these two friendships show how communication is transactional. Chris and I couldn't be competitive without each of us trying to outdo the other. And the vibe between Mik and me is so low key because each of us helps make it that way.

success depends on interaction with others. As he says, "one cannot be 'attractive' without others who are attracted, a 'leader' without others willing to follow, or a 'loving person' without others to affirm with appreciation" (p. 158).

Communication Has a Content Dimension and a Relational Dimension Virtually all exchanges have content and relational dimensions. The **content dimension** involves the information being explicitly discussed: "Please pass the salt," "Not now, I'm tired," "You forgot to buy a quart of milk." In addition to this sort of obvious content, all messages also have a **relational dimension** (Dillard et al., 1999; Watzlawick et al., 1967) that expresses how you feel about the other person: whether you like or dislike the other person, feel in control or subordinate, feel comfortable or anxious, and so on. For instance, consider how many different relational messages you could communicate by simply saying "Thanks a lot" in different ways. You can appreciate the importance of communication's relational dimension by looking at the photo on this page. Regardless what this couple is discussing on the content level, their nonverbal cues suggest the emotional status of their relationship at this point.

Sometimes the content dimension of a message is all that matters. For example, you may not care how the directory assistance operator feels about you as long as you get the phone number you're seeking. In a qualitative sense, however, the relational dimension of a message is often more important than the content under discussion. This explains why disputes over apparently trivial subjects become so important. In such cases we're not really arguing over whose turn it is to take out the trash or whether to play tennis or swim. Instead, we're disputing the nature of the relationship. Who's in control? How important are we to each other? Chapter 9 explores several key relational issues in detail.

Communication Can Be Intentional or Unintentional Some communication is clearly deliberate: You probably plan your words carefully before asking the boss for a raise or offering constructive criticism. Some scholars (e.g., Motley, 1990) argue that only intentional messages like these qualify as communication. However, others (e.g., Baxter & Montgomery, 1996; Buck & VanLear, 2002) suggest that even unintentional behavior is communicative. Suppose, for instance, that a friend overhears you muttering complaints to yourself. Even though you didn't intend for her to hear your remarks, they certainly did carry a message. In addition to these slips of the tongue, we unintentionally send many nonverbal messages. You might not be aware of your sour expression, impatient shifting, or sigh of boredom, but others view them nonetheless.

Even the seeming absence of a behavior has communicative value. Recall the times when you sent an e-mail or left a voice mail message and received no reply. You probably assigned some meaning to the nonresponse. Was the other person angry? Indifferent? Too busy to reply? Whether or not your hunch was correct, the point remains: All behavior has communicative value. "Nothing" never happens.

As noted earlier, scholars have conducted an ongoing argument about whether unintentional behavior should be considered communication (e.g., Clevenger, 1991) and what the relationship is between language and thought (Millikan, 2001). It's unlikely that they will ever settle this issue (Griffin, 2006). In *Interplay* we look at the communicative value of both intentional and unintentional behavior. This book takes the position that whatever you do—whether you speak or remain silent, confront or avoid, show emotion or keep a poker face—you provide information to others about your thoughts and feelings. In this sense, we are like transmitters that can't be shut off.

Communication Is Irreversible We sometimes wish that we could back up in time, erasing words or acts and replacing them with better alternatives. Unfortunately, such reversal is impossible. Sometimes, further explanation can clear up another's confusion or an apology can mollify another's hurt feelings, but other times no amount of explanation can erase the impression you have created. It is no more possible to "unreceive" a message than to "unsqueeze" a tube of toothpaste. Words said and deeds done are irretrievable.

"Let's stop this before we both say a lot of things we mean."

Communication Is Unrepeatable Because communication is an ongoing process, an event cannot be repeated. The friendly smile that worked so well when meeting a stranger last week may not succeed with the person you encounter tomorrow. Even with the same person, it's impossible to re-create an event. Why? Because both you and the other person have changed. You've both lived longer. The behavior isn't original. Your feelings about each other may have changed. You need not constantly invent new ways to act around familiar people, but you should realize that the "same" words and behavior are different each time they are spoken or performed.

COMMUNICATION MISCONCEPTIONS

Now that we've described what communication is, we need to identify some things it is not. Avoiding these common misconceptions (adapted from McCroskey & Richmond, 1996) can save you a great deal of trouble in your personal life.

Not All Communication Seeks Understanding Most people operate on the implicit but flawed assumption that the goal of all communication is to maximize understanding between communicators. While some understanding is necessary for us to coordinate our interaction, there are some types of communication in which understanding as we usually conceive it isn't the primary goal. Consider, for example,

- *The social rituals we enact every day.* "How's it going?" you ask. "Great," the other person replies. The primary goal in exchanges like these is mutual acknowledgment of one another's existence and value (even if the person *isn't* feeling great). The unstated message is "I consider you important enough to notice." There's obviously no serious attempt to exchange information.

- *Many attempts to influence others.* A quick analysis of most television commercials shows that they are aimed at persuading viewers to buy products, not to understand the content of the ad. In the same way, many of our attempts at persuading others to act as we want don't involve a desire to get the other person to understand what we want—just to comply with our wishes.

- *Deliberate ambiguity and deception.* When you decline an unwanted invitation by saying "I can't make it," you probably want to create the impression that the decision is really beyond your control. (If your goal was to be perfectly clear, you might say, "I don't want to get together. In fact, I'd rather do almost anything than accept your invitation.") As Chapter 3 explains in detail, we often lie or hedge our remarks precisely because we want to obscure our true thoughts and feelings.

More Communication Is Not Always Better While failure to communicate effectively can certainly cause problems, *too much* talking also can be a mistake. Sometimes excessive communication is simply unproductive, as when two people "talk a problem to death," going over the same ground again and again without making progress.

There are other times when talking too much actually aggravates a problem. We've all had the experience of "talking ourselves into a hole"—making a bad situation worse by pursuing it too far. As McCroskey and Wheeless (1976, p. 5) put it, "More and more negative communication merely leads to more and more negative results." In one study, college roommates revealed that thinking and talking about conflicts can actually increase relational problems (Cloven & Roloff, 1991). Even when relationships aren't troubled, less communication may be better than more. One study found that coworkers who aren't highly dependent on one another perform better when they don't spend a great deal of time talking with one another (Barrick et al., 2007).

There are even times when *no* interaction is the best course. When two people are angry and hurt, they may say things they don't mean and will later regret. In such cases it's probably best to spend time cooling off, thinking about what to say and how to say it. Chapter 8 will help you decide when and how to share feelings.

Communication Will Not Solve All Problems Sometimes even the best-planned, best-timed communication won't solve a problem. For example, imagine that you ask an instructor to explain why you received a poor grade on a project you believe deserved top marks. The professor clearly outlines the reasons why you received the low grade and sticks to that position after listening thoughtfully to your protests. Has communication solved the problem? Hardly.

Sometimes clear communication is even the cause of problems. Suppose, for example, that a friend asks you for an honest opinion of an expensive outfit he just bought. Your clear and sincere answer, "I think it makes you look fat," might do more harm than good. Deciding when and how to self-disclose isn't always easy. See Chapter 3 for suggestions.

Effective Communication Is Not a Natural Ability Most people assume that communication is something that people can do without the need for training—rather like breathing. Although nearly everyone does manage to function passably without much formal communication training, most people operate at a level of effectiveness far below their potential. In fact, communication skills are rather like athletic ability. Even the most inept of us can learn to be more effective with training and practice, and even the most talented need to "keep in shape."

Interpersonal Communication Defined

Now that you have a better understanding of the overall process of human communication, it's time to look at what makes some types of communication uniquely interpersonal.

QUANTITATIVE AND QUALITATIVE DEFINITIONS

Scholars have characterized interpersonal communication in two ways (Redmond, 1995). Some definitions take a **quantitative** approach that defines interpersonal communication as any interaction between two people. Social scientists call two persons interacting a **dyad**, and they often use the adjective *dyadic* to describe this type of communication. So, in a quantitative sense, the terms *dyadic communication* and *interpersonal communication* can be used interchangeably. Using a quantitative definition, a salesclerk and customer or a police officer ticketing a speeding driver would be examples of interpersonal acts, whereas a teacher and class or a performer and audience would not.

Dyadic communication *is* different from the kind of interaction that occurs in larger groups (Wilmot, 1995). In a group, participants can form coalitions to get support for their positions. In a dyad, though, partners must work matters out with each other. This difference explains why, when a task calls for competition, children prefer to play in three-person groups, and if it calls for cooperation, they prefer to be in dyads (Benenson et al., 2000).

Despite the unique qualities of dyads, you might object to the quantitative definition of interpersonal communication. For example, consider a routine transaction between a salesclerk and customer, or the rushed exchange when you ask a stranger on the street for directions. Communication of this sort hardly seems the same as when you talk with a friend about a personal problem or share your experiences of a year in school with your family.

The impersonal nature of some two-person exchanges—the kind when you think, "I might as well have been talking to a machine"—has led some scholars (e.g., Miller & Steinberg, 1975) to argue that quality, not quantity, is what distinguishes interpersonal communication. Using a **qualitative** approach, interpersonal communication occurs when people treat one another as unique individuals, regardless of the context in which the interaction occurs or the number of people involved. When quality of interaction is the criterion, the opposite of interpersonal communication is *impersonal* interaction, not group, public, or mass communication.

Several features distinguish qualitatively interpersonal communication from less personal exchanges. The first is *uniqueness.* Whereas impersonal exchanges are governed by the kind of social rules we learn from parents, teachers, and etiquette books, the way we communicate in a truly personal relationship is unlike our behavior with anyone else. In one relationship you might exchange good-natured insults, while in another you are careful never to offend your partner. Likewise, you might handle conflicts with one friend or family member by expressing disagreements as soon as they arise, whereas the unwritten rule in another relationship is to withhold resentments until they build up and then clear the air periodically. Communication scholar Julia Wood (2005) coined the term "relational culture" to describe people in close relationships who create their own unique ways of interacting.

A second characteristic of qualitatively interpersonal communication is *irreplaceability.* Because interpersonal relationships are unique, they can't be replaced. This explains why we usually feel so sad when a close friendship or

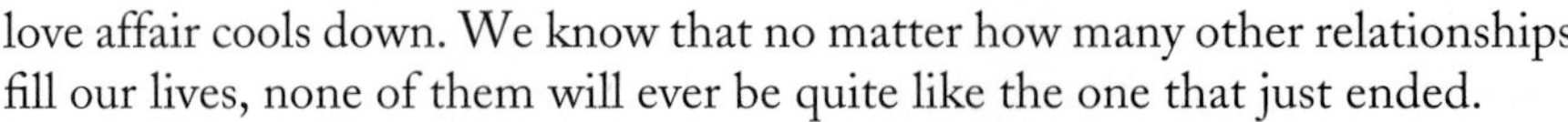

love affair cools down. We know that no matter how many other relationships fill our lives, none of them will ever be quite like the one that just ended.

Interdependence is a third characteristic of qualitatively interpersonal relationships. Here, the fate of the partners is connected. You might be able to brush off the anger, affection, excitement, or depression of someone you're not involved with interpersonally, but in an interpersonal relationship the other's life affects you. Sometimes interdependence is a pleasure, and at other times it is a burden. In either case, interdependence is a fact of life in qualitatively interpersonal relationships.

A fourth yardstick of interpersonal communication is *disclosure* of personal information. In impersonal relationships we don't reveal much about ourselves, but in many interpersonal ones communicators feel more comfortable sharing their thoughts and feelings. This doesn't mean that all interpersonal relationships are warm and caring or that all self-disclosure is positive. It's possible to reveal negative personal information: "I'm really mad at you!"

In impersonal communication we seek payoffs that have little to do with the people involved. You listen to professors in class or talk to potential buyers of your used car in order to reach goals that have little to do with developing personal relationships. By contrast, you spend time in qualitatively interpersonal relationships with friends, lovers, and others because of *intrinsic rewards* that come from your communication. It doesn't matter what you talk about: Developing the relationship is what's important.

Because interpersonal communication is characterized by the qualities of uniqueness, irreplaceability, interdependence, disclosure, and intrinsic rewards, it forms a small fraction of our interaction. The majority of our communication is relatively impersonal. We chat pleasantly with shopkeepers or fellow passengers on the bus or plane; we discuss the weather or current events with most classmates and neighbors; we deal with coworkers and teachers in a polite way; but considering the number of people with whom we communicate, interpersonal relationships are by far the minority. As the Focus on Research box on page 20 illustrates, even in our most intimate relationships, sharing personal information is only a small part of our communication.

The rarity of qualitatively interpersonal communication isn't necessarily unfortunate. Most of us don't have the time or energy to create personal relationships with everyone we encounter. Even with our closest relational partners, deeply personal conversations are rare. In fact, the scarcity of interpersonal communication contributes to its value. Like precious and one-of-a-kind artwork, qualitatively interpersonal communication is special because it is rare.

Personal and Impersonal Communication Are Universal: *Babel*

In the remote Moroccan desert, tragedy strikes when an errant rifle shot seriously injures Susan (Cate Blanchett) as she and her husband, Richard (Brad Pitt), confront the misery of their unhappy marriage. This accident starts a chain of events that connects the lives of people in North Africa, Mexico, Japan, and the United States.

The film's promotional materials proclaim that this complicated story "demonstrates the necessity and importance of human communication." It also dramatically contrasts the difference between impersonal and qualitatively interpersonal communication. In the course of this tale, some relationships shift from impersonal to intensely personal: American Richard bonds with a generous Moroccan villager. A rebellious deaf Japanese teenager lets go of her hostility and connects with both her father and a kind police investigator. Other communication is heartbreakingly impersonal: U.S. Border Patrol officers dispassionately pursue a loving nanny, and the Moroccan police abuse a naive and unsophisticated family.

As you will read throughout this book, there are many ways that communication varies from one culture to another. Nonetheless, the polar opposites of impersonal and qualitatively interpersonal interaction are options for people from all backgrounds.

SELF-ASSESSMENT

How Interpersonal Are Your Relationships?

Select three important relationships to assess. These might include your relationships with people at work or school, or with friends or family. For each relationship, respond to the following items:

1. **To what extent is the relationship characterized by uniqueness? How much is this relationship one of a kind?**
   LOW LEVEL OF UNIQUENESS **1 2 3 4 5 6 7** HIGHLY UNIQUE
2. **To what extent is the relationship irreplaceable?**
   VERY EASY TO REPLACE **1 2 3 4 5 6 7** VERY HARD TO REPLACE
3. **To what extent are you and your relationship partner interdependent; that is, to what extent does one person's actions affect the other?**
   LITTLE INTERDEPENDENCE **1 2 3 4 5 6 7** HIGH INTERDEPENDENCE
4. **To what extent is communication in the relationship marked by high disclosure of personal information?**
   LOW DISCLOSURE **1 2 3 4 5 6 7** HIGH DISCLOSURE
5. **To what extent does the relationship create its own intrinsic rewards?**
   REWARDS ARE EXTRINSIC **1 2 3 4 5 6 7** REWARDS ARE INTRINSIC

Based on your answers, decide how qualitatively interpersonal (or how impersonal) each of the relationships is. (If you have more 5s, 6s, and 7s in your answers, then your relationship is more interpersonal. If you have more 1s, 2s, and 3s, then the relationship is more impersonal.) How satisfied are you with your findings? What can you do to improve your level of satisfaction with these relationships?

PERSONAL AND IMPERSONAL COMMUNICATION: A MATTER OF BALANCE

Now that the differences between qualitatively interpersonal and impersonal communication are spelled out, we need to ask some important questions. Is personal communication better than the impersonal variety? Is more personal communication the goal?

Most relationships aren't either personal or impersonal. Rather, they fall somewhere between these two extremes. Consider your own communication and you'll find that there is often a personal element in even the most impersonal situations. You might appreciate the unique sense of humor of a grocery checker or spend a few moments sharing private thoughts with the person cutting your hair. And even the most tyrannical, demanding, by-the-book boss might show an occasional flash of humanity.

FOCUS ON RESEARCH

Maintaining Relationships through Daily Conversations

What can researchers learn from analyzing 172 hours of couples' daily conversations about mundane topics such as pets, television shows, and weekend plans? According to Jess Alberts and her colleagues, the routine talk that makes up much of everyday life is an important tool that helps couples maintain their relationships.

The research team took on the laborious task of taping, transcribing, and coding the daily interactions of 10 satisfied couples in long-term relationships. They found that more than 40 percent of the couples' conversations involved self-reports (e.g., "I had lunch today with the rep on my new account") or observations ("That clock is slow"). The researchers concluded that relational partners play important roles as "audiences for the articulation of one's experiences and thoughts." In other words, people want and expect their partners to provide a listening ear.

The couples talked about more than just themselves. For example, they discussed other people in their lives (friends, family, colleagues) and television shows (often while watching television together). Time was also spent discussing household tasks and upcoming plans. Were many of these interactions mundane and routine? Certainly. Were they unimportant? Hardly. Alberts and her colleagues concluded that these apparently mundane conversations are "necessary types of interaction for relationship maintenance that form the bedrock on which the relationship is built."

Alberts, J. K., Yoshimura, C. G., Rabby, M., & Loschiavo, R. (2005). Mapping the topography of couples' daily conversation. *Journal of Social and Personal Relationships, 22*, 299–322.

Just as there's a personal element in many impersonal settings, there is also an impersonal side to our relationships with the people we care about most. There are occasions when we don't want to be personal: when we're distracted, tired, busy, or just not interested. In fact, interpersonal communication is rather like rich food—it's fine in moderation, but too much can make you uncomfortable. The blend of personal and interpersonal communication can shift in various stages of a relationship. The communication between young lovers who talk only about their feelings may change as their relationship develops. Several years later their communication has become more routine and ritualized, and the percentage of time they spend on personal, relational issues drops while the conversation about less intimate topics increases. Chapter 9 discusses how communication changes as relationships pass through various stages, and Chapter 3 describes various theories of self-disclosure. As you read this information, you will see even more clearly that, while interpersonal communication can make life worth living, it isn't possible or desirable all the time.

Interpersonal Communication and Technology

Until a generation ago, face-to-face communication seemed essential to starting and maintaining most, if not all, personal relationships. Other channels

existed: The telephone (in an era of expensive long-distance rates and less-than-perfect technology) might have worked during temporary absences, and postal correspondence helped bridge the gap until the people involved could reconnect in person. Nonetheless, interpersonal communication seemed to require physical proximity.

Technological changes have given us new options for communicating personally. Along with easier and more affordable telephone service, **computer-mediated communication (CMC)** provides another way to interact. E-mail is the most popular form of CMC, but it isn't the only one. Text messaging, instant messaging, social networking, and blogging are all tools that friends, family, acquaintances, and even strangers can use to communicate (Lenhart et al., 2007).

MEDIATED VERSUS FACE-TO-FACE COMMUNICATION

At first glance, CMC might seem inferior to face-to-face interaction, since it lacks the rich array of nonverbal cues that are available in person. Even the telephone offers vocal cues. By contrast, CMC—at least the text-based variety—offers almost none of this richness. Some critics (e.g., Putnam, 2000) argue that the almost hypnotic attraction of an Internet connection discourages a sense of community. A small body of research supports this position. Some research indicates that heavy Internet users spend less time talking in person and on the phone with friends and family members (Bower, 1998; Nie, 2001), which can lead to high levels of emotional loneliness (Moody, 2001). These findings are questionable, since people who are already lonely tend to spend time on the Internet (Amichai-Hamburger & Ben-Artzi, 2003). Even when people replace their face-to-face communication with online contacts, some observers claim the quality of the relationship suffers. "E-mail is a way to stay in touch," said one researcher, "but you can't share a coffee or a beer with somebody on e-mail or give them a hug" (Nie & Erbring, 2000, p. 19).

Other research suggests that mediated relationships can be rich and satisfying. A survey of over 3,000 adults in the United States characterized the Internet as a "vibrant social universe" in which relationships can prosper (Horrigan et al., 2001). In that study, 72 percent of the Internet users had communicated with a relative or a friend within the past day, compared with 61 percent for nonusers. The Internet users also were more likely to phone friends and relatives. Almost all parents in one survey reported that the Internet has no effect on their children's interaction with friends (UCLA, 2003).

Even more significant than the amount of communication that occurs online is its quality. Fifty-five percent of Internet users said e-mail improved communications with family, and 66 percent reported that their contact with friends increased because of e-mail. Among women, the rate of satisfaction was even higher: 60 percent reported better contact with family and 71 percent with friends (Horrigan et al., 2001).

REFLECTION

Blogging As Interpersonal Communication

I am a faithful participant in a baseball fan blog. This blog is open to the public, but most of the postings come from a couple dozen regulars. We've all gotten to know each other quite well, even though we have never met in person. Along with discussing baseball in great detail, we talk about the rest of our lives: favorite movies, music, food, and relationships. We know who's married, who has kids, who's young, who's old, etc. We've expressed genuine sympathy when fellow bloggers have had their houses flooded, lost jobs, or gone in the hospital. From this experience, I've found blogging to be very interpersonal.

Other research confirms that CMC can support interpersonal relationships. In a 5-year survey, Internet users reported having more social contacts than nonusers, as well as more community and political involvement (Katz et al., 2001). Almost 60 percent of American teenagers say that their use of the Internet helps their relationships with their friends, and almost a third report that it helps them make new friends (Lenhart et al., 2001).

There are several reasons why CMC can increase both the amount and quality of interpersonal communication (Barnes, 2003). For one thing, it makes communication easier. Busy schedules and long distances can make quality time in face-to-face contact difficult or impossible. The challenge of finding time is especially tough for people who are separated by long distances and multiple time zones. In relationships like this, the *asynchronous* nature of e-mail provides a way to share information that otherwise would be impossible. Instant messaging is another way to keep in touch: Discovering that a friend or relative is online and starting an electronic conversation is "like walking down the street and sometimes running into a friend," said one computer consultant (Marriott, 1998).

Sometimes CMC can profoundly expand the quality of interpersonal communication. Even text-only CMC has the power to stimulate both self-disclosure and direct questioning between strangers, resulting in greater interpersonal attraction (Atheunis et al., 2007). Sociolinguist Deborah Tannen (1996, p. 52) describes how e-mail transformed the quality of two relationships:

> E-mail deepened my friendship with Ralph. Though his office was next to mine, we rarely had extended conversations because he is shy. Face to face he mumbled so, I could barely tell he was speaking. But when we both got on e-mail, I started receiving long, self-revealing messages; we poured our hearts out to each other. A friend discovered that e-mail opened up that kind of communication with her father. He would never talk much on the phone (as her mother would), but they have become close since they both got on line.

Experiences like these help explain why Steve Jobs, the cofounder of Apple Computer, suggested that personal computers be renamed "*inter*-personal computers" (Kirkpatrick, 1992).

FOCUS ON RESEARCH

Less Can Be More: When Online Partners Meet in Person

research

Imagine meeting someone online—in a chat room, on a blog, or through a social networking site like Facebook. After interacting for months using various technologies (e-mail, IM-ing, texting), you find yourself wondering whether getting together in person would enhance your growing relationship. The answer, according to a recent study, might surprise you.

Communication researchers Artemio Ramirez and Shuangyue Zhang placed over 800 previously unacquainted college students into two-person "virtual partnerships." Over a 9-week period, the partners were required to complete a series of tasks together. Some of the duos communicated only online, with no face-to-face contact. Others began their work online but later met in person to finish their tasks. The researchers wanted to know whether "modality switching"—that is, moving from online to face-to-face communication—would affect the way the partners thought and felt about one another.

The findings: Partners who communicated exclusively online actually felt greater intimacy and social attraction to one another than those who met in person. For those who did meet face to face, the longer they delayed getting together, the lower their attraction when they finally met in person. The researchers explained that in online-only relationships, "idealization and heightened expectations can occur"—and that face-to-face meetings sometimes lead to a chilly dose of reality.

These findings raise a cautionary note for communicators who meet online and look forward to their relationship's flourishing in person. While some relationships can handle the transition, this study suggests there are risks involved—and that success is hardly guaranteed.

Ramirez, A., & Zhang, S. (2007). When online meets offline: The effect of modality switching on relational communication. *Communication Monographs, 74,* 287–310.

CHALLENGES OF MEDIATED COMMUNICATION

Nobody would downplay the challenges of communicating in face-to-face situations. But communicating via the Internet or phone presents its own set of issues.

Leaner Messages Social scientists use the term **richness** to describe the abundance of nonverbal cues that add clarity to a verbal message. Face-to-face communication is rich because it abounds with nonverbal cues that help clarify the meanings of one another's words and offer hints about their feelings (Surinder &. Cooper, 2003). By comparison, most mediated communication is a much leaner channel for conveying information.

To appreciate how message richness varies by medium, imagine you haven't heard from a friend in several weeks, and you decide to ask, "Is anything wrong?" Your friend replies: "No, I'm fine." Would that response be more or less descriptive depending on whether you received it:

via text message?
over the phone?
in person?

You almost certainly would be able to tell a great deal more from a face-to-face response because it would contain a richer array of cues: facial expressions, vocal tone, and so on. By contrast, a text message contains only words. The phone message—with its vocal cues but no visual cues—would probably fall somewhere in between.

Because most mediated messages are leaner than the face-to-face variety, they can be harder to interpret with confidence. Irony and attempts at humor can easily be misunderstood; so as a receiver, it's important to clarify your interpretations before jumping to conclusions. And as a sender, think about how to send unambiguous messages so that you aren't misunderstood.

The leanness of mediated messages presents another challenge. Without nonverbal cues, online communicators can create idealized—and sometimes unrealistic—images of one another. As we'll discuss in Chapter 3, the absence of nonverbal cues allows cybercommunicators to manage their identities carefully. After all, it's a world without bad breath, unsightly blemishes, or stammering responses. Such conditions encourage participants to engage in what Joseph Walther (1996) calls *hyperpersonal* communication, accelerating the discussion of personal topics and relational development beyond what normally happens in face-to-face interaction. This may explain why communicators who meet online sometimes have difficulty shifting to a face-to-face relationship (see the Focus on Research box on page 23). People who communicate primarily through lean mediated channels need to monitor their expressiveness, as we'll now discuss.

Disinhibition Sooner or later most of us speak before we think, blurting out remarks that embarrass ourselves and offend others. The tendency to transmit messages without considering their consequences can be especially great in online communication, where we don't see, hear, or sometimes even know the target of our remarks. This **disinhibition** can take two forms.

Sometimes online communicators volunteer personal information that they would prefer to keep confidential from at least some receivers. Consider the example of social networking sites like Facebook, MySpace, and Friendster. A quick scan of home pages there shows that many users post text and images about themselves that could prove embarrassing in some contexts: "Here I am just before my DUI arrest"; "This is me in Cancun on spring break." This is not the sort of information most people would be eager to show a prospective employer or certain family members.

Along with mediated communication's being more personal than the face-to-face variety, it also is more expressive. A growing body of research shows that communicators are more direct—often in a critical way—when using mediated channels than in face-to-face contact (Watts, 2007). Sometimes communicators take disinhibition to the extreme, blasting off angry—even vicious—e-mails, text messages, and website postings. The common term for these outbursts is *flaming*. Here is the account of one writer who was the target of an obscenity-filled e-mail:

> No one had ever said something like this to me before, and no one could have said this to me before: in any other medium, these words would be, literally, unspeakable. The guy couldn't have said this to me on the phone, because I would have hung up and not answered if the phone rang again, and he couldn't have said it to my face, because I wouldn't have let him finish. . . . I suppose the guy could have written me a nasty letter: he probably wouldn't have used the word "rectum," though, and he probably wouldn't have mailed the letter; he would have thought twice while he was addressing the envelope. But the nature of e-mail is that you don't think twice. You write and send. (Seabrook, 1994, p. 71)

Permanence Common decency aside, the risk of hostile e-messages—or any inappropriate mediated messages—is their permanence. It can be bad enough to blurt out a private thought or lash out in person, but at least there is no permanent record of your indiscretion. By contrast, a regrettable text message, e-mail, or web posting can be archived virtually forever. Even worse, it can be retrieved and forwarded in ways that can only be imagined in your worst dreams. The best advice, then, is to take the same approach with mediated messages that you do in person: Think twice before saying something you might later regret. As David Bennehum (2005) put it, "Old e-mail never dies."

CHOOSING THE BEST COMMUNICATION CHANNEL

The information on channel selection in Table 1.1 can help you answer some important questions about channel selection. Is it better to say "I'm sorry" in person or over the phone? What channel is the best for expressing your anger? Should you approach the boss directly or write a memo when asking for a raise? Will asking a merchant for a refund via e-mail work better than an in-person request? As Table 1.1 suggests, each channel has both pros and cons.

Communication Competence

"What does it take to communicate better?" is probably the most important question to ask as you read this book. Answering it has been one of the leading challenges for communication scholars. While all the answers aren't in yet, research has identified a great deal of important and useful information about communication competence.

COMMUNICATION COMPETENCE DEFINED

Defining **communication competence** isn't as easy as it might seem. Although scholars continue to debate a precise definition, most agree that competent communication is both *effective* and *appropriate* (Spitzberg, 2000). To

TABLE 1.1 ***Factors to Consider When Choosing a Communication Channel***

COMMUNICATION CHANNEL	TIME REQUIRED FOR FEEDBACK	RICHNESS OF INFORMATION CONVEYED	SENDER'S CONTROL OVER HOW MESSAGE IS COMPOSED	CONTROL OVER RECEIVER'S ATTENTION	EFFECTIVENESS FOR DETAILED MESSAGES
Face-to-Face	Immediate	High (verbal and nonverbal cues)	Moderate	High	Weak (listeners are likely to forget details of complicated messages)
Telephone	Immediate	Moderate (vocal cues but no visual cues)	Moderate	Moderate	Very Weak
Voice Mail	Delayed	Moderate (vocal cues but no visual cues)	High (since the receiver can't interrupt)	Low	Weak
E-Mail	Delayed	Low (when text only, no formatting)	High	Low	Moderate (messages are often saved)
Text Messaging	Immediate	Low (when text only, no formatting)	High	Low	Weak
Instant Messaging	Potentially quick	Low (when text only, no formatting)	High	Moderate (both parties online at the same time)	Weak
Hard Copy (e.g., handwritten or typed message)	Delayed	Low	Very High	Low	Good

Adapted from Adler, R. B., & Elmhorst, J. (2008). *Communicating at work: Principles and practices for business and the professions* (9th ed., p. 31). New York: McGraw-Hill.

understand these two dimensions, consider how you might handle everyday communication challenges such as declining an unwanted invitation or communicating about a friend's annoying behavior. In cases like these, *effective* communication would get the results you want. *Appropriate* communication would do so in a way that, in most cases, enhances the relationship in which it occurs (Wiemann et al., 1997). You can appreciate the importance of both appropriateness and effectiveness by imagining approaches that would satisfy one of these criteria but not the other. Effectiveness without appropriateness might satisfy your goals, but leave others unhappy. Conversely, appropriateness without effectiveness might leave others content but you frustrated. With the goal of balancing effectiveness and appropriateness, the following paragraphs outline several important characteristics of communication competence.

"How much you puttin' in?"

There Is No Single "Ideal" or "Effective" Way to Communicate Your own experience shows that a variety of communication styles can be effective. Some very successful communicators are serious, while others use humor; some are gregarious, while others are quieter; and some are more straightforward, while others hint diplomatically. Just as there are many kinds of beautiful music or art, there are many kinds of competent communication. Furthermore, a type of communication that is competent in one setting might be a colossal blunder in another. The joking insults you routinely trade with one friend might offend a sensitive family member, and last Saturday night's romantic approach would probably be out of place at work on Monday morning. This means that there can be no surefire list of rules or tips that will guarantee your success as a communicator.

Flexibility is especially important when members of different cultures meet. Some communication skills seem to be universal (Ruben, 1989). Every culture has rules that require speakers to behave appropriately, for example. But the definition of what kind of communication is appropriate in a given situation varies considerably from one culture to another (Arasaratnam, 2007; Ulrey, 2001). On an obvious level, customs like belching after a meal or appearing nude in public that might be appropriate in some parts of the world would be considered outrageous in others. But there are more subtle differences in competent communication. For example, qualities like self-disclosure and straight talking that are valued in the United States are likely to be considered overly aggressive and insensitive in many Asian cultures, where subtlety and indirectness are considered important (Kim et al., 1998). We'll discuss the many dimensions of intercultural competence in Chapter 2.

Competence Is Situational Because competent behavior varies so much from one situation and person to another, it's a mistake to think that communication competence is a trait that a person either possesses or lacks (Spitzberg, 1991). It's more accurate to talk about *degrees* or *areas* of competence.

You and the people you know are probably quite competent in some areas and less so in others. For example, you might deal quite skillfully with peers, while feeling clumsy interacting with people much older or younger, wealthier or poorer, more or less attractive than yourself. In fact, your competence may vary from situation to situation. This means it's an overgeneralization to say, in a moment of distress, "I'm a terrible communicator!" It's more accurate to say, "I didn't handle this situation very well, but I'm better in others."

Competence Can Be Learned To some degree, biology is destiny when it comes to communication style (Beatty, McCroskey, & Heisel, 1998; Bodary, 2000). Studies of identical and fraternal twins suggest traits including sociability, anger, and relaxation seem to be partially a function of our genetic makeup. In addition, a study by Beatty et al. (2001) found that social composure and wit are highly heritable. (The same study showed that articulation ability and appropriate disclosure aren't.)

Fortunately, biology isn't the only factor that shapes how we communicate. Communication competence is, to a great degree, a set of skills that anyone can learn (Fortney et al., 2001). For instance, people with high communication apprehension often benefit from communication skills training (Ayres & Hopf, 1993; Dwyer, 2000). Sometimes even a modest amount of training can produce dramatic results. For example, after only 30 minutes of instruction, one group of observers became significantly more effective in detecting deception in interviews (deTurck & Miller, 1990). Even without systematic training, it's possible to develop communication skills through the processes of observation and trial and error. We learn from our own successes and failures, as well as from observing other models—both positive and negative. One study revealed that education does lead to improved communication skill: College students' communication competence increases over the course of their undergraduate studies (Rubin et al., 1990). And, of course, it's our hope that you will become a more competent communicator as a result of putting the information in this book to work.

CHARACTERISTICS OF COMPETENT COMMUNICATION

Despite the fact that competent communication varies from one situation to another, scholars have identified several common denominators that characterize effective communication in most contexts.

A Large Repertoire of Skills As we've already seen, good communicators don't use the same approach in every situation. They know that sometimes it's best to be blunt and sometimes tactful, that there is a time to speak up and a time to be quiet. They understand that it's sometimes best to be serious and sometimes best to be playful.

The chances of reaching your personal and relational goals increase with the number of options you have about how to communicate. For example, if you want to start a conversation with a stranger, your chances of success increase as you have more options available (Kelly & Watson, 1986). All it might take to get the conversational ball rolling is a self-introduction. In other cases, seeking assistance might work well: "I've just moved here. What kind of neighborhood is the Eastside?" A third strategy is to ask a question about some situational feature: "I've never heard this band before. Do you know anything about them?" You could also offer a sincere compliment and follow it up with a question: "Great shoes! Where did you get them?"

A recent study shows how a large repertoire can help communicators achieve a variety of goals. William Sharkey and his colleagues (2004) found that many people intentionally embarrass themselves in front of others, saying things like "That was a dumb thing for me to do" and "I'm such a klutz!" When pressed for an explanation, people offered several reasons why they deprecate themselves: to socialize in a group (showing modesty and a sense of humor), to deflect embarrassment away from others, to create relational bonds, and to make conversations more fun and interesting. While constant self-flagellation would soon become annoying, it's easy to see how occasional deliberate, strategic self-embarrassment can be a tool.

Many people with disabilities have learned the value of having a repertoire of options available to manage unwanted offers of help (Braithwaite & Eckstein, 2003). Some of those options include performing a task quickly, before anyone has the chance to intervene; pretending not to hear the offer; accepting a well-intentioned invitation, to avoid seeming rude or ungrateful; using humor to deflect a bid for help; declining a well-intentioned offer with thanks; and assertively refusing help from those who won't take no for an answer.

Just as a golfer has a wide range of clubs to use for various situations, a competent communicator has a large array of behaviors from which to choose.

Incompetence Dooms Relationships: *Sideways*

In this tragicomic tale, two clueless friends suffer the consequences of their communicative incompetence during a road trip to California wine country.

Neurotic Miles (Paul Giamatti) is still suffering from a recent divorce. He describes his beloved Pinot Noir wine grape as "thin skinned and temperamental," but he might as well be talking about himself. Jack (Thomas Hayden Church) would rather make another sexual conquest than tell the truth to the women he seduces—that his marriage is less than a week away.

It's easy to laugh at the blunders of this odd pair of friends; but it's clear that Miles' hypersensitivity and Jack's dishonesty appear to doom them to a life of failed relationships. These two sad characters clearly need a larger repertoire of skills, some empathy for the people in their lives, and a healthy dose of self-monitoring.

Adaptability Having a large repertoire of possible behaviors is one ingredient of competent communication, but you have to be able to choose the *right* one for a particular situation (Brashers & Jackson, 1999; Hample & Dallinger, 2000). To repeat: An approach that works well in one situation might be disastrous somewhere else. Effective communication means choosing the right response for the situation.

Ability to Perform Skillfully Once you have chosen the appropriate way to communicate, you have to perform that behavior effectively (Burleson, 2007). In communication, as in other activities, practice is the key to skillful performance. Much of the information in *Interplay* will introduce you to new tools for communicating, and the Skill Builder activities at the end of each chapter will help you practice them.

Involvement Not surprisingly, effective communication occurs when the people care about one another and the topic at hand (Cegala et al., 1982). Rod Hart suggests that this involvement has several dimensions (adapted here from Knapp & Vangelisti, 2006). It includes commitment to the other person and the relationship, concern about the message being discussed, and a desire to make the relationship clearly useful.

Empathy/Perspective Taking People have the best chance of developing an effective message when they understand the other person's point of view

(Ifert & Roloff, 1997; Lobchuk, 2006). Since others aren't always good at expressing their thoughts and feelings clearly, the ability to imagine how an issue might look from another's perspective suggests why listening is such an important communication skill. Not only does it help you understand others, but it also provides information to develop strategies about how to best influence them. Empathy is such an important element of communicative competence that researcher Mark Redmond (1989, p. 594) flatly states that "by definition, a person cannot produce a message that is empathic that is not also communicatively competent."

Cognitive Complexity **Cognitive complexity** is the ability to construct a variety of different frameworks for viewing an issue. Imagine that a longtime friend seems to be angry with you. One possible explanation is that your friend is offended by something you've done. Another possibility is that something has happened in another part of your friend's life that is upsetting. Or perhaps nothing at all is wrong, and you're just being overly sensitive.

Researchers have found that a large number of constructs for interpreting the behavior of others leads to greater "conversational sensitivity," increasing the chances of acting in ways that will produce satisfying results (Burleson & Caplan, 1998; Mohd Salleh, 2008; Waltman, 2002).

Self-Monitoring Psychologists use the term **self-monitoring** to describe the process of paying close attention to one's own behavior and using these observations to shape the way one behaves. Self-monitors are able to detach a part of their consciousness to observe their behavior from a detached viewpoint, making observations such as

"I'm making a fool out of myself."
"I'd better speak up now."
"This approach is working well. I'll keep it up."

It's no surprise that self-monitoring generally increases one's effectiveness as a communicator (Kolb, 1998; Sypher & Sypher, 1983). The ability to ask yourself the question "How am I doing?" and to change your behavior if the answer isn't positive is a tremendous asset for communicators. People with poor self-monitoring skills often blunder through life, sometimes succeeding and sometimes failing, without the detachment to understand why.

How does your behavior as an interpersonal communicator measure up against the standards of competence described in this chapter? Like most people, you will probably find some areas of your life that are very satisfying and others that you would like to change. As you read on in this book, realize that the information in each chapter offers advice that can help your communication become more productive and rewarding.

Although the qualities described here do play an important role in communicative competence, they can be ineffective when carried to excess (Spitzberg, 1994). As the "Dark Side" box on this page shows, too much self-monitoring can be a problem in close relationships. Even in less personal contexts, an excessive concern for appearance ("How do I sound?" "How am I doing?") overshadows the need to be faithful to one's true beliefs. Likewise, an excess of empathy and cognitive complexity can lead you to see all sides of an issue so well that you're incapable of acting. In other words, there is a *curvilinear relationship* among most of the elements described in these pages: Both a deficiency and an excess can lead to incompetent communication.

THE DARK SIDE OF COMMUNICATION

Excessive Self-Monitoring Discourages Intimacy

Although self-monitoring is generally an element of effective communication, some research suggests that paying *too much* attention to how you present yourself can have a dark side. One study revealed that high self-monitors often experience less intimacy, satisfaction, and commitment in their romantic relationships than people who aren't so strategic. On reflection, these results make sense: Communicators who are overly concerned with managing impressions often hide what they really think and feel—hardly a recipe for intimacy.

As a rule of thumb, self-monitoring is a valuable skill in less personal interactions and in the early stages of close relationships. Over time, however, romantic relationships can profit from communication that is a bit less guarded, crafted, and scrutinized.

Wright, C. N., Holloway, A., & Roloff, M. E. (2007). The dark side of self-monitoring: How high self-monitors view their romantic relationships. *Communication Reports, 20,* 101–114.

Summary

Communication is important for a variety of reasons. Besides satisfying practical needs, meaningful communication contributes to physical health, plays a major role in defining our identity, and forms the basis for our social relationships.

Communication is a complex process that can be represented in a communication model. The model presented in this chapter depicts how communicators usually send and receive messages simultaneously. The meaning of these messages resides in the people who exchange them, not in the messages themselves. Environment and noise affect communication, as do the channels we choose for sending our messages.

A variety of principles help explain how communication operates. Communication is transactional—that is, it's a dynamic process that people create through interaction. Messages can be intentional or unintentional, and they almost always have both a content and a relational dimension. Once expressed, messages cannot be withdrawn. Finally, communication is unrepeatable.

Interpersonal communication can be defined quantitatively (by the number of people involved) or qualitatively (by the nature of interaction between them).

In a qualitative sense, interpersonal relationships are unique, irreplaceable, interdependent, and intrinsically rewarding. Qualitatively interpersonal communication is relatively infrequent, even in many close relationships. While some research suggests that computer-mediated communication (CMC) is more impersonal than face-to-face communication, other research shows that it can add to and enhance interpersonal relationships.

To understand the communication process, it is important to recognize and avoid several common misconceptions. Despite the value of self-expression, more communication is not always better. In fact, there are occasions when more communication can increase problems. Sometimes total understanding isn't as important as we might think. Even at its best, communication is not a panacea that will solve every problem. Effective communication is not a natural ability. While some people have greater aptitude at communicating, everyone can learn to interact with others more effectively. Communicating via mediated channels presents its own set of challenges and works most effectively when participants are mindful of them.

Communication competency is the ability to be both effective and appropriate—that is, to get desired results from others in a manner that maintains the relationship on terms that are acceptable to everyone. There is no single ideal way to communicate: Flexibility and adaptability are characteristics of competent communicators, as are skill at performing behaviors, involvement with others, empathy and perspective taking, cognitive complexity, and self-monitoring. The good news is, communication competency can be learned.

Activities

1. Invitation to Insight

How much time do you spend communicating? Conduct an informal study to answer this question by keeping a 2-day log of your activities. Based on your findings, answer the following questions:

a. What percentage of your waking time is spent speaking and listening to others?
b. Using the explanation on pages 16–19, describe what percentage of your entire communication is qualitatively interpersonal.
c. How satisfied are you with your findings? How would you like to change your everyday communication?

2. Critical Thinking Probe

As you read in this chapter, communication is transactional in nature: something we do *with* others and not *to* them. How does face-to-face communication differ from computer-mediated communication, such as e-mail? Are they equally transactional?

3. Invitation To Insight

How competent are you as a communicator? You can begin to answer this question by interviewing people who know you well: a family member, friend, or fellow worker, for example. Interview different people to determine if you are more competent in some relationships than others, or in some situations than others.

a. Describe the characteristics of competent communicators outlined on pages 28–31 of this chapter. Be sure your interviewee understands each of them.
b. Ask your interviewee to rate you on each of the observable qualities. (It won't be possible for others to evaluate internal characteristics, such as cognitive complexity and self-monitoring.) Be sure this evaluation reflects your communication in a variety of situations: It's likely you aren't uniformly competent—or incompetent—in all of them.
c. If your rating is not high in one or more areas, discuss with your partner how you could raise it.

4. Skill Builder

Knowing how you want to communicate isn't the same as being able to perform competently. The technique of behavior rehearsal provides a way to improve a particular communication skill before you use it in real life. Behavior rehearsal consists of four steps:

a. Define your goal. Begin by identifying the way you want to behave.
b. Break the goal into the behaviors it involves. Most goals are made up of several verbal and nonverbal parts. You may be able to identify these parts by thinking about them yourself, by observing others, by reading about them, or by asking others for advice.
c. Practice each behavior before using it in real life. You can practice a new behavior by rehearsing it alone and then with others before you put it into action. Another approach is to picture yourself behaving in new ways. This mental image can boost effectiveness.
d. Try out the behavior in real life. You can increase the odds of success if you follow two pieces of advice when trying out new communication behaviors: Work on only one subskill at a time, and start with easy situations. Don't expect yourself suddenly to behave flawlessly in the most challenging situations. Begin by practicing your new skills in situations in which you have a chance of success.

CHAPTER 2

Culture and Communication

CHAPTER OUTLINE

After studying the material in this chapter . . .

YOU SHOULD UNDERSTAND:

1. The prevalence and importance of intercultural communication in today's world.
2. The role of perception in intercultural communication.
3. Five key values that help shape a culture's communication norms.
4. The factors that shape a culture's verbal codes, nonverbal codes, and decoding of messages.
5. The attitudes, knowledge, and skills required for intercultural communication competence.

YOU SHOULD BE ABLE TO:

1. Identify the range and significance of intercultural contacts you are likely to experience.
2. Describe a set of cultural values, norms, and codes different from yours that could result in different cultural communication patterns.
3. Identify your tolerance for ambiguity and your open-mindedness to different cultural communication patterns.
4. Develop a strategy for interacting with people of cultural backgrounds different from your own.

KEY TERMS

- Achievement culture (49)
- Co-culture (38)
- Collectivistic culture (45)
- Culture (37)
- Ethnocentrism (60)
- High-context culture (44)
- Individualistic culture (45)
- In-group (38)
- Intercultural communication (40)
- Low-context culture (44)
- Nurturing culture (49)
- Out-group (38)
- Power distance (47)
- Prejudice (60)
- Salience (41)
- Social identity (38)
- Uncertainty avoidance (48)

Over a half-century ago, Marshall McLuhan (1964) coined the metaphor of the world as a "global village" where members of every nation are connected by communication technology. Just like members of a traditional village, McLuhan suggested, the affairs and fates of the occupants of planet Earth are connected—for better or worse. This analysis has proven to be increasingly true in the years since McLuhan introduced it. The following factors, outlined by communication scholars Larry Samovar and his colleagues (2007), make the citizens of the world increasingly connected.

Demographic changes are transforming the United States into a microcosm of the global village. Immigration has made North American society increasingly multicultural and multiethnic. (See Figure 2.1.) In the first decade of the new millennium, females, minorities, and immigrants constitute almost 85 percent of those entering the workforce—an enormous change from the mostly white male labor pool of the previous century.

Relatively cheap transportation has reduced the barrier of distance, making international travel easier for more people than ever before. Erla Zwingle

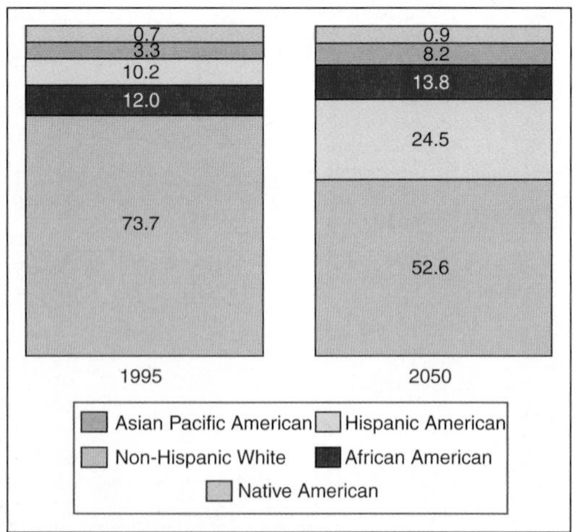

FIGURE 2.1 U.S. Population by Race, 1995 and 2050 (projected)
Adapted from Shinagawa, L. H. (1997). *Atlas of American diversity.* Lanham, MD: Altamira, a division of Rowan & Littlefield, p. 150.

(1999, p. 12) captures the degree to which worldwide travel and communication have blended cultures:

> That I should be sitting in a coffee shop in London drinking Italian espresso served by an Algerian waiter to the strains of the Beach Boys singing "I wish they all could be California girls. . . ." Or hanging around a pub in New Delhi that serves Lebanese cuisine to the music of a Filipino band in rooms decorated with barrels of Irish stout, a stuffed hippo head, and a vintage poster announcing the Grand Ole Opry concert to be given at the high school in Douglas, Georgia. Some Japanese are fanatics for flamenco. Denmark imports five times as much Italian pasta as it did ten years ago. The classic American blond Barbie doll now comes in some 30 national varieties—and this year emerged as Austrian and Moroccan.

Thanks to the growth in communication technology, even stay-at-homes have access to virtually the entire world, and commerce has changed in ways that would have been unimaginable just a generation ago. International telephone service is affordable and efficient. The Internet allows users around the world to share information with one another instantaneously, at a cost no greater than exchanging computer messages with someone in the same town. Organizations span the globe, and their members form virtual teams that "meet" in cyberspace. The extent to which new communication technology has influenced the world is clear from the title of a recent book: *From Rural Village to Global Village: Telecommunications for Development in the Information Age* (Hudson, 2006).

Given these changes, it makes sense to examine how communication operates when members of different cultures interact. Our examination will show that there is, indeed, a cultural dimension to human communication—and that when people from different backgrounds interact, they face a set of challenges different from those that arise when members of the same culture communicate (Olaniran, 2004). In this chapter we outline some of those differences and offer suggestions on how to communicate most effectively when encountering people from other backgrounds.

Fundamental Concepts

Before going any further, we need to clarify two important concepts: *culture* and *intercultural communication.* We also need to look at what distinguishes intercultural communication from interpersonal communication.

CULTURE AND CO-CULTURE

Defining **culture** isn't an easy task. One early survey of scholarly literature revealed 500 definitions, phrasings, and uses of the concept (Kroeber & Kluckholn, 1952). For our purposes, Larry Samovar and Richard Porter (2007) offer a clear and comprehensive definition of *culture:* "the language, values, beliefs, traditions, and customs people share and learn."

FOCUS ON RESEARCH

Communicating in Two Cultures: The Dual Lives of First-Generation College Students

They come from a culture that some of them describe as "supportive but clueless" while daily entering an "alien culture" as "strangers in a strange land." Who are these sojourners? They are first-generation college (FGC) students. According to Mark Orbe and Christopher Groscurth, FGC students are a co-culture in the world of higher education, and their communication patterns change dramatically between school and home.

Because no one in their family has attended college, FGC students often feel a step behind in their preparation for higher education. One way they cope is to engage in *assimilation* behaviors—that is, they go out of their way to fit in with what they view as the "college crowd." Sometimes assimilating requires self-censorship, as FGC students avoid discussions that might reveal their educational or socioeconomic backgrounds. In addition, some FGC students say they overcompensate by studying harder and getting more involved on campus than their non-FGC classmates, just to prove they belong in the college culture.

At home, FGC students also engage in self-censorship—but for different reasons. They are cautious when talking about college life for fear of threatening and alienating their families. In fact, many FGC students say they set up barriers and pull away from family interactions because the rewards of communicating at home don't always outweigh the costs. The only exception is that some feel a need to model their new educational status to younger family members so "they can see that it can be done."

It's clear that many FGC students feel the intercultural strain of "trying to live simultaneously in two vastly different worlds." The good news is that when FGC students achieve their educational goals, their families are often the ones who cheer longest and loudest about their successes.

Orbe, M. P., & Groscurth, C. R. (2004). A co-cultural theoretical analysis of communicating on campus and at home: Exploring the negotiation strategies of first-generation college (FGC) students. *Qualitative Research Reports in Communication, 5,* 41–47.

This definition shows that culture is, to a great extent, a matter of *perception* and *definition.* When you identify yourself as a member of a culture, you must not only share certain characteristics, but you must also recognize yourself and others like you as possessing these features and see others who don't possess them as members of different categories. For example, eye color doesn't seem like a significant factor in distinguishing "us" from "them," while skin color plays a more important role, at least in some cases. It's not hard to imagine a society where the opposite were true. Social scientists use the label **in-groups** to describe groups with which we identify and **out-groups** to label those that we view as different (Tajfel & Turner, 1992). Cultural membership contributes to every person's **social identity**—the part of the self-concept that is based on membership in groups. Your answer to the question "Who are you?" would probably include social categories such as your ethnicity and nationality. Social scientists use the term **co-culture** to describe the perception of membership in a group that is part of an encompassing culture (Orbe

& Spellers, 2005). Members of these co-cultures often develop unique patterns of communication. For example, the Focus on Research profile on page 38 shows how first-generation college students communicate to manage the challenges of fitting into the world of higher education. Co-cultures in North American society include

- age (e.g., teens, senior citizens)
- race/ethnicity (e.g., African American, Latino)
- sexual orientation (e.g., lesbian, gay male)
- nationality (e.g., immigrants from a particular country, expatriates)
- physical disability (e.g., wheelchair users, deaf persons)
- religion (e.g., Church of Jesus Christ of Latter Day Saints, Muslim)
- activity (e.g., biker, gamer)

Membership in co-cultures can be a source of enrichment and pride. But when the group is stigmatized by others, being connected with a co-culture isn't always so fulfilling. For instance, Patrice Buzzanell (1999) describes how members of underrepresented groups are disadvantaged in employment interviews, where the rules are established by the dominant culture. Studies of Jamaican children (Ferguson & Cramer, 2007) and Latino children (Golash-Boza & Darity, 2008) indicate that skin color influences self-identification and self-esteem. In other cases, co-cultures voluntarily embrace the chance to distinguish themselves from society at large—such as teens creating slang that is understood only by members of their in-group. Some scholars (e.g., Tannen, 1990, 1994; Kimmel, 2008; Wood, 2005) and writers in the popular press (e.g., Gray, 1992) have even characterized men and women as belonging to different co-cultures because their communication styles are so different. As you read this chapter, you will notice that many of the communication challenges that arise between members of different cultures also operate when people from different co-cultures interact.

DARK SIDE OF COMMUNICATION

Dangerous Identity: Gangs as Co-cultures

Gangs have been part of the American landscape since the early 19th century, when groups of young immigrants banded together for solidarity and protection. By the first decade of the 21st century, there were almost 25,000 gangs with over 700,000 active members across the United States.

Gangs fit the definition of a co-culture: Members have a well-defined identity, both among themselves and in the outside world. This sense of belonging is often reflected in distinctive language and nonverbal markers, such as clothing, tattoos, and hand signals.

Now, as in the past, gangs provide people who are marginalized by society a sense of identity and security in an often dangerous and hostile world. Sadly, though, these benefits come at considerable cost. When compared to similar youths, gang members have higher rates of delinquency and drug use. They commit more violent offenses and have higher arrest rates.

Gangs are a serious and complicated problem, both for members and for society at large. The challenge is to find ways for young people to gain the same sense of belonging, security, and prestige that everyone wants in a way that is both safe and constructive.

National Youth Violence Prevention Resource Center. (2007, December 20). *Gangs fact sheet.* Available at: http://www.safeyouth.org/scripts/facts/gangs.asp

U.S. Department of Justice. (2002, February). *OJJDP fact sheet: Highlights of the 2000 National Youth Gang Survey.* Washington, DC: Office of Juvenile Justice and Delinquency Prevention. Available at: http://www.ncjrs.gov/pdffiles1/ojjdp/fs200204.pdf

INTERCULTURAL COMMUNICATION

Having defined culture, we can go on to define **intercultural communication** as the process that occurs when members of two or more cultures or co-cultures exchange messages in a manner that is influenced by their different cultural perceptions and symbol systems, both verbal and nonverbal (Samovar et al., 2007).

Since all of us belong to many groups (ethnic, economic, interest-based, age, etc.), you might be asking yourself whether there is any communication that *isn't* intercultural or at least co-cultural. The answer to this question is "yes," for two reasons. First, even in an increasingly diverse world, there are still plenty of relationships in which people share a basically common background. The Irish marchers in a St. Patrick's Day parade, the suburban-bred group of men who play poker every other Friday night, and the members of a college sorority or fraternity are likely to share fundamentally similar personal histories and, therefore, have similar norms, customs, and values.

Even when people with different cultural backgrounds communicate, those differences may not be important (Singer, 1998). David may be a Jewish male whose ancestors came from eastern Europe while Lisa is a third-generation Japanese person whose parents are practicing Christians, but they have created a life together that usually is more significant than their differences and that leaves them able to deal comfortably with those differences when they do arise.

Rather than classifying some exchanges as intercultural and others as free from cultural influences, it's more accurate to talk about *degrees* of cultural significance (Lustig & Koester, 2005). Encounters can fit along a spectrum of "interculturalness." At the "most intercultural" end are situations where differences between the backgrounds and beliefs of communicators are high. A traveler visiting a new country for the first time with

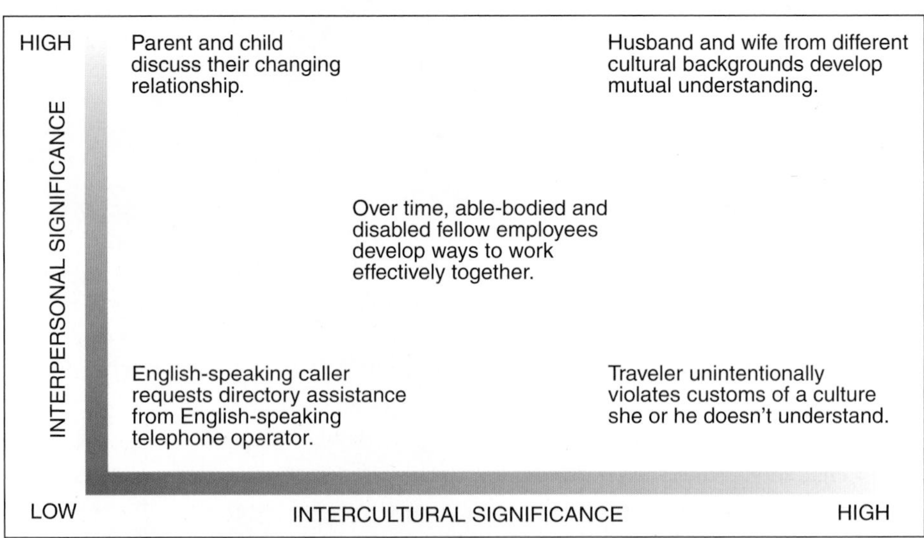

FIGURE 2.2 Some Possible Interactions among Interpersonal and Intercultural Dimensions of Person-to-Person Communication

little knowledge of local society would be an obvious example. At the "least intercultural" end of the spectrum fall exchanges where cultural differences make little difference. A student from Los Angeles who attends a small liberal arts college in the Midwest might find life somewhat different, but the adjustment would be far less difficult than that for the international traveler. In between these extremes falls a whole range of encounters in which culture plays varying roles.

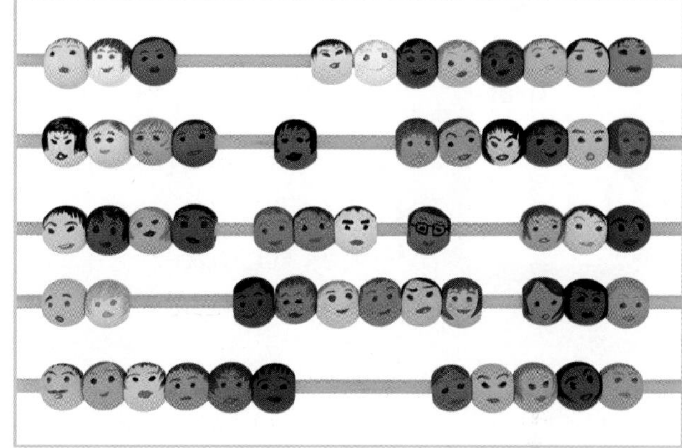

Note that intercultural communication (at least as we'll use the term here) doesn't always occur when people from different cultures interact. The cultural backgrounds, perceptions, and symbol systems of the participants must have a significant impact on the exchange before we can say that culture has made a difference. Social scientists use the term **salience** to describe how much weight we attach to a particular person or phenomenon. Consider a few examples where culture has little or no salience:

- A group of preschool children is playing together in a park. These 3-year-olds don't recognize the fact that their parents may come from different countries, or even that they don't speak the same language. At this point we wouldn't say that intercultural communication is taking place. Only when cultural factors become salient (diet, sharing, or parental discipline, for example) do the children begin to think of one another as different.

- Members of a school basketball team—some Asian, some black, some Latino, and some white—are intent on winning the league championship. During a game, cultural distinctions aren't salient. There's plenty of communication, but it isn't fundamentally intercultural. Away from their games, the players are friendly when they encounter one another, but they rarely socialize. If they did, they might notice some fundamental differences in the way members of each group communicate.

- A husband and wife were raised in homes with different religious traditions. Most of the time their religious heritage makes little difference, and the partners view themselves as a unified couple. Every so often, however—perhaps during the holidays or when meeting members of each other's family—the different backgrounds are more salient. At those times we can imagine the partners feeling quite different from each other—thinking of themselves as members of separate cultures.

These examples show that in order to view ourselves as a member of a culture, there has to be some distinction between "us" and "them," between in- and out-group. We may not always be able to say precisely what the differences are. We may have only a gut feeling that something is going on, and there are occasions when cultural influences are powerful but so subtle that they go unrecognized.

INTERPERSONAL AND INTERCULTURAL COMMUNICATION

What is the relationship between intercultural communication and interpersonal relationships? William Gudykunst and Young Kim (2002) summarize an approach that helps answer this question. They suggest that interpersonal and intercultural factors combine to form a two-by-two matrix in which the importance of interpersonal communication forms one dimension and intercultural significance forms the second one (Figure 2.2). This model shows that some interpersonal transactions (for example, a conversation between two siblings who have been raised in the same household) have virtually no intercultural elements. Other encounters (such as a traveler from Senegal trying to get directions from a Ukrainian taxi driver in New York City) are almost exclusively intercultural, without the personal dimensions that we have discussed throughout this book.

Still other exchanges—the most interesting ones for our purposes—contain elements of both intercultural and interpersonal communication. This range of encounters is broad in the global village: Business people from different backgrounds try to wrap up a deal; U.S. born and immigrant children learn to get along in school; health care educators seek effective ways to serve patients from around the world; neighbors from different racial or ethnic backgrounds look for ways to make their streets safer and cleaner; suburban-bred teachers seek common ground with inner-city students—the list seems almost endless. In situations like these, communicators are trying to establish some degree of relationship and understanding. When they do find ways of connecting that account for, and even transcend, cultural differences, communicators have created what Fred Casmir (1991) calls a "third culture": a unique relationship shared by two or more people.

Where Cultures and Communication Styles Collide: *Spanglish*

As its name implies, *Spanglish* explores communication at the intersection of two cultures. Flor (Paz Vega) is an undocumented Latina immigrant, hired by Deborah and John Clasky (Tea Leoni and Adam Sandler) to take care of their children and the family's upscale homes in Bel-Air and Malibu. After Flor's daughter, Christina (Shelbie Bruce), moves in with the family, Deborah uses all the tools of charm and privilege at her disposal to win the young Latina's affection. (After Deborah takes Christina shopping, the teen declares that Deborah is "the most amazing white woman" she has ever known.) John intervenes in the growing conflict between the two mothers, showing emotion and compassion that surprises Christina, who says, "To someone with firsthand knowledge of Latin machismo, he seemed to have the emotions of a Mexican . . . woman."

It's not hard to see what director James L. Brooks thinks about these characters: John is a sweet but somewhat ineffectual father. Deborah is manic, insensitive, and casually racist. By contrast, Flor is kind, honest, and genuinely loving. Still, *Spanglish* illustrates how cultural background intersects with personality to create a blend of factors that makes communication both fascinating (to observers) and challenging (to those living the story). Reflecting the world beyond Hollywood, *Spanglish* looks at how different cultures approach parenting and gender roles, the challenges of identity and assimilation, and the universal values of pride, influence, self-esteem, and love.

CULTURAL DIFFERENCES AS GENERALIZATIONS

The following pages spell out a variety of ways communication varies from one culture to another. While these variations can sometimes be significant,

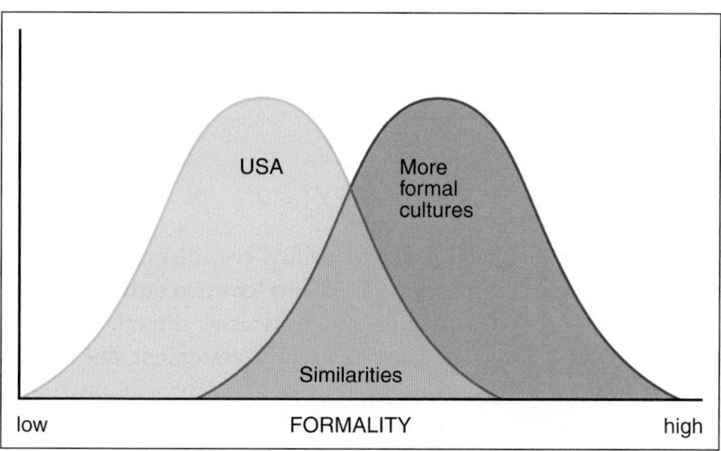

FIGURE 2.3 Differences and Similarities within and between Cultures
Adapted from Trompenaars, F. (1994). *Riding the waves of culture.* New York: McGraw-Hill/Irwin, p. 28.

it's important to remember that cultural practices aren't *totally* different: People from varied backgrounds often share enough common ground to make relationships work. When all the physical and social attributes of human beings are added up, there are far more similarities than differences among the people of the world.

Moreover, there are sometimes greater differences *within* cultures than *between* them. Consider the matter of formality as an example: By most measures, U.S. culture is far more casual than many others. But Figure 2.3 shows that there may be more common ground between a formal American and a casual member of a formal culture than there is between two Americans with vastly differing levels of formality. Furthermore, within every culture, members display a wide range of communication styles. For instance, while most Asian cultures tend to be collectivistic, many members of those cultures would identify themselves as individualists. The parents next door might make decisions for their children with unquestioned authority, while you were raised in a much more egalitarian family. For these reasons, it's important to remember that generalizations—even when accurate and helpful—don't apply to every member of a group.

Cultural Values and Norms

Some cultural influences on communication are obvious. You don't have to be a scholar or researcher to appreciate how different languages or customs can make communication between groups both interesting and challenging. However, in addition to these obvious differences, some far less visible values and norms shape how members of cultures think and act (Gudykunst & Matsumoto, 1996). In this section we look at five of these subtle yet vitally important values and norms that shape the way members of a culture communicate. Unless communicators are aware of these differences, they may see people from other cultures as unusual—or even offensive—without realizing that their apparently odd behavior comes from following a different set of beliefs and unwritten rules about the "proper" way to communicate.

HIGH VERSUS LOW CONTEXT

Anthropologist Edward Hall (1959) identified two distinct ways that members of various cultures deliver messages. A **low-context culture** uses language primarily to express thoughts, feelings, and ideas as directly as possible. To low-context communicators, the meaning of a statement lies in the words spoken. By contrast, a **high-context culture** relies heavily on subtle, often nonverbal cues to maintain social harmony (Ambady et al., 1996; Ishikawa & Yamazaki, 2005). Rather than upsetting others by speaking directly, communicators in these societies learn to discover meaning from the context in which a message is delivered: the nonverbal behaviors of the speaker, the history of the relationship, and the general social rules that govern interaction between people. Table 2.1 summarizes some key differences in how people from low- and high-context cultures use language.

Mainstream culture in the United States, Canada, Northern Europe, and Israel falls toward the low-context end of the scale. Longtime residents generally value straight-talk and grow impatient with "beating around the bush." By contrast, most Asian and Middle Eastern cultures fit the high-context pattern and can be offended by the bluntness of low-context communication styles.

In many Asian societies, for example, maintaining harmony is important, so communicators avoid speaking directly if that threatens another person's "face," or dignity. For this reason, communicators raised in Japanese or Korean cultures are less likely than Americans to offer a clear "no" to an undesirable request. Instead, they would probably use roundabout expressions like "I agree with you in principle, but . . ." or "I sympathize with you. . . ." As T. R. Reid (1999, p. 84) explains, "Japanese people avoid saying 'no,' not because they are dishonest, but because saying a flat 'no' might cause disappointment and ill-feeling. . . . So the Japanese fall back on their arsenal of euphemisms: 'That would be difficult.' 'We'll give your request careful thought.' 'Excuse me, but. . . .'"

Even the interpretation of insults varies from high- to low-context cultures. Laura Leets (2001, 2003) presented European Americans and people of color—Asian American, African American, and Latino—with examples of racist messages, all of which were aimed at people of color. Some of these messages were direct and blatantly offensive, while others were indirect and less overtly racist. Leets found that European American participants judged the directly racist messages as more hurtful, while Asian American respondents rated the indirectly racist comments as more damaging. The researcher concluded that the traditional Asian tendency to favor high-context messages explains why Asian Americans were more offended by indirectly racist speech.

To members of high-context cultures, communicators with a low-context style can appear overly talkative, lacking in subtlety, and redundant. On the

TABLE 2.1 ***High-Context and Low-Context Communication Styles***

LOW CONTEXT	HIGH CONTEXT
Majority of information carried in explicit verbal messages, with less focus on the situational context.	Important information carried in contextual cues such as time, place, relationship, situation. Less reliance on explicit verbal messages.
Self-expression valued. Communicators state opinions and desires directly and strive to persuade others to accept their own viewpoint.	Relational harmony valued and maintained by indirect expression of options. Communicators abstain from saying "no" directly.
Clear, eloquent speech considered praiseworthy. Verbal fluency admired.	Communicators talk "around" the point, allowing the others to fill in the missing pieces. Ambiguity and use of silence admired.

Adapted from Adler, R. B., & Elmhorst, J. (2008). *Communicating at work: Principles and practices for business and the professions* (9th ed., p. 31). New York: McGraw-Hill.

other hand, to people from low-context backgrounds, high-context communicators often seem unexpressive, or even dishonest. It is easy to see how the clash between directness and indirectness can aggravate problems between straight-talking, low-context Israelis and their Arab neighbors, whose high-context culture stresses smooth interaction. Israelis might view their Arab counterparts as evasive, while the Arabs might perceive the Israelis as insensitive and blunt.

INDIVIDUALISM VERSUS COLLECTIVISM

Some cultures value the individual, while others place greater emphasis on the group. Members of an **individualistic culture** view their primary responsibility as helping themselves, whereas communicators in **collectivistic cultures** feel loyalties and obligations to an in-group: one's extended family, community, or even the organization one works for (Triandis, 1995). Individualistic cultures also are characterized by self-reliance and competition, whereas members of a collectivistic culture are more attentive to and concerned with the opinions of significant others. The consequences of a culture's individualistic-collectivistic orientation are so powerful that some scholars (e.g., Andersen, 1999) have labeled it as the most fundamental dimension of cultural differences.

The United States is one of the world's more individualistic countries, along with Canada, Australia, and Great Britain. Latin American and Asian cultures are generally more collectivistic (Hofstede, 1984, 2003). Table 2.2 summarizes some differences between individualistic and collectivistic cultures.

Members of individualistic cultures tend to view themselves in terms of what they *do,* while people in collectivistic cultures are more likely to define

TABLE 2.2 ***The Self in Individualistic and Collectivistic Cultures***

INDIVIDUALISTIC CULTURES	COLLECTIVISTIC CULTURES
Self is separate, unique individual; should be independent, self-sufficient.	People belong to extended families or in-groups; "we" or group orientation.
Individual should take care of himself or herself and immediate family.	Person should take care of extended family before self.
Many flexible group memberships; friendships based on shared interests and activities.	Emphasis on belonging to a very few permanent in-groups, which have a strong influence over the person
Reward for individual achievement and initiative; individual decision encouraged; individual credit and blame assigned.	Reward for contribution to group goals and well-being; cooperation with in-group members; group decisions valued; credit and blame shared
High value on autonomy, change, youth, individual security, equality.	High value on duty, order, tradition, age, group security, status, and hierarchy.

Adapted by Sandra Sudweeks from Triandis, H. C. (1990). Cross-cultural studies of individualism and collectivism. In J. Berman (Ed.), *Nebraska symposium on motivation* (pp. 41–133). Lincoln: University of Nebraska Press; and Hall, E. T. (1959). *Beyond culture.* New York: Doubleday.

themselves in terms of group membership. For instance, members of several cultures were asked to answer the question "Who am I?" 20 times (DeAngelis, 1992b). North Americans were likely to answer by giving individual factors ("I am athletic"; "I am short"). By contrast, members of more collectivistic societies—Chinese, Filipinos, Japanese, and some South Americans, for example—responded in terms of their relationships with others ("I am a father"; "I am an employee of XYZ Corporation").

Individualistic and collectivistic cultures have very different approaches to handling disagreements. Individualistic societies are relatively tolerant of conflicts and use a direct, solution-oriented approach. By contrast, members of collectivistic cultures are less direct and more accommodating (Cai & Fink, 2002; Ting-Toomey, 1988). Collectivistic societies produce team players, while individualistic ones are far more likely to produce and reward superstars. Some research (e.g., Moss et al., 2007) suggests that collectivist groups have a higher sense of teamwork and are more productive than groups of individualistic members.

The difference between individualistic and collectivistic cultures also shows up in the level of comfort or anxiety their respective members feel when communicating. In societies where the need to conform is great, there is a higher degree of communication apprehension. For example, as a group, residents of China, Korea, and Japan exhibit a significantly higher degree of anxiety about speaking out in public than do members of individualistic cultures such as the United States and Australia (Klopf, 1984). It's important to realize that different levels of communication apprehension don't mean that shyness is a "problem" in some cultures. In fact, just the opposite is true: In these societies reticence is valued. When the goal is to avoid being "the nail that sticks out," it's logical to feel nervous when you make yourself appear different by calling attention your way. A self-concept that includes "assertive" might make a Westerner feel proud, but in much of Asia it would more likely be cause for shame.

Struggling for Individuality in a Collectivist Culture: *Whale Rider*

In current-day New Zealand, 12-year-old Pai (Keisha Castle-Hughes) is coming of age in an all-Maori community led by her loving grandfather Koro (Rawiri Paratene).

Koro's most important task is to find and train the next chief. It's Maori tradition that all chiefs are male, but Pai is convinced that she could become the next leader. Despite his love for his granddaughter, Koro fiercely resists her ambition. His disapproving messages cause Pai great pain.

Anyone who appreciates the value of individualism will root for Pai. But from a collectivist perspective, it's easy to sympathize with her grandfather's expectation that his family should act in the best interests of the Maori community by honoring ancient traditions. There are moments when Pai is lost in discouragement and despair, and at one point she is tempted to leave her native community and live with her father in Europe. But she remains steadfast in the belief that her people need her, whether or not her grandfather realizes it.

Despite its focus on Maori culture, *Whale Rider* illustrates a broader theme—the challenge of creating a unique identity in the face of a community with different ideas about who we should be.

POWER DISTANCE

For members of democratic societies, the principle embodied in the U.S. Declaration of Independence that "all men [and women] are created equal" is so fundamental that we accept it without question. However, not all cultures share this belief. Some operate on the assumption that certain groups of people (an aristocracy or an economic class, for example) and some institutions (such as a church or the government) have the right to control the lives of individuals. Geert Hofstede (1984) coined the term **power distance** to describe the degree to which members of a society accept an unequal distribution of power.

Cultures with low power difference believe in minimizing the difference between various social classes. In fact, people from cultures with low power difference, compared with those from a high power culture, actually see fewer distinctions in the verbal and nonverbal behavior of high- and low-status individuals with whom they interact (Kowner & Wiseman, 2003). Rich and poor, educated and uneducated groups may still exist, but there is a pervasive belief in low power difference cultures that one person is as good as another regardless of his or her station in life. Low power difference cultures also support the notion that challenging authority is acceptable—even desirable. Members aren't necessarily punished for raising questions about the status quo. According to Hofstede's research, U.S. and Canadian societies have relatively low power distance, though not the lowest in the world. Austria, Denmark, Israel, and New Zealand proved to be the most egalitarian countries. At the other end of the spectrum are countries with a high degree of power distance: Philippines, Mexico, Venezuela, India, and Singapore.

The degree of power distance in a culture is reflected in key relationships (Lustig & Koester, 1999). Children who are raised in cultures with

high power difference are expected to obey their parents and other authority figures to a degree that would astonish most children raised in the United States or Canada. Power automatically comes with age in many countries. For example, the Korean language has separate terms for *older brother, oldest brother, younger sister, youngest sister,* and so on. Parents in cultures with low power distance don't expect the same degree of unquestioning obedience. They are not surprised when children ask "Why?" when presented with a request or demand.

On-the-job communication is different in low- and high-power-distance societies (Cohen, 2007). In countries with higher degrees of power distance, employees have much less input into the way they perform their work. In fact, workers from these cultures are likely to feel uncomfortable when given freedom to make their own decisions or when a more egalitarian boss asks for their opinion: They prefer to view their bosses as benevolent decision makers. The reverse is true when management from a culture with an egalitarian tradition tries to do business in a country whose workers are used to high power distance. They can be surprised to find that employees do not expect much say in decisions and do not feel unappreciated when they aren't consulted. They may regard dutiful, submissive, respectful employees as lacking initiative and creativity—traits that helped them gain promotions back home. Given these differences, it's easy to understand why multinational companies need to consider fundamental differences in communication values and behavior when they set up shop in a new country.

UNCERTAINTY AVOIDANCE

The desire to resolve uncertainty seems to be a trait shared by people around the world (Berger, 1988). While uncertainty may be universal, cultures have different ways of coping with an unpredictable future. Hofstede (1984, 2003) uses the term **uncertainty avoidance** to reflect the degree to which members of a culture feel threatened by ambiguous situations and how much they try to avoid them. He developed an uncertainty avoidance index (UAI) to measure differing degrees of uncertainty avoidance around the world. Residents of some countries (including Singapore, Great Britain, Denmark, Sweden, Hong Kong, and the United States) proved to be relatively unthreatened by change, while others (such as natives of Belgium, Greece, Japan, and Portugal) found new or ambiguous situations discomfiting.

A culture's degree of uncertainty avoidance is reflected in the way its members communicate. In countries that avoid uncertainty, deviant people and ideas are considered dangerous, and intolerance is high (Samovar &

Porter, 2004). People in these cultures are especially concerned with security, so they have a strong need for clearly defined rules and regulations. It's easy to imagine how most relationships in cultures with a high UAI—family, work, friendships, and romance—are likely to fit a predictable pattern. By contrast, people in a culture that is less threatened by the new and unexpected are more likely to tolerate—or even welcome—people who don't fit the norm. Following established rules and patterns isn't necessarily expected, and different behavior might even be welcomed. This difference shows up in the acceptability of new products and ideas: Innovation is high in countries that are low on uncertainty avoidance, and imitation is high in countries that are high on uncertainty avoidance (Yaveroglu & Donthu, 2002).

When a mainstream North American who is relatively comfortable with change and novelty spends time with someone from a high UAI culture such as Japan, both communicators may find the other behaving in disconcerting ways. The North American is likely to view the Japanese as rigid and overly controlled, while the Japanese would probably regard the North American as undisciplined, overly tolerant, and generally lacking self-control. On the other hand, if the communicators understand how their cultural conditioning affects their style, then they are more likely to understand, and maybe even learn from, the other's different style.

ACHIEVEMENT VERSUS NURTURING

The term **achievement culture** describes societies that place a high value on material success and a focus on the task at hand, while **nurturing culture** is a descriptive term for cultures that regard the support of relationships as an especially important goal. Hofstede (1984, 2003) referred to the first group as "masculine" and the second as "feminine," based on the stereotypical focus of each sex. In some ways, the terms "hard" and "soft" are more descriptive. "Hard" cultures that emphasize achievement include Japan, Switzerland, and Germany. "Softer," more nurturing cultures, include the Scandinavian countries (Norway, Sweden, and Denmark), Spain, and France.

The portrait of an effective communicator varies from one type of culture to another. Most notably, achievement-oriented societies prescribe different roles for women and men. In these cultures, male virtues include assertiveness, independence, and individuality. Women who exhibit these traits may be viewed unfavorably for "acting like a man." By contrast, in nurturing societies there is little difference between the expected behavior for men and women: The ideal profile for both sexes is one of cooperation, and of holding the belief that personal relationships are at least as important as material achievement.

As you think about the cultural values described here, you may realize that they don't just arise between people from different countries. In today's increasingly multicultural society, people from different cultural backgrounds are likely to encounter one another "at home," in the country they share. Consider the United States and Canada in the new millennium: Native Americans;

Latinos from the Caribbean, Mexico, and South America; Middle Easterners; and Asians from China, Japan, Korea, Vietnam, and other countries mingle with first-generation and longtime residents whose ancestors came from Europe. This is a cultural mixture that often seems less like a melting pot than a salad bowl, in which the many "ingredients" retain much of their own identity.

REFLECTION

Power Distance, Achievement, and Nurturing in Two Cultures

I have been a university student in both the United States and China. The contrast in standards and expectations is almost as great as the difference in languages.

In China, the power distance between teachers and students is much larger. We are taught to respect our teachers, and to do whatever they say without challenging. In the U.S, it's more acceptable to ask "why," or even to dispute a teacher's judgment.

Another difference involves achievement and nurturing. In China, you are expected to achieve success through hard work. If you don't succeed, there are plenty of other students who will take your place. In the United States, there is much more support. Students are encouraged to ask for help, and there are many more people in the system ready to offer support.

I'm not sure which system produces better results, but the way teachers and students communicate is certainly different.

Codes and Culture

At this point, you probably have a healthy appreciation for the challenges that arise when two or more people try to communicate with one another. These challenges become even greater when the communicators use different verbal and nonverbal communication systems.

VERBAL CODES

Although there are remarkable similarities between the world's many languages (Brown, 1991), they also differ in important respects that affect the way their speakers communicate with one another and with speakers of other tongues. The following sections outline some of those factors.

Language and Identity If you live in a culture where everyone speaks the same tongue, then language will have little noticeable impact on how you view yourself and others. But when some members of a society speak the dominant language and others speak a minority tongue, or when that second language is not prestigious, the sense of being a member of an out-group is strong. At this point the speaker of a nondominant language can react in one of two ways: either feel pressured to assimilate by speaking the "better" language, or refuse to accommodate to the majority language and maintain loyalty to the ethnic tongue (Giles et al., 1992c). This problem can be acute in countries like the United States, where many students are children of immigrant parents (Chiang & Schmida, 2002). In either case, the impact of language on the self-concept is powerful. On one hand, the feeling is likely to be "I'm not as good as speakers of the native language," and on the other, the belief is "There's something unique and worth preserving in my language" (Bergman et al., 2008).

A case study of Latino managers illustrates the dilemma of speaking a nondominant language (Banks, 1987). The managers, employees in a European American organization, felt their Mexican identity threatened when they found that the road to advancement would be smoother if they deemphasized their Spanish and adopted a more colloquial English style of speaking.

Even the names a culture uses to identify its members reflect its values and shape the way its members relate to one another. When asked to identify themselves, individualistic Americans, Canadians, Australians, and Europeans would probably respond by giving their first name, surname, street, town, and country. Many Asians do it the other way around (Servaes, 1989). If you ask Hindus for their identity, they will give you their caste and village and then their name. The Sanskrit formula for identifying oneself begins with lineage and goes on to state family and house, and ends with one's personal name (Bharti, 1985). The same collectivist orientation is reflected in Chinese written language, where the pronoun *I* looks very similar to the word for *selfish* (Samovar & Porter, 2004). The Japanese language has no equivalent to the English pronoun *I*. Instead, different words are used to refer to one's self depending on the social situation, age, gender, and other social characteristics (Gudykunst, 1993a).

Even within a language system, the labels that members of a co-culture use to define themselves can both reflect and help define their sense of identity (Jandt, 2007). In one study, Linda Larkey and her associates (1993) surveyed a cross-section of African Americans to identify the significance of the labels they used to identify themselves. The most commonly used terms revealed different orientations toward the user's sense of self as a member of a distinct co-culture. Communicators who identified themselves as "black" generally were oriented toward the goals of unity and acceptability, while those who preferred "African American" tended to focus more on their blended heritage. The researchers detected a trend toward use of the term "African American," which they interpreted as a move toward self-determination in meeting the challenge of maintaining a positive identity.

In more recent studies, Niven and Zilber (2000) tested the notion that people who use the term "African American" are more liberal than those who use the term "black." They analyzed 3,103 speeches made by members of the U.S. House of Representatives and Senate and found that, indeed, political liberals were more likely to choose African American than black. Anglin and Whaley (2006) found that college students who labeled themselves as "African American" reported more experiences of growing up that emphasized racial struggle, cultural survival, and the importance of ethnic pride than did students who identified themselves as West Indian/Caribbean, African, or black.

Verbal Communication Styles Using language is more than just a matter of choosing a particular group of words to convey an idea. Each language has its own unique style that distinguishes it from others. Matters like the amount of formality or informality, precision or vagueness, and brevity or detail are major ingredients in speaking competently. When a communicator tries to use the verbal style from one culture in a different one, problems are likely to arise.

Gudykunst and Ting-Toomey (1988) describe three important types of cultural differences in verbal style. One is *directness* or *indirectness.* We have already discussed how low-context cultures use language primarily to express thoughts, feelings, and ideas as clearly, directly, and logically as possible, while high-context cultures may speak less directly, using language to maintain social harmony.

Another way in which language styles can vary across cultures is in terms of whether they are *elaborate* or *succinct.* For instance, speakers of Arabic commonly use language that is much more rich and expressive than normally found in English. Strong assertions and exaggerations that would sound ridiculous in English are a common feature of Arabic. This contrast in linguistic style can lead to misunderstandings between people from different backgrounds:

> First, an Arab feels compelled to overexert in almost all types of communication because others expect him [or her] to. If an Arab says exactly what he [or she] means without the expected assertion, other Arabs may still think that he [or she] means the opposite. For example, a simple "no" from a guest to the host's requests to eat more or drink more will not suffice. To convey the meaning that he [or she] is actually full, the guest must keep repeating "no" several times, coupling it with an oath such as "By God" or "I swear to God." Second, an Arab often fails to realize that others, particularly foreigners, may mean exactly what they say even though their language is simple. To the Arabs, a simple "no" may mean the indirectly expressed consent and encouragement of a coquettish woman. On the other hand, a simple consent may mean the rejection of a hypocritical politician. (Almaney & Alwan, 1982, p. 84)

Succinctness is most extreme in cultures where silence is valued. In many Native American cultures, for example, the favored way to handle ambiguous social situations is to remain quiet (Basso, 1970; Hett, 1993). When you contrast this silent style to the talkativeness that is common when people first meet in mainstream American cultures, it's easy to imagine how the first encounter between an Apache or Navajo and a European American might be uncomfortable for both people.

A third way that languages differ from one culture to another involves *formality* and *informality.* One guidebook for British readers who want to understand how Americans communicate describes the openness and informality that characterizes U.S. culture:

> Visitors may be overwhelmed by the sheer exuberant friendliness of Americans, especially in the central and southern parts of the country. Sit next to an American on an airplane and he will immediately address you by your first name, ask "So—how do you like it in the States?," explain his recent divorce in intimate detail, invite you home for dinner, offer to lend you money, and wrap you in a warm hug on parting. This does not necessarily mean he will remember your name the next day. Americans are friendly because they just can't help it; they like to be neighbourly and want to be liked. (Faul, 1994, pp. 3–4)

The informal approach that characterizes communication in countries like the United States is quite different from the great concern for propriety in many parts of Asia and Africa. Formality isn't so much a matter of using correct grammar as of defining social relationships. For example, there are different degrees of formality for speaking with old friends, nonacquaintances whose background one knows, and complete strangers. One sign of being a learned person in Korea is the ability to use language that recognizes these relational distinctions. When you contrast these sorts of distinctions with the casual friendliness many North Americans use even when talking with complete

FOCUS ON RESEARCH

Nonverbal Elements in Learning a New Language

When students learn a second language, the focus is often on linguistic elements such as vocabulary, grammar, and sentence structure. Communication scholars Anamai Damnet and Helen Borland suspected that learning about nonverbal codes, such as facial expression, eye contact, and body language, is equally important—and they conducted a study to investigate that point.

Two groups of Thai college students in the study attempted to enhance their English communication skills by watching scenes from movies such as *Erin Brockovich* and *While You Were Sleeping*. Prior to watching the clips, one group was given traditional instruction that focused on language issues. The second group was given additional instruction on understanding and interpreting nonverbal codes. Post-tests showed that the students who received nonverbal instruction understood more accurately the communication between the characters in the scenes they viewed.

Chapter 6 will discuss the importance of nonverbal communication in great detail. For now, these results remind us that intercultural communication involves interpreting both verbal and nonverbal codes—and that instruction about these codes can increase a person's intercultural competence.

Damnet, A., & Borland, H. (2007). Acquiring nonverbal competence in English language contexts: The case of Thai learners of English viewing American and Australian films. *Journal of Asian Pacific Communication, 17*, 127–148.

strangers, it's easy to see how a Korean might view American communicators as boorish and how an American might see Koreans as stiff and unfriendly.

NONVERBAL CODES

Many elements of nonverbal communication are shared by all humans, regardless of culture (Matsumoto, 2006; Schiefenhövel, 1997). For instance, people of all cultures convey messages through facial expressions and gestures. Furthermore, some of these physical displays have the same meaning everywhere. Crying is a universal sign of unhappiness or pain, and smiles signal friendly intentions. (Of course, smiles and tears may be insincere and manipulative, but their overt meanings are similar and constant in every culture.) The universality of many basic nonverbal behaviors was demonstrated in one study when inhabitants of the New Guinea rain forest, who had not been exposed to any media from the industrialized world, correctly identified the emotions on photos of U.S. citizens' faces (Ekman et al., 1969; Izard, 1971). The same universality was demonstrated in a study in which respondents in the United States and India (all between the ages of 15 and 60 years) were shown 14 facial expressions, but this time asked to say what had happened to cause the person to make the face (Haidt & Keltner, 1999).

Despite nonverbal similarities, the range of differences in nonverbal behavior is tremendous. For example, the meaning of some gestures varies from one culture to another. Consider the use of gestures such as the "OK" sign made by joining thumb and forefinger to form a circle. This gesture is a cheery affirmation to most Americans, but it has very different meanings in other parts of the world (Knapp & Hall, 2006). In France and Belgium it means "you're worth zero," in Japan it means "money," and in Greece and Turkey it is an insulting or vulgar sexual invitation. Given this sort of cross-cultural ambiguity, it's easy to visualize how an innocent tourist from the United States could wind up in serious trouble overseas without understanding why.

Less obvious cross-cultural differences can damage relationships without the communicators ever recognizing exactly what has gone wrong (Beaulieu, 2004; Hall, 1959). Anglo-Saxons use the largest zone of personal space, followed by Asians. People from the Mediterranean and Latinos use the closest distance. It is easy to visualize the awkward advance and retreat pattern that might occur when two diplomats or businesspeople from these cultures meet. The Middle Easterner would probably keep moving forward to close the gap that feels so wide, while the North American would continually back away. Both would probably feel uncomfortable without knowing why.

When people of different races or ethnicities interact, they sometimes use the space around them in ways that may reflect their attitudes. Randall and Delbridge (2005) found that blacks and whites in one North Carolina county, with a long history of interacting, reported sitting and standing closer to each other than to any other racial or ethnic group, with which they did not share this long history. Also, blacks kept greater distance from Mexicans than did whites, and Mexicans reported greater distance from African Americans than from whites.

Like distance, patterns of eye contact vary around the world. A direct gaze is considered appropriate for speakers in Latin America, the Arab world, and southern Europe. On the other hand, Asians, Indians, Pakistanis, and northern Europeans gaze at a listener peripherally or not at all. In either case, deviations from the norm are likely to make a culturally uneducated listener uncomfortable.

DECODING MESSAGES

Given all the differences in verbal and nonverbal communication systems, it's easy to see how decoding is an especially big challenge for communicators from different cultural backgrounds. The following pages show that the potential for misunderstanding is even greater than it might already seem.

Translation Anyone who has tried to translate ideas from one language to another knows that the potential for misunderstanding is always present. Sometimes the results of a bungled translation can be amusing. For example, the American manufacturers of Pet milk unknowingly introduced their product in French-speaking markets without realizing that the word *pet* in French means "to break wind" (Ricks, 1983).

Even choosing the right words during translation won't guarantee that non-native speakers will use an unfamiliar language correctly. For example, Japanese insurance companies warn their policyholders who are visiting the United States to avoid their cultural tendency to say "excuse me" or "I'm sorry" if they are involved in a traffic accident (Sugimoto, 1991). In Japan, apologizing is a traditional way to express goodwill and maintain social harmony, even if the person offering the apology is not at fault. But in the United States, an apology can be taken as an admission of guilt and result in Japanese tourists being held accountable after accidents for which they may not be responsible.

Difficult as they may be, translation and terminology constitute only one of many communication challenges facing members of different cultures and co-cultures. Now we need to look at some more subtle challenges that can make decoding messages from members of other cultures a challenging task.

Attributional Variations As you'll see in Chapter 4, attribution is the process of making sense of another person's behavior. Attribution is an unavoidable part of communicating: We have to form some sort of interpretation of what others' words and actions mean. But most behavior is so ambiguous that it can be interpreted in several ways. Furthermore, the usual tendency is to stick to the first attribution one makes. It's easy to see how this quick, sloppy attribution process can lead to making faulty interpretations—especially when communicators are from different cultural backgrounds.

In Table 2.3, a supervisor from the United States invites a subordinate from Greece to get involved in making a decision (Triandis, 1975, pp. 42–43). Since U.S. culture ranks relatively low on power distance, the supervisor encourages input from the employee. In Greece, however, the distance between bosses and their subordinates is much greater. Therefore, the Greek employee wants and expects to be told what to do. After all, it's the boss's job to give orders. Table 2.3 shows how the differing cultural beliefs shape both figures' attributions of the other's messages.

Culturally based attributions don't just occur between members of different nationalities. Even different use of dialects or accents by native-born members of the same country can affect a listener's evaluation of a speaker. Most cultures have a "standard dialect," which is spoken by high-status opinion leaders. For the most part, people who use the standard dialect are judged as being competent, intelligent, industrious, and confident (Ng & Bradac, 1993). By contrast, nonstandard speakers are likely to be rated less favorably. The likely attribution is "this person doesn't even speak correctly. There must be something wrong with him or her."

Patterns of Thought The way members of a culture are taught to think and reason shapes the way they interpret others' messages (Gudykunst & Kim,

TABLE 2.3 ***Culture Affects Attributions***

BEHAVIOR	ATTRIBUTION
American: How long will it take you to finish the report?	American: I asked him to participate.
Greek: I do not know. How long should it take?	Greek: His behavior makes no sense. He is the boss. Why doesn't he tell me?
	American: He refuses to take responsibility.
	Greek: I asked him for an order.
American: You are in the best position to analyze time requirements.	American: I press him to take responsibility for his own actions.
Greek: Ten days.	Greek: What nonsense! I better give him an answer.
American: Take fifteen. It is agreed you will do it in fifteen days?	American: He lacks the ability to estimate time; this estimate is totally inadequate.
Greek: These are my orders. Fifteen days.	American: I offer a contract.
American: Where is the report?	American: I am making sure he fulfills his contract.
Greek: It will be ready tomorrow.	Greek: He is asking for the report.
	(Both understand that it is not ready.)
American: But we agreed that it would be ready today.	American: I must teach him to fulfill an agreement.
The Greek hands in his resignation.	Greek: The stupid, incompetent boss! Not only did he give me wrong orders, but he does not appreciate that I did a thirty-day job in sixteen days.
The American is surprised.	Greek: I can't work for such a man.

2002). One important force that affects thinking is a culture's system of logic. Members of individualistic cultures such as the United States prize rationality and linear, logical thinking. They value the ability to be impartial—to analyze a situation from a detached perspective. They rely on facts, figures, and experts to make decisions. Members of individualistic societies tend to see the world in terms of dichotomies: good-bad, right-wrong, happy-sad, and so on. In contrast, members of collectivistic societies are more likely to be intuitive. They prefer to get a feel for the big picture and are less impressed by precision, classification, or detachment. Collectivistic cultures are also less prone to see the world in either-or terms. They accept the fact that people, things, or ideas can be both right and wrong, good and bad at the same time.

Don't misunderstand: These differing ways of thinking don't mean that members of individualistic cultures are never intuitive or that collectivists are never rational. The differences in ways of thinking are a matter of degree. Nonetheless, it's easy to imagine how an individualist raised in mainstream U.S. culture and someone from an extremely collectivistic Asian one could find their relationship perplexing. For instance, consider what might happen when a conflict arises between two romantic partners, friends, or coworkers. "Let's look at this rationally," the individualist might say. "Let's figure out exactly what happened. Once we decide whose fault the problem is, we can fix it." By contrast, the partner with a more collectivistic way of thinking might say, "Let's not get caught up in a lot of details or an argument about who is right or wrong. If we can get a feel for the problem, we can make things more harmonious." Although both partners might be speaking the same language, their modes of thinking about their relationship would be dramatically different.

Developing Intercultural Communication Competence

What distinguishes competent and incompetent intercultural communicators? The rest of this chapter focuses on answering this question. But before we get to the answers, take a moment to complete the Self-Assessment on pages 58–59 to evaluate your intercultural communication sensitivity. The instrument was developed by Guo-Ming Chen and William Starosta (2000).

To a great degree, interacting successfully with strangers calls for the same ingredients of general communicative competence outlined in Chapter 1. It's important to have a wide range of behaviors and to be skillful at choosing and performing the most appropriate ones in a given situation. A genuine concern for others plays an important role. Cognitive complexity and the ability to empathize also help, although empathizing with someone from another culture can be challenging (DeTurk, 2001). Finally, self-monitoring is important, since the need to make midcourse corrections in your approach is often necessary when dealing with people from other cultures.

But beyond these basic qualities, communication researchers have worked long and hard to identify qualities that are unique, or at least especially important, ingredients of intercultural communicative competence (Arasaratnam, 2007; Hajek & Giles, 2003).

MOTIVATION AND ATTITUDE

The desire to communicate successfully with strangers is an important start. For example, people high in willingness to communicate with people from other cultures report a greater number of friends from different backgrounds

SELF-ASSESSMENT

What Is Your Intercultural Sensitivity?

A series of statements concerning intercultural communication follow. There are no right or wrong answers. Imagine yourself interacting with people from a wide variety of cultural groups, not just one or two. Record your first impression to each of the following statements by indicating the degree to which you agree or disagree, using the following scale.

5 strongly agree **4** agree **3** uncertain **2** disagree **1** strongly disagree

_____ **1. I enjoy interacting with people from different cultures.**
_____ **2. I think people from other cultures are narrow-minded.**
_____ **3. I am pretty sure of myself in interacting with people from different cultures.**
_____ **4. I find it very hard to talk in front of people from different cultures.**
_____ **5. I always know what to say when interacting with people from different cultures.**
_____ **6. I can be as sociable as I want to be when interacting with people from different cultures.**
_____ **7. I don't like to be with people from different cultures.**
_____ **8. I respect the values of people from different cultures.**
_____ **9. I get upset easily when interacting with people from different cultures.**
_____ **10. I feel confident when interacting with people from different cultures.**
_____ **11. I tend to wait before forming an impression of people from different cultures.**
_____ **12. I often get discouraged when I am with people from different cultures.**
_____ **13. I am open-minded to people from different cultures.**
_____ **14. I am very observant when interacting with people from different cultures.**
_____ **15. I often feel useless when interacting with people from different cultures.**

than those who are less willing to reach out (Kassing, 1997). But desire alone isn't sufficient (Arasaratnam, 2006). Some other ways of thinking—called "culture-general"—are essential when dealing with people from other backgrounds (Samovar et al., 2007). These culture-general attitudes are necessary when communicating competently with people from any background that is different from one's own.

TOLERANCE FOR AMBIGUITY

As noted earlier, one of the most important concerns facing communicators is their desire to reduce uncertainty about one another (Berger, 1988). When we encounter communicators from different cultures, the level of uncertainty is especially high. Consider the basic challenge of communicating in an unfamiliar language. Pico Iyer (1990, pp. 129–130) captures the ambiguity that

_____ **16. I respect the ways people from different cultures behave.**

_____ **17. I try to obtain as much information as I can when interacting with people from different cultures.**

_____ **18. I would not accept the opinions of people from different cultures.**

_____ **19. I am sensitive to my culturally distinct counterpart's subtle meanings during our interaction.**

_____ **20. I think my culture is better than other cultures.**

_____ **21. I often give positive responses to my culturally different counterpart during our interaction.**

_____ **22. I avoid those situations where I will have to deal with culturally distinct persons.**

_____ **23. I often show my culturally distinct counterpart my understanding through verbal or nonverbal cues.**

_____ **24. I have a feeling of enjoyment toward differences between my culturally distinct counterpart and me.**

SCORING:
To determine your score, begin by reverse-coding items 2, 4, 7, 9, 12, 15, 18, 20, and 22 (if you indicated 5, reverse-code to 1, if you indicated 4, reverse-code to 2, and so on) Higher scores indicate a greater probability of intercultural communication competence.

Sum items 1, 11, 13, 21, 22, 23, and 24__________Interaction Engagement (range is 7–35)
Sum items 2, 7, 8, 16, 18, and 20__________Respect for Cultural Differences (6–30)
Sum items 3, 4, 5, 6, and 10__________Interaction Confidence (5–25)
Sum items 9, 12, and 15__________Interaction Enjoyment (3–15)
Sum items 14, 17, and 19__________Interaction Attentiveness (3–15)
Sum of all the items = __________(24–120, with a midpoint of 48)

Permission to use courtesy of Guo-Ming Chen. Chen, G. M., & Starosta, W. J. (2000). The development and validation of the Intercultural Sensitivity Scale. *Human Communication, 3,* 1-14.

arises from a lack of fluency when he describes his growing friendship with Sachiko, a Japanese woman he met in Kyoto:

> I was also beginning to realize how treacherous it was to venture into a foreign language if one could not measure the shadows of the words one used. When I had told her, in Asuka, "*Jennifer Beals ga suki-desu. Anata mo*" ("I like Jennifer Beals—and I like you"), I had been pleased to find a way of conveying affection, and yet, I thought, a perfect distance. But later I looked up suki and found that I had delivered an almost naked protestation of love. . . .
>
> Meanwhile, of course, nearly all her shadings were lost to me. . . . Once, when I had to leave her house ten minutes early, she said, "I very sad," and another time, when I simply called her up, she said, "I very happy"—and I began to think her unusually sensitive, or else prone to bold and violent extremes, when really she was reflecting nothing but the paucity of her English vocabulary. . . . Talking in a language not one's own was like walking on one leg; when two people did it together, it was like a three-legged waltz.

Competent intercultural communicators accept—even welcome—this kind of ambiguity. Iyer (1990, pp. 220–221) describes the way the mutual confusion he shared with Sachiko actually helped their relationship develop:

> Yet in the end, the fact that we were both speaking in this pared-down diction made us both, I felt, somewhat gentler, more courteous, and more vulnerable than we would have been otherwise, returning us to a state of innocence.

Without a tolerance for ambiguity, the mass of often confusing and sometimes downright incomprehensible messages that bombard intercultural sojourners would be impossible to manage. Some people seem to come equipped with this sort of tolerance, while others have to cultivate it. One way or the other, that ability to live with uncertainty is an essential ingredient of intercultural communication competence (Gudykunst, 1993b).

OPEN-MINDEDNESS

Being comfortable with ambiguity is important, but without an open-minded attitude a communicator will have trouble interacting competently with people from different backgrounds. To understand open-mindedness, it's helpful to consider three traits that are incompatible with it. **Ethnocentrism** is an attitude that one's own culture is superior to others. An ethnocentric person thinks—either privately or openly—that anyone who does not belong to his or her in-group is somehow strange, wrong, or even inferior. Travel writer Rick Steves (1996, p. 9) describes how an ethnocentric point of view can interfere with respect for other cultural practices:

> . . . we [Americans] consider ourselves very clean and commonly criticize other cultures as dirty. In the bathtub we soak, clean, and rinse, all in the same water. (We would never wash our dishes that way.) A Japanese visitor, who uses clean water for each step, might find our way of bathing strange or even disgusting. Many cultures spit in public and blow their nose right onto the street. They couldn't imagine doing that into a small cloth, called a hanky, and storing that in their pocket to be used again and again.
>
> Too often we think of the world in terms of a pyramid of "civilized" (us) on the top and "primitive" groups on the bottom. If we measured things differently (maybe according to stress, loneliness, heart attacks, hours spent in traffic jams, or family togetherness) things stack up differently.

Ethnocentrism leads to an attitude of **prejudice**—an unfairly biased and intolerant attitude toward others who belong to an out-group. (Note that the root term in *prejudice* is "prejudge.") An important element of prejudice is stereotyping. Stereotypical prejudices include the obvious exaggerations that all women are emotional, all men are sex-crazed and insensitive goons, all older people are out of touch with reality, and all immigrants are welfare parasites. Stereotyping can even be a risk when it comes to knowledge of cultural characteristics like individualism or collectivism. Not all members of a group are equally individualistic or collectivistic. For example, a close look at Americans of European and Latin descent showed differences within each group (Oetzel, 1998). Some Latinos were more independent than some European Americans, and vice versa. Chapter 4 has more to say about stereotyping.

It's encouraging to know that open-minded communicators can overcome pre-existing stereotypes and learn to appreciate people from different backgrounds as individuals. In one study, college students who were introduced to strangers from different cultural backgrounds developed attitudes about their new conversational partners based more on their personal behavior than on pre-existing expectations about how people from those backgrounds might behave (Manusov et al., 1997). Open-mindedness is especially important in intercultural work teams (Matveev, 2004)

KNOWLEDGE AND SKILL

Attitude alone isn't enough to guarantee success in intercultural encounters. Communicators need to possess enough knowledge of other cultures to know what approaches are appropriate. For example, research by Mary Jane Collier (1996) revealed how ethnic background influences what people consider the most important qualities in a friendship. Collier found that Latinos were most likely to value relational support and bonding with friends. By contrast, Asian Americans placed a greater value on helping one another achieve personal goals. For African Americans in the study, the most important quality in a friend was respect for and acceptance of the individual. European Americans reported that they valued friends who met their task-related needs, offered advice, shared information, and had common interests.

This and other research studies—for example, Johnson et al.'s (2001) study of what people from different cultures perceive as competent communication behaviors in initial interactions—suggest how knowledge of others' cultural background might help you become a more competent intercultural communicator. If, for example, you understand that a potential friend's background is likely to make displays of respect especially important, you could adjust your communication accordingly.

Unlike the culture-general attitudes we have discussed so far, knowledge of how to communicate with people from different backgrounds is usually culture specific. The rules and customs that work with one group might be quite different from those that succeed with another. For example, Korean and Japanese employees tend to shy away from using e-mail because of the perception that it may be seen by supervisors as rude (Olaniran, 2004). The ability to "shift gears" and adapt one's style to the norms of another culture or co-culture is an essential ingredient of communication competence (Kim et al., 1996).

How can a communicator acquire the culture-specific information that leads to competence? One important element is what Stella Ting-Toomey (1999) and others label as *mindfulness*—awareness of one's own behavior and that of others. Communicators who lack this quality blunder through intercultural encounters *mindlessly,* oblivious of how their own behavior may confuse or offend others, and how behavior that they consider weird may be simply different.

Charles Berger (1979) suggests three strategies for moving toward a more mindful, competent style of intercultural communication. *Passive observation* involves noticing what behaviors members of a different culture use and applying these insights to communicate in ways that are most effective. *Active strategies* include reading, watching films, and asking experts and members of the other culture how to behave, as well as taking academic courses related to intercultural communication and diversity (Carrell, 1997). The third strategy, *self-disclosure,* involves volunteering personal information to people from the other culture with whom you want to communicate. One type of self-disclosure is to confess your cultural ignorance: "This is very new to me. What's the right thing to do in this situation?" This approach is the riskiest of the three described here, since some cultures may not value candor and self-disclosure as much as others. Nevertheless, most people are pleased when strangers attempt to learn the practices of their culture, and they are usually more than willing to offer information and assistance.

Summary

The growing diversity of American culture and the increased exposure to people from around the world make an understanding of intercultural communication essential. Intercultural communication occurs when members of two or more cultures or co-cultures exchange messages in a manner that is influenced by their different cultural perceptions and symbol systems. In other words, intercultural communication requires the perception of differences, not just their existence.

A number of fundamental values shape communication. When members of different cultures interact, these values can affect interaction in ways that may be felt but not understood. These values include an emphasis on high- or low-context communication, individualism or collectivism, high or low power distance, relatively more or less avoidance of uncertainty, and either achievement or nurturing.

The codes that are used by members of a culture are often the most recognizable factors that shape communication between people from different backgrounds. Verbal codes include language spoken and the worldview created by it, as well as verbal communication style. Nonverbal codes also differ significantly, as do the attributions that cultural conditioning generate.

Intercultural communicative competence involves four dimensions: motivation and attitude, tolerance for ambiguity, open-mindedness, and knowledge and skill. These dimensions go hand in hand, since none alone is sufficient. Whereas motivation, attitude, tolerance, and open-mindedness are culture-general, knowledge and skill are usually culture-specific, requiring the active acquisition of information and training to reduce uncertainty about another culture.

Activities

1. Invitation to Insight
What in-groups do you belong to? You can best answer this question by thinking about whom you regard as belonging to out-groups. Based on your observations, consider the criteria you use to define in- and out-groups. Do you rely on race? Ethnicity? Age? Lifestyle? How do your judgments about in- and out-group membership affect your communication with others?

2. Critical Thinking Probe
Identify one of your important interpersonal relationships. Consider how that relationship might be different if you and your partner adopted values and norms that were opposite from the ones you already hold. For example, if your communication is low context, how would things be different if you shifted to a high-context style? If you are tolerant of uncertainty, what might happen if you avoided any surprises? Based on your answers, consider the advantages and disadvantages of the cultural values and norms you hold. Think about the pros and cons of cultures that have differing values and norms.

3. Ethical Challenge
Some cultural differences seem charming. However, others might seem alien—even inhumane. Explore the question of whether there are (or should be) any universal norms of behavior by identifying what rights and practices, if any, should be prohibited or honored universally.

4. Skill Builder
Use the criteria on pages 57–61 to evaluate your intercultural communication competence. Identify one culture with which you currently interact or could interact with in the future. Collect information on communication rules and norms in that culture through library research and personal interviews. Based on your findings, describe the steps you can take to communicate more effectively with the culture's members.

5. Skill Builder
Think about a foreign film or a film that depicts interaction between North Americans and people of another culture. Or observe people who are from a culture other than your own. Describe what you think are the verbal and nonverbal communication behaviors—and rules for communicating—that are different from your own.

CHAPTER

3 Communication and the Self

CHAPTER OUTLINE

After studying the material in this chapter . . .

YOU SHOULD UNDERSTAND:

1. The subjective nature of the self-concept and the communicative influences that shape it.
2. How it is possible to change one's self-concept.
3. The nature and extent of identity management.
4. How and why we engage in self-disclosure, and its benefits and risks.
5. The alternatives to self-disclosure.

YOU SHOULD BE ABLE TO:

1. Describe the influence others have had on shaping your self-concept and the influence you have had on others.
2. Explain the steps you can take to change undesirable elements of your self-concept.
3. Describe the differences between your perceived self and various presenting selves and outline the identity management strategies you use.
4. Explain how the social penetration and Johari Window models represent the level of self-disclosure in one of your relationships.
5. Outline the potential benefits and risks of disclosing in a selected situation.
6. Compose responses to a situation that reflect varying degrees of candor and equivocation.

KEY TERMS

- Benevolent lie (96)
- Cognitive conservatism (73)
- Equivocal language (98)
- Facework (78)
- Identity management (77)
- Johari Window (89)
- Lie (95)
- Perceived self (78)
- Presenting self (78)
- Reference groups (69)
- Reflected appraisal (68)
- Self-concept (66)
- Self-disclosure (87)
- Self-esteem (66)
- Self-fulfilling prophecy (74)
- Significant other (68)
- Social comparison (69)
- Social penetration model (87)

Who are you? Before reading on, take a few minutes to try a simple experiment. First, make a list of the 10 words or phrases that describe the most important features of who you are. Some of the items on your list may involve social roles: student, son or daughter, employee, and so on. Or you could define yourself through physical characteristics: fat, skinny, tall, short, beautiful, ugly. You may focus on your intellectual characteristics: smart, stupid, curious, inquisitive. Perhaps you can best define yourself in terms of moods, feelings, or attitudes: optimistic, critical, energetic. Or you could consider your social characteristics: outgoing, shy, defensive. You may see yourself in terms of belief systems: pacifist, Christian, vegetarian, libertarian. Finally, you could focus on particular skills (or lack of them): swimmer, artist, carpenter. In any case, choose 10 words or phrases that best describe you, and write them down.

Next, choose the one item from your list that is the most fundamental to who you are and copy it on another sheet of paper. Then pick the second most fundamental item and record it as number two on your new list. Continue ranking the 10 items until you have reorganized them all.

Communication and the Self-Concept

The list you created in the exercise you just completed offers clues about your **self-concept:** the relatively stable set of perceptions you hold of yourself. One way to understand the self-concept is to imagine a special mirror that not only reflects physical features, but also allows you to view other aspects of yourself—emotional states, talents, likes, dislikes, values, roles, and so on. The reflection in that mirror would be your self-concept.

Any description of your self-concept that you constructed in this exercise is only a partial one. To make it complete, you'd have to keep adding items until your list ran into hundreds of words. Of course, not every dimension of your self-concept list is equally important. For example, the most significant part of one person's self-concept might consist of social roles, whereas for another it might be physical appearance, health, friendships, accomplishments, or skills.

Self-esteem is the part of the self-concept that involves evaluations of self-worth. A communicator's self-concept might include being quiet, argumentative, or serious. His or her self-esteem would be determined by how he or she feels about these qualities.

High or low self-esteem has a powerful effect on communication behavior, as Figure 3.1 shows. People who feel good about themselves have positive expectations about how they will communicate (Baldwin & Keelan, 1999). These feelings increase the chance that communication will be successful, and successes contribute to positive self-evaluations, which reinforce self-esteem. Of course, the same principle can work in a negative way with communicators who have low self-esteem.

Although high self-esteem has obvious benefits, it doesn't guarantee interpersonal success (Baumeister, 2005; Baumeister et al., 2003). People with high levels of self-esteem may *think* they make better impressions on others and have better friendships and romantic lives, but neither impartial observers nor objective tests verify these beliefs. It's easy to see how people with an inflated sense of self-worth could irritate others by coming across as condescending know-it-alls, especially when their self-worth is challenged (Vohs & Heatherton, 2004). Moreover, people with low self-esteem have the potential to change their self-appraisals (more on that later in this chapter). The point here is that positive self-evaluations can often be the starting point for positive communication with others.

HOW THE SELF-CONCEPT DEVELOPS

Researchers generally agree that the self-concept does not exist at birth (Rosenblith, 1992). An infant lying in a crib has no notion of self, no notion—even if verbal language were miraculously made available—of how to answer the question "Who am I?" At about 6 or 7 months, the child begins to recognize "self" as distinct from surroundings. If you've ever watched children at this age, you've probably marveled at how they can stare with great fascination at a foot, hand, and other body parts that float into view, almost as if they were

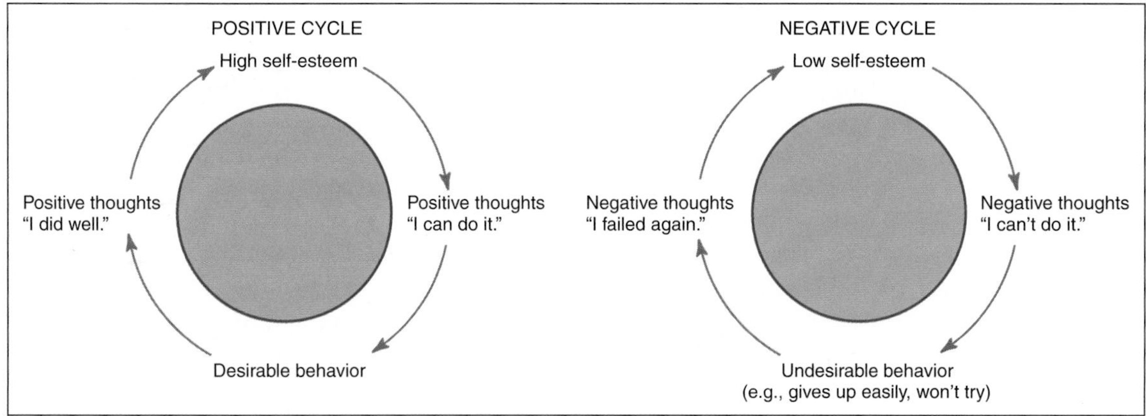

FIGURE 3.1 The Relationship between Self-Esteem and Communication Behavior
Adapted from Johnson, H. M. (1998). *How do I love me?* (3rd. ed.). Salem, WI: Sheffield, pp. 3, 5.

strange objects belonging to someone else. Then the connection is made, almost as if the child were realizing "The hand is me," "The foot is me." These first revelations form the child's earliest concept of self.

As the child develops, this rudimentary sense of identity expands into a much more complete and sophisticated picture that resembles the self-concept of adults. This evolution is almost totally a product of social interaction (Schmidt, 2006; Weigert & Gecas, 2003). Two complementary theories describe how interaction shapes the way individuals view themselves: reflected appraisal and social comparison (Burkitt, 1992; Sedikides & Skowronski, 1995).

Reflected Appraisal Before reading on, try the following exercise: Either by yourself or aloud with a partner, recall someone you know or once knew who helped enhance your self-concept by acting in a way that made you feel accepted, worthwhile, important, appreciated, or loved. This person needn't have played a crucial role in your life, as long as the role was positive. Often one's self-concept is shaped by many tiny nudges as well as a few giant shoves. For instance, you might recall a childhood neighbor who took a special interest in you or a grandparent who never criticized or questioned your youthful foolishness.

After thinking about this supportive person, recall someone who acted in either a big or small way to diminish your self-esteem. For instance, you may have had a coach who criticized you in front of the team, or a teacher who said or implied that you wouldn't amount to much.

After thinking about these two types of people, you should begin to see that everyone's self-concept is to some degree a **reflected appraisal:** a mirroring of the judgments of those around her or him. To the extent that you have received supportive messages, you have learned to appreciate and value yourself. To the degree that you have received critical signals, you are likely to feel less valuable, lovable, and capable (Felson, 1985; Jaret et al., 2005). Your self-concept can be seen, at least in part, as a reflection of the messages you've received throughout your life.

Social scientists use the term **significant other** to describe a person whose evaluations are especially influential. Messages from parents, of course, are an early and important influence on the self-concept. Supportive parents are more likely to raise children with healthy self-concepts. By contrast, parents with poor, negative, or deviant self-concepts tend to have unhappy children who view themselves in primarily negative ways (Fitts, 1971; Salimi et al., 2005), communicate less effectively (Huang, 1999), and go on to have unsatisfying relationships (Vangelisti & Crumley, 1998). Interestingly, if one parent has a good self-concept and the other a poor self-concept, the child is most likely to choose the parent with the more positive self-concept as a model. If neither parent has a strong self-concept, the child may seek an adult outside the family with whom to identify.

Along with family, the messages from many other significant others shape our self-concept (Hergovitch et al., 2002). A teacher from long ago, a special friend or relative, or even a barely known acquaintance whom you respected can all leave an imprint on how you view yourself.

As we grow older, the power of messages from significant others remains (Voss et al., 1999). Some social scientists have coined the phrase "Michelangelo phenomenon" to describe the way significant others sculpt one another's self-concepts (Drigotas, 2002; Rusbult et al., 2005). Romantic partners, people on the job, friends, and many others can speak and act in ways that have a profound effect on the way we view ourselves.

You might argue that not every part of your self-concept is shaped by others, that there are certain objective facts recognizable by self-observation alone. After all, nobody needs to tell you whether you are taller than others, speak with an accent, have curly hair, and so on. Indeed, some features of the self are immediately apparent. But the *significance* we attach to them—that is, the rank we assign them in the hierarchy of our list and the interpretation we give them—depends greatly on the opinions of others.

Social Comparison So far, we have looked at the way others' messages shape the self-concept. In addition to using these messages, we form our self-image by the process of **social comparison:** evaluating ourselves in terms of how we compare with others. We decide whether we are superior or inferior and similar or different by comparing ourselves to what social scientists call **reference groups**—those people we use to evaluate our own characteristics. You might feel ordinary or inferior in terms of talent, friendships, or attractiveness if you compare yourself with an inappropriate reference group (Pahl & Eiser, 2007). For instance, studies have shown that young women who regularly compare themselves with ultra-thin media models develop negative appraisals of their own bodies, in some cases leading to eating disorders (Han, 2003; Harrison & Cantor, 1997). Men, too, who compare themselves to media-idealized male physiques, evaluate their bodies negatively (Strong, 2005). The Focus on Research box in this section describes how television makeover shows can perpetuate a myth of perfection, with consequences for the self-esteem of viewers. You'll read more about how to avoid placing perfectionistic demands on yourself in Chapter 8.

To some degree, we're in control of whom we choose for comparison. It's possible to seek out people with whom we compare favorably. This technique may bring to mind a search for a community of idiots in which you would appear as a genius, but there are healthier ways of changing your standards for comparison. For instance, you might decide that it's foolish to constantly compare your athletic prowess with professionals or campus stars, your looks with movie idols, and your intelligence with members of Phi Beta Kappa.

FOCUS ON RESEARCH

When Making Over Starts Taking Over

research

Makeover programs are a popular genre of TV shows. Some focus on remodeling houses and gardens. Others change participants' physical appearance through clothing, diets, exercise, hairstyle, and even surgery. Self-improvement is generally a good thing, but is it possible that these shows send less-than-subtle messages about not measuring up unless you're "made over"? That's what researchers Kelly Kubic and Rebecca Chory wanted to know.

Kubic and Chory surveyed 155 college students, asking how often they watched shows such as *What Not to Wear*, *Queer Eye for the Straight Guy*, and *Extreme Makeover*. The students also filled out inventories measuring their self-esteem, perfectionism, and body dissatisfaction. As predicted, frequent exposure to makeover programs was negatively related to self-esteem and positively related to perfectionism and body dissatisfaction.

It's important to note that the correlation between viewing makeover shows and these negative traits doesn't clearly spell out a causal relationship. It's certainly possible that the programming shapes the audience's attitudes, but it's also possible that viewers with low self-esteem seek out these programs. In any case, it is wise for fans of TV makeover shows to be sure that the quest for self-improvement doesn't turn into an exercise in self-disdain.

Kubic, K. N., & Chory, R. M. (2007). Exposure to television makeover programs and perceptions of self. *Communication Research Reports, 24,* 283–291.

Once you place yourself alongside a truly representative sample, your self-concept may become more realistic.

CHARACTERISTICS OF THE SELF-CONCEPT

Now that you have a better idea of how your self-concept has developed, we can take a closer look at some of its characteristics.

The Self-Concept Is Subjective The way we view ourselves may be at odds with others' perceptions—and often with the observable facts. For instance, people are notoriously bad judges of their own communication skills. In one study, there was no relationship between the subjects' self-evaluations as interpersonal communicators, public speakers, or listeners and their observed ability to perform well in any of these areas (Carrell & Willmington, 1996). In another study (Myers, 1980), a random sample of men were asked to rank themselves on their ability to get along with others. Defying mathematical laws, all subjects—every last one—put themselves in the top half of the population. Sixty percent rated themselves in the top 10 percent of the population, and an amazing 25 percent believed they were in the top 1 percent. The men had similarly lofty appraisals of their leadership and athletic abilities. Other research shows that these perceptions of superiority tend to increase over time (Kanten & Teigen, 2008).

There are several reasons why some people have a level of self-esteem that others would regard as unrealistically favorable. First, a self-estimation might be based on obsolete information. Perhaps your jokes used to be well received, or your grades were high, or your work was superior, but now the facts have changed. Self-esteem might also be excessively favorable due to distorted feedback from others. A boss may claim to be an excellent manager because assistants pour on false praise in order to keep their jobs. A child's inflated ego may be based on the praise of doting parents.

There are also times when we view ourselves more harshly than the facts warrant. We have all experienced a temporary case of the "uglies," convinced we look much worse than others say that we really appear. Research confirms what common sense suggests—people are more critical of themselves when they are experiencing these negative moods than when they are feeling more positive (Brown & Mankowski, 1993; Sturman & Mongrain, 2008). While everyone suffers occasional bouts of low self-esteem, some people suffer from long-term or even permanent states of excessive self-doubt and criticism (Gara et al., 1993). It's easy to understand how this chronic condition can influence the way these people approach and respond to others.

What are the reasons for such excessively negative self-evaluations? As with unrealistically high self-esteem, one source for an overabundance of self-put-downs is obsolete information. A string of past failures in school or with social relations can linger to haunt a communicator long after they have occurred. Similarly, we've known slender students who still think of themselves as fat, and clear-complexioned people who still behave as if they were acne ridden.

Distorted feedback also can lead to low self-esteem. Growing up in an overly critical family is one of the most common causes of a negative self-image. In other cases, the remarks of cruel friends, uncaring teachers, excessively demanding employers, or even memorable strangers can have a lasting effect. As you read earlier, the impact of significant others and reference groups in forming a self-concept can be great, and their effect on your self-esteem can be just as great.

Along with obsolete information and distorted feedback, another cause for low self-esteem is the myth of perfection that is common in our society. From the time most of us learn to understand language, we are exposed to fairy-tale models who appear to be perfect at whatever they do. Unfortunately, many parents perpetuate the myth of perfection by refusing to admit that they are ever mistaken or unfair. Children, of course, accept this perfectionist façade for a long time, not being in a position to dispute the wisdom of such powerful beings. From the behavior of the adults around them comes the clear message: "A well-adjusted, successful person has no faults." We'll have a great deal to say about perfection and other irrational ideas, both later in this chapter and in Chapter 8.

A final reason people often sell themselves short is also connected to social expectations. Curiously, the perfectionist society to which we belong rewards those people who downplay the strengths we demand they possess (or pretend to possess). We term these people "modest" and find their behavior agreeable. On the other hand, we consider some of those who honestly appreciate their own strengths to be "braggarts" or "egotists," confusing them with the people who boast about accomplishments they do not possess (Miller et al., 1992). This convention leads most of us to talk freely about our shortcomings while downplaying our accomplishments. It's all right to proclaim that you're miserable if you have failed to do well on a project, but it's seen as boastful to express your pride at a job well done.

Self-esteem may be based on inaccurate thinking, but it still has a powerful effect on the way we relate to others. Table 3.1 summarizes some important differences between communicators with positive and negative self-esteem. Differences like these make sense when you realize that people who dislike themselves are likely to believe that others won't like them either. Realistically or not, they imagine that others are constantly viewing them critically, and they accept these imagined or real criticisms as more proof that they are indeed unlikable people. This low self-esteem is sometimes manifested in hostility toward others, who are seen as "perfect," since the communicator takes the approach that the only way to look good is to put others down.

A Healthy Self-Concept Is Flexible People change. From moment to moment, we aren't the same. We wake up in the morning in a jovial mood and turn grumpy before lunch. We find ourselves fascinated by a conversational topic one moment, then suddenly lose interest. You might be a relaxed conversationalist with people you know but at a loss for words with strangers. The self-concepts of most communicators react to these changes ("I'm patient at work;" "I'm not patient at home"), and these changes affect self-esteem ("I'm not as good a person at home as I am in the office").

As we change in these and many other ways, our self-concept must also change in order to stay realistic. An accurate self-portrait today would not be exactly the same as the one we had a year ago, a few months ago, or even yesterday. This does not mean that you change radically from day to day. The fundamental characteristics of your personality will stay the same for years, perhaps for a lifetime. After the age of 30, most people's self-concept doesn't change radically, at least not without a conscious effort, such as psychotherapy (van der Meulen, 2001; Zanobini & Usai, 2002). However, it is likely that in important ways you are changing—physically, intellectually, emotionally, and spiritually.

The Self-Concept Resists Change A realistic self-concept should reflect the way we change over time, but the tendency to resist revision of our self-perception is strong. Once a communicator fastens onto a self-concept, the tendency is to seek out people who confirm it. Numerous studies (e.g., Stets

TABLE 3.1 ***Characteristics of Communicators with Positive and Negative Self-Esteem***

PERSONS WITH POSITIVE SELF-ESTEEM	PERSONS WITH NEGATIVE SELF-ESTEEM
1. Are likely to think well of others.	1. Are likely to disapprove of others.
2. Expect to be accepted by others.	2. Expect to be rejected by others.
3. Evaluate their own performance more favorably.	3. Evaluate their own performance less favorably.
4. Perform well when being watched; are not afraid of others' reactions.	4. Perform poorly when being watched; are sensitive to possible negative reactions.
5. Work harder for people who demand high standards of performance.	5. Work harder for undemanding, less critical people.
6. Are inclined to feel comfortable with others they view as superior in some way.	6. Feel threatened by people they view as superior in some way.
7. Are able to defend themselves against negative comments of others.	7. Have difficulty defending themselves against others' negative comments: are more easily influenced.

Reported by Hamachek, D. E. (1982). *Encounters with others: Interpersonal relationships and you.* New York: Holt, Rinehart & Winston.

& Cast, 2007; Swann et al., 2003) show that both college students and married couples with high self-esteem seek out partners who view them favorably, while those with low self-esteem are more inclined to interact with people who view them unfavorably. This tendency to seek information that conforms to an existing self-concept has been labeled **cognitive conservatism** (Greenwald, 1995; Kihlstrom & Klein, 1994).

We are understandably reluctant to revise a favorable self-concept. If you were a thoughtful, romantic partner early in a relationship, it would be hard to admit that you might have become less considerate and attentive lately. Likewise, if you used to be a serious student, acknowledging that you have slacked off isn't easy.

Curiously, the tendency to cling to an outmoded self-perception holds even when the new image would be more favorable. We can recall scores of attractive, intelligent students who still view themselves as the gawky underachievers they were in the past. The tragedy of this sort of cognitive conservatism is obvious. People with unnecessarily negative self-esteem can become their own worst enemies, denying themselves the validation they deserve and need to enjoy satisfying relationships.

Once the self-concept is firmly rooted, only a powerful force can change it. At least four requirements must be met for an appraisal to be regarded as important (Bergner & Holmes, 2000; Gergen, 1971).

- The person who offers a particular appraisal must be *someone we see as competent to offer it.* Parents satisfy this requirement extremely well because as young children we perceive that our parents know so much about us—sometimes more than we know about ourselves.

- *The appraisal must be perceived as highly personal.* The more the other person seems to know about us and adapts what is being said to fit us, the more likely we are to accept judgments from this person.
- The appraisal must be *reasonable in light of what we believe about ourselves.* If an appraisal is similar to one we give ourselves, we will believe it; if it is somewhat dissimilar, we will probably still accept it; but if it is completely dissimilar, we will probably reject it. (See the Reflection in this section for an example)
- Appraisals that are *consistent* and *numerous* are more persuasive than those that contradict usual appraisals or those that occur only once. As long as only a *few* students yawn in class, a teacher can safely disregard them as a reflection on his or her teaching ability. In like manner, you could safely disregard the appraisal of the angry date who tells you in no uncertain terms what kind of person behaves as you did. Of course, when you get a second or third similar appraisal in a short time, the evaluation becomes harder to ignore.

REFLECTION

Don't They Get It?

One of my guilty pleasures is watching so-called reality TV shows in which people with no musical talent bomb miserably in front of millions of viewers. What's amazing is that most of these contestants honestly believe they're fantastic singers and dancers. It's a classic case of cognitive conservatism—they've surrounded themselves with people who tell them they're great, and they refuse to believe anyone who says otherwise. It's actually a bit sad—but it makes for great entertainment!

THE SELF-FULFILLING PROPHECY AND COMMUNICATION

The self-concept is such a powerful influence on the personality that it not only determines how you see yourself in the present but also can actually affect your future behavior and that of others. Such occurrences come about through a phenomenon called the self-fulfilling prophecy.

A **self-fulfilling prophecy** occurs when a person's expectations of an event, and her or his subsequent behavior based on those expectations, make the outcome more likely to occur than would otherwise have been true (Snyder & Klein, 2005; Watzlawick, 2005). A self-fulfilling prophecy involves four stages:

1. Holding an expectation (for yourself or for others)
2. Behaving in accordance with that expectation
3. The expectation coming to pass
4. Reinforcing the original expectation

Let's use a slightly exaggerated example to illustrate the concept. One morning you read your horoscope, which offers the following prediction: "Today you will meet the person of your dreams, and the two of you will live happily ever after." Assuming you believe in horoscopes, what will you do? You'll probably start making plans to go out on the town that night in search of your "dream person." You'll dress up, groom yourself well, and carefully evaluate every person you encounter. You'll also be attentive, charming, witty, polite, and gracious when you end up meeting your "dream candidate." As a result, that person is likely to be impressed and attracted to you—and lo and behold, the two of you end up living happily ever after. Your conclusion? That horoscope sure had it right!

Upon closer examination, the horoscope—which helped create the Stage 1 expectation—really wasn't the key to your success. While it got the ball rolling, you would still be single if you had stayed home that evening. Stage 2—going out on the town and acting charming—was what led your "dream person" to be attracted to you, bringing about the positive results (Stage 3). While it's tempting to credit the horoscope for the outcome (Stage 4), it's important to realize that *you* were responsible for bringing the prediction to pass—hence the term *self-fulfilling* prophecy.

The horoscope story is fictional, but research shows that self-fulfilling prophecies operate in real-life situations. To see how, read on.

"I don't sing because I am happy. I am happy because I sing."

Types of Self-Fulfilling Prophecies There are two types of self-fulfilling prophecies. Self-imposed prophecies occur when your own expectations influence your behavior. You've probably had the experience of waking up in a cross mood and saying to yourself, "This will be a bad day." Once you made such a decision, you may have acted in ways that made it come true. If you avoid the company of others because you expect they had nothing to offer, your suspicions would have been confirmed—nothing exciting or new is likely to happen. On the other hand, if you approach the same day with the idea that it could be a good one, this expectation may well be met. Smile at people, and they're more likely to smile back. Enter a class determined to learn something, and you probably will—even if it's how not to instruct students! In these cases and other similar ones, your attitude has a great deal to do with what you see and how you behave.

Research has demonstrated the power of self-imposed prophecies. In one study, communicators who believed they were incompetent proved less likely than others to pursue rewarding relationships and more likely to sabotage their existing relationships than did people who were less critical of themselves (Kolligan, 1990). Research also suggests that communicators who feel anxious about giving speeches seem to create self-fulfilling prophecies about doing poorly, which causes them to perform less effectively (MacIntyre & Thivierge, 1995). On the other hand, students who perceive themselves as capable achieve more academically (Zimmerman, 1995).

A second category of self-fulfilling prophecies occurs when one person's expectations govern another's actions (Blank, 1993)—whether those expectations are positive (the Pygmalion effect) or negative (the Golem effect) (Reynolds, 2007). The classic example was demonstrated by Robert Rosenthal and Lenore Jacobson (1968) in a study they described in their book *Pygmalion in the Classroom.* The experimenters told teachers that 20 percent of the children in a certain elementary school showed unusual potential for intellectual growth. The names of the 20 percent were drawn by means of a table of random numbers—much as if they were drawn out of a hat. Eight months later these unusual or "magic" children showed significantly greater gains in IQ than did the remaining children, who had not been singled out for the teachers' attention. The change in the teachers' behavior toward these allegedly "special" children led to changes in their intellectual performance. Among other things, the teachers gave the "smart" students more time to answer questions, and provided more feedback to them. These children did better not because they were any more intelligent than their classmates, but because their teachers—significant others—communicated the expectation that they could.

Notice that it isn't just the observer's *belief* that creates a self-fulfilling prophecy for the person who is the target of the expectations. The observer must *communicate that belief* in order for the prediction to have any effect. If parents have faith in their children but the kids aren't aware of that confidence, they won't be affected by their parents' expectations. If a boss has concerns about an employee's ability to do a job but keeps those worries to herself, the subordinate won't be influenced. In this sense, the self-fulfilling prophecies imposed by one person on another are as much a communication phenomenon as a psychological one.

CHANGING YOUR SELF-CONCEPT

You've probably begun to realize that it is possible to change an unsatisfying self-concept. In the next sections we discuss some methods for accomplishing such a change.

Have Realistic Expectations It's important to realize that some of your dissatisfaction might come from expecting too much of yourself. Nobody is able to handle every conflict productively, to be totally relaxed and skillful in conversations, to ask perceptive questions all the time, or to be 100 percent helpful when others have problems. Expecting yourself to reach such unrealistic goals is to doom yourself to unhappiness at the start.

It's important to judge yourself in terms of your own growth and not against the behavior of others. Rather than feeling miserable because you're not as talented as an expert, realize that you probably are a better, wiser, or more skillful person than you used to be and that this growth is a legitimate source of satisfaction. Perfection is fine as an ideal, but you're being unfair to yourself if you actually expect to reach it.

Have a Realistic Perception of Yourself One source of low self-esteem is inaccurate self-perception. As you've already read, such unrealistic pictures sometimes come from being overly harsh on yourself, believing that you're worse than the facts indicate. Of course, it would be foolish to deny that you could be a better person than you are, but it's also important to recognize your strengths. A periodic session of "bragging"—acknowledging the parts of yourself with which you're pleased and the ways you've grown—is often a good way to put your strengths and shortcomings into perspective.

Unrealistically low self-esteem also can come from the inaccurate feedback of others. Workers with overly critical supervisors, children with cruel "friends," and students with unsupportive teachers are all prone to suffer from low self-esteem due to excessively negative feedback. If you fall into this category, it's important to seek out supportive people who will acknowledge your assets as well as point out your shortcomings. Doing so is often a quick and sure boost to your self-esteem.

Have the Will to Change Often we say we want to change but aren't willing to do the necessary work. In such cases the responsibility for not growing rests squarely on your shoulders. At other times we maintain an unrealistic self-concept by claiming that we "can't" be the person we'd like to be, when in fact we're simply not willing to do what's required (we'll discuss the fallacy of helplessness and ridding yourself of "can't" statements in Chapter 8). You can change in many ways, but only if you are willing to put out the effort.

Have the Skill to Change Trying is often not enough. There are times when you would change if you knew how to do so.

First, you can seek advice—from books such as this one and other printed sources. You also can get advice from instructors, counselors, and other experts, as well as from friends. Of course, not all the advice you receive will be useful, but if you read widely and talk to enough people, you have a good chance of learning the things you want to know.

A second method of learning how to change is to observe models—people who handle themselves in the ways you would like to master. It's often been said that people learn more from models than in any other way, and by taking advantage of this principle you will find that the world is full of teachers who can show you how to communicate more successfully. Become a careful observer. Watch what people you admire do and say, not so you can copy them but so you can adapt their behavior to fit your own personal style.

At this point you might be overwhelmed by the difficulty of changing the way you think about yourself and the way you act. Remember, we never said that this process would be easy (although it sometimes is). But even when change is difficult, it's possible if you are serious. You don't need to be perfect, but you *can* change your self-concept and raise your self-esteem, and, as a result, your communication—*if you choose to.*

Presenting the Self: Communication as Identity Management

So far, we've described how communication shapes the way communicators view themselves. We will now turn the tables and focus on the topic of **identity management**—the communication strategies people use to influence how others view them. In the following pages you will see that many of our messages are aimed at creating desired impressions.

PUBLIC AND PRIVATE SELVES

To understand why identity management exists, we have to discuss the notion of self in more detail. So far, we have referred to the "self" as if each of us had only one identity. In truth, each of us possesses several selves, some private and others public. These selves are often quite different.

The **perceived self** is the person you believe yourself to be in moments of honest self-examination. The perceived self may not be accurate in every respect. For example, you might think you are much more (or less) intelligent than an objective test would measure. Accurate or not, the perceived self is powerful because we believe it reflects who we are. We can call the perceived self "private" because you are unlikely to reveal all of it to another person. You can verify the private nature of the perceived self by thinking of elements of your self-perception that you would not disclose. For example, you might be reluctant to share some feelings about your appearance ("I think I'm rather unattractive"), your goals ("The most important thing to me is becoming rich"), or your motives ("I care more about myself than about others").

In contrast to the perceived self, the **presenting self** is a public image—the way we want to appear to others. In most cases the presenting self we seek to create is a socially approved image: diligent student, loving partner, conscientious worker, loyal friend, and so on. Sociologist Erving Goffman (1959, 1971) used the word **face** to describe this socially approved identity, and he coined the term **facework** to describe the verbal and nonverbal ways in which we act to maintain our own presenting image and the images of others. He argued that each of us can be viewed as a kind of playwright who creates roles that we want others to believe, as well as the performer who acts out those roles.

Goffman suggested that each of us maintains face by putting on a *front* when we are around others whom we want to impress. In contrast, behavior in the *back region*—when we are alone—may be quite different. You can recognize the difference between front- and backstage behavior by recalling a time when you observed a driver, alone in his or her car, behaving in ways that would never be acceptable in public. All of us engage in backstage ways of acting that we would never exhibit in front of others. Just recall how you behave in front of the bathroom mirror when the door is locked, and you will appreciate the difference between public and private behavior. If you knew someone was watching, would you behave differently?

CHARACTERISTICS OF IDENTITY MANAGEMENT

Now that you have a sense of what identity management is, we can look at some characteristics of this process (Domenici & Littlejohn, 2006).

We Strive to Construct Multiple Identities It is an oversimplification to suggest we use identity management strategies to create just one identity. In the course of even a single day, most people play a variety of roles: "respectful student," "joking friend," "friendly neighbor," and "helpful worker," to suggest just a few. We even play a variety of roles around the same person. As you grew up, you almost certainly changed characters as you interacted with your parents. In one context you acted as the responsible adult ("You can trust me with the car!") and at another time you were the helpless child ("I can't find my socks!"). At some times—perhaps on birthdays or holidays—you were a dedicated family member, and at other times you may have played the role of rebel. Likewise, in romantic relationships we switch among many ways of behaving, depending on the context: friend, lover, business partner, scolding critic, apologetic child, and so on. Each of us constructs multiple identities, many of which may be independent of each other, and some of which may even conflict with one another (Spears, 2001). For example, some student-athletes experience tension when the roles of student and athlete seem to have incompatible demands (Yopyk & Prentice, 2005).

The ability to construct multiple identities is one element of communication competence. For example, the style of speaking or even the language itself can reflect a choice about how to construct one's identity. Many bilingual Latinos in the United States understand this principle and often choose whether to use English or Spanish depending on the kind of identity they are seeking in a given conversation (Myers-Scotton, 2000).

Identity Management Is Collaborative As we perform like actors trying to create a front, our "audience" is made up of other actors who are trying to create their own characters. Identity-related communication is a kind of process theater in which we improvise scenes where our character reacts with others. Good-natured teasing only works if the other person appreciates your humor and responds well. (Imagine how your kidding would fall flat if somebody didn't get or enjoy the joking.) Likewise, being a successful romantic can only succeed if the object of your affections plays his or her part.

Identity Management Can Be Deliberate or Unconscious There's no doubt that sometimes we are highly aware of managing impressions. Most job interviews and first dates are clear examples of deliberate identity management. But in other cases we unconsciously act in ways that are really small public performances. For example, experimental participants expressed facial disgust in reaction to eating sandwiches laced with a supersaturated solution of saltwater only when there was another person present; when they were alone, they made no faces upon eating the same snack (Brightman et al., 1975). Another study showed that communicators engage in facial mimicry (such as smiling or looking sympathetic in response to another's message) only in face-to-face settings, when their expressions can be seen by the other person. When they are speaking over the phone and their reactions cannot be seen, they do not make the same expressions (Chovil, 1991). Studies like these suggest that most of our behavior is aimed at sending messages to others—in other words, identity management.

Despite the claims of some theorists, it seems an exaggeration to suggest that *all* behavior is aimed at making impressions. Young children certainly aren't strategic communicators. A baby spontaneously laughs when pleased and cries when sad or uncomfortable, without any notion of creating an impression in others. Likewise, there are almost certainly times when we, as adults, act spontaneously. But when a significant other questions the presenting self we try to present, the likelihood of acting to prop it up increases. This process isn't always conscious: At a nonconscious level of awareness we monitor others' reactions, and swing into action when our "face" is threatened—especially by significant others (Leary & Kowalski, 1990).

People Differ in Their Degree of Identity Management As you read in Chapter 1, some people are much more aware of their identity management behavior than others. There are certainly advantages to being a high self-monitor (Hamachek, 1992). People who pay attention to themselves are generally good "people-readers" who can adjust their behavior to get the desired reaction from others. Along with the advantages, there are some potential drawbacks to being an extremely high self-monitor (Wright et al., 2007). Their analytical nature may prevent them from experiencing events completely, since a portion of their attention will always be viewing the situation from a detached position. High self-monitors' ability to act makes it difficult to tell how they are really feeling. In fact, because high self-monitors change roles often, they may have a hard time knowing *themselves* how they really feel.

By now it should be clear that neither extremely high nor low self-monitoring is the ideal. There are some situations when paying attention to yourself and adapting your behavior can be useful, and other times when reacting without considering the effect on others is a better approach. This need for a range of behaviors demonstrates once again the notion of communicative competence outlined in Chapter 1—flexibility is the key to successful relationships.

WHY MANAGE IMPRESSIONS?

Why bother trying to shape others' opinions? Sometimes we create and maintain a front to follow social rules. As children we learn to act politely, even when bored. Likewise, part of growing up consists of developing a set of manners for various occasions, such as meeting strangers, attending school, and going to church. Young children who haven't learned all the do's and don'ts of polite society often embarrass their parents by behaving inappropriately ("Mommy, why is that man so fat?"), but by the time they enter school, behavior that might have been excusable or even amusing just isn't acceptable. Good manners are often aimed at making others more comfortable. For example, able-bodied people often mask their discomfort upon encountering someone who is disabled by acting nonchalant or stressing similarities between themselves and the disabled person (Coleman & DePaulo, 1991).

Social rules govern our behavior in a variety of settings. For example, it would be impossible to keep a job without meeting certain expectations. Salespeople are supposed to treat customers with courtesy. Employees need to appear reasonably respectful when talking to the boss. Some forms of clothing would be considered outrageous at work. By agreeing to take on a job, you are signing an unwritten contract that dictates you will present a certain face at work, whether or not that face reflects the way you might be feeling at a particular moment.

Even when social roles don't dictate the proper way to behave, we often manage impressions for a second reason: to accomplish personal goals. You might, for example, dress up for a visit to traffic court in the hope that your front (responsible citizen) will convince the judge to treat you sympathetically. You might be sociable to your neighbors so they will agree to your request that they keep their dog off your lawn. To achieve success in some organizations, gay and lesbian employees may manage their sexual identity three different ways (Button, 2004): create a false heterosexual identity, avoid the issue of sexuality altogether, or integrate a gay or lesbian identity into the work context. In cases like these, personal goals may influence how professional impressions are managed.

Identity management sometimes aims at achieving relational goals. For instance, you might act more friendly and lively than you feel upon meeting a new person so that you will appear likable. You might smile and preen to show the attractive stranger at a party that you would like to get better acquainted. In situations like these, you aren't being deceptive as much as "putting your best foot forward."

All these examples show that it is difficult—perhaps even impossible—*not* to create impressions. After all, you have to send some sort of message. If you don't act friendly when meeting a stranger, you have to act aloof, indifferent, hostile, or in some other manner. If you don't act businesslike, you have to behave in an alternative way: casual, goofy, or whatever. Often the question isn't whether or not to present a face to others; it's only which face to present.

Managing Identities under the Sea: *Shark Tale*

The animated feature *Shark Tale* is an amusing illustration of characters who reap the benefits and suffer the consequences of presenting false identities. Oscar (Will Smith) is a fast-talking small fish who changes from nobody to celebrity when he is mistaken for a brazen "shark slayer." Given his newfound fame and happiness, it's not surprising that Oscar is willing to live a lie. Lenny (Jack Black) is a great white shark with a sensitive side and a secret about his identity: He's a vegetarian. When Lenny's secret is revealed, he becomes the object of scorn and ridicule. Both characters find themselves exhausted from managing their false identities and ultimately return to their true nature, which they learn is also preferred by those who love them most.

HOW DO WE MANAGE IMPRESSIONS?

How do we create a public face? In an age in which technology provides many options for communicating, the answer depends in part on the communication channel chosen.

Face-to-Face Identity Management In face-to-face interaction, communicators can manage their front in three ways: manner, appearance, and setting. *Manner* consists of a communicator's words and nonverbal actions. Chapters 5 and 6 will describe in detail how what you say and do creates impressions. Since you have to speak and act, the question isn't whether your manner sends a message; rather, it's whether these messages will be intentional.

A second dimension of identity management is *appearance*—the personal items people use to shape an image. Sometimes clothing is part of creating a professional image. A physician's white lab coat and a police officer's uniform set the wearer apart as someone special. In the business world, a tailored suit creates a very different impression than a rumpled outfit. Off the job, clothing is just as important. We choose clothing that sends a message about ourselves: "I'm stylish," "I'm sexy," "I'm athletic," and a host of other possible messages.

A final way to manage impressions is through the choice of *setting*—physical items we use to influence how others view us. In modern Western society, the car is a major part of identity management. This explains why many people lust after cars that are far more expensive and powerful than they really need. A sporty convertible or fancy imported sedan doesn't just get drivers from one place to another; it also makes statements about the kind of people they are. The physical setting we choose and the way we arrange it is another important way to manage impressions. What colors do you choose for the place you live? What artwork is on your walls? What music do you play? (See the nearby Reflection.) If possible, we choose a setting that we enjoy, but in many cases we create an environment that will present the desired front to others.

REFLECTION

Managing My Musical Identity

When I visit friends' homes, I enjoy looking over their music collections. I can tell a lot about people (or at least I think I can) by a quick review of the artists and songs they like.

After reading the section on impression management, I realized that I carefully monitor what music is in *my* collection, knowing that others might assess me the way I assess them. To be honest, I have some songs and artists on display that I rarely listen to, but I like what they represent—and I've also hidden some that I don't want others to know I enjoy!

Identity Management in Mediated Communication Most of the preceding examples involve face-to-face interaction, but identity management is just as pervasive and important in other types of communication. Consider the care you probably take when drafting a résumé for a potential employer, a thank-you letter in response to a gift, or a love note to a sweetheart. Besides giving careful thought to the wording of your message, you probably make strategic decisions about its appearance. Will you use plain white paper or something more distinctive? Will you type your words or handwrite them? People think carefully about considerations like these because they instinctively know that the way a message is presented can say as much as the words it contains (Sitkin et al., 1992).

At first glance, computer-mediated communication (CMC) seems to limit the potential for identity management. Instant messaging and e-mail, for example, appear to lack the "richness" of other channels. They don't convey the tone of your voice, postures, gestures, or facial expressions. Recently, though, communication scholars have begun to recognize that what is missing in CMC can actually be an advantage for communicators who want to manage the impressions they make (Hancock & Dunham, 2001). John Suler (2002, p. 455) puts it this way:

> One of the interesting things about the Internet is the opportunity it offers people to present themselves in a variety of different ways. You can alter your style of being just slightly or indulge in wild experiments with your identity by changing your age, history, personality, and physical appearance, even your gender. The username you choose, the details you do or don't indicate about yourself, the information presented on your personal web page, the persona or avatar you assume in an online community—all are important aspects of how people manage their identity in cyberspace.

"I loved your E-mail, but I thought you'd be older."

E-mailers and instant messengers can choose the desired level of clarity or ambiguity, seriousness or humor, logic or emotion. Unlike face-to-face communication, electronic correspondence allows a sender to say difficult things without forcing the receiver to respond immediately, and it permits the receiver to ignore a message rather than give an unpleasant response. Options like these show that CMC can serve as a tool for identity management at least as well as face-to-face communication (Suler, 2002; Walther, 1996).

Like other forms of online communication, "broadcasting" on the web is also a tool for managing one's identity. Blogs, personal web pages, and profiles on social networking websites like MySpace, Facebook, and Friendster all provide opportunities for their creators to manage their identities. Every Web surfer has encountered pages "under construction." Some observers have pointed out that the construction involves much more than what appears on the computer screen: Personal home page designers also are constructing their public identities (Chandler, 1998; Cheung, 2000, 2005). The words, images, and sounds that Web designers choose make a statement about who they are—or at least how they want to be regarded by others.

Designers create identity both by what they *include* and what they *exclude* from their home page. Consider how featuring or withholding the following kinds of information affects how Web surfers might regard the creator of a home page: age, personal photo, educational or career accomplishments, sexual orientation, job title, personal interests, personal philosophy and religious beliefs, and organizations to which the page creator belongs. You can easily think of a host of other kinds of material that could be included or excluded, and the effect that each would have on how others regard the page creator.

IDENTITY MANAGEMENT AND HONESTY

At first, identity management might sound like an academic label for manipulation or phoniness. There certainly are situations where people misrepresent themselves to gain the trust of others (Buller & Burgoon, 1996). A manipulative date who pretends to be affectionate in order to gain sexual favors is clearly unethical and deceitful. So are job applicants who lie about their academic records to get hired or salespeople who pretend to be dedicated to customer service when their real goal is to make a quick buck. Lindsy Van Gelder (1996) reports "the strange case of the electronic lover" in which a male computer bulletin board user misrepresented himself as a female therapist named Joan to women who were seeking counseling.

Deception in cyberspace is common. In one survey, 27 percent of respondents had engaged in deceptive behaviors while online (Lenhart et al., 2001). A quarter of teens have pretended to be a different person online, and a third confess they have given false information about themselves while e-mailing, instant messaging, or game playing. Even the selection of an avatar can involve deception (Galanxhi & Nah, 2007). And a surprising number of people represent themselves as members of the opposite sex (Samp et al., 2003; Turkle, 1996).

These examples raise important ethical questions about identity management. Is it okay to omit certain information in an online dating service in an attempt to put your best foot forward? (See the Focus on Research box on page 85.) In a job interview, is it legitimate to act more confident and reasonable than you really feel? Likewise, are you justified in acting attentive in a boring conversation out of courtesy to the other person? Is it sometimes wise to use false names and information on the Internet for your protection and security? Situations like these suggest that managing impressions doesn't necessarily make you a liar. In fact, it is almost impossible to imagine how we could communicate effectively without making decisions about which front to present in one situation or another.

Each of us has a repertoire of faces—a cast of characters—and part of being a competent communicator is choosing the best role for a situation. Imagine yourself in each of the following situations, and choose the most effective way you could act, considering the options:

- You offer to teach a friend a new skill, such as playing the guitar, operating a computer program, or sharpening up a tennis backhand. Your friend is making slow progress with the skill, and you find yourself growing impatient.
- You've been corresponding for several weeks with someone you met online, and the relationship is starting to turn romantic. You have a physical trait that you haven't mentioned.
- At work you face a belligerent customer. You don't believe that anyone has the right to treat you this way.

In each of these situations—and in countless others every day—you have a choice about how to act. It is an oversimplification to say that there is only

FOCUS ON RESEARCH

Online Dating: Balancing the Real and Ideal

An estimated 30 million to 40 million Americans have used an online dating service. One attraction of cyberspace courtship is the ability to carefully craft an attractive identity—even when that online persona is more appealing than the facts suggest. Nicole Ellison and her colleagues interviewed participants of an online dating service to find out how the members manage their self-presentations.

Interviewees acknowledged the delicate task of balancing an ideal online identity against the "real" self behind the profile. Many admitted they sometimes fudged facts about themselves—using outdated photos or "forgetting" information about their age, for instance. But respondents were less tolerant when prospective dates posted inaccurate identities. For example, one date-seeker expressed resentment on learning that a purported "hiker" hadn't hiked in years.

Not all misrepresentations by online daters are intentional. The researchers used the term "foggy mirror" to describe the gap between participants' self-perceptions and a more objective assessment. An online dater who describes himself or herself as being "average" in weight might be engaging in wishful thinking rather than telling an outright lie.

As in all interactions—whether in person or in cyberspace—it can be difficult for online daters to recognize and present less-than-ideal parts of themselves. Still, in online dating the potential for misrepresentation makes the old maxim "Buyer beware!" especially valid.

Ellison, N., Heino, R., & Gibbs, J. (2006). Managing impressions online: Self-presentation processes in the online dating environment. *Journal of Computer-Mediated Communication, 11*(2), article 2. http://jcmc.indiana.edu/vol11/issue2/ellison.html

one honest way to behave in each circumstance and that every other response would be insincere and dishonest. Instead, identity management involves deciding which face—which part of yourself—to reveal. For example, when teaching a new skill you may choose to display the "patient" side of yourself instead of the "impatient" side. In the same way, at work you have the option of being either hostile or nondefensive in difficult situations. With strangers, friends, or family you can choose whether or not to disclose your feelings. Which face to show to others is an important decision, but in any case you are sharing a real part of yourself.

Disclosing the Self: Choosing What to Reveal

What we choose to disclose about ourselves is an important component of identity management. So what constitutes self-disclosure? You might argue that aside from secrets, it's impossible *not* to make yourself known to others. After all, every time you open your mouth to speak, you're revealing your tastes, interests, desires, opinions, beliefs, or some other bit of information about yourself. In addition, Chapter 6 will describe how each of us communicates nonverbally even when we're not speaking. For instance, a yawn may mean that you're tired or bored, a shrug of your shoulders may indicate uncertainty or indifference, and how close or how far you choose to stand from your listener may be taken as a measure of your friendliness or comfort.

If every verbal and nonverbal behavior in which you engage is self-revealing, how can self-disclosure be distinguished from any other act of communication? Psychologist Paul Cozby (1973) offers an answer. He suggests that in order for a communication act to be considered self-disclosing, it must (1) contain personal information about the sender, (2) the sender must communicate this information verbally, and (3) another person must be the target. Put differently, the subject of self-disclosing communication is the *self,* and information about the self is *purposefully communicated to another person.*

Although this definition is a start, it ignores the fact that some messages intentionally directed toward others are not especially revealing. For example, telling an acquaintance "I don't like clams" is quite different from announcing "I don't like you." Let's take a look at several factors that further distinguish self-disclosure from other types of communication.

HONESTY It almost goes without saying that true self-disclosure has to be honest. It's not revealing to say "I've never felt this way about anyone before" to every Saturday night date, or to preface every lie with the statement "Let me be honest. . . ."

As long as you are honest and accurate to the best of your knowledge, communication can qualify as an act of self-disclosure. On the other hand, painting an incomplete picture of yourself (telling only part of what's true) is not genuine disclosure. We'll talk more about the relationship between honesty and disclosure later in this chapter.

DEPTH A self-disclosing statement is generally regarded as being personal—containing relatively "deep" rather than "surface" information. Of course, what is personal and intimate for one person may not be for another. You might feel comfortable admitting your spotty academic record, short temper, or fear of spiders to anyone who asks, whereas others would be embarrassed to do so. Even basic demographic information, such as age, can be extremely revealing for some people.

AVAILABILITY OF INFORMATION Self-disclosing messages must contain information that the other person is not likely to know at the time or be able to obtain from another source. For example, describing your conviction for a drunk-driving accident might feel like an act of serious disclosure because the information concerns you, is offered intentionally, is honest and accurate, and is considered personal. However, if the other person could obtain that information elsewhere without much trouble—from a glance at the morning newspaper or from various gossips, for example—your communication would not be especially self-disclosing.

CONTEXT OF SHARING Sometimes the self-disclosing nature of a statement comes from the setting in which it is uttered. For instance, relatively innocuous information about family life seems more personal when a student shares it with the class (Myers, 1998), when an athlete tells it to her coach (Officer & Rosenfeld, 1985), or when it's shared online (Stritzke et al., 2004).

We can summarize our definitional tour by saying that **self-disclosure** (1) has the self as subject, (2) is intentional, (3) is directed at another person, (4) is honest, (5) is revealing, (6) contains information generally unavailable from other sources, and (7) gains much of its intimate nature from the context in which it is expressed.

Although many acts of communication may be self-revealing, this definition makes it clear that few of our statements may be classified as self-disclosure. Pearce and Sharp (1973) estimate that as little as 2 percent of our communication qualifies as self-disclosure. Other research confirms this. For example, most conversations—even among friends—focus on everyday mundane topics and disclose little or no personal information (Dindia et al., 1997; Duck & Miell, 1986). Even partners in intimate relationships don't talk about personal matters with a high degree of frequency (Alberts et al., 2005).

MODELS OF SELF-DISCLOSURE

Now that we've defined self-disclosure, let's take a look at two models that help us better understand how self-revelations operate in our relationships with others.

Degrees of Self-Disclosure: The Social Penetration Model Social psychologists Irwin Altman and Dalmas Taylor (1973; Taylor & Altman, 1987) describe two ways in which communication can be more or less disclosing. Their social penetration model is pictured in Figure 3.2. The first dimension

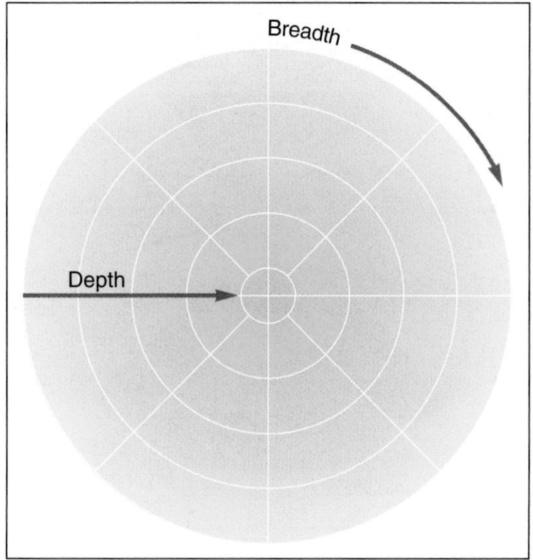

FIGURE 3.2 Social Penetration Model

of self-disclosure in this model involves the breadth of information volunteered—the range of subjects being discussed. For example, the breadth of disclosure in your relationship with a fellow worker will expand as you begin revealing information about your life away from the job, as well as on-the-job details. The second dimension of disclosure is the depth of the information being volunteered—the shift from relatively nonrevealing messages to more personal ones.

Depending on the breadth and depth of information shared, a relationship can be defined as casual or intimate. In a casual relationship, the breadth may be great, but not the depth. A more intimate relationship is likely to have high depth in at least one area. The most intimate relationships are those in which disclosure is great in both breadth and depth. Altman and Taylor see the development of a relationship as a progression from the periphery of their model to its center, a process that typically occurs over time. Each of your personal relationships probably has a different combination of breadth of subjects and depth of revelation. Figure 3.3 pictures a student's self-disclosure in one relationship.

One way to classify the depth of disclosure is to look at the types of information that can be revealed. *Clichés* are ritualized, stock responses to social situations—virtually the opposite of self-disclosure: "How are you doing?" "Fine." Although hardly revealing, clichés can serve as a valuable kind of shorthand that makes it easy to keep the social wheels greased.

Another kind of message involves communicating *facts.* Not all factual statements qualify as self-disclosure. To qualify they must fit the criteria of

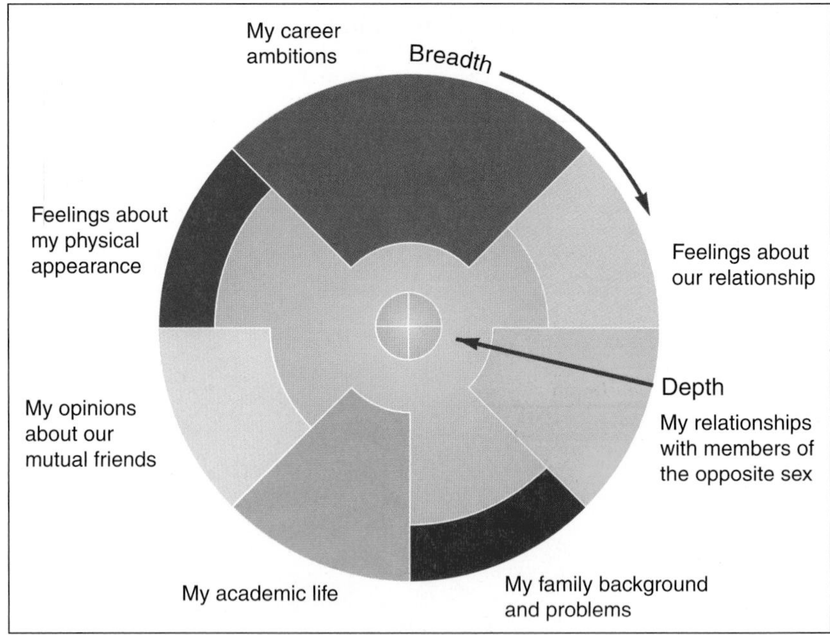

FIGURE 3.3 Sample Model of Social Penetration

being intentional, significant, and not otherwise known: "This isn't my first try at college. I dropped out a year ago with terrible grades." Disclosing personal facts like these often signals a desire to move a relationship to a new level of intimacy.

Opinions can be a kind of self-disclosure since they often reveal more about a person than facts alone do. Every time you offer a personal opinion, you are giving others valuable information about yourself.

The fourth level of self-disclosure—and usually the most revealing one—involves the expression of *feelings.* At first glance, feelings might appear to be the same as opinions, but there's a big difference. "I don't think you're telling me about what's on your mind" is an opinion. Notice how much more we learn about the speaker by looking at three different feelings that could accompany this statement: "I don't think you're telling me what's on your mind . . .

and I'm suspicious."
and I'm angry."
and I'm hurt."

Awareness of Self-Disclosure: The Johari Window Model Another way to illustrate how self-disclosure operates in communication is to look at a model called the **Johari Window**, developed by Joseph Luft and Harry Ingham (Janas, 2001; Luft, 1969).

Imagine a frame that contains everything there is to know about you: your likes and dislikes, your goals, your secrets, your needs—everything. This frame could be divided into information you know about yourself and things you don't know. It could also be split into things others know about you and things they don't know. Figure 3.4 reflects these divisions.

Part 1 represents the information of which both you and the other person are aware. This part is your *open area.* Part 2 represents the *blind area:* information of which you are unaware but that the other person knows. You learn about information in the blind area primarily through feedback

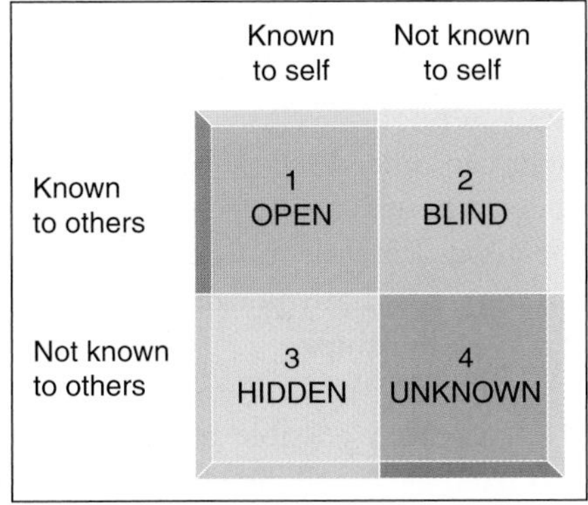

FIGURE 3.4 Johari Window

Luft, J. *Group process: An introduction to group dynamics.* © 1963, 1970 by Joseph Luft. Used with permission of Mayfield Publishing Company.

from others. Part 3 of the Johari Window represents your *hidden area:* information that you know but aren't willing to reveal to others. Items in this hidden area become public primarily through self-disclosure, which is the focus of this section. Part 4 of the Johari Window represents information that is *unknown* to both you and to others. At first the unknown area seems impossible to verify. After all, if neither you nor others know what it contains, how can you be sure it exists at all? We can deduce its existence because we are constantly discovering new things about ourselves. For example, it is not unusual to discover that you have an unrecognized talent, strength, or weakness. Items move from the unknown area into the open area when you share your insight, or into the hidden area, where it becomes a secret.

The relative size of each area in our personal Johari Windows changes from time to time according to our moods, the subject we are discussing, and our relationship with the other person. Despite these changes, a single Johari Window could represent most people's overall style of disclosure.

BENEFITS AND RISKS OF SELF-DISCLOSURE

By now it should be clear that neither all-out disclosure nor complete privacy is desirable. On one hand, relationships suffer when people keep important information from one another (Caughlin & Golish, 2002; Mashek & Sherman, 2004). On the other hand, revealing deeply personal information can threaten the stability—or even the survival—of a relationship. In the following pages we will outline both the benefits and risks of opening yourself to others.

Benefits of Self-Disclosure Modern culture, at least in the United States, places high value on self-disclosure (Katriel & Philipsen, 1981; Marshall, 2008) and warns about the dangers of keeping secrets (Cooks, 2000; Kelly, 1999). There is evidence that revealing secrets can have important benefits (Agne et al., 2000; Kelly, 1999). We can build upon this work by listing some potential benefits of revealing personal information:

CATHARSIS Sometimes you might disclose information in an effort to "get it off your chest." Catharsis can indeed relieve the burden of pent-up emotions (Pennebaker, 1997), but when it's the *only* goal of disclosure, the results of opening up may not be good. Later in this chapter you'll read guidelines for disclosing that increase the odds that you can achieve catharsis in a way that helps, instead of harming relationships.

SELF-CLARIFICATION It is often possible to clarify your beliefs, opinions, thoughts, attitudes, and feelings by talking about them with another person. This sort of gaining insight by "talking the problem out" occurs in many psychotherapies, but it also goes on in other relationships, ranging from good friends to interaction with bartenders or hairdressers.

SELF-VALIDATION If you disclose information with the hope of seeking the listener's agreement ("I think I did the right thing"), you are seeking validation of your behavior—confirmation of a belief you hold about yourself. On a deeper level, this sort of self-validating disclosure seeks confirmation of important parts of your self-concept. For instance, self-validation is an important part of the "coming out" process through which gay people recognize their sexual orientation and choose to disclose this knowledge in their personal, family, and social lives (Han, 2001; Savin-Williams, 2001).

RECIPROCITY A well-documented conclusion from research is that one person's act of self-disclosure increases the odds that the other person will reveal personal information (Derlega et al., 1993; Dindia, 2000b, 2002). There is no guarantee that revealing personal information will trigger self-disclosures by others, but your own honesty can create a climate that makes the other person feel safer, and perhaps even obligated to match your level of candor ("I've been bored with our relationship lately" might get a response of "Wow, me, too!"). Reciprocity doesn't always occur on a turn-by-turn basis: Telling a friend today about your job-related problems might help her feel comfortable opening up to you later about her family history, when the time is right for this sort of disclosure.

IMPRESSION FORMATION Sometimes we reveal personal information to make ourselves more attractive, and research shows that this strategy seems to work. One study revealed that both men's and women's attractiveness was associated with the amount of self-disclosure in conversations (Stiles et al., 1996). Consider a couple on their first date. It's not hard to imagine how one or both partners might share personal information to appear more sincere, interesting, sensitive, or curious about the other person. The same principle applies in other situations. A salesperson might say, "I'll be honest with you" primarily to show that she is on your side.

RELATIONSHIP MAINTENANCE AND ENHANCEMENT Research demonstrates that we like people who disclose personal information to us. In fact, the relationship between self-disclosure and liking works in several directions: We like people who disclose personal information to us; we reveal more about ourselves to people we like; and we tend to like others more after we have disclosed to them (Dindia, 2000b).

Appropriate self-disclosure is positively related to marital satisfaction (Rosenfeld & Bowen, 1991; Waring & Chelune, 1983). Disclosing spouses give their relationships higher evaluations and have more positive expectations than do partners who disclose less. In one sample of 50 couples, the amount of overall disclosure in their relationships was a good predictor of whether the partners remained together over the 4 years in which they were studied (Sprecher, 1987). And a number of studies have demonstrated that increased self-disclosure can improve troubled marriages (Vito, 1999; Waring, 1981). With the guidance of a skilled counselor or therapist, partners can learn constructive ways to open up.

SELF-ASSESSMENT

Analyzing Your Self-Disclosure Choices

PART 1: WHY YOU DISCLOSE

Use the following scale to indicate your reasons for self-disclosing. These reasons are likely to vary for each relationship you analyze, so you may choose to repeat this self-assessment more than once. Keep one relationship in mind as you complete the self-assessment.

1 = This is *definitely not* a reason I self-disclose.
2 = This is *probably not* a reason I self-disclose.
3 = I am *unsure* whether this is a reason I self-disclose.
4 = This is *probably* a reason I self-disclose.
5 = This is *definitely* a reason I self-disclose.

_____ **1. I disclose as a means to get something off my chest—to vent my feelings.**
_____ **2. I disclose as a way to clarify what my beliefs, feelings, opinions, thoughts, and so on are—to use the other person as a "sounding board."**
_____ **3. I disclose to get the other person to agree with me about how I see the situation.**
_____ **4. I disclose as a way to encourage the other person to talk to me.**
_____ **5. I disclose certain pieces of information so as to create a particular impression of myself.**
_____ **6. I disclose to keep the other person current with what is happening to me, so that our relationship "doesn't fall behind."**
_____ **7. I disclose to be able to achieve some particular goal—for example, to increase my control over the other person, the situation, or our relationship.**
_____ **8. I disclose so I can get advice, support, or assistance from this person.**
_____ **9. I disclose because I "owe it" to this person, feel obligated, because this person has the right to know.**
_____ **10. I disclose to the other person because we care for each other, trust one another, and support one another.**

PART 2: REASONS FOR NOT DISCLOSING

Use the following scale to identify your reasons for not disclosing personal information. As before, you may choose to repeat this self-assessment for each of your important relationships, but keep one relationship in mind for each evaluation.

1 = This is *definitely not* a reason I avoid self-disclosing.
2 = This is *probably not* a reason I avoid self-disclosing.
3 = I am *unsure* whether this is a reason I avoid self-disclosing.
4 = This is *probably* a reason I avoid self-disclosing.
5 = This is *definitely* a reason I avoid self-disclosing.

_____ **1. I can't find the opportunity to self-disclose.**
_____ **2. I don't want to upset or hurt the person—perhaps put the person's life in an uproar.**

_____ **3. I can't think of a way to self-disclose.**
_____ **4. The information I disclose might be used against me in some way.**
_____ **5. I might be treated differently after I self-disclose.**
_____ **6. I might be treated as if I were "crazy" after I self-disclose.**
_____ **7. I don't think I'll get support if I self-disclose.**
_____ **8. I might not be understood.**
_____ **9. My self-disclosure might hurt our relationship.**
_____ **10. What I self-disclose might be told to people I would prefer not know.**
_____ **11. I don't self-disclose because our relationship isn't close enough.**
_____ **12. What I self-disclose might be told to people I would prefer to tell myself.**
_____ **13. I don't know how to put what I want to say into words.**

What are your most important or usual reasons for disclosing? What are your most important or usual reasons for not disclosing? What does this information reveal to you about how you use self-disclosure in your relationships, and the kinds of relationships you have?

MORAL OBLIGATION Sometimes we disclose personal information out of a sense of moral obligation. People who are HIV-positive, for example, are often faced with the choice of whether they should tell their health care providers and their partner. One study (Agne et al., 2000) found that patients typically did disclose their HIV status to their health care provider because they felt it was the responsible thing to do for themselves (to help fight their illness) and to protect the provider. Another study (Derlega et al., 2000) found that people who are HIV-positive often see disclosing their status "as a duty" and as a way to educate the partner—as an obligation.

SOCIAL INFLUENCE Self-disclosure can be an effective compliance-gaining strategy. For example, a valued employee who tells the boss that another firm has made overtures probably will have an increased chance of getting raises and improvements in working conditions.

In addition to disclosing to help ourselves, people sometimes reveal personal information to help others. This behavior is common in self-help groups such as Alcoholics Anonymous (Hegelson & Gottlieb, 2000). On a larger scale, one study revealed that guests who chose to self-disclose on a particular television talk show indicated that their primary motive was "evangelical": They felt a calling to address injustices and remedy stereotypes (Priest & Dominick, 1994).

SELF-DEFENSE Sometimes you may choose to self-disclose something before someone else discloses it for you. A review of the social influence literature by Williams and Dolnik (2001) suggests that self-disclosing negative or damaging information is frequently used as an adaptive social influence strategy called "stealing thunder."

Risks of Self-Disclosure While the benefits of disclosing are certainly important, opening up can also involve risks that make the decision to disclose a difficult and sometimes painful one (Afifi & Caughlin, 2007; Cline & McKenzie, 2000). The risks of self-disclosure fall into several categories (Derlega et al., 2000; Greene et al., 2006; Rosenfeld, 1979, 2000).

REJECTION In answering the question that forms the title of his book *Why Am I Afraid to Tell You Who I Am?* John Powell (1969) summed up the risks of disclosing: "I am afraid to tell you who I am because if I tell you who I am, you may not like who I am, and that's all I have." The fear of disapproval is powerful. Sometimes it is exaggerated and illogical, but there are real dangers in revealing personal information:

A: I'm starting to think of you as more than a friend. To tell the truth, I think I love you.
B: I think we should stop seeing one another.

NEGATIVE IMPRESSION Even if disclosure doesn't lead to total rejection, it can create a negative impression.

A: You know, I've never had a relationship with a woman that lasted more than a month.
B: Really? I wonder what that says about you.

DECREASE IN RELATIONAL SATISFACTION Besides affecting others' opinions of you, disclosure can lead to a decrease in the satisfaction that comes from a relationship. Consider a scenario like this, where the incompatible wants and needs of each person become clear through disclosure:

A: Let's get together with Wes and Joanne on Saturday night.
B: To tell you the truth, I'm tired of seeing Wes and Joanne. I don't have much fun with them, and I think Wes is kind of a jerk.
A: But they're my best friends!

LOSS OF INFLUENCE Another risk of disclosure is a potential loss of influence in the relationship. Once you confess a secret weakness, your control over how the other person views you can be diminished.

A: I'm sorry I was so sarcastic. Sometimes I build myself up by putting you down.
B: Is that it? I'll never let you get away with that again!

LOSS OF CONTROL Revealing something personal about yourself means losing control of the information. What might happen if the person tells others what you disclosed, people you prefer not know, or who you would like to tell yourself?

A: I never really liked Leslie. I agreed to go out because it meant a good meal in a nice restaurant.
B: Really? Leslie would sure like to know that!

HURT THE OTHER PERSON Even if revealing hidden information leaves you feeling better, it might hurt others—cause them to be upset, for example. It's probably easy to imagine yourself in a situation like this:

A: Well, since you asked, I have felt less attracted to you lately. I know you can't help it when your skin breaks out, but it is kind of a turnoff.
B: I know! I don't see how you can stand me at all!

ALTERNATIVES TO SELF-DISCLOSURE

While self-disclosure plays an important role in interpersonal relationships, it isn't the only type of communication available. To understand why complete honesty isn't always an easy or ideal choice, consider some familiar dilemmas:

- You have grown increasingly annoyed with some habits of the person you live with. You fear that bringing up this topic could lead to an unpleasant conversation, and maybe even damage the relationship.
- Your friend, who is headed out the door for an important job interview, says, "I know I'll never get this job! I'm really not qualified, and besides I look terrible." You agree with your friend's assessment.
- You've just been given a large, extremely ugly lamp as a gift by a relative who visits your home often. How would you respond to the question, "Where will you put it?"

Situations like these highlight some of the issues that surround deceptive communication.

Although honesty is desirable in principle, it often has risky, potentially unpleasant consequences. It's tempting to sidestep situations where self-disclosure would be difficult, but examples like the ones you just read show that avoidance isn't always possible. Research and personal experience show that communicators—even those with the best intentions—aren't always completely honest when they find themselves in situations when honesty would be uncomfortable (O'Hair & Cody, 1993). Four common alternatives to self-disclosure are silence, lying, equivocation, and hinting. We will take a closer look at each one.

Silence One alternative to self-disclosure is to keep your thoughts and feelings to yourself. As the cartoon on page 96 shows, there are many times when keeping information to yourself can seem like the best approach, both for you and the other person.

You can get a sense of how much you rely on silence instead of disclosing by keeping a record of when you do and don't express your opinions. You're likely to find that withholding thoughts and feelings is a common approach for you.

Lying A **lie** is a deliberate attempt to hide or misrepresent the truth. At first glance, lying seems to be an obvious breach of ethics. In fact, extensive use of lying is typically a sign of relational distress (Cole, 2001).

Lying to gain unfair advantage over an unknowing victim seems clearly wrong, but another kind of mistruth—the "benevolent lie"—isn't so easy to dismiss as completely unethical. **Benevolent lies** are defined (at least by the people who tell them) as not being malicious—and perhaps they are even helpful to the person to whom they are told. You can almost certainly recall times when you have been less than truthful in order to avoid hurting someone you care for.

Whether or not they are innocent, benevolent lies are certainly common. In several studies spanning four decades, a significant majority of people surveyed acknowledge that even in their closest relationships, there are times when lying is justified (Knapp, 2006). In one study, 130 subjects were asked to keep track of the truthfulness of their everyday conversational statements (Turner et al., 1975). Only 38.5 percent of these statements—slightly more than a third—proved to be totally honest. Another study (DePaulo & Kashy, 1998) found that both community leaders and undergraduate students lied about once in every 10 conversations with people they were close to, such as romantic partners, best friends, and family members. More of the lies told to best friends and friends, however, were benevolent rather than self-serving, and the reverse was true of lies told to acquaintances and strangers, a finding replicated in a recent study (Ennis et al., 2008).

Most people think benevolent lies are told for the benefit of the recipient. For example, the majority of subjects in the DePaulo et al. (1996) study claimed such lying was "the right thing to do." Other research paints a less flattering picture of who benefits most from lying. One study found that two out of every three lies are told for "selfish reasons" (Hample, 1980). Other research, by Paula Lippard (1988), seems to indicate that this figure is too conservative. Of 322 lies recorded, 75.8 percent were for the benefit of the

TABLE 3.2 ***Some Reasons for Lying***

REASON	EXAMPLE
Save face for others	"Don't worry—I'm sure nobody noticed that stain on your shirt."
Save face for self	"I wasn't looking at the files—I was accidentally in the wrong drawer."
Acquire resources	"Oh, *please* let me add this class. If I don't get in, I'll never graduate on time!"
Protect resources	"I'd like to lend you the money, but I'm short myself."
Initiate interaction	"Excuse me, I'm lost. Do you live around here?"
Be socially gracious	"No, I'm not bored—tell me more about your vacation."
Avoid conflict	"It's not a big deal. We can do it your way. Really."
Avoid interaction	"That sounds like fun, but I'm busy Saturday night."
Leave taking	"Oh, look what time it is! I've got to run!"
Present a competent image	"Sure I understand. No problem."
Increase social desirability	"Yeah, I've done a fair amount of skiing."
Exaggeration	"You think *this* is cold? Let me tell you about how cold it was on that trip. . . ."

liar. Less than 22 percent were for the benefit of the person hearing the lie, while a mere 2.5 percent were intended to aid a third person. Table 3.2 identifies various reasons for lying, adapted from Camden et al. (1984) and other studies cited in this section.

Not all lies are equally devastating. Feelings like dismay and betrayal are greatest when the relationship is most intense, the importance of the subject is high, and when there was previous suspicion that the other person wasn't being completely honest. Of these three factors, the importance of the information lied about proved to be the key factor in provoking a relational crisis (McCornack & Levine, 1990). We may be able to cope with "misdemeanor" lying, but "felonies" are a grave threat—often leading to the end of a relationship.

The lesson here is clear: Lying about major parts of your relationship can have the gravest of consequences. If preserving a relationship is important to you, then honesty—at least about important matters—really does appear to be the best policy.

Equivocation Lying isn't the only alternative to self-disclosure. When faced with the choice between lying and telling an unpleasant truth, communicators can—and often do—equivocate. **Equivocal language** has two or more equally plausible meanings.

Sometimes we send equivocal messages without meaning to, resulting in confusion. "I'll meet you at the apartment" could refer to more than one place. But other times we are deliberately vague. For instance, when a friend asks what you think of an awful outfit, you could say, "It's really unusual—one of a kind!" Likewise, if you are too angry to accept a friend's apology but don't want to appear petty, you might say, "Don't mention it."

The value of equivocation becomes clear when you consider the alternatives. Consider the dilemma of what to say when you've been given an unwanted present—an ugly painting, for example—and the giver asks what you think of it. How can you respond? On the one hand, you need to choose between telling the truth and lying. At the same time, you have a choice of whether to make your response clear or vague. Figure 3.5 displays these choices.

A study by Sandra Metts and her colleagues (1992) shows how equivocation can save face in difficult situations. Several hundred college students were asked how they would turn down unwanted sexual overtures from a person whose feelings were important to them: a close friend, a prospective date, or a dating partner. The majority of students chose a diplomatic reaction ("I just don't think I'm ready for this right now") as being more

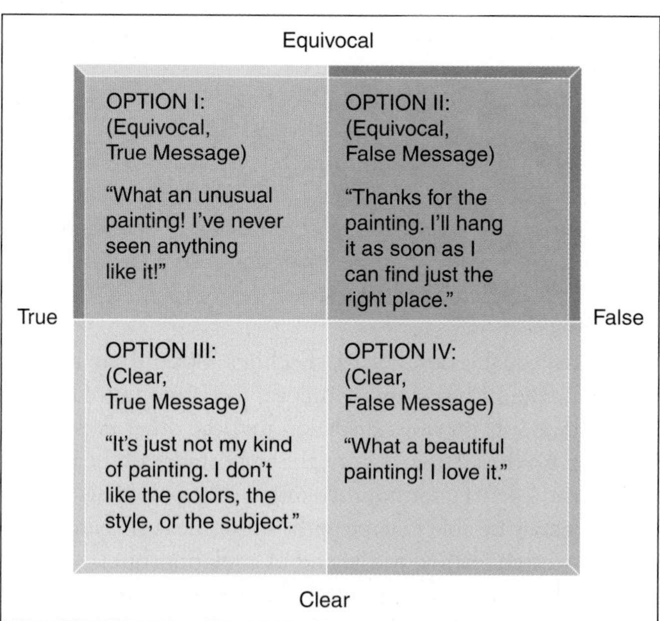

FIGURE 3.5 Dimensions of Truthfulness and Equivocation

face-saving and comfortable than a direct statement like "I just don't feel sexually attracted to you." The diplomatic reaction seemed sufficiently clear to get the message across, but not so blunt as to embarrass or humiliate the other person.

Equivocal language also may save the speaker from being caught lying. If a potential employer asks about your grades during a job interview, you would be safe saying "I had a *B* average last semester," even though your overall grade average is closer to *C*. The statement isn't a complete answer, but it is honest as far as it goes. As Bavelas et al. (1990, p. 171) put it, "Equivocation is neither a false message nor a clear truth, but rather an alternative used precisely when both of these are to be avoided."

The underlying point of equivocal messages is often not lost on their recipients. Renee Edwards and Richard Bello (2001; Bello & Edwards, 2005) explored how receivers interpreted equivocal statements, such as telling a friend that his or her speech was "interesting" instead of saying "You messed up." Besides regarding the equivocal statements as more polite, they had no trouble discerning the intended meaning—that the speech was poor, to use our example.

Given the advantages of equivocation, it's not surprising that most people usually will choose to equivocate rather than tell a lie. In a series of experiments, subjects chose between telling a face-saving lie, the truth, and equivocating (Bavelas et al., 1990). Only 6 percent chose the lie, and between 3 and 4 percent chose the hurtful truth. By contrast, over 90 percent chose the equivocal response. People may say they prefer truth-telling to equivocating, but given the choice, they usually finesse the truth (Robinson et al., 1998).

Hinting Hints are more direct than equivocal statements. Whereas an equivocal message isn't necessarily aimed at changing another's behavior, a hint seeks to get the desired response from the other person. As Michael Motley (1992) suggests, some hints are designed to save the receiver from embarrassment:

Direct Statement	Face-Saving Hint
You're too overweight to be ordering dessert.	These desserts are terribly overpriced.
I'm too busy to continue with this conversation. I wish you would let me go.	I know you're busy; I'd better let you go.

Other hints are less concerned with protecting the receiver than with saving the sender from embarrassment:

Direct Statement	Face-Saving Hint
Please don't smoke here; it bothers me.	I'm pretty sure that smoking isn't permitted here.
I'd like to invite you out for lunch, but I don't want to risk a "no" answer to my invitation.	Gee, it's almost lunch time. Have you ever eaten at that new Italian restaurant around the corner?

The success of a hint depends on the other person's ability to pick up the unexpressed message. Your subtle remarks might go right over the head of an insensitive receiver, or one who chooses not to respond to them. If this happens, you still have the choice to be more direct. If the costs of a straightforward message seem too high, you can withdraw without risk.

The Ethics of Evasion It's easy to see why people often choose hints, equivocations, and benevolent lies instead of complete self-disclosure. These strategies provide a way to manage difficult situations that is easier than the alternatives for both the speaker and the receiver of the message. In this sense, successful liars, equivocators, and hinters can be said to possess a certain kind of communicative competence. On the other hand, there *are* times when honesty is the right approach, even if it's painful. At times like these, evaders could be viewed as lacking either the competence or the integrity to handle a situation effectively.

Are hints, benevolent lies, and equivocations ethical alternatives to self-disclosure? Some of the examples in these pages suggest the answer is a qualified "yes." Many social scientists and philosophers agree. For example, researchers David Buller and Judee Burgoon (1994) argue that the morality of a speaker's motives for lying ought to be judged, not the deceptive act itself. Another approach is to consider whether the effects of a lie will be worth the deception. Ethicist Sissela Bok (1978) offers some circumstances where deception may be justified: doing good, avoiding harm, and protecting a larger truth. One example is when a patient asks, "How am I doing?"; if a nurse perceives that telling the truth could be harmful, it would violate the obligation to "do good and avoid harm," and honesty would be less important than caring (Tuckett, 2005). Perhaps the right questions to ask, then, are whether an indirect message is truly in the interests of the receiver and whether this sort of evasion is the only effective way to behave. Bok suggests another way to check the justifiability of a lie: Imagine how others would respond if they knew what you were really thinking or feeling. Would they accept your reasons for not disclosing?

Bending the Truth: *Bend It Like Beckham*

Jess Bhamra (Parminder Nagra) is a young woman caught in the middle of conflicting goals, relationships, and cultures. Her parents want her to embrace her Indian heritage and traditional Sikh upbringing, but she would rather play soccer in the parks of London. When she's invited to try out for a local soccer team, Jess knows her parents would never allow her to participate—so she doesn't tell them. She makes the team and attends their practices and games in secret.

Secrets are a central theme of this movie. Several characters choose not to disclose important information for a variety of reasons, ranging from saving face to saving relationships. As their stories unfold, discovered secrets often lead to hurt and a sense of betrayal—yet it's easy to see that most of the secrets are kept for good reasons.

The title of the film is a reference to the kicking style of soccer star David Beckham, whom Jess idolizes. It is also a metaphor for the communication style of many of the movie's characters. For Jess, while she sometimes bends the truth, she is also trying to get her parents to bend their ways. The key, as they all learn, is to discover how to "bend without breaking."

GUIDELINES FOR SELF DISCLOSURE

Self-disclosure is a special kind of sharing that is not appropriate for every situation. Let's take a look at some guidelines that can help you recognize how to express yourself in a way that's rewarding for you and for the others involved (Greene et al., 2006).

Is the Other Person Important to You? There are several ways in which someone might be important. Perhaps you have an ongoing relationship deep enough so that sharing significant parts of yourself justifies keeping your present level of togetherness intact. Perhaps the person to whom you're considering disclosing is someone with whom you've previously related on a less personal level. Now you see a chance to grow closer, and disclosure may be the path toward developing that personal relationship.

Is the Risk of Disclosing Reasonable? Most people intuitively calculate the potential benefits of disclosing against the risks of doing so (Fisher, 1986; Vangelisti et al., 2001). Even if the probable benefits are great, opening yourself up to almost certain rejection may be asking for trouble. For instance, it might be foolhardy to share your important feelings with someone you know is likely to betray your confidences or ridicule them. On the other hand, knowing that your partner will respect the information makes the prospect of speaking out more reasonable.

Revealing personal thoughts and feelings can be especially risky on the job (Eisenberg, 1990; Eisenberg & Witten, 1987)—particularly if the subject involves sexual orientation (Ragins & Singh, 2007). The politics of the workplace sometimes require communicators to keep feelings to themselves in order to accomplish both personal and organizational goals. For example, you might find the opinions of a boss or customer personally offensive but decide to bite your tongue rather than risk your job or lose goodwill for the company.

DARK SIDE OF COMMUNICATION

Brutal Honesty

Sometimes honesty can be a weapon, wielded deliberately with the intention to cause pain. Lyricist Paul Simon captured the tone of heartless candor in his song "Tenderness":

You say you care for me
But there's no tenderness
Beneath your honesty.

Pain-inducing candor isn't always deliberate. Sometimes we may be thoughtlessly honest, causing pain due to carelessness rather than premeditated malice. Whether intentional or not, imagine the consequences if you shared every thought that crossed your mind: "I'm bored." "I don't believe you." "You look terrible!"

Whether it's malicious or just insensitive, brutal honesty is hard to justify. The challenge we face is knowing when and how to tell the truth appropriately.

Is the Self-Disclosure Appropriate? Self-disclosure isn't an all-or-nothing proposition. It's possible to reveal information in some situations and keep it to yourself in others. One important variable is the relational stage (VanLear, 1987; Won-Doornick, 1979). Research shows that sharing personal information is appropriate during the integrating stage of a relationship, where partners grow closer by disclosing. But once the same relationship has reached a maintenance stage, the frequency of personal disclosures drops (Sillars et al., 1987). This makes sense, for by now the partners have already shared much of their private selves. Even the closest long-term relationships are a mixture of much everyday, nonintimate information and less frequent but more personal messages. Finally, realize that even intimate partners need to be sensitive to the timing of a message. If the other person is tired, preoccupied, or grumpy, it may be a good idea to postpone an important conversation.

Is the Disclosure Relevant to the Situation at Hand? The kind of disclosure that is often a characteristic of highly personal relationships usually isn't appropriate in less personal settings. For instance, a study of classroom communication revealed that sharing all feelings—both positive and negative—and being completely honest resulted in less cohesiveness than a "relatively" honest climate in which pleasant but superficial relationships were the norm (Rosenfeld & Gilbert, 1989).

Is the Disclosure Reciprocated? There's nothing quite as disconcerting as talking your heart out to someone, only to discover that the other person has yet to say anything to you that is half as revealing. You think to yourself, "What am I doing?" Unequal self-disclosure creates an unbalanced relationship, one with potential problems.

The reciprocal nature of effective disclosure doesn't mean that you are obliged to match another person's revelations on a tit-for-tat basis. You might reveal personal information at one time, while the other person could open up at a later date. There are even times when reciprocal self-disclosure can be taken as stage hogging. For instance, if a close friend is talking about his opinion of your relationship, it's probably better to hear him out and bring up your perspective later, after he's made his point.

There are few times when one-way disclosure is acceptable. Most of them involve formal, therapeutic relationships in which a client approaches a trained professional with the goal of resolving a problem. For instance, you wouldn't necessarily expect your physician, during an office visit, to begin sharing information with you on her or his personal ailments—although it's been known to happen, sometimes to the chagrin of the patient (McDaniel et al., 2007).

Will the Effect Be Constructive? Self-disclosure can be a vicious tool if it's not used carefully. Every person has a psychological "beltline," and below that beltline are areas about which the person is extremely sensitive. Jabbing at an area "below the belt" is a surefire way to disable another person, usually at great cost to the relationship. It's important to consider the effects of your candor before opening up to others. Comments such as "I've always thought you were pretty unintelligent" or "Last year I made love to your best friend" may sometimes resolve old business and thus be constructive, but they also can be devastating—to the listener, to the relationship, and to your self-esteem.

Summary

The self-concept is a relatively stable set of perceptions individuals hold about themselves. It begins to develop soon after birth, being shaped by the appraisals of significant others and by social comparisons with reference groups. The self-concept is subjective and can vary substantially from the way a person is perceived by others. Although the self may evolve over time, the self-concept resists change.

A self-fulfilling prophecy occurs when a person's expectations of an event and subsequent behavior influence the event's outcome. One type of prophecy consists of predictions by others, while another category is self-imposed. It is possible to change one's self-concept in ways that lead to more effective communication.

Identity management consists of an individual's strategic communication designed to influence others' perceptions. Identity management aims at presenting one or more faces to others, which may be different from private, spontaneous behavior that occurs outside of others' presence. Some communicators are high self-monitors who are highly conscious of their own behavior, while others are less aware of how their words and actions affect others. Communicating through mediated channels can enhance a person's ability to manage impressions. Since each person has a variety of faces that she or he can reveal, choosing which one to present is a central concern of competent communicators.

Self-disclosure consists of honest, revealing messages about the self that are intentionally directed toward others. Disclosing communication contains information that is generally unavailable via other sources.

The percentage of messages that are truly self-disclosing is relatively low. A number of factors govern whether a communicator will be judged as being a high- or low-level discloser.

Two models for describing self-disclosure are the social penetration model and the Johari Window model. The social penetration model describes two dimensions of self-disclosure: breadth and depth. The Johari Window illustrates the amount of information that an individual reveals to others, hides, is blind to, and is unaware of.

Communicators disclose personal information for a variety of reasons. There also are several reasons to choose not to self-disclose, some of which serve primarily the interests of the nondiscloser, and others of which are intended to benefit the target. Four alternatives to revealing self-disclosures are silence, lies (both benevolent and self-serving), equivocations, and hints. These may be ethical alternatives to self-disclosure; however, whether they are or not depends on the speaker's motives and the effects of the deception. When deciding whether or not to disclose, communicators should consider a variety of factors detailed in the closing section of the chapter.

Activities

1. Invitation to Insight/Ethical Challenge

Choose someone with whom you have an important interpersonal relationship, and explore how you influence each other's self-concepts.

a. Interview your partner to discover how your words and deeds influence his or her self-concept. Identify specific incidents to illustrate these influences, and discuss which specific parts of the self-concept you have affected.

b. Now share with your partner how his or her behaviors have affected your self-concept. Again, be specific about identifying the incidents and the parts of your self-concept that were affected.
c. Once you recognize the power you have to shape another's self-concept, ask yourselves what responsibility each of you has to treat the other person in a supportive manner when you are faced with delivering a potentially critical message.
d. Based on the information exchanged so far, discuss whether you are satisfied with the way you have affected each other's self-concepts. Identify any ways you could communicate more effectively.

2. Invitation to Insight

What reference groups do you use to define your self-concept? You can recognize your social comparison groups by answering several questions:

a. Select one area in which you compare yourself to others. In what area is the comparison made? (For example, is the comparison based on wealth, intelligence, or social skill?)
b. In the selected area, ask yourself, "Which people am I better or worse than?"
c. In the selected area, ask yourself, "Which people am I the same as or different from?"

What is the effect of using these groups as a basis for judging yourself? How might you view yourself differently if you used other reference groups as a basis for comparison?

3. Invitation to Insight

Describe two incidents in which self-fulfilling prophecies you have imposed on yourself have affected your communication. Explain how each of these predictions shaped your behavior, and describe how you might have behaved differently if you had made a different prediction. Next, describe two incidents in which you imposed self-fulfilling prophecies on others. What effect did your prediction have on these people's actions?

4. Skill Builder

Identify one communication-related part of your self-concept you would like to change. Use the guidelines on pages 76–77 to describe how you could make that change.

a. Decide whether your expectations for change are realistic. Don't expect to become a new person: Becoming a *better* one should be enough.
b. Recognize your strengths as well as your shortcomings. You may not be as bad as you think you are!
c. Decide whether you are willing to make the necessary effort to change. Good intentions are an important start, but hard work also is necessary.
d. Develop a specific plan to change the way you behave. You may want to consult books and experts as well as observe models to gain a clear idea of your new goals and how to achieve them.

5. Ethical Challenge

You can gain a clearer sense of the ethical implications of impression management by following these directions:

a. Make a list of the different presenting selves you try to communicate at school or work, to family members, to friends, and to various types of strangers—in either face-to-face communication or via computer-mediated communication.
b. Which of these selves are honest, and which are deceptive?
c. Are any deceptive impressions you try to create justified? What would be the consequences of being completely candid in the situations you have described?
d. Based on your answers to these questions, develop a set of guidelines to distinguish ethical and unethical impression management.

6. Ethical Challenge

Recall three recent situations in which you used each of the following evasive approaches: benevolent lying, equivocating, and hinting. Write an anonymous written description of each situation on a separate sheet of paper. Submit the cases to a panel of "judges" (most likely fellow students), who will use the criteria of justifiable motives and desirable effects to evaluate the morality of this deception. Invite the "judges" to consider how they would feel if they knew someone used these evasive approaches with them.

7. Skill Builder

Use the guidelines on pages 100–102 to develop one scenario in which you *might* reveal a self-disclosing message. Create a message of this type, and use the information in this chapter to discuss the risks and benefits of sharing the message.

CHAPTER

4 Perceiving Others

CHAPTER OUTLINE

After studying the material in this chapter . . .

YOU SHOULD UNDERSTAND:

1. The difference between first- and second-order realities, and how the processes of selection, organization, interpretation, and negotiation affect a communicator's perception of others.
2. How physiological, psychological, social, and cultural factors lead communicators to perceive one another and other phenomena differently.
3. The common tendencies in perception that can sometimes lead to misperceptions.
4. The value of empathy in interpersonal communication and relationships.

YOU SHOULD BE ABLE TO:

1. Describe the factors that shape your perceptions of important people and events, and explain how these and other factors could lead another person to perceive the same people and events differently.
2. Describe an interpersonal issue from the other person's point of view, showing how and why the other person experiences the issue differently.
3. Use perception checking to clarify your understanding of another person's point of view.

KEY TERMS

- Androgynous (120)
- Attribution (122)
- Confirmation bias (125)
- Empathy (130)
- First-order realities (109)
- Gender (120)
- Halo effect (124)
- Interpretation (112)
- Narrative (114)
- Negotiation (114)
- Organization (111)
- Perception checking (129)
- Psychological sex type (120)
- Punctuation (112)
- Second-order realities (109)
- Selection (110)
- Self-serving bias (125)
- Standpoint theory (119)
- Stereotyping (123)

"Look at it my way. . . ."
"Put yourself in my shoes. . . ."
"YOU DON'T UNDERSTAND ME!"

Statements like these reflect one of the most common communication challenges. We can talk to (or at) one another until we're hoarse and exhausted, yet we still don't really understand one another. Research confirms this fact: Typical dyads can interpret and explain only 25–50 percent of each other's behavior accurately (Spitzberg, 1994), and spouses consistently overestimate the degree to which they agree with their partners (Sillars et al., 1992). Some communication scholars (e.g., Eisenberg & Goodall, 2001) have suggested complete understanding could lead to more disagreement and dissatisfaction, not smoother relationships. Nonetheless, failing to share each other's view of the world can leave us feeling isolated and frustrated, despairing that our words don't seem able to convey the depth and complexity of what we think and feel.

Just like the boxes in Figure 4.1, virtually every interpersonal situation can be seen from many points of view. Take a minute to study that figure. How many ways can you discover to view this image? If you only see one or two, keep looking. (You can see at least four ways of viewing the image by looking at Figure 4.2.) If making quick and accurate sense of simple drawings is a difficult task, imagine the challenge involved in trying to understand the perspectives of other human beings, who are far more complex and multidimensional.

This chapter provides tools for communicating in the face of perceptual differences. It begins by explaining that reality is constructed through communication. Then it introduces some of the many reasons why the world appears so

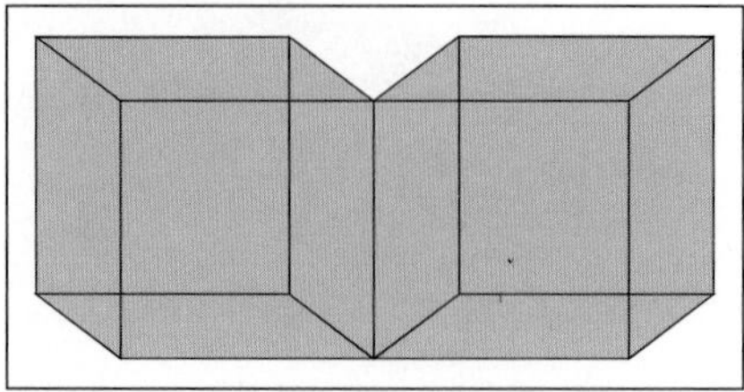

FIGURE 4.1 Two Cubes Touching

FIGURE 4.2 Four Sets of Two Cubes Touching

different to each of us. After examining the perceptual factors that make understanding so difficult, we will look at tools for bridging the perceptual gap.

The Perception Process

How do our perceptions affect our communication with others? We begin to answer these questions by taking a look at the way we make sense of the world.

REALITY IS CONSTRUCTED

Most social scientists agree that the world we know isn't "out there." Rather, we create our reality with others through communication (DeCapua, 2007; O'Brien, 2005). This may seem hard to accept until we recognize that there are two levels of reality, which have been labeled "first-order" and "second-order" (Watzlawick, 1984, 1990). **First-order realities** are physically observable qualities of a thing or situation. For example, the fact that your grandmother wrapped you in a big hug would be obvious to any observer. Likewise, there probably wouldn't be an argument about what word was uttered if a friend called you a "bonehead." By contrast, **second-order realities** involve our *attaching meaning* to first-order things or situations. Second-order realities don't reside in objects or events, but rather in our minds.

Life runs most smoothly when we share second-order realities:

First-order reality:	Your grandma gives you a hug.
Shared second-order reality:	It's appropriate for grandparents to hug their grandchildren.
First-order reality:	A job interviewer asks you how your day has been going.
Shared second-order reality:	This is a reasonable question for the situation.

Communication becomes more problematic when we have different second-order realities. For example:

First-order reality:	Your friend calls you a "bonehead."
Your second-order reality:	Your friend is being critical.
Friend's second-order reality:	The remark was an affectionate joke.
First-order reality:	A job interviewer asks whether you are married.
Your second-order reality:	The question has nothing to do with the job and is inappropriate.
Interviewer's second-order reality:	The interviewer is trying to make conversation.

As the cartoon below shows, communication problems arise when we don't share second-order realities. This is especially true when we don't realize that these views of the world are personal constructions, not objective facts. This chapter explores many of the factors that cause us to experience and make sense of the world in different ways. Perhaps more importantly, it introduces you to some communication tools that can help bridge the gap between differing perceptions, and in so doing improve relationships.

STEPS IN THE PERCEPTION PROCESS

We attach meanings to our experiences in four steps: selection, organization, interpretation, and negotiation.

Selection Since we're exposed to more input than we can possibly manage, the first step in perception is the **selection** of which data we will attend to. There are several factors that cause us to notice some messages and ignore others.

Stimuli that are *intense* often attract our attention. Something that is louder, larger, or brighter stands out. This explains why—other things being equal—we're more likely to remember extremely tall or short people and why someone who laughs or talks loudly at a party attracts more attention (not always favorable) than do more quiet guests.

Repetitious stimuli, repetitious stimuli, repetitious stimuli, repetitious stimuli, repetitious stimuli, repetitious stimuli also attract attention.* Just as a quiet but steadily dripping faucet can come to dominate our awareness, people to whom we're frequently exposed become noticeable.

Attention is also frequently related to *contrast* or *change* in stimulation. Put differently, unchanging people or things become less noticeable. This principle offers an explanation (excuse?) for why we take consistently wonderful people for granted when we interact with them frequently. It's only when they stop being so wonderful or go away that we appreciate them.

Later in this chapter, we'll look at a variety of other factors—physiological, psychological, social, and cultural—that lead us to pay attention to certain people and events while ignoring others.

Organization After selecting information from the environment, we must arrange it in some meaningful way in order to make sense of the world. We call this stage **organization**. The raw sense data we perceive can be organized in more than one way. (See Figure 4.2 for a visual example of this principle.) We do this by using *perceptual schema,* cognitive frameworks that allow us to give order to the information we have selected (Macrae & Bodenhausen, 2001).

We use four types of schema to classify others (Andersen, 1999). As you read about each one, think about how you use it to organize your perceptions.

Physical constructs classify people according to their appearance: beautiful or ugly, fat or thin, young or old, and so on.

Role constructs use social position, such as student, attorney, wife.

* The graphic demonstrations of factors influencing perception in this and the following paragraphs are borrowed from Coon (2009).

Interaction constructs focus on social behavior: friendly, helpful, aloof, or sarcastic, for example.

Psychological constructs refer to internal states of mind and dispositions: confident, insecure, happy, neurotic, and so on.

Once we have selected an organizing scheme to classify people, we use that scheme to make generalizations about members of the groups who fit our categories. For example, if you are especially aware of a person's sex, you might be alert to the differences between the way men and women behave or the way they are treated. You might even misremember or distort information that doesn't fit with your beliefs on the subject (Frawley, 2008). If religion plays an important part in your life, you might think of members of your faith differently than you do others. If ethnicity is an important issue for you, you probably tune into the differences between members of various ethnic groups. There's nothing wrong with generalizations about groups as long as they are accurate. In fact, it would be impossible to get through life without them. But faulty overgeneralizations can lead to problems of stereotyping, which you'll read about in a few pages.

Perceptual differences don't just involve the general categories we use to classify others. We also can organize specific communication transactions in different ways, and these differing organizational schemes can have a powerful effect on our relationships. Communication theorists have used the term **punctuation** to describe the determination of causes and effects in a series of interactions (Watzlawick et al., 1967). You can begin to understand how punctuation operates by visualizing a running quarrel between a husband and wife. The husband accuses the wife of being a nag, while she complains that he is withdrawing from her. Notice that the order in which each partner punctuates this cycle affects how the dispute looks. The husband begins by blaming the wife: "I withdraw because you nag." The wife organizes the situation differently, starting with the husband: "I nag because you withdraw." Once the cycle gets rolling, it is impossible to say which accusation is accurate, as Figure 4.3 indicates. The answer depends on how the sequence is punctuated.

Anyone who has seen two children argue about "who started it" can understand that haggling over causes and effects isn't likely to solve a conflict. In fact, the kind of finger pointing that goes along with assigning blame will probably make matters worse (Caughlin & Huston, 2002). Rather than argue about whose punctuation of an event is correct, it's far more productive to recognize that a dispute can look different to each person and then move on to the more important question of "What can we do to make things better?"

REFLECTION

Problematic Punctuation

When I was living with my parents, my father always was asking where I was going or where I had been. I interpreted his questions as too nosy, and I usually responded with hostility or silence. This made him even more concerned about what I was doing.

Now I recognize that each of us was punctuating this situation differently. He saw me as being the problem: "I ask you what you're doing because you never tell me." I saw him as the cause of the problem: "I never tell you what I'm doing because you're always pestering me." Who started the cycle? Either way, we both lost.

Interpretation Once we have selected and organized our perceptions, we interpret them in a way that makes some sort of sense. **Interpretation** plays a role in virtually every interpersonal act. Is the person who smiles at you across a crowded room interested in romance or simply being polite? Is a friend's kidding a sign of affection or irritation? Should you take an invitation to "drop by any time" literally or not?

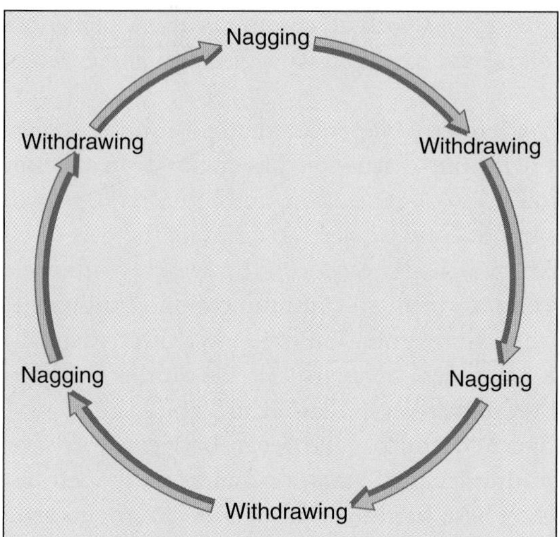

FIGURE 4.3 The way a communication sequence is punctuated affects its perceived meaning. Which comes first, the nagging or the withdrawing?

There are several factors that cause us to interpret a person's behavior in one way or another. *Relational satisfaction* is a powerful one: The behavior that seems positive when you are happy with a partner might seem completely different when the relationship isn't satisfying. For example, couples in unsatisfying relationships are more likely than satisfied partners to blame one another when things go wrong (Bradbury & Fincham, 1990; Manusov, 1993).

Expectation is another factor that shapes our interpretations (Burgoon & Burgoon, 2001). For instance, if you go into a conversation expecting a hostile attitude, you're likely to hear a negative tone in the other person's voice—even if that tone isn't there (Hample et al., 2007). We'll talk more about how expectations affect perception later in this chapter.

A third factor that influences interpretations is *personal experience.* For instance, if you've been taken advantage of by landlords in the past, you might be skeptical about an apartment manager's assurances that careful housekeeping will ensure the refund of your cleaning deposit.

Assumptions about human behavior also influence interpretations. Do you assume people are lazy, dislike work, avoid responsibility, and must be coerced to do things, or do you believe people exercise self-direction and self-control, possess creativity, and seek responsibility? Imagine the differences in a boss who assumes workers fit the first description versus one who assumes they fit the second (McGregor, 1960; Neuliep, 1996).

Although we have talked about selection, organization, and interpretation separately, these three phases of perception can occur in differing sequences. For example, a parent's or babysitter's past interpretations (such as "Jason is a troublemaker") can influence future selections (his behavior becomes especially noticeable) and the organization of events (when there's a fight, the assumption is that Jason started it). As with all communication, perception is an ongoing process in which it is hard to pin down beginnings and endings.

Negotiation In Chapter 1 you read that meaning is created both *in* and *among* people. So far our discussion has focused on the inner components of perception—selection, organization, and interpretation—that take place in each individual's mind. Now we need to examine the part of our sense-making that occurs *among* people. The process by which communicators influence each other's perceptions through communication is known as **negotiation**.

One way to explain negotiation is to view interpersonal communication as the exchange of stories. Scholars call the stories we use to describe our personal worlds **narratives** (Allan et al., 2002; Shaw, 1997). Just as the boxes in Figure 4.1 on page 108 can be viewed in several ways, virtually every interpersonal situation can be described by more than one narrative. These narratives often differ in their casting of characters as "heroes" and "villains" (Aleman, 2005). For instance, consider a conflict between a boss and employee. If you ask the employee to describe the situation, she might depict the manager as a "heartless bean counter" while she sees herself as a worker who "always gets the job done." The manager's narrative might cast the roles quite differently: the "fair boss" vs. the "clock watcher who wants to leave early." Similarly, children may say their parents are too controlling, while the parents talk about their children as irresponsible and naive. Stepmothers and mothers-in-law who see themselves as "helpful" might be portrayed as "meddlesome" in the narratives of stepdaughters and daughters-in-law (Christian, 2005; Sandel, 2004). People who value cleanliness and order may label their housemates as "dirty and sloppy," while those housemates describe a concern for tidiness as "obsessive."

REFLECTION

Negotiating New Roles

Ever since I left our family business to try my hand at being a professional musician, my father and I have had a rough relationship. During a recent argument I blurted out, "I'm tired of being the bad son!" My father immediately responded, "And I'm tired of being the mean parent!"

After a long pause, my dad said, "I'd rather be the 'Concerned Father.'" I replied, "I'd rather be the 'Creative Son.'" We agreed it was time to renegotiate our roles—and our perceptions of each other.

As the Reflection on this page shows, when our narratives clash with those of others we can either hang on to our own point of view and refuse to consider anyone else's (usually not productive) or try to negotiate a narrative that creates at least some common ground.

Shared narratives provide the best chance for smooth communication. For example, romantic partners who celebrate their successful struggles against relational obstacles are happier than those who don't have this shared appreciation (Flora & Segrin, 2000). Likewise, couples that agree about the important turning points in their relationships are more satisfied than those who have different views of which incidents were most important (Baxter & Pittman, 2001).

Shared narratives don't have to be accurate to be powerful (Martz et al., 1998; Murray et al., 1996). Couples who report being happily married after 50 or more years seem to collude in a relational narrative that doesn't always jibe with the facts (Miller et al., 2006). They agree that they rarely have conflict, although objective analysis reveals that they have had their share of disagreements and challenges. Without overtly agreeing to do so, they choose to blame outside forces or unusual circumstances for problems, instead of attributing responsibility to one another. They offer the most charitable interpretations of one another's behavior, believing that their spouse acts with good intentions when

"I know what you're thinking, but let me offer a competing narrative."

things don't go well. They seem willing to forgive, or even forget transgressions. Examining this research, Judy Pearson (2000) asks:

> Should we conclude that happy couples have a poor grip on reality? Perhaps they do, but is the reality of one's marriage better known by outside onlookers than by the players themselves? The conclusion is evident. One key to a long happy marriage is to tell yourself and others that you have one and then to behave as though you do! (p. 186)

Influences on Perception

How we select, organize, interpret, and negotiate data about others is influenced by a variety of factors. Some of our perceptual judgments are affected by physiology, others by cultural and social factors, and still others by psychological factors (Hochberg, 1998).

PHYSIOLOGICAL INFLUENCES

Sometimes differing perspectives come from our physical environment and the ways that our bodies differ from others.

The Senses The differences in how each of us sees, hears, tastes, touches, and smells stimuli can affect interpersonal relationships (Clark, 2000). Consider a few examples arising from physiological differences:

> "Turn down that radio! It's going to make me go deaf."
> "It's not too loud. If I turn it down, it will be impossible to hear it."

"It's freezing in here."
"Are you kidding? We'll suffocate if you turn up the heat!"

"Why don't you pass that truck? The highway is clear for half a mile."
"I can't see that far, and I'm not going to get us killed."

Age Older people view the world differently than younger ones because of a greater scope and number of experiences. Developmental differences also shape perceptions. Developmental psychologists (Lourenco & Machado, 1996; Piaget, 1952) describe ways in which younger children are incapable of performing mental feats that are natural to the rest of us. Until they approach the age of seven, for example, they aren't able to take another person's point of view. This fact helps explain why youngsters often seem egocentric, selfish, and uncooperative. A parent's exasperated "Can't you see I'm too tired to play?" just won't make sense to a 4-year-old full of energy, who imagines that everyone else must feel the same.

Health and Fatigue Recall the last time you came down with a cold, flu, or some other ailment. Health can have a strong impact on how you relate to others. It's good to realize that someone else may be behaving differently because of illness. In the same way, it's important to let others know when you feel ill so they can give you the understanding you need.

FOCUS ON RESEARCH

Is "Gaydar" Real?

research

Despite shopworn stereotypes about gay and lesbian behavior, most social scientists argue that sexual orientation is something you can't identify by simply looking at a person. In fact, many gay men and lesbians describe the surprised reactions they hear when they "come out" and publicly declare their sexual orientation. On the other hand, folk wisdom among many gay and lesbian people includes the belief that their "gaydar" is quite accurate and that they can spot kindred spirits at a glance.

In an effort to determine whether gaydar is a real phenomenon, Lisa Woolery reviewed research on this controversial subject. She found some evidence that, compared to self-identified heterosexuals, lesbians and gay men are more accurate at spotting the orientation of target individuals when provided a "thin slice" of information in the form of a photograph or brief video. On the other hand, the intuition of gay and lesbian subjects varied widely, and the gap between them and heterosexual observers vanished as more information became available.

Citing research that has been popularized in books like Malcolm Gladwell's *Blink*, Woolery concludes that personal familiarity with gay and lesbian communities can turn observers into "experts" whose experience gives them an edge in making quick judgments that can appear to outsiders as intuition. She looks forward to the day when society will become tolerant enough that guessing will be unnecessary and it will be easy simply to ask another person about his or her sexual orientation.

Woolery, Lisa M. (2007). Gaydar: A social-cognitive analysis. *Journal of Homosexuality, 53*(3), 9–17.

Likewise, fatigue can affect relationships. When you've been working long hours or studying late for an exam, the world can seem quite different than when you are well rested. People who are sleep deprived, for example, perceive time intervals as longer than they really are. So the 5 minutes you're waiting for a friend to show up may seem longer, leaving you feeling more impatient than you otherwise would be (Miró et al., 2003).

Hunger Your own experience probably confirms that being hungry (and getting grumpy) or having overeaten (and getting tired) affects how we interact with others. For example, a study by Katherine Alaimo and her colleagues (2001) found that teenagers who reported that their family did not get enough food to eat were almost three times as likely to have been suspended from school, almost twice as likely to have difficulty getting along with others, and four times as likely to have no friends. While the exact nature of the causes and effects in this study are hard to pin down, one thing is clear: Hunger can affect our perception and communication.

Biological Cycles Are you a "morning person" or a "night person"? Each of us has a daily cycle in which all sorts of changes constantly occur, including variations in body temperature, sexual drive, alertness, tolerance to stress, and mood (Maguire, 2005; Touitou, 1998). These cycles can affect the way we relate toward each other. For example, Jeffrey Larson and his associates (1991) discovered that couples with mismatched waking and sleeping patterns (e.g., an evening person and a morning person) reported significantly more conflict, less sexual intimacy, and less time spent conversing on important topics than couples with matched sleeping patterns.

Neurobehavioral Challenges Some differences in perception are rooted in neurology. For instance, people with AD-HD (attention-deficit–hyperactivity disorder) are easily distracted from tasks and have difficulty delaying gratification (Goldstein, 2008; Tripp et al., 2007). It's easy to imagine how those with AD-HD might find a long lecture boring and tedious, while other audience members are fascinated by the same lecture (Von Briesen, 2007). People with bipolar disorder experience significant mood swings in which their perceptions of events, friends, and even family members shift dramatically. The National Institute of Mental Health (2008) estimates that between 5 million and 7 million Americans are affected by these two disorders alone—and there are many other psychological conditions that influence people's perceptions.

PSYCHOLOGICAL INFLUENCES

Along with physiology, our psychological state also influences the way we perceive others.

Mood Our emotional state strongly influences how we view people and events, and therefore how we communicate (Forgas & Bower, 2001). An early experiment using hypnotism dramatically demonstrated this fact (Lebula & Lucas, 1945). Each subject was shown the same series of six pictures, each time having been put in a different mood. The descriptions of the pictures differed radically depending on the emotional state of the subject. For example, these are descriptions by one subject in various emotional states while describing a picture of children digging in a swampy area:

> *Happy mood:* "It looks like fun, reminds me of summer. That's what life is for, working out in the open, really living—digging in the dirt, planting, watching things grow."
>
> *Anxious mood:* "They're going to get hurt or cut. There should be someone older there who knows what to do in case of an accident. I wonder how deep the water is."
>
> *Critical mood:* "Pretty horrible land. There ought to be something more useful for kids of that age to do instead of digging in that stuff. It's filthy and dirty and good for nothing."

Such evidence shows that our judgments often say more about our own attitudes than about the other people involved.

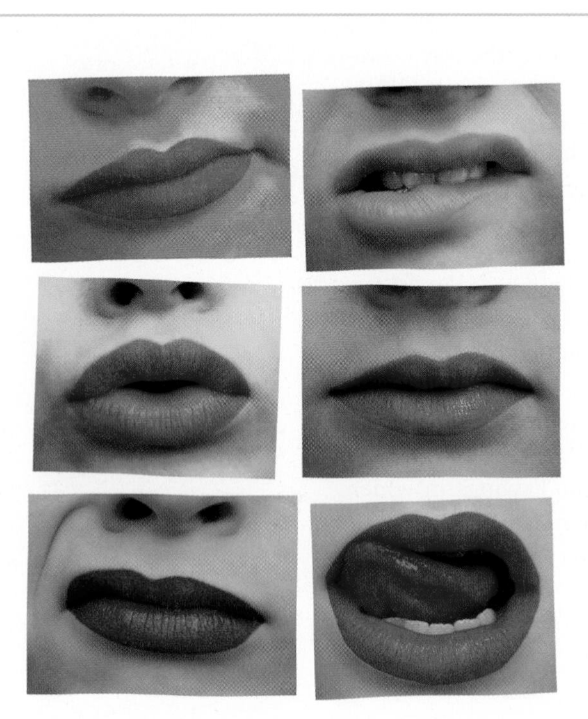

Although there's a strong relationship between mood and happiness, it's not clear which comes first: the perceptual outlook or the amount of relational satisfaction. There is some evidence that perception leads to satisfaction rather than the opposite order (Fletcher et al., 1987). In other words, the attitude/expectation we bring to a situation shapes our level of happiness or unhappiness. Once started, this process can create a spiral. If you're happy about your relationship, you will be more likely to interpret your partner's behavior in a charitable way. This, in turn, can lead to greater happiness. Of course, the same process can work in the opposite direction. One study revealed that spouses who felt uncertain about the status of their marriage saw relational threats in conversations their partners had with strangers that seemed quite ordinary to outsiders (Knobloch et al., 2007).

One remedy to serious distortions—and unnecessary conflicts—is to monitor your own moods. If you're aware of being especially critical or sensitive, you can avoid overreacting to others.

Self-Concept Another factor that influences perception is the self-concept (Hinde et al., 2001). For example, the recipient's self-concept has proven to be the single greatest factor in determining whether people who are being teased interpret the teaser's motives as being friendly or hostile, and whether they respond with comfort or defensiveness (Alberts et al., 1996). As discussed in Chapter 3, the way we think and feel about ourselves strongly influences how we interpret others' behavior.

SOCIAL INFLUENCES

Within a culture, our personal point of view plays a strong role in shaping perceptions. Social scientists have developed **standpoint theory** to describe how a person's position in a society shapes her or his view of society in general, and of specific individuals (Litwin & Hallstein, 2007; Orbe, 1998). Standpoint theory is most often applied to the difference between the perspectives of privileged social groups and people who have less power, and to the perspectives of women and men (Dougherty, 2001). Unless one has been disadvantaged, it can be difficult to imagine how the world might look to someone who has been treated badly because of race, ethnicity, gender, biological sex, sexual orientation, or socioeconomic class. After some reflection, though, you probably can understand how being marginalized can make the world seem like a very different place.

Sex and Gender Roles Physiological and psychological differences aren't the only factors that shape the differing perceptions of men and women. Personal experiences and social expectations also are powerful. For example, women and men judge the same behaviors quite differently (e.g., Diekman & Eagly, 2000); and women react differently depending on their age and marital status (Hanzal et al., 2008). Some types of behavior that men find innocuous have been judged as being harassing by women (Dougherty, 2001). Not surprisingly, much of the difference comes from experience: Women who report having been harassed are more likely to find harassment in subsequent interactions (Singer et al., 1998). Experience isn't the only factor, though: Younger women are more likely to perceive harassment than older ones who, presumably, have a different set of expectations about what kinds of communication are and aren't appropriate. Also, attitudes play a role: People who disapprove of socializing and dating between coworkers are more likely to perceive harassment than those who accept this sort of relationship (Solomon & Williams, 1997).

The Power of a Shared Narrative: *Lars and the Real Girl*

Lars (Ryan Gosling) is a kind and decent but painfully shy 27-year-old. By choice, he lives alone in a garage and avoids conversation and contact with others as much as possible.

Everyone in his small, close-knit town is stunned when Lars introduces his new girlfriend, Bianca—an anatomically correct silicone mannequin. Understandably worried about Lars' mental health, his brother and sister-in-law seek the help of their family doctor, who advises them to play along with his delusion and to see what happens. Soon the entire town buys into the shared narrative that Bianca and Lars are a real couple. Bianca volunteers at the local hospital, "reads" stories to schoolchildren, and even wins a seat on the school board.

While this plot might seem farfetched, critics and moviegoers have agreed that this tender drama-comedy showcases the power of a community to support one of its own. The obvious fiction they conspire to construct takes on its own reality, illustrating how communication can be a powerful tool for creating shared narratives.

"How is it gendered?"

Early theorizing by Sandra Bem (1974) suggested that stereotypical masculine and feminine behaviors are not opposite poles of a single continuum, but rather two separate sets of behavior. With this view, a person—regardless of her or his biological sex—can act in a masculine manner or a feminine manner, or exhibit both types of characteristics. The masculine-feminine dichotomy, then, is replaced with four **psychological sex types**, including masculine, feminine, **androgynous** (combining masculine and feminine traits), and undifferentiated (neither masculine nor feminine). The word **gender** is a shorthand term for psychological sex type. Combining the four psychological sex types with the traditional biological sex types produces four categories for men: Masculine males, feminine males, androgynous males, and undifferentiated males; and four categories for women: Masculine females, feminine females, androgynous females, and undifferentiated females. Although there are women and men who fit into all of the categories, in general, people see themselves as either sex-typed (masculine male/feminine female) or androgynous (Korabik & McCreary, 2000).

Each of these eight combined psychological/biological sex types perceives interpersonal relationships differently. For example, masculine males probably see their interpersonal relationships as opportunities for competitive interaction, as opportunities to win something. Feminine females probably see their interpersonal relationships as opportunities to be nurturing, to express their feelings and emotions. Androgynous males and females, on the other hand, probably differ little in their perceptions of their interpersonal relationships. For example, feminine females and androgynous individuals, both male and female, give more sympathy to grieving people than do masculine males (Versalle & McDowell, 2004-2005).

Androgynous individuals tend to see their relationships as opportunities to behave in a variety of ways, depending on the nature of the relationships themselves, the context in which a particular relationship takes place, and the myriad other variables affecting what might constitute appropriate behavior. These variables are usually ignored by the sex-typed masculine males and feminine females, who have a smaller repertoire of behaviors.

Occupational Roles The kind of work we do also governs our view of the world. Imagine five people taking a walk through a park. One, a botanist, is fascinated by the variety of trees and plants. The zoologist is on the lookout for interesting animals. The third, a meteorologist, keeps an eye on the sky, noticing changes in the weather. The fourth, a psychologist, is totally unaware of the goings-on of nature, concentrating instead on the interaction among the people in the park. The fifth, a pickpocket, quickly takes advantage of the others' absorption to collect their wallets. There are two lessons in this little story: The first, of course, is to watch your wallet carefully. The second is that our occupational roles frequently govern our perceptions.

Perhaps the most dramatic illustration of how occupational roles shape perception occurred in the early 1970s. Stanford psychologist Philip Zimbardo (1971, 2007) recruited a group of well-educated middle-class young men. He randomly chose 11 to serve as "guards" in a mock prison set up in the basement of Stanford's psychology building. He issued the guards uniforms, handcuffs, whistles, and billy clubs. The remaining 10 participants became "prisoners" and were placed in rooms with metal bars, bucket toilets, and cots.

Zimbardo let the guards establish their own rules for the experiment. The rules were tough: no talking during meals and rest periods and after lights out. They took head counts at 2:30 A.M. Troublemakers received short rations.

Faced with these conditions, the prisoners began to resist. Some barricaded their doors with beds. Others went on hunger strikes. Several ripped off their identifying number tags. The guards reacted to the rebellion by clamping down hard on protesters. Some turned sadistic, physically and verbally abusing the prisoners. The experiment was scheduled to go on for 2 weeks, but after 6 days Zimbardo realized that what had started as a simulation had become too intense. It seems that *what* we are is determined largely by society's designation of *who* we are.

CULTURAL INFLUENCES

Cultural selection, organization, interpretation, and negotiation exert a powerful influence on the way we view others' communication. Even beliefs about the very value of talk differ from one culture to another (Giles et al., 1992a). Western cultures tend to view talk as desirable and use it for social purposes as well as to perform tasks. Silence has a negative value in these cultures. It is likely to be interpreted as lack of interest, unwillingness to communicate, hostility, anxiety, shyness, or a sign of interpersonal incompatibility. Westerners are uncomfortable with silence, which they find embarrassing and awkward.

On the other hand, Asian cultures tend to perceive talk quite differently. For thousands of years, Asian cultures have discouraged the expression of thoughts and feelings. Silence is valued, as Taoist sayings indicate: "In much talk there is great weariness" or "One who speaks does not know; one who knows does not speak." Unlike Westerners, who are uncomfortable with silence, Japanese and Chinese people believe that remaining quiet is the proper state when there is nothing to be said. To Asians, a talkative person is often considered a show-off or a fake.

It's easy to see how these different views of speech and silence can lead to communication problems when people from different cultures meet. Both the "talkative" Westerner and the "silent" Asian are behaving in ways they believe are proper, yet each views the other with disapproval and mistrust. Only when they recognize the different standards of behavior can they adapt to one another, or at least understand and respect their differences.

The valuing of talk isn't the only way culture shapes perceptions. Author Anne Fadiman (1997) explains why Hmong immigrants from the mountains of Laos preferred their traditional shamanistic healers, called *txiv neeb,* to American doctors—and perceived their behaviors very differently:

> A *txiv neeb* might spend as much as eight hours in a sick person's home; doctors forced their patients, no matter how weak they were, to come to the hospital, and then might spend only twenty minutes at their bedsides. *Txiv neebs* were polite and never needed to ask questions; doctors asked about their sexual and excretory habits. *Txiv neebs* could render an immediate diagnosis; doctors often demanded samples of blood (or even urine or feces, which they liked to keep in little bottles), took X rays, and waited for days for the results to come back from the laboratory—and then, after all that, sometimes they were unable to identify the cause of the problem. *Txiv neebs* never undressed their patients; doctors asked patients to take off all their clothes, and sometimes dared to put their fingers inside women's vaginas. *Txiv neebs* knew that to treat the body without treating the soul was an act of patent folly; doctors never even mentioned the soul. (p. 33)

Perceptual differences don't just occur between residents of different countries. Within a single national culture, regional and ethnic co-cultures can create very different realities. In a fascinating series of studies, Peter Andersen and colleagues (1987a, 1987b) discovered that climate and geographic latitude were remarkably accurate predictors of communication predispositions. People living in southern latitudes of the United States were found to be more socially isolated, less tolerant of ambiguity, higher in self-esteem, more likely to touch others, and more likely to verbalize their thoughts and feelings than their northern counterparts. This sort of finding helps explain why communicators who travel from one part of a country to another find that their old patterns of communicating don't work as well in their new location. A southerner whose relatively talkative, high-touch style seemed completely normal at home might be viewed as pushy and aggressive in a new, northern home.

Of course, geography isn't the only factor that shapes perception. The gap between cultures often extends beyond dissimilar norms to a wide range of different experiences and feelings. Chapter 2 described the multitude of factors that lead people from different cultural backgrounds to experience the world in ways that often bear little resemblance to one another.

Common Tendencies in Perception

By now it's obvious that many factors distort the way we interpret the world. Social scientists use the term **attribution** to describe the process of attaching meaning to behavior. We attribute meaning to both our own actions and to the actions of others, but we often use different yardsticks. Research has uncovered several perceptual tendencies that may lead to inaccurate attributions (Hamachek, 1992).

WE MAKE SNAP JUDGMENTS

Our ancestors often had to make quick judgments about whether strangers were likely to be dangerous, and there are still times when this ability can be a survival skill (Flora, 2004). But there are many cases when judging others without enough knowledge or information can get us into trouble. In the most serious cases, innocent people are gunned down by shooters who make inaccurate snap decisions about "intruders" or "enemies." On a more personal level, most of us have felt badly misjudged by others who made unfavorable snap judgments about us. If you've ever been written off by a potential employer in the first few minutes of an interview, or have been unfairly rebuffed by someone you just met, then you know the feeling.

Despite the risks of rash decision making, in some circumstances people can make surprisingly good choices in the blink of an eye (Gladwell, 2004). The best snap judgments come from people whose decisions are based on expertise and experience. For example, psychologist John Gottman (1995) can watch a couple talking for just 12 minutes and predict with 90 percent accuracy whether they will still be married in 15 years.

Sometimes even nonexperts can be good at making split-second decisions. For example, students who watched a silent, 2-second video of a professor they never met and were asked to rate the teacher's effectiveness came up with ratings very similar to those of students who were in the professor's class for a semester (Ambady & Rosenthal, 1993). And many people who have tried the technique called "speed dating" are able to determine in just a few minutes whether a person they have just met will become a romantic partner (Kurzban & Weeden, 2005).

Snap judgments become particularly problematic when they are based on **stereotyping**—exaggerated beliefs associated with a categorizing system. Stereotypes, which people automatically make on "primitive categories" like race, sex, and age (Nelson, 2005), may be founded on a kernel of truth, but they go beyond the facts at hand and make claims that usually have no valid basis.

Three characteristics distinguish stereotypes from reasonable generalizations. The first involves *categorizing others on the basis of easily recognized but not necessarily significant characteristics.* For example, perhaps the first thing you notice about a person is his or her skin color—but that may not be nearly as significant as the person's intelligence or achievements. The second feature that characterizes stereotypes is *ascribing a set of characteristics to most or all members of a group.* For example, you might unfairly assume that all older people are doddering or that all men are insensitive to women's concerns (Hummert et al., 2004). Finally, stereotyping involves *applying the generalization to a*

Farcus by David Waisglass Gordon Coulthart

"There are two types of people in this world ... those who generalize, and those who don't."

particular person. Once you believe all old people are geezers or all men are jerks, it's a short step to considering a particular senior citizen as senile or a particular man as a sexist slob.

Stereotypes can plague interracial communication (Buttny, 1997; Hughes & Baldwin, 2002). Surveys of college student attitudes show that many blacks characterize whites as "demanding" and "manipulative," while many whites describe blacks as "loud" and "ostentatious." Many black women report having been raised with stereotypical characterizations of whites (e.g., "most whites cannot be trusted"). One black college professor reported a personal story revealing a surprising set of stereotypical assumptions from a white colleague. "As the only African American at a university-sponsored party for faculty a few years ago, I was appalled when a white professor (whom I had just met) asked me to sing a Negro spiritual" (Hecht et al., 1993). Although it's possible that behavior like this can be motivated by a desire to be friendly, it is easy to see how it can be insensitive and offensive.

By adulthood, we tend to engage in stereotyping frequently, effortlessly, and often unconsciously (Zenmore et al., 2000). Once we create and hold stereotypes, we seek out isolated behaviors that support our inaccurate beliefs. For example, men and women in conflict with each other often remember only behaviors of the opposite sex that fit their stereotypes (Allen, 1998). They then point to these behaviors—which might not be representative of how the other person typically behaves—as "evidence" to suit their stereotypical and inaccurate claims: "Look! There you go criticizing me again. Typical for a woman!"

One way to avoid the kinds of communication problems that come from excessive stereotyping is to "decategorize" others, giving yourself a chance to treat people as individuals instead of assuming that they possess the same characteristics as every other member of the group to which you assign them.

WE CLING TO FIRST IMPRESSIONS

Snap judgments can be dangerous because we tend to cling to them—whether or not they're correct. If our impressions are accurate, they can be useful ways of deciding how to respond best to people in the future. However, problems arise when our initial assessments are inaccurate; for once we form an opinion of someone, we tend to hang onto it and make any conflicting information fit our image.

Social scientists have coined the term **halo effect** to describe the tendency to form an overall positive impression of a person on the basis of one positive characteristic. Most typically, the positive impression comes from physical attractiveness, which can lead people to attribute all sorts of other virtues to the good-looking person (Dion et al., 1972; van Leeuwen & Macrae, 2004). For example, employment interviewers rate mediocre but attractive job applicants higher than their less attractive candidates (Watkins & Johnston, 2000). The first impression can also come from something you're told about a person. For example, in one study (Pentok-Voak et al., 2007), women who were told that a man liked children perceived him as more attractive and social.

Once we form a first impression—whether it's positive or negative—we tend to seek out and organize our impressions to support that opinion. Psychologists use the term **confirmation bias** to describe this process. For example, once a potential employer forms a positive impression, the tendency is to ask questions that confirm the employer's image of the applicant (Dougherty et al, 1994). The interviewer might ask leading questions aimed at supporting her positive views ("What lessons did you learn from that setback?"), interpret answers in a positive light ("Ah, taking time away from school to travel was a good idea!"), encourage the applicant ("Good point!"), and sell the company's virtues ("I think you would like working here"). Likewise, applicants who create a negative first impression are operating under a cloud that may be impossible to dispel.

The power of first impressions is also important in personal relationships. A study of college roommates found that those who had positive initial impressions of each other were likely to have positive subsequent interactions, manage their conflicts constructively, and continue living together (Marek et al., 2004). The converse was also true: Roommates who got off to a bad start tended to spiral negatively. This reinforces the wisdom and importance of the old adage, "You never get a second chance to make a first impression."

WE JUDGE OURSELVES MORE CHARITABLY THAN WE DO OTHERS

While we may evaluate others critically, we tend to judge ourselves in the most generous terms possible (Farah & Atoum, 2002; Pal, 2007). Social scientists have labeled this tendency **self-serving bias**. On the one hand, when others suffer, we often blame the problem on their personal qualities. On the other hand, when we're the victims we find explanations outside ourselves (Floyd, 2000; Sedikides et al., 1998); Consider a few examples:

- When *they* botch a job, we think they weren't listening well or trying hard enough; when *we* make the mistake, the problem was unclear directions or not enough time.
- When *she* lashes out angrily, we say she's being moody or too sensitive; when *we* blow off steam, it's because of the pressure we've been under.
- When *he* gets caught speeding, we say he should have been more careful; when *we* get the ticket, we deny we were driving too fast or say, "Everybody does it."
- When *she* uses profanity, it's because of a flaw in her character; when *we* swear, it's because the situation called for it (Young, 2004).
- If *he* wins the lottery, we predict he'll make many negative changes to his life; if *we* win the lottery, changes we make to our lives will be positive (Nelson & Beggan, 2004).

Not surprisingly, self-serving bias is especially common in troubled relationships. In one study (Schütz, 1999), couples in conflict were more likely to blame their partner for the problem than to accept responsibility for their role in the problem. The researchers point out that these results came from couples dealing with ordinary relational challenges. They observe that self-serving bias is likely to be even stronger in troubled relationships.

When people are aware of both the positive and negative characteristics of another person, they tend to be more influenced by the undesirable traits (Baumeister et al., 2001; Kellermann, 1989). This attitude sometimes makes sense. If the negative quality clearly outweighs any positive ones, you would be foolish to ignore it. For example, a surgeon with shaky hands and a teacher who hates children would be unsuitable for their jobs, whatever their virtues. But much of the time it's a bad idea to pay excessive attention to negative qualities and overlook good ones.

WE ARE INFLUENCED BY OUR EXPECTATIONS

Suppose you took a class and were told in advance that the instructor is terrific. Would this affect the way you perceive the teacher? Research shows that it almost certainly would. In one study, students who read positive comments about instructors on a website viewed those teachers as more credible and attractive than did students who were not exposed to the same comments (Edwards et al., 2007). In situations like these and others, our expectations influence our perceptions.

Expectations don't always lead to more positive appraisals. There are times when we raise our expectations so high that we are disappointed with the events that occur. If you are told that someone you are about to meet is extremely attractive, you may create a picture in your mind of a professional model, only to be let down when the person doesn't live up to your unrealistic expectations. What if you had been told that the person isn't very good looking? In that case, you might have been pleasantly surprised by the person's appearance, and perhaps you would rate the person's attractiveness more positively. The point is, our expectations influence the way we see others, both positively and negatively.

The knowledge that expectations influence our perceptions is important when making decisions about others. Many professions require that

The Tragedy of Distorted Perceptions: *Atonement*

On a sweltering summer afternoon at her family's English country estate, 13-year-old Briony Tallis (Saoirse Ronan) spies two encounters between her older sister, Cecilia (Keira Knightley), and Robbie Turner (James McAvoy), the son of the family's housekeeper. Driven by her overactive imagination and a jealous crush on Robbie, Briony jumps to mistaken conclusions and accuses Robbie of a crime he did not commit. Briony's indictment destroys three lives, including her own. She spends the rest of her days atoning for her accusations.

The film presents crucial scenes in the story several times; first from Briony's point of view, and then as Cecilia and Robbie experience them. By the end, we have viewed a powerful lesson in the varieties of perception, and the danger of assuming one's own point of view is the definitive, accurate representation of what "really happened."

proposals be evaluated through "blind review"—that is, the person submitting the proposal is not allowed to offer identifying information that might influence the evaluator's appraisal. In the same way, you can probably think of times when it would be wise to avoid advance information about another person so that you perceive the person as neutrally as possible.

WE ARE INFLUENCED BY THE OBVIOUS

Being influenced by what is most obvious is understandable. As you read earlier, we select stimuli from our environment that are noticeable—that is, intense, repetitious, unusual, or otherwise attention grabbing. The problem is that the most obvious factor is not necessarily the only cause—or the most significant one—of an event. For example:

- When two children (or adults, for that matter) fight, it may be a mistake to blame the one who lashes out first. Perhaps the other one was at least equally responsible, teasing or refusing to cooperate.
- You might complain about an acquaintance whose malicious gossiping or arguing has become a bother, forgetting that by putting up with that kind of behavior you have been at least partially responsible.
- You might blame an unhappy work situation on the boss, overlooking other factors beyond her control, such as a change in the economy, the policy of higher management, or demands of customers or other workers.

These examples show that it is important to take time to gather all the facts before arriving at a conclusion.

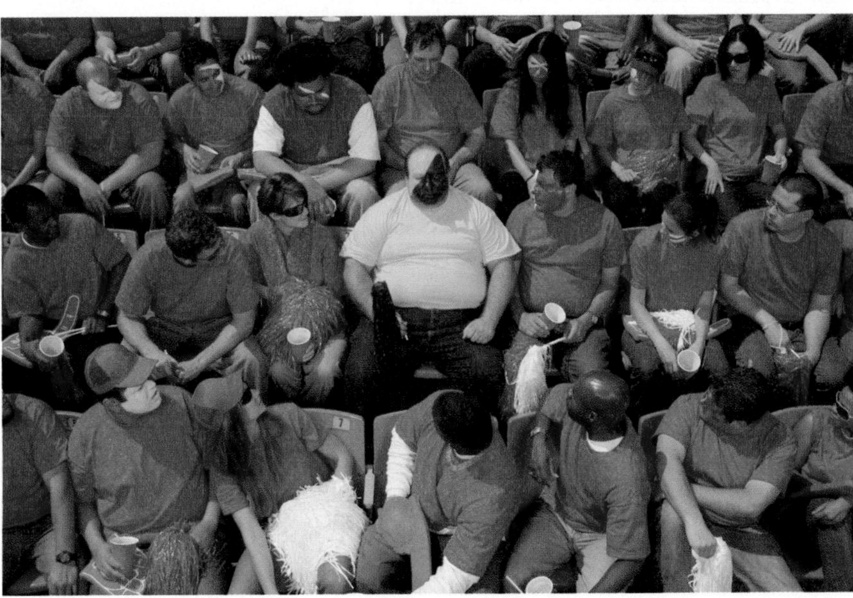

WE ASSUME OTHERS ARE LIKE US

We commonly imagine that others possess the same attitudes and motives that we do. The frequently mistaken assumption that others' views are similar to our own applies in a wide range of situations. For example:

- You've heard a slightly raunchy joke that you found funny. You assume that it won't offend a friend. It does.
- You've been bothered by an instructor's tendency to get off the subject during lectures. If you were a professor, you'd want to know if you were creating problems for your students; so you decide that your instructor will probably be grateful for some constructive criticism. Unfortunately, you're wrong.
- You lost your temper with a friend a week ago and said some things you regret. In fact, if someone said those things to you, you would consider the relationship finished. Imagining that your friend feels the same way, you avoid making contact. In fact, your friend feels that he was partly responsible and has avoided you because he thinks you're the one who wants to end things.

These examples show that others don't always think or feel the way we do and that assuming similarities can lead to problems. Sometimes you can find out the other person's real position by asking directly, sometimes by checking with others, and sometimes by making an educated guess after you've thought the matter out. All these alternatives are better than simply assuming everyone would react the way you do.

We don't always fall into the kind of perceptual tendencies described in this section. Sometimes, for instance, people *are* responsible for their misfortunes, or our problems *are not* our fault. Likewise, the most obvious interpretation of a situation may be the correct one. Nonetheless, a large amount of research has shown again and again that our perceptions of others are often distorted in the ways we have described. The moral, then, is clear: Don't assume your appraisals of others are accurate or unbiased.

Synchronizing Our Perceptions

After reading this far, you can appreciate how out of synch our perceptions of one another can be. It's easy to understand how these mismatched perceptions can interfere with our communication. What we need, then, are tools to help others understand our perceptions and for us, in turn, to understand theirs. The following section introduces two such tools.

PERCEPTION CHECKING

With the likelihood for perceptual errors so great, it's easy to see how a communicator can leap to the wrong conclusion and make inaccurate assumptions. Consider the defense-arousing potential of incorrect accusations like these:

"Why are you mad at me?" (Who said I was?)
"What's the matter with you?" (Who said anything was the matter?)
"Come on now. Tell the truth." (Who said you were lying?)

Even if your interpretations are correct, these kinds of mind-reading statements are likely to generate defensiveness. The skill of **perception checking** provides a better way to check and to share your interpretations. A complete perception check has three parts:

1. A description of the behavior you noticed;
2. Two possible interpretations of the behavior;
3. A request for clarification about how to interpret the behavior.

Perception checks for the preceding three examples would look like this:

"When you stomped out of the room and slammed the door [behavior], I wasn't sure whether you were mad at me [first interpretation] or just in a hurry [second interpretation]. How did you feel? [request for clarification]"

"You haven't laughed much in the last couple of days [behavior]. It makes me wonder whether something's bothering you [first interpretation] or whether you're just being quiet [second interpretation]. What's up? [request for clarification]"

"You said you really liked the job I did [behavior], but there was something about your voice that made me think you may not like it [first interpretation]. Maybe it's just my imagination, though [second interpretation]. How do you really feel? [request for clarification]"

Perception checking is a tool to help us understand others accurately instead of assuming that our first interpretation is correct. Because its goal is mutual understanding, perception checking is a cooperative approach to communication. Besides leading to more accurate perceptions, it signals an attitude of respect and concern for the other person, saying, in effect, "I know I'm not qualified to judge you without some help."

Sometimes an effective perception check won't need all of the parts listed in the preceding example to be effective:

"You haven't dropped by lately. Is anything the matter?" [single interpretation].

"I can't tell whether you're kidding me about being cheap or if you're serious [behavior combined with interpretations]. Are you mad at me?"

"Are you sure you don't mind driving? I can use a ride if it's no trouble, but I don't want to take you out of your way" [request for clarification comes first; no need to describe behavior].

The straightforward approach of perception checking has the best chance of working in what Chapter 2 identifies as *low-context cultures,* ones in which members use language as clearly and logically as possible. The dominant cultures of North America and Western Europe fit into this category, and members of these groups are most likely to appreciate the kind of straight talking that perception checking embodies. On the other hand, members of *high-context cultures* (more common in Latin America and Asia) value social harmony over clarity. High-context communicators are more likely to regard candid approaches like perception checking as potentially embarrassing, preferring instead less direct ways of understanding one another. Thus, a "let's get this straight" perception check might work well with a European American manager who was raised to value clarity but it could be a serious mistake with a Mexican American or Asian American boss who has spent most of his or her life in a high-context culture.

Along with clarifying meaning, perception checking can sometimes be a face-saving way to raise an issue without directly threatening or attacking the other person. Consider these examples:

> "Are you planning on doing those dishes later, or did you forget that it's your turn?
>
> "Am I boring you, or do you have something else on your mind?"

In the first case you might have been quite confident that the other person had no intention of doing the dishes, and in the second that the other person was bored. Even so, a perception check is a less threatening way of pointing out their behavior than direct confrontation. Remember—one element of competent communication is the ability to choose the best option from a large repertoire, and perception checking can be a useful strategy at times.

BUILDING EMPATHY

Perception checking can help you decode messages more accurately, but it doesn't provide enough information for us to claim that we fully understand another person. For example, a professor who uses perception checking might learn that a student's reluctance to ask questions is due to confusion and not lack of interest. This information would be helpful, but imagine how much more effective the professor would be if she could get a sense of how it feels to be confused, and consider how the material that is so familiar to her appears to the student who is examining it for the first time. Likewise, parents whose perception checks reveal that their teenager's outlandish behavior grows from a desire to be accepted by others don't necessarily understand (or perhaps recall) what it feels like to crave that acceptance.

"How would you feel if the mouse did that to you?"

Empathy Defined What we need, then, to understand others more completely is **empathy**—the ability to re-create another person's perspective, to experience the world from his or her point of view. It is impossible to achieve total empathy, but with enough effort and skill, we can come closer to this goal (Bonvicini, 2008; Long et al., 1999).

FOCUS ON RESEARCH

Developing Empathy through Virtual Reality

research

As the well-known aphorism suggests, the best way to appreciate another person's perspective is by walking a mile in his or her shoes. Stanford University communication researchers Nick Yee and Jeremy Bailenson have taken this principle into the digital age.

Yee and Bailenson wanted to know whether young people would become more tolerant toward the elderly after experiencing the world as a senior. The researchers created an "immersive virtual environment" in which college-age subjects took on the identity of an elderly "avatar," viewing themselves as a walking, speaking character of advanced age. Other subjects inhabited avatars of young people.

After only a few minutes of self-observation and conversation with a research assistant, the students took a variety of tests to measure their attitudes toward the elderly. Subjects who had just acted as elderly people displayed significantly more positive attitudes toward the aged than did those whose avatars were more youthful.

It's hard to imagine the world of someone who is different from us. Research like this suggests that digital technology offers a valuable tool for boosting empathy.

Yee, N., & Bailenson, J. N. (2006, August). Walk a mile in digital shoes: The impact of embodied perspective-taking on the reduction of negative stereotyping in immersive virtual environments. *Proceedings of PRESENCE 2006: The 8th Annual International Workshop on Presence.* Cleveland, OH. Available at: http://www.temple.edu/ispr/prev_conferences/proceedings/2006/confindex.html

As we'll use the term here, empathy has three dimensions (Stiff et al., 1988). On one level, empathy involves *perspective taking*—the ability to take on the viewpoint of another person. This understanding requires a suspension of judgment so that for the moment you set aside your own opinions and take on those of the other person. Besides cognitive understanding, empathy also has an affective dimension—what social scientists term *emotional contagion.* In everyday language, emotional contagion means that we experience the same feelings that others have. We know their fear, joy, sadness, and so on. A third ingredient of empathy is a genuine *concern* for the welfare of the other person. Not only do we think and feel as others do, but we have a sincere interest in their well-being. Full empathy requires both intellectual understanding of the other person's position and an affective understanding of the other's feelings (Kerem et al., 2001).

The linguistic roots of the word *empathy* shed light on the word's meaning. *Empathy* is derived from two Greek words that mean "feeling (in)side," which suggests that empathy means *experiencing* the other's perception—in effect, temporarily becoming that person. This kind of understanding is very different from sympathy. The Greek roots for *sympathy* mean "feeling with." As this definition implies, when you feel sympathetic you stand beside the other person. You feel compassion, but you do not share the other person's emotions. Despite your concern, sympathy involves less identification than does empathy. When you sympathize, the confusion, joy, or pain belongs to another. When you empathize, the experience becomes your own, at least for the moment.

The Value of Empathy The recipient of empathy receives several payoffs. The first is increased *self-esteem.* Others usually respond to your point of view with judgments such as "That's right . . ." or "No, it's not that way at all. . . ." An empathic response is different: It suggests the listener is willing to accept you as you are, without any evaluations. It's flattering to find that someone is interested enough in your position to hear you out without passing judgment. The act of being understood also can be very *comforting,* whether or not the other person's reflections offer any additional help. When others empathize, a common thought is "I'm not alone." Finally, the target of empathy learns to *trust* the empathizer in a way that probably would not be otherwise possible.

Empathy and Ethics The "golden rule" of treating others as we want to be treated points to the clear relationship between the ability to empathize and the ethical principles that enable society to function in a matter that we consider civilized. Martin Hoffman (1991) and Frans de Waal (2008) cite research showing the link between empathy and ethical altruism. Bystanders who feel empathy for victims are more likely to intervene and offer help than those who are indifferent. On a larger scale, studies in the United States and Germany have revealed a relationship between feelings of empathy and the willingness of people to favor the moral principle that resources should be allocated according to people's needs.

A look at criminal behavior also demonstrates the link between empathy and ethics. Typically, people who commit the most offensive crimes against others, such as rape and child abuse, are not inhibited by any sense of how their offenses affect the victims (Goleman, 1995). Promising new treatments attempt to change behavior by instilling the ability to imagine how others are feeling. In one program, offenders read emotional descriptions of crimes similar to the ones they have committed and watch videotapes of victims describing what it was like to be assaulted. They also write accounts of what their offense must have felt like to the victim, read these stories to others in therapy groups, and even experience simulated reenactments of the crime in which they play the role of the victim. Through strategies like these, therapists try to help offenders de-

DARK SIDE OF COMMUNICATION

Empathy Fatigue: When Helpers Need Help

Empathy is a powerful way to offer social support. But for many in the helping professions—counselors, health care professionals, social workers, police, firefighters, and emergency personnel—providing this form of support can take a toll. *Empathy fatigue* (sometimes called *compassion fatigue*) is a type of burnout that results in physical, mental, and emotional exhaustion. Ironically, one of the side effects of empathy fatigue is that caregivers may become emotionally hardened and lose the compassion they would normally feel for others.

There are a variety of prescriptions for those with empathy fatigue, including time off, diet and exercise regimens, and creating boundaries between personal and professional worlds. Those prescriptions are probably good advice for anyone who typically gives more empathy and compassion than he or she receives.

Stebnicki, M. A. (2007). Empathy fatigue: Healing the mind, body, and spirit of professional counselors. *American Journal of Psychiatric Rehabilitation, 10,* 317–338.

SELF-ASSESSMENT

Empathy in Friendships

This instrument can help you determine the degree to which empathy is part of your friendships. Think of one of your close personal friendships and, with that friendship in mind, respond to each statement according to how much you agree with it.

If you agree completely, mark the statement **4.**
If you agree a great deal but not completely, mark the statement **3.**
If you agree somewhat, mark the statement **2.**
If you agree very little, mark the statement **1.**
If you do not agree, mark the statement **0.**

_____ **1. I understand what my friend says.**
_____ **2. I understand how my friend feels.**
_____ **3. I appreciate what my friend's experiences feel like to her or him.**
_____ **4. I try to see things through my friend's eyes.**
_____ **5. I ask my friend questions about what his or her experiences mean to him or her.**
_____ **6. I ask my friend questions about what she or he is thinking.**
_____ **7. I ask my friend questions about how he or she is feeling.**
_____ **8. My friend understands what I say.**
_____ **9. My friend understands how I feel.**
_____ **10. My friend appreciates what my experiences feel like to me.**
_____ **11. My friend tries to see things through my eyes.**
_____ **12. My friend asks me questions about what my experiences mean to me.**
_____ **13. My friend asks me questions about what I'm thinking.**
_____ **14. My friend asks me questions about how I'm feeling.**

SCORING:
Add your scores for items 1–7: This figure represents your perception of your empathy for your friend.
Add your scores for items 8–14: This represents your perception of your friend's empathy for you.

Each sum can range from 0 to 28. The higher the sum, the greater the empathy.
Now have your friend respond to the items, and compare your answers. The results might well contribute to greater empathy in your relationship.

velop the ethical compass that makes it more difficult to be indifferent to causing pain in others.

Requirements for Empathy Empathy may be valuable, but it isn't always easy to achieve. In fact, research shows that it's hardest to empathize with people who are radically different from us: in age, sex, socioeconomic status, intelligence, and so forth (Cronkhite, 1976). In order to make such perceptual leaps, you need to develop several skills and attitudes: open-mindedness, imagination, and commitment.

Perhaps the most important characteristic of an empathic person is the ability and disposition to be *open-minded*—to set aside for the moment your own beliefs, attitudes, and values and to consider those of the other person. Open-mindedness is especially difficult when the other person's position is radically different from your own. The temptation is to think (and sometimes say) "That's crazy!" "How can you believe that?" or "I'd do it this way. . . ."

Being open-minded is often difficult because people confuse *understanding* another's position with *accepting* it. These are quite different matters. To understand why a friend disagrees with you, for example, doesn't mean you have to give up your position and accept hers.

Being open-minded often isn't enough to allow empathy. You also need enough *imagination* to be able to picture another person's background and thoughts. A happily married or single person needs imagination to empathize with the problems of a friend considering divorce. A young person needs it to empathize with a parent facing retirement. A teacher needs it to understand the problems facing students, just as students can't be empathic without trying to imagine how their instructor feels.

Because empathizing is often difficult, a third necessary quality is *commitment,* a sincere desire to understand another person. Listening to unfamiliar, often confusing information takes time and isn't always fun. If you aim to be empathic, be willing to face the challenge.

By now, you can see the tremendous challenges that face us when we want to understand one another. Physiological distortion, psychological interference, and social and cultural conditioning all insulate us from our fellow human beings. But the news isn't all bad: With a combination of determination and skill, we can do a better job of spanning the gap that separates us and, as a result, enjoy more satisfying interpersonal relationships.

Summary

Many communication challenges arise because of differing perceptions. The process of interpersonal perception is a complex one, and a variety of factors cause each person's view of reality to vary.

The reality we perceive is constructed through communication with others. First-order realities involve things and events that are tangible; second-order realities are the meanings we assign to those things and events. Interpersonal perception involves four phases: selection, organization, interpretation, and negotiation. A number of influences can affect how we perceive others' behavior. Physiological factors include our senses, age, health, fatigue, hunger, and biological cycles. Psychological factors such as mood and self-concept also have a strong influence on how we regard others. In addition, social influences such as sex and gender roles and occupational roles, play an important part in the way we view those with whom we interact. Finally, cultural influences shape how we recognize and make sense of others' words and actions.

Our perceptions are often affected by common perceptual tendencies. We tend to make snap judgments and cling to first impressions, even if they are mistaken. We are more likely to blame others than ourselves for misfortunes. We are influenced by our expectations. We also are influenced by obvious stimuli, even if they are not the most important factors. Finally, we assume others are similar to us.

One way to coordinate our interpretations with others is through perception checking. Instead of jumping to conclusions, communicators who check their perceptions describe the behavior they noticed, offer two equally plausible interpretations, and ask for clarification from their partner.

Empathy is the ability to experience the world from another person's perspective. There are three dimensions to empathy: perspective taking, emotional involvement, and concern for the other person. Empathy has benefits for both the empathizer and the recipient. Some evidence suggests that there may be hereditary influences on the ability to empathize but that this ability can be developed with practice. Requirements for empathy include open-mindedness, imagination, and commitment.

Activities

1. Critical Thinking Probe

Complete the following sentences:

a. Women ______________________________

____

b. Men ______________________________

____

c. Latinos ______________________________

____

d. European Americans ______________________________

____

e. African Americans ______________________________

____

f. Older people ______________________________

____

Now ask yourself the degree to which each of your responses was a stereotype and/or a generalization. Is it possible to make generalizations about these groups? How could your answers to these questions change the way you perceive and respond to people in these groups?

2. Invitation to Insight

You can get a better appreciation of the importance of punctuation by using the format pictured in Figure 4.3 to diagram the following situations:

a. A father and daughter are growing more and more distant. The daughter withdraws because she interprets her father's coolness as rejection. The father views his daughter's aloofness as a rebuff and withdraws further.
b. The relationship between two friends is becoming strained. One jokes to lighten up the tension, and the other becomes more tense.
c. A couple is on the verge of breaking up. One partner frequently asks the other to show more affection. The other withdraws physical contact.

Explain how each of these situations could be punctuated differently by each participant. Next, use the same procedure to identify how an event from your experience could be punctuated in at least two different ways. Describe the consequences of failing to recognize the plausibility of each of these punctuation schemes.

3. Invitation to Insight

Choose one of the following situations, and describe how it could be perceived differently by each person. Be sure to include the steps of selection, organization, and interpretation. What might their narratives sound like as they negotiate their perceptions? List any relevant physiological, psychological, social, and cultural influences, as well as suggesting how the communicators' self-concepts might have affected their perceptions.

a. A customer complains to a salesperson about poor service in a busy store.
b. A parent and teenager argue about the proper time for returning home after a Saturday night date.
c. A quiet student feels pressured when called upon by an instructor to speak up in class.
d. A woman and a man argue about whether to increase balance in the workplace by making special efforts to hire employees from underrepresented groups.

4. Invitation to Insight

Pages 122–128 of this chapter outline several common perceptual tendencies. Describe instances in which you committed each of them, and explain the consequences of each one. Which of these perceptual tendencies are you most prone to make, and what are the potential results of making it? How can you avoid these tendencies in the future?

5. Skill Builder

Improve your perception-checking ability by developing complete perception-checking statements for each of the following situations. Be sure your statements include a description of the behavior, two equally plausible interpretations, and a request for verification.

a. You made what you thought was an excellent suggestion to your boss. He or she said, "I'll get back to you about that right away." It's been 3 weeks, and you haven't received a response yet.
b. You haven't received the usual weekly phone call from your family in over a month. Last time you spoke, you had an argument about where to spend the holidays.

6. Skill Builder

You can develop your empathy skills by putting yourself in the shoes of someone with whom you have an interpersonal relationship. With that person's help, describe *in the first person* how the other person views an issue that is important to him or her. In other words, try as much as possible to become that person and see things from his or her perspective. Your partner will be the best judge of your ability to make this perceptual jump, so use his or her feedback to modify your account. After completing the exercise, describe how your attempt changed the way you might relate to the other person.

CHAPTER

5 Language

CHAPTER OUTLINE

After studying the material in this chapter . . .

YOU SHOULD UNDERSTAND:

1. The symbolic nature of language.
2. That meanings are in people, not words.
3. The types of rules that govern the use of language.
4. How language affects worldview.
5. The influence of language on identity, credibility and status, affiliation, power, and attitudes about sexism and racism.
6. The factors that influence precision and vagueness in language.
7. The language patterns that reflect a speaker's level of responsibility for his or her statements.
8. Three forms of disruptive language.
9. Varying positions about the relationship between gender and language.

YOU SHOULD BE ABLE TO:

1. Identify cases in which you have attributed meanings to words instead of people.
2. Analyze a real or potential misunderstanding in terms of semantic or pragmatic rules.
3. Describe how principles presented in the section of this chapter titled "The Impact of Language" operate in your life.
4. Construct a message at the optimal level of specificity or vagueness for a given situation.
5. Construct statements that acknowledge your responsibility for the content of messages.
6. Rephrase disruptive statements in less inflammatory terms.
7. Identify similarities and differences in male and female language use, and provide explanations for such differences.

KEY TERMS

- Abstraction ladder (154)
- Ambiguous language (153)
- "But" statement (159)
- Convergence (147)
- Divergence (148)
- Emotive language (163)
- Euphemism (156)
- Factual statement (162)
- "I" language (159)
- Inferential statement (163)
- "It" statement (159)
- Linguistic relativism (144)
- Opinion statement (162)
- Phonological rules (141)
- Powerless speech mannerisms (149)
- Pragmatic rules (142)
- Racist language (152)
- Relative language (156)
- Sapir–Whorf hypothesis (144)
- Semantic rules (142)
- Sexist language (151)
- Static evaluation (158)
- Syntactic rules (141)
- "We" language (159)
- "You" language (159)

"I don't know what you mean by 'glory,'" Alice said.

Humpty Dumpty smiled contemptuously. "Of course you don't—till I tell you. I meant 'there's a nice knock-down argument for you!'"

"But 'glory' doesn't mean 'a nice knock-down argument,'" Alice objected.

"When I use a word," Humpty Dumpty said, in a rather scornful tone, "it means just what I choose it to mean—neither more nor less."

"The question is," said Alice, "whether you can make words mean so many different things."

"The question is," said Humpty Dumpty, "which is to be master—that's all."

—LEWIS CARROLL, *THROUGH THE LOOKING GLASS*

Like Alice, at one time or another everyone has felt trapped in a linguistic wonderland. Words shift meanings until we don't know what others, or even we ourselves, are saying. Even when we think we understand one another, there's a good chance we are overestimating how clearly and completely others understand us (Keyser & Henley, 2002). Although language is an imperfect vessel with which to convey ideas, it also is a marvelous tool that we often take for granted. Only when we consider life without the ability to connect linguistically does the wonder of the everyday exchange of messages become apparent. Consider the powerful story of Carly Fleischmann, a teenager with severe autism who is unable to speak. After years of living in silence and isolation, Carly suddenly started typing words on her computer, unleashing thoughts and feelings she had been holding all her life. According to her father, Carly's use of language gave them access to the "articulate, intelligent, emotive person that we had never met" (McKenzie, 2008). Carly's story evokes the memory of Helen Keller, who broke through the isolation imposed by deafness and blindness, learning a form of tactile language that first enabled her to communicate with her teacher and ultimately with the world at large (Keller, 2005).

In this chapter we explore the relationship between words and ideas. We describe some important characteristics of language and show how these characteristics affect our day-to-day communication. We outline several types of troublesome language and show how to replace them with more effective kinds of speech. Finally, we look at the degree to which gender influences the way we use language.

The Nature of Language

We begin our survey by looking at some features that characterize all languages. These features explain both why language is such a useful tool and why it can be so troublesome.

LANGUAGE IS SYMBOLIC

Words are arbitrary symbols that have no meaning in themselves. For example, the word *five* is a kind of code that represents the number of fingers on your hand only because we agree that it does. As Bateson and Jackson (1964) point out, "There is nothing particularly five-like in the number 'five'" (p. 271). To a speaker of French, the symbol *cinq* would convey the same meaning; to a computer, the same value would be represented by the electronically coded symbol *00110101.*

Even sign language, as "spoken" by most deaf people, is symbolic in nature and not the pantomime it might seem (Tolar et al., 2008). Because this form of communication is symbolic and not literal, there are hundreds of different sign languages used around the world that have evolved independently, whenever significant numbers of deaf people have come in contact (Sacks, 1989). These distinct languages include American Sign Language, Mexican Sign Language, British Sign Language, French Sign Language, Danish Sign Language, Chinese Sign Language, and Australian Aboriginal and Mayan sign languages—and communicating across different sign languages can be as difficult as it is across different spoken languages (Quinto-Pozos, 2008).

LANGUAGE IS RULE-GOVERNED

The only reason symbol-laden languages work at all is that people agree on how to use them. The linguistic agreements that make communication possible can be codified in rules. Languages contain several types of rules. **Phonological rules** govern how sounds are combined to form words. For instance, the words *champagne, double,* and *occasion* have the same meaning in French and English, but are pronounced differently because the languages have different phonological rules.

"What part of oil lamp next to double squiggle over ox don't you understand?"

Whereas phonological rules determine how spoken language sounds, **syntactic rules** govern the way symbols can be arranged. Notice that the following statements contain the same words, but the shift in syntax creates quite different meanings:

> Whiskey makes you sick when you're well.
> Whiskey, when you're sick, makes you well.

Although most of us aren't able to describe the syntactic rules that govern our language (Parisse, 2005), it's easy to recognize their existence when they are violated. A humorous example is the way the character Yoda speaks in the *Star Wars* movies. Phrases such as "the dark side are they" or "your father he is" often elicit a chuckle because they bend syntactical norms. Sometimes, however, apparently ungrammatical speech is simply following a different set of syntactic rules, reflecting regional or co-cultural dialects. Linguists believe it is crucial to view such dialects as *different* rather than *deficient* forms of English (Wolfram & Schilling-Estes, 2005).

Semantic rules also govern our use of language. Whereas syntax deals with structure, semantics governs the meaning of statements. Semantic rules are what make it possible for us to agree that "bikes" are for riding and "books" are for reading, and they help us know whom we will encounter when we use restrooms marked "men" and "women." Without semantic rules, communication would be impossible: Each of us would use symbols in unique ways, unintelligible to others.

Semantic rules help us understand the meaning of individual words, but they often don't explain how language operates in everyday life. Consider the statement "Let's get together tomorrow." The semantic meaning of the words in this sentence is clear enough, yet the statement could be taken in several ways. It could be a request ("I hope we can get together"), a polite command ("I want to see you"), or an empty cliché ("I don't really mean it"). We learn to distinguish the accurate meanings of such speech acts through **pragmatic rules** that tell us what uses and interpretations of a message are appropriate in a given context. When these rules are understood by all players in the language game, smooth communication is possible. For example, one rule specifies that the relationship between communicators plays a large role in determining the meaning of a statement. Our example, "I want to see you," is likely to mean one thing when uttered by your boss and another entirely when it comes from your lover. Likewise, the setting in which the statement is made plays a role. Saying "I want to see you" will probably have a different meaning at the office than the same words uttered at a cocktail party—although the nonverbal behaviors that accompany a statement help us decode its meaning.

The *coordinated management of meaning* (CMM) theory describes some types of pragmatic rules that operate in everyday conversations. It suggests that we use rules at several levels to create our own messages and interpret others' statements (Cronen & Chetro-Szivos, 2001; Pearce, 2005). Table 5.1 uses a CMM framework to illustrate how two people might wind up confused because they are using different rules at several levels. In situations like this, it's important to make sure that the other person's use of language matches yours before jumping to conclusions about the meaning of his or her statements. The skill of perception checking described in Chapter 3 can be a useful tool at times like these.

TABLE 5.1 ***Pragmatic Rules Govern the Use and Meaning of a Statement***

Notice how the same message ("You look very pretty today") takes on different meaning depending on which of a variety of rules are used to formulate and interpret it.

	BOSS	EMPLOYEE
Content Actual words	"You look very pretty today."	
Speech Act The intent of a statement	Compliment an employee	Unknown
Relational Contract The perceived relationship between communicators	Boss who treats employees like family members	Subordinate employee, dependent on boss's approval for advancement
Episode Situation in which the interaction occurs	Casual conversation	Possible come-on by boss?
Life Script Self-concept of each communicator	Friendly guy	Woman determined to succeed on own merits
Cultural Archetype Cultural norms that shape member's perceptions and actions	Middle-class American	Working-class American

Adapted from Pearce, W. B., & Cronen, V. (1980). *Communication, action, and meaning.* New York: Praeger. Used by permission.

LANGUAGE IS SUBJECTIVE

If the rules of language were more precise and if everyone followed them, we would suffer from fewer misunderstandings. You respond to a "while you were out" note and spend a full day trying to reach Ashley, only to find you called the wrong one of your two friends with that name. You have an hour-long argument about "feminism" only to discover that you were using the term in different ways and that you really were in basic agreement. You tease a friend in what you mean to be a playful manner, but he takes you seriously and is offended.

These problems occur because people attach different meanings to the same message. Ogden and Richards (1923) illustrated this point graphically in their well-known "triangle of meaning" (see Figure 5.1). This model shows that there is only an indirect relationship—indicated by a broken line—between a word and the thing or idea it represents.

The Ogden and Richards model is oversimplified in that not all words refer to physical "things" or referents. For instance, some referents are abstract ideas (such as *love*), while others (like *angry* or *exciting*) aren't even nouns. Despite these shortcomings, the triangle of meaning is useful since it clearly demonstrates that meanings are in people, not words. Hence, an important task

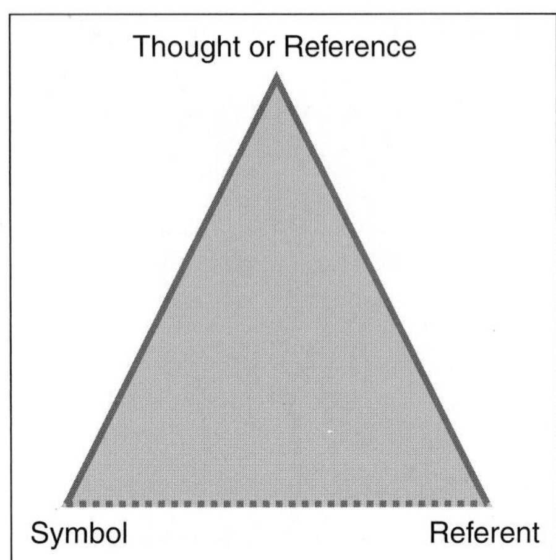

FIGURE 5.1 Ogden and Richards' Triangle of Meaning

facing communicators is to establish a common understanding of the words they use to exchange messages. In this sense, communication—at least the effective kind—requires us to negotiate the meaning of our language (Duck, 1994; Fine & Beim, 2007). This brings us back to a familiar theme: Meaning is both *in* and *among* people.

LANGUAGE AND WORLDVIEW

For almost 150 years, theorists have put forth the notion of **linguistic relativism:** that the worldview of a culture is shaped and reflected by the language its members speak. For instance, bilingual speakers seem to think differently when they change languages (Giles & Franklyn-Stokes, 1989). In one study, French Americans were asked to interpret a series of pictures. When they spoke in French, their descriptions were far more romantic and emotional than when they used English to describe the same kind of images. Likewise, when students in Hong Kong were asked to complete a values test, they expressed more traditional Chinese values when they answered in Cantonese than when they spoke in English. In Israel, both Arab and Jewish students saw bigger distinctions between their group and "outsiders" when using their native language than when they spoke in English, a neutral tongue. Examples like these show the power of language to shape cultural identity—sometimes for better and sometimes for worse.

The best-known declaration of linguistic relativism is the **Sapir–Whorf hypothesis**, formulated by Benjamin Whorf, an amateur linguist, and anthropologist Edward Sapir (Whorf, 1956; Widlok, 2008). Following Sapir's theoretical work, Whorf found that the language spoken by Hopi Native Americans represented a view of reality that is dramatically different from most tongues. For example, the Hopi language makes no distinction between nouns and verbs. Therefore, the people who speak it describe the entire world as being constantly in process. Whereas English speakers use nouns to characterize people or objects as being fixed or constant, the Hopi language represents them more as verbs, constantly changing. In this sense, English represents the world rather like a collection of snapshots, whereas Hopi reflects a worldview that is more like a motion picture.

Some languages contain terms that have no English equivalents (Rheingold, 1988). For example, consider a few words in other languages that have no simple translation in English:

"You'll have to phrase it another way. They have no word for 'fetch'"

- *Nemawashi* (Japanese): the process of informally feeling out all the people involved with an issue before making a decision
- *Lagniappe* (French/Creole): an extra gift given in a transaction that wasn't expected by the terms of a contract
- *Lao* (Mandarin): respectful term used for older people, showing their importance in the family and in society
- *Dharma* (Sanskrit): each person's unique, ideal path in life and the knowledge of how to find it
- *Koyaanisquatsi* (Hopi): nature out of balance; a way of life so crazy it calls for a new way of living

It's possible to imagine concepts like these without having specific words to describe them; but linguistic relativism suggests that the terms do shape the thinking and actions of people who use them. Thus, speakers of a language that includes the notion of *lao* would probably be more inclined to treat its older members respectfully, and those who are familiar with *lagniappe* might be more generous. As author David Malouf observes,

> It is all very well to regard language as simply "a means of communication. . . ." But for most of us it is also a machine for thinking; and what can be thought and felt . . . is different, both in quality and kind, from one language to the next. (2003, p. 44)

The Impact of Language

Besides simply describing the world, language can have a strong effect on our perceptions and how we regard one another. In the following pages we will examine some of the many ways language can impact our lives.

NAMING AND IDENTITY

"What's in a name?" Juliet asked rhetorically. If Romeo had been a social scientist, he would have answered, "A great deal." Research has demonstrated that names are more than just a simple means of identification: They shape the way others think of us, the way we view ourselves, and the way we act (Lieberson, 2000).

For more than a century, researchers have studied the impact of rare and unusual names on the people who bear them (Christenfeld & Larsen, 2008). Early studies claimed that people with non-normative names suffered everything from psychological and emotional disturbance to failure in college. More recent studies have shown that people often have negative appraisals not only of unusual names, but also of unusual name spellings (Mehrabian, 2001). Of course, what makes a name (and its spelling) unusual changes with time. In 1900, the 20 most popular names for baby girls included Bertha, Mildred, and Ethel. By 2007, top 20 names included Madison, Addison, and Alyssa—names that would have been highly unusual a century earlier (Social Security Administration, 2008).

Some people regard unique names as distinctive rather than unusual. You can probably think of four or five unique names—of celebrities, sports stars, or even personal friends—that make the person easily recognizable and memorable. Sometimes the choice of unique names is connected with cultural identity. For example, in recent decades a large percentage of names given to African American babies have been distinctively black (Fryer & Levitt, 2004). In California, over 40 percent of black girls born recently have names that not a single white baby born in the entire state was given. Researchers suggest that distinctive names like these are a symbol of solidarity with the African American community. Conversely, choosing a less distinctive name can be a way of integrating the baby into the majority culture.

Names aren't just a reflection of ethnic identity: They can also be an indicator of status. Steven Levitt and Stephen Dunbar (2005) used Census data to show the link between children's names and socioeconomic status. Once a name catches on among high-income, highly educated parents, it starts working its way down the socioeconomic ladder as it is bestowed on children of parents with less education and lower income. Thus, it's possible to speculate about the socioeconomic status of people once you know their name and date of birth.

REFLECTION

Sharing a Name

I was named after my father, who was named after his father. When I was growing up, I didn't always like sharing a name with my dad and grandpa. Sometimes it got confusing, and I often got called "Little Stevie" (which I detested) at family gatherings.

But now that I'm older, I like the shared name a lot more. When people who know my dad hear my name and ask if we're related, I feel a real sense of pride and connection. It's not just my name; it's *our* name—and I'm okay with that.

Many women in Western society, aware of the power of names to influence identity, view the name they choose to identify themselves after marriage as a significant decision. They may choose to take their husband's last name, hyphenate their own name and their husband's, or keep their birth name. One study by Karen Foss and Belle Edison (1989) revealed that a woman's choice is likely to reveal a great deal about herself and her relationship with her husband. Surveys revealed that women who took their husband's names placed the most importance on relationships, with social expectations of how they should behave rated second and issues of self coming last. On the other hand, women who kept their birth names put their personal concerns ahead of relationships and social expectations. Women with hyphenated names fell somewhere between the other groups, valuing self and relationships equally.

Some research suggests that the results of name-keeping or name-changing aren't as profound as they might seem. For example, one study (Stafford & Kline, 1996) analyzed 110 well-educated married women, both name-changers and name-keepers. Contrary to what linguistic reformers might have expected, there were no significant differences between name-changers and name-keepers in terms of self-esteem, relationship dependency, autonomy, or feelings about the balance of control in their marriages. Another study, which analyzed *New York Times* wedding announcements, Harvard alumni records, and Massachusetts birth records, indicated that women most likely to keep their surname held advanced degrees, worked in the arts and writing, and had longer careers before marriage (Goldin & Shim, 2004).

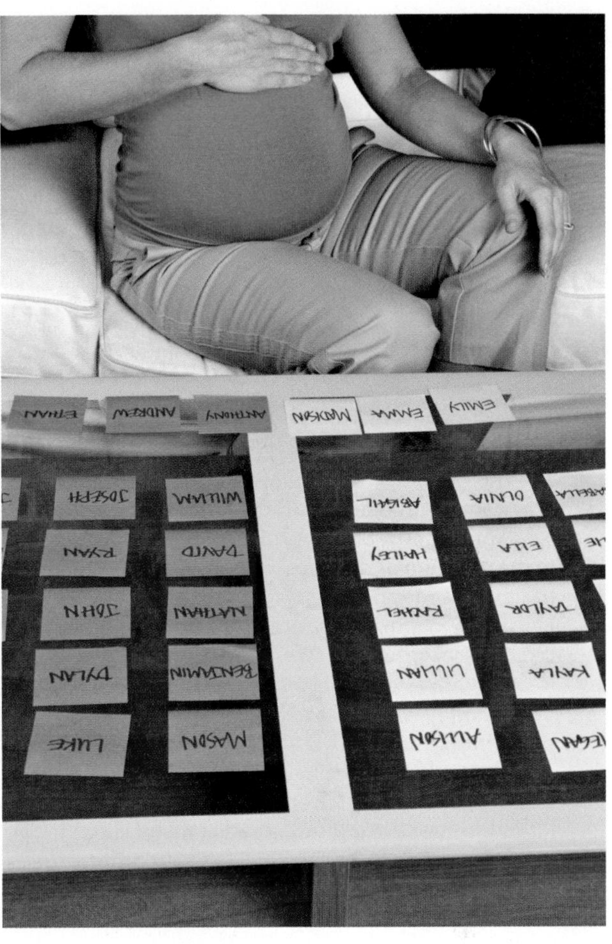

AFFILIATION

Along with expressing ideas and feelings, speech can be a way of building and demonstrating solidarity with others. An impressive body of research has demonstrated that communicators who want to show affiliation with one another adapt their speech in a variety of ways, including their choice of vocabulary, rate of talking, number and placement of pauses, and level of politeness (Aune & Kikuchi, 1993; Giles et al., 1992c). On an individual level, close friends and lovers often develop a set of special terms that serve as a way of signifying their relationship (Bell et al., 1987; Bell & Healey, 1992). Using the same vocabulary serves to set these people apart from others, reminding themselves and the rest of the world of their relationship. The same process works among members of larger groups, ranging from street gangs to military personnel. Communication researchers call the process of adapting one's speech style to match that of others with whom the communicator wants to identify **convergence**.

Communicators can experience convergence in cyberspace as well as in face-to-face interactions. Members of online communities often develop a shared language and conversational style, and their affiliation with each other can be seen in increased uses of the pronoun *we* (Cassell & Tversky, 2005). On a larger scale, IM and e-mail users create and use shortcuts that mark them as Internet-savvy. If you know what ROTFL, IMHO, and JK mean, you're probably part of that group. (For the uninitiated, those acronyms mean, respectively, "Rolling on the floor laughing," "In my humble opinion," and "Just kidding"). Interestingly, IMers may find that their cyberlanguage creeps into everyday conversations (have you ever said "LOL" instead of the words "laughing out loud"—or instead of actually laughing out loud?).

When two or more people feel equally positive about one another, their linguistic convergence will be mutual. But when communicators want or need approval, they often adapt their speech to accommodate the other person's style, trying to say the "right thing" or speak in a way that will help them fit in. We see this process when immigrants who want to gain the reward of material success in a new culture strive to master the host language. Likewise, employees who seek advancement tend to speak more like their superiors, supervisors adopt the speech style of managers, and managers converge toward their bosses. One study even showed that adopting the swearing patterns of bosses and coworkers can help people feel connected on the job (Baruch & Jenkins, 2006).

Divide or Unite: *The N Word*

It is possibly the most inflammatory word in American culture—so much so that the letter *N* is substituted for the actual word in most public discussions of the term. But as this documentary shows, the "N word" has many and varied meanings, ranging from a degrading slur to a term of endearment. A host of scholars and celebrities (including Chris Rock, Whoopi Goldberg, George Carlin, Ice Cube, and Quincy Jones) discuss and debate when, where, how, by whom, and even whether the "N word" should be used.

The film offers a vivid illustration of how pragmatic rules and linguistic convergence/divergence operate in interpersonal and intercultural communication. It also shows how failing to know and abide by cultural meanings and rules can lead to significant misunderstandings and conflict.

The principle of speech accommodation works in reverse, too. Communicators who want to set themselves apart from others adopt the strategy of **divergence**, speaking in a way that emphasizes their differences. For example, members of an ethnic group, even though fluent in the dominant language, might use their own dialect as a way of showing solidarity with one another—a sort of "we're proud of our heritage" strategy. The same can occur across age lines, such as teens who adopt the slang of subcultures other than their own to show divergence with adults and convergence with their peers (Reyes, 2005). Of course, communicators need to be careful about when—and when not—to converge their language with others. Most of us can remember the embarrassment of hearing a parent use youthful slang and thinking, "You're too old to be saying that." On a more serious level, using ethnic/racial epithets when you're not a member of that in-group can be inappropriate and even offensive. One of the pragmatic goals of divergence is the creation of norms about who has the "right" to use certain words and who does not. (See the Film Clip on this page for an example of this issue.)

POWER

Communication researchers have identified a number of language patterns that add to or detract from a speaker's power to influence others. Notice the difference between these two statements:

> Excuse me, sir. I hate to say this, but I . . . uh . . . I guess I won't be able to turn in the assignment on time. I had a personal emergency and . . . well . . . it was just impossible to finish it by today. I'll have it in your mailbox on Monday, OK?
>
> I won't be able to turn in the assignment on time. I had a personal emergency and it was impossible to finish it by today. I'll have it in your mailbox on Monday.

Whether or not the instructor finds the excuse acceptable, it's clear that the second one sounds more confident, whereas the tone of the first is apologetic and uncertain. Table 5.2 (below) identifies several **powerless speech mannerisms** illustrated in the statements you just read. A number of studies have shown that speakers whose talk is free of these mannerisms are rated as more competent, dynamic, and attractive than speakers who sound powerless (Ng & Bradac, 1993; Reid & Ng, 1999). The effects of powerful versus powerless speech styles also are apparent on employment interview outcomes: a powerful speech style results in more positive attributions of competence and employability than a powerless one (Parton et al., 2002). Even a single type of powerless speech mannerism, such as hedges, appears to make a person appear less authoritative or socially attractive (Hosman, 1989; Hosman & Siltanen, 2006).

Powerful speech that gets the desired results in mainstream North American and European culture doesn't succeed everywhere with everyone (Samovar & Porter, 2004). In Japan, saving face for others is an important goal, so communicators there tend to speak in ambiguous terms and use hedge words and qualifiers. In most Japanese sentences the verb comes at the end of the sentence so the "action" part of the statement can be postponed. Traditional Mexican culture, with its strong emphasis on cooperation, also uses hedging to smooth over interpersonal relationships. By not taking a firm stand with their speech mannerisms, Mexicans believe they will not make others feel ill at ease. The Korean culture represents yet another group of people who prefer "indirect" (for example, *perhaps, could be*) over "direct" speech.

Even in North American culture, simply counting the number of powerful or powerless statements won't always reveal who has the most control in

TABLE 5.2 ***Examples of Less Powerful Language***

TYPE OF USAGE	EXAMPLE
Hedges	"I'm kinda disappointed . . ." "I think we should . . ." "I guess I'd like to . . ."
Hesitations	"Uh, can I have a minute of your time?" "Well, we could try this idea . . ." "I wish you would—er—try to be on time."
Polite forms	"Excuse me, sir . . ."
Tag questions	"It's about time we got started, isn't it?" "Don't you think we should give it another try?"
Disclaimers	"I probably shouldn't say this, but . . ."

Adapted from Adler, R. B., & Elmhorst, J. (2008). *Communicating at work: Principles and practices for business and the professions* (9th ed., p. 31). New York: McGraw-Hill.

FOCUS ON RESEARCH

"I Don't Mean to Antagonize You, But . . ."

research

We use disclaimers to ward off a negative reaction by distancing ourselves from the unwelcome remarks we're about to utter. For example, you might preface a critical message by saying "I don't mean to sound judgmental, but . . ." and then go on to express your disapproval.

Disclaimers lower a speaker's credibility and attractiveness, which is why they are classified as a form of powerless speech (See Table 5.2). Despite this disadvantage, it might be worth using them if the payoff is preserving a positive relationship. To explore whether this trade-off of power for harmony is a valid option, a research team led by Amani El-Alayli explored whether disclaimers can, in fact, inoculate a speaker from the disapproval for delivering an unwelcome message.

The researchers found that disclaimers actually *increase* negative judgments about precisely the qualities the speaker is trying to downplay. For instance, the disclaimer "I don't mean to sound arrogant . . ." followed by a high-handed comment led subjects to regard the speaker as *more* arrogant. Disclaimers involving other negative qualities such as laziness and selfishness produced similar results.

It seems that disclaimers backfire because they sensitize listeners to look for—and find—precisely the qualities that the speaker is trying to disavow.

El-Alayli, A., Myers, C. J., Petersen, T. L., & Lystad, A. L. (2008). "I don't mean to sound arrogant, but . . ." The effects of using disclaimers on person perception. *Personality and Social Psychology Bulletin, 34,* 130–143.

a relationship. Social rules often mask the real distribution of power. A boss who wants to be pleasant might say to a secretary, "Would you mind getting this file?" In truth, both boss and secretary know this is an order and not a request, but the questioning form makes the medicine less bitter. Sociolinguist Deborah Tannen (1994, p. 101) describes how politeness can be a face-saving way of delivering an order:

> I hear myself giving instructions to my assistants without actually issuing orders: "Maybe it would be a good idea to . . . ;" "It would be great if you could . . ." all the while knowing that I expect them to do what I've asked right away. . . . This rarely creates problems, though, because the people who work for me know that there is only one reason I mention tasks—because I want them done. I *like* giving instructions in this way; it appeals to my sense of what it means to be a good person . . . taking others' feelings into account.

As this quotation suggests, high-status speakers—especially higher-status women, according to Tannen—often realize that politeness is an effective way to get their needs met while protecting the dignity of the less-powerful person. The importance of achieving both content and relational goals helps explain why a mixture of powerful and polite speech is usually most effective (Geddes, 1992). The key involves adapting your style to your conversational partner. If the other person is likely to perceive politeness as weakness, it may be necessary to shift to a more powerful speaking style. Conversely, if the person sees powerful speech as rude and insensitive, it might be best to use a more polite approach. As always, competent communication requires flexibility and adaptability.

SEXISM AND RACISM

Sexist language "includes words, phrases, and expressions that unnecessarily differentiate between females and males *or* exclude, trivialize, or diminish" either sex (Parks & Robertson, 2000, p. 415). This type of speech can affect the self-concepts of women and men, which is why one author (Lillian, 2007) argues that it is a form of hate speech. Suzanne Romaine (1999) offers several examples of how linguistic terms can subtly stereotype men and women. To say that a woman *mothered* her children focuses on her nurturing behavior, but to say that a man *fathered* a child talks only about his biological role. We are familiar with terms like *working mother,* but there is no term *working father* because we assume (perhaps inaccurately) that men are the breadwinners.

Beyond just stereotyping, sexist language can stigmatize women. For example, the term *unmarried mother* is common, but we do not talk about *unmarried fathers* because for many people there is no stigma attached to this status for men. Whereas there are over 200 English words for promiscuous women, there are only 20 for men (Stanley, 1977).

There are at least two ways to eliminate sexist language (Rakow, 1992). The first circumvents the problem altogether by eliminating sex-specific terms or substituting neutral terms. For example, using the plural *they* eliminates the necessity for *he, she, she and he,* or *he and she.* When no sex reference is appropriate, you can substitute neutral terms. For example: *mankind* may be replaced with *humanity, human beings, human race,* and *people; man-made* may be replaced with *artificial, manufactured,* and *synthetic; manpower* may be replaced with *labor, workers,* and *workforce;* and *manhood* may be replaced with *adulthood.* In the same way, *Congressmen* are *members of Congress; firemen* are *firefighters; chairmen* are *presiding officers, leaders,* and *chairs; foremen* are *supervisors; policemen* and *policewomen* are both *police officers;* and *stewardesses* and *stewards* are both *flight attendants.* Of course, some terms refer to things that could not possibly have a sex—so, for example, a *manhole* is a *sewer lid.*

The second method for eliminating sexism is to mark sex clearly—to heighten awareness of whether the reference is to a female or a male. For example, rather than substitute "chairperson" for "chairman," use the terms chairman and chairwoman to specify whether the person is a man or a woman. (Note, also, that there is nothing sacred about putting he before she; in fact, putting *she, her,* and *hers* after *he, him,* and *his,* without changing the order, continues to imply that males are the more important sex and should come first.)

"Sorry, Chief, but of course I didn't mean 'bimbo' in the pejorative sense."

While sexist language usually defines the world as made up of superior men and inferior women,

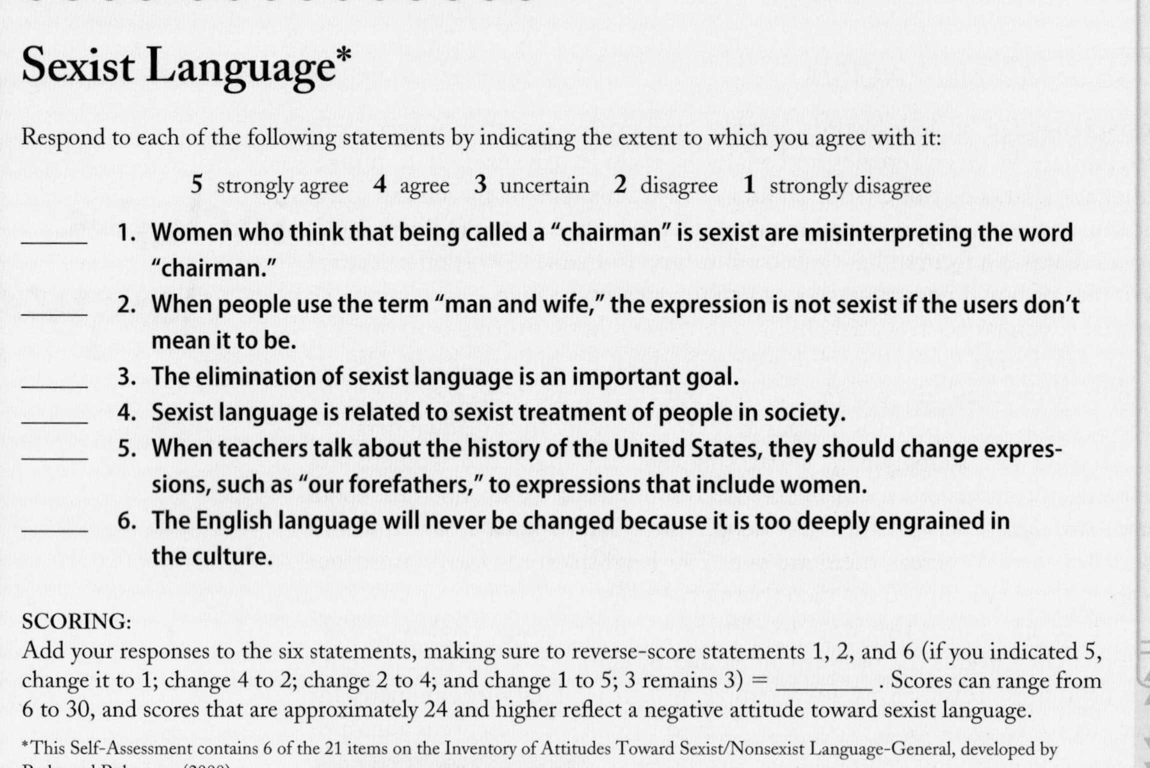

SELF-ASSESSMENT

Sexist Language*

Respond to each of the following statements by indicating the extent to which you agree with it:

5 strongly agree **4** agree **3** uncertain **2** disagree **1** strongly disagree

_____ **1. Women who think that being called a "chairman" is sexist are misinterpreting the word "chairman."**

_____ **2. When people use the term "man and wife," the expression is not sexist if the users don't mean it to be.**

_____ **3. The elimination of sexist language is an important goal.**

_____ **4. Sexist language is related to sexist treatment of people in society.**

_____ **5. When teachers talk about the history of the United States, they should change expressions, such as "our forefathers," to expressions that include women.**

_____ **6. The English language will never be changed because it is too deeply engrained in the culture.**

SCORING:
Add your responses to the six statements, making sure to reverse-score statements 1, 2, and 6 (if you indicated 5, change it to 1; change 4 to 2; change 2 to 4; and change 1 to 5; 3 remains 3) = ________ . Scores can range from 6 to 30, and scores that are approximately 24 and higher reflect a negative attitude toward sexist language.

*This Self-Assessment contains 6 of the 21 items on the Inventory of Attitudes Toward Sexist/Nonsexist Language-General, developed by Parks and Robertson (2000).

racist language reflects a worldview that classifies members of one racial group as superior and others as inferior (Asante, 2002). Not all language that might have racist overtones is deliberate. For example, the connotations of many words favor whites over people of color, as noted by Aaron Smith-McLallen and his colleagues (2006):

> In the United States and many other cultures, the color white often carries more positive connotations than the color black. . . . Terms such as "Black Monday," "Black Plague," "black cats," and the "black market" all have negative connotations, and literature, television, and movies have traditionally portrayed heroes in white and villains in black. The empirical work of John E. Williams and others throughout the 1960s demonstrated that these positive and negative associations with the colors black and white, independent of any explicit connection to race, were evident among white and black children as young as 3 years old . . . as well as among adults. (pp. 47–48)

An obvious step toward eliminating racist language is to make sure your communication is free of offensive labels and slurs—even those "innocent" uses of racist language that are not meant to be taken seriously but are used to maintain relationship solidarity (Guerin, 2003). Some troublesome language will be easy to identify, while other problematic speech will be more subtle. For instance, you may be unaware of using racial and ethnic modifiers when describing others, such as "black professor" or "Pakistani merchant" (or modifiers identifying sex, such as "female doctor" or "male secretary"). Modifiers like these usually aren't necessary, and they can be subtle indicators of racism/sexism. If you wouldn't typically use the phrases "white professor," "European American merchant," "male doctor," or "female secretary," then modifiers that identify race and sex might be indicators of attitudes and language that need to be changed.

Uses (and Abuses) of Language

By now, it's apparent that language can shape the way we perceive and understand the world. Next we will look at some specific types of usage and explore both the value and the potential problems that can arise.

PRECISION AND VAGUENESS

Most people assume that the goal of language is to make our ideas clear to one another. When clarity *is* the goal, we need language skills to make our ideas understandable to others. Sometimes, however, we want to be less than perfectly clear. The following pages will point out some cases where vagueness serves useful purposes as well as cases where perfect understanding is the goal.

Ambiguous Language **Ambiguous language** consists of words and phrases that have more than one commonly accepted definition. Some ambiguous language is amusing, as the following newspaper headlines illustrate:

Police Begin Campaign to Run Down Jaywalkers
Teacher Strikes Idle Kids
20-Year Friendship Ends at the Altar

Many misunderstandings that arise from ambiguity are trivial. We recall eating dinner at a Mexican restaurant and ordering a "tostada with beans." Instead of being served a beef tostada with beans on the side, we were surprised to see the waiter bring us a plate containing a tostada *filled* with beans. As with most such misunderstandings, hindsight showed that the phrase *tostada with beans* has two equally correct meanings.

Other misunderstandings involving ambiguous messages can be more serious. A nurse gave one of her patients a scare when she told him that he "wouldn't be needing" his robe, books, and shaving materials anymore. The patient became quiet and moody. When the nurse inquired about the odd behavior, she discovered that the poor man had interpreted her statement to mean he was going to die soon. In fact, the nurse meant he would be going home shortly.

For another example of ambiguous language, consider the word *love.* J. A. Lee (1973; see also Hendrick et al., 1998) points out that people commonly use that term in six very different ways: *eros* (romantic love), *ludus* (game-playing love), *storge* (friendship love), *mania* (possessive, dependent love), *pragma* (logical love), and *agape* (all-giving, selfless love). These boil down to two basic notions (Fehr & Broughton, 2001): passionate love (intense arousal, attraction, and emotions) and companionate love (a bond of trust, caring, and respect). Imagine the conflicts that would occur between a couple who sincerely pledged their love to one another, each with a different kind of love in mind. We can imagine them asking one another, "If you really love me, why are you acting like this?" without realizing that each of them views the relationship differently (e.g., Olson, 2003).

It's difficult to catch and clarify every instance of ambiguous language. For this reason, the responsibility for interpreting statements accurately rests in large part with the receiver. Feedback of one sort or another—for example, paraphrasing and questioning—can help clear up misunderstandings: "You say you love me, but you want to see other people. In my book, 'love' is exclusive. What about you?"

Despite its obvious problems, ambiguous language has its uses (Eisenberg, 2007). For example, when a hospital system defined the nursing role of "care coordinator" in a strategically ambiguous way, some nurses were excited and exhilarated by the challenge of crafting a new role (Miller et al., 2000). As discussed in Chapter 3, using language that is open to several interpretations can help you avoid the kind of honesty and clarity that can embarrass both the speaker and listener. For example, if a friend proudly shows you a newly completed painting and asks your opinion about it, you might respond equivocally by saying, "Gee, it's really unusual. I've never seen anything like it," instead of giving a less ambiguous but more hurtful response such as "This may be the ugliest thing I've ever seen!" See the discussion of euphemism on page 156 for more information on the value of ambiguity.

Abstraction High-level abstractions are convenient ways of generalizing about similarities between several objects, people, ideas, or events. Figure 5.2 is an **abstraction ladder** that shows how to describe the same phenomenon at various levels of abstraction.

We use higher-level abstractions all the time. For instance, rather than saying "Thanks for washing the dishes," "Thanks for vacuuming the rug," and "Thanks for making the bed," it's easier to say "Thanks for cleaning up." In such everyday situations, abstractions are a useful kind of verbal shorthand.

Like ambiguity, high-level abstractions also can help communicators find face-saving ways to avoid confrontations and embarrassment by being deliberately unclear (Eisenberg, 1984; Eisenberg & Witten, 1987). If a friend apologizes for arriving late for a date, you can choose to brush off the incident instead of making it an issue by saying "Don't worry. It wasn't the end of the world"— a true statement, but less specific than saying "To tell you the truth, I was mad at the time, but I've cooled off now." If your boss asks your opinion of a new idea that you think is weaker than your own approach but you don't

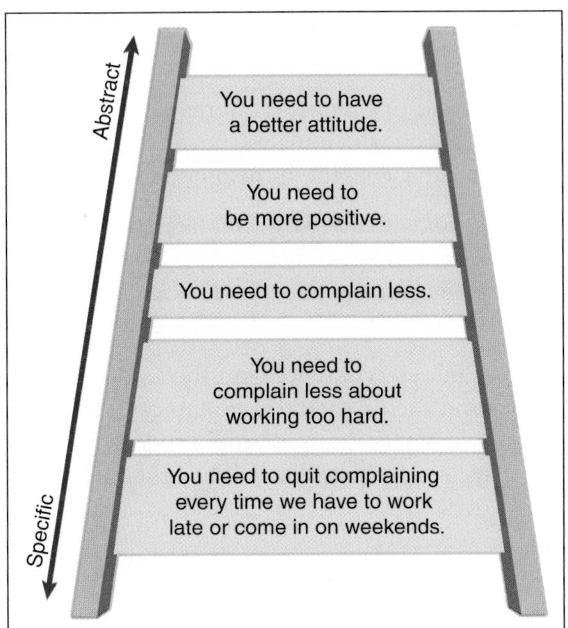

FIGURE 5.2 Abstraction Ladder
A boss gives feedback to an employee about career advancement at various levels of specificity.

want to disagree, you could respond with a higher-level abstraction by saying "I never thought of it that way."

Although vagueness does have its uses, highly abstract language can cause several types of problems. At the most basic level, the vagueness of some abstract language makes it hard to understand the meaning of a message. Overly abstract language can also lead to stereotyping. Imagine someone who has had one bad experience and, as a result, blames an entire group: "Marriage counselors are worthless"; "New Yorkers are all rude"; or "Men are no good." Overly abstract expressions like these can cause people to think in generalities, ignoring uniqueness. As you learned in Chapter 3, expecting people to act in a certain way can become a self-fulfilling prophecy. If you expect the worst of people, you have a good chance of getting it.

Besides narrowing your own options, excessively abstract language also can confuse others. Telling the hairstylist "not too short" or "more casual" might produce the look you want, or it might lead to an unpleasant surprise, just as telling the boss "Having several ideas to test is better than having just one" might give her the impression you like her idea.

Overly abstract language can lead to problems of a more serious nature. For instance, accusations of sexual assault can arise because one person claims to have said "no" when the other person insists no such refusal was ever conveyed. In response to this sort of disagreement, specific rules of sexual conduct have become more common in work and educational settings. Perhaps the best-known code of this type is the one developed at Antioch College (2006) in Ohio. The policy uses low-level abstractions to minimize the chances of anyone claiming confusion about a partner's willingness. For example, the code states:

- If sexual contact and/or conduct is not mutually and simultaneously initiated, then the person who initiates sexual contact/conduct is responsible for getting verbal consent of the other individual(s) involved.
- Verbal consent [for sexual activity] should be obtained with each new level of physical and/or sexual behavior. . . . Asking "Do you want to have sex with me?" is not enough. The request for consent must be specific to each act.
- If someone has initially consented but then stops consenting during a sexual interaction, she/he should communicate withdrawal of consent verbally (example: saying "no" or "stop") and/or through physical resistance (example: pushing away). The other individual(s) must stop immediately.

Some critics have ridiculed rules like these as being unrealistically legalistic and chillingly inappropriate for romantic relationships. Whatever their weaknesses, the Antioch code illustrates how low-level abstractions can reduce the chances of a serious misunderstanding. Specific language may not be desirable or necessary in many situations, but in an era when misinterpretations can lead to accusations of physical assault, it does seem to have a useful place.

You can make your language—and your thinking—less abstract and more clear by learning to make *behavioral descriptions* of your problems, goals, appreciations, complaints, and requests. We use the word *behavioral* because such descriptions move down the abstraction ladder to describe the specific, observable objects and actions we're thinking about. Table 5.3 (page 157) shows how behavioral descriptions are much more clear and effective than vague, abstract statements.

Euphemism **Euphemisms** (from a Greek word meaning "to use words of good omen") are innocuous terms substituted for blunt ones. A euphemism avoids a direct, literal reference to an event (such as "She died"), substituting terms describing its consequences ("She's no longer with us"), related events ("She took her last breath"), metaphors ("She jumped the last hurdle"), or other, more abstract associations (McGlone et al., 2006). Euphemisms are typically used to soften the impact of information that might be unpleasant. It's easy to imagine how a relational breakup might be easier to handle with the explanation "I'm not ready for commitment" than with "I want to date other people." We tend to use euphemisms more when talking with people of higher status, probably as a way to avoid offending them (Makin, 2004). When choosing how to broach difficult subjects, the challenge is to be as kind as possible without sacrificing either your integrity or the clarity of your message

Relative Language **Relative language** gains meaning by comparison. For example, do you attend a large or a small school? This depends on what you compare it to. Alongside a campus such as Ohio State University, with more

TABLE 5.3 ***Abstract and Behavioral Descriptions***

	ABSTRACT DESCRIPTION	BEHAVIORAL DESCRIPTION			REMARKS
		WHO IS INVOLVED	IN WHAT CIRCUMSTANCES	SPECIFIC BEHAVIORS	
Problem	I'm no good at meeting strangers.	People I'd like to date	At parties and in school	I think, "They'd never want to date me." Also, I don't originate conversations.	Behavioral description more clearly identifies thoughts and behaviors to change.
Goal	I'd like to be more assertive.	Telephone and door-to-door solicitors	When I don't want the product or can't afford it	Instead of apologizing, I want to keep saying "I'm not interested" until they go away.	Behavioral description clearly outlines how to act; abstract description doesn't.
Appreciation	"You've been a great boss."	(no clarification necessary)	When I've needed to change my schedule because of school exams or assignments	"You've rearranged my hours cheerfully."	Give both abstract and behavioral descriptions for best results.
Complaint	"I don't like some of the instructors around here."	Professors A and B	In class, when students ask questions the professors think are stupid	They either answer in a sarcastic voice (you might demonstrate) or accuse us of not studying hard enough.	If talking to A or B, use only behavioral description. With others, use both abstract and behavioral descriptions.
Request	"Quit bothering me!"	You and your friends, X and Y	When I'm studying for exams	"Instead of asking me again and again to party with you, I wish you'd accept my comment that I need to study tonight."	Behavioral description will reduce defensiveness and make it clear that you don't always want to be left alone.

than 50,000 students, your school may look small, but compared with a smaller institution, it may seem quite large. Relative words such as fast and slow, smart and stupid, short and long are clearly defined only through comparison.

Using relative terms without explaining them can lead to communication problems. Have you ever responded to someone's question about the weather by saying it was warm, only to find out the person thought it was cold? Have you followed a friend's advice and gone to a "cheap" restaurant, only to find that it was twice as expensive as you expected? Have classes you heard were "easy" turned out to be hard? The problem in each case resulted from failing to link the relative word to a more measurable term.

One way to make words more measurable is to turn them into numbers. Health care practitioners have learned that patients often use vague wording when describing their pain: "It hurts a little"; "I'm pretty sore." The use of a numeric pain scale can give a more precise response—and lead to a better diagnosis (Prentice, 2005). When patients are asked to rank their pain from 1 to 10, with 10 being the most severe pain they've ever experienced, the number 7 is much more concrete and specific than "It aches a bit." The same technique can be used when asking people to relate anything from the movies they've seen to their job satisfaction.

Static Evaluation "Mark is a nervous guy." "Karen is short-tempered." "You can always count on Wes." Descriptions or evaluations that use the word *is* contain a **static evaluation**—the usually mistaken assumption that people or things are consistent and unchanging. Instead of labeling Mark as permanently and completely nervous, it would probably be more accurate to outline the situations in which he behaves nervously: "Mark acts nervously until you get to know him." The same goes for Karen, Wes, and the rest of us: We are more changeable than the way static, everyday language describes us.

Edward Sagarian (1976) writes about an unconscious language habit that imposes a static view of others. Why is it, he asks, that we say, "He has a cold" but say, "He is a convict" or a genius, a slow learner, or any other set of behaviors that are also not necessarily permanent? Sagarian argues that such linguistic labeling leads us to typecast others and in some cases forces them to perpetuate behaviors that could be changed.

Alfred Korzybski (1933) suggested the linguistic device of *dating* to reduce static evaluation. He proposed adding a subscript whenever appropriate to show the transitory nature of a referent. For example, a teacher might write the following as an evaluation of a student: "Susan$_{\text{May 12}}$ had difficulty cooperating with her classmates." Although the actual device of subscripting is awkward in writing and impractical in conversation, the idea it represents can still be used. Instead of saying "I'm shy," a more accurate statement might be "I haven't approached any new people since I moved here." The first statement implies that your shyness is an unchangeable trait, rather like your height, while the second one suggests that you are capable of changing.

THE LANGUAGE OF RESPONSIBILITY

Besides providing a way to make the content of a message clear or obscure, language reflects the speaker's willingness to take responsibility for her or his beliefs, feelings, and actions. This acceptance or rejection of responsibility says a great deal about the speaker, and it can shape the tone of a relationship. To see how, read on.

"It" Statements Notice the difference between the sentences of each set:

"It bothers me when you're late."
"I'm worried when you're late."

"It's nice to see you."
"I'm glad to see you."

"It's a boring class."
"I'm bored in the class."

As their name implies, **"it" statements** replace the personal pronoun *I* with the less immediate construction *it's*. By contrast, **"I" language** clearly identifies the speaker as the source of a message. Communicators who use "it" statements avoid responsibility for ownership of a message, instead attributing it to some unidentified body. This habit isn't just imprecise; more important, it's an unconscious way to avoid taking a position. You can begin to appreciate the increased directness of "I" language by trying to use it instead of the less direct and more evasive "it" statements in your own conversations.

"But" Statements Statements that take the form "X-but-Y" can be quite confusing. A closer look at the **"but" statement** explains why. *But* has the effect of canceling the thought that precedes it:

"You're really a great person, but I think we ought to stop seeing each other."
"You've done good work for us, but we're going to have to let you go."
"This paper has some good ideas, but I'm giving it a grade of *D* because it's late."

"Buts" *can* be a face-saving strategy worth using at times. When the goal is to be absolutely clear, however, the most responsible approach will deliver the central idea without the distractions that can come with "but" statements. Breaking statements like the foregoing into two sentences and explaining each one as necessary lets you acknowledge both parts of the statement without contradicting yourself.

"I," "You," and "We" Language We've already seen that "I" language is a way of accepting responsibility for a message. **"You" language** is quite different. It expresses a judgment of the other person. Positive judgments ("You look great today!") rarely cause problems, but notice how each of the following critical "you" statements implies that the subject of the complaint is doing something wrong:

"You left this place a mess!"
"You didn't keep your promise!"
"You're really crude sometimes!"

It's easy to see why "you" language can arouse defensiveness. A "you" statement implies that the speaker is qualified to judge the target—not an idea that most listeners are willing to accept, even when the evaluation is correct.

"I" language provides a more accurate and less provocative way to express a complaint (Kubany et al., 1992; Winer & Majors, 1981). "I" language shows that the speaker takes responsibility for the accusation by describing his or her reaction to the other's behavior without making any judgments about its worth. A complete "I" statement has three parts: It describes (1) the other person's behavior, (2) your feelings, and (3) the consequences the other's behavior has for you:

"I get embarrassed [feeling] when you talk about my bad grades in front of our friends [behavior]. I'm afraid they'll think I'm stupid [consequence]."

"When you didn't pick me up on time this morning [behavior], I was late for class and wound up getting chewed out by the professor [consequences]. That's why I got so angry [feeling]."

"I haven't been very affectionate [consequence] because you've hardly spent any time with me in the past few weeks [behavior]. I'm confused [feeling] about how you feel about me."

When the chances of being misunderstood or getting a defensive reaction are high, it's a good idea to include all three elements in your "I" message. In some cases, however, only one or two of them will get the job done:

"I went to a lot of trouble fixing this dinner, and now it's cold. Of course I'm annoyed!" (The behavior is obvious.)

"I'm worried because you haven't called me up." ("Worried" is both a feeling and a consequence in this statement.)

As the "Cathy" cartoon on page 161 suggests, even the best-constructed and best-delivered "I" message won't always receive a nondefensive response (Bippus & Young, 2005). As Thomas Gordon (1970) points out, "nobody welcomes hearing that his behavior is causing someone a problem, no matter how the message is phrased" (p. 145). Furthermore, "I" language in large doses can start to sound egotistical (Proctor, 1989). Research shows that self-absorbed people, also known as "conversational narcissists," can be identified by their constant use of first-person singular pronouns (Raskin & Shaw, 1988; Vangelisti et al., 1990). For this reason, "I" language works best in moderation.

One way to avoid overuse of "I" language is to consider the pronoun *we*. **"We" language** implies that the issue is the concern and responsibility of both the speaker and receiver of a message. Consider a few examples:

"We have a problem. We can't seem to talk about money without fighting."

"We aren't doing a very good job of keeping the apartment clean, are we?"

"We need to talk to your parents about whether we'll visit them for the holidays."

It's easy to see how "we" language can help build a constructive climate. It suggests a kind of "we're in this together" orientation, a component of what is known as *verbal immediacy* (Gorham, 1988). Couples who use "we"

language are more satisfied than those who rely more heavily on "I" and "you" pronouns (Honeycutt, 1999; Sillars et al., 1997). On the other hand, using the pronoun "we" can be presumptuous since you are speaking for the other person as well as for yourself. It's easy to imagine someone responding to the statement "We have a problem . . ." by saying "Maybe *you* have a problem, but don't tell me *I* do!"

As Table 5.4 (page 162) summarizes, all three pronouns—*I, you,* and *we*—have their advantages and drawbacks. Given this fact, what advice can we give about the most effective pronouns to use in interpersonal communication? A study by Russell Proctor and James Wilcox (1993) offers an answer. The researchers found that "I"/"we" combinations (for example, "I think that we . . ." or "I would like to see us . . .") were strongly endorsed by college students, particularly for confrontational conversations in romantic relationships. Anita Vangelisti and her associates (1990) made a similar observation: Unlike conversational narcissists, nonnarcissists combine their "I" references with references to other persons, objects, and events. Since too much of any pronoun comes across as inappropriate, combining pronouns is generally a good idea. If your "I" language reflects your position without being overly self-absorbed, your "you" language shows concern for others without judging them, and your "we" language includes others without speaking for them, you will probably come as close as possible to the ideal mix of pronouns.

DISRUPTIVE LANGUAGE

Not all linguistic problems come from misunderstandings. Sometimes people understand one another perfectly and still wind up in conflict. Of course, not all disagreements can, or should be, avoided. But eliminating three harmful linguistic habits from your communication repertoire can minimize the kind

TABLE 5.4 ***Pronoun Uses and Their Effects***

PRONOUN	PROS	CONS	RECOMMENDATION
"I" Language	• Takes responsibility for personal thoughts, feelings, and wants. • Less defense-provoking than evaluative "you" language	• Can be perceived as egotistical, narcissistic, and self-absorbed.	• Use descriptive "I" messages in conflicts when the other person does not perceive a problem. • Combine "I" with "we" language in conversations.
"We" Language	• Signals inclusion, immediacy, cohesiveness, and commitment.	• Can speak improperly for others.	• Combine with "I" language, particularly in personal conversations. • Use in group settings to enhance sense of unity. • Avoid when expressing personal thoughts, feelings, and wants.
"You" Language	• Signals other-orientation, particularly when the topic is positive.	• Can sound evaluative and judgmental, particularly during confrontations.	• Use "I" language during confrontations. • Use "you" language when praising or including others.

of clashes that don't need to happen, allowing you to save your energy for the unavoidable and important struggles.

Fact–Opinion Confusion **Factual statements** are claims that can be verified as true or false. By contrast, **opinion statements** are based on the speaker's beliefs. Unlike matters of fact, they can never be proven or disproven. Consider a few examples of the difference between factual and opinion statements:

Fact	**Opinion**
It rains more in Seattle than in Portland.	The climate in Portland is better than in Seattle.
Kareem Abdul-Jabbar is the all-time leading scorer in the National Basketball Association.	Kareem is the greatest basketball player in the history of the game!
The United States is the only industrialized country without universal health care.	The quality of life in the United States is lower than in any other industrial country when it comes to health care.

When factual and opinion statements are set side by side like this, the difference between them is clear. In everyday conversation, however, we often present our opinions as if they were facts, and in doing so we invite an unnecessary argument. For example:

"That was a dumb thing to say!"
"Spending that much is a waste of money!"
"You can't get a fair shake in this country unless you're a white male."

Notice how much less antagonistic each statement would be if it were prefaced by a qualifier such as "In my opinion . . ." or "It seems to me. . . ."

Fact–Inference Confusion Labeling your opinions can go a long way toward relational harmony, but developing this habit won't solve all linguistic problems. Difficulties also arise when we confuse factual statements with **inferential statements**—conclusions arrived at from an interpretation of evidence.

Arguments often result when we label our inferences as facts:

A: Why are you mad at me?
B: I'm not mad at you. Why have you been so insecure lately?
A: I'm not insecure. It's just that you've been so critical.
B: What do you mean, "critical"? I haven't been critical. . . .

Instead of trying to read the other person's mind, a far better course is to identify the observable behaviors (facts) that have caught your attention and to describe the interpretations (inferences) that you have drawn from them. After describing this train of thought, ask the other person to comment on the accuracy of your interpretation:

"When you didn't return my phone call [fact], I got the idea that you're mad at me [inference]. Are you?" (question)

"You've been asking me a lot lately whether I still love you [fact], and that makes me think you're feeling insecure [inference]. Is that right?" (question)

DARK SIDE OF COMMUNICATION

Compulsive Talkers: Too Much of a Good Thing

Speech is a marvelous tool that connects us with others—but like most good things, it's best when used in moderation. Most of us are familiar with people who talk too much. Communication researchers refer to them as "compulsive communicators" and measure their behavior on a "Talkaholic Scale."

Studies have yielded some interesting findings about compulsive communicators:

- Most of them are quite aware of how much they talk, but they often feel like they can't—or don't want to—restrain themselves.
- They typically don't see their talkativeness as a problem—they think it's simply a part of their personality that helps them accomplish their goals.
- Others *do* see compulsive communication as a problem. And when it occurs in a classroom, students believe that teachers need to "rein in" those who talk too frequently.

The next two chapters in this book—on nonverbal communication and listening—will offer important alternatives for compulsive talkers.

McPherson, M. B., & Liang, Y. (2007). Students' reactions to teachers' management of compulsive communicators. *Communication Education, 56,* 18–33.

McCroskey, J. C., & Richmond, V. P. (1995). Correlates of compulsive communication: Quantitative and qualitative characteristics. *Communication Quarterly, 43,* 39–52.

Emotive Language **Emotive language** seems to describe something but really announces the speaker's attitude toward it (Hansson, 1996; Richards, 1948). If you approve of a friend's roundabout approach to a difficult subject, you might call her "tactful"; if you don't like it, you might accuse her of "beating around the bush." Whether the approach is good or bad is more a matter of opinion than of fact, although this difference is obscured by emotive language.

You can appreciate how emotive words are really editorial statements when you consider these examples:

If You Approve, Say	**If You Disapprove, Say**
thrifty	cheap
traditional	old-fashioned
extrovert	loudmouth
cautious	coward
progressive	radical
information	propaganda
eccentric	crazy

Not surprisingly, research shows that the relational climate suffers when communicators use emotive language. A study by Jess Alberts (1988) indicated that when dealing with problems, dissatisfied couples were more likely to use personal, emotive comments but that satisfied partners described the other's behaviors in neutral terms.

Gender and Language

So far we have discussed language usage as if it were identical for both women and men. Are there differences between male and female language use? If so, how important are they? For answers to these questions, read on.

EXTENT OF GENDER DIFFERENCES

Given the obvious physical differences between the sexes and the differences in how men and women are regarded in most societies, it's not surprising that the general public has been captivated by the topic of gender differences in language use. Some people believe that men and women communicate in fundamentally different ways, while others find far more similarities than differences. We'll outline three approaches that represent three different sides in the gender and language debate.

Approach 1: Fundamental Differences In 1992, John Gray argued that men and women are so fundamentally different that they might as well have come from separate planets. In his best-selling book *Men Are from Mars, Women Are from Venus,* he claimed that

> men and women differ in all areas of their lives. Not only do men and women communicate differently but they think, feel, perceive, react, respond, love, need, and appreciate differently. They almost seem to be from different planets, speaking different languages and needing different nourishment. (p. 5)

Gray's work is based largely on anecdotes and conjecture and lacks scholarly support. However, social scientists have acknowledged that there are some fundamental differences in the way men and women behave socially (Eagly & Wood, 1999; Palomares, 2008; Wood & Eagly, 2002). This has led some scholars to describe males and females as members of distinct cultures, with their differences arising primarily from socialization rather than biology. The best known advocate of this "two-culture" theory is sociolinguist Deborah Tannen (1990, 1994, 2001). She suggests that men and women grow up learning different rules about how to speak and act. Tannen cites research (e.g., Maltz & Borker, 1982) reporting that from an early age girls play with one another in a way that is cooperative and nonconfrontational. By contrast, boys' play is more competitive and status-oriented. According to the two-culture theory, gender differences carry over into adulthood. Women tend to seek close relationships through talk and deal with conflict in nonconfrontational ways. By contrast, men are more likely to seek conversational dominance and try to get their way through competition.

Despite these differences, Tannen believes that satisfying communication between men and women is possible if they follow principles similar to the intercultural competence guidelines discussed in Chapter 2 of this textbook:

> The answer is for both men and women to try to take each other on their own terms rather than applying the standards of one group to the behavior of the other. . . . Women and men would both do well to learn strategies more typically used by members of the other group—not to switch over entirely, but to have more strategies at their disposal. (Tannen, 1990, pp. 120–122)

Approach 2: Important Differences While not all communication scholars endorse the two-culture theory of gender differences, most acknowledge that there are some significant differences in the way men and women use language. Consider for example the content of everyday conversation. While there is obviously variation within each sex, on the average men and women discuss a different range of topics. Over almost a century, research shows that the topics have stayed remarkably similar (Bischoping, 1993; Fehr, 1996). Certain subjects are common to both sexes: Work, movies, and television proved to be frequent topics for both groups. However, there are significant differences in the conversations of men and women, especially when talking to friends. Female friends spend much more time discussing relationship problems; family, health, and reproductive matters; weight; food; clothing; and men. Women also report discussing other women frequently. Men, on the other hand, are more likely to discuss sports, hobbies, and activities.

In addition to conversational topics, there are also some significant differences in the reasons men and women have for communicating. Both men and women, at least in the dominant cultures of the United States and Canada, use language to build and maintain social relationships. *How* men and women accomplish these goals, though, is often different. Although most communicators try to make their interaction enjoyable, men are more likely than women to emphasize making conversation fun. Their discussions are more likely to involve joking and good-natured teasing. By contrast, women's conversations focus more frequently on feelings, relationships, and personal problems (Burleson et al., 1996; Samter et al., 1994). When a group of women was surveyed to find out what kinds of satisfaction they gained from talking with their friends, the most common theme mentioned was a feeling of empathy—"To know you're not alone," as some put it (Sherman & Haas, 1984).

Whereas men commonly described same-sex conversations as something they *liked,* females characterized their woman-to-woman talks as a kind of contact they *needed.*

There are also some notable differences in the conversational style of men and women (for summaries, see Turner et al., 1995; Wood, 2005). For example, Mulac (2006) reports that men are more likely than women to speak in sentence fragments ("Nice photo."). Men typically talk about themselves with "I" references ("I have a lot of meetings") and use judgmental language. They are also more likely to make directive statements. By contrast, Mulac found that female speech is more tentative, elaborate, and emotional. For instance, women's sentences are typically longer than men's. Women also make more reference to feelings and use intensive adverbs ("He's *really* interested") that paint a more complete verbal picture than the characteristically terse masculine style. In addition, female speech is often less assertive. It contains more statements of uncertainty ("It seems to be . . ."), hedges ("We're *kind of* set in our ways."), and tag questions ("Do you think so?"). Some theorists have argued that such differences cause women's speech to be less powerful than men's.

Other studies have revealed that men and women behave differently in different conversational settings. For example, in mixed-sex dyads men talk longer than women, while in same-sex situations women speak for a longer time. Women speak more tentatively than men when they are in mixed-sex conversations, although their speech is just as confident as men's in same-sex situations. In larger groups men talk more, while in smaller settings women do more of the speaking (Mulac et al., 1988, 2001).

REFLECTION

Different Roles, Different Language

As the first woman in a formerly all-male architectural firm, I feel like something of a guinea pig. Most of the partners and associates have made me feel welcome, but a small group treats me with what seems like a condescending attitude. The structural, mechanical, and electrical engineers we use as consultants are even worse. I don't think they've ever worked with a woman who wasn't a secretary. I've found that with these guys I have changed the way I speak. I try to use more powerful language, with fewer hesitations and hedges. I make more statements and ask fewer questions. In other words, I sound more like a stereotypical man.

I don't know yet whether this approach will make any difference. The point is, I sound like a different person when I'm at work than in any other setting. It's not really an act: It's more an effort to sound professional. I guess if someone dresses differently when they go to work, there's nothing wrong with sounding different too.

Approach 3: Minor Differences Despite the differences in the way men and women speak, the link between sex and language use isn't as clear-cut as it might seem. One analysis of over 1,200 research studies found that only 1 percent of variance in communication behavior resulted from sex differences (Canary & Hause, 1993). An analysis of 30 studies looking at power differences in women's and men's speech found that differences were small and, for the most part, not important (Timmerman, 2002). Other studies have found no significant difference between male and female speech in use of qualifiers such as "I guess" or "this is just my opinion," tag questions, and vocal fluency (Grob et al., 1997; Nemati & Bayer, 2007; Zahn, 1989). And the popular myth that women are more talkative than men doesn't hold up under scientific scrutiny—researchers have found that men and women speak roughly the same number of words per day (Mehl et al., 2007).

In a recent study, Kristen Precht (2008) compared women's and men's use of "stance" words—the expression of attitude, emotion, certainty, doubt,

FOCUS ON RESEARCH

Gender Differences in Instant Messages

You're working at your computer when an instant message (IM) pops onto your screen. If you paid attention only to the message's content without looking at the sender's name, could you guess the person's gender? According to one study, the answer is "probably"—if you know what to look for.

Annie Fox and her colleagues recruited 35 college students and gave them tools for recording their IM exchanges. Participants were asked to select six of their IM conversations—three with men and three with women—and to submit them to the researchers for analysis.

The results showed that messages written by women were more expressive than ones composed by men. They were more likely to contain laughter ("hehe") emoticons (smiley faces), emphasis (italics, boldface, repeated letters), and adjectives. However, a number of other variables—such as questions, words per turn, and hedges—revealed no significant gender differences.

The verdict is similar to other research discussed in this chapter. While there are differences in the language styles of men and women, they aren't as drastic as some might think.

Fox, A. B., Bukatko, D., Hallahan, M., & Crawford, M. (2007). The medium makes a difference: Gender similarities and differences in instant messaging. *Journal of Language and Social Psychology, 26,* 389–397.

and commitment—by analyzing 900,000 words of informal conversation in social and work settings. She found no differences between the sexes in their use of many types of words—for example, opinion and attitude words (e.g., "amazing," "happy," "funny," and "interesting"), certainty, doubt, and factuality words (e.g., "of course," "right?," and "sure"), emphatic words (e.g., "absolutely" and "never"), and hedges (e.g., "almost" and "usually"). Only expletives (e.g., "cool," "damn," and "wow") showed a significant difference between men and women (men use more of them).

In light of the considerable similarities between the sexes and the relatively minor differences, communication researcher Kathryn Dindia (2006) suggests that the "men are from Mars, women are from Venus" claim should be replaced by the metaphor that "men are from North Dakota, women are from South Dakota." Where differences do exist, they are often small and are matters of degree and not kind. Women may be *somewhat* more expressive, and men may use humor *slightly* more, but gender differences aren't as dramatic as books like Gray's suggest. Tannen's arguments that young girls and boys live in different cultures are, in many cases, based on small studies using limited data (Edwards & Hamilton, 2004; Goldsmith & Fulfs, 1999). Scholars like Dindia argue that focusing on relatively minor sex differences while overlooking the larger number of similarities can perpetuate inaccurate stereotypes of both women and men. Polarized characterizations of both sexes, she claims, aren't just sloppy thinking: They create unnecessary friction and contribute to inequalities between the sexes.

ACCOUNTING FOR GENDER DIFFERENCES

By now you might be confused by what seem like contradictory views of how large and important the differences are between male and female speech. A growing body of research helps reconcile some of the apparent contradictions by pointing out factors other than communicator sex that influence language use. For instance, occupation can trump gender as an influence on speaking style. As an example, male day care teachers' speech to their students resembles the language of female teachers more closely than it resembles the language of fathers at home (Gleason & Greif, 1983). Research also shows that male and female athletes communicate in similar ways (Sullivan, 2004). A close study of trial transcripts showed that the speaker's experience on the witness stand and occupation had more to do with language use than did biological sex. The researcher concluded, "So-called women's language is neither characteristic of all women nor limited only to women" (O'Barr, 1982).

Another powerful force that influences the way individual men and women speak is their *gender role.* Recall the various sex types described in Chapter 4 (pages 119–120): masculine, feminine, and androgynous. Remember that these sex types don't necessarily line up neatly with biological sex. There are "masculine" females as well as "feminine" females, "feminine" males as well as "masculine" males, and androgynous communicators who combine traditionally masculine and feminine characteristics. Research shows that these gender roles can influence a communicator's style more than his or her biological sex. Donald Ellis and Linda McCallister (1980) found that masculine subjects used significantly more dominance language than did either feminine or androgynous group members. Feminine members expressed slightly more submissive behaviors and more equivalence behaviors than the androgynous group members, and their submissiveness and equivalence were much greater than the masculine subjects'.

Another factor that trumps sex differences is *power.* For instance, in gay and lesbian relationships, the conversational styles of partners

Gender Stereotypes in Conversation: *When Harry Met Sally*

Harry Burns (Billy Crystal) and Sally Albright (Meg Ryan) are strangers who first get together for purely functional reasons: a cross-country car ride in which they share gas costs and driving. She sizes him up as crude and insensitive; he views her as naive and obsessive. By the time they finish their journey, they are glad to part ways.

But the car ride is just the start of their relationship—and the beginning of a look at stereotypical male and female communication styles. In their conversations, Harry and Sally often exhibit communication patterns that support the notion that men and women are from different cultures. For instance, Harry tends to treat discussions as debates. He regularly tells jokes and enjoys having the first and last word. He rarely asks questions but is quick to answer them. Harry self-discloses with his buddy Jess (Bruno Kirby), but only while watching a football game or taking swings in a batting cage.

Sally, on the other hand, self-discloses with her female friends at restaurants, by phone, while shopping—just about anyplace. She regularly asks questions of Harry but seems troubled by his competitive answers and approach to sex (Sally: "So you're saying that a man can be friends with a woman he finds unattractive?" Harry: "No, you pretty much want to nail them too"). In the language of Deborah Tannen, Sally's communication is about "rapport" while Harry's is about "report."

The story ends with a strong sense of hope for cross-sex communication. This is due in part to Harry's defying gender stereotypes. The rancor of his early interactions with Sally softens when he expresses empathy (much to her surprise) in a chance bookstore meeting. Near the movie's end, he offers warm and detailed descriptions of why he enjoys being with and around her. Clearly, they are friends as well as lovers, which seems to make their communication stronger. It also helps them fulfill a goal of most movies: the ending suggests they have a good chance to live "happily ever after."

reflect power differences in the relationship (e.g., who is earning more money) more than the biological sex of the communicators (Steen & Schwartz, 1995). There are also few differences between the way men and women use powerful speech (specifically, threats) when they have the same amount of bargaining strength in a negotiation (Scudder & Andrews, 1995). Findings like this suggest that characteristically feminine speech has been less a function of gender or sex than of women's historically less powerful positions in some parts of the social world.

Even when no gender differences exist or when the existing differences are overwhelmed by similarities, we may *perceive* that there is a strong gender effect in speech. There are several reasons for this perception (Dindia, 2006). The popular media emphasizes differences over similarities. (For example, see the Film Clip on page 168.) Parents may socialize their children to believe that boys and men are fundamentally different than girls and women. Even speech habits themselves can contribute to the perception of differences. For instance, referring to members of the "opposite sex" (rather than the "other sex") suggests Mars and Venus more than North Dakota and South Dakota (Kahn &Yoder, 1989). As men and women grow to have equal opportunities and more similar social experiences, we can expect that there will be fewer differences—both real and perceived—in the ways they speak.

Summary

Language is both a marvelous communication tool and the source of many interpersonal problems. Every language is a collection of symbols governed by a variety of rules. Because of its symbolic nature, language is not a precise vehicle: Meanings rest in people, not in words themselves. Finally, the very language we speak can shape our worldview.

Besides conveying meanings about the content of a specific message, language both reflects and shapes the perceptions of its users. Terms used to name people influence the way they are regarded. Language also reflects the level of affiliation communicators have with each other. In addition, language patterns reflect and shape a speaker's perceived power. Language reflects and influences sexist and racist attitudes.

When used carelessly, language can lead to a variety of interpersonal problems. The level of precision or vagueness of messages can affect a receiver's understanding of them. Both precise messages and vague, evasive messages have their uses in interpersonal relationships, and a competent communicator has the ability to choose the optimal level of precision for the situation at hand. Language also acknowledges or avoids the speaker's acceptance of responsibility for his or her positions, and competent communicators know how to use "I," "you," and "we" statements to accept the optimal level of responsibility and relational harmony. Some language habits—confusing facts with opinions or inferences and using emotive terms—can lead to unnecessary disharmony in interpersonal relationships.

The relationship between gender and language is a complex one. While some writers in the popular press have argued that men and women are radically different and thus speak different languages, this position isn't supported by scholarship. Some theorists have argued that important but less dramatic differences in language usage arise because men and women occupy different cultures. A growing body of research suggests that what differences do exist are relatively minor in light of the similarities between the sexes. Many of the language differences that first appear to be gender-related are actually due to other factors such as occupation, gender roles, and interpersonal power.

Activities

1. Invitation to Insight

For each of the following scenes, describe one syntactic, one semantic, and one pragmatic rule:

a. Asking an acquaintance out for a first date.
b. Declining an invitation to a party.
c. Responding to a stranger who has just said "excuse me" after bumping into you in a crowd.

2. Invitation to Insight

Recall an incident in which you were misunderstood. Explain how this event illustrated the principle "Meanings are in people, not words."

3. Ethical Challenge

The information about the impact of language on pages 145–153 shows how the words a communicator chooses can shape others' perceptions. Create two scenarios for each type of linguistic influence in the following list. The first should describe how the type of influence could be used constructively, and the second should describe an unethical application of this knowledge.

a. Naming and identity
b. Affiliation
c. Power
d. Sexism and racism

4. Invitation to Insight

Because meanings reside in people and not in words, one way to understand the nature of offensive language is to explore the reactions of people who may be offended by words that others speak or write without malice. Explore this by interviewing several people from various groups that perceive themselves to be marginalized because of factors such as religion, ethnicity, sexual orientation, gender, or political philosophy. Ask your subjects what language, if any, they find offensive and what interpretation they place on such language. Based on your findings, explore ways in which you and others could adapt speech to get across ideas in a way that is less likely to offend others.

5. Skill Builder

Translate the following into behavioral language:

- An abstract goal for improving your interpersonal communication (for example, "Be more assertive" or "Stop being so sarcastic").
- A complaint you have about another person (for instance, that he or she is "selfish" or "insensitive").

In both cases, describe the person or people involved, the circumstances in which the communication will take place, and the precise behaviors involved. What difference will using the behavioral descriptions be likely to make in your relationships?

6. Invitation to Insight

Are there ever situations in your life when it is appropriate to be less clear and more vague? Use the information on pages 153–154 to answer this question and to decide whether vagueness is the most competent approach to the situation.

7. Skill Builder

You can develop your skill at delivering "I" and "we" messages by following these steps:

a. Visualize situations in your life when you might have sent each of the following messages:
   "You're not telling me the truth!"
   "You only think of yourself!"
   "Don't be so touchy!"
   "Quit fooling around!"
   "You don't understand a word I'm saying!"
b. Write alternatives to each statement, using "I" language.
c. Think of three "you" statements you could make to people in your life. Transform each of these statements into "I" and "we" language, and rehearse them with a classmate.

8. Invitation to Insight

What roles do the types of disruptive language described on pages 161–163 play in your life? Recall incidents when you have confused facts and opinions, confounded facts and inferences, and used emotive language. Discuss the consequences of each type of language use, and describe how the results might have been different if you had used language more carefully.

9. Invitation to Insight

Some authors believe that differences between male and female communication are so great that they can be characterized as "men are from Mars, women are from Venus." Other researchers believe the differences aren't nearly so dramatic and would describe them as "men are from North Dakota, women are from South Dakota." Which approach seems more accurate to you? Offer experiences from your life to support your point of view.

CHAPTER

6 Nonverbal Communication

CHAPTER OUTLINE

After studying the material in this chapter . . .

YOU SHOULD UNDERSTAND:

1. The distinguishing characteristics of nonverbal communication.
2. The functions that nonverbal communication can serve.
3. The various ways in which nonverbal messages are communicated.

YOU SHOULD BE ABLE TO:

1. Describe your nonverbal behavior in any situation.
2. Identify nonverbal behavior that creates/maintains relationships, regulates interaction, influences others, conceals/deceives, or manages identity.
3. Monitor and manage your nonverbal cues in ways that achieve your goals.
4. Share appropriately your interpretation of another's nonverbal behavior.

KEY TERMS

- Chronemics (197)
- Disfluencies (192)
- Emblems (180)
- Haptics (190)
- Intimate distance (195)
- Kinesics (188)
- Manipulators (189)
- Nonverbal communication (175)
- Oculesics (188)
- Paralanguage (191)
- Personal distance (195)
- Personal space (194)
- Proxemics (194)
- Public distance (196)
- Regulators (183)
- Social distance (195)
- Territory (196)

P*eople don't always say what they mean . . . but their body gestures and movements tell the truth!*

Will he ask you out? Is she encouraging you?

Know what is really happening by understanding the secret language of body signals. You can:

Improve your sex life . . .
Pick up your social life . . .
Better your business life . . .

Read Body Language *so that you can penetrate the personal secrets, both of intimates and total strangers . . .*

Does her body say that she's a loose woman?
Does her body say that she's a phony?
Does her body say that she's a manipulator?
Does her body say that she's lonely?

Unless you've been trapped in a lead mine or doing fieldwork in the Amazon Basin, claims like these are probably familiar to you. Almost every pharmacy, supermarket, and airport bookrack has its share of "body language" paperbacks. They promise that, for only a few dollars and with a fifth-grade reading ability, you can learn secrets that will change you from a fumbling social failure into a self-assured mind reader who can uncover a person's deepest secrets at a glance.

Observations like these are almost always exaggerations or fabrications. Don't misunderstand: There *is* a scientific body of knowledge about nonverbal communication, and it *has* provided many fascinating and valuable clues to human behavior. That's what this chapter is about. It's unlikely the next few pages will turn you instantly into a rich, sexy, charming communication superstar, but don't go away. Even without glamorous promises, a quick look at some facts about nonverbal communication shows that it's an important and valuable field to study.

Nonverbal Communication Defined

If *non* means "not" and *verbal* means "with words," then it seems logical that *nonverbal communication* would involve "communication without words." This definition is an oversimplification, however, because it fails to distinguish between *vocal* communication (by mouth) and *verbal* communication (with words). Some nonverbal messages have a vocal element. For example, the words "I love you" have different meanings depending on the way they are spoken. Furthermore, some nonspoken forms of communication, including sign languages used in the deaf community, are actually linguistic and not really nonverbal in the sense most social scientists use the term. A better definition of **nonverbal communication** is "messages expressed by nonlinguistic means."

These nonlinguistic messages are important because what we *do* often conveys more meaning than what we *say*. Psychologist Albert Mehrabian (1972) claimed that 93 percent of the emotional impact of a message comes from a nonverbal source, whereas only a paltry 7 percent is verbal. Anthropologist Ray Birdwhistell (1970) described a 65–35 percent split between actions and words, respectively. Although social scientists have disputed these figures and the relative importance of verbal versus nonverbal cues (e.g., Lapakko, 1997; Stern, 2002), the point remains: Nonverbal communication contributes a great deal to shaping perceptions.

You might ask how nonverbal communication can be so powerful. At first glance, it seems as if meanings come from words. To answer this question, recall a time when you observed speakers of an unfamiliar language communicating. Although you can't understand the words being spoken, there are plenty of clues that give you an idea of what is going on in the exchange. By tuning into their facial expressions, postures, gestures, vocal tones, and other behaviors you probably can make assumptions about the way the communicators feel about one another at the moment and get some ideas about the nature of their relationship. Researchers have found that subjects who hear content-free speech—ordinary speech that has been electronically manipulated so that the words are unintelligible—can consistently recognize the emotion being expressed, as well as identify its strength (Knapp & Hall, 2006).

Characteristics of Nonverbal Communication

The many types of nonverbal communication share some characteristics. As Table 6.1 shows, these characteristics are quite different from verbal, linguistic means of communication. We will now take a look at some of the fundamental characteristics of nonverbal communication.

TABLE 6.1 ***Some Differences between Verbal and Nonverbal Communication***

VERBAL COMMUNICATION	NONVERBAL COMMUNICATION
• Mostly voluntary and conscious	• Often unconscious
• Usually content-oriented	• Usually relational
• Can be clear or vague	• Inherently ambiguous
• Primarily shaped by culture	• Primarily shaped by biology
• Discontinuous/intermittent	• Continuous
• Single channel (words only)	• Multichanneled

Adapted from p. 16 of Andersen, P. A. (1999). *Nonverbal communication: Forms and functions.* Mountain View, CA: Mayfield.

ALL BEHAVIOR HAS COMMUNICATIVE VALUE

Some theorists have suggested that *all* nonverbal behavior communicates information. They argue that it is impossible *not* to communicate. You can understand the impossibility of noncommunication by considering what you would do if someone told you not to communicate any messages at all. What would you do? Close your eyes? Withdraw into a ball? Leave the room? You can probably see that even these behaviors communicate messages that mean you're avoiding contact. One study (DePaulo, 1992) took just this approach. When communicators were told not to express nonverbal clues, others viewed them as dull, withdrawn, uneasy, aloof, and deceptive.

The impossibility of not communicating is significant because it means that each of us is a kind of transmitter that cannot be shut off. No matter what we do, we send out messages that say something about ourselves and our relationships with others. If, for instance, others were observing you now, what nonverbal clues would they get about how you're feeling? Are you sitting forward or reclining back? Is your posture tense or relaxed? Are your eyes wide open, or do they keep closing? What does your facial expression communicate now? Can you make your face expressionless? Don't people with expressionless faces communicate something to you? Even uncontrollable behaviors can convey

Not Acting Her Age: *13 Going On 30*

Jenna Rink (Jennifer Garner) is a 13-year-old girl with two wishes—to grow up quickly and to be cool. After a humiliating birthday party, Jenna's wish is granted. She becomes a gorgeous 30-year-old: Single, successful, and a certified member of the New York in-crowd.

From a communication perspective, the movie is interesting because many of adult Jenna's nonverbal behaviors are really those of a perky young teenager. The scene in which she leads her coworkers in the demons-do-the-hustle chorus line number from Michael Jackson's "Thriller" video is worth the price of admission. It also illustrates that certain nonverbal behaviors are—and sometimes aren't—"age appropriate."

a message. You may not intend to show that you're embarrassed, but your blushing can still be a giveaway. Of course, not all behaviors (intentional or not) will be interpreted correctly: Your trembling hands might be taken as a sign of nervousness when you're really just shivering from the cold. But whether or not your behavior is intentional, and whether or not it is interpreted accurately, all nonverbal behavior has the potential to create messages.

Although nonverbal behavior reveals information, reviews of research show we aren't always conscious of what we and others are communicating nonverbally (Byron, 2008; Choi et al., 2005; Lakin, 2006). In one study, less than a quarter of experimental participants who had been instructed to show increased or decreased liking of a partner could describe the nonverbal behaviors they used (Palmer & Simmons, 1995). Furthermore, just because communicators are nonverbally expressive doesn't mean that others will tune in to the abundance of unspoken messages that are available. One study comparing the richness of e-mail to in-person communication confirmed the greater amount of information available in face-to-face conversations, but it also showed that some communicators (primarily men) failed to recognize these messages (Dennis et al., 1999).

NONVERBAL COMMUNICATION IS PRIMARILY RELATIONAL

Some nonverbal messages serve utilitarian functions. For example, a police officer directs the flow of traffic, or a team of street surveyors uses hand motions to coordinate their work. But nonverbal communication also serves in a far more common (and more interesting) series of *social* functions.

Along with identity management, nonverbal communication allows us to define the kind of relationships we want to have with others (Burgoon & Le Poire, 1999). You can appreciate this fact by thinking about the wide range of ways you could behave when greeting another person. You could wave, shake hands, nod, smile, clap the other person on the back, give a hug, or avoid all contact. Each one of these behaviors sends a message about the nature of your relationship with the other person.

Nonverbal messages perform another valuable social function: They convey emotions that we may be unwilling or unable to express, or ones we may

not even be aware of. In fact, nonverbal communication is much better suited to expressing attitudes and feelings than it is ideas. You can prove this for yourself by imagining how you could express each item on the following list nonverbally:

1. "I'm tired."
2. "I'm in favor of capital punishment."
3. "I'm attracted to another person in the group."
4. "I think prayer in the schools should be allowed."
5. "I'm angry at someone in this room."

REFLECTION

Sad or Mad?

I'm an elementary school teacher who puts "smiley faces" next to good answers on the papers I grade. I also put "frowning faces" near questions that students don't answer, indicating that I'm sad to see them left blank.

One of my students came to me after class wanting to know why I was mad at her. Surprised, I said I wasn't mad at her at all. She then pulled out her paper and showed me the "frowning face." I said, "Oh no, honey, that's not mad—it's sad"—and I tried to explain the difference. I'm not sure she got it. It reminded me that even hand-drawn nonverbal expressions are ambiguous.

This experience shows that, short of charades, ideas (such as statements 2 and 4) don't lend themselves to nonverbal expressions nearly as well as attitudes and feelings (statements 1, 3, and 5). This explains why it's possible to understand the attitudes or feelings of others, even if you aren't able to understand the subject of their communication.

As technology develops, an increasing number of Internet messages will include visual and vocal dimensions, making communication richer and enhancing understanding (Ramirez & Burgoon, 2004; Walther, 2006). Until then, e-mail messages offer fewer nonverbal cues about the speaker's feelings than do face-to-face encounters, or even telephone conversations. New e-mail users soon learn that their messages can be and often are misunderstood. Probably the biggest problems arise from joking remarks taken as serious statements. To solve these problems, e-mail correspondents have developed a series of symbols—called *emoticons* or *smileys*—that can be created using keyboard characters to simulate nonverbal dimensions of a message (Walther & D'Addario, 2001). The following list contains some of the most common ones. (Because of formatting limitations that come with e-mail, emoticons appear sideways instead of in an up-and-down orientation.) Note that, like most nonverbal messages, emoticons can have multiple meanings.

:-)	Basic smile. Most commonly used to indicate humorous intent ("no offense intended").
:-D	Big smile.
;-)	Wink and grin. Sometimes used to indicate sarcasm or for saying "Don't hit me for what I just said."
:-(	Frown.
:-I	Indifference.
:-@	Screaming, swearing, very angry.
:-||	Disgusted, grim.
:~-(	Crying.
:-/ or :-	Skeptical.
:- O	Surprised, yelling, realization of an error ("Oops!").
+o(	Sick.
:-| or :|	Disappointed.

Symbols like these may be helpful, but they wouldn't seem to be an adequate substitute for the rich mixture of nonverbal messages that flow in face-to-face exchanges, or even in telephone conversations. Despite this fact, some research (e.g., Walther, 2006; Walther et al., 2005) suggests that it is possible to convey a rich array of emotional messages online. In any case, as Internet technology improves, more and more computer users will be able to see one another as they communicate.

NONVERBAL COMMUNICATION IS AMBIGUOUS

Chapter 5 pointed out how some language can be ambiguous. (For example, the statement "That nose piercing really makes you stand out" could be a compliment or a criticism, and the vague statement "I'm almost done" could mean you have to wait a few minutes or an hour.) Most nonverbal behavior has the potential to be even more ambiguous than verbal statements like these. To understand why, consider how you would interpret silence from your companion during an evening together. Think of all the possible meanings of this nonverbal behavior: warmth, anger, preoccupation, boredom, nervousness, thoughtfulness—the possibilities are many.

The ambiguity of nonverbal behavior was illustrated when one supermarket chain tried to emphasize its customer-friendly approach by instructing employees to smile and make eye contact with customers. Several clerks filed grievances when some customers mistook the service-with-a-smile approach as sexual come-ons. As this story suggests, nonverbal cues are much more ambiguous than verbal statements when it comes to expressing a willingness to become physically involved (Lim & Roloff, 1999). Romantic partners typically interpret nonverbal cues as signs of sexual willingness. However, these nonverbal messages are far less likely to be misunderstood when accompanied by verbal statements. Using clearer and less ambiguous verbal messages could reduce a variety of unfortunate outcomes, ranging from a spoiled evening to lawsuits and accusations of sexual assault.

Summarizing studies on emotion recognition within and across cultures, Elfenbein and Ambady (2002) found that while emotions were universally recognized at better-than-chance levels, accuracy was higher when emotions were both expressed and recognized by members of the same national, ethnic, or regional group, suggesting an in-group advantage. However, not all nonverbal behavior is equally identifiable. In laboratory settings, subjects are better at identifying positive facial expressions, such as happiness, love, surprise, and interest, than negative ones, like fear, sadness, anger, and disgust (Druckmann et al., 1982). In real life, though, spontaneous nonverbal expressions are so ambiguous that observers are frequently unable to identify accurately what they mean (Motley, 1993).

Because nonverbal behavior is so ambiguous, caution is wise when you are responding to nonverbal cues. Rather than jumping to conclusions about the meaning of a sigh, smile, slammed door, or yawn, it's far better to use the kind of perception-checking approach described in Chapter 4. "When you yawned, I got the idea I might be boring you. But maybe you're just tired. What's going on?" The ability to consider more than one possible interpretation for nonverbal behavior illustrates the kind of cognitive complexity that Chapter 1 identified as an element of communication competence. Popular advice on the subject notwithstanding, it's usually not possible to read a person like a book.

NONVERBAL COMMUNICATION IS INFLUENCED BY CULTURE

In 2005, many television viewers were surprised to see televised news clips of U.S. President George W. Bush holding hands with Saudi Arabia's Crown Prince Abdullah during the Arab leader's visit to the president's Texas ranch. Man-to-man hand-holding didn't seem to fit with the usual image of Texan masculinity, but most Saudis probably found it quite normal. In the Arab world, this gesture is a sign of solidarity and kinship between men, with none of the homosexual connotations that Americans might read into it (Khuri, 2001).

Cultures have different nonverbal languages as well as verbal ones (Matsumoto & Yoo, 2005). Fiorello LaGuardia, legendary mayor of New York from 1933 to 1945, was fluent in English, Italian, and Yiddish. Researchers who watched films of his campaign speeches with the sound turned off found that they could tell which language he was speaking by the changes in his nonverbal behavior (Birdwhistell, 1970).

As Chapter 2 explained in detail, the meaning of some gestures varies from one culture to another. Communicators become more tolerant of others once they understand that unusual nonverbal behaviors are the result of cultural differences. In one study, American adults were presented with videotaped scenes of speakers from the United States, France, and Germany (Warnecke et al., 1992). When the sound was cut off, viewers judged foreigners more negatively than their fellow citizens. But when the speakers' voices were added (allowing viewers to recognize that they were from a different country), the ratings of the speakers improved.

Some nonverbal behaviors—called **emblems**— are culturally understood substitutes for verbal expressions. Nodding the head up and down is an accepted way of saying "yes" in most cultures. Likewise, a side-to-side head shake is a nonverbal way of saying "no," and a shrug of the shoulders is commonly understood as meaning "I don't know" or "I'm not sure." Remember, however, that some emblems—such as the thumbs-up gesture—vary from one culture to another (it means "Good job!" in the United States, the number 1 in Germany, and the number 5 in Japan). Other nonverbal signs can be ambiguous even within a single culture. For example, a wink might mean something entirely different to the person on the receiving end than it does to the person winking (Lindsey & Vigil, 1999).

Despite differences like these, many nonverbal behaviors are universal. Certain expressions have the same meanings around the world. Smiles and laughter are a universal signal of positive emotions, for example, while the same sour expressions convey displeasure in every culture. Charles Darwin believed that expressions like these are the result of evolution, functioning as survival mechanisms that allowed early humans to convey emotional states before the development of language. The innateness of some facial expressions becomes even more clear when we examine the behavior of children born deaf and blind (Eibl-Eibesfeldt, 1972). Despite a lack of social learning, these children display a broad range of expressions. They smile, laugh, and cry in ways virtually identical to seeing and hearing infants.

While nonverbal expressions like these may be universal, the way they are used varies widely around the world (Matsumoto, 2006). In some cultures display rules discourage the overt demonstration of feelings like happiness or anger. In other cultures the same feelings are perfectly appropriate. Thus, a Japanese person might appear much more controlled and placid than an Arab, when in fact their feelings might be identical (Leathers, 1992).

It's important to note that the *culture* in which people live is far more important than their *nationality* or *ethnicity*. For example, the facial expressions of Japanese nationals and Japanese Americans differ in ways that reflect their cultural backgrounds (Marsh et al., 2003).

The same principle operates closer to home among co-cultures (Dovidio et al., 2006). For example, observations have shown that black women in all-black groups are nonverbally more expressive and interrupt one another more than white women in all-white groups (Booth-Butterfield & Jordan, 1989). This doesn't mean that black women always feel more intensely than their white counterparts. A more likely explanation is that the two groups follow different cultural rules. The researchers found that in racially mixed groups both black and white women moved closer to each others' style. This nonverbal convergence shows that skilled communicators can adapt their behavior when interacting with members of other cultures or co-cultures in order to make the exchange more smooth and effective.

Functions of Nonverbal Communication

Now that you understand what nonverbal communication is, we need to explore the functions it serves in relationships. As you'll read, nonverbal cues play several important roles in the way we relate with others.

CREATING AND MAINTAINING RELATIONSHIPS

As you will read in Chapter 9, communication is our primary means for beginning, maintaining, and ending relationships. Nonverbal behavior plays an important role during every relational stage.

Consider the importance of nonverbal communication during the very first stage of a relationship. When we first meet another person, our initial goal is to reduce our uncertainty about her or him (Berger, 1987). We ask ourselves questions like "Would I like to know this person better?" and "Is she (or he) interested in me?" One of the first ways we answer these questions is by observing nonverbal cues including facial expression, eye contact, posture, gesture, and tone of voice (Berger & Kellermann, 1994). This process occurs quite rapidly—often in a matter of seconds (Sudnow, 1972).

At the same time we are sizing up others, we are providing nonverbal cues about our attitude toward them. We rarely share these thoughts and feelings

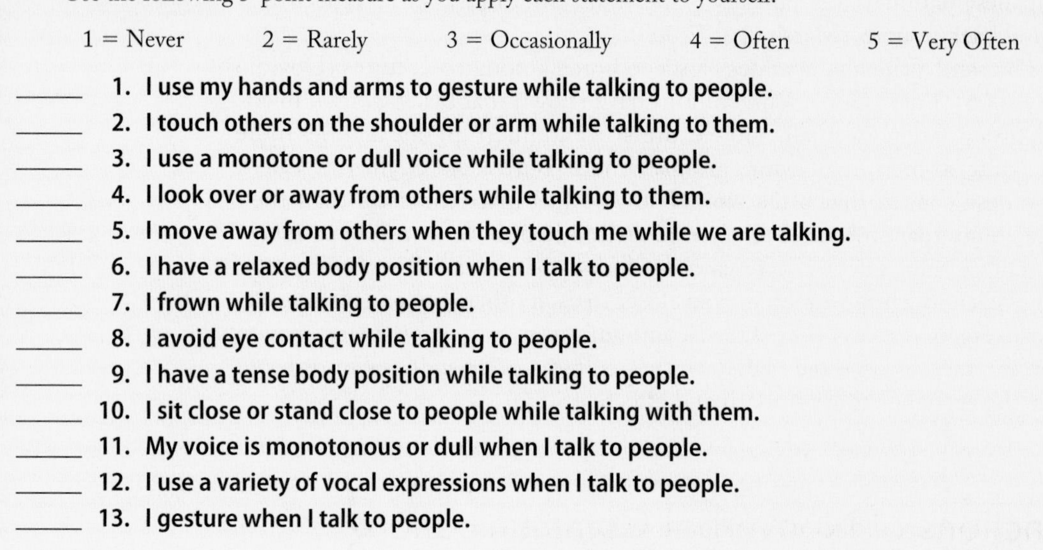
SELF-ASSESSMENT

Nonverbal Immediacy Behaviors

Most communication researchers agree that *nonverbal immediacy*—the display of involvement signaled by physical closeness, eye contact, and movement, and touch—is an important ingredient of communication competence. You can measure your immediacy by completing this self-assessment. Indicate the degree to which you believe each statement applies to you.

Use the following 5-point measure as you apply each statement to yourself:

1 = Never 2 = Rarely 3 = Occasionally 4 = Often 5 = Very Often

_____ **1. I use my hands and arms to gesture while talking to people.**
_____ **2. I touch others on the shoulder or arm while talking to them.**
_____ **3. I use a monotone or dull voice while talking to people.**
_____ **4. I look over or away from others while talking to them.**
_____ **5. I move away from others when they touch me while we are talking.**
_____ **6. I have a relaxed body position when I talk to people.**
_____ **7. I frown while talking to people.**
_____ **8. I avoid eye contact while talking to people.**
_____ **9. I have a tense body position while talking to people.**
_____ **10. I sit close or stand close to people while talking with them.**
_____ **11. My voice is monotonous or dull when I talk to people.**
_____ **12. I use a variety of vocal expressions when I talk to people.**
_____ **13. I gesture when I talk to people.**

overtly. Imagine how odd it would be to say or hear words like "I'm friendly and relaxed" or "You look pretty interesting, but I won't pursue this unless you give me a sign that you're interested too." Messages like these are much more safely expressed via nonverbal channels. Of course, it's important to remember that nonverbal cues are ambiguous, and that you may be misinterpreting them (Levesque & Kenny, 1993). In cases when you're considering moving the relationship forward, you may want to use the perception-checking skill outlined in Chapter 4 to verify your hunches.

Nonverbal cues are just as important in established, ongoing relationships, where they both create and signal the emotional climate. For example, the amount and coordination of ongoing touch is a strong measure of a couple's degree of commitment to one another (Johnson & Edwards, 1991). In families, nonverbal cues offer a clear sign of relational satisfaction (Rogers, 2001), as well as who controls interaction and decision making (Siegel et al., 1992). On the job, supervisors who offer nonverbal cues of liking can increase subordinates' job motivation, job satisfaction, and liking of their boss (Richmond & McCroskey, 2000).

______ **14. I am animated when I talk to people.**
______ **15. I have a bland facial expression when I talk to people.**
______ **16. I move closer to people when I talk to them.**
______ **17. I look directly at people while talking to them.**
______ **18. I am stiff when I talk to people.**
______ **19. I have a lot of vocal variety when I talk to people.**
______ **20. I avoid gesturing while I am talking to people.**
______ **21. I lean toward people when I talk to them.**
______ **22. I maintain eye contact with people when I talk to them.**
______ **23. I try not to sit or stand close to people when I talk with them.**
______ **24. I lean away from people when I talk to them.**
______ **25. I smile when I talk to people.**
______ **26. I avoid touching people when I talk to them.**

SCORING:
Step 1. Start with a score of 78. To that, add the scores from the following items: 1, 2, 6, 10, 12, 13, 14, 16, 17, 19, 21, 22, and 25.
Step 2. Add the scores from the following items: 3, 4, 5, 7, 8, 9, 11, 15, 18, 20, 23, 24, and 26.
Total Score = Step 1 minus Step 2. (Scores can range from a low of 26 to a high of 130.)

Men and women differed in their self-evaluations using this scale, with women perceiving themselves as engaging in more nonverbal immediacy behaviors then men. College-age women had an average score of 102, with most scores between 91 and 113. College-age men had an average score of 93.8, with most scores between 83 and 105.

Richmond, V. P., McCroskey, J. C., & Johnson, A. D. (2003). Development of the Nonverbal Immediacy Scale (NIS): Measures of self- and other-perceived nonverbal immediacy. *Communication Quarterly, 51,* 504–517.

You can test the power of nonverbal behavior in relationships for yourself. First, observe the interaction of people in relationships without paying attention to their words. Watch couples or families in restaurants or other public places. Focus on fellow employees in the workplace. Observe professors and their students interacting in and outside of class. See how parents treat their children, and vice versa. You are likely to see a multitude of cues that suggest the quality of each relationship. Chances are good that you could make educated guesses about whether the people you're watching are satisfied with each other—and whether their relationship is beginning, maintaining, or ending.

REGULATING INTERACTION

Nonverbal **regulators** are cues that help control verbal interaction. The best example of such regulation is the wide array of turn-taking signals in everyday conversation (Drummond & Hopper, 1993; Rosenfeld, 1987). Three nonverbal signals that indicate a speaker has finished talking and is ready to yield to a listener are (1) changes in vocal intonation—a rising or falling in pitch at the end of a clause, (2) a drawl on the last syllable or the stressed syllable in a clause, and (3) a drop in vocal pitch or loudness when speaking a common expression such as "you know." You can see how these regulators work by observing almost any conversation.

Eye contact is another way of regulating verbal communication (Bavelas et al., 2002). In conversations, the person listening typically looks more at the speaker than the reverse. When the speaker seeks a response, he or she signals by looking at the listener, creating a brief period of mutual gaze called a "gaze window." At this point, the listener is likely to respond with a nod, "uh-huh," or other reaction, after which the speaker looks away and continues speaking. Children (and some socially insensitive adults) have not learned all the subtle signals of such turn taking. Through a rough series of trial and error, children finally learn how to "read" other people well enough to avoid interrupting behaviors.

INFLUENCING OTHERS

How we look, act, and sound can be more important in meeting our goals than the words we speak. The influence of nonverbal behavior comes in many forms. It can capture attention, show or increase liking, generate power, and boost credibility (Cesario & Higgins, 2008; Kopacz, 2006). Sometimes deliberately and sometimes without thought, we use nonverbal behaviors in ways that get others to satisfy our wants and needs. For example, people are more willing to do our bidding when we look them directly in the eye (Segrin, 1993), wear high-status clothing (Bushman, 1988), and use open body postures (Burgoon et al. 1990). As you'll read later in this chapter, touching others—even strangers—in appropriate ways can increase their compliance.

CONCEALING/DECEIVING

We may value and honor the truth, but the majority of messages we exchange are not completely truthful. Sometimes we keep silent, sometimes we hedge, and sometimes we downright lie. As you read in Chapter 3, not all deception is self-serving or malicious: Much of it is aimed at saving the "face" of the communicators involved. For example, you might pretend to have a good time at a family celebration or business event, even though you are bored senseless. Likewise, you might act graciously when socializing with someone you'd rather never see again. In situations like these and many others, it's easy to see how nonverbal factors can make the face-saving deception either succeed or fail.

FOCUS ON RESEARCH

Conversation Regulation among Blind Adults

Nonverbal turn-taking cues are the lubricant that keeps conversation moving smoothly. Since many of these cues are visual, researcher Anna-Karin Magnusson explored the question of how blind communicators manage the flow of conversation.

Magnusson video-recorded a series of conversations between pairs of strangers. At least one of the partners in each dyad was blind. The researcher was not interested in the content of these conversations. Rather, her focus was on how the blind subjects managed the back-and-forth shifts from speaker to listener.

Not surprisingly, Magnusson found that the blind conversationalists relied heavily on vocal cues, such as changes in pitch and extended drawls at the end of a speaker's comments. More surprisingly, she discovered that some (though not all) blind conversationalists displayed visual cues such as smiling, nodding, and body leaning to signal willingness to let the other person continue speaking—even when talking to blind partners. When they wanted to hold on to their speaking turn, blind speakers again relied heavily on vocal cues. But several also used visual signals: furrowing the eyebrows, turning the face away from the partner, and using hand gestures.

Magnusson was struck by the fact that the turn-taking cues of blind conversationalists were almost as different from one another as they were from sighted people. With that finding in mind, she urges communicators with sight to regard blind people in conversation as unique individuals and not as disabled partners who need to be treated differently.

Magnusson, A. (2006). Nonverbal conversation-regulating signals of the blind adult. *Communication Studies*, *57*, 421–433.

Some people are better at hiding deceit than others. High self-monitors are usually better at hiding their deception than communicators who are less self-aware (Burgoon et al., 1994), and raters judge highly expressive liars as more honest than those who are more subdued (Burgoon et al., 1995). Not surprisingly, people whose jobs require them to act differently than they feel, such as actors, lawyers, diplomats, and salespeople, are more successful at deception than the general population (Riggio & Friedman, 1983).

Table 6.2 outlines some conditions under which liars are likely to betray themselves nonverbally. See if they match your personal experience.

Decades of research have revealed that there are no surefire nonverbal clues that indicate deception. As one writer put it, "There is no unique telltale signal for a fib. Pinocchio's nose just doesn't exist, and that makes liars difficult to spot" (Lock, 2004, p. 72). This may explain why most observers have only a coin-flip's chance of knowing when they're being told a fib (Vrij et al., 2004). With training, however, the accuracy of catching deceit can increase to over 75 percent (Akehurst et al., 2004; Vrij et al., 2000). Some nonverbal cues offer more important information about lying than others. In addition, these cues manifest themselves more clearly during "high-stake lies," when deceivers are under greater levels of mental and emotional stress.

TABLE 6.2 ***Circumstances in which a Deceiver Leaks Nonverbal Clues to Deception***

LEAKAGE MOST LIKELY	LEAKAGE LEAST LIKELY
Wants to hide emotions being experienced at the moment	Wants to hide information unrelated to emotions
Feels strongly about the information being hidden	Has no strong feelings about the information being hidden
Feels apprehensive about the deception	Feels confident about the deception
Feels guilty about being deceptive	Experiences little guilt about the deception
Gets little enjoyment from being deceptive	Enjoys the deception
Needs to construct the message carefully while delivering it	Knows the deceptive message well and has rehearsed it

Based on material from Ekman, P. (1981). Mistakes when deceiving. In T. A. Sebeok & R. Rosenthal (Eds.), *The Clever Hans phenomenon: Communication with horses, whales, apes, and people* (pp. 269–278). New York: New York Academy of Sciences.

Despite the challenges, there are some clues that may reveal less-than-totally-honest communication (Andersen, 1999). For example, deceivers typically make more speech errors than truth-tellers: stammers, stutters, hesitations, false starts, and so on. Vocal pitch often rises when people tell lies, and liars hesitate more (Rockwell et al., 1997). Liars also make fewer hand and finger movements, have more speech disturbances, and pause longer before offering answers than do truth-tellers (Sporer & Schwandt, 2007; Vrij et al., 2000). Even with clues like these, it's a mistake to assume that every tongue-tied, fidgeting, eye-blinking person is a liar.

The bottom line is that nonverbal cues offer important information for detecting deception, but most lies aren't detected through snap judgments of a facial expression or a shift in posture. Instead, people who suspect a lie tend to collect a variety of clues (including information from third parties and physical evidence) over a period of days, weeks, or even longer (Park et al., 2002). Jumping to conclusions based on limited information isn't wise communication, and it may lead to relational difficulties. Handle this material about deception detection with care and good judgment.

"I knew the suspect was lying because of certain telltale discrepancies between his voice and non verbal gestures. Also his pants were on fire."

MANAGING IDENTITY

Chapter 3 (see pages 77–85) explained that one major goal of communicating is identity management: getting others to view us as we want to be seen. In many cases, nonverbal cues can be more important than verbal messages in creating impressions (DePaulo, 1992; Zuckerman et al., 1999). To appreciate how we manage impressions via nonverbal means, consider what happens when you meet strangers you would like to know better. Instead of projecting your image verbally ("Hi! I'm attractive, friendly, and easygoing"), you behave in ways that will present this identity. For example, you might dress fashionably, smile a lot, and perhaps try to strike a relaxed pose.

There are several ways of managing identity nonverbally. Sandra Metts and Erica Grohskopf (2003) reviewed professional trade journal articles on constructing good impressions and found examples of each of the following categories (their examples are in parentheses in the following list):

- *Manner* refers to the way we act: How we deliberately stand and move, the way we control facial expressions, and the adjustments we make in our voice. ("Stand tall and walk proudly"; "When meeting others, make direct eye contact and use a firm but friendly handshake.")
- *Appearance* involves the way we dress, the artifacts we wear, hair, makeup, scents, and so on. ("Dress how you wish to be remembered: with assurance, some spark of originality, and in a way that makes you feel comfortable and confident.")
- *Setting* involves the physical items we surround ourselves with: personal belongings, vehicles, and even the place we live. ("Mat and frame awards and certificates and display them in your office.")

Managing Identity for Romance: *Hitch*

Alex "Hitch" Hitchens (Will Smith) is a New York "date doctor" who teaches men how to romance the women of their dreams. His latest client is Albert Brenneman (Kevin James), a nerdy accountant who needs to improve his style to win the affections of the wealthy and beautiful Allegra Cole (Amber Valletta).

Hitch coaches Albert on a variety of nonverbal behaviors, including how to walk, stand, and dance, so that Albert can attract his dream woman. Despite the importance of self-presentation, Hitch's own love life shows that romantic success depends on more than manipulating a few nonverbal cues.

Types of Nonverbal Communication

So far, we've talked about the role nonverbal communication plays in our interpersonal relationships. Now it's time to look at the many types of nonverbal communication.

FACE AND EYES

The face and eyes are probably the most noticeable parts of the body. However, the nonverbal messages from the face and eyes are not the easiest to read (Carroll & Russell, 1996). The face is a tremendously complicated channel of expression to interpret, for several reasons.

"Spare a little eye contact?"

First, it's hard to describe the number and kind of expressions commonly produced by the face and eyes. For example, researchers have found that there are at least 8 distinguishable positions of the eyebrows and forehead, 8 more of the eyes and lids, and 10 for the lower face (Ekman & Friesen, 1974a, 1975). When you multiply this complexity by the number of emotions we experience, you can see why it would be almost impossible to compile a dictionary of facial expressions and their corresponding emotions.

The study of how the eyes can communicate is sometimes known as **oculesics**. Gazes and glances are usually signals of the looker's interest. However, the *type* of interest can vary. Sometimes, as mentioned earlier, looking is a conversational turn-taking signal that says, "I'm finished talking. Now it's your turn." Gazing also is a good indicator of liking (Druckmann et al., 1982). Sometimes, eye contact *reflects* liking that already exists, and at other times it actually creates or *increases* liking—hence the expression "making eyes." In other situations, eye contact indicates interest, but not attraction or approval, such as when a teacher glares at a rowdy student or a police officer "keeps an eye on" a suspect.

In addition to influencing verbal responses, research by Stephen Davis and Jamie Kieffer (1998) details at least one effect of eye contact on an important nonverbal behavior: tipping. They found that customers in both small towns and urban areas leave larger tips when their servers (whether male or female) maintain eye contact with them. The authors speculate that good eye contact makes the atmosphere of the restaurant friendlier, and makes the customers feel as if they are dining at home.

BODY MOVEMENT

Another way we communicate nonverbally is through the physical movement of our bodies: our posture, gestures, physical orientation to others, and so on. Social scientists use the term **kinesics** to describe the study of how people communicate through bodily movements.

Some social scientists claim that a language of gestures was the first form of human communication, preceding speech by tens of thousands of years (Corballis, 2002). To appreciate the communicative value of kinesic messages, stop reading for a moment and notice how you're sitting. What does your position say nonverbally about how you feel? Are there any other people near you now? What messages do you get from their present posture? By paying attention to the postures of those around you, as well as to your own, you'll find another channel of nonverbal communication that reveals how people feel about themselves and others.

The English language indicates the deep links between posture and communication. English is full of expressions that tie emotional states with body postures:

"I won't take this lying down!"
"Stand on your own two feet."
"Take a load off your back."
"You're all wrapped up in yourself."
"Don't be so uptight!"

Phrases like these show an awareness of posture, even if it's often unconscious. The main reason we miss most posture messages is that they aren't too obvious. It's seldom that people who feel weighed down by a problem hunch over dramatically. When we're bored, we usually don't lean back and slump enough to embarrass the person with whom we're bored. In interpreting posture, then, the key is to look for small changes that might be shadows of the way people feel.

Gestures are a fundamental element of communication—so fundamental, in fact, that people who have been blind from birth use them (Iverson, 1999; Iverson & Goldin-Meadow, 1997). Gestures are sometimes intentional—for example, a cheery wave or thumbs-up. In other cases, however, our gestures are unconscious. Occasionally an unconscious gesture will consist of an unambiguous emblem, such as a shrug that clearly means "I don't know." More often, however, there are several possible interpretations to gestures (Krauss et al., 1991). A group of ambiguous gestures consists of what we usually call *fidgeting*—movements in which one part of the body grooms, massages, rubs, holds, pinches, picks, or otherwise manipulates another part. Social scientists call these behaviors **manipulators**. Social rules may discourage us from performing more manipulators in public, but people still do so without noticing.

Research reveals what common sense suggests—that an increased use of manipulators is often a sign of discomfort (Ekman & Friesen, 1974b). But not *all* fidgeting signals uneasiness. People also are likely to use manipulators when relaxed. When they let their guard down (either alone or with friends), they will be more likely to fiddle with an earlobe, twirl a strand of hair, or clean their fingernails.

The amount and type of gesturing a person uses can be a measure of power and status (Andersen, 1999). For example, people who gesture more are rated by observers as being in positions of control and power, whereas those who gesture less are judged by observers as being subordinate. Head bowing is generally perceived as a submissive gesture and head raising as a dominant gesture (Mignault & Chaudhuri, 2003). Head nodding occurs more often when speaking with a person of higher status than of equal status; for example, a student nods more when talking with a professor than with another student (Helweg et al., 2004). And pointing is judged by observers as one indicator of power, since it implies at least some ability to order other people around.

Gestures can produce a wide range of reactions in receivers (Druckmann et al., 1982). In many situations, the right kinds of gestures can increase persuasiveness. Increasing hand and arm movements, leaning forward, fidgeting less, and keeping limbs open all make a speaker more effective at influencing others (Leathers, 1992). Even more interesting is the fact that persuasiveness increases when one person mirrors another's movements (Van Swol, 2003). When persuader and audience are reasonably similar, reciprocating the other person's gestures has a positive effect, whereas acting in a contrary manner is likely to have the opposite result.

As with almost any nonverbal behavior, the context in which gestures occur makes all the difference in the results they produce. Animated movements that are well received in a cooperative social setting may seem like signals of aggression or attempts at domination in a more competitive setting. Fidgeting that might suggest deviousness in a bargaining session could be appropriate when you offer a nervous apology in a personal situation. In any case, trying to manufacture insincere, artificial gestures (or any other nonverbal behaviors) will probably backfire. A more useful goal is to recognize the behaviors you find yourself spontaneously delivering and to consider how they reflect the attitudes you already feel.

TOUCH

Social scientists use the term **haptics** to distinguish the study of touching. Contemporary research confirms the value of touch for infants (Field, 2003). Studies at the University of Miami's School of Medicine, for example, have shown that premature babies grow faster and gain more weight when massaged (Adler, 1993). The same institute's researchers demonstrated that massage can help premature children gain weight, make colicky children sleep better, and boost the immune function of cancer and HIV patients. Massage helps newborn babies thrive, and it also helps depressed mothers of newborns feel better and smoothes the delivery process (Mwakalyelye & DeAngelis, 1995). Studies show that touch between therapists and clients has the potential to encourage a variety of beneficial changes: more self-disclosure, client self-acceptance, and better client-therapist relationships (Driscoll et al., 1988). In addition, patients with dementia who were administered hand massage on each hand, along with intermittent gentle touch on the arm and shoulder and calm soothing speech, decreased their anxiety and dysfunctional behavior (Kim & Buschmann, 1999).

Touch also plays a large part in how we respond to others. For instance, in a laboratory task, participants evaluated partners more positively when they were touched (appropriately, of course) by them (Burgoon et al., 1992). Besides increasing liking, touch also boosts compliance. In a study by Chris Kleinke (1977), participants were approached by a female confederate who requested that they return a dime left in the phone booth from which they had just emerged. When the request was accompanied by a light touch on the participant's arm, the probability that he or she would return the dime increased significantly. In a similar experiment (Willis & Hamm, 1980), participants were asked by a male or female confederate to sign a petition or complete a rating scale. Again, participants were more likely to cooperate when they were touched lightly on the arm. In the rating-scale variation of the study, the results were especially dramatic: 70 percent of those who were touched complied, whereas only 40 percent of the untouched participants were willing to cooperate.

Arguing that these small solicitations hardly get at the power of touch, Guéguen and Fischer-Lokou (2002) conducted an experiment in which confederates asked passersby to look after a large and very excited dog for 10 minutes so the owner could go into a pharmacy where animals were prohibited. In half of the cases, the passerby was touched during the request. Results confirmed that touch has a large effect on compliance: when touched, 55 percent agreed with the request, whereas only 35 percent in the no-touch condition agreed.

An additional power of touch is its on-the-job utility. Studies show that even fleeting touches on the hand or forearm can result in larger tips for restaurant servers (Crusco & Wetzel, 1984; Guéguen & Jacob, 2005). And a server who touches a patron's arm while suggesting a meal choice increases the probability of the patron's making the recommended choice (Guéguen et al., 2007). The effect extends to alcohol consumption: both women and men in taverns, whether in same-sex or different-sex dyads, increase their alcohol consumption when touched (appropriately, of course) by the server (Kaufman & Mahoney, 1999).

In contemporary society, unwanted touching is cause for concern, and even legal action. In the United States, touching is generally more appropriate for women than for men (Derlega et al., 1989; Jones, 1986). Males touch their male friends less than they touch their female friends, and also less than females touch their female friends. Although women are generally more comfortable about touching than men, biological sex isn't the only factor that shapes contact. In general, the degree of touch comfort goes along with openness to expressing intimate feelings, an active interpersonal style, and satisfactory relationships (Fromme et al., 1989).

The amount of touching usually decreases with age (Knapp & Hall, 2006). Sixth-graders touch each other less than do first-graders. Parents touch their older children less often than their younger ones. As young children, most North Americans receive at least a modest amount of physical contact from their parents. The next time most can expect to receive this level of physical caring won't come until they have chosen a partner. Even then, the nurturing seemingly brought by physical contact will most often come only from that partner—a heavy demand for one person to carry.

VOICE

Social scientists use the term **paralanguage** to describe the way a message is spoken. Vocal rate, pronunciation, pitch, tone, volume, and emphasis can give the same word or words many meanings. For example, note how many meanings come from a single sentence just by shifting the emphasis from one word to another:

> *This* is a fantastic communication book.
> (Not just any book, but *this* one in particular.)
>
> This is a *fantastic* communication book.
> (This book is superior, exciting.)

This is a fantastic *communication* book.
(The book is good as far as communication goes; it may not be so great as literature or as drama.)

This is a fantastic communication *book.*
(It's not a play or record; it's a book.)

Along with tone, speed, pitch, volume, and emphasis, paralanguage includes length of pauses and **disfluencies** (such as stammering and use of "uh," "um," and "er"). All these factors can do a great deal to reinforce or contradict the message that words convey.

The impact of paralinguistic cues is strong. In fact, listeners pay more attention to paralanguage than to the content of the words when asked to determine a speaker's attitudes (Burns & Beier, 1973). Furthermore, when vocal factors contradict a verbal message (as when a speaker shouts "I am *not* angry!"), listeners tend to judge the speaker's intention from the paralanguage, not the words themselves (Mehrabian & Weiner, 1967). Vocal changes that contradict spoken words are not easy to conceal. If the speaker is trying to hide fear or anger, the voice will probably sound higher and louder, and the rate of talk may be faster than normal. Sadness produces the opposite vocal pattern: quieter, lower-pitched speech delivered at a slower rate (Ekman, 1985). Vocal cues can signal how to interpret a verbal message. For example, Salvatore Attardo and his colleagues (2003) found that when a television character is being ironic or sarcastic, that attitude is signaled by a contrasting change of pitch (along with a blank facial expression).

Paralanguage can affect behavior in many ways, some of which are rather surprising. Studies by David Buller and Kelly Aune (1988, 1992) reveal that communicators are most likely to comply with requests delivered by speakers whose rate is similar to their own. However, speaking rate isn't constant. For example, it changes when a speaker's first message doesn't seem to get the desired results. Charles Berger and Patrick diBattista (1993) discovered that when communicators gave directions that weren't followed, the wording of their

DARK SIDE OF COMMUNICATION

Accents and Stigmas

In the musical *My Fair Lady,* Professor Henry Higgins transforms Eliza Doolittle from a humble flower girl into a high-society woman by replacing her Cockney accent with an upper-crust British speaking style. Although the story (based on George Bernard Shaw's play *Pygmalion*) is fictional, the notion that we judge people by their accents is all too real.

Several decades of research show that judgments of attractiveness and status are strongly influenced by style of speech. In one study, jurors in the United States found testimony less believable when delivered by witnesses speaking with German, Mexican, or Middle Eastern accents. In another experiment, researchers asked human resource professionals to rate the intelligence, initiative, and personality of job applicants after hearing a 45-second recording of their voices. The speakers with identifiable regional accents—Southern or New Jersey, for example—were recommended for lower-level jobs, while those with less pronounced speech styles were tagged for higher-level jobs that involved more public contact.

It's common knowledge that we shouldn't judge a book by its cover or people by superficial characteristics—but, unfortunately, we do so all the time. Remember when listening to people whose accent is different from yours to stay focused on what they're saying, not how they're saying it.

Bailey, R. W. (2003). Ideologies, attitudes, and perceptions. *American Speech, 88,* 115–142.

Frumkin, L. (2007). Influences of accent and ethnic background on perceptions of eyewitness testimony. *Psychology, Crime & Law, 13,* 317–331.

second attempts didn't change significantly. Instead, they simply slowed down and spoke louder.

Sarcasm is one approach in which we use both emphasis and tone of voice to change a statement's meaning to the opposite of its verbal message. Experience this reversal yourself with the following three statements. First say them literally, and then say them sarcastically.

"You look terrific!"
"I really had a wonderful time on my blind date."
"There's nothing I like better than calves' brains on toast."

As with other nonverbal messages, people often ignore or misinterpret the vocal nuances of sarcasm. Members of certain groups—children, people with weak intellectual skills, poor listeners, and people with certain forms of brain damage—are more likely to misunderstand sarcastic messages than are others (Andersen, 1992; Shamay et al., 2002).

Young children in particular have difficulty making sense of mixed messages. In one study (Morton & Trehub, 2001), youngsters ages 4–8 years old were presented with a series of positive and negative statements. When positive statements (such as "Dad gave me a new bike for my birthday") were delivered in a sad tone of voice, the children gauged the speaker as happy because they paid attention to the words rather than the vocal cues. When negative statements were read in an upbeat tone, children interpreted the message as negative—again, relying more on the content than the paralanguage. There was a direct relationship between age and sensitivity to nonverbal cues, with the youngest children relying most heavily on the words spoken. Preschool children (ages 3–5 years old) have the hardest time decoding mixed messages. The only time they can do so is when there is an exaggerated difference between the verbal and nonverbal meanings (Eskritt & Lee, 2003).

Communication through paralanguage isn't always intentional. Our voices often give us away when we're trying to create an impression different from our actual feelings. For example, you've probably had the experience of trying to sound calm and serene when you were really seething with inner nervousness. Maybe your deception went along perfectly for a while—just the right smile, no telltale fidgeting of the hands, posture appearing relaxed—and then, without being able to do a thing about it, right in the middle of your relaxed comments, your voice squeaked! The charade was over.

In addition to reinforcing or contradicting messages, some vocal factors influence the way a speaker is perceived by others (Castelan-Cargile & Bradac, 2001). For example, surgeons whose voices were regarded as dominating and indifferent were more likely to be sued for malpractice than those with a less threatening vocal style (Ambady et al., 2002). People who speak more slowly are judged as having greater conversational control than fast talkers (Tusing & Dillard, 2000), and people who judge a speaker's speech rate as similar to their own perceive the speaker as more competent and socially attractive than when the rate is different (Feldstein et al., 2001). Communicators with more attractive voices are rated more highly than those whose speech sounds less attractive

REFLECTION

Vocal Confidence

Last summer I worked in a call center where I was basically a telephone salesperson. We spent an entire day of training rehearsing the vocal parts of our sales pitch. We practiced how to control the speed, tone, and volume of our voice. For example, our boss pointed out that we would be most effective by ending sentences on a downward note when we were describing our products. He explained that this made us sound confident, whereas ending on an upward note sounds much more tentative. We were instructed to sound as if we were already occupied as we took each call (to create the impression that there was a high demand for our service).

When I think back on the experience it all sounds quite manipulative. But these techniques did work, and they show that the voice can make a huge difference in how people think of us.

(Francis & Wales, 1994; Zuckerman & Driver, 1989). Just what makes a voice attractive can vary. As Figure 6.1 shows, culture can make a difference. Surveys indicate that there are both similarities and differences between what Mexicans and U.S. citizens view as the "ideal" voice. Howard Giles and his associates (1992b) found that age combines with accent to form preferences by listeners. Older-sounding communicators whose language was accent-free were rated as most competent, while older-sounding speech by people who did not speak in a culturally standard way was judged least competent.

DISTANCE

Proxemics is the study of how communication is affected by the use, organization, and perception of space and distance. Each of us carries around a sort of invisible bubble of **personal space** wherever we go. We think of the area inside this bubble as our own—almost as much a part of us as our own bodies. Our personal bubbles vary in size according to the culture in which we were raised, the person we're with, and the situation. It's precisely the varying size of our personal space—the distance we put between ourselves and others—that gives a nonverbal clue to our feelings (Sommer, 2002).

D. Russell Crane (1987) and other researchers tested over 100 married couples, asking partners to walk toward one another and stop when they reached a "comfortable conversational distance." Then they gave each partner a battery of tests to measure their marital intimacy, desire for change, and potential for divorce. The researchers discovered that there was a strong relationship between distance and marital happiness. The average space between distressed couples was about 25 percent greater than that between satisfied partners. On average, the happy couples stood 11.4 inches apart, while the distance between unhappy spouses averaged 14.8 inches.

In another study, Mark Snyder (1980) reported that the distance participants unconsciously placed between themselves and others was a good indication of their prejudices. All the participants were polled on their attitudes about homosexuality. Half the interviewers, who were confederates of the experimenter, wore "Gay and Proud" buttons and mentioned their membership in the Association of Gay Psychologists. The other interviewers wore no buttons and simply identified themselves as graduate students. Despite their expressions of tolerance, participants seated themselves almost a foot farther away from the apparently gay interviewers of the same sex.

Preferred spaces are largely a matter of cultural norms (Beaulieu, 2004). For example, people living in hyperdense Hong Kong manage to live in crowded residential quarters that most North Americans would find intolerable (Chan, 1999). Looking at the distances that North American communicators use in everyday interaction, Hall (1969) found four, each of which reflects a different way we feel toward others at a given time. By "reading" which distance people select, we can get some insight into their feelings.

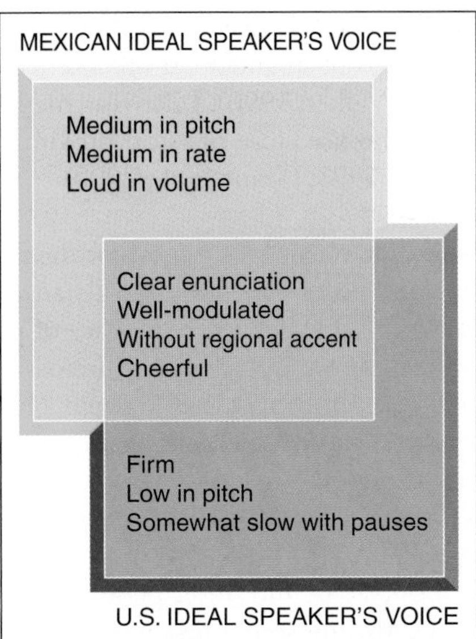

FIGURE 6.1 A Comparison of the Ideal Speaker's Voice Types in Mexico and the United States

Reproduced from p. 62 of Valentine, C. A., & Saint Damian, B. (1988). Communicative power: Gender and culture as determinants of the ideal voice. In C. A. Valentine & N. Hoar (Eds.), *Women and communicative power: Theory, research, and practice.* Washington, DC: National Communication Association.

Intimate Distance The first of Hall's zones begins with skin contact and ranges out to about 18 inches. We usually use **intimate distance** with people who are emotionally close to us, and then mostly in private situations—making love, caressing, comforting, protecting. By allowing people to move into our intimate distance, we let them enter our personal space. When we let them in voluntarily, it's usually a sign of trust: We've willingly lowered our defenses. On the other hand, when someone invades this most personal area without our consent, we usually feel threatened.

Personal Distance The second spatial zone, **personal distance**, ranges from 18 inches at its closest point to 4 feet at its farthest. Its closer phase is the distance at which most couples stand in public. If someone thought to be sexually attractive stands this near one partner at a party, the other partner is likely to become alert. This "moving in" often is taken to mean that something more than casual conversation is taking place. The far range of personal distance runs from about 2½ to 4 feet. It's the zone just beyond the other person's reach. As Hall puts it, at this distance we can keep someone "at arm's length." His choice of words suggests the type of communication that goes on at this range: The contacts are still reasonably close, but they're much less personal than the ones that occur a foot or so closer.

Social Distance The third zone is **social distance.** It ranges from 4 to about 12 feet out. Within this zone, the distance between communicators can have a powerful effect on how we regard and respond to others. For example, students are more satisfied with teachers who reduce (at appropriate levels, of course) the distance between themselves and their classes. They also are more satisfied with the course itself and are more likely to follow the teacher's instructions (Hackman & Walker, 1990). Likewise, medical patients are more satisfied with physicians who use close physical proximity to convey warmth and concern (Conlee et al., 1993; Grant et al., 2000).

Public Distance **Public distance** is Hall's term for the farthest zone, running outward from 12 feet. The closer range of public distance is the one that most teachers use in the classroom. In the farther reaches of public space—25 feet and beyond—two-way communication is almost impossible. In some cases it's necessary for speakers to use public distance to reach a large audience, but we can assume that anyone who chooses to use it when more closeness is possible is not interested in a dialogue.

When our spatial bubble is invaded we experience stress, and we respond with *barrier behaviors,* strategies designed to create a barrier (or fix a broken one) between ourselves and other people (Evans & Wener, 2007; Kanaga & Flynn, 1981). Invade someone's personal space, and notice the reaction. At first the person is most likely simply to back away, probably without realizing what is happening. Next your partner might attempt to put an object between you, such as a desk, a chair, or some books clutched to the chest, all in an effort to get some separation. Then the other person will probably decrease eye contact (the "elevator syndrome," in which we can crowd in and even touch one another so long as we avoid eye contact). Furthermore, your reluctant partner might sneeze, cough, scratch, and exhibit any variety of behaviors to discourage your antisocial behavior. In the end, if none of these behaviors achieves the desired goal of getting some space between the two of you, the other person might leave or "counterattack," gently at first ("Move back, will you?"), then more forcefully (probably with a shove).

TERRITORIALITY

While personal space is the invisible bubble we carry around, the area that serves as an extension of our physical being, **territory** remains stationary (Hidalgo & Hernandez, 2001). Robert Sommer (1969) watched students in a college library and found that there's a definite pattern for people who want to study alone. While the library was uncrowded, students almost always chose corner seats at one of the empty rectangular tables. After each table was occupied by one reader, new readers would choose a seat on the opposite side and at the far end, thus keeping the maximum distance between themselves and the other readers. One of Sommer's associates tried violating these "rules" by sitting next to and across from other female readers when more distant seats were available. She found that the approached women reacted defensively, signaling their discomfort through shifts in posture, gesturing, or moving away.

How you respond depends on *who* enters and uses your territory (a friend is less threatening than a stranger), *why* she or he enters or uses it (for instance, a "mistake" is less important than a "planned attack"), *what* territory is entered or used (you may care more about a territory over which you have exclusive rights, such as your bedroom, than about a territory in a public area, such as your seat in class), and *how* it is entered or used (an invasion is more threatening than a violation).

TIME

Social scientists use the term **chronemics** to describe the study of how humans use and structure time. The way we handle time can express both intentional and unintentional messages. Social psychologist Robert Levine (1988) describes several ways that time can communicate. For instance, in cultures like those of the United States, Canada, and northern Europe, which value time highly, waiting can be an indicator of status. "Important" people (whose time is supposedly more valuable than others) may be seen by appointment only, while it is acceptable to intrude without notice on lesser beings. To see how this rule operates, consider how natural it is for a boss to drop into a subordinate's office unannounced, while the employee would never intrude into the boss's office without an appointment. A related rule is that low-status people must never make more important people wait. It would be a serious mistake to show up late for a job interview, although the interviewer might keep you cooling your heels in the lobby. Important people are often whisked to the head of a restaurant or airport line, while presumably less exalted ones are forced to wait their turn.

The use of time depends greatly on culture. In some cultures, punctuality is critically important, while in others it is barely considered (Levine & Norenzayan, 1999). Punctual mainlanders often report welcoming the laid-back Hawaiian approach to time. One psychologist discovered the difference between North and South American attitudes when teaching at a university in Brazil (Levine, 1988). He found that some students arrived halfway through a 2-hour class and that most of them stayed put and kept asking questions when the class was scheduled to end. A half hour after the official end of the period, the professor finally closed off discussion, since there was no indication that the students intended to leave. This flexibility of time is quite different from what is common in most North American colleges and universities!

Even within a culture, rules of time vary. Sometimes the differences are geographic. In New York City, the party invitation may say 9:00 P.M., but nobody would think of showing up before 10:30 P.M. In Salt Lake City, guests are expected to show up on time, or perhaps even a bit early. Even within the same geographic area, different groups establish their own rules about the use of time. Consider your own experience. In school, some instructors begin and end class punctually, while others are more casual. With some people, you feel comfortable talking for hours in person or on the phone, while with others time seems precious and not to be "wasted."

Differences also may be associated with health. For example, children with attention-deficit/hyperactivity disorder (ADHD) have an impaired time perception when compared to children without ADHD (Meaux, 2002).

PHYSICAL ATTRACTIVENESS

The importance of beauty has been emphasized in the arts for centuries. More recently, social scientists have begun to measure the degree to which physical attractiveness affects interaction between people (Swami & Furnham, 2008). Recent findings, summarized by Knapp and Hall (2006), indicate that women who are perceived as attractive have more dates, receive higher grades in college, persuade males with greater ease, and receive lighter court sentences. Both men and women whom others view as attractive are rated as being more sensitive, kind, strong, sociable, and interesting than their less fortunate brothers and sisters. There is even some evidence that parents favor their good-looking children over their less attractive offspring (Harrell, 2005).

The influence of attractiveness begins early in life (Dion, 1973). For example, preschoolers were shown photographs of children their own age and asked to choose potential friends and enemies. The researchers found that children as young as age 3 agreed as to who was attractive ("cute") and unattractive ("homely"). Furthermore, they valued their attractive counterparts—both of the same and the opposite sex—more highly. Also, preschool children rated by their peers as pretty were most liked, and those identified as least pretty were least liked. Children who were interviewed rated good-looking children as having positive social characteristics ("He's friendly to other children") and unattractive children negatively ("He hits other children without reason").

Teachers also are affected by students' attractiveness. Vicki Ritts and her colleagues (1992) found that physically attractive students are usually judged more favorably—more intelligent, friendly, and popular. Even the parents of attractive students benefit from their children's good looks: They are judged by strangers as caring more about education than are parents of less attractive youngsters.

Fortunately, attractiveness is something we can control without having to call the plastic surgeon. If you aren't totally gorgeous or handsome, don't

FOCUS ON RESEARCH

Communication Enhances Physical Attractiveness

How can you make yourself more physically attractive to a romantic partner? Most of us think of ways to change our appearance, such as a new hairstyle or wardrobe and trips to the gym. Communication professor Kelly Albada and her associates have explored a different approach, which they have labeled Interaction Appearance Theory (IAT). IAT predicts that rewarding interactions with a partner will make him or her see you as more physically attractive.

Albada and her colleagues collected data to test IAT in three different ways: a series of interviews with people in romantic relationships, a survey of college students in newly formed dating relationships, and an analysis of diaries kept by romantic partners.

Time and again, the researchers found support for the notion that partners find one another more physically attractive as they communicate with one another in positive ways, such as offering compliments, expressing affection, and buying gifts. Here is how one man in the study recounts the shift in his appraisal of the woman he eventually married:

> Initially, I saw her as pretty average in physical attractiveness. . . . But after we dated and I fully appreciated how well we related to each other, I saw her as much more physically attractive. I actually saw her differently. Now, I can't see her as any less physically attractive.

IAT suggests that physical attractiveness is not a static property of an individual; instead, it is a perception that can be enhanced through good communication skills.

Albada, K. F., Knapp, M. L., & Theune, K. E. (2002). Interaction Appearance Theory: Changing perceptions of physical attractiveness through social interaction. *Communication Theory, 12,* 8–40.

despair: Evidence suggests that, as we get to know more about people and like them, we start to regard them as better looking (Bazil, 1999). (See the Focus on Research box on this page for further evidence of this phenomenon.) Moreover, we view others as beautiful or ugly not just on the basis of their "original equipment," but also on *how they use that equipment.* Posture, gestures, facial expressions, and other behaviors can increase the attractiveness of an otherwise unremarkable person. Finally, the way we dress can make a significant difference in the way others perceive us, as you'll now see.

CLOTHING

Besides protecting us from the elements, clothing is a means of nonverbal communication. One writer has suggested that clothing conveys at least 10 types of messages to others (Thourlby, 1978):

1. Economic level
2. Educational level

3. Trustworthiness
4. Social position
5. Level of sophistication
6. Economic background
7. Social background
8. Educational background
9. Level of success
10. Moral character

We do make assumptions about people based on their style of clothing. For example, the way people are dressed affects judgments of their credibility. In one experiment, college students judged victims of sexual harassment differently depending on their attire. Victims dressed in black were rated as less honest and more aggressive than those dressed in light colors (Vrij & Akehurst, 1999). Not surprisingly, the perception of a female actor's sexual intent increased when she wore more revealing clothes, although this effect was greater for men in the study (Koukounas & Letch, 2001). In another study, a man and a woman were stationed in a hallway so that anyone who wished to go by had to avoid them or pass between them. In one condition the conversationalists wore "formal daytime dress"; in the other, they wore "casual attire." Passersby behaved differently toward the couple, depending on the style of clothing: They responded positively to the well-dressed couple and showed more annoyance when the same people were casually dressed (Fortenberry et al., 1978). Similar results in other situations show the influence of clothing. For example, a table-tennis opponent wearing clothing specific to the sport is more intimidating than one wearing general sportswear (Greenlees et al., 2005).

Attire makes a difference in the classroom too. College students' perceptions of their graduate teaching associate's (GTA) expertise decreases as the GTA's attire becomes more casual. On the other hand, GTAs who dress casually are seen as more interesting, extroverted, and sociable than those who dress more formally (Morris et al., 1996; Roach, 1997). Dressing up may be more important for men than for women when it comes to perceptions of status. Observers rely more on women's nonverbal behavior as cues to their social position, whereas men are rated more on their attire (Mast & Hall, 2004).

Judgments based on what a person wears, like other perceptions, need to be made carefully. For example, while many Americans believe a *hijab*—a "veil" or "headscarf"—functions to oppress women, veiled women see their hijab as helping them define their Muslim identity, resist sexual objectification, and afford more respect (Droogsma, 2007).

PHYSICAL ENVIRONMENT

We conclude our look at nonverbal communication by examining how physical settings, architecture, and interior design affect communication. Begin by recalling the different homes you've visited lately. Were some of these homes more comfortable to be in than others? Certainly a lot of your feelings were shaped by the people you were with, but there are some houses in which it seems impossible to relax, no matter how friendly the hosts. We've spent what seemed like endless evenings in what Knapp and Hall (2006) call "unliving rooms," where the spotless ashtrays, furniture coverings, and plastic lamp covers send nonverbal messages telling us not to touch anything, not to put our feet up, and not to be comfortable. People who live in such houses probably wonder why nobody ever seems to relax and enjoy themselves at their parties. One thing is quite certain: They don't understand that the environment they have created can communicate discomfort to their guests.

The impressions that home designs communicate can be remarkably accurate. Edward Sadalla (1987) showed 99 students slides of the insides or outsides of 12 upper-middle-class homes and then asked them to infer the personality of the owners from their impressions. The students were especially accurate after glancing at interior photos. The decorating schemes communicated accurate information about the homeowners' intellectualism, politeness, maturity, optimism, tenseness, willingness to take adventures, family orientations, and reservedness. The home exteriors also gave viewers accurate perceptions of the owners' artistic interests, graciousness, privacy, and quietness.

Besides communicating information about the designer, an environment can also shape the kind of interaction that takes place in it. In one experiment, participants working in a "beautiful" room were more positive and energetic than those working in "average" or "ugly" spaces (Maslow & Mintz, 1956). Inner-city adults and children who have access to landscaped public spaces interact in ways that are much more prosocial than do those who have to interact in more barren environments (Taylor et al., 1998). Kuo and Sullivan (2001a, 2001b) found that public housing inner-city residents living in relatively barren buildings reported more mental fatigue, aggression, and violence than did their counterparts in buildings with nearby grass and trees.

Students see professors who occupy well-decorated offices as being more credible than those occupying less attractive work areas (Teven & Comadena, 1996). Physicians have shaped environments to improve the quality of interaction with their patients. According to environmental psychologist Robert Sommer (1969), simply removing a doctor's desk made patients feel almost five times more at ease during office visits. Sommer also found that redesigning a convalescent ward of a hospital greatly increased the interaction between patients. In the old design, seats were placed shoulder to shoulder around the edges of the ward. By grouping the chairs around small tables so that patients faced each other at a comfortable distance, the amount of conversations doubled.

Summary

Nonverbal communication consists of messages expressed by nonlinguistic means. Nonverbal communication is pervasive; in fact, nonverbal messages are always available as a source of information about others. Most nonverbal behavior suggests messages about relational attitudes and feelings, in contrast to verbal statements, which are better suited to expressing ideas. Messages that are communicated nonverbally are usually more ambiguous than verbal communication.

Nonverbal communication serves many functions. It can help in the creating and maintaining of relationships. Nonverbal communication also serves to regulate interaction and to influence others. Nonverbal communication can be used as a tool to enhance the success of deceptive verbal messages. Finally, we use nonverbal cues to manage our identity and impressions with others.

Nonverbal messages can be communicated in a variety of ways: Through the use of face and eyes, body movement, touch, voice, distance, territory, time, physical appearance, clothing, and environment. Culture plays a significant role in determining the rules and meanings for each of these factors.

Activities

1. Invitation to Insight

Demonstrate for yourself that it is impossible to avoid communicating nonverbally by trying *not* to communicate with a friend or family member. (You be the judge of whether to tell the other person about this experiment beforehand.) See how long it takes for your partner to inquire about what is going on and to report on what he or she thinks you might be thinking and feeling.

2. Critical Thinking Probe

Interview someone from a culture different from your own, and learn at least three ways in which nonverbal codes differ from the environment where you were raised. Together, develop a list of ways you could violate unstated but important rules about nonverbal behavior in your partner's culture in three of the following areas:

Eye contact
Posture
Gesture
Facial expression
Distance
Territory
Voice
Touch
Time
Clothing
Environmental design
Territory

Describe how failure to recognize different cultural codes could lead to misunderstandings, frustrations, and dissatisfaction. Discuss how awareness of cultural rules can be developed in an increasingly multicultural world.

3. Invitation to Insight

Using the videotape of a television program or film, identify examples of the following nonverbal functions:

Creating and maintaining relationships
Regulating interaction
Influencing others
Concealing or deceiving
Managing identity

If time allows, show these videotaped examples to your classmates.

4. Skill Builder

Sharpen your ability to distinguish between *observing* and *interpreting* non-verbal behaviors by following these directions:

Sit or stand opposite a partner at a comfortable distance. For a 1-minute period, report your observations of the other person's behavior by repeatedly completing the statement "Now I see (*nonverbal behavior*)." For example, you might report "Now I see you blinking your eyes . . . now I see you looking down at the floor . . . now I see you fidgeting with your hands. . . ." Notice that no matter what your partner does, you have an unending number of nonverbal behaviors to observe.

For a second 1-minute period, complete the sentence "Now I see (*nonverbal behavior*), and I think ______," filling in the blank with your interpretation of the other person's nonverbal behavior. For instance, you might say "Now I see you look away, and I think you're nervous about looking me in the eye . . . now I see you smiling and I think you're imagining that you agree with my interpretation. . . ." Notice that by clearly labeling your interpretation, you give the other person a chance to correct any mistaken hunches.

Repeat the first two steps, switching roles with your partner.

5. Invitation to Insight

How satisfied are you with the way your body looks? For each of the body parts below, mark your level of satisfaction as follows:

7 Extremely satisfied
6 Satisfied
5 Slightly satisfied
4 Neither satisfied nor unsatisfied
3 Slightly unsatisfied
2 Unsatisfied
1 Extremely unsatisfied

hair	overall body appearance
nose	mouth
eyes	chest/breasts
stomach	back
sex organs	teeth
hips	cheeks
arms	chin
forearms	wrists
elbows	fingers
thighs	hands
calves	buttocks
knees	weight
overall facial attractiveness	height

How does your feeling about a particular body part affect how you behave? How is your self-esteem affected by your physical appearance?

6. Invitation to Insight

Learn more about the nonverbal messages you send by interviewing someone who knows you well: a friend, family member, or coworker. Ask your interview participant to describe how he or she knows when you are feeling each of the following emotions, even though you may not announce your feelings verbally:

Anger or irritation
Boredom or indifference
Happiness
Sadness
Worry or anxiety

Which of these nonverbal behaviors do you display intentionally, and which are not conscious? Which functions do your nonverbal behaviors perform in the situations your partner described: creating/maintaining relationships, regulating interaction, influencing others, concealing/deceiving, and/or managing your identity?

7. Invitation to Insight

Explore your territoriality by listing the spaces you feel you "own," such as your parking space, parts of the place you live, and seats in a particular classroom. Describe how you feel when your territory is invaded and identify things you do to "mark" it.

8. Invitation to Insight

This activity requires you to observe how people use space in a particular setting and to note reactions to violations of spatial expectations. Select a supermarket, department store, college bookstore, or some other common setting in which people shop for things and then pay for them on a checkout line. Observe the interaction distances that seem usual between salesclerks and customers, between customers as they shop, and between customers in the checkout line.

a. What are the average distances between the people you observed?
b. How do people respond when one person comes too close to another or when one person touches another? How do people react to these violations of their space? How could they avoid violating each other's personal space?
c. Try to observe people from a culture other than your own in this store. Describe their use of spatial distance. If this is not possible in the store, think back to a foreign film or a film that contains interaction between North Americans and people of another culture, as well as people from that same culture.

CHAPTER 7

Listening: Understanding and Supporting Others

CHAPTER OUTLINE

After studying the material in this chapter . . .

YOU SHOULD UNDERSTAND:

1. The importance of listening.
2. The definition of listening.
3. The error of common myths which suggest that listening is easy.
4. The habits of people who listen ineffectively.
5. The components of the listening process.
6. The differences among the listening responses introduced in this chapter.
7. The advantages and disadvantages of various listening styles.

YOU SHOULD BE ABLE TO:

1. Identify the situations in which you listen mindfully and those when you listen mindlessly, and evaluate the appropriateness of each style.
2. Identify the circumstances in which you listen ineffectively, and the poor listening habits you use in these circumstances.
3. Identify the response styles you commonly use when listening to others.
4. Demonstrate a combination of listening styles you could use to respond effectively to another person.

KEY TERMS

- Advising (236)
- Ambushing (216)
- Analyzing (232)
- Attending (217)
- Closed questions (222)
- Counterfeit questions (223)
- Defensive listening (216)
- Empathizing (227)
- Evaluating (232)
- Filling in gaps (216)
- Hearing (210)
- Insulated listening (216)
- Listening (210)
- Listening fidelity (212)
- Mindful listening (211)
- Mindless listening (210)
- Open questions (222)
- Paraphrasing (224)
- Pseudolistening (216)
- Questioning (222)
- Remembering (219)
- Responding (219)
- Selective listening (216)
- Silent listening (221)
- Sincere questions (223)
- Stage hogging (216)
- Supporting (229)
- Understanding (218)

The grizzled army sergeant faced a roomful of new Signal Corps cadets about to begin their training as radio operators.

"The equipment is a snap to operate," he explained. "All you have to do to send a message is to push this button on the microphone, and your voice goes out to anyone who's tuned in. Go ahead . . . give it a try."

Each recruit picked up a microphone and began speaking. The sound of 30 amplified voices all transmitting at the same time created a loud, painful squeal.

"OK, soldiers," the sergeant announced. "You just learned the first principle of radio communication. Any fool can send a message. The only way communication works is if you're willing and able to receive one, too."

The sergeant's lesson is a good one for every communicator. Speaking is important, but without listening, a message might as well never be sent. In this chapter you will learn just how important listening is in interpersonal communication. You will learn about the many factors that make good listening difficult and find reasons for tackling those challenges. You will learn what really happens when listening takes place. Finally, you will read about a variety of listening responses that you can use to increase your own understanding, improve your relationships, and help others.

The Nature of Listening

When it comes to the subject of listening, plenty of people have advice on how to do it better, such as "close your mouth and open your ears." While such advice is a good start, simplistic prescriptions like these don't capture the complex nature of listening. We'll begin our exploration of this subject by describing the importance of listening in interpersonal communication.

THE IMPORTANCE OF LISTENING

How important is listening? If we use frequency as a measure, it ranks at the top of the list. Surveys (Barker et al., 1981; Emanuel et al., 2008) show that as much as 55 percent of college students' communication time is spent listening (see Figure 7.1). The business world yields similar numbers: Execu-

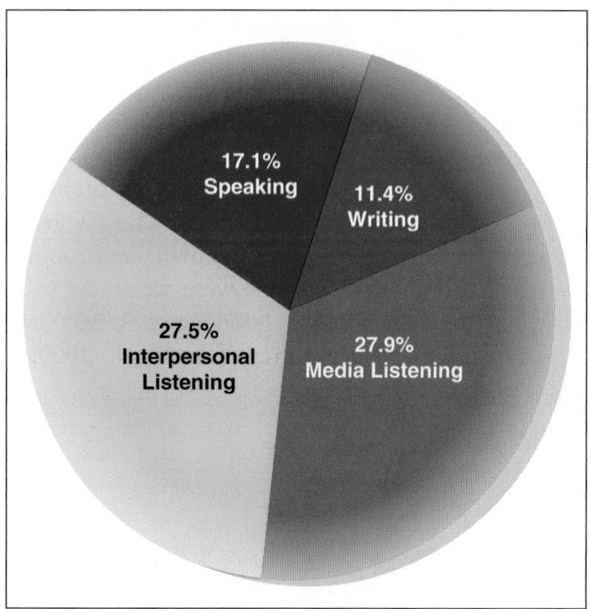

FIGURE 7.1 Time Devoted to Communication Activities

Emanuel, R., Adams, J., Baker, K., Daufin, E. K., Ellington, C., Fitts, E., Himsel, J., Holladay, L., & Okeowo, D. (2008). How college students spend their time communicating. *International Journal of Listening, 22,* 13–28.

tives spend approximately 60 percent of their communication time listening (Brown, 1982; Steil, 1996).

Besides being the most frequent form of communication, listening is arguably a more valued skill than speaking. Andrew Wolvin, Carolyn Coakley, and Carolyn Gwynn (1999; Wolvin & Coakley, 1991) summarize numerous studies that find listening to be the most important communication skill for entry-level workers, subordinates, supervisors, and managers on several dimensions: job and career success, productivity, upward mobility, communication training, and organizational effectiveness. When several hundred human resource executives were asked to identify skills of the ideal manager, the ability to listen effectively ranked at the top of the list (Winsor et al., 1997). In problem-solving groups, effective listeners are judged as having the most leadership skills (Johnson & Bechler, 1998). Senior executives, students, and employers, when asked what skills were most important on the job, identified listening more often than any other skill, including technical competence, computer knowledge, creativity, and administrative talent (Gabric & McFadden, 2001; Landrum & Harrold, 2003).

The business world is not the only setting in which listening is vital. When a group of adults was asked to rank various communication skills according to their importance, listening topped the family/social list as well as the career list (Wolvin, 1984). In committed relationships, listening to personal information in everyday conversations is considered an important ingredient of satisfaction (Prager & Buhrmester, 1998). John Gentile (2004) argues that listening to one another's personal narratives (see Chapter 4) is fundamental to our humanity and sense of well-being.

Unfortunately, there is no connection between how well most communicators *think* they listen and how competent they really are in their ability to understand others (Carrell & Willmington, 1996). A study by Judi Brownell (1990) illustrates this point vividly. A group of managers in her study were asked to rate their listening skills. Astonishingly, not one of the managers described himself or herself as a "poor" or "very poor" listener, while 94 percent rated themselves as "good" or "very good." The favorable self-ratings contrasted sharply with the perceptions of the managers' subordinates, many of whom said their bosses' listening skills were weak. As you'll soon read, some poor listening is inevitable. The good news is that listening can be improved through instruction and training (Lane et al., 2000; McNaughton et al., 2008).

LISTENING DEFINED

So far we have used the term "listening" as if it needs no explanation. Actually, there's more to this concept than meets the eye (or should we say, "the ear"). We will define **listening**—at least the interpersonal type—as the process of making sense of others' spoken messages. As you'll soon see, this definition excludes some behavior that most people would consider listening.

Hearing versus Listening Listening and hearing aren't identical. **Hearing** is the process in which sound waves strike the eardrum and cause vibrations that are transmitted to the brain. *Listening* occurs when the brain reconstructs these electrochemical impulses into a representation of the original sound and then gives them meaning (Fernald, 2001; Robinshaw, 2007). Barring illness, injury, or cotton plugs, you can't stop hearing. Your ears will pick up sound waves and transmit them to your brain whether you want them to or not.

"You're not listening to what you're hearing."

Listening, however, isn't automatic. Many times we hear but do not listen. Sometimes we automatically and unconsciously block out irritating sounds, such as a neighbor's lawn mower or the roar of nearby traffic. We also stop listening when we find a subject unimportant or uninteresting. Boring stories, television commercials, and nagging complaints are common examples of messages we may tune out.

Mindless Listening When we move beyond hearing and start to listen, researchers note that we process information in two very different ways (Chaiken & Trope, 1999; Todorov et al., 2002). Ellen Langer (1990) uses the terms "mindless" and "mindful" to describe these different ways of listening. **Mindless listening** occurs when we react to others' messages automatically and routinely, without much mental investment. Words like "superficial" and "cursory" describe mindless listening better than terms like "ponder" and "contemplate."

While the term *mindless* may sound negative, this sort of low-level information processing is a potentially valuable type of communication, since it frees us to focus our minds on messages that require our careful attention (Burgoon et al., 2000). Given the number of messages to which we're exposed, it's impractical to listen carefully and thoughtfully 100 percent of the time. It's unrealistic to devote your attention to long-winded stories, idle chatter, or remarks you've heard many times before. The only realistic way to manage the onslaught of messages is to be "lazy" toward many of them (Griffin, 2006). In situations like these, we forgo careful analysis and fall back on the schemas—and sometimes the stereotypes—described in Chapter 4 to make sense of a message. If you stop right now and recall the messages you have heard today, it's likely that you processed most of them mindlessly.

Mindful Listening By contrast, **mindful listening** involves giving careful and thoughtful attention and responses to the messages we receive. You tend to listen mindfully when a message is important to you, and also when someone you care about is speaking about a matter that is important to him or her. Think of how your ears perk up when someone starts talking about your favorite hobby, or how you tune in carefully when a close friend tells you about the loss of a loved one. In situations like these, you want to give the message-sender your complete and undivided attention.

Sometimes we respond mindlessly to information that deserves—and even demands—our mindful attention. Ellen Langer's determination to study mindfulness began when her grandmother complained about headaches coming from a "snake crawling around" beneath her skull. The doctors quickly diagnosed the problem as senility—after all, they reasoned, senility comes with old age and makes people talk nonsense. In fact, the grandmother had a

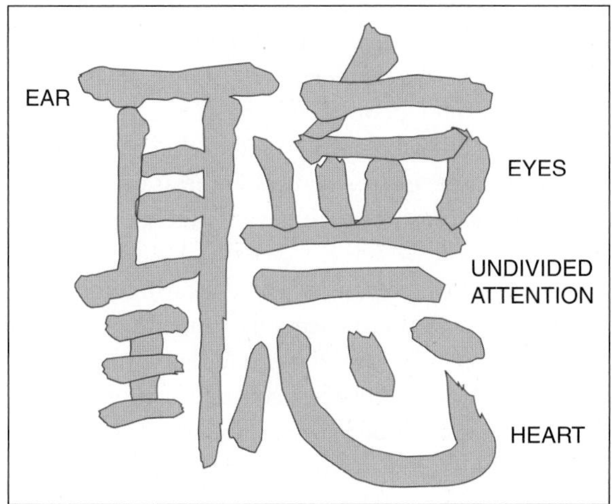

FIGURE 7.2 The Chinese characters that make up the verb "to listen" tell us something significant about this skill.

brain tumor that eventually killed her. The event made a deep impression on Langer (1990, p. 3):

> For years afterward I kept thinking about the doctors' reactions to my grandmother's complaints, and about our reactions to the doctors. They went through the motions of diagnosis, but were not open to what they were hearing. Mindsets about senility interfered. We did not question the doctors; mindsets about experts interfered.

Most of our daily decisions about whether to listen mindfully don't have life-and-death consequences, but the point should be clear: There are times when we need to consciously and carefully listen to what others are telling us. That kind of mindful listening will be the focus of the remainder of this chapter.

REASONS FOR LISTENING

There are several different reasons to listen, and each one requires a different set of attitudes and skills.

To Understand The most obvious reason for listening is *to understand and retain information*. You need to comprehend information from a lecture to earn the grade you're seeking. You have to understand your boss's feedback to succeed on the job. You want to grasp the advice from your coach so that you can do better in your favorite sport. Communication researchers use the term **listening fidelity** to describe the degree of congruence between what a listener understands and what the message sender was attempting to communicate (Fitch-Hauser et al., 2007; Powers & Bodie, 2003).

Even people who are highly motivated to listen carefully often lack the skill to understand others' messages. For example, more than half of medical patients fail to grasp their doctors' instructions about medication and other treatments. Likewise, physicians often fail to understand their patients' concerns (Christensen, 2004; Scholz, 2005).

When the issue isn't a matter of personal concern, the lack of desire to understand others can be even stronger. Carl Trosset (1998) presented about 200 college students with a list of sensitive topics, such as "whether race is an important difference between people." Then the students were asked whether they thought it was possible to have an open exchange of ideas on these topics. The majority of students expressed little interest in wanting to understand others' views on these issues; they merely wanted to persuade others to see the world as they did.

Of course there's nothing wrong with advocating your strongly held beliefs, but one would assume that an equally valuable goal would be to learn something new. Yet only 5 of the 200 students in the study said they approached their conversations with what communication theorists Sonja Foss and Cindy Griffin (1995; Foss & Foss, 2003) have called an *invitational* attitude: to learn more about perspectives other than their own.

To Evaluate A second type of listening involves *evaluating the quality of messages*. Not all evaluations are equal. Most people judge messages mindlessly,

relying on their pre-existing beliefs and a superficial analysis of the issue at hand (O'Keefe, 2002). If you listen to most people arguing about politics or religion, you're likely to recognize this knee-jerk type of responding.

A more justified and mindful evaluation involves several elements. First, it requires the *motivation* to expend the considerable energy required to think through an issue carefully. Second, mindful evaluation requires the *ability* to analyze the other person's comments. Finally, mindful evaluation requires a willingness to be *impartial* and listen open-mindedly instead of viewing the other person's comments through the lenses of our pre-existing attitudes and beliefs. Try to recall the last time you dedicated yourself to listening thoughtfully and sincerely to another's position—or the last time someone did you this favor—and you'll appreciate how rare and valuable this approach can be.

To Build and Maintain Relationships A third reason for listening is especially relevant for interpersonal communication: *building and maintaining relationships*. Research shows that effective listening "builds better relationships, and poor listening weakens relationships, or prevents relationships from developing at all" (Kaufmann, 1993, p. 4). In one survey, marital counselors identified "failing to take the other's perspective when listening" as one of the most frequent communication problems in the couples with which they work (Vangelisti, 1994; see also Long et al., 1999). Roger McIntire (1999) argues that listening well is the first and most important habit parents need in order to build a good relationship with their children. Listening is just as important in commercial settings. For example, customers shopping for a new car are most disposed to do business with salespeople who seem to be listening thoughtfully (Ramsey & Sohi, 1997), and Conor McGrath (2006) found that good lobbyists, like good salespeople, possess well-developed listening skills.

To Help Others A fourth type of listening involves *helping others,* another important interpersonal skill. Listening is an essential tool professionals use to help their clients. Doctors, lawyers, teachers, managers, supervisors, clergy, and therapists must listen carefully so they can offer sound and appropriate assistance. Professionals aren't the only people we call on for help; we also seek the counsel of friends and family. When others listen to us with understanding and concern, we can gain different and useful perspectives for solving problems (Bender & Messner, 2003; Welch, 2003).

The Challenge of Listening

By now you can see that mindful listening is important. Even with the best intentions, though, listening carefully is a challenge. Now we'll take a look at some of the obstacles we need to overcome when we want to listen carefully.

LISTENING IS NOT EASY

There are numerous obstacles that must be hurdled to become an effective listener, and doing so sometimes involves time, concentration, and work. Researchers have identified several barriers to listening (Golen, 1990; Hulbert, 1989). A look at some of these barriers will show why good listening is so tough.

Information Overload The sheer amount of information most of us encounter every day makes it impossible to listen carefully to everything we hear. We're bombarded with messages not only in face-to-face interaction, but also from the Internet, the media, cell phones, and various other sources (Arsenault, 2007). Given this barrage of information, it's virtually impossible for us to keep our attention totally focused for so long. As a result, we often choose—understandably and sometimes wisely—to listen mindlessly rather than mindfully.

"I'm not convinced that's the best strategy. Then again, I wasn't listening."

Personal Concerns A second reason we don't always listen carefully is that we're often wrapped up in personal concerns of more immediate importance to us than the messages others are sending. It's hard to pay attention to someone else when you're anticipating an upcoming test or thinking about the wonderful time you had last night. When we still feel that we have to "listen" politely to others, listening becomes mindless at best, and often a polite charade.

Rapid Thought Careful listening is also difficult because our minds are so active. Although we're capable of understanding speech at rates up to 600 words per minute (Drullman & Smoorenburg, 1997; Versfeld & Dreschler, 2002), the average person speaks much more slowly—between 100 and 140 words per minute. Therefore, we have a lot of "spare time" to spend with our minds while someone is talking. The temptation is to use this time in ways that don't relate to the speaker's ideas, such as thinking about personal interests, daydreaming, planning a rebuttal, and so on. The trick is to use this spare time to understand the speaker's ideas better, rather than let your attention wander.

Noise Finally, our physical and mental worlds often present distractions that make it hard for us to pay attention. The sounds of other conversations, traffic, and music, as well as the kinds of psychological noise discussed in Chapter 1, all interfere with our ability to listen well. For example, research has supported the commonsense suspicion that background noise, such as from a television set, reduces the ability of a communicator to understand messages (Armstrong et al., 1991; Jones et al., 2007). Also, fatigue or other forms of discomfort can distract us from paying attention to a speaker's remarks. For instance, consider how the efficiency of your listening decreases when you are seated in a crowded, hot, stuffy room full of moving people and other noises. In such circumstances, even the best intentions aren't enough to ensure cogent understanding.

ALL LISTENERS DO NOT RECEIVE THE SAME MESSAGE

When two or more people are listening to a speaker, we tend to assume that each hears and understands the same message. In fact, such uniform comprehension isn't the case. Recall our discussion of perception in Chapter 4, where we pointed out the many factors that cause each of us to perceive an event in a different manner. Physiological factors, social roles, cultural background, personal interests, and needs all shape and distort the raw data we hear into very different messages. Because every person interprets data uniquely, we have to accept the fact that we can never completely understand another person. As John Stewart (1983) and Benjamin Broome (1991) note, even the most active, empathic listener cannot actually "lay aside" the self and truly "walk in another's shoes." We bring our personal perspective and experiences with us into every interaction, and they affect the way we make sense of others' words and actions. It's no wonder that dyads typically achieve only 25 to 50 percent accuracy in interpreting or representing each other's behavior (Spitzberg, 1994). Our listening is always colored and limited by our unique, and fairly consistent, view of the world (Robins et al., 2004).

POOR LISTENING HABITS

Most people possess one or more bad habits that keep them from understanding others' messages. As you read about the following poor listening behaviors, see which ones describe you.

Pseudolistening is only an imitation of the real thing. Pseudolisteners give the appearance of being attentive: They look you in the eye, and they may even nod and smile, but their minds are in another world.

When **stage hogging**, people are interested only in expressing their ideas and don't care about what anyone else has to say. These individuals allow you to speak from time to time, but only so they can catch their breath and use your remarks as a basis for their own babbling. Research on "conversational narcissism" (Vangelisti et al., 1990) shows that self-centered stage hogs ask questions, but not other-oriented, information-seeking ones. Rather, these conversational narcissists ask counterfeit questions to demonstrate their superiority and hold the floor (we'll talk more about counterfeit versus sincere questions later in this chapter).

The Boss From Hell: *The Devil Wears Prada*

Miranda Priestly (Meryl Streep) is every employee's nightmare. She's a self-centered, domineering, hard-driven boss who treats the people who work for her like slaves.

Priestly exemplifies every poor listening habit. She attends only to things that matter to her ("The details of your incompetence do not interest me") and does so insensitively ("Bore someone else with your questions"). Pseudolistening, defensive listening, and stage hogging? She does them all. She also interrupts, rolls her eyes when she doesn't like what she's hearing, and walks out on her subordinates in mid-conversation.

Priestly may be a successful businesswoman, but she fails on many other counts—especially as a listener.

With selective listening, people respond only to the parts of a speaker's remarks that interest them, rejecting everything else. Unless and until you bring up one of these pet subjects, you might as well be talking to a tree.

People **filling in gaps** like to think that what they remember makes a whole story. These people manufacture information so that when they retell what they listened to, they can give the impression they "got it all." The message that's left is actually a distorted (not merely incomplete) version of the real message.

The habit of **insulated listening** is almost the opposite of selective listening. Instead of looking for something, these listeners avoid it. Whenever a topic arises they'd rather not deal with, insulated listeners simply fail to hear or acknowledge it.

People who engage in **defensive listening** take innocent comments as personal attacks. It's fair to assume that many defensive listeners are suffering from shaky self-images, and they avoid facing this by projecting their own insecurities onto others.

A person who engages in **ambushing** will listen carefully to you, but only because he or she is collecting information that will be used to attack what you have to say. Needless to say, using this kind of strategy will justifiably initiate defensiveness from the other person.

Components of Listening

By now, you can begin to see that there is more to listening than sitting quietly while another person speaks. In truth, listening—especially *mindful* listening—

consists of five separate elements: hearing, attending, understanding, remembering, and responding.

> **DARK SIDE OF COMMUNICATION**
>
> **Hearing Loss and Relational Stress**
>
> Over 22 million Americans have some form of impaired hearing. While hearing loss can be challenging for those who experience it, recent research suggests it can also affect their relationships. One survey explored the feelings of adults who have spouses with hearing loss. Nearly two thirds of the respondents said they feel annoyed when their partner can't hear them clearly. Almost a quarter said that beyond just being annoyed, they felt ignored, hurt, or sad. Many of the respondents believe their spouses are in denial about their condition, which makes the problem even more frustrating.
>
> Once a hearing problem has been diagnosed, it's often possible to treat it. If you suspect that you or someone you know might have a hearing loss, it's wise to have a physician or audiologist perform an examination. The results may lead to more satisfying relationships.
>
> Listen to this: Hearing problems can stress relationships. (2008). Available at: http://www.energizer.com/livehealthy/#listentothis
>
> Shafer, D. N. (2007). Hearing loss hinders relationships. *ASHA Leader, 12*(9), 5–7.

HEARING

As we have already discussed, hearing is the physiological aspect of listening. It is the nonselective process of sound waves impinging on the ear. Hearing is obviously vital to listening because it's the starting point of the process. It can be diminished by physiological disorders, background noise, or auditory fatigue, which is a temporary loss of hearing caused by continuous exposure to the same tone or loudness. People who spend an evening at a rock concert or hearing fireworks may experience auditory fatigue and, if they are exposed often enough, permanent hearing loss (5.2 Million Young Americans, 2001). It's wise to heed the warnings of the Dark Side box on this page and protect your hearing—for your own sake as well as for the sake of your relationships.

ATTENDING

While hearing is a physiological process, **attending** is a psychological one, and it is part of the process of selection that we described in Chapter 4. As discussed earlier in this chapter, it's especially hard to focus on messages—even important ones—when we are bombarded by information. Face-to-face messages come from friends, family, work, and school. Personal media—text messages, phone calls, e-mails, and instant messages—demand your attention. Along with these personal channels, we are awash in messages from the mass media. This deluge of communication has made the challenge of attending tougher than at any time in human history (Hansen, 2007).

We would go crazy if we attended to every thing we hear, so we filter out some messages and focus on others. Not surprisingly, we attend most carefully to messages when there's a payoff for doing

"If you can hear me, give me a sign."

so (Burleson, 2007; Smeltzer & Watson, 1984). If you're planning to see a movie, you'll listen to a friend's description more carefully than you otherwise would. And when you want to get better acquainted with others, you'll pay careful attention to almost anything they say, in hopes of improving the relationship. If you care about another person's problems, you're more likely to attend thoughtfully to his or her laments.

As you read in Chapter 6, skillful communicators attend to both speakers' words and their nonverbal cues. If you asked a friend "How's it going?" you can easily imagine two ways he or she could answer "Fine": One set of nonverbal behaviors (big smile, enthusiastic vocal tone) would reinforce the verbal statement, while another (downcast eyes, slumped posture, dejected vocal tone) would contradict it. Some people are simply inattentive to nonverbal cues, but others suffer from a physiological syndrome called nonverbal learning disorder (Palombo, 2006). Due to a processing deficit in the right hemisphere of the brain, people with this disorder have trouble making sense of many nonverbal cues. Whether due to insensitivity or physiology, it's easy to see how failing to attend to nonverbal cues is a listening deficit.

Surprisingly, attending doesn't just help the listener: It also benefits the message-sender. Participants in one study viewed brief movie segments and then described them to listeners who varied in their degree of attentiveness to the speaker. Later on, the researchers tested the speakers' long-term recall of details from the movie segment. Those who had recounted the movie to attentive listeners remembered more details of the movie (Pasupathi et al., 1998).

One way to attend better to important messages is to screen out distractions. Some companies now hold "laptopless" meetings, prohibiting computer use that might distract participants (Guynn, 2008). You may be familiar with other public forums—including some classrooms—where cell phone interruptions are not welcome (Campbell, 2006). While new technology has greatly increased our ability to communicate with others, it's important to be mindful of when it intrudes on attentive listening.

UNDERSTANDING

Paying attention—even close attention—to a message doesn't guarantee that you'll understand what's being said. **Understanding** is composed of several elements. First, of course, you must be aware of the syntactic and grammatical rules of the language. But beyond this basic ability, understanding a message depends on several other factors. One is your knowledge about the source of the message. Such background will help you decide, for example, whether a friend's insulting remark is a joke or a serious attack. The context of a message also helps you understand what's being said. A yawning response to your comments would probably have a different meaning at midnight than at noon.

Finally, understanding often depends on the listener's mental abilities. Generally speaking, the ability to make sense of messages is closely related to the listener's intelligence (Bostrom & Waldhart, 1980). As early as 1948, Ralph Nichols related successful understanding to factors that included verbal ability, intelligence, and motivation. Timothy Plax and Lawrence Rosenfeld (1979) found that the personality traits of listeners also affect their ability to understand messages. People good at interpreting disorganized messages were especially secure, sensitive to others, and willing to understand the speaker. Listeners successful at understanding disorganized speech proved to be more insightful and versatile in their thinking.

REMEMBERING

The ability to recall information once we've understood it, or **remembering**, is a function of several factors: the number of times the information is heard or repeated, how much information there is to store in the brain, and whether the information may be "rehearsed" or not.

Early research on listening revealed that people remember only about half of what they hear immediately after hearing it, even when they listen mindfully (Barker, 1971). Within 2 months, 50 percent of the originally remembered portion is forgotten, bringing what we remember down to about 25 percent of the original message. However, this loss doesn't take 2 months: People start forgetting immediately (within 8 hours, the 50 percent remembered drops to about 35 percent). Of course, these amounts vary from person to person and depend on the importance of the information being recalled (Cowan & AuBuchon, 2008).

Whatever the particular amounts we remember may be, given the abundance of information we process every day—from teachers, friends, radio, television, and other sources—the residual message (what we remember) is a small fraction of what we hear.

RESPONDING

All the steps we have discussed so far—hearing, attending, understanding, and remembering—are internal activities. A final part of the listening process involves **responding** to a message—giving observable feedback to the speaker (Bostrom, 1996; Cooper et al., 1997). One study of 195 critical incidents in banking and medical settings showed that a major difference between effective and ineffective listening was the kind of feedback offered (Lewis & Reinsch, 1988). Good listeners showed that they were attentive by nonverbal behaviors such as keeping eye contact and reacting with appropriate facial expressions. Their verbal behavior—for example, answering questions and exchanging ideas—also demonstrated their attention. It's easy to imagine how other responses would signal less effective listening. A slumped posture, bored expression, and yawning send a clear message that you are not tuned in to the speaker.

Adding responsiveness to our listening model demonstrates the fact we discussed in Chapter 1, that communication is transactional in nature. Listening isn't just a passive activity. As listeners, we are active participants in a communication transaction. At the same time that we receive messages, we also send them.

Types of Listening Responses

Of the five components of listening described in the preceding section, it's responding that lets us know if others are truly tuned in to what we're saying. Think for a moment of someone you consider a good listener. Why did you choose that person? It's probably because of the way she or he behaves while you are speaking: making eye contact and nodding when you're talking, staying attentive while you're telling an important story, reacting with an exclamation when you say something startling, expressing empathy and support when you're hurting, and offering another perspective or advice when you ask for it (Bippus, 2001). As Figure 7.3 illustrates, listening responses like these range from reflective feedback that invites the speaker to talk without concern of evaluation, to more directive responses that evaluate the speaker's messages. We'll spend the remainder of the chapter looking at each of these response styles in detail.

SILENT LISTENING

There are times when the best response is to say nothing. This is certainly true when you don't want to encourage a speaker to keep talking. For instance, recall times when a boss or instructor droned on and on when you needed to leave for an appointment, or instances when a friend retold the story of a love affair gone bad for what seemed like the tenth time. In situations like these, a verbal response would only encourage the speaker to continue—precisely the opposite reaction you would be seeking. The best response in these cases may

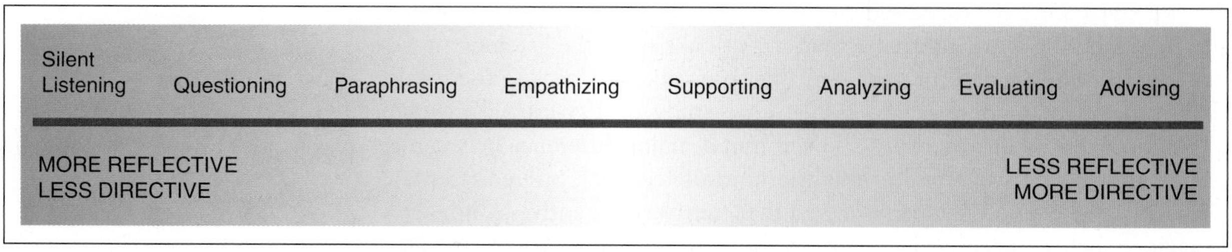

Silent Listening	Questioning	Paraphrasing	Empathizing	Supporting	Analyzing	Evaluating	Advising

MORE REFLECTIVE / LESS DIRECTIVE ⟶ LESS REFLECTIVE / MORE DIRECTIVE

FIGURE 7.3 Types of Listening Responses

be **silent listening**—staying attentive and nonverbally responsive without offering any verbal feedback.

Silent listening isn't just an avoidance strategy. It also can be the right approach when you are open to the other person's ideas but your interjections wouldn't be appropriate. If you are part of a large audience hearing a lecture, asking questions and offering comments would probably be disruptive. On a more personal level, when a friend tells you a joke, butting in to ask for clarification ("There was a priest, a rabbi, and a *what*?") would probably spoil your friend's rhythm.

There are even times when silent listening can help others solve their problems. Sonia Johnson (1987) describes a powerful activity she calls "hearing into being." The process is simple: In brainstorming sessions, each participant has a half hour of uninterrupted floor time. "When we are free to talk without threat of interruption, evaluation, and the pressure of time," notes Johnson, "we move quickly past known territory out into the frontiers of our thought" (p. 132). Johnson, who uses the technique in feminist seminars, reports that some women burst into tears when they first experience "hearing into being" because they are not used to being listened to so seriously and completely. Ask yourself: When was the last time you talked, uninterrupted, to an attentive partner for more than a few minutes? How would you like the chance to develop your ideas without pausing for another's comments? Silent listening is a response style that many of us could profit from using—and receiving—more often.

FOCUS ON RESEARCH

Reflective or Directive: The Value of Different Styles

research

Figure 7.3 (page 220) shows that some listening styles (such as paraphrasing and empathizing) are more reflective, while others (such as advising and evaluating) are more directive. This might raise the question: Which approach is better? The answer, according to one study, is that both are important—and that they work well in combination.

Raymond Young and Carl Cates surveyed first-year students in a college orientation course about the listening abilities of their peer mentors. More specifically, the researchers asked the students to assess their mentors' reflective (or "emotional") and directive listening styles and how well those approaches helped the students fit in at their university.

Not surprisingly, the students said they liked and had greater closeness with mentors who possessed strong reflective listening skills. At the same time, they appreciated helpful direction and advice. The results showed that the ideal mentor used both reflective and directive listening responses and that both styles were vital for helping socialize the new students.

As you read through the remainder of this chapter, keep in mind that each type of listening response has value and that a competent communicator knows when, where, and how to use them all.

Young, R. W., & Cates, C. M. (2004). Emotional and directive listening in peer mentoring. *International Journal of Listening, 18*, 21–33.

QUESTIONING

Regarded as "the most popular piece of language" (Goodman & Esterly, 1990), **questioning** occurs when the listener asks the speaker for additional information. There are several reasons to ask sincere, nondirective questions:

- *To clarify meanings.* By now you know that people who share words do not always share meanings. Good listeners don't assume they know what their partners mean; they ask for clarification with questions such as these: "What did you mean when you said he had been 'unfair' to you?" "You said she's 'religious'—how do you define that term?" "You said you were going 'fast'—could you be more specific?" Of course, be sure to use an appropriate tone of voice when asking such questions, or else they might sound like an inquisition (Tracy, 2002).

- *To learn about others' thoughts, feelings, and wants.* A caring listener may want to inquire about more than just "the facts." Opinions, emotions, needs, and even hopes are buried inside many messages; with sensitivity, a sincere question can draw these out. "What do you think about the new plan?" "How did you feel when you heard the news?" and "Were you hoping for something different?" are examples of such probes. When inquiring about personal information, it is usually best to ask **open questions** that allow a variety of extended responses rather than **closed questions** that only allow a limited range of answers. For instance, "How did you feel?" is an open question that allows a variety of responses, while "Did you feel angry?" is a closed question that requires only a yes or no answer (and may direct respondents toward feelings they weren't experiencing).

- *To encourage elaboration.* People are sometimes hesitant to talk about themselves, or perhaps they aren't sure if others are interested. Remarks such as "Tell me more about that," "Try me again—I'm not sure I understand," and "Keep going—I'm following you" convey concern and involvement. Notice that none of these examples ends with a question mark. Unlike the television show *Jeopardy,* questioning responses need not be phrased in the form of a question. We can encourage elaboration simply by acknowledging that we are listening.

- *To encourage discovery.* People in the helping professions—clergy, counselors, therapists, and so on—often ask questions to prod their clients into discovering solutions for their problems (Watts et al., 2005). "Playing counselor" can be a dangerous game, but there are times when you can use questions to encourage others to explore their thoughts and feelings. "So, what do you see as your options?" may prompt an employee to come up with creative problem-solving alternatives. "What would be your ideal solution?" might help a friend get in touch with various wants and needs. Most importantly, encouraging discovery rather than dispensing advice indicates you have faith in others' ability to think for themselves. This may be the most important message that you can communicate as an effective listener.

- *To gather more facts and details.* Just because your conversational partner tells you something doesn't mean you understand the whole story. As long as your questions aren't intrusive (and you'll need to monitor others' nonverbal behavior to determine this), people often appreciate listeners who want to learn more. Questions such as "What did you do then?" and "What did she say after that?" can help a listener understand the big picture.

Not all questions are genuine requests for information. Whereas **sincere questions** are aimed at understanding others, **counterfeit questions** are really disguised attempts to send a message, not receive one. As such, they really fit better at the "more directive" end of the listening response continuum pictured in Figure 7.3 on page 220. It's also likely that they'll lead to a defensive communication climate, as discussed in Chapter 10.

Counterfeit questions come in several varieties:

- *Questions that trap the speaker.* When your friend says, "You didn't like that movie, did you?" you're being backed into a corner. It's clear that your friend disapproves, so the question leaves you with two choices: You can disagree and defend your position, or you can devalue your reaction by lying or equivocating—"I guess it wasn't terrific." Consider how much easier it would be to respond to the sincere question, "What did you think of the movie?"

  Adding a tag question such as "Did you?" or "Isn't that right?" to the end of a question can be a tip-off that the asker is looking for agreement, not information. While some listeners use these tag endings to confirm and facilitate understanding (Coates, 1986), our concern here is when tags are used to coerce agreement: "You said you'd call at five o'clock, but you forgot, didn't you?" Similarly, questions that begin with "Don't you" (such as "Don't you think she would make a good boss?") direct others toward a desired response. As a simple solution, changing "Don't you?" to "Do you?" makes the question less leading.

  Leading questions not only signal what the desired answer is, they also affect memory, especially in children. David Bjorklund and his colleagues (2000) showed children and adults a video of a theft and then interviewed them several days later, using both leading and neutral questions. While the adults were unaffected by the type of question asked, the children who were asked leading questions had less accurate recall of the video than those who were asked free recall questions.

- *Questions that make statements.* "Are you *finally* off the phone?" is more of a statement than a question—a fact unlikely to be lost on the targeted person. Emphasizing certain words also can turn a question into a statement: "You lent money to *Tony?*" We also use questions to offer advice. The person who asks, "Are you going to stand up to him and give him what he deserves?" has clearly stated an opinion about what should be done.

- *Questions that carry hidden agendas.* "Are you busy Friday night?" is a dangerous question to answer. If you say "No," thinking the person has something fun in mind, you won't like hearing "Good, because I need some help moving my piano." Obviously, such questions are not designed to enhance understanding; they are setups for the proposal that follows. Other examples include "Will you do me a favor?" and "If I tell you what happened, will you promise not to get mad?" Because they are strategic rather than spontaneous, these questions are likely to provoke defensiveness (Gibb, 1961). Wise communicators answer questions that mask hidden agendas cautiously with responses such as "It depends" or "Let me hear what you have in mind before I answer."

- *Questions that seek "correct" answers.* Most of us have been victims of question-askers who only want to hear a particular response. "Which shoes do you think I should wear?" can be a sincere question—unless the asker has a predetermined preference. When this happens, the asker isn't interested in listening to contrary opinions, and "incorrect" responses get shot down. Some of these questions may venture into delicate territory. "Honey, do you think I'm overweight?" is usually a request for a "correct" answer—and the listener must have a fair amount of discretion and good judgment to determine an appropriate response.
- *Questions based on unchecked assumptions.* "Why aren't you listening to me?" assumes the other person isn't paying attention. "What's the matter?" assumes that something is wrong. As Chapter 4 explained, perception checking is a much better way of confirming assumptions. As you recall, a perception check offers a description of behavior and interpretations, followed by a sincere request for clarification: "When you kept looking over at the television, I thought you weren't listening to me, but maybe I was wrong. Were you paying attention?"

No question is inherently sincere or counterfeit since the meaning and intent of any statement is shaped by its context. Moreover, a slight change in tone of voice or facial expression can turn a sincere question into a counterfeit one, and vice versa. Nonetheless, the types of questions in the preceding list are usually closer to statements than requests for information.

It's also worth noting that counterfeit questions aren't all bad: They can be powerful tools for making a point. Lawyers use them to get confessions in the courtroom (Cotterill, 2004), and journalists ask them to uncover concealed information. Our point is that they usually get in the way of effective listening and relationship building—after all, most people don't like feeling trapped or "grilled" in a conversation.

PARAPHRASING

Paraphrasing is feedback that restates, in your own words, the message you thought the speaker sent. You may wonder, "Why would I want to restate what's already been said?" Consider this simple exchange:

"Let's make plans to get together next weekend."
"So you want to chat next week to make plans for Saturday?"

"No, what I meant is that we should check our calendars now to see if we're free to go to the game on Sunday."

By paraphrasing, the listener learned that the speaker wanted to make plans now, not later—and that "weekend" meant Sunday, not Saturday. Note that the listener rephrased rather than repeated the message. In effective paraphrasing you restate what you think the speaker has said in your own words as a way of checking the meaning you've assigned to the message. It's important that you paraphrase, not "parrot-phrase." If you simply repeat the speaker's comments verbatim, you'll sound foolish or hard-of-hearing—and just as important, you still might misunderstand what's been said.

Types of Paraphrasing Statements Restating another person's message in a way that sounds natural can sometimes be a difficult skill to master. Here are three approaches to get you started:

1. Change the speaker's wording.

   Speaker: "Bilingual education is just another failed idea of bleeding-heart liberals."
   Paraphrase: "Let me see if I've got this right. You're mad because you think bilingual ed sounds good, but it doesn't work?"

2. Offer an example of what you think the speaker is talking about.
   When the speaker makes an abstract statement, you may suggest a specific example or two to see if your understanding is accurate.

   Speaker: "Lee is such a jerk. I can't believe the way he acted last night."
   Paraphrase: "You think those jokes were pretty offensive, huh?"

3. Reflect the underlying theme of the speaker's remarks.
   When you want to summarize the theme that seems to have run through another person's conversation, a complete or partial perception check is appropriate:

   Paraphrase: You keep reminding me to be careful. Sounds like you're worried that something might happen to me. Am I right?"

There are several reasons why paraphrasing assists listening. First, as the preceding examples illustrate, paraphrasing allows you to find out if the message received is the message the sender intended. Second, paraphrasing often draws out further information from the speaker, much like questioning. (In fact, a good paraphrase often ends with a question such as "Is that what you meant?") Third, paraphrasing is an ideal way to take the heat out of intense discussions. When conversations begin to boil, it is often because the people involved believe they aren't being heard. Rather than escalating the conflict, try paraphrasing what the other person says: "OK, let me be sure I understand you. It sounds like you're concerned about . . ." Paraphrasing usually short-circuits a defensive spiral because it assures the other person of your involvement and concern. When you take the time to restate and clarify a speaker's message, your commitment to mindful listening is hard to deny.

There are two levels at which you can paraphrase messages. The first involves feedback of factual information; the second involves reflecting personal information.

REFLECTION

Letting Others Give Themselves Advice

Last week my roommate and her boyfriend were arguing. It seemed to me that she was making a much bigger deal of the situation than she should have, but I knew it would be a mistake to tell her my opinion. Besides, I could have been wrong.

So, instead of telling her what I thought (as I usually would have done), I decided to paraphrase back what she was saying. All of a sudden she stopped talking and smiled and said, "Gosh, I am being really dumb. This isn't even worth wasting my time on." I was amazed! This was exactly what I had been thinking, but she got there on her own.

This approach worked especially well with my roommate because she is the kind of person who gets defensive if you come out and tell her your opinion. I think I'll use paraphrasing more often—it sure seems better than giving advice that people don't want to hear.

Paraphrasing Factual Information Summarizing facts, data, and details is important during personal or professional conversations. "We've agreed that we'll take another few days to think about our choices and make a decision on Tuesday—right?" might be an effective way to conclude a business lunch. A questioning tone should be used; a listener wants to be sure that meaning has been shared. Even personal topics are sometimes best handled on a factual level: "So your main problem is that our friends take up all the parking spaces in front of your place. Is that it?" While this "neutral" response may be difficult when you are under attack, it helps to clarify facts before you offer your reaction. It is also a good idea to paraphrase instructions, directions, and decisions before acting on what you *think* has been said.

Paraphrasing Personal Information While restating factual information is relatively easy, it takes a sensitive ear to listen for others' thoughts, feelings, and wants. The "underlying message" is often the more important message, and effective listeners try to reflect what they hear at this level. Listening for thoughts, feelings, and wants addresses the cognitive (rational), affective (emotional), and behavioral (desired action) domains of human experience. Read the following statement as if a married, female friend is talking to you, and listen for all three components in her message:

> Bob has hardly been home all week—he's been so busy with work. He rushes in just long enough to eat dinner, then he buries himself at his desk until bedtime. Then he tells me today that he's going fishing Saturday with his buddies. I guess men are just like that—job first, play second, family third.

What is the speaker thinking, feeling, and wanting? Paraphrasing can help you find out: "Sounds like you're unhappy (feeling) because you think Bob's ignoring you (thought) and you want him to spend more time at home (want)." Recognize that you may not be accurate; the speaker might reply, "No, I really don't want him to spend more time at home—I just want him to pay attention to me when he's here." Recognize also that you could identify an entirely different think-feel-want set: "So you're frustrated (feeling) because you'd like Bob to change (want), but you think it's hopeless because men have different priorities (thought)." The fact that these examples offer such different interpretations of the same message demonstrates the value of paraphrasing.

Your paraphrases don't have to be as long as the examples in the preceding paragraph. It's often a good idea to mix paraphrasing with other listening responses. In many cases, you'll want to reflect only one or two of the think-feel-want components. The key is giving feedback that is appropriate for the situation and offering it in a way that assists the listening process. Because paraphrasing is an unfamiliar way of responding, it may feel awkward at first. If you start by paraphrasing occasionally and then gradually increase the frequency of such responses, you can begin to see the benefits of this method.

EMPATHIZING

Empathizing is a response style listeners use when they want to show that they *identify* with a speaker. As discussed in Chapter 4, empathy involves perspective taking, emotional contagion, and genuine concern. When listeners put the attitude of empathy into verbal and nonverbal responses, they engage in empathizing. Sometimes these responses can be quite brief: "Uh-huh," "I see," "Wow!" "Ouch!" "Whew!" "My goodness." In other cases, empathizing is expressed in statements like these:

"I can see that really hurts."
"I know how important that was to you."
"It's no fun to feel unappreciated."
"I can tell you're really excited about that."
"Wow, that must be rough."
"I think I've felt that way, too."
"Looks like that really made your day."
"This means a lot to you, doesn't it?"

Even statements like these may not fully capture the feeling of effective empathizing, which is not reducible to a technique or skill, but something that emerges from a relationship (Myers, 2000). Genuine empathizing ideally requires genuine identification with another person (Malle & Hodges, 2005).

Empathizing falls near the middle of the listening response continuum pictured in Figure 7.3. It is different from the more reflective responses at the left end of the spectrum, which attempt to gather information neutrally. It is also different from the more evaluative styles at the right end of the spectrum, which offer more direction than reflection. To understand how empathizing compares to other types of responses, consider these examples:

"So your boss isn't happy with your performance and you're thinking about finding a new job." (Paraphrasing)
"Ouch—I'll bet it hurt when your boss said you weren't doing a good job." (Empathizing)
"Hey, you'll land on your feet—your boss doesn't appreciate what a winner you are." (Supporting)

Notice that empathizing identifies with the speaker's emotions and perceptions more than paraphrasing does, yet offers less evaluation and agreement than supporting responses. In fact, it's possible to empathize with others while disagreeing with them. For instance, the response "I can tell that this issue is important to you" legitimizes a speaker's feelings without assenting to that person's point of view (note that it could be said to either a friend or a foe at a business meeting). Empathizing is therefore an important skill not only for interacting with people with whom you agree, but also for responding to those who see the world differently than you.

Perhaps a better way to explain empathizing is to describe what it *doesn't* sound like. Many listeners believe they are empathizing when, in fact, they are offering responses that are evaluative and directive—providing what has been called "cold comfort" (Burleson, 2003; Hample, 2006). Listeners are probably *not* empathizing when they display the following behaviors:

- *Denying others the right to their feelings.* Consider this common response to another person's problem: "Don't worry about it." While the remark may be intended as a reassuring comment, the underlying message is that the speaker wants the person to feel differently. The irony is that the direction probably won't work—after all, it's unlikely that people can or will stop worrying just because you tell them to do so. Other examples of denying feelings are "It's nothing to get so upset about" and "That's a silly way to feel." Research suggests that men are more likely than women to offer these kinds of responses (Goldsmith & Fulfs, 1999). Research also shows that empathizing is more effective than denying the feelings and perspectives of others (Burleson & Samter, 1985, 1994).

- *Minimizing the significance of the situation.* Think about the times someone said to you, "Hey, it's only _____." You can probably fill in the blank a variety of ways: "a game," "words," "a test," "a party." How did you react? You probably thought the person who said it just didn't understand. To someone who has been the victim of verbal abuse, the hurtful message wasn't "just words"; to a child who didn't get an invitation, it wasn't "just a party" (see Burleson, 1984); to a student who has flunked an important exam, it wasn't "just a test" (see Burleson & Samter, 1985). When you minimize the significance of someone else's experience, you aren't empathizing. Instead, you are interpreting the event from your perspective and then passing judgment—rarely a helpful response.

- *Self-defending.* When your response to others' concerns is to defend yourself ("Don't blame me; I've done my part"), it's clear you are more concerned with yourself than with the other person. Chapter 10 offers detailed advice for responding nondefensively to criticism.

- *Raining on the speaker's parade.* Most of the preceding examples deal with difficult situations or messages about pain. However, empathizing involves identifying with others' joys as well as their sorrows. Many of us can recall coming home with exciting news, only to be told "A 5 percent raise? That isn't so great." "An *A minus*? Why didn't you get an *A*?" "Big deal—I got one of those years ago." Taking the wind out of someone's sails is the opposite of empathizing.

Authors Florence Wolff and Nadine Marsnik (1993) believe that empathizing requires "fine skill and exquisite tuning to another's moods and feelings" (p. 100). Research suggests that cognitive complexity and flexibility are needed to offer these nonjudgmental, other-oriented responses (Applegate, 1990). Fortunately, research also indicates that the ability to offer such responses can be learned by both children and adults (Vancleave, 2008; Wei & Li, 2001). The exercises at the end of this chapter can offer you valuable practice in developing your skill as an empathic communicator.

SUPPORTING

So far, we have looked at listening responses that put a premium on being reflective and nonevaluative. However, there are times when other people want to hear more than a reflection of how *they* feel: They would like to know how *you* feel about *them*. **Supporting** responses reveal the listener's solidarity with the speaker's situation. Brant Burleson (2003) describes supporting as "expressions of care, concern, affection, and interest, especially during times of stress or upset" (p. 552). There are several types of supportive responses:

Agreement	"You're right—the landlord is being unfair." "Yeah, that class was tough for me too."
Offers to help	"I'm here if you need me." "Let me try to explain it to him."
Praise	"I don't care what the boss said: I think you did a great job!" "You're a terrific person! If she doesn't recognize it, that's her problem."
Reassurance	"The worst part seems to be over. It will probably get easier from here." "I know you'll do a great job."
Diversion	"Let's catch a movie and get your mind off this." "That reminds me of the time we. . . ."

There's no question about the value of receiving support when faced with personal problems. "Comforting ability" and social support have been shown to be among the most important communication skills a friend—or a teacher, or a coach, or a parent—can have (Cunningham & Barbee, 2000; Robbins & Rosenfeld, 2001). Supportive responses have been shown to enhance the psychological, physical, and relational health of those who receive them (Burleson, 2003; Jones & Wirtz, 2006). For example, support helps buffer the effects of anxiety, depression, and even financial strain. It increases the optimism of people feeling troubled enough to seek counseling (Hatchett & Park, 2004). Support can boost the sense of well-being for people living in poverty (Ramirez-Ponce, 2005). Reassurance has encouraged older adults to take better physical care of themselves (Fitzpatrick et al., 2005; Resnick et al., 2002). Evidence suggests that people who benefit from emotional support recover more quickly from injuries and disease, and may even live longer (Burleson, 2003).

Loving through Listening: *Dead Man Walking*

Sister Helen Prejean (Susan Sarandon) is a nun who serves in an inner-city neighborhood. She receives a letter from death row inmate Matthew Poncelet (Sean Penn) and decides to visit him in prison. He fills the profile for everything she is not: uneducated, angry, bigoted, rude, and insecure. Nonetheless, Sister Helen agrees to help Poncelet appeal his murder conviction and death sentence—and her world turns upside down.

Sister Helen's highest goal is to get Matthew to take responsibility for his actions and to come to peace with God, the murder victims' parents, and himself. She does this not by pushing or persuading, but by giving him her time and her ear. In their early meetings, Prejean comes with no agenda; she tells Poncelet, "I'm here to listen. Whatever you want to talk about is fine with me." She asks open-ended questions and allows Poncelet to arrive at his own conclusions. He admits to being surprised that she "didn't come down here preaching fire and brimstone," so he slowly opens his life to her.

As time goes on, Sister Helen comes to realize that Poncelet is, indeed, guilty of the awful crimes for which he has been convicted. Her pain is obvious as she confronts the grieving families of his victims, none of whom can understand or accept why she is willing to help a murderer. What they don't appreciate is that she never wavers in her abhorrence for his deeds, but she remains steadfast in separating her hate for the crime from her concern and love for Poncelet. As such, she provides viewers with proof that unconditional positive regard can be achieved, and can heal.

Men and women differ in the way they act when the opportunity to support others arises. Women are more prone than men to give supportive responses when presented with another person's problem (Burleson et al., 2005; Hale et al., 1997) and are more skillful at composing such messages (Burleson, 1982). By contrast, men tend to respond to others' problems by offering advice, or by diverting the topic (Barbee et al., 1990; Derlega et al., 1994). In a study of sororities and fraternities, Woodward and his colleagues (1996) found that sorority women frequently respond with emotional support when asked to help; also, they rated their sisters as being better at listening nonjudgmentally, and on comforting and showing concern for them. Fraternity men, on the other hand, fit the stereotypical pattern of offering help by challenging their brothers to evaluate their attitudes and values.

Although women and men may tend to offer different kinds of support, both sexes respond well to the same types of comforting messages. Both men and women are most comforted by messages that feel highly personal, and which are delivered with nonverbal immediacy (such as touching and maintaining eye contact) (Jones & Burleson, 2003).

For social support to be effective, it must match the other person's needs (Sarason et al., 1990). This means that even though you might be doing your best to help someone, you might be wasting your effort if what you offer isn't what's needed. In one study, hospice workers who received emotional support from their coworkers experienced an increase in stress, whereas those who received technical support experienced a decrease (Richman & Rosenfeld, 1987). The emotional support communicated "you're right to feel overwhelmed," while the technical challenge support communicated "you're smart and motivated to solve the problem," and pushed the workers to develop solutions. And with children and adolescents, companionship and diversion ("Let's go do something fun") is sometimes more helpful than trying to talk through a difficult situation (Clark et al., 2008).

Even the most sincere supportive efforts don't always help. Mourners suffering from the recent death of a loved one often report that a majority of the statements made to them are unhelpful (Davidowitz & Myrick, 1984; Glanz, 2007). Most of these unhelpful statements are advice: "You've got to get out more" and "Don't question God's will." Another frequent response is reassurance, such as "She's out of pain now." Far more helpful are expressions that acknowledge the mourner's feelings, such as "I know this is a painful loss for you." One American Red Cross grief counselor explained to survivors of the September 11, 2001, terrorist attacks on the United States how simply being present can be more helpful than trying to reassure grief-stricken family members who had lost loved ones in the tragedy.

> Don't say anything. Saying "it'll be okay," or "I know how you feel" can backfire. Right now that's not what a victim wants to hear. They want to know people are there and care about them if you need them. Be there, be present, listen. The clergy refer to it as a ministry of presence. You don't need to do anything, just be there or have them know you're available. ("Attacks on U.S. Soil," 2001)

As with the other helping styles, supporting can be beneficial, but only under certain conditions (Goldsmith & Fitch, 1997; Halone & Pecchioni, 2001):

- *Make sure your expression of support is sincere.* Phony agreement or encouragement is probably worse than no support at all, since it adds the insult of your dishonesty to whatever pain the other person is already feeling.
- *Be sure the other person can accept your support.* Sometimes people are so upset that they aren't ready or able to hear anything positive. When you know a friend is going through a difficult time, it's important not to be overly intrusive before that person is ready to talk and receive your support (Clark & Delia, 1997).
- *Focus on "here and now" rather than "then and there."* While it's sometimes true that "You'll feel better tomorrow," it sometimes isn't (you can probably remember times when you felt worse the next day). More importantly, focusing on the future avoids supporting in the present. Even if the prediction that "ten years from now, you won't even remember her name" proves correct, it gives little comfort to someone experiencing heartbreak today. "Everything is going to turn out fine" and "There are other fish in the sea—you'll land one soon" are variations on the same theme—they are promises that may not come true and that tell the person to stop feeling the way she or he

"There you go again, trying to solve my problems. I'm not asking you to do that. I just need you to listen."

feels. The intentions of people who offer these sentiments may be good, but they usually don't offer the support that's needed.

ANALYZING

In **analyzing** a situation, the listener offers an interpretation of a speaker's message ("I think what's really bothering you is . . ."; "She's doing it because . . ."; or "Maybe the problem started when he . . ."). Interpretations are often effective in helping people who have problems seeing alternative meanings of a situation—meanings they would have never thought of without your assistance. Sometimes an analysis helps clarify a confusing problem, providing an objective understanding of the situation. Research suggests that analytic listeners are able to hear the concerns of emotionally upset others without experiencing similar emotions, which can be an advantage in problem solving (Weaver & Kirtley, 1995).

In other cases, an analysis can create more problems than it solves. There are two reasons why: First, your interpretation may not be correct, in which case the problem holder may become even more confused by accepting it. Second, even if your analysis is accurate, sharing it with the problem holder might not be useful. There's a chance that it will arouse defensiveness (analysis implies being superior and in a position to evaluate). Besides, the problem holder may not be able to understand your view of the problem without working it out personally.

How can you know when it's helpful to offer an analysis? There are several guidelines to follow:

- *Offer your interpretation in a tentative way rather than as absolute fact.* There's a big difference between saying "Maybe the reason is . . ." and insisting "This is the truth."
- *Your analysis ought to have a reasonable chance of being correct.* An inaccurate interpretation—especially one that sounds plausible—can leave a person more confused than before.
- *Make sure that the other person will be receptive to your analysis.* Even if you're completely accurate, your thoughts won't help if the problem holder isn't ready to consider them. Pay attention to the other person's verbal and nonverbal cues to see how your analysis is being received.
- *Be sure that your motive for offering an analysis is truly to help the other person.* It can be tempting to offer an analysis to show how brilliant you are or even to make the other person feel bad for not having thought of the right answer in the first place. Needless to say, an analysis offered under such conditions isn't helpful.

EVALUATING

An **evaluating** response appraises the sender's thoughts or behaviors in some way. The evaluation may be favorable ("That's a good idea" or "You're on the right track now") or unfavorable ("An attitude like that won't get you anywhere"). In either case, it implies that the person evaluating is in some way qualified to pass judgment on the speaker's thoughts or actions.

Sometimes negative evaluations are purely critical. How many times have you heard responses such as "Well, you asked for it!" or "I told you so!" or "You're just feeling sorry for yourself"? Although such comments can sometimes serve as a verbal slap that "knocks sense" into the problem holder, they usually make matters worse by arousing defensiveness in that person. After all, suggesting that someone is foolish or mistaken is an attack on the presenting image that most people would have a hard time ignoring or accepting.

Other times, negative evaluations are less critical. These involve what we usually call constructive criticism, which is intended to help the problem holder improve in the future. Friends give this sort of response about the choice of everything from clothing, to jobs, to friends. A common setting for constructive criticism is school, where instructors evaluate students' work in order to help them master concepts and skills. Even constructive criticism can

FOCUS ON RESEARCH

Problem Solving or Solace? Supporting Victims of Sexual Harassment

Imagine that you're a college student and you believe you've been sexually harassed by a professor. Research shows that you may seek out the support of someone you trust—and that person might be another professor. What kind of response are you likely to get? According to Shereen Bingham and Karen Battey, the trusted professor will probably offer more problem solving than emotional support.

Professors in the study were asked to respond to a scenario in which a student tells them about being harassed by another faculty member. Most of the helpers' responses fell into two categories: "Solve" (providing informational and/or tangible support to help solve the problem) and "Solace" (providing emotional and/or esteem support to help the victim feel more positive and cared for). Some of the professors provided responses that fell into both categories, but every instructor—100 percent—offered at least one response that fell into the "Solve" category. By contrast, less than 40 percent offered "Solace" responses.

The researchers note that problem solving is an important component of social support, and that there are a variety of constraints that might keep professors from offering solace. However, Bingham and Battey would like to see universities "empower professors to combine their problem-solving advice and information with more emotionally sensitive and tangible assistance for students." In other words, both "Solve" and "Solace" are important responses in traumatic situations.

Bingham, S. G., & Battey, K. M. (2005). Communication of social support to sexual harassment victims: Professors' responses to a student's narrative of unwanted sexual attention. *Communication Studies, 56,* 131–155.

SELF-ASSESSMENT

Your Listening Responses

Learn more about your helping style by indicating how you would most likely respond to each of the statements below. Don't try to guess the "right" response: Choose the response that is closest to what you would probably say after hearing each statement.

1. "I think I understand the material, but I don't know where I stand in the course. I'm not sure what the instructor expects of me, and she doesn't tell me how I'm doing. I wish I knew where I stood."

a) "Has your instructor ever given you any indication of what she thinks of your work?"
b) "If I were you, I'd discuss it with her."
c) "She's probably just trying to give everyone in the class a lot of freedom to do what they want to do."
d) "It sounds like you're worried about your grade. Is that it?"
e) "Don't take it so seriously. Most of the time in school you don't know where you stand."
f) "What do you think you can do to solve this situation? What have you tried?"
g) "I've had teachers like that, and it's a lousy situation."

2. "The policy in the chemistry department is supposed to be to hire lab assistants from people in the advanced chem classes. And now I find that this person from a beginning class is getting hired. I had my eyes on that job; I've been working hard for it. I know I could be a terrific assistant if I had a chance."

a) "I can tell how disappointed you are."
b) "Why do you think they hired the person from the beginning class?"
c) "If not getting the job means not having enough money to make it through the semester, I can help out with a loan."
d) "Getting ahead is very important to you, and it sounds like you feel cheated that someone else got the job as lab assistant."
e) "You should take some more chemistry classes to help you advance."
f) "I told you not to get your hopes up."
g) "You shouldn't complain—they probably hired the best person to be an assistant."

3. "I'm really tired of this. I'm taking more classes than anyone I know, and then on the same day three of my teachers tell me that there's another assignment due on top of what's already due. I've got so many people asking me to do things that I just can't keep up, and it bothers me. I like my teachers, and my classes are interesting, but I am getting overwhelmed."

a) "With so many teachers asking you to do extra assignments, it's difficult for you to accomplish all of it, and the pressure gets you down."
b) "Are all these requests from your teachers required work?"
c) "I'm really sorry you feel so overwhelmed."
d) "You seem to have too much work. Why don't you talk it over with your teachers?"

e) "Yikes! Sounds like things are pretty hectic for you right now."
f) "You're probably overworked because you're not organized."
g) "Who told you to take so many classes?"

4. "My teacher tells the class that he would appreciate getting term projects as soon as possible to help him with grading. So I work like mad to get it completed and on his desk early. What's my reward for helping him out? Nothing! No thanks, no nothing. In fact, I think my project will sit on his desk until all the projects are handed in."
a) "How often do teachers do this to you?"
b) "Don't be a baby. You don't need a pat on the back for every good thing you do."
c) "You ought to tell him how you feel."
d) "You feel resentful because you think he's taking advantage of you?"
e) "I hate when teachers do that to us!"
f) "I hear you! Been there, felt that—it's no fun."
g) "I think your professor was trying to teach the value of doing work before the last minute."

5. "He used to be one of the guys until he was made the team's coach. Now, it's like he's not my friend anymore. I don't mind being told about my mistakes, but he doesn't have to do it in front of the rest of the team. Whenever I get the chance, he's going to get his!"
a) "Revenge is only one way of handling this."
b) "I'll bet that really upset you."
c) "To be told about your mistakes in front of the rest of the team is embarrassing, especially by a person you once considered a friend."
d) "If you didn't make so many mistakes, the coach wouldn't have to tell you about them."
e) "Why don't we talk it over with a few other people on the team and then go talk to him about this situation?"
f) "How often does he criticize you in front of the others?"
g) "Seems like he's on a power trip."

Listed below are the possible response types for each of the five situations. For example, if you indicated answer a in situation number 1, note that this is a "questioning response." If you indicated answer b, note that this is an "advising response." Do this for your five responses.

Questioning response: 1a, 2b, 3b, 4a, 5f
Advising response: 1b, 2e, 3d, 4c, 5e
Analyzing response: 1c, 2g, 3f, 4g, 5g
Paraphrasing response: 1d, 2d, 3a, 4d, 5c
Evaluating response: 1e, 2f, 3g, 4b, 5d
Supportive response: 1f (technical challenge support), 2c (tangible support), 3c (emotional support), 4f (listening support), 5a (emotional challenge support)
Empathizing response: 1g, 2a, 3e, 4e, 5b

Do you have a particular way of responding? What does this tell you about how you listen, that is, the kinds of information you listen for? When is your typical way of responding most and least useful? What do you think is the most useful—needed—response in each of the five situations?

arouse defensiveness because it may threaten the self-concept of the person at whom it is directed. Chapter 10 provides guidelines for offering constructive criticism in ways that protect the self-concept of the recipient.

Evaluations have the best chance of being received when two conditions exist:

- *The person with the problem should have requested an evaluation from you.* Occasionally, an unsolicited judgment may bring someone to his or her senses, but more often this sort of uninvited evaluation will trigger a defensive response.
- *Your evaluation should be genuinely constructive and not designed as a put-down.* If you are tempted to use evaluations as a weapon, don't fool yourself into thinking that you are being helpful. Often, statements such as "I'm telling you this for your own good" simply aren't true.

ADVISING

When approached with another's problem, the most common reaction is **advising** (Notarius & Herrick, 1988). We're all familiar with advising responses: "If you're so unhappy, you should just quit the job." "Just tell him what you think." "You should take some time off." Advice can be offered in at least three conditions. The first type comprises advice that is requested in a straightforward manner: "What do you think I should do?" In other cases, an ambiguous statement might sound like a request for suggestions. Ambiguous statements of this sort include requests for opinions ("What do you think of Jeff?"), soliciting information ("Would that be an example of sexual harassment?"), and announcement of a problem ("I'm really confused . . ."). Finally, advice is sometimes offered even when it hasn't been solicited ("You look awful. You ought to get more sleep!"). Research suggests that the first two methods are usually the most effective (Goldsmith & MacGeorge, 2000; MacGeorge et al., 2002).

Even when advice is requested and offered in a face-saving manner, there are several reasons why it often isn't helpful. First, it may not offer the best suggestion about how to act. In fact, it might even be harmful. There's often a temptation to tell others how you would behave in their place, but it's important to realize that what's right for one person may not be right for another. A related consequence of advising is that it often allows others to avoid responsibility for their decisions. A partner who follows a suggestion of yours that doesn't work out can always pin the blame on you. Finally, people often don't want advice: They may not be ready to accept it, and instead may simply need to talk out their thoughts and feelings.

Before offering advice, then, be sure four conditions are present:

- *Be sure the other person really wants to hear your suggestions.* The best indicator is a clear request for advice. If you're not sure whether the other person is seeking your opinion, it may be best to ask.

- *Consider whether the person seeking your advice is truly ready to accept it.* This way, you can avoid the frustration of making good suggestions, only to find that the person with the problem had another solution in mind all the time.
- *Be confident that your advice is correct.* Resist the temptation to act like an authority on matters you know little about or to make suggestions when you aren't positive that they are the best choice. Realize that while a particular course of action worked for you, it probably won't be correct for everybody.
- *Be certain that the receiver won't blame you if the advice doesn't work out.* You may be offering the suggestions, but the choice and responsibility for accepting them is up to the recipient of your advice.

WHICH STYLE TO USE?

By now, it should be clear that there are many ways to respond as a listener. You also can see that each style has advantages and disadvantages. This leads to the important question: Which style is best? There isn't a simple answer to this question. All response styles have the potential to help others accept their situation, feel better, and have a sense of control over their problems (Imhof, 2003; Young & Cates, 2004).

As a rule of thumb, it's probably wise to begin with responses from the left and middle of the listening response continuum: silent listening, questioning, paraphrasing, empathizing, and supporting. Once you've gathered the facts and demonstrated your interest and concern, it's likely that the speaker will be more receptive to (and perhaps even ask for) your analyzing, evaluating, and advising responses.

You can boost the odds of choosing the best style in each situation by considering three factors. First, think about the *situation,* and match your response to the nature of the problem. People sometimes need your advice. In other cases your encouragement and support will be most helpful, and in still other instances your analysis or judgment may be truly useful. And, as you have seen, there are times when your questioning and paraphrasing can help others find their own answer.

Besides considering the situation, you also should think about the *other person* when deciding which approach to use. It's important to be sure that the other person is open to receiving *any* kind of help. Furthermore, you need to be confident that you will be regarded as someone whose support is valuable. The same response that would be accepted with gratitude when it comes from one communicator can be regarded as unhelpful when it's offered by the wrong person (Clark et al., 1998; Sullivan, 1996).

It's also important to match the type of response you offer with the style of the person to whom it is directed (Bippus, 2001). Some people are able to consider advice thoughtfully, while others use suggestions to avoid making their own decisions. Many communicators are extremely defensive and aren't capable of receiving analysis or judgments without lashing out. Still

REFLECTION

Asking Which Style to Use

I often have trouble figuring out what kind of listening response my girlfriend wants from me. I sometimes give her advice she doesn't appreciate, and sometimes I'm quiet when she's looking for my enthusiastic support.

Lately I've been asking her what kind of response she wants with questions like "Are you looking for advice, or just a listening ear?" That approach has saved us a lot of misunderstandings—and it's also made me a better listener.

others aren't equipped to think through problems clearly enough to profit from questioning and paraphrasing. Sophisticated listeners choose a style that fits the person.

Finally, think about *yourself* when deciding how to respond. Most of us reflexively use one or two styles (did you notice this when you completed the Self-Assessment on pages 234–235?). You may be best at listening quietly, posing a question, or paraphrasing from time to time. Or perhaps you are especially insightful and can offer a truly useful analysis of the problem. Of course, it's also possible to rely on a response style that is *unhelpful.* You may be overly judgmental or too eager to advise, even when your suggestions aren't invited or productive. As you think about how to respond to another's problems, consider your weaknesses as well as your strengths.

Summary

Listening is both more frequent and less emphasized than speaking. Despite its relative invisibility, listening is at least as important as speaking. Research shows that good listening is vital for both personal and professional success.

Listening is the process of making sense of others' spoken messages. We listen to many messages mindlessly, but it's important to listen mindfully in a variety of situations. There are several reasons why we listen to others. At the most basic level, we listen to understand and retain information. Perhaps more importantly, we listen to build and maintain our interpersonal relationships. We may listen to help others, and also to evaluate their messages.

Most peoples' understanding of listening is based on poor listening habits and also on several misconceptions that communicators need to correct. Mindful listening is not easy; rather, it is a challenge that requires much effort and talent. Several barriers can hamper effective listening: personal concerns, information overload, rapid thought, and both internal and external noise. Even careful listening does not mean that all listeners will receive the same message. A wide variety of factors discussed in this chapter can result in widely varying interpretations of even simple statements.

Listening consists of several components: hearing, attending to a message, understanding the statement, recalling the message after the passage of time, and responding to the speaker. Listening responses are important because they let us know if others are truly tuned in to what we're saying. Listening responses can be placed on a continuum. More reflective/less directive responses include silent listening, questioning, paraphrasing, and empathizing. These put a premium on gathering information and showing interest and concern. Less reflective/more directive responses include supporting, analyzing, evaluating, and advising. These put a premium on offering input and direction. It is possible to use the "more reflective" listening responses to help people arrive at their own decisions without offering advice or evaluation. The most effective listeners use several styles, depending on the situation, the other person, and their own personal skills and motivation.

Activities

1. Invitation to Insight

You can start to overcome bad listening habits by recalling specific instances when:

a. you heard another person's message but did not attend to it.
b. you attended to a message but forgot it almost immediately.
c. you attended and remembered a message but did not understand it accurately.
d. you understood a message but did not respond sufficiently to convey your understanding to the sender.

For each situation, describe how you could have listened more effectively.

2. Invitation to Insight

Keep a 3-day journal of your listening behavior, noting the time you spend listening in various contexts. In addition, analyze your reasons for listening. Which goal(s) were you trying to achieve?

a. To understand and retain information
b. To build and maintain relationships
c. To help
d. To evaluate

3. Critical Thinking Probe

Communication problems can arise from factors that aren't easily observed. Based on your experience, decide which of the following steps in the listening process cause the greatest difficulties for you:

a. Hearing
b. Attending
c. Understanding
d. Remembering
e. Responding

Discuss your findings with your friends, and develop a list of remedies that can help minimize listening problems in the areas you identified.

4. Skill Builder

Explore the benefits of silent listening by using a "Talking Stick." Richard Hyde (1993) developed this exercise from the Native American tradition of "council." Gather a group of people in a circle, and designate a particular item as the talking stick. Participants will then pass the stick around the circle. Participants may speak

a. only when holding the stick;
b. for as long as they hold the stick; and
c. without interruption from anyone else in the circle.

When a member is through speaking, the stick passes to the left and the speaker surrendering the stick must wait until it has made its way around the circle before speaking again.

After each member of the group has had the chance to speak, discuss how this experience differs from more common approaches to listening. Decide how the desirable parts of this method could be introduced in everyday conversations.

5. Ethical Challenge

What responsibility do communicators have to listen as carefully and thoughtfully as possible to other speakers? Are there ever cases where the poor listening habits listed on pages 215–216 (for example, pseudolistening, stage hogging, and defensive listening) are justified? How would you feel if you knew that others weren't listening to you?

6. Skill Builder

Practice your ability to paraphrase in order to understand others by following these steps.

a. Choose a partner, and designate one of yourselves as A and the other as B. Find a subject on which you and your partner seem to disagree—a personal dispute, a philosophical or moral issue, or perhaps a matter of personal taste.
b. A begins by making a statement on the subject. B's job is to paraphrase the idea. In this step B should feed back only what he or she heard A say, without adding any judgment or interpretation. B's job here is simply to *understand* A—not to agree or disagree with A.
c. A responds by telling B whether or not the response was accurate, and by making any necessary additions or corrections to clarify the message.
d. B then paraphrases the revised statement. This process should continue until A is sure that B understands him or her.
e. Now B and A reverse roles and repeat the procedure in steps a–d. Continue the conversation until both partners are satisfied that they have explained themselves fully and have been understood by the other person.

After the discussion has ended, consider how this process differed from typical conversations on controversial topics. Was there greater understanding here? Do the partners feel better about one another? Finally, ask yourself how your life might change if you used more paraphrasing in everyday conversations.

7. Skill Builder

Explore the various types of listening responses by completing the following steps.

a. Join with two partners to form a trio. Designate members as A, B, and C.

b. A begins by sharing a current, real problem with B. The problem needn't be a major life crisis, but it should be a real one. B should respond in whatever way seems most helpful. C's job is to categorize each response by B as silent listening, questioning, paraphrasing, empathizing, supporting, analyzing, evaluating, or advising.
c. After a 4- to 5-minute discussion, C should summarize B's response styles. A then describes which of the styles were most helpful and which were not helpful.
d. Repeat the same process two more times, switching roles so that each person has been in all of the positions.
e. Based on their findings, the threesome should develop conclusions about what combination of response styles can be most helpful.

CHAPTER 8 Emotions

After studying the material in this chapter . . .

YOU SHOULD UNDERSTAND:

1. The four components of emotion.
2. The influence of culture and gender on emotional expressiveness and sensitivity.
3. The relationships among activating events, thoughts, emotions, and communication behavior.
4. Seven fallacies leading to unnecessarily debilitative emotions that can interfere with effective communication.
5. The steps in the rational-emotive approach for coping with debilitative emotions.

YOU SHOULD BE ABLE TO:

1. Observe the physical and cognitive manifestations of some of the emotions you experience.
2. Label your own emotions accurately.
3. Identify the degree to which you express your emotions and the consequences of this level of expression.
4. Follow the guidelines in this chapter in deciding when and how to express your emotions in an important relationship.
5. Realize which of your emotions are facilitative and which are debilitative.
6. Identify the fallacious beliefs that have caused you to experience debilitative emotions in a specific situation.
7. In a specific situation, apply the rational-emotive approach to managing your debilitative emotions.

KEY TERMS

- Communication apprehension (261)
- Debilitative emotions (260)
- Emotional contagion (254)
- Facilitative emotions (260)
- Fallacy of approval (264)
- Fallacy of catastrophic expectations (268)
- Fallacy of causation (266)
- Fallacy of helplessness (267)
- Fallacy of overgeneralization (266)
- Fallacy of perfection (263)
- Fallacy of should (265)
- Rumination (269)
- Self-talk (263)

Imagine how different life would be if you lost your ability to experience emotions. An emotionless world would be free of boredom, frustration, fear, and loneliness. But the cost of such a pain-free existence would be the loss of emotions like joy, pride, and love. Few of us would be willing to make that sort of trade-off.

The role of emotions in human affairs is apparent to social scientists and laypeople alike. When Yale University psychologist Robert Sternberg (1985) asked people to describe an "intelligent person," one of the skills listed was the ability to understand and get along with others. This ability to get along was described by psychologist Daniel Goleman (1995; Cherniss et al., 2006) as one aspect of *emotional intelligence*—the ability to understand and manage one's own emotions and to be sensitive to others' feelings. Goleman makes the claim that intellectual ability is not the only way to measure one's talents, and that success in the world depends in great part on emotional intelligence.

Because emotions are such an important part of human communication, we will take a close look at them in the following pages. We will explore what feelings are, discuss the ways they are handled in contemporary society, and see how recognizing and expressing them can improve relationships. We will look at some guidelines that should give you a clearer idea of when and how to express your emotions constructively. Finally, we will explore a method for coping with troublesome, debilitating feelings that inhibit rather than help your communication.

What Are Emotions?

Suppose an extraterrestrial visitor asked you to explain emotions. How would you answer? You might start by saying that emotions are things that we feel. But this doesn't say much, for in turn you would probably describe feelings as synonymous with emotions. Social scientists generally agree that there are several components to the phenomena we label as an emotion (Baumeister, 2005; Planalp et al., 2006).

PHYSIOLOGICAL CHANGES

When a person has strong emotions, many bodily changes occur (Rochman & Diamond, 2008). For example, the physical components of fear include an increased heartbeat, a rise in blood pressure, an increase in adrenaline secretions, an elevated blood sugar level, a slowing of digestion, and a dilation of pupils. Marriage researcher John Gottman notes that symptoms like these also occur when couples are in intense conflicts (Gottman & Silver, 1999). He calls the condition "flooding" and has found that it impedes effective problem solving. Some of these changes are recognizable to the person having them. These physiological messages can offer a significant clue to your emotions once you become aware of them. A churning stomach or tense jaw can be a signal that something is wrong.

NONVERBAL REACTIONS

Not all physical changes that accompany emotions are internal. Feelings are often apparent by observable changes. Some of these changes involve a person's appearance, such as blushing or perspiring. Other changes involve behavior: a distinctive facial expression, posture, gestures, different vocal tone and rate, and so on.

Although it's reasonably easy to tell when someone is feeling a strong emotion, it's more difficult to be certain exactly what that emotion might be. A slumped posture and sigh may be a sign of sadness, or it may signal fatigue. Likewise, trembling hands might indicate excitement, or they may be an outward sign of fear. As you learned in Chapter 6, nonverbal behavior

is usually ambiguous, and it's dangerous to assume that it can be "read" with much accuracy.

Although we usually think of nonverbal behavior as the reaction to an emotional state, there may be times when the reverse is true—when nonverbal behavior *causes* emotions. Research shows that people can actually create emotional states by altering their facial expressions. When volunteers in one study were coached to smile, they reported feeling better, and when they altered their expressions to look unhappy, they felt worse than before (Kleinke et al., 1998). Previous research by Paul Ekman and his colleagues (1983; see also Levenson et al., 1990) produced similar results, with subjects feeling afraid, angry, disgusted, amused, sad, surprised, and contemptuous when they created facial expressions that mimicked those feelings. As behavioral scientists like to say, it can be easier to act yourself into new ways of feeling than to feel yourself into new ways of acting.

COGNITIVE INTERPRETATIONS

Although there may be cases in which there is a direct connection between physical behavior and emotional states, in most situations the mind plays an important role in determining how we feel (Genov, 2001). As noted earlier, some physiological components of fear are a racing heart, perspiration, tense muscles, and elevated blood pressure. Interestingly enough, these symptoms are similar to the physical changes that accompany excitement, joy, and other emotions. In other words, if we were to measure the physical condition of someone having a strong emotion, we would have a hard time knowing whether that person was trembling with fear or quivering with excitement. For example, Stephen Mallalieu and his colleagues (2003) found that some athletes experiencing precompetition stress labeled their feelings in positive emotional terms and interpreted their emotion as facilitating their work, while other athletes experiencing the same stress labeled it negatively.

The recognition that the bodily components of most emotions are similar led some psychologists to conclude that the experience of fright, joy, or anger comes primarily from the labels—and the accompanying cognitive interpretations—we give to our physical symptoms (Valins, 1966). Psychologist Philip Zimbardo (1977, p. 53) offers a good example of this principle:

> I notice I'm perspiring while lecturing. From that I infer I am nervous. If it occurs often, I might even label myself a "nervous person." Once I have the label, the next question I must answer is "Why am I nervous?" Then I start to search for an appropriate explanation. I might notice some students leaving the room, or being inattentive. I am nervous because I'm not giving a good lecture. That makes me nervous. How do I know it's not good? Because I'm boring my audience. I am nervous because I am a boring lecturer and I want to be a good lecturer. I feel inadequate. Maybe I should open a delicatessen instead. Just then a student says, "It's hot in here, I'm perspiring and it makes it tough to concentrate on your lecture." Instantly, I'm no longer "nervous" or "boring."

In his book *Shyness* (1977), Zimbardo discusses the consequences of making inaccurate or exaggerated attributions such as these. In a survey of more than 5,000 people, over 80 percent described themselves as having been shy at some time in their lives, whereas more than 40 percent considered themselves presently shy. Most significantly, those who labeled themselves "not shy" behaved in virtually the same way as their shy counterparts. They would blush, perspire, and feel their hearts pounding in certain social situations. The biggest difference between the two groups seemed to be the label with which they described themselves. This is a significant difference. Someone who notices the symptoms we've described and thinks "I'm such a shy person!" will most likely feel more uncomfortable and communicate less effectively than another person with the same symptoms who thinks "Well, I'm a bit shaky (or excited) here, but that's to be expected."

We'll take a closer look at ways to reduce unpleasant emotions through cognitive processes later in this chapter.

VERBAL EXPRESSION

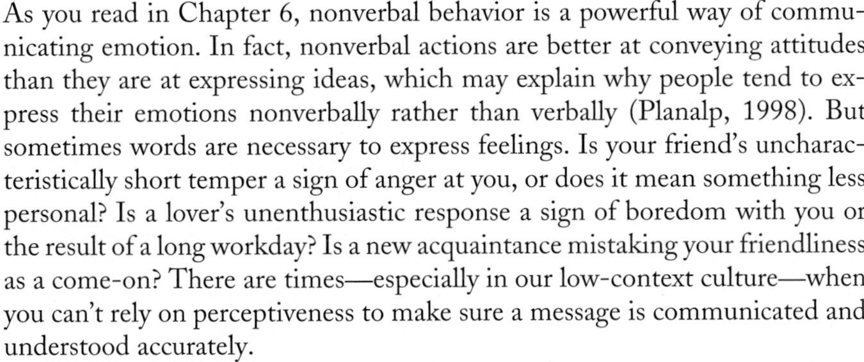

As you read in Chapter 6, nonverbal behavior is a powerful way of communicating emotion. In fact, nonverbal actions are better at conveying attitudes than they are at expressing ideas, which may explain why people tend to express their emotions nonverbally rather than verbally (Planalp, 1998). But sometimes words are necessary to express feelings. Is your friend's uncharacteristically short temper a sign of anger at you, or does it mean something less personal? Is a lover's unenthusiastic response a sign of boredom with you or the result of a long workday? Is a new acquaintance mistaking your friendliness as a come-on? There are times—especially in our low-context culture—when you can't rely on perceptiveness to make sure a message is communicated and understood accurately.

Some researchers believe there are several "basic" or "primary" emotions (Panksepp, 2007; Plutchik, 1984). However, there isn't much agreement among scholars about what those emotions are, or about what makes them "basic" (Ekman, 1999; Ortony & Turner, 1990). Moreover, emotions that are primary in one culture may not be primary in others, and some emotions may have no equivalent in other cultures (Ferrari & Koyama, 2002). For example, "shame" is a central emotion in the Chinese experience (Shaver et al., 1992), while it's much less central to most people from Western cultures, and Japanese *amae* (parental indulgence of a child) is often equated by Westerners as spoiling. Despite this debate, most scholars acknowledge that *anger, joy, fear,* and *sadness* are common and typical human emotions.

We experience most emotions with different degrees of intensity—and we use specific emotion words to represent these differences. Figure 8.1 illustrates this point clearly. To say you're "annoyed" when a friend breaks an important promise, for example, would probably be an understatement. In other cases, people chronically overstate the strength of their feelings. To them, everything is "wonderful" or "terrible." The problem with this sort of exaggeration is that when a truly intense emotion comes along, they have no

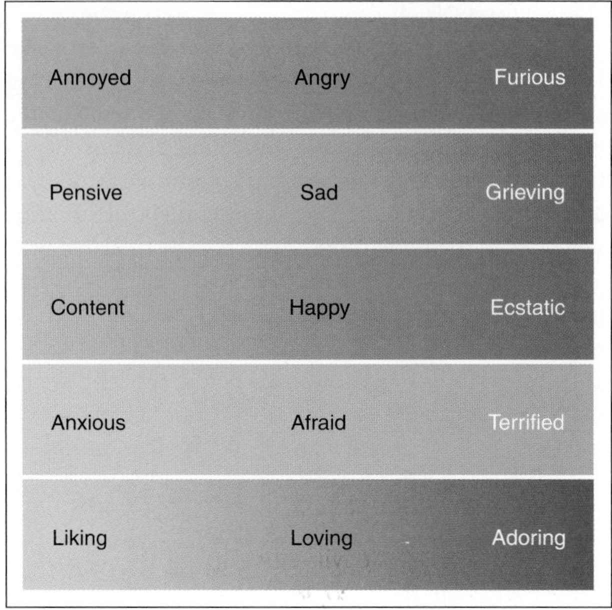

FIGURE 8.1 Intensity of Emotions

words left to describe it adequately. If chocolate chip cookies from the local bakery are "fantastic," how does it feel to fall in love?

The ability to communicate clearly about feelings has been characterized as part of "emotional intelligence," which we discussed earlier in this chapter. Social scientists have identified a wide range of problems that arise for people who aren't able to talk about emotions constructively, including social isolation, unsatisfying relationships, feelings of anxiety and depression, and misdirected aggression (Cherniss et al., 2006; Whiffen et al., 2007).

The way parents talk to their children about emotions has a powerful effect on the children's development. John Gottman and his associates (1997) identified two distinct parenting styles, "emotion coaching" and "emotion dismissing." They show how the coaching approach gives children skills for communicating about feelings in later life that lead to much more satisfying relationships. Children who grow up in families where parents dismiss emotions are at higher risk for behavior problems than those who are raised in families that practice emotion coaching (Lunkenheimer et al., 2007). Later in this chapter you will find some guidelines for communicating effectively about emotions.

Influences on Emotional Expression

Each of us is born with the disposition to reveal our emotions, at least nonverbally. But over time, a wide range of differences develops in emotional expression. In the next few pages, we will look at some influences that shape how people communicate their feelings.

PERSONALITY

Science has established an increasingly clear relationship between personality and the way people experience and communicate emotions (Gross et al., 1998; McCroskey et al., 2004). For example, extroverted people—those with a tendency to be upbeat, optimistic, and to enjoy social contact—report more positive emotions in everyday life than more introverted individuals (Lucas et al., 2008). Conversely, people with neurotic personalities—those with a tendency to worry, be anxious, and feel apprehensive—report more negative emotions than less neurotic individuals.

These personality traits are at least partially biological in nature. Psychologist Turhan Canli and his colleagues (2001) used magnetic imaging to measure the relationship between personality type and brain activity. Experimental subjects who tested high on measures of extroversion also had greater brain reactivity to positive stimuli than less extroverted people. Those who scored high on neuroticism measures had more brain reactions to negative stimuli. In other words, people's brains amplified some aspects of experience over others—while all the participants saw very positive and very negative scenes, some reacted by emphasizing the positive aspects and some reacted by emphasizing the negative.

While personality can be a powerful force, it doesn't have to govern your communication satisfaction. Consider shyness, which can be considered the opposite of extroversion. Introverted people can devise comfortable and effective strategies for reaching out. For example, the Internet has proven to be an effective way for reticent communicators to make contact. Chat rooms, instant messaging, e-mail, and computer dating services all provide a low-threat way to approach others and get acquainted (Kelly et al., 2001; Scharlott & Christ, 1995). Online relationships shouldn't be a way to avoid in-person communication (Ebeling-Witte et al., 2007); but they can be a rewarding way to gain confidence that will pay off in more satisfying face-to-face relationships.

Acknowledging Suppressed Emotions: *Garden State*

Andrew Largeman (Zach Braff) is living an emotionally numb life. This numbness is due in part to the debilitating guilt he carries from a childhood accident in which he may have been responsible for a paralyzing injury to his mother. When his mother dies, Andrew returns home to New Jersey for the first time in nine years—and he confronts the ghosts of his past.

While home, Zach meets a young woman named Sam (Natalie Portman) and falls for her quirky charm. With the help of Sam and some of his friends, Andrew realizes that he must acknowledge and purge the pain he's been carrying. Andrew also discovers that the road to emotional health runs through his father, Gideon (Ian Holm). Despite the fact that he is a psychiatrist, Gideon has many unresolved issues of his own. He represses his own feelings of anger and pain and holds Andrew responsible for the breach between them, failing to take responsibility for the guilt and disconfirmation he has heaped on his son through the years.

Andrew tells his father that even negative feelings are better than suppressed ones: "What I want more than anything in the world is for it to be okay with you for me to feel something again, even if it's pain." By the film's end, Andrew is transformed. He discovers that confronting pain can lead to joy, and that the road to emotional health is most easily traveled with loving companions.

CULTURE

While people around the world experience the same emotions, the same events can generate quite different feelings in different cultures. The notion of eating snails might bring a smile of delight to some residents of France, though it would cause many North Americans to grimace in disgust. More to the point of this book, research has shown that fear of strangers and risky situations is more likely to frighten people living in the United States and Europe than those in Japan, while Japanese are more apprehensive about relational communication than are Americans and Europeans (Ting-Toomey, 1991).

There are also differences in the degree to which people in various cultures display their feelings (Cole et al., 2002; Matsumoto, 2006). For example, social scientists have found support for the notion that people from warmer climates are more emotionally expressive than those who live in cooler places (Pennebaker et al., 1996). Over 2,900 respondents representing 26 nationalities reported that people from the southern part of their countries were more emotionally expressive than northerners.

Cultural background influences the way we interpret others' emotions as well as the way we express our own. In one experiment (Matsumoto, 1993), an ethnically varied group of students—European American, Latinos, African American, and Asian American—identified the type, intensity, and appropriateness of emotional expression in 56 photos representing eight social situations (e.g., alone, with a friend, in public, with someone of higher status). Results indicated that ethnicity led to considerable differences in the way subjects gauged others' emotional states. For example, blacks perceived the emotions in the photos as more intense than the European American,

FOCUS ON RESEARCH

Saying "I Love You": Different Cultures, Different Rules

research

It's been said that love is the universal language. To the contrary, Richard Wilkins and Elisabeth Gareis found that saying "I love you" (or its equivalent in other languages) has very different meanings around the world.

Wilkins and Gereis surveyed college students from a variety of countries and cultures. They found significant differences about when, where, how often, and with whom the phrase "I love you" is used. The investigation revealed that Americans say "I love you" more frequently and with more people than do members of most other cultures. By contrast, Middle Easterners in the survey believed that "I love you" should only be expressed between spouses. They warned that American men who use the phrase casually with Middle Eastern women might be misinterpreted as making a marriage proposal. Participants from several other cultures (e.g., Eastern Europe, India, Korea) also reported saying "I love you" sparingly, believing that the power of expressing their love would be diminished if used too often. Interestingly, many participants for whom English is a second language said they were more likely to make declarations of love in English than in their native tongues.

This line of research shows that while love may be a universal emotion, the rules for *communicating* that sentiment vary greatly from culture to culture.

Wilkins, R., & Gareis, E. (2006). Emotion expression and the locution "I love you": A cross-cultural study. *International Journal of Intercultural Relations, 30,* 51–75.

Asian American, and Latino respondents; Asian Americans perceived them as the least intense. Also, blacks reported a greater frequency of anger expressions than the other groups. Ethnicity also shaped ideas about appropriate rules for expressing one's own emotions. For example, European Americans perceived the display of emotions as more appropriate than did the other groups; Asian Americans perceived their display as least appropriate. These findings remind us that, in a multicultural society, one element of communicative competence is the ability to understand our own cultural filters when judging others' emotion-related behaviors.

"If I were a car, you could find the words."

One of the most significant factors influencing emotional expression is the position of a culture on the individualism-collectivism spectrum (Kim-Prieto & Eid, 2004; Markus & Kitayama, 1991). Members of collectivistic cultures (such as Japan and India) prize harmony among members of their "in-group" and discourage expression of any negative emotions that might upset relationships among people who belong to it. By contrast, members of highly individualistic cultures like the United States and Canada feel comfortable revealing their feelings to people with whom they are close (Gallois, 1993; Matsumoto, 1991). Individualists and collectivists also handle emotional expression with members of out-groups differently: Whereas individualists are quite frank about expressing negative emotions toward outsiders, collectivists are more likely to hide emotions such as disliking (Triandis, 1994). It's easy to see how differences in display rules can lead to communication problems. For example, individualistic North Americans might view collectivistic Asians as less than candid, whereas a person raised in Asia could easily regard North Americans as overly demonstrative.

GENDER

Even within our culture, gender roles often shape the ways in which men and women experience and express their emotions (Guerrero et al., 2006; Wester et al., 2002). In fact, according to Swenson and Casmir (1998), biological sex is the best predictor of the ability to detect and interpret emotional expressions—better than academic background, amount of foreign travel, cultural similarity, or ethnicity. For example, research suggests that women are faster than men at recognizing both positive and negative emotions from facial cues (Hampson et al., 2006) and better at recognizing multiple emotions (Hall & Matsumoto, 2004) and that in general they are more physiologically attuned to emotions than men (Canli et al., 2002).

Research on emotional expression suggests that there is also some truth in the cultural stereotype of the inexpressive male and the more demonstrative female. On the whole, women seem more likely than men to verbally and nonverbally express a wide range of feelings (Burgoon & Bacue, 2003; Palomares, 2008). On the Internet, the same differences between male and female emotional expressiveness apply. For example, women are more likely to use emoticons to clarify their feelings (Witmer & Katzman, 1997), whereas men are more likely to use emoticons sarcastically (Wolf, 2000).

Whether on the Internet or in face-to-face conversations, men tend to be less emotionally expressive, particularly when it comes to revealing feelings of vulnerability, including fear, sadness, loneliness, and embarrassment. On the other hand, men are less bashful about revealing their strengths and positive emotions, and both sexes feel and express anger equally (Goldsmith & Fulfs, 1999). Moreover, research shows that some married men become more emotionally expressive later in life (Dickson & Walker, 2001).

SOCIAL CONVENTIONS AND ROLES

In mainstream U.S. society, the unwritten rules of communication discourage the direct expression of most emotions (Rabinowitz & Cochran, 1994; Shimanoff, 1984, 1985). Count the number of genuine emotional expressions you hear over a 2- or 3-day period and you'll discover that such expressions are rare. People are generally comfortable making statements of fact and often delight in expressing their opinions, but they rarely disclose how they feel.

Not surprisingly, the emotions that people do share directly are usually positive (although, as Duck, 1992, points out, social rules even discourage too much expression of positive feelings). Communicators are reluctant to send messages that embarrass or threaten the "face" of others (Shimanoff, 1988). Historians offer a detailed description of the ways contemporary society discourages expressions of anger. When compared to past centuries, North Americans today strive to suppress this "unpleasant" emotion in almost every context, including child rearing, the workplace, and personal relationships (Stearns & Stearns, 1986). Research supports this analysis. One study of married couples revealed that the partners shared complimentary feelings ("I love you") or face-saving ones ("I'm sorry I yelled at you"). They also willingly disclosed both positive and negative feelings about absent third parties ("I like Fred," "I'm uncomfortable around Gloria"). On the other hand, the husbands

and wives rarely verbalized face-threatening feelings ("I'm disappointed in you") or hostility ("I'm mad at you") (Shimanoff, 1985).

Expression of emotions is also limited by the requirements of many social roles. Salespeople are taught always to smile at customers, no matter how obnoxious. Firefighters are socialized to manage their emotions and how they display them (Scott & Myers, 2005). Teachers are portrayed as paragons of rationality, supposedly representing their field of expertise and instructing their students with total impartiality. Students are often rewarded for asking "acceptable" questions and otherwise being submissive creatures (McMullen et al., 2007; Trenholm & Rose, 1980).

Just as a muscle withers away when it is unused, our capacity to recognize and act on certain emotions decreases without practice. It's hard to cry after spending most of one's life fulfilling the role society expects of a man, even when the tears are inside (Pollack, 1999). After years of denying anger, the ability to recognize that feeling takes real effort. For someone who has never acknowledged love for one's friends, accepting that emotion can be difficult indeed.

FEAR OF SELF-DISCLOSURE

In a society that discourages the expression of feelings, emotional self-disclosure can seem risky. For a parent, boss, or teacher whose life has been built on the image of confidence and certainty, it may be frightening to say, "I'm sorry. I was wrong."

Moreover, someone who musters up the courage to share feelings such as these still risks unpleasant consequences. Others might

Social Rules and Emotions: *3:10 to Yuma*

Dan Evans (Christian Bale) is a beleaguered man. Crippled by a Civil War injury, beset by cattle rustlers, and harassed by the railroad company that wants his land, Evans struggles to eke out a living for his family in the harsh Arizona territory. To regain the respect of his wife and oldest son, Evans signs on to help deliver the wily and dangerous outlaw Ben Wade (Russell Crowe) to the federal penitentiary in Yuma.

Expressing emotions directly wasn't the norm in the 19th-century American west, and the film reflects this convention. But the powerful feelings the characters have about one another are nonetheless apparent in their nonverbal behaviors: the contempt of Evans' son for his father, the attraction his wife feels toward the outlaw Wade, the devotion Wade's lieutenant feels for his boss, and, above all, Evans' determination to behave honorably in situations where compromising his principles would be the easy way out.

The characters in *3:10 to Yuma* remind us that even when emotions aren't expressed overtly, they play a powerful role in interpersonal relationships.

misunderstand: An expression of affection might be construed as a romantic invitation (Erbert & Floyd, 2004), and a confession of uncertainty might appear to be a sign of weakness. Another risk is that emotional honesty might make others feel uncomfortable. Finally, there's always a chance that emotional honesty could be used against you, either out of cruelty or thoughtlessness. Chapter 3 discussed alternatives to complete disclosure and suggests circumstances when it can be both wise and ethical to keep your feelings to yourself.

EMOTIONAL CONTAGION

Along with cultural rules, social roles, and self-induced fears, our emotions are also affected by the feelings of those around us through **emotional contagion**, the process by which emotions are transferred from one person to another (Hatfield et al., 1984). As Daniel Goleman (1995, p. 115) observed, "We catch feelings from one another as though they were some kind of social virus." There is evidence that students "catch" the mood of their teachers (Bakker, 2005), that husbands and wives influence each other's emotions directly (Goodman & Shippy, 2002), and that coworkers can affect each other's emotions—especially positive ones—with their online communications (Belkin, 2008).

Although people differ in the extent to which they're susceptible to emotional contagion (Doherty, 1997; Lundqvist, 2008), most of us recognize the degree to which emotions are "infectious." You can probably recall instances in which being around a calm person leaves you feeling more at peace, or when your previously sunny mood was spoiled by contact with a grouch. Researchers have demonstrated that this process can occur quickly, and with little or no verbal communication. In one study (Sullins, 1991), two volunteers completed a survey that identified their moods. They spent 2 unsupervised minutes together, ostensibly waiting for the researcher to return to the room. At the end of that time, they completed another emotional survey. Time after time, the brief exposure resulted in the less expressive partner's moods coming to resemble the feelings of the more expressive one. If an expressive communicator can shape another person's feelings with so little input in such a short time, it's easy to understand how emotions can be even more "infectious" with prolonged contact.

REFLECTION

"If Momma Ain't Happy . . ."

There's a sign hanging on our kitchen wall that captures the concept of emotional contagion quite well. It says, "If momma ain't happy, ain't nobody happy." My dad bought it a few years ago and the whole family had a good laugh when we first saw it. Even mom admits that when she's in a bad mood, she can make the rest of us pretty miserable. The good news is that when she's happy, we're usually happy, too!

Guidelines for Expressing Emotions

A wide range of research supports the value of expressing emotions appropriately. At the most basic physiological level, people who know how to share their feelings are healthier than those who don't. On one hand, underexpression of feelings can lead to serious ailments. Inexpressive people—those who value rationality and self-control, try to control their feelings and impulses, and deny distress—are more likely to get a host of ailments, including cancer, asthma, and heart disease (Consedine et al., 2002; Mayne, 1999). On the other hand, people who are overly expressive also suffer physiologically. When people lash out verbally, their blood pressure jumps an average of 20 points, and in some people it increases by as much as 100 points (Mayne, 1999; Siegman & Snow, 1997). The key to health, then, is to learn how to express emotions *constructively.* In a few pages, you will find guidelines for this important communication skill.

Beyond the physiological benefits, another advantage of expressing emotions effectively is the chance of improving relationships (Graham et al. 2008; Kennedy-Moore & Watson, 1999). As Chapter 9 explains, self-disclosure is one path (though not the only one) to intimacy. Even on the job, many managers and organizational researchers are contradicting generations of tradition by suggesting that constructively expressing emotions can lead to career success as well as helping workers feel better (Nelton, 1996). Of course, the rules for expressing emotions on the job are usually stricter than those in personal relationships—especially when it comes to the expression of anger (Kramer & Hess, 2002; Brescoll & Uhlmann, 2008).

Despite its benefits, expressing emotions effectively isn't a simple matter (Fussell, 2002). It's obvious that showing every feeling of boredom, fear, anger, or frustration would get you in trouble. Even the indiscriminate sharing of positive feelings—love, affection, and so on—isn't always wise. On the other hand, withholding emotions can be personally frustrating and can keep relationships from growing and prospering.

The following suggestions can help you decide when and how to express your emotions. Combined with the guidelines for self-disclosure in Chapter 3, they can improve the effectiveness of your emotional expression.

RECOGNIZE YOUR FEELINGS

Answering the question "How do you feel?" isn't as easy for some people as for others (Peper, 2000). Communication researchers Melanie Booth-Butterfield and Steven Booth-Butterfield (1998) found that some people (whom they term "affectively oriented") are much more aware of their own emotional states and use information about those feelings when making important decisions. By contrast, people with a low affective orientation are usually unaware of their emotions, and tend to reject feelings as useful, important information. The researchers summarize studies showing a relationship between awareness of feelings and a wide range of valuable traits, including positive relationships between parents and children, the ability to comfort others, sensitivity to nonverbal cues, and even skillful use of humor. In other words, being aware of one's feelings is an important ingredient in skillful communication.

Beyond being *aware* of one's feelings, research shows that it's valuable to be able to *identify* one's emotions. Lisa Barrett and her colleagues (2001) found that college students who could pinpoint the negative emotions they experienced (such as "nervous," "angry," "sad," "ashamed," and "guilty") also had the best strategies for managing those emotions. Studies like this led Grewal and Salovey (2005) to conclude that the ability to distinguish and label emotions is a vital component of emotional intelligence.

SELF-ASSESSMENT

Identifying Your Emotions

Circle the emotions that you experience often. Then place a *plus mark* next to those that you express effectively, and a *check mark* next to the ones that you communicate in less-than-satisfactory ways. (If one or more of your most-used or expressed emotions isn't on this list, feel free to add it.)

_____ **affectionate**
_____ **afraid**
_____ **aggravated**
_____ **amazed**
_____ **ambivalent**
_____ **angry**
_____ **annoyed**
_____ **anxious**
_____ **apathetic**
_____ **ashamed**
_____ **bashful**
_____ **bewildered**
_____ **bored**
_____ **calm**
_____ **comfortable**
_____ **concerned**
_____ **confident**
_____ **confused**
_____ **content**
_____ **curious**
_____ **defensive**
_____ **delighted**
_____ **depressed**
_____ **desperate**
_____ **detached**
_____ **devastated**
_____ **disappointed**
_____ **disgusted**
_____ **disturbed**
_____ **eager**
_____ **ecstatic**
_____ **edgy**
_____ **elated**
_____ **embarrassed**
_____ **empty**
_____ **enthusiastic**
_____ **excited**
_____ **exhausted**
_____ **exhilarated**
_____ **fidgety**
_____ **foolish**
_____ **forlorn**
_____ **frustrated**
_____ **furious**
_____ **glad**
_____ **glum**
_____ **grateful**
_____ **guilty**
_____ **happy**
_____ **hateful**
_____ **helpless**
_____ **hopeful**
_____ **hopeless**
_____ **horrible**
_____ **hurt**
_____ **hyper**
_____ **impatient**
_____ **inhibited**
_____ **insecure**
_____ **irritable**
_____ **isolated**
_____ **jealous**
_____ **joyful**
_____ **lazy**
_____ **lonely**
_____ **love-struck**
_____ **loving**
_____ **mad**
_____ **mean**
_____ **melancholy**
_____ **miserable**
_____ **mortified**
_____ **nervous**
_____ **overwhelmed**
_____ **passionate**
_____ **peaceful**
_____ **pessimistic**
_____ **playful**
_____ **pleased**
_____ **possessive**
_____ **preoccupied**
_____ **pressured**
_____ **quiet**
_____ **regretful**
_____ **relieved**
_____ **remorseful**
_____ **repulsed**
_____ **resentful**
_____ **restless**
_____ **sad**
_____ **secure**
_____ **sentimental**
_____ **sexy**
_____ **shaky**
_____ **shocked**
_____ **shy**
_____ **silly**
_____ **smug**
_____ **sorry**
_____ **stubborn**
_____ **stupid**
_____ **subdued**
_____ **surprised**
_____ **suspicious**
_____ **sympathetic**
_____ **tense**
_____ **terrified**
_____ **tired**
_____ **touchy**
_____ **trapped**
_____ **uneasy**
_____ **unsure**
_____ **useless**
_____ **vulnerable**
_____ **wacky**
_____ **warm**
_____ **weak**
_____ **weary**
_____ **worried**
_____ **zany**

What lessons do your responses show? In what ways are you satisfied with your emotional expression? In what areas would you like to improve it? Keep your findings in mind as you continue reading this chapter.

As you read earlier in this chapter, there are a number of ways in which feelings become recognizable. Physiological changes can be a clear sign of your emotional state. Monitoring nonverbal behaviors is another excellent way to keep in touch with your feelings. You can also recognize your emotions by monitoring your thoughts, as well as the verbal messages you send to others. It's not far from the verbal statement "I hate this!" to the realization that you're angry (or bored, nervous, or embarrassed).

"What's the word I want for that disposition of yours?"

CHOOSE THE BEST LANGUAGE

Most people suffer from impoverished emotional vocabularies. Ask them how they're feeling and the response will almost always include the same terms: *good* or *bad, terrible* or *great,* and so on. Take a moment now and see how many feelings you can write down. After you've done your best, look at the Self-Assessment activity on page 256 and see which ones you've missed from this admittedly incomplete list.

Many communicators think they are expressing feelings when, in fact, their statements are emotionally counterfeit. For example, it sounds emotionally revealing to say "I feel like going to a show" or "I feel we've been seeing too much of each other." But in fact, neither of these statements has any emotional content. In the first sentence the word *feel* really stands for an intention: "I *want* to go to a show." In the second sentence the "feeling" is really a thought: "I *think* we've been seeing too much of each other." You can recognize the absence of emotion in each case by adding a genuine word of feeling to it. For instance, "I'm *bored* and I want to go to a show" or "I think we've been seeing too much of each other and I feel *confined.*"

Relying on a small vocabulary of feelings is as limiting as using only a few terms to describe colors. To say that the ocean in all its moods, the sky as it varies from day to day, and the color of your true love's eyes are all "blue" only tells a fraction of the story. Likewise, it's overly broad to use a term like *good* or *great* to describe how you feel in situations as different as earning a high grade, finishing a marathon, and hearing the words "I love you" from a special person.

There are several ways to express a feeling verbally:

- Through *single words:* "I'm angry" (or "excited," "depressed," "curious," and so on).
- By describing *what's happening to you metaphorically:* "My stomach is tied in knots," "I'm on top of the world."
- By describing *what you'd like to do:* "I want to run away," "I'd like to give you a hug," "I feel like giving up."

Finally, you can improve emotional expression by making it clear that your feeling is centered on a specific set of circumstances, rather than the whole relationship. Instead of saying "I resent you," say "I get resentful when you don't keep your promises." Rather than "I'm bored with you," say "I get bored when you talk about money."

SHARE MULTIPLE FEELINGS

Many times the feeling you express isn't the only one you're experiencing. For example, you might often express your anger but overlook the confusion, disappointment, frustration, sadness, or embarrassment that preceded it. To understand the importance of expressing multiple emotions, consider the following examples. For each one, ask yourself two questions: How would I feel? What feelings might I express?

- An out-of-town friend has promised to arrive at your house at 6 o'clock. When your guest hasn't arrived by 9 o'clock, you are convinced that a terrible accident has occurred. Just as you pick up the phone to call the police and local hospitals, your friend breezes in the door with an offhand remark about getting a late start.
- You and your companion have a fight just before leaving for a party. Deep inside, you know you were mostly to blame, even though you aren't willing to admit it. When you arrive at the party, your companion leaves you to flirt with several other attractive guests.

In situations like these you would probably feel several emotions. Consider the case of the overdue friend. Your first reaction to his arrival would probably be relief—"Thank goodness, he's safe!" But you would also be likely to feel anger—"Why didn't he phone to tell me he'd be late?" The second example would probably leave you with an even greater number of emotions: guilt at contributing to the fight, hurt and perhaps embarrassment at your friend's flirtations, and anger at this sort of vengefulness.

Despite the commonness of experiencing several emotions at the same time (Oatley & Duncan, 1992), we often communicate only one feeling—usually, the most negative one. In both of the preceding examples you might show only your anger, leaving the other person with little idea of the full range of your feelings. Consider the different reaction you would get by describing *all* your emotions in these situations as well as others. (See the Reflection on this page.)

REFLECTION

Choosing the Emotion to Express First

Not long ago our 17-year-old daughter spent the entire night out—without telling us about her plans to stay at a friend's. By 2:00 A.M. we were in a panic. We frantically called the police and the local hospitals, but she couldn't be found anywhere. My wife and I spent the entire sleepless night praying that she was all right and imagining all the awful things that might have happened to her.

When our daughter's car came up the driveway at 7:30 A.M., I was never so relieved in my life! But as soon as she walked in the door and I realized she was OK, I really let her have it. "What were you thinking? How irresponsible can you be?" You can imagine how I sounded, and how defensively she reacted.

After a couple of minutes I could see our "conversation" headed in the wrong direction, and that it was at least partly my fault. I had only shared my anger, and not the feelings of relief, concern, and love that were even more important. "Let's start over," I suggested. Then I explained to her how worried we were all night long, and how relieved we were to know that she was safe. What a difference! Our daughter still knew how angry we were, but she also understood that the anger came from love and concern. This experience taught me how important it is to share mixed feelings. Hearing the positive ones makes negative feelings a lot easier to accept.

RECOGNIZE THE DIFFERENCE BETWEEN FEELING AND ACTING

Just because you feel a certain way doesn't mean you must always act on it. In fact, there is compelling evidence that people who act out angry feelings—even by hitting an inanimate punching bag—actually feel worse than those who experience anger without lashing out (Bushman et al., 1999). More to the point of this book, researchers have discovered that people who deal with negative feelings by venting them indiscriminately have above-average levels of anxiety in their interpersonal relationships (Jerome & Liss, 2005).

Recognizing the difference between feeling and acting can liberate you from the fear that getting in touch with certain emotions will commit you to some disastrous course of action. If, for instance, you think "I'm so nervous about the interview that I want to cancel it and pretend that I'm sick," it becomes possible to explore why you feel so anxious and then work to remedy the problem. Pretending that nothing is the matter, on the other hand, will do nothing to diminish your anxiety, which can then block your chances for success.

ACCEPT RESPONSIBILITY FOR YOUR FEELINGS

As you'll soon read, people don't *make us* like or dislike them, and believing that they do denies the responsibility each of us has for our own emotions. It's important to make sure that your emotional expressions don't blame others for the way you feel (Bippus & Young, 2005). The "I" language described in Chapter 5 makes it clear that you own your feelings. For example, instead of saying "You're making me angry," it's more accurate to say, "I'm feeling angry." Instead of "You hurt my feelings," a more responsible statement is, "I feel hurt when you do that."

CHOOSE THE BEST TIME AND PLACE TO EXPRESS YOUR FEELINGS

Often the first flush of a strong feeling is not the best time to speak out. If you're awakened by the racket caused by a noisy neighbor, storming over to complain might result in your saying things you'll regret later. In such a case, it's probably wiser to wait until you have thought out carefully how you might express your feelings in a way that would be most likely to be heard.

THE DARK SIDE OF COMMUNICATION

Virtually Unfaithful: Emotional Infidelity in Cyberspace

Infidelity has been a fact of life as long as romance has existed. In the digital age, some people are "virtually unfaithful," carrying on romantic relationships via e-mail, online chats, and other mediated channels. In recent years, researchers have begun to study how mediated infidelity is similar to and different from the in-person variety.

In an effort to learn about perceptions of "cybercheating," researcher Monica Whitty asked 234 university students to imagine how a person would feel after discovering that his or her partner had developed a romantic relationship with someone over the Internet.

The majority of students—both men and women—believed that infidelity in an online relationship was just as much of a betrayal as cheating in person. Most significantly, emotional dishonesty was regarded as just as disloyal as sexual infidelity.

Research like this provides a cautionary note about the dangers of online romance. Making emotional connections with someone in cyberspace—even if there is no physical involvement—can jeopardize committed face-to-face relationships.

Whitty, M. T. (2005). The realness of cybercheating: Men's and women's representations of unfaithful Internet relationships. *Social Science Computer Review, 23,* 57–67.

Even after you've waited for the first flush of feeling to subside, it's still important to choose the time that's best suited to the message. Being rushed or tired or disturbed by some other matter is probably a good reason for postponing the expression of your feeling. Often, dealing with your emotions can take a great amount of time and effort, and fatigue or distraction will make it difficult to follow through on the matter you've started. In the same manner you ought to be sure that the recipient of your message is ready to hear you out before you begin.

There are also cases where you may choose never to express your feelings. Even if you're dying to tell an instructor that her lectures leave you bored to a stupor, you might decide it's best to answer her question "How's class going?" with an innocuous "OK." And even though you may be irritated by the arrogance of a police officer stopping you for speeding, the smartest approach might be to keep your feelings to yourself. In cases where you experience strong emotions but don't want to share them verbally (for whatever reason), writing out your feelings and thoughts has been shown to have mental, physical, and emotional benefits (Burton & King, 2008; Pennebaker, 2004). For instance, one study found that writing about feelings of affection can actually reduce one's cholesterol level (Floyd et al., 2007).

Managing Difficult Emotions

Perceiving others more accurately isn't the only challenge communicators face. At times we view *ourselves* in a distorted way. These distorted self-perceptions can generate a wide range of feelings—insecurity, anger, and guilt, to name a few—that interfere with effective communication. To begin understanding how this process works, read on.

FACILITATIVE AND DEBILITATIVE EMOTIONS

We need to make a distinction between **facilitative emotions**, which contribute to effective functioning, and **debilitative emotions**, which hinder or

prevent effective performance. A classic example of a debilitative emotion is **communication apprehension**—feelings of anxiety that plague some people at the prospect of communicating in an unfamiliar or difficult context, such as giving a speech, meeting strangers, or interviewing for a job. Not surprisingly, debilitative emotions like communication apprehension can lead to a variety of problems in personal, business, educational, and even medical settings (Bourhis & Allen, 1992; Butler, 2005).

The difference between facilitative and debilitative emotions often isn't one of quality so much as degree. For instance, a certain amount of anger or irritation can be constructive, since it often stimulates a person to improve the unsatisfying conditions. Rage, on the other hand, usually makes matters worse. The same is true for fear. A little bit of nervousness before a job interview may boost you just enough to improve your performance (mellow athletes or actors usually don't do well), but a job candidate who is visibly nervous isn't likely to impress potential employers (Ayres & Crosby, 1995). One big difference, then, between facilitative and debilitative emotions is their *intensity*.

A second characteristic of debilitative feelings is their extended *duration*. Feeling depressed for a while after the breakup of a relationship or the loss of a job is natural. Spending the rest of one's life grieving over the loss accomplishes nothing. In the same way, staying angry at someone for a wrong inflicted long ago can be just as punishing to the grudge holder as to the wrongdoer.

THOUGHTS CAUSE FEELINGS

The goal, then, is to find a method for getting rid of debilitative feelings while remaining sensitive to the more facilitative emotions. Fortunately, such a method—termed a *rational-emotive* approach—does exist (Ellis, 2001, 2004; Ellis & Dryden, 1997). This method is based on the idea that the key to changing feelings is to change unproductive thinking. Let's see how it works.

For most people, emotions seem to have a life of their own. People wish they could feel calm when approaching strangers, yet their voices quiver. They try to appear confident when asking for a raise, but their eyes twitch nervously. Many people would say that the strangers or the boss *makes* them feel nervous, just as they would say that a bee sting causes them to feel pain:

Activating Event	→	**Consequence**
bee sting	→	physical pain
meeting strangers	→	nervous feelings

When looking at emotions in this way, people may believe they have little control over how they feel. However, the causal relationship between activating events and emotional discomfort (or pleasure) isn't as great as it seems. Cognitive psychologists and therapists argue that it is not events, such as meeting strangers or being jilted by a lover, that cause people to feel poorly, but rather the *beliefs they hold* about these events.

Albert Ellis tells a story that clarifies this point. Imagine yourself walking by a friend's house and seeing your friend come to a window and call you a string of vile names. (You supply the friend and the names.) Under the circumstances, it's likely that you would feel hurt and upset. Now imagine that instead of walking by the house, you were passing a mental institution when the same friend, who was obviously a patient there, shouted the same offensive names at you. In this case, your reaction would probably be quite different; most likely, you'd feel sadness and pity.

In this story the activating event—being called names—was the same in both cases, yet the emotional consequences were very different. The reason for different feelings has to do with the pattern of thinking in each case. In the first instance you would most likely think that your friend was angry with you and that you must have done something terrible to deserve such a response. In the second case you would probably assume that your friend had experienced some psychological difficulty, so you would probably feel sympathetic. This example illustrates that people's *interpretations* of events determine their feelings:

Activating Event	→	**Thought or Belief**	→	**Consequences**
being called names	→	"I've done something wrong."	→	hurt, upset
being called names	→	"My friend must be sick."	→	pity, sympathy

The same principle applies in more common situations. For example, the words "I love you" can be interpreted in a variety of ways. They could be taken at face value, as a genuine expression of deep affection. They might also be decoded in a variety of other ways: for example, as an attempt at manipulation, a sincere but mistaken declaration uttered in a moment of passion, or an attempt to make the recipient feel better. It's easy to imagine

how different interpretations of a statement like "I love you" can lead to different emotional reactions:

Event	→	**Thought**	→	**Feeling**
hearing "I love you"	→	"This is a genuine statement."	→	delight (perhaps)
hearing "I love you"	→	"She's (he's) just saying this to manipulate me."	→	anger

The key, then, to understanding and changing feelings lies in the pattern of thought, which manifests itself through **self-talk** (Vocate, 1994)—the nonvocal, internal monologue that is our process of thinking. To understand how self-talk works, pay attention to the part of you that, like a little voice, whispers in your ear. Take a moment now and listen to what the voice is saying.

Did you hear the voice? It was quite possibly saying "What little voice? I don't hear any voices!" This little voice talks to you almost constantly:

"Better pick up a loaf of bread on the way home."
"I wonder when he's going to stop talking."
"It sure is cold today!"
"Are there two or four cups in a quart?"

At work or at play, while reading the paper or brushing our teeth, we all tend to think. This thinking voice rarely stops. It may fall silent for a while when you're running, riding a bike, or meditating, but most of the time it rattles on.

IRRATIONAL THINKING AND DEBILITATIVE EMOTIONS

This process of self-talk is essential to understanding the debilitative feelings that interfere with effective communication (Cohen, 2007). Many debilitative feelings come from accepting a number of irrational thoughts—we'll call them *fallacies* here—that lead to illogical conclusions and, in turn, to debilitating feelings. We usually aren't aware of these thoughts, which makes them especially powerful (Bargh, 1988).

The Fallacy of Perfection People who accept the **fallacy of perfection** believe that a worthwhile communicator should be able to handle any situation with complete confidence and skill. Although such a standard of perfection can serve as a goal and a source of inspiration (rather like making a hole in one for a golfer), it's totally unrealistic to expect that you can reach or maintain this level of behavior. The truth is, people simply aren't perfect. Perhaps the myth of the perfect communicator comes from believing too strongly in novels, television, or films. In these media, perfect characters are often depicted—the perfect mate or child, the totally controlled and gregarious host, the incredibly competent professional. Although these fabrications are certainly appealing, real people will inevitably come up short compared to them.

People who believe that it's desirable and possible to be a perfect communicator come to think that people won't appreciate them if they are imperfect. Admitting mistakes, saying "I don't know," or sharing feelings of uncertainty or discomfort thus seem to be social defects. Given the desire to be valued and appreciated, these people are tempted at least to try to *appear* perfect. They assemble a variety of social masks, hoping that if they can fool others into thinking that they are perfect, perhaps they'll find acceptance. The costs of such deception are high. If others ever detect that this veneer of confidence is false, then the person hiding behind it is considered a phony. Even if the facade goes undetected, the performance consumes a great deal of psychological energy and diminishes the rewards of approval.

Not only can subscribing to the myth of perfection keep others from liking you, but it also acts as a force to diminish self-esteem. How can you like yourself when you don't measure up to your own standards?

You become more liberated each time you comfortably accept the idea that you are not perfect. For example, like everyone else, you sometimes have a hard time expressing yourself. Like everyone else, you make mistakes from time to time, and there is no reason to hide it. You are honestly doing the best you can to realize your potential, to become the best person you can be.

The Fallacy of Approval Another mistaken belief is based on the idea that it is vital—not just desirable—to obtain everyone's approval. Communicators who subscribe to the **fallacy of approval** go to incredible lengths to seek acceptance from others, even to the extent of sacrificing their own principles and happiness. Adherence to this irrational myth can lead to some ludicrous situations, such as feeling nervous because people you really don't like seem to disapprove of you, or feeling apologetic when you are not at fault.

The myth of approval is irrational. It implies that some people are more respectable and more likable because they go out of their way to please others. Often, this implication simply isn't true. How respectable are people who have compromised important values simply to gain acceptance? Are people highly regarded when they repeatedly deny their own needs as a means of buying approval? Genuine affection and respect are hardly due such characters. In addition, striving for universal acceptance is irrational because it is simply not possible.

Don't misunderstand: Abandoning the fallacy of approval doesn't mean living a life of selfishness. It's still important to consider the needs of others. It's also pleasant—one might even say necessary—to strive for the respect of certain people. The point is that the price is too high if you must abandon your own needs and principles in order to gain this acceptance.

The Fallacy of Should One huge source of unhappiness is the inability to distinguish between what *is* and what *should be,* or the **fallacy of should**. For instance, imagine a person who is full of complaints about the world:

"There should be no rain on weekends."
"People ought to live forever."
"Money should grow on trees."
"We should all be able to fly."

Beliefs such as these are obviously foolish. However pleasant such wishing may be, insisting that the unchangeable should be altered won't affect reality one bit. Yet many people torture themselves by engaging in this sort of irrational thinking: They confuse "is" with "ought." They say and think:

"That guy should drive better."
"She shouldn't be so inconsiderate."
"They ought to be more friendly."
"He should work harder."

In each of these cases, the person *prefers* that people behave differently. Wishing that things were better is perfectly legitimate, and trying to change them is, of course, a good idea, but it is unreasonable for people to insist that the world operate just as they want it to. Parents wish that their children were always considerate and neat. Teachers wish that their students were totally fascinated with their subjects and willing to study diligently. Consumers wish that inflation weren't such a problem. As the old saying goes, those wishes and a quarter (now you'd need much more) will get you a cup of coffee.

Becoming obsessed with shoulds yields three bad consequences. First, this preoccupation leads to unnecessary unhappiness. People who are constantly dreaming about the ideal are seldom satisfied with what they have. For instance, partners in a marriage who focus on the ways in which their mate could be more considerate, sexy, or intelligent have a hard time appreciating the strengths that drew them together in the first place.

Second, the obsession keeps you from changing unsatisfying conditions. One employee, for example, constantly complains about the problems on the job: There should be better training, pay ought to be higher, the facilities should be upgraded, and so on. This person could be using the same energy to improve such conditions. Of course, not all problems have solutions, but when they do, complaining is rarely very productive. As one college manager puts it, "Rather than complain about the cards you are dealt, play the hand well."

Finally, this obsession tends to build a defensive climate in others. Imagine living around someone who insisted that people be more punctual, work harder, or refrain from using certain language. This kind of carping is obviously irritating. It's much easier to be around people who comment without preaching.

Rather than demanding that people behave the way you wish they would and feeling overly disappointed when they don't, it can be more realistic to think to yourself "I *wish* she (he) would behave the way I want, and it's probably reasonable to ask for change, but if the other person won't meet my expectations, I'm just setting myself up for disappointment if I expect change to happen."

The Fallacy of Overgeneralization The **fallacy of overgeneralization** occurs when a person bases a belief on a *limited amount of evidence.* Consider the following statements:

"I'm so stupid! I can't understand how to do my income tax."
"Some friend I am! I forgot my best friend's birthday."

In these cases people have focused on a single shortcoming as if it represented everything. Sometimes people forget that despite their difficulties, they have solved tough problems, and that although they can be forgetful, they're often caring and thoughtful.

A second, related category of overgeneralization occurs when we *exaggerate shortcomings:*

"You *never* listen to me."
"You're *always* late."
"I can't think of *anything.*"

Upon closer examination, such absolute statements are almost always false and usually lead to discouragement or anger. It's better to replace overgeneralizations with more accurate messages:

"You often don't listen to me."
"You've been late three times this week."
"I haven't had any ideas I like today."

The Fallacy of Causation People who live their lives in accordance with the **fallacy of causation** believe they should do nothing that can hurt or in any way inconvenience others because it will cause undesirable feelings. For example, you might visit friends or family out of a sense of obligation rather than a genuine desire to see them because, you believe, not to visit them will hurt their feelings. Did you ever avoid objecting to behavior that you found troublesome because you didn't want to cause anger? You may, on occasion, have pretended to be attentive—even though you were running late for an appointment and in a rush—because you didn't want a person to feel embarrassed for "holding you up." Then there were the times when you substituted praise for more honest negative responses in order to avoid causing hurt.

A reluctance to speak out in such situations often results from assuming that one person can cause another's emotions—that others, for example, are responsible for your feeling disappointed, confused, or irritated, or that you are responsible for others feeling hurt, angry, or upset. Actually, this assumption is incorrect. We may *act* in provocative ways, but each person is responsible for the way he or she *reacts.*

To understand why each person is responsible for his or her own feelings, consider how strange it sounds to suggest that people *make* you fall in love with them. Such a statement simply doesn't make sense. It would be more correct to say that people first act in one way or another; then you may or may not fall in love as a result of these actions.

In the same way, it's not accurate to say that people *make* you angry, upset, or even happy. Behavior that upsets or pleases one person might not bring any reaction from another. If you doubt this fact, think about people you know who respond differently to the same behaviors that you find so bothersome. (You may scream "Idiot!" when you're driving and someone switches lanes in front of you without signaling, while the person with you in the car may not even notice, or may notice but not care.) The contrast between others' reactions and yours shows that responses are determined more by our own temperament and thinking than by others' behavior.

One way to avoid the debilitative feelings that often accompany the fallacy of causation is to use responsible language, as discussed in Chapter 5. Instead of saying "He makes me so angry," reframe it as your reaction to the other person's behavior: "I don't like when he talks about me behind my back." Instead of saying, "I had to visit my parents this weekend; they gave me no option," take responsibility for your choices: "I decided to visit my parents this weekend, but I may choose differently next time." Taking ownership for your actions and reactions can often lead to a sense of empowerment.

The Fallacy of Helplessness The **fallacy of helplessness** suggests that forces beyond our control determine satisfaction in life. People with this outlook continually see themselves as victims:

> "There's no way a woman can get ahead in this society. It's a man's world, and the best thing I can do is to accept it."
>
> "I was born with a shy personality. I'd like to be more outgoing, but there's nothing I can do about that."
>
> "I can't tell my boss that she is putting too many demands on me. If I did, I might lose my job."

The error in such statements becomes apparent once a person realizes that few paths are completely closed. In fact, most "can't" statements may be more correctly restated in one of two ways.

The first is to say that you *won't* act in a certain way, that you choose not to do so. For instance, you may choose not to stand up for your rights or to follow unwanted requests, but it is usually inaccurate to claim that some outside force keeps you from doing so. The other way to rephrase a "can't" is to say that you *don't know how* to do something. Examples of such a situation include not knowing how to complain in a way that reduces defensiveness, or not being aware of how to conduct a conversation. Many difficulties a person claims can't be solved do have solutions: The task is to discover those solutions and to work diligently at applying them.

When viewed in this light, many "can'ts" are really rationalizations to justify an unwillingness to change. Research supports the dangers of helpless thinking (Marangoni & Ickes, 1989). Lonely people tend to attribute their poor interpersonal relationships to uncontrollable causes. "It's beyond my control," they think. For example, lonely people are more negative than nonlonely ones about ever finding a mate. Also, they expect their relational partners to reject them. Notice the self-fulfilling prophecy in this attitude: Believing that your relational prospects are dim can lead you to act in ways that make you an unattractive prospect. Once you persuade yourself that there's no hope, it's easy to give up trying. On the other hand, acknowledging that there is a way to change—even though it may be difficult—puts the responsibility for the predicament on your shoulders. Knowing that you can move closer to your goals makes it difficult to complain about the present. You *can* become a better communicator.

The Fallacy of Catastrophic Expectations Some fearful people operate on the assumption that if something bad can happen, it probably will. This is the **fallacy of catastrophic expectations**—a position similar to Murphy's Law. These statements are typical of such an attitude:

> "If I invite them to the party, they probably won't want to come."
> "If I speak up in order to try to resolve a conflict, things will probably get worse."
> "If I apply for the job I want, I probably won't be hired."
> "If I tell them how I really feel, they'll probably just laugh at me."

Once you start imagining terrible consequences, a self-fulfilling prophecy can begin to build. One study revealed that people who believed that their romantic partners would not change for the better were likely to behave in ways that contributed to the breakup of the relationship (Metts & Cupach, 1990).

FOCUS ON RESEARCH

The "Pessimism Bias:" A Recipe for Relational Misery

Sooner or later, uncertainty crops up in most romantic relationships. Was your partner just being friendly, or was she flirting with that stranger at last night's party? Is his silence a normal desire for solitude or a sign of displeasure?

Leanne Knobloch and her colleagues believe that a "pessimism bias" causes people who are unsure about the status of their relationship to overreact in the face of ambiguous messages. To test their hypothesis, they analyzed the conversations of 125 married couples after asking each spouse to describe the degree of uncertainty he or she was feeling about the relationship.

The researchers found that relational uncertainty did indeed lead spouses to process messages negatively. Uncertain partners perceived threats that were not apparent to outside observers. While it's fair to assume that some of the insecure spouses had good reason to worry about their relationships, it's likely that many others imagined threats that didn't exist.

Once a pessimism bias sets in, it's easy to imagine the kinds of irrational self-talk that can create misery for both an insecure communicator and his or her partner.

Knobloch, L. K., Miller, L. E., Bond, B. J., & Mannone, S. E. (2007). Relational uncertainty and message processing in marriage. *Communication Monographs, 74,* 154–180.

Catastrophic thinking often takes the form of **rumination**—recurrent thoughts not demanded by the immediate environment. For example, jealous lovers who dwell on imagined transgressions of their partners feel more distressed than necessary and act in counterproductive ways toward their partners (Carson & Cupach, 2000b). Likewise, teenage girls who ruminate about problems with their friends have an increased risk of suffering from anxiety and depression (Rose et al., 2007). And sometimes ruminating can be used to sustain anger in preparation for retaliation—not a healthy approach (Knobloch-Westerwick & Alter, 2006).

MINIMIZING DEBILITATIVE EMOTIONS

How can you overcome irrational thinking? Social scientists have developed a simple yet effective approach (Cohen, 2007; Ellis, 2001). When practiced conscientiously, it can help you cut down on the self-defeating thinking that leads to many debilitative emotions.

Monitor Your Emotional Reactions The first step is to recognize when you're having debilitative emotions. (Of course, it's also nice to be aware of pleasant feelings when they occur!) As we suggested earlier, one way to notice feelings is through physical stimuli: butterflies in the stomach, racing heart, hot flashes, and so on. Although such reactions might be symptoms of food poisoning, more often they reflect a strong emotion. You also can recognize certain ways of behaving that suggest your feelings: stomping instead of walking normally, being unusually quiet, and speaking in a sarcastic tone of voice are some examples.

It may seem strange to suggest that it's necessary to look for emotions—they ought to be immediately apparent. However, the fact is that we often suffer from debilitative feelings for some time without noticing them. For example, at the end of a trying day you've probably caught yourself frowning and realized that you've been wearing that face for some time without knowing it.

Remember the two key characteristics of debilitating emotions, intensity (they are *too* intense) and duration (they last *too* long), and use them to guide your assessment.

Note the Activating Event Once you're aware of how you're feeling, the next step is to figure out what activating event triggered your response. Sometimes it is obvious. If your sweetheart keeps calling you by the name of a former lover, you're likely to become upset. Research shows that dating couples can develop "social allergies" to each other, becoming hypersensitive about their partner's annoying behaviors (Cunningham et al., 2005). In these cases, it's easy to identify what triggers a given response. In other cases, however, the activating event isn't so apparent.

Sometimes there isn't a single activating event, but rather a series of small incidents that finally build toward a critical mass and trigger a debilitative feeling. This sort of thing happens when someone teases you over and over about the same thing, or when you suffer a series of small disappointments.

The best way to begin tracking down activating events is to notice the circumstances in which you have debilitative feelings. Perhaps they occur when you're around *specific people*. For example, you may feel tense or angry every time you encounter a person with whom you have struggled in the past (Gayle & Preiss, 1999). Until those issues are dealt with, feelings about past events can trigger debilitative emotions, even in apparently innocuous situations.

In other cases, you might discover that being around certain *types of individuals* triggers debilitative emotions. For instance, you might become nervous around people who seem more intelligent or self-confident than you are. In other cases, certain *settings* can stimulate unpleasant emotions: parties, work, school. Sometimes the *topic of conversation* is the factor that sets you off, whether politics, religion, sex, or some other subject. Recognizing your activating events is an important step in minimizing debilitative emotions.

Record Your Self-Talk This is the point at which you analyze the thoughts that are the link between the activating event and your feelings. If you're serious about getting rid of debilitative emotions, it's important to actually write down your self-talk when first learning to use this method. Putting your thoughts on paper will help you see whether or not they make any sense.

Monitoring your self-talk might be difficult at first. This is a new skill, and any new activity seems awkward. If you persevere, however, you'll find you will be able to identify the thoughts that lead to your debilitative feelings. Once you get in the habit of recognizing this internal monologue, you'll be able to identify your thoughts quickly and easily.

Dispute Your Irrational Beliefs Disputing your irrational beliefs is the key to success in the rational-emotive approach. Use the discussion of irrational fallacies on pages 263–268 to find out which of your internal statements are based on mistaken thinking.

You can do this most effectively by following three steps. First, decide whether each belief you've recorded is rational or irrational. Next, explain why the belief does or doesn't make sense. Finally, if the belief is irrational, write down an alternative way of thinking that is more sensible and that can leave you feeling better when faced with the same activating event in the future.

After reading about this method for dealing with unpleasant emotions, some readers have objections:

"*This rational-emotive approach sounds like nothing more than trying to talk yourself out of feeling bad.*" This accusation is totally correct. After all, since we talk ourselves into feeling bad, what's wrong with talking ourselves out of bad feelings, especially when they are based on irrational thoughts?

"*The kind of disputing we just read sounds phony and unnatural. I don't talk to myself in sentences and paragraphs.*" There's no need to dispute your irrational beliefs in any special literary style. You can be just as colloquial as you want. The important thing is to clearly understand what thoughts led you into your debilitative feeling so you can clearly dispute them. When the technique is new to you, it's a good idea to write or talk out your thoughts in order to make them clear. After you've had some practice, you'll be able to do these steps in a quicker, less formal way.

"*This approach is too cold and impersonal. It seems to aim at turning people into cold-blooded, calculating, emotionless machines.*" This is simply not true. A rational thinker can still dream, hope, and love: There's nothing necessarily irrational about feelings like these. Rational people usually indulge in a bit of irrational thinking once in a while. But they usually know what they're doing. Like healthy eaters who occasionally treat themselves to a snack of junk food, rational thinkers occasionally indulge themselves in irrational thoughts, knowing that they'll return to their healthy lifestyle soon with no real damage done.

"*This technique promises too much. There's no chance I could rid myself of all unpleasant feelings, however nice that might be.*" We can answer this by assuring you that rational-emotive thinking probably won't totally solve your emotional problems. What it can do is to reduce their number, intensity, and duration. This method is not the answer to all your problems, but it can make a significant difference—which is not a bad accomplishment.

Summary

Emotions have several dimensions. They are signaled by internal physiological changes, manifested by verbal and nonverbal reactions, and defined in most cases by cognitive interpretations.

There are several reasons why people do not verbalize many of the emotions they feel. Certain personality types respond to emotions more negatively than others. Some cultures encourage and others discourage the expression of emotions. Biological sex and gender roles also shape the way people experience and express emotions. Social rules discourage the expression of some feelings, particularly negative ones. Many social roles do not allow expression of certain feelings. Some people express emotions so rarely that they lose the ability to recognize when they are feeling them. Fear of the consequences of disclosing some emotions leads people to withhold expression of them. Finally, exposure to others' emotions can shape the way we feel ourselves, through the process of emotional contagion.

Since total expression of feelings is not appropriate for adults, several guidelines help define when and how to share emotions effectively. Self-awareness, clear language, and expression of multiple feelings are important, as is the ability to recognize the difference between feeling and acting. Willingness to accept responsibility for feelings instead of blaming them on others leads to better reactions. Choosing the proper time and place to share feelings is also important.

While some emotions are facilitative, other, debilitative feelings inhibit effective functioning. Many of these debilitative emotions are caused by various types of irrational thinking. It is often possible to communicate more confidently and effectively by identifying troublesome emotions, identifying the activating event and self-talk that triggered them, and replacing any irrational thoughts with a more logical analysis of the situation.

Activities

1. Invitation to Insight

The Self-Assessment exercise on page 256 explored your "favorite" emotions without focusing on any particular relationship. What happens when you have a specific relationship in mind? Using the list of emotions in the Self-Assessment, complete the following steps:

a. Focus on an important personal relationship.
b. Identify the few emotions that play the most important role for *you* in the relationship.
c. Identify the few emotions that you think play the most important role for the *other person* in the relationship.
d. Identify how you express each emotion you identified as most important for you. Focus on the frequency with which you express each feeling, the circumstances in which you express it, and the ways you express it.
e. Identify how the other person expresses each emotion you identified as most important for her or him. Focus on the frequency with which the other person expresses each feeling, the circumstances in which it is expressed, and how she or he expresses it.
f. What have you learned about yourself, the other person, and your relationship by conducting this analysis?

If possible, invite the other person to complete the same analysis and compare your results.

2. Skill Builder

Choose an important emotion you experience in one of your relationships. This relationship needn't be highly personal. You might, for example, focus on an employer, a professor, or a neighbor. Use the guidelines on pages 254–260 to determine whether and how you might express this emotion.

3. Ethical Challenge

According to the rational-emotive approach, we cause our own feelings by interpreting an event in one way or another. If this is true, it is a fallacy to claim we "make" others feel happy or sad. Do you accept this position? To what degree are you responsible for communicating in ways hat "cause" others to feel happy or sad? Use a specific incident from your life to illustrate your answer.

4. Invitation to Insight

Explore whether you subscribe to the fallacy of helplessness by completing the following lists. Describe two important (to you) communication-related difficulties you have for each of the following: communicating with family members, people at school or at work, strangers, and friends. Use the following format for each difficulty:

I can't ______________
because ______________.

Now read the list, but with a slight difference. For each "can't," substitute the word "won't." Note which statements are actually "won'ts."

Read the list again, only this time substitute "I don't know how to" for your original "can't." Rewrite any statements that are truly "don't know hows," and decide what you could do to learn the skill that you presently lack.

Based on your experience, decide whether you subscribe to the fallacy of helplessness, and what you could do to eliminate this sort of debilitative thinking from your life.

5. Skill Builder

Choose an important situation in which you experience debilitative emotions that interfere with your ability to communicate effectively. Use the four steps on pages 269–271 to challenge the rationality of your beliefs. Report on how the rational-emotive approach affects your communication in this important situation.

CHAPTER 9 Dynamics of Interpersonal Relationships

CHAPTER OUTLINE

After studying the material in this chapter . . .

YOU SHOULD UNDERSTAND:

1. The reasons people choose others as potential relational partners.
2. The importance of intimacy and commitment in interpersonal relationships.
3. The stages of relational development and maintenance and the characteristics of movement between these stages.
4. The dialectical tensions that can arise as communicators attempt to satisfy conflicting needs.
5. The ways content and relational messages are communicated in interpersonal relationships.
6. The strategies for maintaining healthy relationships and for repairing damaged ones.

YOU SHOULD BE ABLE TO:

1. Identify the bases of interpersonal attraction in one of your relationships.
2. Identify the intimate and committed relationships in your life and ways to keep them strong.
3. Describe the current stage of an important personal relationship and the prospects for the relationship's moving to a different stage.
4. Identify the dialectical tensions that influence your communication goals, the strategies you use to manage these tensions, and alternative strategies you might consider using.
5. Describe ways to maintain your healthy relationships and repair those that have been damaged.

KEY TERMS

- Avoiding (294)
- Bonding (292)
- Circumscribing (294)
- Comparison level (CL) (280)
- Comparison level of alternatives (CL_{alt}) (280)
- Connection-autonomy dialectic (297)
- Conventionality-uniqueness dialectic (299)
- Dialectical tensions (296)
- Differentiating (293)
- Experimenting (290)
- Expression-privacy dialectic (299)
- Inclusion-seclusion dialectic (298)
- Initiating (290)
- Integrating (292)
- Integration-separation dialectic (297)
- Intensifying (291)
- Intimacy (283)
- Metacommunication (303)
- Openness-closedness dialectic (299)
- Predictability-novelty dialectic (298)
- Relational commitment (288)
- Relational maintenance (289)
- Relational transgressions (306)
- Revelation-concealment dialectic (299)
- Stability-change dialectic (298)
- Stagnating (294)
- Terminating (295)

"I'm looking for a meaningful relationship."
"Our relationship has changed lately."
"The relationship is good for both of us."
"This relationship isn't working."

Relationship is one of those words that people use all the time but have trouble defining. Even scholars who have devoted their careers to studying relationships don't agree on what the term means (Guerrero et al., 2007). Their definitions include words like "closeness," "influence," "commitment," and "intimacy"—but coming up with a single definition can be (as the old adage goes) like nailing Jell-O to a wall.

One useful way to distinguish interpersonal relationships from less personal ones is to look for the characteristics you read about in Chapter 1 (pages 16–18): uniqueness, irreplaceability, interdependence, disclosure, and rewards. Even the closest relationships don't always reflect all of these qualities, but, taken together, they are a good measure of where a relationship fits on the impersonal–interpersonal spectrum.

This chapter will explore some of the dynamics that characterize interpersonal relationships and the communication that occurs within them. After reading it, you will see that relationships aren't fixed or unchanging. Rather, they can, and often do, change over time. In other words, a relationship is less a *thing* than a *process.* We'll look at why we form relationships, the dynamics of those relationships, and how to maintain them.

Why We Form Relationships

Why do we form relationships with some people and not with others? Sometimes we have no choice: Children can't select their parents, and most workers aren't able to choose their colleagues. In many other cases, however, we seek out some people and actively avoid others. In this section, we'll look at reasons we form relationships: interpersonal attraction, a desire for intimacy, and a quest for commitment.

ATTRACTION

Social scientists have collected an impressive body of research on interpersonal attraction (e.g., Byrne, 1997; Tadinac & Hromatko, 2004). The following are some of the factors they have identified that influence our choice of relational partners.

Appearance Most people claim that we should judge others on the basis of how they act, not how they look. However, the reality is quite the opposite (Mehrabian & Blum, 2003; Swami & Furnham, 2008). Appearance is especially important in the early stages of a relationship. In one study, a group of over 700 men and women were matched as blind dates, allegedly for a "computer dance." After the party was over, they were asked whether or not they would like to date their partners again. The result? The more physically attractive the person (as judged in advance by independent raters), the more likely he or she was seen as desirable. Other factors—social skills and intelligence, for example—didn't seem to affect the decision (Walster et al., 1966).

Although we might assume that attractive people are radically different from those who are less attractive, the truth is that we view the familiar as beautiful. Langlois and Roggman (1990) presented raters with two types of photos: Some were images of people from North European, Asian, and Latino backgrounds, while others were computer-generated images that combined the characteristics of several individuals. Surprisingly, the judges consistently preferred the composite photos of both men and women. When the features of eight individuals were combined into one image, viewers rated the picture as more attractive than the features of a single person or of a smaller combination of people. Thus, we seem to be drawn to people who represent the most average qualities of ourselves and those people we know. In other words, beautiful people aren't different from the rest of us. Rather, they're "radically similar."

Even if your appearance isn't beautiful by societal standards, consider these encouraging facts: First, after initial impressions have passed, ordinary-looking people with pleasing personalities are likely to be judged as attractive (Berscheid & Walster, 1978), and perceived beauty can be influenced by traits such as liking, respect, familiarity, and social interaction (Albada et al., 2002; Kniffin & Wilson, 2004). Second, physical factors become less important as a relationship progresses. As Don Hamachek (1982, p. 59) puts it, "Attractive features may open doors, but apparently, it takes more than physical beauty to keep them open."

Similarity It's comforting to know someone who likes the same things you like, has similar values, and may even be of the same race, economic class, or educational standing. The basis for this sort of relationship, commonly known as the *similarity thesis,* is the most frequently discussed and strongly supported determinant of relationship formation (Buss, 1985; Yun, 2002). For example, the more similar a married couple's personalities are, the more likely they are to report being happy and satisfied in their marriage (Luo & Klohnen, 2005). Friends in middle and high school report being similar to each other in many ways, including having mutual friends, enjoying the same sports, liking the same social activities, and using (or not using) alcohol and cigarettes to the same degree (Aboud & Mendelson, 1998; Urberg et al., 1998). For adults, similarity is more important to relational happiness than even communication ability:

Friends who have similarly low levels of communication skills are just as satisfied with their relationships as are friends having high levels of skills (Burleson & Samter, 1996).

There are several reasons why similarity is a strong foundation for relationships. First, similarities can be validating. The fact that another person shares your beliefs, tastes, and values can be a form of ego support. One study described the lengths to which "implicit egotism" may unconsciously affect perceptions of attractiveness (Jones et al., 2004). Results showed that people are disproportionately likely to marry others whose first or last names resemble their own, and they're also attracted to those with similar birthdays and even jersey numbers.

Second, when someone is similar to you, you can make fairly accurate predictions—whether the person will want to eat at the Mexican restaurant or hear the concert you're so excited about. This ability to make confident predictions reduces uncertainty and anxiety (Duck & Barnes, 1992).

There's a third explanation for the similarity thesis. It may be that when we learn that other people are similar to us, we assume they'll probably like us, so we in turn like them. The self-fulfilling prophecy creeps into the picture again.

Similarity turns from attraction to dislike when we encounter people who are like us in many ways but who behave in a strange or socially offensive manner (Cooper & Jones, 1969; Taylor & Mette, 1971). For instance, you have probably disliked people others have said were "just like you" but who talked too much, were complainers, or had some other unappealing characteristic. In fact, there is a tendency to have stronger dislike for similar but offensive people than for those who are offensive but different. One likely reason is that such people threaten our self-esteem, causing us to fear that we may be as unappealing as they are. In such circumstances, the reaction is often to put as much distance as possible between ourselves and this threat to our ideal self-image.

Complementarity The old saying "opposites attract" seems to contradict the principle of similarity we just described. In truth, though, both are valid. Differences strengthen a relationship when they are *complementary*—when each partner's characteristics satisfy the other's needs. Research suggests that attraction to partners who have complementary temperaments might be rooted in biology (Fisher, 2007). In addition, some studies show that couples are more likely to be attracted to each other when one partner is dominant and the other passive (Nowicki & Manheim, 1991; Swami & Furnham, 2008). Relationships also work well when the partners agree that one will exercise control in certain areas ("You make the final decisions about money") and the other will take the lead in different ones ("I'll decide how we ought to decorate the place"). Strains occur when control issues are disputed.

Studies that have examined successful and unsuccessful couples over a 20-year period show the interaction between similarities and differences (Klohnen & Luo, 2003). When partners are radically different, the dissimilar qualities that at first appear intriguing later become cause for relational breakups (Amodio & Showers, 2005; Felmlee, 2001). Partners in successful marriages were similar enough to satisfy each other physically and mentally, but were different enough to meet each other's needs and keep the relationship interesting. The successful couples found ways to keep a balance between their similarities and differences while adjusting to the changes that occurred over the years.

Rewards Some relationships are based on an economic model called *exchange theory* (Jeffries, 2002; Thibaut & Kelley, 1959). This approach suggests that we often seek out people who can give us rewards that are greater than or equal to the costs we encounter in dealing with them. Social exchange theorists define rewards as any outcomes we desire. They may be tangible (a nice place to live, a high paying job) or intangible (prestige, emotional support, companionship). Costs are undesirable outcomes: unpleasant work, emotional pain, and so on. A simple formula captures the social exchange explanation for why we form and maintain relationships:

$$\text{Rewards} - \text{Costs} = \text{Outcome}$$

According to social exchange theorists, we use this formula (often unconsciously) to calculate whether a relationship is a "good deal" or "not worth the effort," based on whether the outcome is positive or negative.

At its most blatant level, an exchange approach seems cold and calculating, but in some types of relationships it seems quite appropriate. A healthy business relationship is based on how well the parties help one another, and some friendships are based on an informal kind of barter: "I don't mind listening to the ups and downs of your love life because you rescue me when the house needs repairs." Even close relationships have an element of exchange. Friends and lovers often tolerate each other's quirks because the comfort and enjoyment they get make the less-than-pleasant times worth accepting. However, when one partner feels "underbenefited," it often leads to relational disruption or termination (DeMaris, 2007).

"I'd like to buy everyone a drink. All I ask in return is that you listen to my shallow and simplistic views on a broad range of social and political issues."

Costs and rewards don't exist in isolation: We define them by comparing a certain situation with alternatives. For example, consider a hypothetical woman, Gloria, who is struggling to decide whether to remain in a relationship with Raymond, her longtime boyfriend. Raymond does love Gloria, but he's not perfect: He has a hair-trigger temper, and he has become verbally abusive from time to time. Also, Gloria knows that Raymond was unfaithful to her at least once. In deciding whether or not to stay with Raymond, Gloria will use two standards.

The first standard is her **comparison level (CL)**—her minimum standard of what behavior is acceptable. If Gloria believes that relational partners have an obligation to be faithful and treat one another respectfully at all times, then Raymond's behavior will fall below her comparison level. This will be especially true if Gloria has had positive romantic relationships in the past (Merolla et al., 2004). On the other hand, if Gloria adopts a "nobody's perfect" standard, she is more likely to view Raymond's behavior as meeting or exceeding her comparison level.

Gloria also will rate Raymond according to her **comparison level of alternatives (CL_{alt})**. This standard refers to a comparison between the rewards she is receiving in her present situation and those she could expect to receive in others (Overall & Sibley, 2008). If, for example, Gloria doesn't want to be alone and she thinks, "If I don't have Raymond I won't have anyone," then her CL_{alt} would be lower than her present situation; but if she is confident that she could find a kinder partner, her CL_{alt} would be higher than the status quo.

Weighing the Alternatives: *Waitress*

Jenna (Keri Russell) is a small-town waitress who creates delicious pies for the customers at Joe's Diner. Unfortunately, she feels stuck in an unhappy marriage to a controlling and abusive husband. Social exchange theory explains why Jenna stays in the relationship—and it also describes why she wants to get out. She is not alone: Virtually every character in the film makes relational choices based on rewards, costs, and comparisons with alternatives. For the folks who frequent Joe's Diner, social exchange is as much a part of their everyday lives as Jenna's scrumptious pies.

Social exchange theorists suggest that communicators unconsciously use this calculus to decide whether to form and stay in relationships. At first this information seems to offer little comfort to communicators who are in unsatisfying relationships, such as when the partner's behavior is below the CL and there are no foreseeable alternatives (CL_{alt}). But there are other choices than being stuck in situations where the costs outweigh the rewards. First, you might make sure that you are judging your present relationship against a realistic comparison level. Expecting a situation to be perfect can be a recipe for unhappiness. (Recall the discussion of the "fallacy of shoulds" in Chapter 8.) If you decide that your present situation truly falls below your comparison level, you might explore whether there are other alternatives you haven't considered. And finally, the skills introduced throughout this book may help you negotiate a better relationship with the other person.

Competency We like to be around talented people, probably because we hope their skills and abilities will rub off on us. On the other hand, we are uncomfortable around those who are too competent—probably because we look bad by comparison. Elliot Aronson and his associates (1966) demonstrated how competence and imperfection combine to affect attraction by having subjects evaluate tape recordings of candidates for a quiz program. One was a "perfect" candidate who answered almost all the questions correctly and modestly admitted that he was an honor student, athlete, and college yearbook editor. The "average" candidate answered fewer questions correctly, had average grades, was a less successful athlete, and was a low-level member of the yearbook staff. Toward the end of half the tapes, the candidates committed a blunder, spilling coffee all over themselves. The remaining half of the tapes contained no such blunder. These, then, were the four experimental conditions: (1) a person with superior ability who blundered; (2) a person with superior ability who did not blunder; (3) an average person who blundered; and (4) an average person who did not blunder. The students who rated the attractiveness of these four types of people revealed an interesting and important principle of interpersonal attraction. The most attractive person was the superior candidate who blundered. Next was the superior person who did not blunder. Third was the average person who did not blunder. The least attractive person was the average person who committed the blunder.

Aronson's conclusion was that we like people who are somewhat flawed because they remind us of ourselves. However, there are some qualifications to this principle. People with especially positive or negative self-esteem find "perfect" people more attractive than those who are competent but flawed (Helmreich et al., 1970). Furthermore, women tend to be more impressed by uniformly superior people, whereas men find desirable but "human" subjects especially attractive (Deaux, 1972). On the whole, though, the principle stands: The best way to gain the liking of others is to be good at what you do but also to admit your mistakes.

Proximity As common sense suggests, we are likely to develop relationships with people with whom we interact frequently (Flora, 2005). In many cases, proximity leads to liking. For instance, we're more likely to develop friendships with close neighbors—whether near where we live or in adjacent seats in our classrooms (Back et al., 2008)—than with distant ones. Chances are also good that we'll choose a mate with whom we cross paths often. Proximity even has a role in computer-mediated communication, where sharing a portion of cyberspace—a chat room, or instant messaging connection, for example—constitutes virtual proximity (Levine, 2000). Facts like these are understandable when we consider that proximity allows us to get more information about other people and benefit from a relationship with them. Also, people in close proximity may be more similar to us than those not close—for example, if we live in the same neighborhood, odds are we share the same socioeconomic status.

Familiarity, on the other hand, can breed contempt. Evidence to support this fact comes from police blotters as well as university laboratories. Thieves frequently prey on nearby victims, even though the risk of being recognized is greater. Most aggravated assaults occur within the family or among close neighbors. The same principle holds in more routine contexts: You are likely to develop strong personal feelings, either positive or negative, toward others you encounter frequently.

Disclosure Chapter 3 described how telling others important information about yourself can help build liking (Derlega et al., 1993; Dindia, 2002). Sometimes the basis of this attraction comes from learning about ways we are similar, either in experiences ("I broke off an engagement myself") or in attitudes ("I feel nervous with strangers, too"). Self-disclosure also increases liking because it indicates regard. Sharing private information is a form of respect and trust—a kind of liking that we've already seen increases attractiveness.

Not all disclosure leads to liking. Research shows that the key to satisfying self-disclosure is *reciprocity:* getting back an amount and kind of information equivalent to that which you reveal (Dindia, 2000a). A second important ingredient in successful self-disclosure is *timing.* It's probably unwise to talk about your sexual insecurities with a new acquaintance or express your pet peeves to a friend at your birthday party. The information you reveal ought to be appropriate for the setting and stage of the relationship (Archer & Berg, 1978; Wortman et al., 1976). (See the Dark Side box on this page for other concerns about self-disclosing too quickly in a relationship.)

DARK SIDE OF COMMUNICATION

Abusing Those Who Disclose

As Chapter 3 explained (and as your own experience may confirm), self-disclosure has both benefits and risks. Revealing information about yourself can be a means for building and maintaining relationships, but those revelations can also leave you vulnerable.

A recent study asked college students to describe their levels of self-disclosure in an unpleasant dating relationship. The participants also reported on incidents of psychological abuse in the relationship: insulting and spiteful comments, false accusations, stomping out during conversations, and other demeaning behaviors.

Results showed that participants with strong self-disclosure orientations were also more frequently the targets of psychological abuse. This doesn't mean that sharing personal information will always lead to problems—after all, the only subjects in this study were those reporting on unpleasant relationships. Still, the results raise a cautionary note: In a new relationship, the wisest course may be to reveal personal information cautiously until you are confident that you and your disclosures will be treated with respect.

Shirley, J. A., Powers, W. G., & Sawyer, C. R. (2007). Psychologically abusive relationships and self-disclosure orientations. *Human Communication, 10,* 289–301.

INTIMACY

The musical group Three Dog Night said it well: One *can* be the loneliest number. For most of us, the desire to connect with others is a powerful force that leads us to seek out and form relationships. As Chapter 1 explained, strong attachments with others not only make us happier, they also can make us healthier and help us live longer.

In their book *Intimacy: Strategies for Successful Relationships,* C. Edward Crowther and Gayle Stone (1986) offer a reminder of just how important close relationships can be. As part of a study of people who were dying in hospices and hospitals in the United States and England, Crowther and Stone asked each person what mattered most in his or her life. Fully 90 percent of these terminally ill patients put intimate relationships at the top of the list. Similarly, Christopher Peterson (2006) summarizes research showing that close relationships "may be the *single most important* source of life satisfaction and emotional well-being, across different ages and cultures" (p. 261). With this in mind, let's take a closer look at what it means to have intimate relationships with others.

Dimensions of Intimacy When researchers asked several hundred college students to identify their "closest, deepest, most involved, and most intimate relationship" (Berscheid et al., 1989), the answers were varied. Roughly half (47 percent) identified a romantic partner. About a third (36 percent) chose a friendship. Most of the rest (14 percent) cited a family member.

Intimacy comes in many forms (Laurenceau & Kleinman, 2006; Lippert & Prager, 2001). One type is *emotional*: sharing important information and feelings. Chapters 3 and 8 described these kinds of self-disclosures in detail. Sometimes emotional intimacy comes from talking about feelings, such as acknowledging when you're hurt and embarrassed or saying "I love you." In other cases, emotional intimacy develops as a result of topics that are discussed—personal information, secrets, or delicate subjects. One such subject can be money, which has led some self-help authors to use the term *financial intimacy* to describe how couples need to be open, honest, and in sync on this important topic (Hayes, 2006; Orman, 2005).

Another form of intimacy is *physical*. Even before birth, the developing fetus experiences a kind of physical closeness with its mother that will never happen again: "Floating in a warm fluid, curling inside a total embrace, swaying to the undulations of the moving body and hearing the beat of the pulsing heart" (Morris, 1973, p. 7). As they grow up, fortunate children are continually nourished by physical intimacy: being rocked, fed, hugged, and held. As we grow older, the opportunities for physical intimacy are less regular, but still possible and important. Some physical intimacy is sexual, but this category also can include affectionate hugs, kisses, and even struggles. Companions who have endured physical challenges together—for example, in athletics or during emergencies—form a bond that can last a lifetime.

In other cases, intimacy comes from *intellectual* sharing (Cowan & Mills, 2004; Schaefer & Olson, 1981). Not every exchange of ideas counts as intimacy, of course. Talking about next week's midterm with your professor or classmates isn't likely to forge strong relational bonds. But when you engage another person in an exchange of important ideas, a kind of closeness develops that can be powerful and exciting.

Shared activities can provide a fourth way to emotional closeness (Wood & Inman, 1993). Not all shared activities lead to intimacy. You might work with a colleague for years without feeling any sort of emotional connection. But some shared experiences—struggling together against obstacles or living together as housemates are good examples—can create strong bonds. Play is one valuable form of shared activity. Leslie Baxter (1992) found that both same-sex friendships and opposite-sex romantic relationships were characterized by several forms of play. Partners invented private codes, fooled around by acting like other people, teased one another, and played games—everything from having punning contests to arm wrestling.

The amount and type of intimacy can vary from one relationship to another (Speicher, 1999). Some intimate relationships exhibit all four qualities: emotional disclosure, physical intimacy, intellectual exchanges, and shared activities. Other intimate relationships exhibit only one or two. Of course, some relationships aren't intimate in any way. Acquaintances, roommates, and coworkers may never become intimate. In some cases, even family members develop smooth but relatively impersonal relationships.

Not even the closest relationships always operate at the highest level of intimacy. At some times, you might share all of your thoughts or feelings with a friend, family member, or lover; at other times, you might withdraw. You might freely share your feelings about one topic and stay more distant regarding another one. The same principle holds for physical intimacy, which waxes and wanes in most relationships.

Despite the fact that no relationship is *always* intimate, living without *any* sort of intimacy is hardly desirable. For example, people who fear intimacy in dating relationships anticipate less satisfaction in a long-term relationship and report feeling more distant from even longtime dating partners. A great deal of evidence supports the conclusion that fear of intimacy can cause major problems in both creating relationships and sustaining them (Greenberg & Goldman, 2008; Vangelisti & Beck, 2007).

Gender and Intimacy Until recently, most social scientists believed that women were more concerned with and better than men at developing and maintaining intimate relationships (Impett & Peplau, 2006). Most research *does* show that women (taken as a group, of course) are more interested than men in achieving emotional intimacy (Cross & Madson, 1997; Eldridge & Christensen, 2002), more willing to make emotional commitments (Rusbult & Van Lange, 1996), and somewhat more willing to share their most personal thoughts and feelings (Dindia & Allen, 1992; Stafford et al., 2000), although the differences aren't as dramatic as most people believe (Dindia, 2000b, 2002). In some settings, such as therapist-patient, there appear to be no differences at all (Roe, 2001).

Many social scientists who explored the relationship between biological sex, gender, and communication interpreted the relatively lower rate of male self-disclosure as a sign that men were unwilling or unable to develop close relationships. Some (e.g., Weiss & Lowenthal, 1975) argued that the female trait of disclosing personal information and feelings made them more "emotionally mature" and "interpersonally competent" than men. The title of one book captured this attitude of female superiority and male deficiency: *The Inexpressive Male: A Tragedy of American Society* (Balswick, 1988). Personal growth programs and self-help books urged men to achieve closeness by learning to open up and share their feelings.

But more recent scholarship has begun to show that emotional expression isn't the *only* way to develop close relationships (Floyd, 1996; Zorn & Gregory, 2005). Whereas women place a somewhat higher value on talking about personal matters as a measure of closeness, men are more likely to create and express closeness by doing things together—often in groups rather than in one-on-one interactions (Baumeister, 2005). In one study, more than 75 percent of the men surveyed said that their most meaningful experiences with friends came from shared activities (Swain, 1989). They reported that through shared activities they "grew on one another," developed feelings of interdependence, showed appreciation for one another, and demonstrated mutual liking. Likewise, men regarded practical help as a measure of caring. Findings like these show that, for many men, closeness grows from activities that don't always depend heavily on disclosure: A friend is a person who does things *for* you and *with* you. Of course, it's important not to assume that all men who value shared activities are reluctant to share feelings, or that doing things together isn't important to women. Recent scholarship offers convincing evidence that, in many respects, the meaning of intimacy is more similar than different for men and women (Goldsmith & Fulfs, 1999; Radmacher & Azmitia, 2006).

Whatever differences do exist between male and female styles of intimacy help explain some of the stresses and misunderstandings that can arise between the sexes. For example, a woman who looks for emotional disclosure as a measure of affection may overlook an inexpressive man's efforts to show he cares by doing favors or spending time with her. Fixing a leaky faucet or taking a hike may look like ways to avoid getting close, but to the man who proposes them, they may be measures of affection and bids for intimacy. Likewise, differing ideas about the timing and meaning of sex can lead to misunderstandings. Whereas many women think of sex as a way to *express* an intimacy that has already developed, men are more likely to see it as a way to *create* that intimacy (Reissman, 1990). In this sense, the man who encourages sex early in a relationship or after a fight may not just be a testosterone-crazed lecher: He may view the shared activity as a way to build closeness. By contrast, the woman who views personal talk as the pathway to intimacy may resist the idea of physical closeness before the emotional side of the relationship has been discussed.

As with all research looking at women's and men's communication, it's important to realize that no generalization applies to every person. Furthermore, stereotypes are changing. For example, an analysis of prime-time television sitcoms revealed that male characters who disclose personal information generally receive favorable responses from other characters (Good et al., 2002).

FOCUS ON RESEARCH

Friends with Benefits: The Communication Challenges of Not-So-Casual Sex

It's more than casual sex and less than a committed relationship. *Friends with benefits* (FWB) is a popular term for nonromantic heterosexual friendships that include sexual activity. In separate studies conducted at different universities, nearly 60 percent of the students surveyed said they had participated in at least one FWB relationship.

Research conducted by Kristen McGinty and her colleagues found that men and women are equally likely to be in FWB relationships—but often for different reasons. Whereas the majority of men viewed their relationships as primarily sexual, women were much more likely to be emotionally involved. The researchers concluded that in FWB relationships, women are typically more focused on being "friends" while men are more likely to be interested in the "benefits."

A study by communication researchers Melissa Bisson and Timothy Levine sheds additional light on the FWB experience. A common reason the surveyed students have FWBs is that those relationships offer trust and comfort while avoiding romantic commitment. However, a common concern for both men and women is that sexual activity might lead to unreciprocated desires for romantic commitment. Given this tension, it would seem logical that FWB partners would regularly discuss the status of their relationship—but the researchers found that FWBs routinely avoid explicit communication about this important topic. Bisson and Levine conclude that "FWB relationships are often problematic for the same reasons that they are attractive."

Bisson, M. A., & Levine, T. R. (2007) Negotiating a friends with benefits relationship. *Archives of Sexual Behavior*. Available at: http://www.springerlink.com/content/t22037j0215j4367/fulltext.pdf

McGinty, K., Knox, D., & Zusman, M. E. (2007). Friends with benefits: Women want "friends," men want "benefits." *College Student Journal, 41*, 1128–1131.

In addition, researchers Mark Morman and Kory Floyd (2002) note that a cultural shift is occurring in the U.S. in which fathers are becoming more affectionate with their sons than they were in previous generations—although some of that affection is still expressed through shared activities.

Culture and Intimacy Historically, the notions of public and private behavior have changed dramatically (Adamopoulos, 1991; Gadlin, 1977). What would be considered intimate behavior today was quite public at times in the past. For example, in 16th-century Germany, the new husband and wife were expected to consummate their marriage upon a bed carried by witnesses who would validate the marriage! Conversely, in England as well as in colonial America, the customary level of communication between spouses was once rather formal—not much different from the way acquaintances or neighbors spoke to one another.

Today, the notion of intimacy varies from one culture to another (Adams et al., 2004; Marshall, 2008). In one study, researchers asked residents of Great Britain, Japan, Hong Kong, and Italy to describe their use of 33 rules that regulated interaction in social relationships (Argyle & Henderson, 1985). The rules governed a wide range of communication behaviors: everything from the use of humor, to handshaking, to the management of money. The results showed that the greatest differences between Asian and European cultures involved the rules for dealing with intimacy, including showing emotions, expressing affection in public, engaging in sexual activity, and respecting privacy.

While some of these distinctions continue to hold true, cultural differences in intimacy are becoming less prominent as the world becomes more connected through the media, travel, and technology. For instance, romance and passionate love were once seen as particularly "American" concepts of intimacy. However, recent evidence shows that men and women in a variety of cultures—individualist and collectivist, urban and rural, rich and poverty-stricken—may be every bit as romantic as Americans (Hatfield & Rapson, 2006). These studies suggest that the large differences that once existed between Western and Eastern cultures may be fast disappearing.

Chapter 2 offers detailed information about intercultural communication competence. A principle to keep in mind when communicating with people from different cultures is that it's important to consider their norms for appropriate intimacy. On one hand, don't mistakenly judge them according to your own standards. Likewise, be sensitive about honoring their standards when talking about yourself. In this sense, choosing the proper level of intimacy isn't too different from choosing the appropriate way of dressing or eating when encountering members of a different culture: What seems familiar and correct at home may not be suitable with strangers.

Computer-Mediated Communication and Intimacy A few decades ago, it would have been hard to conceive that the words *computer* and *intimacy* could be positively linked. Computers were viewed as impersonal machines that couldn't transmit important features of human communication, such as facial expression, tone of voice, and touch. However, as Chapters 1 and 3 described, researchers now know that computer-mediated communication (CMC) can be just as personal as face-to-face (FtF) interaction. In fact, studies show that relational intimacy may develop more quickly through CMC than in FtF communication (Hian et al., 2004) and that CMC enhances verbal, emotional, and social intimacy in friendships (Hu et al., 2004).

Your own experience probably supports these claims. The relative anonymity of chat rooms, blogs, and online dating services fosters a freedom of expression that might not occur in FtF meetings (Ben-Ze'ev, 2003), giving relationships a chance to get started. In addition, instant messaging, e-mailing, and text messaging offer more constant contact with friends, family, and partners than might otherwise be possible (Boase et al., 2006). The potential for developing and maintaining intimate relationships via computer is captured well by one user's comment (which has a fun double meaning): "I've never clicked this much with anyone in my life" (Henderson & Gilding, 2004, p. 505).

This doesn't mean that all cyber-relationships are (or will become) intimate. Just as in face-to-face relationships, communicators choose varying levels of self-disclosure with their cyberpartners. Some online relationships are relatively impersonal; others are highly interpersonal. In any case, CMC is an important component in creating and maintaining intimacy in contemporary relationships.

The Limits of Intimacy It's impossible to have a close relationship with everyone you know—nor is that necessarily desirable. Social psychologist Roy Baumeister (2005) makes a compelling case that, on average, most people want four to six close, important relationships in their lives at any given time. While fewer than four such relationships can lead to a sense of social deprivation, more than six leads to diminishing returns. "It is possible," notes Baumeister, "that people simply do not have the time or energy to pursue emotional closeness with more than a half dozen people" (p. 113).

Even if we could seek intimacy with everyone we encounter, few of us would want that much closeness. Consider the range of everyday contacts that don't require any sort of intimacy. Some are based on economic exchange (the people at work or the shopkeeper you visit several times a week), some are based on group membership (church or school), some on physical proximity (neighbors, carpooling), and some grow out of third-party connections (mutual friends, child care). Simply engaging in conversational give-and-take with both strangers and acquaintances can be enjoyable.

Some scholars have pointed out that an *obsession* with intimacy can lead to *less* satisfying relationships (Bellah et al., 1985; Parks, 1982). People who consider intimate communication as the only kind worth pursuing place little value on relationships that don't meet this standard. This can lead them to regard interaction with strangers and casual acquaintances as superficial, or at best as the groundwork for deeper relationships. When you consider the pleasure that can come from polite but distant communication, the limitations of this view become clear. Intimacy is definitely rewarding, but it isn't the only way of relating to others.

COMMITMENT

How important is the role of commitment in personal relationships? Sentiments like the following suggest an answer: "I'm looking for a committed relationship." "Our relationship didn't work because my partner wasn't committed." "I'm just not ready for commitment."

Relational commitment involves a promise—sometimes implied and sometimes explicit—to remain in a relationship and to make that relationship successful. Commitment is important in every type of interpersonal relationship, whether it's a friendship ("Friends for life!"), family ("We're always here for you"), a close-knit working team ("I've got you covered"), or a romantic relationship ("Till death do us part").

As these examples suggest, commitment is both formed and reinforced through communication. Table 9.1 spells out commitment indicators in romantic relationships. You can probably imagine how similar indicators of commitment would operate in other sorts of close relationships.

As Table 9.1 indicates, words alone aren't a surefire measure of true commitment. Deeds are also important. Simply saying "You can count on me" doesn't guarantee loyalty. But without language, commitment may not be clear. For this reason, ceremonies formalizing relationships are an important way to recognize and cement commitment. We'll discuss such ceremonies more in the discussion of bonding on pages 292–293.

TABLE 9.1 ***Major Indicators of a Committed Romantic Relationship***

• Providing affection
• Providing support
• Maintaining integrity
• Sharing companionship
• Making an effort to communicate regularly
• Showing respect
• Creating a relational future
• Creating a positive relational atmosphere
• Working on relationship problems together
• Reassuring one's commitment

Source: Weigel, D. J. (2008). Mutuality and the communication of commitment in romantic relationships. *Southern Communication Journal, 73,* 24–41.

Communication and Relational Dynamics

Even the most stable relationships vary from day to day and over longer periods of time. Communication scholars have attempted to describe and explain how communication creates and reflects the changing dynamics of relational interaction. The following pages describe two very different characterizations of relational development and interaction.

DEVELOPMENTAL MODELS OF INTERPERSONAL RELATIONSHIPS

One of the best-known models of relational stages was developed by Mark Knapp (Knapp & Vangelisti, 2006; see also Avtgis et al., 1998; Welch & Rubin, 2002), who broke the waxing and waning of relationships into 10 steps. Other researchers have suggested that in addition to coming together and coming apart, any model of relational communication ought to contain a third area, **relational maintenance**—communication aimed at keeping relationships operating smoothly and satisfactorily (we'll discuss relational maintenance in more detail later in this chapter). Figure 9.1 shows how Knapp's 10 stages fit into this three-part view of relational communication. This model seems most appropriate for describing communication between romantic partners, but in some cases it can depict other types of

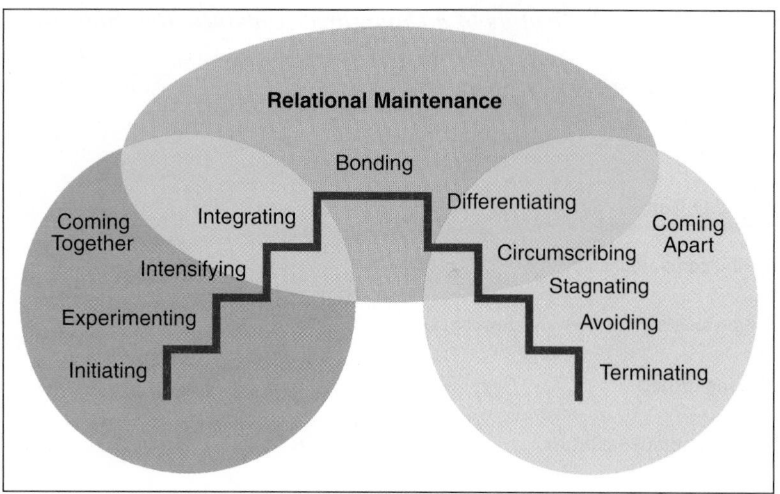

FIGURE 9.1 Stages of Relationship Development
From Mark L. Knapp & Anita L. Vangelisi, *Interpersonal communication and human relationships* (4th ed.). Published by Allyn & Bacon, Boston, MA. Copyright © 2000 by Pearson Education. Reprinted by permission of the publisher.

close relationships. As you read the following section, consider how the stages could describe a long-term friendship (Johnson et al., 2004), a couple in love, or even business partners.

Initiating The goals in the **initiating** stage are to show that you are interested in making contact and to demonstrate that you are a person worth talking to. Communication during this stage is usually brief, and it generally follows conventional formulas: handshakes, remarks about innocuous subjects such as the weather, and friendly expressions. Such behavior may seem superficial and meaningless, but it is a way of signaling that you're interested in building some kind of relationship with the other person. It allows us to say, without saying, "I'm a friendly person, and I'd like to get to know you."

Initiating relationships—especially romantic ones—can be particularly difficult for people who are shy. Computer-mediated communication can make it easier for reticent people to strike up a relationship (Sheeks & Birchmeier, 2007). One study of an online dating service found that participants who identified themselves as shy expressed a greater appreciation for the system's anonymous, non-threatening environment than did non-shy users (Scharlott & Christ, 1995). The researchers found that many shy users employed the online service specifically to help them overcome their inhibitions about initiating relationships in face-to-face settings.

Experimenting After making contact with a new person, we generally begin the search for common ground. This search usually starts with the basics: "Where are you from? What's your major?" From there we look for other similarities: "You're a runner too? How many miles do you run a week?"

It usually doesn't take long for communicators who are interested in one another to move from initiating to **experimenting**. The shift seems to occur even more rapidly in cyberspace than in person (Pratt et al., 1999; Tidwell & Walther, 2002). People who develop relationships via e-mail begin asking questions about attitudes, opinions, and preferences more quickly than those in face-to-face contact. It probably helps that e-mailers can't see each others' nonverbal reactions—they don't have to worry about blushing, stammering, or looking away if they realize that they asked for too much information too quickly.

The hallmark of experimenting is small talk. We tolerate the ordeal of small talk because it serves several functions. First, it is a useful way to find out what interests we share with the other person. It also provides a way to "audition" the other person—to help us decide whether a relationship is worth pursuing. In addition, small talk is a safe way to ease into a relationship. You haven't risked much as you decide whether to proceed further. Finally, small talk does provide some kind of link to others. It's often better than being alone.

The kind of information we look for during the experimentation stage depends on the nature of the relationship we are seeking (Miller, 1998; Stewart et al., 2000). For example, both men and women who are seeking short-term relationships look for someone with an exciting personality and a good sense of humor. Qualities of being trustworthy and romantic become more important when people seek long-term relationships.

Intensifying When a relationship begins **intensifying**, the kind of qualitatively interpersonal relationship defined in Chapter 1 starts to develop. In friendships, intensifying often includes participating in shared activities, hanging out with mutual friends, or taking trips together (Johnson et al., 2004). Dating couples use a wide range of strategies to communicate that their relationship is intensifying (Tolhuizen, 1989). About a quarter of the time they

express their feelings directly to discuss the state of the relationship, such as saying "I love you" (Brantley et al., 2002; Owen, 1987). More often they use less direct methods of communication: spending an increasing amount of time together, asking for support from one another, doing favors for the partner, giving tokens of affection, hinting and flirting, expressing feelings nonverbally, getting to know the partner's friends and family, and trying to look more physically attractive (Richmond et al., 1987).

The intensifying stage is usually a time of relational excitement and even euphoria. For romantic partners, it's often filled with starstruck gazes, goose bumps, and daydreaming. As a result, it's a stage that's regularly depicted in movies and romance novels—after all, we love to watch lovers in love. The problem, of course, is that the stage doesn't last forever. Sometimes romantic partners who stop feeling goose bumps begin to question whether they're still in love. While it's possible that they're not, it also could be that they've simply moved on to a different stage in their relationship—such as integrating.

Integrating As the relationship strengthens, the individuals enter an **integrating** stage. They begin to take on an identity as a social unit. Invitations begin to come addressed to a couple. Social circles merge. The partners share each other's commitments: "Sure, we'll spend Thanksgiving with your family." Common property may begin to be designated—our apartment, our car, our song (Baxter, 1987). Partners develop their own personal idioms (Bell & Healey, 1992) and forms of play (Baxter, 1992). They develop routines and rituals that reinforce their identity as a couple—jogging together, eating at a favorite restaurant, expressing affection with a goodnight kiss, and worshipping together (Afifi & Johnson, 1999; Bruess & Pearson, 1997). As these examples illustrate, the stage of integrating is a time when we give up some characteristics of our former selves and become different people.

As we become more integrated with others, our sense of obligation to them grows (Roloff et al., 1988). We feel obliged to provide a variety of resources, such as class notes and money, whether or not the other person asks for them. When intimates do make requests of one another, they are relatively straightforward. Gone are the elaborate explanations, inducements, and apologies. In short, partners in an integrated relationship expect more from one another than they do in less intimate associations.

As integration increases and as we become more intimate, uncertainty about our relationship decreases: We become clearer about relationship norms, and about what behaviors are appropriate and inappropriate. In addition, our ability to influence each other's daily activities increases, such as the amount of time spent with friends and doing schoolwork (Solomon & Knobloch, 2001). Reducing uncertainty about our partner and the relationship enhances attraction and feelings of closeness (Knobloch & Solomon, 2002).

REFLECTION

Culture and Relational Stages

I think Knapp's model does a good job of describing relational stages in Western culture, but it doesn't work everywhere in the world. My parents were born in India, and their families arranged their marriage when my mother and dad were children. They hardly knew one another when they were married, so most of the experimenting, integrating, and intensifying actually came after their official bonding (i.e., marriage), not before. I'm happy to say that they do love one another, but it happened in a very different way than it usually does in this part of the world.

Bonding During the **bonding** stage, partners make symbolic public gestures to show the world that their relationship exists. These gestures can take the form of a contract between business partners or a license to be married.

Bonding typically generates social support for the relationship. Custom and law impose certain obligations on partners who have officially bonded.

What constitutes a bonded, committed relationship is not always easy to define (Foster, 2008). Terms such as *common-law*, *cohabitation*, and *life partners* have been used to describe relationships that don't have the full support of custom and law but still involve an implicit or explicit bond. Nonetheless, given the importance of bonding in validating relationships and taking them to another level, it's not surprising that the gay and lesbian communities are striving to have legally sanctioned and recognized marriages.

For our purposes here, we'll define bonded relationships as those involving a significant measure of public commitment. These can include engagement or marriage, sharing a residence, a public ceremony, or a written or verbal pledge. The key is that bonding is the culmination of a developed relationship—the "officializing" of a couple's integration.

Relationships don't have to be romantic to achieve bonding. Consider, for instance, authors contracting to write a book together or a student being initiated into a sorority. As Lillian Rubin (1985) notes, in some cultures there are rituals for friends to mark their bonded status through a public commitment:

> Some Western cultures have rituals to mark the progress of a friendship and to give it public legitimacy and form. In Germany, for example, there's a small ceremony called *Duzen*, the name itself signifying the transformation in the relationship. The ritual calls for the two friends, each holding a glass of wine or beer, to entwine arms, thus bringing each other physically close, and to drink up after making a promise of eternal brotherhood with the word *Bruderschaft*. When it's over, the friends will have passed from a relationship that requires the formal *Sie* mode of address to the familiar *du*.

Bonding usually marks an important turning point in relationships. Up to now the relationship may have developed at a steady pace: Experimenting gradually moved into intensifying and then into integrating. Now, however, there is a spurt of commitment. The public display and declaration of exclusivity make this a critical period in the relationship.

Differentiating Now that the two people have formed this commonality, they need to reestablish individual identities. How are we different? How am I unique? **Differentiating** often occurs when a relationship begins to experience the first, inevitable feelings of stress. This often shows up in a couple's pronoun usage. Instead of talking about "our" weekend plans, differentiating conversations focus on what "I" want to do. Relational issues that were once agreed upon (such as "You'll be the breadwinner and I'll manage the home") now become points of contention: "Why am *I* stuck at home when I have better career potential than *you*?" The root of the term *differentiating* is the word *different*, suggesting that change plays an important role in this stage.

Differentiation also can be positive, for people need to be individuals as well as part of a relationship. And as the model on page 290 shows, differentiating is often a part of normal relational maintenance, in which partners manage the inevitable challenges that come their way. The key to successful differentiation is maintaining commitment to a relationship while creating the space for being individuals as well (we'll describe this later in the chapter as the connection-autonomy dialectic).

Circumscribing So far, we have been looking at the growth of relationships. Although some reach a plateau of development, going on successfully for as long as a lifetime, others pass through several stages of decline and dissolution. In the **circumscribing** stage, communication between members decreases in quantity and quality (Duck, 1987). Subtle hints of dissatisfaction grow more evident. Working later at the office, seeking less and less romance, and more and more arguing begin to form a pattern that is hard to ignore (Kellermann et al., 1991). Ironically, both partners in a circumscribed relationship still cooperate in one way: suppressing the true status of the relationship. They hide its decline from others and even from themselves (Vaughn, 1987). Restrictions and restraints characterize this stage, and dynamic communication becomes static. Rather than discuss a disagreement (which requires some degree of energy on both parts), members opt for withdrawal: either mental (silence or daydreaming and fantasizing) or physical (where people spend less time together). Circumscribing doesn't involve total avoidance, which comes later. Rather, it entails a shrinking of interest and commitment.

Stagnating If circumscribing continues, the relationship begins to stagnate. Members behave toward each other in old, familiar ways without much feeling. No growth occurs. The **stagnating** relationship is a hollow shell of its former self. We see stagnation in many workers who have lost enthusiasm for their job yet continue to go through the motions for years. The same sad event occurs for some couples who unenthusiastically have the same conversations, see the same people, and follow the same routines without any sense of joy or novelty.

Slowly Coming Apart: *The Break-Up*

When we meet Brooke Meyers (Jennifer Aniston) and Gary Grobowski (Vince Vaughn), they appear to be living happily together. Unfortunately for them, it's all downhill from there. *The Break-Up* chronicles the disintegration of their relationship in ways that closely match the "coming apart" stages noted in this chapter. We watch their communication pass through the stages of circumscribing (quite literally, as they cordon off their own spaces in the apartment), stagnating, avoiding, and eventually terminating. The movie also illustrates the dialectical tension between connection and autonomy—with Brooke wanting more of the former and Gary wanting more of the latter.

While the movie is billed as a comedy, it's easy to see the pain that Brooke and Gary feel as their relationship falls apart. This film dramatizes the message in the familiar song lyrics—breaking up is hard to do.

Avoiding When stagnation becomes too unpleasant, people in a relationship begin to create distance between each other by **avoiding**. Sometimes they do it under the guise of excuses ("I've been sick lately and can't see you") and sometimes directly ("Please don't call me; I don't want to see you now"). In either case, by this point the handwriting is on the wall about the relationship's future.

Research by Jon Hess (2000) reveals that there are several ways we gain distance. One way is *expressing detachment,* such as avoiding the other person altogether, or zoning out. A second way is *avoiding involvement,* such as leaving the room, ignoring the person's questions, steering clear of touching, and being superficially polite. *Showing antagonism* is a third technique, which includes behaving in a hostile way and treating the other person as a lesser person. A fourth strategy is to *mentally dissociate* from the other person, such as by thinking about the other person as less capable, or as unimportant. A vicious cycle gets started when avoiding the other person: the more one person avoids the other, the greater the odds the other will reciprocate. And the more topics that are avoided, the less satisfactory is the relationship (Sargent, 2002).

Terminating Not all relationships end: Many partnerships, friendships, and marriages last for a lifetime once they're established. But many do deteriorate and reach the final stage of **terminating**. The process of terminating has its own distinguishable pattern (Battaglia et al., 1998; Conlan, 2008). Characteristics of this stage include summary dialogues of where the relationship has gone and the desire to dissociate. The relationship may end with a cordial dinner, a note left on the kitchen table, a phone call, or a legal document stating the dissolution. Depending on each person's feelings, this terminating stage can be quite short or it may be drawn out over time, with bitter jabs at each other. In either case, termination doesn't have to be totally negative. Understanding each other's investments in the relationship and needs for personal growth may dilute the hard feelings.

How do the individuals deal with each other after a romantic relationship has ended? The best predictor of whether the individuals will become friends after the relationship is terminated is whether they were friends before their romantic involvement (Metts et al., 1989). The way the couple splits up also makes a difference. It's no surprise to find that friendships are most possible when communication during the breakup was positive: expressions that there were no regrets for time spent together and other attempts to minimize hard feelings. When communication during termination is negative (manipulative, complaining to third parties), friendships are less likely.

Terminating a relationship is, for many people, a learning experience. Ty Tashiro and Patricia Frazier (2003) asked college students who recently had a romantic relationship breakup to describe the positive things they learned that might help them in future romantic relationships. Responses fell into four categories: "person positives," such as gaining self-confidence and that it's all right to cry; "other positives," such as learning more about what is desired in a partner; "relational positives," such as how to communicate better and how not to jump into a relationship too quickly; and "environment positives," such as learning to rely more on friends and how to better balance relationships and school work.

Limits of Developmental Models While Knapp's model offers insights into relational stages, it doesn't describe the ebb and flow of communication in every relationship. For instance, many relationships don't progress from one stage to another in a predictable manner as they develop and deteriorate. One study found that some terminated friendships did indeed follow a pattern similar to the one described by Knapp and pictured in Pattern One of Figure 9.2 (Johnson et al., 2004). However, several other patterns of development and deterioration were also identified, as seen in Patterns Two through Five.

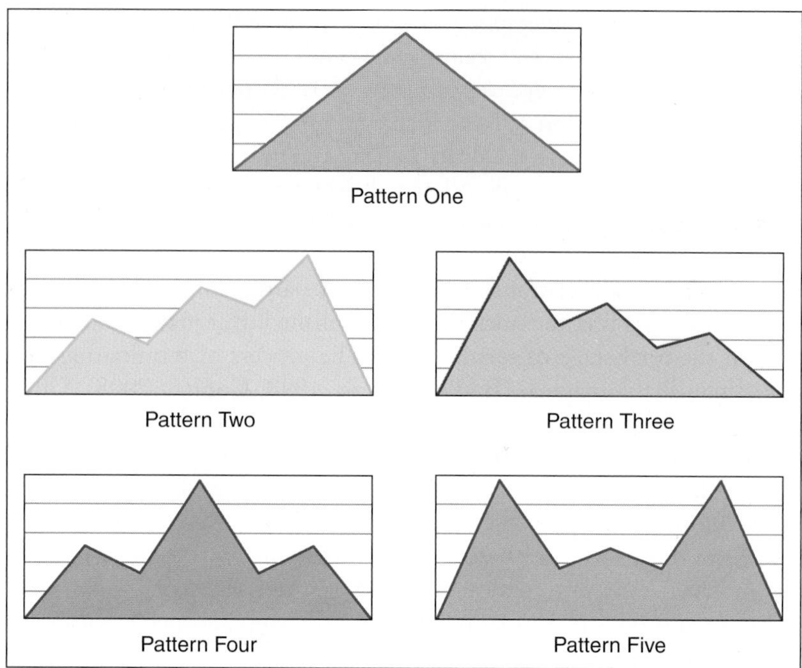

FIGURE 9.2 Patterns of Relational Development and Deterioration
Adapted from Johnson, A., Wittenberg, E., Haigh, M., Wigley, S., Becker, J., Brown, K., & Craig, E. (2004). The process of relationship development and deterioration: Turning points in friendships that have terminated. *Communication Quarterly, 52,* 54–67.

Knapp's model suggests that a relationship exhibits only the most dominant traits of just one of the 10 stages at any given time. Despite this fact, elements of other stages are usually present. For example, two lovers deep in the throes of integrating may still do their share of experimenting ("Wow, I never knew that about you!") and have differentiating disagreements ("I need a weekend to myself"). Likewise, family members who spend most of their energy avoiding each other may have an occasional good spell in which their former closeness briefly intensifies. The notion that relationships can experience features of both "coming together" and "coming apart" at the same time is explored in the following section, on relational dialectics.

DIALECTICAL PERSPECTIVES ON RELATIONAL DYNAMICS

Not all theorists agree that relational stages are the best way to explain interaction in relationships. Some suggest that communicators grapple with the same kinds of challenges whether a relationship is brand new or has lasted decades. Their focus, then, is on the ongoing maintenance of relationships (Lee, 1998). They argue that communicators seek important but apparently incompatible goals. The struggle to achieve these goals creates **dialectical tensions:** conflicts that arise when two opposing or incompatible forces exist simultaneously.

Communication scholars such as Leslie Baxter and Barbara Montgomery (1996) and William Rawlins (1992) have identified several dialectical forces that make successful communication challenging. They suggest that the struggle to manage these dialectical tensions creates the most powerful dynamics in relational communication. In the following pages we will discuss three influential dialectical tensions, which are summarized in Table 9.2. As the table shows, we experience dialectical challenges both *internally,* that is, within the relationship, and *externally* as we and our relational partners face other people whose desires clash with our own.

Integration versus Separation No one is an island. Recognizing this fact, we seek out involvement with others. But, at the same time, we are unwilling to sacrifice our entire identity to even the most

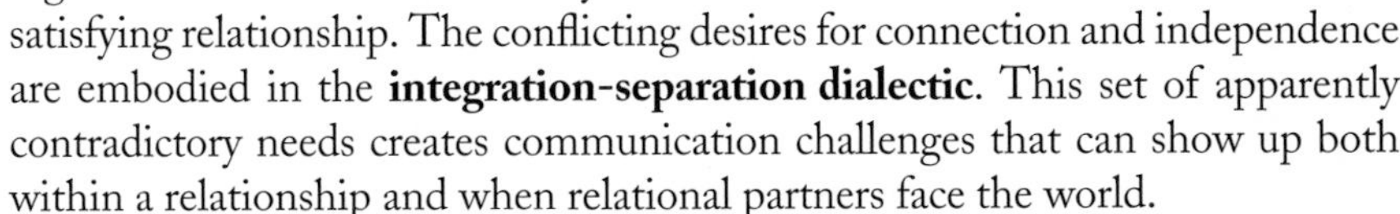

satisfying relationship. The conflicting desires for connection and independence are embodied in the **integration-separation dialectic**. This set of apparently contradictory needs creates communication challenges that can show up both within a relationship and when relational partners face the world.

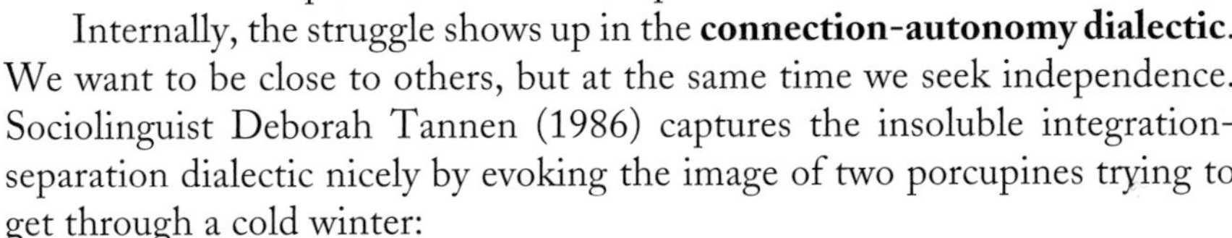

Internally, the struggle shows up in the **connection-autonomy dialectic**. We want to be close to others, but at the same time we seek independence. Sociolinguist Deborah Tannen (1986) captures the insoluble integration-separation dialectic nicely by evoking the image of two porcupines trying to get through a cold winter:

> They huddle together for warmth, but their sharp quills prick each other, so they pull away. But then they get cold. They have to keep adjusting their closeness and distance to keep from freezing and from getting pricked by their fellow porcupines—the source of both comfort and pain.
>
> We need to get close to each other to have a sense of community, to feel we're not alone in the world. But we need to keep our distance from each other to preserve our independence, so others don't impose on or engulf us. This duality reflects the human condition. We are individual and social creatures. We need other people to survive, but we want to survive as individuals.

Baxter (1994) describes the consequences for relational partners who can't successfully manage the conflicting needs for connection and autonomy. Some of the most common reasons for relational breakups involve failure of partners to satisfy one another's needs for connection: "We barely spent any time together"; "My partner wasn't committed to the relationship"; "We had different needs." But other relational complaints involve excessive demands for connection: "I was feeling trapped"; "I needed freedom." Perhaps not surprisingly, research suggests that in heterosexual romantic relationships, men often want more autonomy and women typically want more connection and commitment (Buunk, 2005; Feeney, 1999).

In accounts of relational turning points, both men and women in heterosexual romantic pairs cited the connection-autonomy dialectic as one of

TABLE 9.2 ***Dialectical Tensions***

	DIALECTIC OF INTEGRATION-SEPARATION	DIALECTIC OF STABILITY-CHANGE	DIALECTIC OF EXPRESSION-PRIVACY
Internal Manifestations	Connection-Autonomy	Predictability-Novelty	Openness-Closedness
External Manifestations	Inclusion-Seclusion	Conventionality-Uniqueness	Revelation-Concealment

From Baxter, L. A. (1994). A dialogic approach to relationship maintenance. In D. J. Canary & L. Stafford (Eds.), *Communication and relational maintenance* (p. 240). San Diego, CA: Academic Press.

the most significant factors affecting their relationship (Baxter & Erbert, 1999). This dialectical tension was crucial in negotiating turning points related to commitment, conflict, disengagement, and reconciliation. Research also shows that managing the dialectical tension between connection and autonomy is as important during divorce as it is at the beginning of a marriage, as partners seek ways to salvage and reconcile the unbreakable bonds of their personal history (including finances, children, and friends) with their new independence (Pam & Pearson, 1998).

Parents and children must deal constantly with the conflicting tugs of connection and autonomy. These struggles don't end when children grow up and leave home. Parents experience the mixed feelings of relief at their new freedom and longings to stay connected to their adult children. Likewise, grown children typically feel excitement at being on their own, and yet miss the bonds that had been taken for granted since the beginning of their lives (Blacker, 1999; Fulmer, 1999).

The tension between integration and separation also operates externally, when people within a relationship struggle to meet the competing needs of the **inclusion-seclusion dialectic**. They struggle to reconcile a desire for involvement with the "outside world" with the desire to live their own lives, free of what can feel like interference from others. For example, when the end of a busy week comes, does a couple accept the invitation to a party (and sacrifice the chance to spend quality time with one another), or do they decline the invitation (and risk losing contact with valued friends)? Does a close-knit nuclear family choose to take a much anticipated vacation together (disappointing their relatives), or do they attend a family reunion (losing precious time to enjoy one another without any distractions)?

REFLECTION

One Plus One Makes Three

I've been to a lot of weddings in the last few years, and several couples have included a ceremony that got me thinking about dialectical challenges in a marriage. There are usually three candles in a holder—two that are lit on the outsides and a center one that isn't. The bride and groom each take an outside candle and light the center one, symbolizing that they've created a new union together.

The part that comes next is most interesting to me. Some couples blow out their own individual candles, leaving only the center one burning. Others leave their own individual candles burning.

I like the symbolism of leaving all three candles burning. It reminds me of the autonomy-connection tension we talked about in class. If only the center one is burning, there's connection without autonomy. If only the outside ones are burning, it's autonomy without connection. Leaving all three lit says to me that being a couple is important, but so is being an individual.

Stability versus Change Stability is an important need in relationships, but too much of it can lead to feelings of staleness. The **stability-change dialectic** operates both between partners and when they face others outside the relationship. Within a relationship, the **predictability-novelty dialectic** captures another set of tensions. While nobody wants a completely unpredictable relational partner ("You're not the person I married!"), humorist Dave Barry (1990, p. 47) exaggerates only slightly when he talks about the boredom that can come when husbands and wives know each other too well:

> After a decade or so of marriage, you know *everything* about your spouse, every habit and opinion and twitch and tic and minor skin growth. You could write a seventeen-pound book solely about the way your spouse eats. This kind of intimate knowledge can be very handy in certain situations—such as when you're on a TV quiz show where the object is to identify your spouse from the sound of his or her chewing—but it tends to lower the passion level of a relationship.

At an external level, the **conventionality-uniqueness dialectic** captures the challenges that people in a relationship face when trying to meet others' expectations as well as their own. On one hand, stable patterns of behavior do emerge that enable others to make useful judgments like "happy family" or "dependable organization." But those blanket characterizations can stifle people in relationships, who may sometimes want to break away from the expectations others hold of them. For example, playing the conventional role of "happy family" or "perfect couple" during a time of conflict can be a burden, when the couple feels the need to behave in less stereotypical ways.

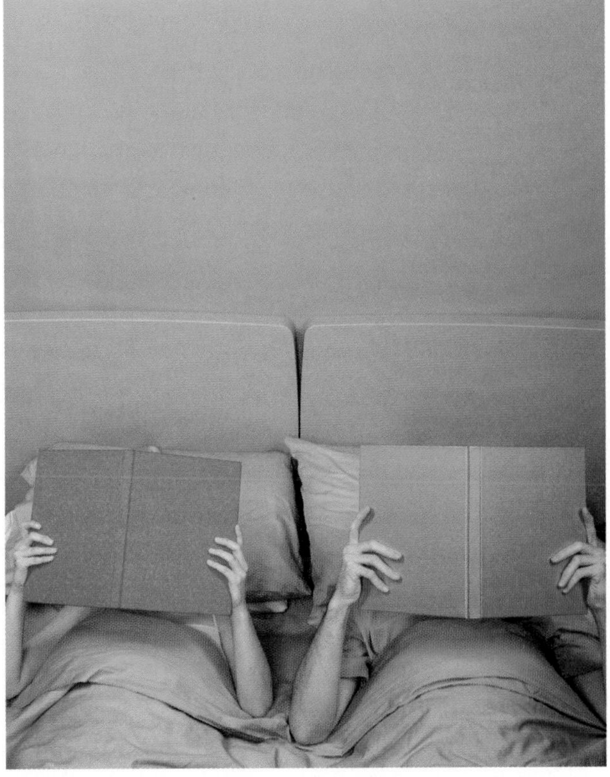

Expression versus Privacy Disclosure is one characteristic of interpersonal relationships. Yet, along with the drive for intimacy, we have an equally important need to maintain some space between ourselves and others. These sometimes conflicting drives create the **expression-privacy dialectic**.

The internal struggle between expression and privacy shows up in the **openness-closedness dialectic**. What do you do in an intimate relationship when a person you care about asks an important question that you don't want to answer? "Do you think I'm attractive?" "Are you having a good time?" Your commitment to the relationship may compel you toward honesty, but your concern for the other person's feelings and a desire for privacy may lead you to be less than completely honest. Partners use a variety of strategies to gain privacy from each other (Burgoon et al., 1989; Petronio, 2000). For example, they may confront the other person directly and explain that they don't want to continue a discussion, or they may be less direct and offer nonverbal cues, change the topic, or leave the room. As you read in Chapter 3, there are both benefits and risks in self-disclosing.

The same conflicts between openness and privacy operate externally in the **revelation-concealment dialectic**. If you and a longtime fellow worker haven't been getting along, do you answer the boss's question "How's it going?" honestly, or do you keep your disagreement to yourselves? If your family has had a run of bad (or good) financial luck and a friend asks to borrow (or lend) money, do you share your situation or keep quiet? If you're part of a lesbian couple but you're not sure your relationship will be endorsed by others, when and how do you go "public" with that information? (Suter et al., 2006; Suter & Daas, 2007). All of these questions speak to tensions related to concealing versus revealing.

For many couples, the revelation-concealment dialectic centers on decisions about how much news to share about their relationship. "Should we tell our friends that we're dating?" or "Is it time for you to meet my family?" are questions they might ask about sharing positive relational information with others. For some couples, however, the concealed news isn't so pleasant. Lara Dieckmann (2000) looked into the world of battered women and found that most of them wrestle with the dialectic of staying private or going public about the abuse in their relationships. A word that Dieckmann used to describe the women's experience is balance—the need to constantly juggle the competing demands of privacy and publicity, secrecy and disclosure, safety and danger. Telling others about partner abuse can be the first step in disengaging from a violent relationship, but it can also threaten a woman's self-esteem, security, and very life.

Although all of the dialectical tensions play an important role in managing relationships, some occur more frequently than others. In one study (Pawlowski, 1998), young married couples reported that connection-autonomy was the most frequent tension (30.8 percent of all reported contradictions). Predictability-novelty was second (occurring 21.7 percent of the time), and inclusion-seclusion was third (21.4 percent). Less common were tensions between openness-closedness (12.7 percent), conventionality-uniqueness (7.5 percent), and revelation-concealment (6 percent). Of all the dialectical tensions, connection-autonomy and openness-closedness seem to be the most important ones to manage, at least in romantic relationships (Baxter & Erbert 1999; Erbert, 2000).

Strategies for Managing Dialectical Tensions Managing the dialectical tensions outlined in these pages presents communication challenges. There are at least eight ways these challenges can be managed (Baxter & Braithwaite, 2006).

- *Denial* In the strategy of denial, communicators respond to one end of the dialectical spectrum and ignore the other. For example, a couple caught between the conflicting desires for stability and novelty might find their struggle for change too difficult to manage and choose to follow predictable, if unexciting patterns of relating to one another.
- *Disorientation* In this mode, communicators feel so overwhelmed and helpless that they are unable to confront their problems. In the face of dialectical tensions they might fight, freeze, or even leave the relationship. A couple who discovers soon after the honeymoon that living a

"happily ever after " conflict-free life is impossible might become so terrified that they would come to view their marriage as a mistake.

- *Alternation* Communicators who use this strategy choose one end of the dialectical spectrum at some times, and the other end on different occasions. Friends, for example, might manage the connection-autonomy dialectic by alternating between times when they spend a large amount of time together and other periods when they live independent lives.

- *Segmentation* Partners who use this tactic compartmentalize different areas of their relationship. For example, a couple might manage the openness-closedness dialectic by sharing almost all their feelings about mutual friends with one another, but keeping certain parts of their past romantic histories private.

- *Balance* Communicators who try to balance dialectical tensions recognize that both forces are legitimate and try to manage them through compromise. As Chapter 12 points out, compromise is inherently a situation in which everybody loses at least a little of what he or she wants. A couple caught between the conflicting desires for predictability and novelty might seek balance by compromising with a lifestyle that is neither as predictable as one wants nor as surprise-filled as the other seeks—not an ideal outcome.

- *Integration* With this approach, communicators simultaneously accept opposing forces without trying to diminish them. Barbara Montgomery (1993) describes a couple who accept both the needs for predictability and novelty by devising a "predictably novel" approach: Once a week they would do something together that they had never done before. Similarly, Dawn Braithwaite and her colleagues (1998) found that stepfamilies often manage the tension between the "old family" and the "new family" by adapting and blending their family rituals.

- *Recalibration* Communicators can respond to dialectical challenges by reframing them so that the apparent contradiction disappears. Consider how a couple who felt hurt by one another's unwillingness to share parts of their past might redefine the secrets as creating an attractive aura of mystery instead of being a problem to be solved. The desire for privacy would still remain, but it would no longer compete with a need for openness about every aspect of the past.

- *Reaffirmation* This approach acknowledges that dialectical tensions will never disappear. Instead of trying to make them go away, reaffirming communicators accept—or even embrace—the challenges they present. The metaphorical view of relational life as a kind of roller-coaster reflects this orientation, and communicators who use reaffirmation view dialectical tensions as part of the ride.

Which of these strategies do you use to manage the dialectical tensions in your life? How successful is each one? Which strategies might serve your communication better? Since dialectical tensions are a part of life, choosing how to communicate about them can make a tremendous difference in the quality of your relationships.

Maintaining Relationships through Communication

Just as gardens need tending, cars need tune-ups, and bodies need exercise, relationships need ongoing maintenance to keep them successful and satisfying. Maintenance-related communication aims to sustain the features that make the relationship successful and satisfying: enjoyment, love, commitment, trust, and so forth (Canary & Stafford, 1992; Sahlstein, 2004). The communication involved in maintaining relationships may not always be exciting, but handling it effectively accounts for as much as 80 percent of the difference between satisfying and unsatisfying relationships (Weigel & Ballard-Reisch, 1999). In this section we'll look at how we communicate about relationships, some strategies for maintaining relationships, and some tips for repairing damaged relationships.

COMMUNICATING ABOUT RELATIONSHIPS

By now it is clear that relationships are complex, dynamic, and important. How do communicators address relational issues with one another?

Content and Relational Messages In Chapter 1 you read that every message has a *content* and a *relational* dimension. The most obvious component of most messages is their content—the subject being discussed. The content of statements like "It's your turn to do the dishes" or "I'm busy Saturday night" is obvious.

Content messages aren't the only information being exchanged when two people communicate. In addition, every message—both verbal and nonverbal—also has a second, relational dimension, which makes statements about how the communicators feel toward one another (Dillard et al., 1999; Knobloch & Solomon, 2003; Watzlawick et al., 1967). These relational messages deal with one or more social needs: intimacy, affinity, respect, and control. Consider the two examples we just mentioned:

- Imagine two ways of saying "It's your turn to do the dishes," one that is demanding and another that is matter-of-fact. Notice how the different nonverbal messages make statements about how the sender views control in this part of the relationship. The demanding tone says, in effect, "I have a right to tell you what to do around the house," whereas the matter-of-fact one suggests, "I'm just reminding you of something you might have overlooked."

- You can easily imagine two ways to deliver the statement "I'm busy Saturday night," one with little affection and the other with much liking.

Like these messages, every statement we make goes beyond discussing the subject at hand and says something about the way the speaker feels about the recipient. You can prove this fact by listening for the relational messages implicit in your own statements to others and theirs to you.

Most of the time we are unaware of the relational messages that bombard us every day. Sometimes these messages don't capture our awareness because they match our belief about the amount of control, liking, or intimacy that is appropriate in a relationship. For example, you probably won't be offended if your boss tells you to drop everything and tackle a certain job, because you agree that supervisors have the right to direct employees. However, if your boss delivered the order in a condescending, sarcastic, or abusive tone of voice, you would probably be offended. Your complaint wouldn't be with the order itself, but with the way it was delivered. "I may work for this company," you might think, "but I'm not a slave or an idiot. I deserve to be treated like a human being."

Expression of Relational Messages Exactly how are relational messages communicated? As the boss-employee example suggests, they are usually expressed nonverbally. To test this fact for yourself, imagine how you could act while saying "Can you help me for a minute?" in a way that communicates each of the following relationships:

superiority
helplessness
friendliness
aloofness
sexual desire
irritation

Although nonverbal behaviors are a good source of relational messages, remember that they are ambiguous. The sharp tone you take as a personal insult might be due to fatigue, and the interruption you take as an attempt to ignore your ideas might be a sign of pressure that has nothing to do with you. Before you jump to conclusions about relational clues, it is a good idea to verify the accuracy of your interpretation with the other person: "When you cut me off, I got the idea you're angry at me. Is that right?"

Not all relational messages are nonverbal. Social scientists use the term **metacommunication** to describe messages that refer to other messages (Dindia & Baxter, 1987; Tracy, 2004). In other words, metacommunication is communication about communication. Whenever we discuss a relationship with others, we are metacommunicating: "I wish we could stop arguing so much," or "I appreciate how honest you've been with me." Verbal metacommunication is an essential ingredient in successful relationships and relational repair (Becker et al., 2008). Sooner or later, there are times when it becomes

"She's texting me, but I think she's also subtexting me."

necessary to talk about what is going on between you and the other person. The ability to focus on the kinds of issues described in this chapter can be the tool for keeping your relationship on track.

Despite its importance, overt metacommunication isn't a common feature of most relationships (Fogel & Branco, 1997; Wilmot, 1987). In fact, there seems to be an aversion to it, even among many intimates. When 90 people were asked to identify the taboo subjects in their personal relationships, the most frequent topics involved metacommunication (Baxter & Wilmot, 1985). For example, people were reluctant to discuss the state of their current relationships and the norms ("rules") that governed their lives together. Other studies suggest that when metacommunication does occur, it sometimes threatens the recipient and provokes conflict (Hocker & Wilmot, 1997). See the Focus on Research boxes "Friends with Benefits" (p. 286) and "Honest but Hurtful Messages" (p. 324) for examples of couples' tendencies to avoid metacommunicating—even when it could probably benefit them.

RELATIONAL MAINTENANCE STRATEGIES

Stafford and Canary (1991) identified five strategies for maintaining romantic relationships:

- *Positivity:*: Keeping things pleasant by being polite, cheerful, and upbeat and also by avoiding criticism.
- *Openness:* Talking directly about the nature of the relationship and disclosing your personal needs and concerns.
- *Assurances:* Letting the other person know that he or she matters to you.
- *Sharing tasks:* Helping one another take care of life's chores and obligations.
- *Social networks:* Relying on friends and family to provide support and relief that helps relational partners understand and appreciate one another, as well as giving them other sources of companionship that take some load off of the relationship.

These maintenance strategies can also be used in nonromantic relationships. One study (Johnson et al., 2008) analyzed college students' e-mail to see which strategies they employed in messages to their family members, friends, and romantic partners. With family and friends, two strategies were used most: *openness* ("Things have been a little crazy for me lately") and *social networks* ("How are you and Sam? Hopefully good"). With romantic partners, however, *assurances* ("This is just a little e-mail to say I love you") was

FOCUS ON RESEARCH

Maintaining Online Romances: The Agony and the Ecstasy

Online romances are no longer novel or unusual. Estimates suggest that millions of people have sought and even found love on the Internet. To learn more about the communication challenges of these relationships, researchers Susan Wildermuth and Sally Vogl-Bauer asked 202 people to write narratives describing their online romances. The participants' stories spoke to both the joys and the heartaches of cyberlove.

Emotional intensity was common in the participants' narratives, as in comments like this: "It's a very special, deep, emotional attraction." Many participants also noted that because their romances were based primarily on "linguistic connections," physical attraction was not a concern to them: "We've talked so long that we are past the point where looks actually matter."

On the downside, some said their emotional involvement left them open to deception by their cyberpartners ("I was infatuated and didn't pick up on the clues"). Others acknowledged that they or their cyberpartner were having an online affair because of an unhappy marriage in "real life." And even cyberlovers who enjoyed their online romance admitted that it wasn't always enough: "The lack of the physical is the hardest part. We talk up a storm but it is never the same."

Although online communication can't always meet the physical needs of its participants, it's clear from the narratives in this study that many people experience powerful attraction, affection, and even love on the Internet.

Wildermuth, S. M., & Vogl-Bauer, S. (2007). We met on the net: Exploring the perceptions of online romantic relationship participants. *Southern Communication Journal, 72*, 211–227.

the most-used maintenance device. The study shows not only that different relationships call for different types of maintenance but that e-mail can be a helpful tool for maintaining interpersonal relationships.

In successful relationships it's important for both partners to use relational maintenance strategies (Canary & Wahba, 2006). Both men and women do a roughly equal amount of relational maintenance work. Women contribute somewhat more effort in joint tasks—especially household chores—and they share personal thoughts and feelings more than men (Aylor & Dainton, 2004). As in most relational matters, the *perception* that both partners are working equally hard at maintaining the relationship is perhaps more important than the reality. When one partner feels like the other isn't doing his or her share, the relationship is headed for trouble (Canary & Stafford, 2001).

REPAIRING DAMAGED RELATIONSHIPS

Sooner or later, even the strongest relationships hit a bumpy patch. Some problems arise from outside forces: work, finances, competing relationships, and so on. At other times, problems arise from differences and disagreements within the relationship. Chapter 11 offers guidelines for dealing with these sorts of challenges.

A third type of relational problem comes from **relational transgressions**, when one partner violates the explicit or implicit terms of the relationship, letting the other one down in some important way.

Types of Relational Transgressions Table 9.3 lists some types of relational transgressons. Violations like these fall into different categories (Emmers-Sommer, 2003).

MINOR VERSUS SIGNIFICANT Some of the items listed in Table 9.3 aren't inherently transgressions, and in small doses they can actually aid relationships. For instance, a *little* distance can make the heart grow fonder, a *little* jealousy can be a sign of affection, and a *little* anger can start the process of resolving a gripe. In large and regular doses, however, these acts become serious transgressions that can damage personal relationships.

SOCIAL VERSUS RELATIONAL Some transgressions violate *social rules* shared by society at large. For example, almost everyone would agree that ridiculing or humiliating a friend or family member in public is a violation of a fundamental social rule regarding saving others' face. Other rules are *relational* in nature—unique norms constructed by the parties involved. For instance, some families have a rule stating "If I'm going to be more than a little bit late, I'll let you know so that you don't worry." Once such a rule exists, failure to honor it feels like a violation, even though outsiders might not view it as such.

DELIBERATE VERSUS UNINTENTIONAL Some transgressions are unintentional. You might reveal something about a friend's past without realizing that this disclosure would be embarrassing. Other violations, though, are intentional. In a fit of anger, you might purposely lash out with a cruel comment, knowing that it will hurt the other person's feelings.

ONE-TIME VERSUS INCREMENTAL The most obvious transgressions occur in a single episode: an act of betrayal, a verbal assault, or walking out in anger. But more subtle transgressions can occur over time. Consider emotional withdrawal: Everybody has times when they retreat into themselves, and we usually give one another the space to do just that. But if the withdrawal slowly becomes pervasive, it becomes a violation of the fundamental rule in most relationships that partners should be available to one another.

Strategies for Relational Repair Research confirms the commonsense notion that a first step to repairing a transgression is to talk about the violation (Dindia & Baxter, 1987). Chapter 5 offers tips for sending clear, assertive "I-messages" when you believe you've been wronged, ("I was really embarrassed when you yelled at me in front of everybody last night"). In other cases, you might be responsible for the transgression and want to raise it for discussion:

TABLE 9.3 ***Some Types of Relational Transgressions***

Lack of Commitment
Failure to honor important obligations (e.g., financial, emotional, task-related)
Self-serving dishonesty
Unfaithfulness
Distance
Physical separation (beyond what is necessary)
Psychological separation (avoidance, ignoring)
Disrespect
Criticism (especially in front of third parties)
Problematic Emotions
Jealousy
Unjustified Suspicion
Rage
Aggression
Verbal hostility
Physical violence

"What did I do that you found so hurtful?" "Why was my behavior a problem for you?" Asking questions like these—and listening nondefensively to the answers—can be an enormous challenge. Chapter 7 offers guidelines for listening, and Chapter 10 provides tips about how to manage criticism.

Not surprisingly, some transgressions are harder to repair than others. One study of dating partners found that sexual infidelity and breaking up with the partner were the two least forgivable offenses (Bachman & Guerrero, 2006). For the best chance of repairing a seriously damaged relationship, an apology needs to be offered—ideally containing these three elements (Kelley & Waldron, 2005):

- An explicit acknowledgement that the transgression was wrong: "I acted like a selfish jerk."
- A sincere apology: "I'm really sorry. I feel awful for letting you down."
- Some type of compensation: "No matter what happens, I'll never do anything like that again."

An apology will be convincing only if the speaker's nonverbal behaviors match his or her words. Even then, it may be unrealistic to expect immediate forgiveness. Sometimes, especially with severe transgressions, expressions of regret and promises of new behavior will only be accepted conditionally, with a need for them to be demonstrated over time before the aggrieved party regards them as genuine (Merolla, 2008).

Given the challenges and possible humiliation involved in apologizing, is it worth the effort? Research suggests yes. Participants in one study con-

sistently reported that they had more remorse over apologies they *didn't* offer than about those they did (Exline et al., 2007).

Forgiving Transgressions Many people think of forgiveness as a topic for theologians and philosophers. However, social scientists have found that forgiving others has both personal and relational benefits. On a personal level, forgiveness has been shown to reduce emotional distress and aggression (Eaton & Struthers, 2006; Orcutt, 2006) as well as to improve cardiovascular functioning (Lawler et al., 2003). Interpersonally, extending forgiveness to lovers, friends, and family can help restore damaged relationships (Waldron & Kelley, 2005). Moreover, research shows that transgressors who have been forgiven are less likely to repeat their offenses than those who have not received forgiveness (Wallace et al., 2008).

Even when a sincere apology is offered, forgiving others can be difficult. Research shows that one way to improve your ability to forgive is to recall times when you have mistreated or hurt others in the past—in other words, to remember that you, too, have wronged others and needed their forgiveness (Exline et al., 2008; Takaku, 2001). Given that it's in our own best interest to be forgiving, communication researcher Douglas Kelley (1998) encourages us to remember these words from R. P. Walters: "When we have been hurt we have two alternatives: be destroyed by resentment, or forgive. Resentment is death; forgiving leads to healing and life" (p. 324).

Granting forgiveness to others can sometimes be done through nonverbal displays, such as replacing frowns with smiles or physical affection. More serious cases might require discussion and negotiation or even an explicit statement of forgiveness. The Self-Assessment on page 309 can help you recognize how you typically express forgiveness to others.

SELF-ASSESSMENT

Forgiveness-Granting Strategies

Presented here is a list of behaviors a person might use to respond to someone seeking forgiveness. To what extent do you use each strategy? Rate each one on a scale from 0 to 7, where 0 = "never use," 4 = "use moderately," and 7 = "use extensively."

NEVER USE **0 1 2 3 4 5 6 7** USE EXTENSIVELY

_____ **1. I touch my partner in a way that communicates forgiveness.**
_____ **2. I say I would forgive my partner if the offense never happened again.**
_____ **3. I tell my partner it was no big deal.**
_____ **4. I initiate discussion about the offense.**
_____ **5. The expression on my face says, "I forgive you."**
_____ **6. I tell my partner not to worry about it.**
_____ **7. I say I would forgive my partner only if things changed.**
_____ **8. I discuss the offense with my partner.**
_____ **9. I tell my partner, "I forgive you."**

Add your responses to items 1 and 5:	_______	Nonverbal display of forgiveness
Add your responses to items 2 and 7:	_______	Forgiveness with contingencies
Add your responses to items 3 and 6:	_______	Minimize the consequences of the transgression
Add your responses to items 4 and 8:	_______	Talk about the offense
Record your response to item 9:	_______	Explicit forgiveness

Your scores should give you an indication of which strategies you use most frequently.

Adapted from Waldron, V. R., & Kelley, D. L (2005). Forgiving communication as a response to relational transgressions. *Journal of Social and Personal Relationships, 22,* 723–742.

Summary

There are several explanations for why we form relationships with some people and not with others. These explanations include appearance (physical attractiveness), similarity, complementarity, rewards, competency, proximity, and disclosure. We also form relationships to achieve various forms of intimacy: emotional, physical, intellectual, and shared activities. Intimacy is influenced by gender and culture and can even take place through computer-mediated communication. Finally, we form relationships with others in quest of relational commitment.

Some theorists argue that interpersonal relationships may go through as many as 10 stages of growth and deterioration. They suggest that communication may reflect more than one stage at a given time, although one stage will be dominant. Other models describe the dynamics of interpersonal communication in terms of dialectical tensions: mutually opposing, incompatible desires that can never be completely resolved. These dialectical tensions include integration-separation, stability-change, and expression-privacy.

Relationships are maintained through communication. Messages have both content and relational dimensions. Relational messages sometimes are expressed overtly via verbal metacommunication; however, more frequently they are conveyed nonverbally. Scholars have identified several strategies for maintaining relationships. Some relationships become damaged over time; others are hurt by relational transgressions. There are several strategies for repairing damaged relationships, with apologies and forgiveness being particularly important.

Activities

1. Critical Thinking Probe

Scholars have argued for years as to whether similarity ("Birds of a feather flock together") or complementarity ("Opposites attract") offers the best explanation for relational attraction and formation. Based on your own experience, which do you think is more valid? Are there cases where both are true? Offer examples to support your position.

2. Invitation to Insight

What kinds of intimacy characterize your relationships? Answer the questions that follow as you think about your relationship with an important person in your life:

a. What is the level of physical intimacy in your relationship?
b. What intellectual intimacy do you share?
c. How emotionally intimate are you? Is your emotional intimacy deeper in some ways than in others?
d. What shared activities occupy an important role in this relationship?
e. Has your intimacy level changed over time? If so, in what ways?

After answering these questions, ask yourself how satisfied you are with the amount of intimacy in this relationship. Identify any changes you would like to occur, and describe the steps you could take to make them happen.

3. Critical Thinking Probe

Some critics claim that Knapp's model of relational stages is better suited to describing romantic relationships than it is other types. Use a variety of romantic and nonromantic interpersonal relationships from your experience to evaluate the breadth of his model. If the model does not describe the developmental path of all types of interpersonal relationships, can you suggest alternative models (such as one of the models depicted in Figure 9.2 on p. 296)?

4. Invitation to Insight

How do you manage the dialectical tensions in your important relationships? Is there a pattern to what you and the other person do, or does it depend on the type of relationship you have? Identify at least two dialectical tensions in two different relationships—one relationship, perhaps, with a person with whom you work closely, and the other with a romantic partner. How is each tension managed? Which approach do you and your partner tend to use (denial, disorientation, alternation, segmentation, balance, integration, recalibration, or reaffirmation)? What seem to be the conditions that determine which method you and your partner use?

5. Skill Builder

Identify three unexpressed relational messages in one or more of your interpersonal relationships.

a. Describe how you could have used metacommunication to express each one. Consider skills you learned in other chapters, such as perception checking, "I" language, and paraphrasing.
b. Discuss the possible benefits and drawbacks of this kind of metacommunication in each of the situations you identified. Based on your discussion here, what principles do you believe should guide your decision about whether and when to focus explicitly on relational issues?

6. Invitation to Insight

Which of the maintenance strategies described on pages 304–305 do you use to keep one of your relationships functioning successfully? Can you think of any way to use these strategies to make the relationship more successful and satisfying?

7. Invitation to Insight

a. Identify transgressions you have made in one important relationship. Describe whether these transgressions were social or relational, deliberate or unintentional, and one-time or incremental. (If you think the relationship can handle it, consider asking the "victim" of your transgression to describe your behavior and its effects.)
b. Consider (or ask the other person) whether it's necessary to repair your transgression. Examine the strategies described earlier, and decide how you could put them into action.

CHAPTER

10 Communication Climate

CHAPTER OUTLINE

After studying the material in this chapter . . .

YOU SHOULD UNDERSTAND:

1. The definition of communication climate.
2. The importance of being valued and confirmed.
3. The characteristics of confirming, disagreeing, and disconfirming messages.
4. The nature of positive and negative communication spirals.
5. The relationship between presenting self (face) and defensiveness.
6. The types of messages that are likely to create positive communication climates.
7. The various ways to transform negative communication climates.

YOU SHOULD BE ABLE TO:

1. Identify confirming, disagreeing, and disconfirming messages and patterns in your own relationships.
2. Identify the parts of your presenting self (face) that you defend, and the consequences of doing so.
3. Create messages that are likely to build supportive rather than defensive communication climates.
4. Create appropriate nondefensive responses to real or hypothetical criticisms.

KEY TERMS

- Aggressiveness (320)
- Ambiguous response (322)
- Argumentativeness (318)
- Certainty (332)
- Communication climate (314)
- Complaining (320)
- Confirming communication (315)
- Controlling communication (329)
- Defensiveness (323)
- Description (328)
- Disagreeing message (318)
- Disconfirming communication (315)
- Empathy (331)
- Equality (332)
- Evaluation (327)
- Face (323)
- Face-threatening acts (323)
- Impersonal response (322)
- Impervious response (321)
- Incongruous response (323)
- Interrupting response (321)
- Irrelevant response (322)
- Neutrality (331)
- Presenting self (323)
- Problem orientation (329)
- Provisionalism (333)
- Sandwich method (334)
- Spiral (325)
- Spontaneity (330)
- Strategy (330)
- Superiority (332)
- Tangential response (322)

How would you describe your most important relationships? Fair and warm? Stormy? Hot? Cold? Just as physical locations have characteristic weather patterns, interpersonal relationships have unique climates, too. You can't measure the interpersonal climate by looking at a thermometer or glancing at the sky, but it's there nonetheless. Every relationship has a feeling, a pervasive mood that colors the goings-on of the participants.

What Is Communication Climate?

The term **communication climate** refers to the social tone of a relationship. A climate doesn't involve specific activities as much as the way people feel about each other as they carry out those activities. For example, consider two interpersonal communication classes. Both meet for the same length of time and follow the same syllabus. It's easy to imagine how one of these classes might be a friendly, comfortable place to learn, whereas the other could be cold and tense—even hostile. It's not the course content that differs—it's the way the people in the classroom feel about and treat each other.

Just as every classroom has a unique climate, so does every relationship. Romances, friendships, and families—just like neighborhoods, cities, and countries—can be defined by their social tone. Another obvious context for observing climate's impact is the workplace, which may explain why the topic is so widely studied (Scarpero, 2000; Sopow, 2008). Think for a moment: Have you ever held a job where backbiting, criticism, and suspicion were the norm? Or have you been lucky enough to work where the atmosphere was positive, encouraging, and supportive? If you've experienced both, you know what a difference climate makes. Other studies (e.g., Anderson et al., 2004; Odden & Sias, 1997) reinforce the fact that employees have a higher level of commitment at jobs in which they experience a positive communication climate, especially to their work group if not the organization as a whole (Bartels et al., 2008).

Like their meteorological counterparts, communication climates are shared by everyone involved. It's rare to find one person describing a relationship as open and positive while another characterizes it as cold and hostile. Also, just like the weather, communication climates can change over

time. A relationship can be overcast at one time and sunny at another. Carrying the analogy to its conclusion, we should say that communication climate forecasting is not a perfect science. Unlike the weather, however, people can change their communication climates—and that's why it's important to understand them. We'll look at several climate issues in this chapter: how communication climates develop, how and why we respond defensively in certain climates, and what can be done to create positive climates and transform negative ones.

How Communication Climates Develop

Why does some communication create a positive climate while other behavior has the opposite effect? A short but accurate answer is that communication climate is determined by the degree to which people see themselves as *valued.* Communicators who perceive others as liking, appreciating, and respecting them react positively, whereas those who feel unimportant or abused react negatively. Social scientists use the term **confirming communication** to describe messages that convey valuing. In one form or another, confirming messages say "you exist," "you matter," "you're important." By contrast, **disconfirming communication** signals a lack of regard. In one form or another, disconfirming messages say, "I don't care about you," "I don't like you," "You're not important to me."

FOCUS ON RESEARCH

Positive Work Climates and Cordial E-mails

research

Sometimes it's hard to determine what makes an organization's climate friendly or frosty. Researchers look for telltale signs in a company's communication patterns. A recent study shows that these indicators can be as subtle as the greetings and sign-offs in e-mail messages.

Joan Waldvogel gathered extensive data from two organizations in New Zealand. Company A had recently been through restructuring and was suffering from low morale and high levels of distrust. Company B had a much more positive, family-like organizational culture. An analysis of hundreds of e-messages sent within the two organizations revealed a trend: Employees of Company B regularly used more and warmer greetings and closings in their e-messages than did employees at Company A. The greetings were more likely to address the recipient by name and use friendly salutations such as "Hi!" The closings usually included the message-sender's name and often a farewell formula such as "Cheers," "Thanks," or "Have a nice day."

It's hard to establish whether these greetings and closings are symptoms or causes of an organization's culture. In either case, it appears that a little cordiality and politeness is one sign of a positive communication climate.

Waldvogel, J. (2007). Greetings and closings in workplace email. *Journal of Computer-Mediated Communication, 12*, 456–477.

As we have stressed throughout this book, every message has a relational dimension along with its content. This means that we send and receive confirming and disconfirming messages virtually whenever we communicate. It isn't what we communicate about that shapes a relational climate as much as *how* we speak and act toward one another. Choosing *not* to speak to someone can also communicate disconfirmation. Stephen Cox (1999) found that one way employees nudge unwanted coworkers to quit their jobs is to avoid interaction with them, creating a chilly communication climate.

It's hard to overstate the importance of confirming messages and the impact of disconfirming ones. Children who lack confirmation suffer a broad range of emotional and behavioral problems (Osterman, 2001), while those who feel confirmed have more open communication with their parents, higher self-esteem, and lower levels of stress (Dailey, 2006; Schrodt et al., 2006). In the classroom, confirming communication by teachers has been shown to enhance student learning and participation while reducing negative behaviors (Goodboy & Myers, 2008). A confirming climate is also important in marriage, where it is the best predictor of marital satisfaction (Clarke, 1973; Veroff et al., 1998). Satisfied couples have a 5:1 ratio of positive to negative statements, while the ratio for dissatisfied partners is 1:1 (Gottman, 2003; see also Canary & Emmers-Sommer, 1997).

Like beauty, the decision about whether a message is confirming or disconfirming is in the eyes of the beholder (Vangelisti & Crumley, 1998). Consider, for example, times when you took a comment that might have sounded unsupportive to an outsider ("You turkey!") as a sign of affection within the context of your personal relationship. Likewise, a comment that the sender might have meant to be helpful ("I'm telling you this for your own good . . .") could easily be regarded as a disconfirming attack.

LEVELS OF MESSAGE CONFIRMATION

Figure 10.1 shows that the range of confirming and disconfirming communication includes several categories of messages, which are described in the following pages.

Confirming Messages There's no guarantee that others will regard even your best attempts at confirming messages the way you intend them, but research shows that three increasingly positive types of messages have the best chance of being perceived as confirming (Cissna & Sieberg, 1999).

RECOGNITION The most fundamental act of confirmation is to recognize the other person. Recognition seems easy and obvious, yet there are many times when we do not respond to others on this basic level. Failure to write to or visit a friend is a common example. So is failure to return a phone message. Likewise, avoiding eye contact and not approaching someone you know can send a negative message. Of course, this lack of recognition may simply be an oversight. You may not notice your friend, or the pressures of work and school may prevent you from staying in touch. Nonetheless, if the other person *perceives* you as avoiding contact, the message has the effect of being disconfirming.

ACKNOWLEDGMENT Acknowledging the ideas and feelings of others is a stronger form of confirmation than simple recognition. Listening is probably the most common form of acknowledgment. Silently and attentively paying attention to another person's words is one measure of your interest. Not surprisingly, employees give high marks to managers who solicit their opinions—even when the managers don't accept every suggestion (Allen, 1995). As you read in Chapter 7, reflecting the speaker's thoughts and feelings can be a powerful way to offer support when others have problems.

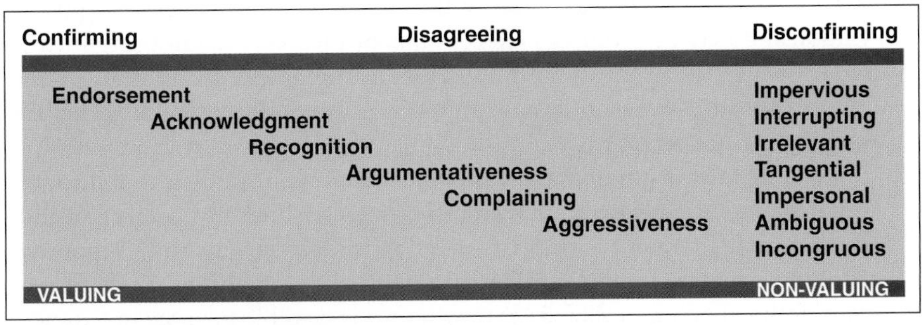

FIGURE 10.1 Confirmation–Disconfirmation Continuum

ENDORSEMENT Whereas acknowledgment communicates you are interested in another person, endorsement means that you agree with her or him or otherwise find her or him important. It's easy to see why endorsement is the strongest type of confirming message, since it communicates the highest form of valuing. The most obvious form of endorsement is agreeing, but it isn't necessary to agree completely with other people in order to endorse their message. You can probably find something in the message that you endorse. "I can see why you were so angry," you might reply to a friend, even if you don't approve of his or her outburst. Of course, outright praise is a strong form of endorsement, one you can use surprisingly often once you look for opportunities to compliment others. Nonverbal endorsement also can enhance the quality of a relational climate. For example, simple acts like maintaining eye contact and nodding while someone speaks can confirm the value of a speaker's idea. On a more intimate level, hugs and embraces can sometimes communicate endorsement in ways that words cannot.

Disagreeing Messages Between confirming and disconfirming lies a type of message that isn't always easy to categorize. A **disagreeing message** essentially says, "You're wrong." In its most constructive form, disagreement includes two of the confirming components we just discussed: recognition and acknowledgment. At its worst, a brutal disagreeing message can so devastate another person that the benefits of recognition and acknowledgment are lost. Because there are better and worse ways to disagree with others, disagreeing messages need to be put on a positive-to-negative scale. We will do just that in this section as we discuss three types of disagreement: argumentativeness, complaining, and aggressiveness.

ARGUMENTATIVENESS Normally when we call a person "argumentative," we're making an unfavorable evaluation. However, the ability to create and deliver a sound argument is something we admire in lawyers, talk-show participants, letters to the editor, and political debates. Taking a positive approach to the term, communication researchers define **argumentativeness** as presenting and defending positions on issues while attacking positions taken by others (Infante & Rancer, 1996). Rather than being a negative trait, argumentativeness—at least in the United States—is associated with a number of positive attributes, such as enhanced self-concept (Rancer et al., 1992), leadership emergence (Limon & LaFrance, 2005), and communicative competence (Onyekwere et al., 1991). In the classroom, research shows a positive relationship between students' perceptions of their instructor as argumentative (not aggressive) and their motivation, learning, and satisfaction (Myers, 2002). You can assess your level of argumentativeness by completing the Self-Assessment on page 319.

The key for maintaining a positive climate while arguing a point is the *way* you present your ideas. It is crucial to attack issues, not people. In addition, a sound argument is better received when it's delivered in a supportive, affirming manner (Infante & Gorden, 1989). The supportive kinds of messages outlined on pages 327–333 show how it is possible to argue in a respectful, constructive way.

SELF-ASSESSMENT

Argumentativeness and Verbal Aggression

The following items are from two instruments, one developed by Infante and Rancer (1982) and the other by Infante and Wigley (1986). Use the following scale to indicate how true each statement is for you.

1 = Almost never true 2 = Rarely true 3 = Occasionally true 4 = Often true 5 = Almost always true

PART 1

_____ **1. While in an argument, I worry that the person I am arguing with will form a negative impression of me.**
_____ **2. Arguing over controversial issues improves my intelligence.**
_____ **3. Once I finish an argument, I promise myself that I will not get into another.**
_____ **4. Arguing with a person creates more problems than it solves.**
_____ **5. I have a pleasant, good feeling when I win a point in an argument.**
_____ **6. When I finish arguing with someone I feel nervous and upset.**
_____ **7. I enjoy a good argument over a controversial issue.**
_____ **8. I have the ability to do well in an argument.**
_____ **9. I try to avoid getting into arguments.**
_____ **10. I enjoy defending my point of view on an issue.**

PART 2

_____ **1. I am extremely careful to avoid attacking individuals' intelligence when I attack their ideas.**
_____ **2. When individuals are very stubborn, I use insults to soften the stubbornness.**
_____ **3. I try to make people feel good about themselves, even when their ideas are stupid.**
_____ **4. When people refuse to do a task I know is important, without good reason, I tell them they are unreasonable.**
_____ **5. When people criticize my shortcomings, I take it in good humor and do not try to get back at them.**
_____ **6. When people simply will not budge on a matter of importance, I lose my temper and say rather strong things to them.**
_____ **7. I refuse to participate in arguments when they involve personal attacks.**
_____ **8. I like poking fun at people who do things that are very stupid in order to stimulate their intelligence.**
_____ **9. When an argument shifts to personal attacks, I try very hard to change the subject.**
_____ **10. When I am not able to refute others' positions, I try to make them feel defensive in order to weaken their positions.**

SCORING:

For Part 1, add your scores on items 2, 5, 7, 8, and 10. This is your tendency to approach argumentative situations. Now, add your scores on 1, 3, 4, 6, and 9. This is your tendency to avoid argumentative situations. To compute your argumentativeness score, subtract the second sum from the first. The higher your score, the greater your predisposition to be argumentative (the possible range is from 0 to 20, with a midpoint of 10).

For Part 2, sum the scores on the 10 items after reversing the scoring for items 1, 3, 5, 7, and 9 (i.e., 5 = 1, 4 = 2, 3 = 3, 2 = 4, and 1 = 5). This is your verbal aggressiveness score—the higher the score, the greater your tendency to be verbally aggressive (the possible range is 10 to 50, with a midpoint of 30).

COMPLAINING When communicators aren't prepared to argue, but still want to register dissatisfaction, they often complain. As is true of all disagreeing messages, some ways of **complaining** are better than others. Jess Alberts (1988, 1990) found that satisfied couples tend to offer behavioral complaints ("You always throw your socks on the floor"), while unsatisfied couples make more complaints aimed at personal characteristics ("You're a slob"). Personal complaints are more likely to result in an escalated conflict episode (Alberts & Driscoll, 1992). The reason should be obvious—complaints about personal characteristics attack a more fundamental part of the presenting self. Talking about socks deals with a habit that can be changed; calling someone a slob is a character assault that is unlikely to be forgotten when the conflict is over. Marriage researcher John Gottman (2000) has found that complaining is not a sign of a troubled relationship—in fact, it's usually healthy for spouses to get their concerns out in the open. However, when couples' communication is filled with disrespectful criticism and contempt, it is often a symptom of a marriage headed for divorce.

AGGRESSIVENESS The most destructive way to disagree with another person is through **aggressiveness**. Dominic Infante and his associates (1992, p. 116) define verbal aggressiveness as the tendency to "attack the self-concepts of other people in order to inflict psychological pain." Unlike argumentativeness, aggressiveness demeans the worth of others. Name calling, put-downs, sarcasm, taunting, yelling, badgering—all are methods of "winning" disagreements at others' expense.

It should come as no surprise that aggressiveness has been found to have a variety of serious consequences (Rancer & Avtgis, 2006). Aggressive behavior is especially hurtful when it comes from people who are close to us (Martin et al., 1996). Research shows it is associated with physical violence in marriages (Infante et al., 1989), juvenile delinquency (Atkin et al., 2002; Straus & Field, 2003), depression (Segrin & Fitzpatrick, 1992), a negative climate in the workplace (Infante & Gorden, 1985, 1987, 1989), lower organizational commitment (Houghton, 2001), and a negative climate in the classroom (Myers & Rocca, 2001). Myers and Rocca compared argumentativeness and verbal aggressiveness and found that "when instructors are perceived to engage in argumentativeness, they promote student . . . motivation; when instructors are perceived to engage in verbal aggressiveness, they contribute negatively to student perceptions of classroom climate and diminish student . . . motivation" (p. 131). In a follow-up study, Myers and his colleagues (2007) found that students who perceive their

Receiving Overdue Confirmation: *Antwone Fisher*

Antwone Fisher (Derek Luke) is an angry young sailor. A shipboard fight lands him in the office of psychiatrist Jerome Davenport (Denzel Washington), whose job is to help Antwone manage his temper. After several sessions of stubborn silence, Antwone reveals that he was abandoned at birth by his imprisoned mother. He never knew his father, who was murdered 2 months before he was born. Raised by a cruel and disconfirming foster family, Antwone feels rootless and mad at the world.

Over time, Dr. Davenport becomes a father figure to Antwone and assures him of his value and worth. Antwone also locates his birth father's family, who didn't know Antwone existed before he shows up on their doorstep. Much to his amazement and relief, they welcome him into their family with open arms. The movie, which is based on a true story, offers hope for turning around a tough life through loving and confirming communication.

instructor as verbally aggressive are less likely to ask questions, interact in the classroom, or seek out-of-class communication.

It's possible to send clear, firm messages that are assertive (standing up for yourself) rather than aggressive (putting others down). For instructions on creating "I" statements, refer to Chapter 5. For details on win-win vs. win-lose approaches to conflict management, see Chapter 11. Later in this chapter, we'll provide tips on offering constructive criticism.

Disconfirming Messages Disconfirming messages are subtler than disagreeing ones but potentially more damaging. Disconfirming communication implicitly says, "You don't exist; you are not valued."

Disconfirming messages, unfortunately, are part of everyday life. While an occasional disconfirming message may not injure a relationship, a pattern of them usually indicates a negative communication climate. Sieberg and Larson (1971) found it was easiest to identify disconfirming communication by observing *responses* to others' messages. They noted seven types of disconfirming responses:

IMPERVIOUS RESPONSE An **impervious response** fails to acknowledge the other person's communicative attempt, either verbally or nonverbally. Failing to return a phone call is an impervious response, as is not responding to another's letter or e-mail message. Impervious responses also happen in face-to-face settings. They are especially common when adults and children communicate. Parents often become enraged when they are ignored by their children; likewise, children feel diminished when adults pay no attention to their questions, comments, or requests. Impervious responses also bother students, who, when ignored, report feeling that their self-esteem is being threatened (Sommer et al., 2001). Most experts concur that being ignored by significant others is psychologically damaging (Holte & Wichstrom, 1990; Laing, 1961). This explains why the "silent treatment" can be so disturbing, and why the cruelest punishment children and adults can bestow on others is to ignore them.

INTERRUPTING RESPONSE As its name implies, an **interrupting response** occurs when one person begins to speak before the other is through making a point.

> *Customer:* I'm looking for an outfit I can wear on a trip I'm . . .
> *Salesperson:* I've got just the thing. It's part wool and part polyester, so it won't wrinkle at all.
> *C:* Actually, wrinkling isn't that important. I want something that will work as a business outfit and . . .
> *S:* We have a terrific blazer that you can dress up or down, depending on the accessories you choose.
> *C:* That's not what I was going to say. I want something that I can wear as a business outfit, but it ought to be on the informal side. I'm going to . . .
> *S:* Say no more. I know just what you want.
> *C:* Never mind. I think I'll look in some other stores.

IRRELEVANT RESPONSE It is disconfirming to respond with an **irrelevant response**, making comments totally unrelated to what the other person was just saying.

A: What a day! I thought it would never end. First the car overheated and I had to call a tow truck, and then the computer broke down at work.
B: Listen, we have to talk about a present for Ann's birthday. The party is on Saturday, and I only have tomorrow to shop for it.
A: I'm really beat. You won't believe what the boss did. Like I said, the computer was down, and in the middle of that mess he decided he absolutely had to have the sales figures for the last 6 months.
B: I just can't figure what would suit Ann. She's been so generous to us, and I can't think of anything she needs.
A: Why don't you listen to me? I beat my brains out all day and you don't give a damn.
B: And you don't care about me!

TANGENTIAL RESPONSE Unlike the three behaviors just discussed, a **tangential response** does acknowledge the other person's communication. However, the acknowledgment is used to steer the conversation in a new direction. Tangents can come in two forms. One is the "tangential shift," which is an abrupt change in conversation. For example, a young boy runs into the house excited, showing his mother the rock he found. She says, "Wash you hands; that rock is dirty." In a "tangential drift" the speaker makes a token connection with what the other person is saying and then moves the conversation in another direction entirely. In the same scenario, the mother might look at the rock, say "Hmmm, nice rock," and then immediately add, "Go wash your hands before dinner."

"Go ask your search engine."

IMPERSONAL RESPONSE In an **impersonal response**, the speaker conducts a monologue filled with impersonal, intellectualized, and generalized statements. The speaker never really interacts with the other on a personal level.

Employee: I've been having some personal problems lately, and I'd like to take off early a couple of afternoons to clear them up.
Boss: Ah, yes. We all have personal problems. It seems to be a sign of the times.

AMBIGUOUS RESPONSE An **ambiguous response** contains a message with more than one meaning. The words are highly abstract or have meanings private to the speaker alone.

A: I'd like to get together with you soon. How about Tuesday?
B: Uh, maybe so. Anyhow, see you later.

C: How can I be sure you mean it?
D: Who knows what anybody means?

INCONGRUOUS RESPONSE An **incongruous response** contains two messages that seem to deny or contradict each other, one at the verbal level and the other at the nonverbal level.

He: Darling, I love you!
She: I love you too. (*giggles*)

Teacher: Did you enjoy the class?
Student: Yes. (*yawns*)

It's important to note again that disconfirming messages, like virtually every other type of communication, are a matter of perception. A message that might not be intended to devalue the other person can be interpreted as disconfirming. For example, your failure to return a phone call or respond to the e-mail of an out-of-town friend might simply be the result of a busy schedule, but if the other person views the lack of contact as a sign that you don't value the relationship, the effect will be just as strong as if you had deliberately intended to convey a slight.

DEFENSIVENESS

It's no surprise that disconfirming and disagreeing messages can pollute a communication climate. Perhaps the most predictable reaction to a hostile or indifferent message is defensiveness.

The word *defensiveness* suggests protecting yourself from attack, but what kind of attack? Seldom when you become defensive is a physical threat involved. If you're not threatened by bodily injury, what *are* you guarding against? To answer this question, we need to talk more about notions of **presenting self** and **face**, both of which were introduced in Chapter 3. Recall that the presenting self consists of the physical traits, personality characteristics, attitudes, aptitudes, and all the other parts of the image you want to present to the world. Actually, it is a mistake to talk about a single face: We try to project different selves to different people. For instance, you might try to impress a potential employer with your seriousness but want your friends to see you as a joker.

When others are willing to accept and acknowledge important parts of our presenting image, there is no need to feel defensive. On the other hand, when others confront us with **face-threatening acts**—messages that we perceive as challenging the image we want to project—we are likely to resist what they say. **Defensiveness**, then, is the process of protecting our presenting self, our face.

You can understand how defensiveness operates by imagining what might happen if an important part of your presenting self were attacked. For instance, suppose an instructor criticized you for making a stupid mistake. Or consider

FOCUS ON RESEARCH

Honest but Hurtful: Face-Threatening Messages in Romantic Relationships

research

"The truth hurts" is a familiar adage that is especially true in close relationships. Although most people say they value honesty and openness, they also dislike hearing negative evaluations of themselves, especially from the people whose opinions they value most. Communication researchers Shuangyue Zhang and Laura Stafford studied "honest but hurtful" (HBH) messages in romantic relationships and found that some such messages are seen as more face-threatening than others.

Participants in the study were asked to reconstruct an HBH message they had received in a current romantic relationship. The researchers found that HBH comments about relational shortcomings (e.g., "You don't pay enough attention to me") were perceived as the most face-threatening—more so than comments about personality characteristics (e.g., "You're too nosy"), personal appearance (e.g., "You need to tone up a bit"), or behaviors not related to the relationship (e.g. "You spend too much money").

Zhang and Stafford say these results are consistent with previous research showing that romantic couples dislike talking about the state of their relationships, especially if there is a problem. An HBH message about a romantic relationship is apparently perceived as threatening both to the recipient and to the relationship itself.

Zhang, S., & Stafford, L. (2008). Perceived face threat of honest but hurtful evaluative messages in romantic relationships. *Western Journal of Communication, 72,* 19–39.

how you would feel if a friend called you self-centered or your boss labeled you as lazy. You would probably feel threatened if these attacks were untrue. But your own experience will probably show that you sometimes respond defensively even when you know that others' criticism is justified. For instance, you have probably responded defensively at times when you *did* make a mistake, act selfishly, or cut corners in your work. In fact, we often feel most defensive when criticism is right on target (Becker et al., 2008; Stamp et al., 1992).

The topics that trigger defensiveness also vary. Sometimes sensitive topics are personal. You might feel a strong need to protect your image of athletic skill or intelligence, while another person might be more concerned with appearing fashionable or funny. Some research suggests that defense-provoking topics can vary by sex. In one study, men interpreted messages about mental or physical errors (such as misfiling a file or tripping on a carpet) more defensively than women did. Males and females got equally defensive about messages about their clothes and hair, but women got more defensive about messages regarding weight (Futch & Edwards, 1999). And professional women report a variety of face-threatening interactions in the workplace, particularly with men in traditionally male occupations (Irizarry, 2004).

Who offers the potentially defense-arousing remark or criticism also matters. Matthew Hornsey and his colleagues (2002) conducted three experiments examining group members' responses to criticism from in-group (other

Australians) and out-group (people from another country) members. They found that in-group criticisms were tolerated surprisingly well, while out-group criticisms were met with defensiveness—probably because in-group criticisms are seen as more legitimate and more constructive.

So far, we have talked about defensiveness as if it is only the responsibility of the person who feels threatened. If this were the case, then the prescription would be simple: Grow a thick skin, admit your flaws, and stop trying to manage impressions. This approach isn't just unrealistic—it also ignores the role played by those who send face-threatening messages. In fact, competent communicators protect others' face needs as well as their own. For example, the people college students judge as close friends are those who provide "positive face support" by endorsing the presenting image of others (Cupach & Messman, 1999). Findings like this make it clear that defensiveness is *interactive:* all communicators contribute to the climate of a relationship.

As a practical example of these concepts, communication researcher Sarah Tracy (2002) analyzed emergency call-center interactions to understand better how and why these conversations sometimes turn into contentious struggles. Tracy concluded that callers become defensive when they perceive call-takers' questions to be face-threatening, and she offered suggestions for making the climate more supportive. For instance, changing a question from "Tell me if . . ." to "Can you tell me if . . ." adds only a few words—but those words soften the inquiry and make it more of a request than a demand. Changes like this take very little extra time, and they have the potential to keep the climate supportive rather than defensive—and in 911 calls, that's a small investment that can save a life.

CLIMATE PATTERNS

Once a communication climate is formed, it can take on a life of its own. The pattern can be either positive or negative. In one study of married couples, each spouse's response in conflict situations was found to be similar to the other's statement (Burggraf & Sillars, 1987). Conciliatory statements (for example, support, accepting responsibility, agreeing) were likely to be followed by conciliatory responses. Confrontive acts (for example, criticism, hostile questions, faultfinding) were likely to trigger an aggressive response. The same pattern held for other kinds of messages: Avoidance led to avoidance, analysis evoked analysis, and so on. This was also found in a study on disagreements of married couples (Newton & Burgoon, 1990). Video-taped interactions revealed that accusations from one partner triggered accusations in response, and that communication satisfaction was highest when both partners used supportive rather than accusatory tactics.

This reciprocal pattern can be represented as a **spiral** (Wilmot, 1987). Some spirals are negative. In poorly adjusted and abusive couples, for example, one spouse's complaint is likely to produce a countercomplaint or denial by the other (Sabourin & Stamp, 1995; Sutter & Martin, 1999). The cartoon on page 326 provides an amusing but sad image of how negative spirals can take on a life of their own.

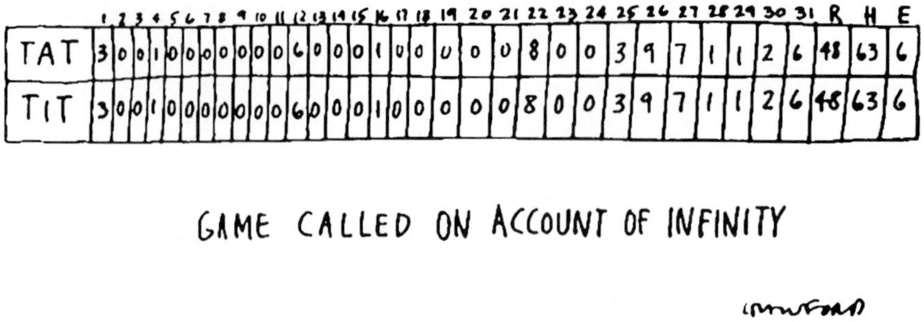

GAME CALLED ON ACCOUNT OF INFINITY

Dudley Cahn (1992) summarizes studies showing that even among well-adjusted couples, negative communication is more likely to be reciprocated than positive—and that once hostility is expressed, it usually escalates. You can probably recall this sort of negative spiral from your own experience: One attack leads to another, until a skirmish escalates into a full-fledged battle:

A: (*mildly irritated*) Where were you? I thought we agreed to meet here a half-hour ago.

B: (*defensively*) I'm sorry. I got hung up at the library. I don't have as much free time as you do, you know.

A: I wasn't *blaming* you, so don't get so touchy. I do resent what you just said, though. I'm plenty busy. And I've got lots of better things to do than wait around for you!

B: Who's getting touchy? I just made a simple comment. You've sure been defensive lately. What's the matter with you?

Fortunately, spirals can also work in a positive direction. One confirming behavior can lead to a similar response from the other person, which in turn leads to further confirmation by the first person (Le Poire & Yoshimura, 1999).

Spirals—whether positive or negative—rarely go on indefinitely. When a negative spiral gets out of hand, the partners might agree to back off from their disconfirming behavior. "Hold on," one might say, "this is getting us nowhere." At this point there may be a cooling-off period, or the partners might work together more constructively to solve their problem (Becker et al., 2008). This ability to "rebound" from negative spirals and turn them in a positive direction is a hallmark

DARK SIDE OF COMMUNICATION

Cyberbullying: Electronic Character Assassination

It's bad enough to be ridiculed and humiliated by a known attacker. But cyberbullies hide behind a veil of anonymity, using e-mails, text messaging, social networking websites, blogging, and other communication technologies to ridicule, threaten, and lie about their victim. In a typical incident, one high schooler was stunned to discover that he was the subject of a web page titled "Welcome to the Page That Makes Fun of Dave Knight."

The consequences of cyberbullying can be devastating. Perhaps the most infamous case is that of Megan Meier, a 13-year-old middle school student who committed suicide after a prolonged bullying campaign coordinated by the mother of a teenage neighbor who had parted ways with Megan. Cases like these show that the climate created by cyberbullying is more than just chilly—it's downright cold and cruel.

Li, Q. (2007). New bottle but old wine: A research of cyberbullying in schools. *Computers in Human Behavior, 23*(4). 1777–1791.

of successful relationships (Gottman & Levenson, 1999). However, if the partners pass "the point of no return" and continue spiraling downward, the relationship may end. As you read in Chapter 1, it's impossible to take back a message once it has been sent, and some exchanges are so lethal that the relationship can't survive them. Positive spirals also have their limit: Even the best relationships go through rocky periods in which the climate suffers. However, the accumulated goodwill and communication ability of the partners can make these times less frequent and intense.

Creating Positive Climates

Even the "best" message isn't guaranteed to create a positive climate. A comment of praise can be interpreted as sarcasm; an innocent smile can be perceived as a sneer; an offer to help can be seen as condescension. Because human communication is so complex, there aren't any foolproof words, phrases, or formulas for creating positive climates. Nonetheless, research suggests that there *are* strategies that can increase the odds of expressing yourself in ways that lead to positive relational climates—even when the message you're delivering is a tough one.

REDUCING DEFENSIVENESS

Several decades ago, psychologist Jack Gibb published a helpful study (1961) that isolated six types of defense-arousing communication and six contrasting behaviors that seem to reduce the level of threat and defensiveness. These "Gibb categories" are listed in Table 10.1. Gibb's findings have commonsense appeal and multiple applications. As a result, they've played an important part in communication textbooks, training seminars, journals, and research studies (e.g., Becker et al., 2008; Proctor & Wilcox, 1993). We'll use them here to discuss how positive climates can be created by sending supportive rather than defense-provoking messages.

Evaluation versus Description The first type of defense-arousing message Gibb identified is **evaluation**. An evaluative message judges the other person, usually in a negative way. For instance, consider this message: "You don't care about me!" Evaluative messages like this possess several characteristics that make them so face-threatening. They judge what the other person is feeling rather than describing the speaker's thoughts, feelings, and wants. They don't explain how the speaker arrived at his or her conclusion, and they lack specifics. Furthermore, they're often phrased in the kind of defense-arousing "you" language described in Chapter 5. It's easy to understand why evaluative statements often trigger a defensive spiral.

Do the climate-threatening properties of evaluative messages mean that it's impossible to tell others how some of the things that they do bother you? No: It simply means that you must be alert to more constructive ways to do

TABLE 10.1 *The Gibb Categories of Defensive and Supportive Behaviors*

DEFENSIVE BEHAVIORS	SUPPORTIVE BEHAVIORS
1. Evaluation	1. Description
2. Control	2. Problem Orientation
3. Strategy	3. Spontaneity
4. Neutrality	4. Empathy
5. Superiority	5. Equality
6. Certainty	6. Provisionalism

so. **Description** is a way to offer your thoughts, feelings, and wants without judging the listener. Descriptive messages make documented observations that are specific and concrete. As we mentioned earlier when discussing complaining, description focuses on behavior that can be changed rather than on personal characteristics that cannot. In addition, descriptive messages often use "I" language, which tends to provoke less defensiveness than "you" language (Heydenberk & Heydenberk, 2007; Proctor & Wilcox, 1993). Contrast the evaluative "You don't care about me" with this more descriptive message: "I'm sorry that we don't spend as much time together as we did during the summer. When we don't talk during the week, I sometimes feel unimportant. Maybe we could set up a phone-call time on Wednesdays—that would mean a lot to me."

Let's look at more examples of the difference between evaluative and descriptive messages:

Evaluation	**Description**
You're not making any sense.	I don't understand the point you're trying to make.
You're inconsiderate.	I would appreciate it if you'd let me know when you're running late—I was worried.
That's an ugly tablecloth.	I'm not crazy about big blue stripes: I like something more subtle.

Note several characteristics of these descriptive messages. First, their focus is on the speaker's thoughts, feelings, and wants, with little or no judgment of the other person. Second, the messages address specific behaviors rather than making sweeping character generalizations (for example, "you don't care"). The messages also provide information about how the speaker arrived at these conclusions. Finally—and perhaps most important—notice that each of the descriptive statements is just as honest as their evaluative counterparts. Once you have learned to speak descriptively, you can be as direct and straightforward as ever, while avoiding personal attacks that can poison a climate.

Control versus Problem Orientation A second defense-provoking message involves some attempt to control another. **Controlling communication** occurs when a sender seems to be imposing a solution on the receiver with little regard for the receiver's needs or interests. The object of control can involve almost anything: where to eat dinner, how to spend a large sum of money, or whether to remain in a relationship. Whatever the situation, people who act in controlling ways create a defensive climate. None of us likes to feel that our ideas are worthless and that nothing we say will change other people's determination to have their way—yet this is precisely the attitude a controller communicates. Whether done with words, gestures, tone of voice, or through some other channel, whether control is accomplished through status, insistence on obscure or irrelevant rules, or physical power, the controller generates hostility wherever he or she goes. The unspoken message such behavior communicates is "I know what's best for you, and if you do as I say, we'll get along."

In **problem orientation**, however, communicators focus on finding a solution that satisfies both their own needs and those of the others involved. The goal here isn't to "win" at the expense of your partner but to work out some arrangement in which everybody feels like a winner. (Chapter 11 has a great deal to say about "win-win" problem solving as a way to find problem-oriented solutions.) Problem orientation is often typified by "we" language (see Chapter 5), which suggests the speaker is making decisions *with* rather than *for* other people. University chairpersons found to be most effective by members of their departments were best characterized as using few control communications and adopting a problem orientation (Czech, 2007).

Here are some examples of how some controlling and problem-orientation messages might sound:

Controlling	**Problem Oriented**
Get off the phone—now!	I need to make an important call. If you can give me 5 minutes, I'll let you know when I'm off.
There's only one way to handle this problem . . .	Looks like we have a problem. Let's work out a solution we can both live with.
Either you start working harder, or you're fired!	The production in your department hasn't been as high as I'd hoped. Any ideas on what we could do?

Strategy versus Spontaneity Gibb uses the word **strategy** to characterize defense-arousing messages in which speakers hide their ulterior motives. The terms *dishonesty* and *manipulation* reflect the nature of strategy. Even if the intentions that motivate strategic communication are honorable, the victim of deception who discovers the attempt to deceive is likely to feel offended at being played for a sucker.

As we discussed in Chapter 7, counterfeit questions are a form of strategic communication because they try to trap others into desired responses. Many sales techniques are strategic, for they give customers limited information and then make it difficult to say no. This is not to say that all sales techniques are wrong or unethical, but most strategic ones aren't well-suited for interpersonal relationships. If you've ever gotten defensive when you thought a friend was doing a "sales job" on you, you understand the concept.

Spontaneity is the behavior that contrasts with strategy. Spontaneity simply means being honest with others rather than manipulating them. What it doesn't mean is blurting out what you're thinking as soon as an idea comes to you. As we discussed in Chapter 3, there are appropriate (and inappropriate) times for self-disclosure. You would undoubtedly threaten others' presenting selves if you were "spontaneous" about every opinion that crossed your mind. That's not what Gibb intended in using the term spontaneity. What he was after was setting aside hidden agendas that others both sense and resist. You can probably recall times when someone asked you a question and you suspiciously responded with "Hmmm . . . why do you want to know?" Your defensive antennae were up because you detected an underlying strategy. If the person had told you up-front why he or she was asking the question, then your defenses probably would have been lowered. That's what we mean by spontaneity. Here are some examples:

Defensive—with Good Reason: *Meet the Parents*

Meeting your future in-laws has the potential to be nerve-wracking. But things can get really stressful when your prospective father-in-law is a suspicious ex-CIA agent who doubts that any man is good enough for his daughter.

Greg Focker (Ben Stiller) tries hard to impress the parents of his fiancée, Pam (Teri Polo); but Pam's father, Jack (Robert DeNiro), turns the weekend into a nightmare by using every type of defense-arousing communication described in these pages. Every question Jack asks is strategic ("Are you a pothead, Focker?"); every comment he makes is controlling and contemptuous ("I have nipples, Greg. Could you milk me?"). Jack exudes superiority and certainty in virtually every exchange (Jack: "Can you really trust another human being?" Greg: "Yeah, I think so." Jack: "No. The answer is you cannot."). Greg's defensiveness leads to a series of blunders: He ends up threatening the life of the family cat, flooding the septic tank, burning down the house, and almost ending his relationship with Pam.

The hijinks in this comedy are definitely over the top—but Jack's tactics offer a hilarious illustration of how defense-arousing communication can jeopardize relationships.

Strategy	**Spontaneity**
What are you doing Friday after work?	I have a piano I need to move Friday after work. Can you give me a hand?
Have you ever considered another line of work?	I'm concerned about your job performance over the last year; let's set up a time to talk about it.
Ali and Kasey go out to dinner every week.	I'd like to go out for dinner more often.

This is a good place to pause and talk about larger issues regarding the Gibb model. First, Gibb's emphasis on being direct is better suited for a low-context culture like the United States, which values straight-talk, than for high-context cultures. Second, there are ways in which each of the communication approaches Gibb labels as "supportive" can be used to exploit others and, therefore, violate the spirit of positive climate building. For instance, consider spontaneity. Although it sounds paradoxical at first, spontaneity can be a strategy, too. Sometimes you'll see people using honesty in a calculating way, being just frank enough to win someone's trust or sympathy. This "leveling" is probably the most defense-arousing strategy of all because once we've learned someone is using frankness as a manipulation, there's almost no chance we'll ever trust that person again.

Neutrality versus Empathy Gibb used the term **neutrality** to describe a fourth behavior that arouses defensiveness. Probably a better word would be indifference. For example, 911 emergency telephone dispatchers are taught to be neutral in order to calm down the caller, but they shouldn't communicate indifference or a lack of caring (Shuler, 1998). Using Gibb's terminology, a neutral attitude is disconfirming because it communicates a lack of concern for the welfare of another and implies that the other person isn't very important to you. This perceived indifference is likely to promote defensiveness because people do not like to think of themselves as worthless, and they'll protect a self-concept that sees them as worthwhile.

The poor effects of neutrality become apparent when you consider the hostility that most people have for the large, impersonal organizations with which they have to deal: "They think of me as a number instead of a person"; "I felt as if I were being handled by computers and not human beings." These common statements reflect reactions to being handled in an indifferent, neutral way.

The behavior that contrasts with neutrality is **empathy**. Gibb found that empathy helps rid communication of the quality of indifference. When people show that they care for the feelings of another, there's little chance that the person's self-concept will be threatened. Empathy means accepting another's feelings, putting yourself in another's place. This doesn't mean you need to agree with that person. By simply letting someone know about your care and respect, you'll be acting in a supportive way. Gibb noted the importance of nonverbal messages in communicating empathy. He found that facial and bodily expressions of concern are often more important to the receiver than the words used.

We addressed the concept of empathy in Chapter 4 and the skill of empathizing in Chapter 7; let's see what empathic messages look like when contrasted with neutral ones:

Neutrality	**Empathy**
This is what happens when you don't plan properly.	Ouch—looks like this didn't turn out the way you expected.
Sometimes things just don't work out. That's the way it goes.	I know you put a lot of time and effort into this project.
Don't get too excited—Everybody gets promoted sooner or later.	I'll bet you're pretty excited about the promotion.

Superiority versus Equality A fifth behavior creating a defensive climate involves **superiority**. Jake Harwood and his associates (Harwood et al., 1997; Harwood & Giles, 1996) summarize a body of research that describes how patronizing messages irritate receivers ranging from young students to senior citizens. Any message that suggests "I'm better than you" is likely to arouse feelings of defensiveness in the recipients.

Many times in our lives we communicate with people who possess less talent or knowledge than we do, but it isn't necessary to convey an attitude of superiority in these situations. Gibb found ample evidence that many who have superior skills and talents are capable of projecting feelings of **equality** rather than superiority. Such people communicate that although they may have greater talent in certain areas, they see other human beings as having just as much worth as themselves.

Charles and Elizabeth Beck (1996) observe that equality is put to the test when a person doesn't have superior skills, yet is in a position of authority. Supervisors sometimes have less expertise in certain areas than their subordinates but believe it would be beneath them to admit it. Think for a moment: You've probably been in situations where you knew more about the subject than the person in charge—be it a boss, a teacher, a parent, or a salesperson—yet this person acted as if he or she knew more. Did you feel defensive? No doubt. Did that person feel defensive? Probably. You both were challenging each other's presenting self, so the climate most likely became hostile. A truly secure person can treat others with equality even when there are obvious differences in knowledge, talent, and status. Doing so creates a positive climate in which ideas are evaluated not on the basis of who contributed them, but rather on the merit of the ideas themselves.

REFLECTION

Be Careful How You Give the Boss a Suggestion

My brother is a pretty smart guy, especially when it comes to running a business, but he got into trouble when he tried to give his boss advice. As my brother tells it, he went to the head of the company and gave a short speech about how things were not run well and what could be done to make the business more efficient. When my brother was through, the boss said, "You're right, Allan—everything you said is true—but nobody talks to me that way. You're fired." My brother came off as superior to the owner of the company. He virtually told him, "I'm smarter than you are"—which was not a smart move on his part.

What does equality sound like? Here are some examples:

Superiority	Equality
When you get to be in my position someday, *then* you'll understand.	I'd like to hear how the issue looks to you. Then I can tell you how it looks to me.
You don't know what you're talking about.	I'm not sure I agree.
No, that's not the right way to do it!	I'd be happy to help if you'd like—just let me know.

Certainty versus Provisionalism Have you ever run into people who are positive they're right, who know that theirs is the only or proper way of doing something, who insist that they have all the facts and need no additional information? If you have, you've met individuals who project the defense-arousing behavior Gibb calls **certainty**.

How do you react when you're the target of such certainty? Do you suddenly find your energy directed to proving the dogmatic individual wrong? If you do, you're reacting normally—if not very constructively.

Communicators who regard their own opinions with certainty while disregarding the ideas of others demonstrate a lack of regard for others. It's likely the receiver will take the certainty as a personal affront and react defensively.

In contrast to dogmatic certainty is **provisionalism**, in which people may have strong opinions but are willing to acknowledge that they don't have a corner on the truth and will change their stand if another position seems more reasonable. Provisionalism often surfaces in a person's word choice. While certainty regularly uses the terms *can't, never, always, must,* and *have to,* provisionalism uses *perhaps, maybe, possibly, might,* and *may.* It's not that provisional people are spineless; they simply recognize that discussion is aided by open-minded messages. Winer and Majors (1981) found that provisional word choice does indeed enhance communication climate.

"What do you mean 'Your guess is as good as mine'? My guess is a hell of a lot better than your guess!"

Let's look at some examples:

Certainty	**Provisionalism**
That will *never* work!	My guess is that you'll run into problems with that approach.
You'll hate that class! Stay away from it!	I didn't like that class very much; I'm not sure you would, either.
You won't get anywhere without a college education: Mark my words.	I think it's important to get that degree. I found it was hard to land an interview until I had one.

You've probably noticed a great deal of overlap between the various Gibb components. For instance, look at the final example under "Provisionalism." The statement is likely to create a positive climate, not only because it is provisional rather than certain, but also because it is descriptive rather than evaluative, problem-oriented rather than controlling, and equal rather than superior. You may also have noticed a tone underlying all of the supportive examples: *respect.* By valuing and confirming others—even if you disagree with them—you create a respectful climate that helps enhance a positive communication climate, both now and in future interactions. Communication scholars Sonja Foss and Cindy Griffin (1995; Foss & Foss, 2003) use the term *invitational rhetoric* to describe this sort of respectful approach that strives to understand others and invite them to see your point of view, rather than dominating them in defense-provoking ways. There are no guarantees of your achieving positive responses or outcomes, but by sending supportive messages, your odds for interpersonal success should improve.

OFFERING CONSTRUCTIVE CRITICISM

Gibb's supportive behaviors can work in a variety of situations, including times when you have a message that's likely to be taken as criticism. But along with being descriptive, problem-oriented, honest, empathic, egalitarian, and open-minded, you can exhibit attitudes and skills that are especially helpful when you want or need to offer constructive criticism.

Check Your Motives There are times when telling others what you think, feel, and want is primarily for *your* own good, not theirs. In those cases, it's more appropriate to use assertive "I" messages, described in Chapter 5 (pp. 159–161).

Unlike criticism aimed at benefiting yourself, the goal of *constructive* criticism is to offer information that both helps the other person and preserves the relationship. It isn't about venting pent-up anger, unloading for catharsis, or trying to get even. Before offering constructive criticism, you would do well to check your motives to be sure you have the other person's interests in mind—or at the very least, that you're not motivated by ill will or revenge.

Choose a Good Time Although it's tempting to "teach someone a lesson" the moment they've done something that bothers you, that's often the worst time to do so. At those moments, both the other person's embarrassment and your frustration are probably running high. Marriage researcher John Gottman (Gottman & Silver, 1999) says that a "harsh startup" is a key predictor of conversations that turn into destructive fights, so getting off on the right foot is crucial. Ideally, it's best to wait for a time—or perhaps even arrange one—when both parties can calmly and rationally discuss the issue of concern.

Buffer Negatives with Positives One way start off on the right foot is to focus on positives. A popular approach for offering constructive criticism is known as the **sandwich method** (e.g., Iannone & Iannone, 2000; Kohn & O'Connell, 2005). The idea is to sandwich your issue of concern between two positive comments. Here's an example in which one coworker approaches another:

- *Positive comment:* "It's been great being on the same shift the past few months. You're a hard worker and we've had a lot of fun."
- *Issue of concern:* "There's one thing, though: The past two weeks, you've showed up a half hour late almost every day. I know it's tough to get here early in the morning—for me, too—but it means that I end up doing both your work and mine, so we can open at noon."
- *Positive comment:* "I really hope we can figure out a way to resolve this because I want to keep working together on the same shift."

Research shows that buffering criticism with praise is effective because it helps the recipient perceive the comments as constructive and well intentioned (Hornsey et al., 2008). The same study showed that criticism is also better received when the message-sender acknowledges having similar shortcomings ("for me, too"). Doing so communicates Gibb's supportive climate components of equality and empathy.

It's important to note that methods like the sandwich can easily turn into hackneyed and insincere techniques. When that happens, they ring of Gibb's defensive components of strategy and control. For the sandwich approach to work, it's vital that the praise being offered is genuine—and that the criticism is a clear behavioral description. Moreover, if the *only* time you praise people is prior to criticizing them, they will likely grow leery of your positive comments, assuming the other shoe is about to drop. Rather than viewing the sandwich method as a technique to use rigidly, it's better to understand and follow its underlying principle: Positive comments and praise make criticism easier to swallow. As the well-known song accurately suggests, a spoonful of sugar *does* help the medicine go down.

Follow Up Constructive criticism shouldn't be a "hit-and-run" event. If the recipient makes positive changes as a result of your discussion, it's important to acknowledge them. Of course, it's also vital not to sound patronizing when doing so, which will likely generate a defensive response. Simple descriptions offered in supportive tones can go a long way toward reinforcing positive behaviors that enhance relationships:

"Thanks for being on time this week—it sure made things less crazy in the kitchen."

"I appreciate your forwarding me fewer e-mails—it helped me focus on the important ones you sent my way."

"Thanks for cutting back on the complaining—it makes a big difference for me."

Transforming Negative Climates

The world would be a happier place if everyone communicated supportively. But how can you respond nondefensively when others use evaluation, control, superiority, and all the other attacking behaviors Gibb identified? Despite your best intentions, it's difficult to be reasonable when you're faced with a torrent of criticism. Being attacked is hard enough when the critic is clearly being unfair, but it's often even more threatening when the judgments are on target. Despite the accuracy of your critic, the tendency is either to counterattack defensively with a barrage of verbal aggression or to withdraw nonassertively. If criticism, defensiveness, and withdrawal continue as a pattern, it's a sure sign of a relationship that's in trouble (Gottman & Silver, 1999). Since these responses aren't likely to resolve a dispute, we need alternative ways of behaving. There are two such methods. Despite their apparent simplicity, they have proven to be among the most valuable skills communicators can learn.

SEEK MORE INFORMATION

The response of seeking more information makes good sense when you realize that it's foolish to respond to a critical attack until you understand what the other person has said. Even comments that on first consideration appear to be totally unjustified or foolish often prove to contain at least a grain of truth and sometimes much more.

Many readers object to the idea of asking for details when they are criticized. Their resistance grows from confusing the act of *listening open-mindedly* to a speaker's comments with *accepting* them. Once you realize that you can listen to, understand, and even acknowledge the most hostile comments without necessarily accepting them, it becomes much easier to hear another person out. If you disagree with a speaker's objections, you will be in a much better position to explain yourself once you understand the criticism. On the other hand, after carefully listening to the other person's remarks, you might just see that they are valid, in which case you have learned some valuable information about yourself. In either case, you have everything to gain and nothing to lose by paying attention to the critic.

Of course, after years of instinctively resisting criticism, learning to listen to the other person will take some practice. To make matters clearer, here are several ways in which you can seek additional information from your critics.

Ask for Specifics Often the vague attack of a critic is virtually useless, even if you sincerely want to change. Abstract accusations such as "you're being unfair" or "you never help out" can be difficult to understand. In such cases it is a good idea to request more specific information from the sender. "What do I *do* that's unfair?" is an important question to ask before you can judge whether the accusation is correct. "When haven't I helped out?" you might ask before agreeing with or disputing the accusation.

If you already solicit specifics by using questions and are still accused of reacting defensively, the problem may be in the *way* you ask. Your tone of voice and facial expression, posture, or other nonverbal clues can give the same words radically different connotations. For example, think of how you could use the question "Exactly what are you talking about?" to communicate either a genuine desire to know or your belief that the speaker is crazy. It's important to request specific information only when you genuinely want to learn more from the speaker; asking under any other circumstances will only make matters worse.

Guess about Specifics On some occasions even your sincere and well-phrased requests for specific details won't meet with success. Sometimes your critics won't be able to define precisely the behavior they find offensive. In these instances, you'll hear such comments as, "I can't tell you exactly what's wrong with your sense of humor—all I can say is that I don't like it." In other cases, your critics may know the exact behaviors they don't like, but for some reason they seem to get a perverse satisfaction out of making you struggle to figure them out. In instances like these, you can often learn more clearly what is bothering your critic by *guessing* at the specifics of a complaint. In a sense you become both detective and suspect, the goal being to figure out exactly what "crime" you have committed. Like the technique of asking for specifics, guessing must be done with goodwill if it's to produce satisfying results. You need to convey to the critic that for both of your sakes you're truly interested in finding out what is the matter. Once you have communicated this intention, the emotional climate generally becomes more comfortable because, in effect, both you and the critic are seeking the same goal.

Here are some typical questions you might hear from someone guessing about the details of another's criticism:

"So you object to the language I used in writing the paper. Was my language too formal?"

"OK, I understand that you think the outfit looks funny. What is it that's so bad? Is it the color? Does it have something to do with the fit? The design?"

"When you say that I'm not doing my share around the house, do you mean that I haven't been helping enough with the cleaning?"

Paraphrase the Speaker's Ideas Another strategy is to draw out confused or reluctant speakers by paraphrasing their thoughts and feelings, using the reflective listening skills described in Chapter 7. Paraphrasing is especially good in helping others solve their problems—and since people generally criticize you because your behavior creates some problem for them, the method is especially appropriate at such times.

One advantage of paraphrasing is that you don't have to guess about the specifics of your behavior that might be offensive. By clarifying or amplifying what you understand critics to be saying, you'll learn more about their objections. A brief dialogue between a disgruntled customer and a store manager who is an exceptional listener might sound like this:

Customer: The way you people run this store is disgusting! I just want to tell you that I'll never shop here again.

Manager: (*reflecting the customer's feeling*) It seems that you're quite upset. Can you tell me your problem?

Customer: It isn't *my* problem; it's the problem your salespeople have. They seem to think it's a great inconvenience to help a customer find anything around here.

Manager: So you didn't get enough help locating the items you were looking for, is that it?

Customer: Help? I spent 20 minutes looking around in here before I even talked to a clerk. All I can say is that it's a lousy way to run a store.

Manager: So what you're saying is that the clerks seemed to be ignoring the customers?

Customer: No. They were all busy with other people. It just seems to me that you ought to have enough help around to handle the crowds that come in at this hour.

Manager: I understand now. What frustrated you the most was the fact that we didn't have enough staff to serve you promptly.

Customer: That's right. I have no complaint with the service I get once I'm waited on, and I've always thought you had a good selection here. It's just that I'm too busy to wait so long for help.

Manager: Well, I'm glad you brought this to my attention. We certainly don't want loyal customers going away mad. I'll try to see that it doesn't happen again.

This conversation illustrates two advantages of paraphrasing. First, the critic often reduces the intensity of the attack once the attacker realizes that the complaint is being heard. Criticism often grows from the frustration of unmet needs—which in this case was partly a lack of attention. As soon as the manager genuinely demonstrated interest in the customer's plight, the customer began to feel better and was able to leave the store relatively calmly. Of course, paraphrasing won't always mollify your critic, but even when it doesn't there's still another benefit that makes the technique worthwhile. In the sample conversation, for instance, the manager learned some valuable information by taking time to understand the customer. As you read earlier, even apparently outlandish criticism often contains at least a grain of truth, and thus a person who is genuinely interested in improving would be wise to hear it out—especially when the complaint is coming from a valued customer (Homburg & Furst, 2007).

Ask What the Critic Wants Sometimes your critic's demand will be obvious:

"Turn down that music!"
"I wish you'd remember to tell me about phone messages."
"Would you clean up your dirty dishes *now?!*"

In other cases, however, you'll need to do some investigating to find out what the critic wants from you:

A: I can't believe you invited all those people over without asking me first!
B: Are you saying you want me to cancel the party?
A: No, I just wish you'd ask me before you make plans.

C: You're so critical! It sounds like you don't like *anything* about this paper.
D: But you asked for my opinion. What do you expect me to do when you ask?
C: I want to know what's wrong, but I don't just want to hear criticisms. If you think there's anything good about my work, I wish you'd tell me that too.

This last example illustrates the importance of accompanying your questions with the right nonverbal behavior. It's easy to imagine two ways D could have said, "What do you expect me to do when you ask?" One would show a genuine desire to clarify what C wanted, while the other would have been clearly hostile and defensive. As with all of the styles in this section, your responses to criticism have to be sincere in order to work.

Ask about the Consequences of Your Behavior As a rule, people complain about your actions only when some need of theirs is not being met. One way to respond to this kind of criticism is to find out exactly what troublesome consequences your behavior has for them. You'll often find that actions that seem perfectly legitimate to you cause some difficulty for your critic; once you have understood this, comments that previously sounded foolish take on a new meaning:

Neighbor A: You say that I ought to have my cat neutered. Why is that important to you?
Neighbor B: Because at night he picks fights with my cat, and I'm tired of paying the vet's bills.

Worker A: Why do you care whether I'm late to work?
Worker B: Because when the boss asks, I feel obligated to make up some story so you won't get in trouble, and I don't like to lie.

Husband: Why does it bother you when I lose money at poker? You know I never gamble more than I can afford.
Wife: It's not the cash itself. It's that when you lose, you're in a grumpy mood for 2 or 3 days, and that's no fun for me.

Ask What Else Is Wrong It might seem crazy to invite more criticism, but sometimes asking about other complaints can uncover the real problem:

A: Are you mad at me?
B: No, why are you asking?
A: Because the whole time we were at the picnic you hardly spent any time talking to me. In fact, it seemed like whenever I came over to where you were, you went off somewhere else.
B: Is anything else wrong?
A: Well, to be honest, I've been wondering lately if you're tired of me.

This example shows that asking if anything else bothers your critic isn't just an exercise in masochism. If you can keep your defensiveness in check, probing further can lead the conversation to issues that are the source of the critic's real dissatisfaction.

Soliciting more information from a critic sometimes isn't enough. For instance, what do you do when you fully understand the other person's objections and still feel a defensive response on the tip of your tongue? You know that if you try to protect yourself, you'll wind up in an argument; on the other hand, you simply can't accept what the other person is saying about you. The solution to such a dilemma is outrageously simple and is discussed in the following section.

AGREE WITH THE CRITIC

But, you protest, how can I honestly agree with comments I don't believe are true? The following pages will answer this question by showing that there's virtually no situation in which you can't honestly accept the other person's point of view and still maintain your position. To see how this can be so, you need to realize that there are several different types of agreement, one of which you can use in almost any situation.

Agree with the Truth Agreeing with the truth is easy to understand, though not always easy to practice. You agree with the truth when another person's criticism is factually correct:

"You're right; I am angry."
"I suppose I was just being defensive."
"Now that you mention it, I did get pretty sarcastic."

Agreeing with the facts seems quite sensible when you realize that certain matters are indisputable. If you agree to be somewhere at 4:00 P.M. and don't show up until 5:00, you are late, no matter how good your explanation for tardiness is. If you've broken a borrowed object, run out of gas, or failed to finish a job you started, there's no point in denying the fact. In the same way, if you're honest you will have to agree with many interpretations of your behavior, even when they're not flattering. You do get angry, act foolishly, fail to listen, and behave inconsiderately. Once you rid yourself of the myth of perfection, it's much easier to acknowledge these truths.

If it's so obvious that the descriptions others give of your behaviors are often accurate, why is it so difficult to accept them without being defensive? The answer to this question lies in a confusion between agreeing with the *facts* and accepting the *judgment* that so often accompanies them. Most critics don't merely describe the action that offends them; they also evaluate it, and it's the evaluation that we resist:

"It's silly to be angry."
"You have no reason for being defensive."
"You were wrong to be so sarcastic."

It's such judgments that we resent. By realizing that you can agree with—even learn from—the descriptive part of many criticisms and still not accept the accompanying evaluations, you'll often have a response that is both honest and nondefensive. A conversation between a teacher and a student illustrates this point:

Teacher: Look at this paper! It's only two pages long, and it contains 12 misspelled words. I'm afraid you have a real problem with your writing.
Student: You're right. I know I don't spell well at all.
T: I don't know what's happening in the lower grades. They just don't seem to be turning out people who can write a simple, declarative sentence.
S: You're not the first person I've heard say that.
T: I should think you'd be upset by the fact that after so much time in English composition classes you haven't mastered the basics of spelling.
S: You're right. It does bother me.

REFLECTION

Agreeing with a Critic Can Be Liberating

I've always been a very thrifty person. Sometimes I wish I was more of a free and easy spender, but I'm just not. When my roommates and I shop for food, I'm always looking for bargains.

Just after we covered the part of our textbook that talked about agreeing with a critic, we were in the market and I was doing my usual "we can't afford that" routine. One of my housemates said "Jeez, you are really a tightwad!" Instead of arguing, I agreed with the truth of his accusation and said "You're right, I am!" This surprised us both, and we both started to laugh. It felt great to acknowledge the reality of his claim without getting defensive.

Notice that in agreeing with the teacher's comments the student did not in any way demean herself. Even though there might have been extenuating circumstances to account for her lack of skill, the student didn't find it necessary to justify her errors because she wasn't saddled with the burden of pretending to be perfect. By simply agreeing with the facts, she was able to maintain her dignity and avoid an unproductive argument.

Of course, in order to reduce defensiveness it's important that your agreement with the facts be honest and admitted without malice. It's humiliating to accept inaccurate descriptions, and maliciously pretending to agree with these only leads to trouble. You can imagine how unproductive the above conversation would have been if the student had spoken the same words in a sarcastic tone. Agree with the facts only when you can do so sincerely. Although it won't always be possible, you'll be surprised at how often you can use this simple response.

Agreeing with criticism is fine, but by itself it isn't an adequate response to your critic. For instance, once you've admitted to another that you are defensive, habitually late, or sarcastic, you can expect the other to ask what you intend to do about this behavior. Such questions are fair. In most cases it would be a mistake simply to understand another's criticism, to agree with the accusations, and then to go on behaving as before. Such behavior makes it clear that you have no concern for the speaker. The message that comes through is "Sure, now I understand what I've done to bother you. You're right, I have been doing it and I'll probably keep on doing it. If you don't like the way I've been behaving, that's tough!" Such a response might be appropriate for dealing with people you genuinely don't care about—manipulative solicitors, abusive strangers, and so on—but it is clearly not suitable for people who matter to you.

Before reading on, then, understand that responding nondefensively to criticism is only the *first* step in resolving the conflicts that usually prompt another's attack. In order to resolve your conflicts fully, you'll need to learn the conflict resolution skills described in Chapter 11.

Agree with the Odds Sometimes a critic will point out possible unpleasant consequences of your behavior:

"If you don't talk to more people, they'll think you're a snob."
"If you don't exercise more, you'll wind up having a heart attack one of these days."
"If you run around with that crowd, you'll probably be sorry."

Often such comments are genuinely helpful suggestions that others make for your own good. In other cases, however, they are really devices for manipulating you into behaving the way your critic wants you to. For instance, "If we go to the football game, you might catch cold" could mean "I don't want to go to the football game." "You'll probably be exhausted tomorrow if you stay up late" could be translated as "I want you to go to bed early." Chapter 11 will have more to say about such methods of indirect aggression, but for now it is sufficient to state that such warnings often generate defensiveness. A mother-son argument shows this outcome:

Mother: I don't see why you want to ride that motorcycle. You could wind up in an accident so easily. (*states the odds for an accident*)

Son: Oh, don't be silly. I'm a careful driver, and besides you know that I never take my bike on the freeway. (*denies the odds*)

M: Yes, but every time I pick up the paper I read about someone being hurt or killed. There's always a danger that some crazy driver will miss seeing you and run you off the road. (*states the odds of an injury*)

S: Oh, you worry too much. I always look out for the other driver. And besides, you have a lot better maneuverability on a motorcycle than in a car. (*denies the odds for an injury*)

M: I know you're careful, but all it takes is one mistake and you could be killed. (*states the odds for being killed*)

S: Somebody is killed shaving or taking a shower every day, but you don't want me to stop doing those things, do you? You're just exaggerating the whole thing. (*denies the odds for being killed*)

From this example you can see that it's usually counterproductive to deny another's predictions. You don't convince the critic, and your opinions stay unchanged as well. Notice the difference when you agree with the odds (though not the demands) of the critic:

M: I don't see why you want to drive that motorcycle. You could wind up in an accident so easily. (*states the odds for an accident*)

S: I suppose there is a chance of that. (*agrees with the odds*)

M: You're darned right. Every time I pick up the newspaper, I read about someone being hurt or killed. There's always a danger that some crazy driver will miss seeing you and run you off the road. (*states the odds for an injury*)

S: You're right; that could happen (*agrees with the odds*), but I don't think the risk is great enough to keep me off the bike.

M: That's easy for you to say now. Someday you could be sorry you didn't listen to me. (*states the odds for regret*)

S: That's true. I really might regret driving the bike someday—but I'm willing to take that chance. (*agrees with the odds*)

Notice how the son simply considers his mother's predictions and realistically acknowledges the chance that they might come true. While such responses might at first seem indifferent and callous, they can help the son avoid the pitfall of indirect manipulation. Suppose the conversation were a straightforward one in which the mother was simply pointing out to her son the dangers of motorcycle riding. He acknowledged that he understood her concern and even agreed with the possibility that her prediction could come true. If, however, her prediction were really an indirect way of saying "I don't want you to ride anymore," then the son's response would force her to clarify her demand so that he could deal with it openly. At this point they might be able to figure out a solution that lets the son satisfy his need for transportation and excitement and at the same time allows his mother to alleviate her concern.

In addition to bringing hidden agendas into the open for resolution, agreeing with the odds also helps you become aware of some possible previously unconsidered consequences of your actions. Instead of blindly denying the chance that your behavior is inappropriate, agreeing with the odds will help you look objectively at whether your course of action is in fact the best one. You might agree with your critic that you really should change your behavior.

Agree in Principle Criticism often comes in the form of abstract ideals against which you're unfavorably compared:

> "I wish you wouldn't spend so much time on your work. Relaxation is important too, you know."
> "You shouldn't expect so much from your kids. Nobody's perfect."
> "What do you mean, you're not voting? The government is only going to get better when people like you take more of an interest in it."
> "You mean you're still upset by that remark? You ought to learn how to take a joke better."

In cases like these, you can accept the principle upon which the criticism is based and still behave as you have been. After all, some rules do allow occasional exceptions, and people often are inconsistent. Consider how you might sincerely agree with the criticisms above without necessarily changing your behavior:

> "You're right. I am working hard now. It probably is unhealthy, but finishing the job is worth the extra strain to me."
> "I guess my expectations for the kids are awfully high, and I don't want to drive them crazy. I hope I'm not making a mistake."
> "You're right: If everybody stopped voting, the system would fall apart."
> "Maybe I *would* be happier if I could take a joke in stride. I'm not ready to do that, though, at least not for jokes like that one."

Agree with the Critic's Perception What about times when there seems to be no basis whatsoever for agreeing with your critics? You've listened carefully and asked questions to make sure you understand the objections, but the more you listen, the more positive you are that they are totally out of line: There is no truth to the criticisms, you can't agree with the odds, and you can't even accept the principle the critics are putting forward. Even here there's a way of agreeing—this time not with the critics' conclusions, but with their right to perceive things their way:

> *A:* I don't believe you've been all the places you were just describing. You're probably just making all this up so that we'll think you're hot stuff.
> *B:* Well, I can see how you might think that. I've known people who lie to get approval.

> *C:* I want to let you know right from the start that I was against hiring you for the job. I think the reason you got it was because you're a woman.
> *D:* I can understand why you'd believe that with all the antidiscrimination laws on the books. I hope that after I've been here for a while you'll change your mind.

E: I don't think you're being totally honest about your reasons for wanting to stay home. You say that it's because you have a headache, but I think you're avoiding Mary and Walt.

F: I can see why that would make sense to you since Mary and I got into an argument the last time we were together. All I can say is that I do have a headache.

Such responses tell critics that you're acknowledging the reasonableness of their perceptions, even though you don't agree or wish to change your behavior. This coping style is valuable, for it lets you avoid debates over who is right and who is wrong, which can turn an exchange of ideas into an argument. Notice the difference in the following scenes.

DISPUTING THE PERCEPTION:

A: I don't see how you can stand to be around Josh. The guy is so crude that he gives me the creeps.

B: What do you mean, crude? He's a really nice guy. I think you're just touchy.

A: Touchy! If it's touchy to be offended by disgusting behavior, then I'm guilty.

B: You're not guilty about anything. It's just that you're too sensitive when people kid around.

A: Too sensitive, huh? I don't know what's happened to you. You used to have such good judgment about people. . . .

AGREEING WITH THE PERCEPTION:

A: I don't see how you can stand to be around Josh. The guy is so crude that he gives me the creeps.

B: Well, I enjoy being around him, but I guess I can see how his jokes would be offensive to some people.

A: You're damn right! I don't see how you can put up with him.

B: Yeah. I guess if you didn't appreciate his humor, you wouldn't want to have much to do with him.

Notice how in the second exchange B was able to maintain his own position without attacking A's in the least. Such acceptance is the key ingredient for successfully agreeing with your critics' perceptions: Using acceptance, you clarify that you are in no way disputing their views. Because you have no intention of attacking your critics' views, your critics are less likely to be defensive.

All these responses to criticism may appear to buy peace at the cost of denying your feelings. However, as you can see by now, counterattacking usually makes matters worse. The nondefensive responses you have just learned won't solve problems or settle disputes by themselves. Nevertheless, they *will* make a constructive dialogue

REFLECTION

Coping with Criticism as a Martial Art

I've been taking self-defense lessons for a year, and I think there are a lot of similarities between judo and agreeing with your critic. In both techniques you don't resist your attacker. Instead you use the other person's energy to your advantage. You let your opponent defeat himself.

Last week I used "verbal judo" on a very judgmental friend who called me a hypocrite because I'm a vegetarian but still wear leather shoes. I knew that nothing I could say would change his mind, so I just agreed with his perception by saying, "I can see why you think I'm not consistent." (I really could see how my lifestyle looks hypocritical to him, although I don't agree.) No matter what he said, I replied (in different ways), "I understand why it looks that way to you." And each time I meant it. I won't always agree with my critics this way, any more than I'll always use judo. But it sure is a useful approach to have at my disposal.

possible, setting the stage for a productive solution. How to achieve productive solutions is the topic of Chapter 11.

Summary

Communication climate refers to the social tone of a relationship. The most influential factor in shaping a communication climate is the degree to which the people involved see themselves as being valued and confirmed. Messages have differing levels of confirmation. We can categorize them as confirming, disagreeing, or disconfirming.

Confirming messages, which communicate "you exist and are valued," involve recognition, acknowledgment, or endorsement of the other party. Disagreeing messages, which communicate "you are wrong," use argumentativeness, complaining, or aggressiveness. Disconfirming messages, which communicate "you do not exist and are not valued," include responses that are impervious, interrupting, irrelevant, tangential, impersonal, ambiguous, or incongruous. Over time, these messages form climate patterns that often take the shape of positive or negative spirals.

Defensiveness is at the core of most negative spirals. Defensiveness occurs when individuals perceive that their presenting self is being attacked by face-threatening acts. We get particularly defensive about flaws that we don't want to admit and those that touch on sensitive areas. Both the attacker and the person attacked are responsible for creating defensiveness, since competent communicators protect others' face needs as well as their own.

Jack Gibb suggested a variety of ways to create a positive and nondefensive communication climate. These include being descriptive rather than evaluative, problem-oriented rather than controlling, spontaneous rather than strategic, empathic rather than neutral, equal rather than superior, and provisional rather than certain. When offering constructive criticism, it's important to check your motives, choose a good time, blend positive and negative comments, and follow up afterwards.

When faced with criticism by others, there are two alternatives to responding defensively: seeking additional information from the critic and agreeing with some aspect of the criticism. When performed sincerely, these approaches can transform an actual or potentially negative climate into a more positive one.

Activities

1. Invitation to Insight

Identify three personal relationships that matter to you. For each relationship,

a. Come up with a weather phrase that describes the current climate of the relationship.
b. Come up with a weather phrase that forecasts the climate of the relationship over the next year.

c. Consider why you chose the phrases you did. In particular, identify how feeling valued and confirmed played a part in the climates you perceived and predicted.

2. Critical Thinking Probe

Mental health experts generally believe it is better to have others disagree with you than ignore you. Express your opinion on this matter, using specific examples from personal experiences to support your position. Next, discuss whether (and how) it is possible to disagree without being disconfirming.

3. Skill Builder

Develop your ability to communicate supportively instead of triggering defensive reactions in others. Restate each of the following evaluative "you" statements as descriptive "I" messages. Use details from your own personal relationships to create messages that are specific and personally relevant.

a. "You're only thinking of yourself."
b. "Don't be so touchy."
c. "Quit fooling around!"
d. "Stop beating around the bush and tell me the truth."
e. "You're a slob!"

4. Ethical Challenge

Gibb argues that spontaneous rather than strategic communication reduces defensiveness. However, in some situations a strategic approach may hold the promise of a better climate than a completely honest message. Consider situations such as these:

a. You don't find your partner very attractive. He or she asks, "What's the matter?"
b. You intend to quit your job because you hate your boss, but you don't want to offend him or her. How do you explain the reasons for your departure?
c. You are tutoring a high school student in reading or math. The student is sincere and a hard worker, but is perhaps the most dull-witted person you have ever met. What do you say when the teenager asks, "How am I doing?"

Describe at least one situation from your experience where complete honesty increased another person's defensiveness. Discuss whether candor or some degree of strategy might have been the best approach in this situation. How can you reconcile your approach with Gibb's arguments in favor of spontaneity?

5. Invitation to Insight

Review the Gibb behaviors discussed on pages 327–333, and then answer the following questions:

a. Which defense-provoking behavior do you find most annoying?
b. Who in your life uses that behavior most often?
c. What part of your presenting self is threatened by that behavior?
d. How do you normally respond to that behavior?

e. What behavior do you wish that person would use instead?
f. How could you respond to avoid a negative spiral?

6. Skill Builder

Try your hand at offering constructive criticism in the following situations, using the sandwich method described on pages 334–335:

a. Your partner rarely says "thank you" when you do favors for her or him.
b. Your good friend wears unflattering clothing that embarrasses you in public
c. Your sibling doesn't show up at important family events.
d. Your coworker tells offensive jokes in front of customers.

7. Skill Builder

Practice your skill at responding nondefensively to critical attacks by following these steps:

a. Identify five criticisms you are likely to encounter from others in your day-to-day communication. If you have trouble thinking of criticisms, invite one or more people who know you well to supply some real, sincere gripes.
b. For each criticism, write one or more nondefensive responses using the alternatives on pages 336–339. Be sure your responses are sincere and that you can offer them without counterattacking your critic.
c. Practice your responses, either by inviting a friend or classmate to play the role of your critics or by approaching your critics directly and inviting them to share their gripes with you.

CHAPTER 11

Managing Conflict

CHAPTER OUTLINE

After studying the material in this chapter . . .

YOU SHOULD UNDERSTAND:

1. The five elements of conflict.
2. That conflict is natural and inevitable.
3. The characteristics of functional and dysfunctional conflicts.
4. The differences between avoidance, accommodation, competition, compromise, and collaboration.
5. The influence of gender and culture on interpersonal conflict.
6. The ways individuals interact to create relational conflict systems.

YOU SHOULD BE ABLE TO:

1. Recognize and accept the inevitability of conflicts in your life.
2. Identify the behaviors that characterize your dysfunctional conflicts and suggest more functional alternatives.
3. Identify the conflict styles you use most commonly and evaluate their appropriateness.
4. Describe the relational conflict system in one of your important relationships.
5. Use the win-win problem-solving approach to resolve an interpersonal conflict.

KEY TERMS

- Accommodation (360)
- Avoidance (359)
- Collaboration (363)
- Competition (360)
- Complementary conflict style (369)
- Compromise (362)
- Conflict (351)
- Conflict ritual (371)
- De-escalatory spiral (369)
- Direct aggression (362)
- Dysfunctional conflict (353)
- Escalatory spiral (369)
- Functional conflict (353)
- Parallel conflict style (369)
- Passive aggression (361)
- Relational conflict style (368)
- Symmetrical conflict style (369)
- Win-win problem solving (364)

Once upon a time, there was a world without conflicts. The leaders of each nation recognized the need for cooperation and met regularly to solve any potential problems before they could grow. They never disagreed on matters needing attention or on ways to handle these matters, and so there were never any international tensions, and of course there was no war.

Within each nation things ran just as smoothly. The citizens always agreed on who their leaders should be, so elections were always unanimous. There was no social friction among various groups. Age, race, and educational differences did exist, but each group respected the others, and all got along harmoniously.

Human relationships were always perfect. Strangers were always kind and friendly to each other. Neighbors were considerate of each other's needs. Friendships were always mutual, and no disagreements ever spoiled people's enjoyment of one another. Once people fell in love—and everyone did—they stayed happy. Partners liked everything about each other and were able to fully satisfy each other's needs. Children and parents agreed on every aspect of family life and never were critical or hostile toward each other. Each day was better than the one before.

Of course, everybody lived happily ever after.

This story is obviously a fairy tale. Regardless of what we may wish for or dream about, a conflict-free world just doesn't exist. Even the best communicators, the luckiest people, are bound to wind up in situations when their needs don't match the needs of others. Money, time, power, sex, humor, aesthetic taste, and a thousand other issues arise and keep us from living in a state of perpetual agreement.

For many people the inevitability of conflict is a depressing fact. They think that the existence of ongoing conflict means that there's little chance for happy relationships with others. Effective communicators know differently. They realize that although it's impossible to *eliminate* conflict, there are ways to *manage* it effectively. The skillful management of conflict can open the door to healthier, stronger, and more satisfying relationships as well as to increased mental and physical health (Canary, 2003; Malis & Roloff, 2007).

What Is Conflict?

Stop reading for a moment and make a list of as many different conflicts as you can think of that you've experienced personally. The list will probably show you that conflict takes many forms. Sometimes there's angry shouting, as when parents yell at their children. In other cases, conflicts involve restrained discussion, as in labor-management negotiations or court trials. Sometimes conflicts are carried on through hostile silence, as in the unspoken feuds of angry couples. Finally, conflicts may wind up in physical fighting between friends, enemies, or even total strangers.

Whatever forms they may take, all interpersonal conflicts share certain similarities. William Wilmot and Joyce Hocker (2007) provide a thorough definition of conflict. They state that **conflict** is an expressed struggle between at least two interdependent parties who perceive incompatible goals, scarce resources, and interference from the other party in achieving their goals. The various parts of this definition can help you gain a better understanding of how conflict operates in everyday life.

EXPRESSED STRUGGLE

In order for conflict to exist, all the people involved must know that some disagreement exists. You may be upset for months because a neighbor's loud music keeps you awake at night, but no conflict exists until the neighbor learns about your problem. An expressed struggle doesn't have to be verbal. You can show your displeasure with someone without saying a word. A dirty look, the silent treatment, and avoiding the other person are all ways of expressing yourself. One way or another, both people must know that a problem exists before it fits our definition of conflict.

PERCEIVED INCOMPATIBLE GOALS

All conflicts look as if one person's gain would be another's loss. For instance, consider the neighbor whose music keeps you awake at night. It appears that someone has to lose: If the neighbor turns down the noise, then he loses the enjoyment of hearing the music at full volume; but if the neighbor keeps the volume up, then you're still awake and unhappy.

The goals in this situation really aren't completely incompatible—solutions do exist that allow both people to get what they want. For instance, you could achieve peace and quiet by closing your windows or getting the neighbor to close his. You might use a pair of earplugs, or perhaps the neighbor could get a set of earphones, which would allow the music to play at full volume without bothering anyone. If any of these solutions prove workable, then the conflict disappears.

Unfortunately, people often fail to see mutually satisfying answers to their problems. As long as they *perceive* their goals to be mutually exclusive, the conflict is real, albeit unnecessary.

PERCEIVED SCARCE RESOURCES

Conflicts also exist when people believe there isn't enough of something to go around: affection, money, space, and so on. Time is often a scarce commodity. As authors, teachers, and family men, the writers of this textbook are constantly in the middle of struggles about how to use the limited time we have at home. Should we work on this book? Spend time with our families? Enjoy the luxury of being alone? With only 24 hours in a day, we're bound to wind up in conflicts with our families, editors, students, colleagues, and friends—all of whom want more of our time than we have available to give.

INTERDEPENDENCE

However antagonistic they might feel, the people in a conflict are dependent upon each other. The welfare and satisfaction of one depends on the actions of another. If this were not true, then there would be no need for conflict, even in the face of scarce resources and incompatible goals. In fact, many conflicts remain unresolved because the people fail to understand their interdependence. One of the first steps toward resolving a conflict is to take the attitude that "we're all in this together."

INEVITABILITY

Conflicts are bound to happen, even in the best relationships. College students who kept diaries of their relationships reported that they take part in about seven arguments per week (Benoit & Benoit, 1987). Other surveys show that conflicts with friends are typical, with an average of one or two disagreements a day (Samter & Cupach, 1998; Tuval-Mashiach & Shulman, 2006). Among families, conflict can be even more frequent. Researchers recorded dinner conversations for 52 families and found an average of 3.3 "conflict episodes" per meal (Vuchinich, 1987). This doesn't mean that families have "knock down, drag out" fights at the dinner table every night—but they regularly have disagreements and points of contention.

A Conflict of Interests: *Juno*

Along with being smart and witty, teenager Juno MacGuff (Ellen Page) could well be described as "independent"—until she learns she is pregnant. From that point on, Juno faces a series of difficult decisions that affect a variety of people. Her life and choices become intertwined with her family, with the couple who wants to adopt her baby, and with Paulie (Michael Cera), the teenage father of her child. These interdependent stakeholders struggle over scarce resources and perceived incompatible goals.

After considering the concerns of everyone involved, Juno does what she believes is best for herself and her baby. Along the way, the conflicts that arise actually help several characters learn important things about themselves and their relationships.

Since it is impossible to *avoid* conflicts, the challenge is to handle them effectively when they do arise. Decades of research shows that people in both happy and unhappy relationships have conflicts, but that they perceive them and manage them in very different ways (Simon et al., 2008; Wilmot & Hocker, 2007). Unhappy couples argue in ways cataloged in this book as destructive. They are more concerned with defending themselves than with being problem-oriented; they fail to listen carefully to one another, have little or no empathy for their partners, use evaluative "you" language, and ignore each other's relational messages.

Many satisfied couples handle their conflicts more effectively. They recognize disagreements as healthy and know that conflicts need to be faced (Crohan, 1992; Ridley et al., 2001). While they may argue vigorously, they use skills like perception checking to find out what the other person is thinking, and they let the other person know that they understand the other side of the dispute (Canary et al., 1991). These people are willing to admit their mistakes, a habit that contributes to a harmonious relationship and also helps solve the problem at hand. With this in mind, let's take a closer look at what makes some conflicts more functional than others.

Functional and Dysfunctional Conflicts

Some bacteria are "good," aiding digestion and cleaning up waste, whereas others are "bad," causing infection. There are helpful forest fires, which clean out dangerous accumulations of underbrush, and harmful ones, which threaten lives and property. In the same way, some conflicts can be beneficial. They provide a way for relationships to grow by solving the problem at hand and often improving other areas of interaction. Other conflicts can be harmful, causing pain and weakening a relationship. Communication scholars usually describe harmful conflicts as dysfunctional and beneficial ones as functional (Canary & Messman, 2000). In a **dysfunctional conflict**, the outcomes fall short of what is possible and have a damaging effect on the relationship. By contrast, participants in a **functional conflict** achieve the best possible outcome, even strengthening the relationship.

What makes some conflicts functional and others dysfunctional? Usually, the difference doesn't rest in the subject of the conflict, for it's possible to have good or poor results on almost any issue. Certain individual styles of communication can be more productive than others. In other cases, the success or failure of a conflict will depend on the method of resolution the communicators choose. We'll talk more about types of conflict resolution later in this chapter. Now, though, we will describe some characteristics that distinguish functional from dysfunctional conflicts.

INTEGRATION VERSUS POLARIZATION

In a dysfunctional conflict, participants regard each other as polar opposites. They see themselves as "good" and the other person as "bad," their actions

as "protective" and the other's as "aggressive," their behavior as "open and trustworthy" and the other's as "sneaky and deceitful." Alan Sillars and his colleagues (2000) found that in severe conflicts and dissatisfied relationships, married people saw their spouses as more blameworthy than themselves. Researchers Robert Blake and Jane Mouton (1964) found that people engaged in this kind of polarization underestimate the commonalties shared with the other person and miss areas of agreement and goodwill.

By contrast, participants in a functional conflict recognize they are integrated—that they're in the difficult situation together. They don't think of the other person as necessarily "wrong" or "bad"; rather, they think of that person as a partner with whom to work. To use Gibb's language (see Chapter 10), they are *problem-oriented,* focused on solving the problem in a way that works for everybody rather than on controlling the other person. Integration is most likely when people in conflict appreciate each other's differences (Brown, 2004).

COOPERATION VERSUS OPPOSITION

Participants in a dysfunctional conflict see each other as opponents and view the other's gain as their loss: "If you win, I lose" is the attitude. This belief keeps partners from looking for ways to agree or finding solutions that can satisfy them both. People in opposition rarely try to redefine the situation in more constructive ways, and they seldom give in, even on noncritical issues (Deutsch, 2006).

A more functional approach recognizes that cooperation may bring about an answer that leaves everyone happy (Lewis, 2006). Even nations basically hostile to each other often recognize the functional benefits of cooperating.

For example, although many member countries of the United Nations have clear-cut differences in certain areas, they work together to alleviate world hunger and to encourage peaceful solutions to world conflict. Such cooperation is also possible in interpersonal conflicts. We have more to say about cooperative problem solving later in this chapter.

CONFIRMATION VERSUS DISCONFIRMATION

In functional conflicts, the people involved may disagree but they are not disagreeable. By using the supportive behaviors described on pages 327–333 in Chapter 10 (description instead of evaluation, provisionalism instead of certainty, etc.), it is possible to tackle the problem at hand without attacking the person with whom you share it. When partners treat one another with affection and without trying to dominate one another, relational satisfaction increases—even in the face of conflict (Ebesu-Hubbard, 2001).

AGREEMENT VERSUS COERCION

In destructive conflicts, the participants rely heavily on coercion to get what they want (Tuval-Mashiach & Shulman, 2006). "Do it my way, or else" is a threat commonly stated or implied in dysfunctional conflicts. Money, favors, friendliness, sex, and sometimes even physical coercion become tools for forcing the

FOCUS ON RESEARCH

Emotional Intelligence and Conflict Management

research

Chapter 8 introduced the concept of emotional intelligence, the ability to understand and manage one's own emotions and to be sensitive to others' feelings. Research has linked emotional intelligence (EI) with a variety of positive outcomes, including physical and mental health. Lynn Smith and her colleagues wanted to know if EI also helps couples' interpersonal health—and more specifically, their ability to manage conflict constructively.

The researchers recruited 82 heterosexual cohabitating couples and gave them survey instruments measuring their EI, conflict communication patterns, and relational satisfaction. Not surprisingly, there was a strong correlation between couples' emotional intelligence and their ability to effectively manage conflict. Of particular interest was the finding that avoidance and withdrawing during conflict were *negatively* related to EI and relational satisfaction (see the Dark Side box on p. 359 for further discussion of this concept).

Many of the functional approaches to conflict mentioned in this section—focusing, foresight, and cooperation, for instance—have been linked with emotional intelligence. It seems clear that an important component of managing conflicts is the management of their accompanying emotions.

Smith, L., Heaven, P. C. L., & Ciarrochi, J. (2008). Trait emotional intelligence, conflict communication patterns, and relationship satisfaction. *Personality and Individual Differences, 44,* 1314–1325.

other person to give in. Needless to say, victories won with such power plays don't do much for a relationship.

More enlightened communicators realize that power plays are usually a bad idea, not only on ethical grounds but because they can often backfire. Rarely is a person in a relationship totally powerless; it's often possible to win a battle only to lose the war. One classic case of the dysfunctional consequences of using power to resolve conflicts occurs in families where authoritarian parents turn their children's requests into "unreasonable demands." It's easy enough to send 5-year-olds out of a room for some real or imagined misbehavior, but when they grow into teenagers they acquire many ways of striking back.

REFLECTION

E-Mail De-Escalates Conflict Spiral

My dad is a family law attorney who specializes in divorce cases. He says that e-mail has been a good way to get angry couples to communicate. Some husbands and wives can't be in the same room without getting into a shouting match, but e-mail slows things down and gives them a chance to think before they respond to one another. My dad asks each person in a divorcing couple to wait overnight before responding to the other's message, which cuts down on the angry and hurtful replies.

My dad says that e-mail doesn't save failing marriages, but it sure makes the breakup more civilized and less painful.

DE-ESCALATION VERSUS ESCALATION

In destructive conflicts, the problems seem to grow larger instead of smaller (Alberts & Driscoll, 1992). As you read in Chapter 10, defensiveness is reciprocal: The person you attack is likely to strike back even harder. We've all seen a small incident get out of hand and cause damage out of proportion to its importance.

One clear sign of functional conflict is that in the long run the behaviors of the participants solve more problems than they create. We say "long run" because facing up to an issue instead of avoiding it will usually make life more difficult for a while. In this respect, handling conflicts functionally is rather like going to the dentist: You may find it a little (or even a lot!) painful for a short time, but you're only making matters worse if you don't face the problem.

FOCUSING VERSUS DRIFTING

In dysfunctional conflicts, the partners often bring in issues having little or nothing to do with the original problem. Take, for example, a couple having trouble deciding whether to spend the holidays at his or her parents' home. As they begin to grow frustrated at their inability to solve the dilemma, their interaction sounds like this:

A: Your mother is always trying to latch onto us!

B: If you want to talk about latching on, what about your folks? Ever since they loaned us that money, they've been asking about every dime we spend.

A: Well, if you could ever finish with school and hold down a decent job, we wouldn't have to worry about money so much. You're always talking about wanting to be an equal partner, but I'm the one paying all the bills around here.

You can imagine how the conversation would go from here. Notice how the original issue became lost as the conflict expanded. Such open-ended hostility is unlikely to solve any of the problems it brings up, not to mention its potential for creating problems that didn't even exist before.

One characteristic of communicators who handle conflict well is their ability to keep focused on one subject at a time. Unlike those dysfunctional battlers whom George Bach and Peter Wyden (1968) call "kitchen sink fighters," skillful communicators might say, "I'm willing to talk about how my parents have been acting since they made us that loan, but first let's settle the business of where to spend the holidays." In other words, for functional problem solving the rule is "one problem at a time."

FORESIGHT VERSUS SHORTSIGHTEDNESS

Shortsightedness can produce dysfunctional conflicts even when partners do not lose sight of the original issue. One common type of shortsightedness occurs when disputants try to win a battle and wind up losing the war. Friends might argue about who started a fight, but if you succeed in proving that you were "right" at the cost of the friendship, then the victory is a hollow one. In another type of shortsightedness, partners are so interested in defending their own solution to a problem that they overlook a different solution that would satisfy both their goals. A final type of shortsightedness occurs when one or both partners jump into a conflict without thinking about how they can approach the issue most constructively. In a few pages, we have more to say about preventing these last two types of shortsightedness.

Foresight is a feature of functional conflicts because it helps participants "pick their battles" wisely ("If I keep this up, I'm going to lose a friend—and I don't want that to happen"). It also helps partners see that their relationship is usually more important than the issue being disputed.

POSITIVE VERSUS NEGATIVE RESULTS

So far, we have looked at the differences between the *processes* of functional and dysfunctional conflicts. Now we will compare the *results* of these different styles.

Dysfunctional conflict typically has two consequences. First, no one is likely to get what was originally sought. In the short run, it may *look* as if one person might win a dispute while the other person loses, but today's victor is likely to suffer tomorrow at the hands of the original loser. Second, dysfunctional conflicts can threaten the future of a relationship. Family members, lovers, friends, neighbors, or fellow workers usually are bound together by webs of commitments and obligations that aren't easy to break. If they can't find satisfactory ways of resolving their differences, their connections will become strained and uncomfortable. Even when it is possible, dissolving a relationship in the face of a conflict is hardly a satisfying pattern.

In contrast to these dismal outcomes, functional conflicts have positive results. One benefit of skillfully handling issues is the reward of successfully facing a challenge. Finding a solution that works for you and the other person can leave partners feeling better about themselves and each other. Partners learn more about each other's needs and how they can be satisfied. Feelings are clarified. Backgrounds are shared. The relationship grows deeper and stronger. Of course, growth can occur in non-conflict situations too, but the point here is that dealing with problems can be an opportunity for getting to know each other better and appreciate each other more. Constructive conflict also provides a safe outlet for the feelings of frustration and aggression that are bound to occur. Without this kind of release, partners can build up a "gunnysack" of grudges that interfere with their everyday functioning and their goodwill toward one another.

Conflict Styles

Most people have "default" styles of handling conflict—characteristic approaches they take when their needs appear incompatible with what others want. While our habitual styles work sometimes, they may not work at all in other situations. What styles do you typically use to deal with conflict? Find out by thinking about how two hypothetical characters—Chris and Pat—manage a problem.

Chris and Pat have been roommates for several years, and every fall they have weekly conflicts about television viewing. Chris is a big sports fan and loves watching football on Monday nights. Pat doesn't like sports, but really enjoys a particular show that's broadcast on—you guessed it—Monday nights. Chris and Pat have only one television, so every week they have a conflict over what they will (and won't) watch on Monday evenings. Here are five ways they could handle their conflict, representing five different conflict styles:

- Chris and Pat don't discuss the issue—they don't want another fight. When show time rolls around, neither Pat nor Chris makes a move for the remote control. Neither show gets watched.
- Pat gives in and lets Chris watch football. It's a kind gesture and a gracious way to treat a good friend. Pat hopes Chris will return the favor next week.
- Chris tries to convince Pat that the football game is far more important than Pat's show. Pat tries to convince Chris that football is mindless entertainment, while Pat's favorite show is witty and intelligent. Both want the other person to give up and give in.
- Pat and Chris agree to alternate weeks—one week Chris gets football, the next week Pat gets the TV show. No exceptions will be made to this schedule.
- Chris and Pat brainstorm and decide that getting a second television would be the best way to resolve the conflict. They agree to raise the funds by working together at a campus concession stand that weekend.

These approaches represent the five styles depicted in Figure 11.1, each of which is described in the following paragraphs.

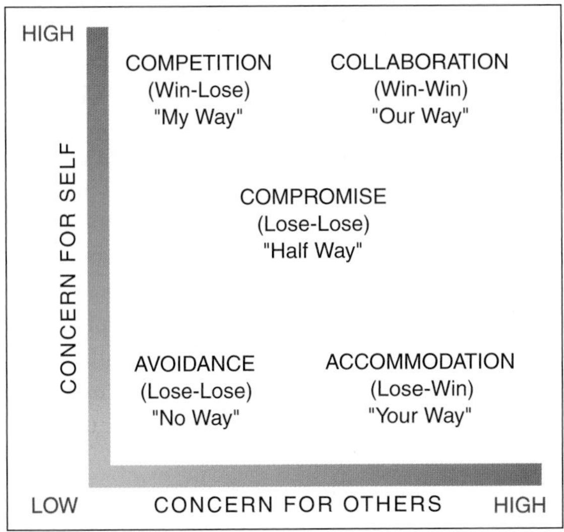

FIGURE 11.1 Conflict Styles
Adapted from Wilmot, W. W., & Hocker, J. L. (2007). *Interpersonal conflict* (7th ed.). New York: McGraw-Hill.

AVOIDANCE (LOSE-LOSE)

Avoidance occurs when people nonassertively ignore or stay away from conflict. Avoidance can be physical (steering clear of a friend after having an argument) or conversational (changing the topic, joking, or denying that a problem exists).

Avoidance reflects a pessimistic attitude about conflict. This approach reflects the belief that there is no good way to resolve the issue at hand. Avoiders usually believe it's easier to put up with the status quo than to face the problem head-on and try to solve it. In the case of Chris and Pat, avoidance means that, rather than having another fight, neither of them will watch television. Their "solution" illustrates how avoidance often produces lose-lose results.

Although avoiding important issues can keep the peace temporarily, it typically leads to unsatisfying relationships (Caughlin & Golish, 2002). Chronic misunderstandings, resentments, and disappointments pile up and contaminate the emotional climate. For this reason, we can say that avoiders have both a low concern for their own needs and for the interests

DARK SIDE OF COMMUNICATION

When Silence Isn't Golden

"Silence is golden," says the well-known maxim. There certainly are times when keeping resentments to yourself can be a smart approach. But a certain kind of silence—labeled *stonewalling* by family communication researcher John Gottman—is anything but golden. Stonewalling occurs when one person in a relationship withdraws from the interaction, shutting down dialogue—and any chance of resolving the problem in a mutually satisfactory way.

Gottman has found that it's healthy for couples to express their anger and complaints, as long as they do so without criticism and contempt. When couples *stop* voicing their concerns, Gottman predicts, they are headed for divorce. As another family therapist once put it, "More marriages are killed by silence than by violence."

Gottman, J. (1994). *Why marriages succeed or fail and how you can make yours last.* New York: Simon & Schuster.

of the other person, who is also likely to suffer from unaddressed issues (see Figure 11.1).

Despite its obvious shortcomings, avoidance isn't always a bad idea (Caughlin & Arr, 2004; Oduro-Frimpong, 2007). You might choose to avoid certain topics or situations if the risk of speaking up is too great, such as getting fired from a job you can't afford to lose, being humiliated in public, or even risking physical harm. You might also avoid a conflict if the relationship it involves isn't worth the effort. Even in close relationships, though, avoidance has its logic. If the issue is temporary or minor, you might let it pass. These reasons help explain why the communication of many happily married couples is characterized by "selectively ignoring" the other person's minor flaws (Cahn, 1992). This doesn't mean that a key to successful relationships is avoiding *all* conflicts. Instead, it suggests that it's smart to save energy for the truly important ones.

ACCOMMODATION (LOSE-WIN)

Accommodation occurs when we allow others to have their own way rather than asserting our own point of view. Figure 11.1 depicts accommodators as having low concern for themselves and high concern for others, resulting in lose-win, "we'll do it your way" outcomes. In our hypothetical scenario, Pat accommodates to Chris by letting Chris watch football—even though it means missing Pat's favorite show.

The motivation of an accommodator plays a significant role in this style's effectiveness. If accommodation is a genuine act of kindness, generosity, or love, then chances are good that it will enhance the relationship. Most people appreciate those who "take one for the team," "treat others as they want to be treated," or "lose the battle to win the war." However, people are far less appreciative of those who habitually use this style to play the role of "martyr, bitter complainer, whiner, or saboteur" (Wilmot & Hocker, 2007).

We should pause here to mention the important role that culture plays in perceptions of conflict styles. People from high-context, collectivistic backgrounds (such as many Asian cultures) are likely to regard avoidance and accommodation as face-saving and noble ways to handle conflict (Georgakopoulos, 2004; Oetzel & Ting-Toomey, 2003). In low-context, individualistic cultures (such as the United States), avoidance and accommodation are often viewed less positively. For instance, think of the many unflattering terms that Americans use for people who give up or give in during conflicts ("pushover," "yes man," "doormat," "spineless"). As you will read later in this chapter, collectivistic cultures have virtuous words and phrases to describe these same traits. The point here is that all conflict styles have value in certain situations, and that culture plays a significant role in determining how each style is valued.

COMPETITION (WIN-LOSE)

The flip side of accommodation is **competition**, a win-lose approach to conflict that involves high concern for self and low concern for others. As Figure 11.1

shows, competition seeks to resolve conflicts "my way." When Chris and Pat make their cases that one show is better than the other, trying to get each other to concede, they are using a competitive approach.

Many North Americans default to a competitive approach because it's ingrained in their culture, as Laura Tracy (1991, p. 4) observes:

> whether we like it or not, we live in a competitive society. Our economy is competitive by design, and as a nation, we see in competition a challenge to develop our resources and ourselves.

Just as competition can develop an economy, it can sometimes develop a relationship. Susan Messman and Rebecca Mikesell (2000) found that some men and women in satisfying dating relationships used competition to enrich their interaction. For example, some found satisfaction by competing in play (who's the better racquetball player?), in achievement (who gets the better job offer?), and in altruism (who's more romantic?). These satisfied couples developed a shared narrative (see Chapter 4) that defined competition as a measure of regard, quite different from conflict that signaled a lack of appreciation and respect. Of course, it's easy to see how these arrangements could backfire if one partner became a gloating winner or a sore loser. It's also easy to see how feeling like you've been defeated can leave you wanting to get even, creating a downward competitive spiral that degrades to a lose-lose relationship (Olson & Braithwaite, 2004; Singleton & Vacca, 2007).

If you feel your way is the best one, you may feel justified in trying to control the situation, but it's likely that the other person won't view your bid for control so charitably (Gross et al., 2004). The dark side of competition is that it often breeds aggression (Warren et al., 2005). Sometimes aggression is obvious, but at other times it can be more subtle. To understand how, read on.

Passive Aggression **Passive aggression** occurs when a communicator expresses dissatisfaction in a disguised manner. In the case of Pat and Chris, perhaps the "loser" runs the vacuum cleaner loudly during the other person's show—or joins in watching the program but makes sarcastic jokes about it the entire time. Passive aggression can take the form of "crazymaking" (Bach & Wyden, 1968)—tactics designed to punish another person without direct confrontation. Crazymaking takes its name from the effect such behavior usually has on its target. There are a number of crazymaking ways to deal with conflict. One is through guilt: "Never mind. I'll do all the work myself. Go ahead and have a good time. Don't worry about me." Another crazymaker is when someone agrees with you to your face but has a different agenda behind your back—such as the teenager who says he'll clean his room, then doesn't do so as a means of getting back at the parent who grounded him. Some passive aggression is nonverbal: a loud sigh, a pained expression, or a

"It's not enough that we succeed. Cats must also fail."

disdainful laugh can get a message across. If the target of these messages asks about them, the passive aggressor can always deny the conflict exists. Even humor—especially sarcasm—can be used as passive aggression.

Direct Aggression A directly aggressive communicator lashes out to attack the source of displeasure. Dominic Infante (1987) identified nine types of **direct aggression:** character attacks, competence attacks, physical appearance attacks, maledictions (wishing the other bad fortune), teasing, ridicule, threats, swearing, and nonverbal emblems (fist-shaking, waving arms, etc.). Like all types of relational communication, direct aggression has both verbal and nonverbal dimensions. In the case of Chris and Pat, the conflict about which show to watch might turn into an ugly shouting match, with denigrating comments about how only an "idiot" could like such a "stupid" program.

The results of direct aggression can have a severe impact on the target. There is a significant connection between verbal aggression and physical aggression (Atkin et al., 2002; Infante et al., 1989). Even if the attacks never lead to blows, the psychological effects can be harmful, or even devastating. Recipients can feel embarrassed, inadequate, humiliated, hopeless, desperate, or depressed (Infante, 1987). These results can lead to decreased effectiveness in personal relationships, on the job, and in families (Beatty et al., 1996; Doss et al, 2008; Muñoz-Rivas et al., 2007). Verbal aggression can affect the relationship as well as the target. One aggressive remark can lead to an equally combative reaction, starting a destructive spiral that can expand beyond the original dispute and damage the entire relationship (Olson & Braithwaite, 2004; Turk & Monahan, 1999).

COMPROMISE (NEGOTIATED LOSE-LOSE)

A **compromise** gives both people at least some of what they want, although both sacrifice part of their goals. People usually settle for a compromise when it seems that partial satisfaction is the best they can hope for. In the case of Pat and Chris, they strike a "halfway" deal by alternating weeks for watching their shows. Unlike avoidance, where both parties lose because they don't address their problem, compromisers actually negotiate a lose-lose solution.

Although a compromise may be better than losing everything, this approach hardly seems to deserve the positive image it has with some people. In his valuable book on conflict resolution, Albert Filley (1975, p. 23) makes an interesting observation about our attitudes toward this method. Why is it, he asks, that if someone says, "I will compromise my values," we view the action unfavorably, yet we talk admiringly about people in a conflict who compromise to reach a solution? Although compromises may be the best obtainable result in some conflicts, it's important to realize that both people in a dispute can often work together to find much better solutions. In such cases, *compromise* is a negative word.

Most of us are surrounded by the results of bad compromises. Consider a common example: the conflict between one person's desire to smoke

cigarettes and another's need for clean air. The win-lose outcomes on this issue are obvious: Either the smoker abstains or the nonsmoker gets polluted lungs—neither option a very satisfying one. But a compromise in which the smoker gets to enjoy only a rare cigarette or must retreat outdoors and in which the nonsmoker still must inhale some fumes or feel like an ogre is hardly better. Both sides have lost a considerable amount of both comfort and goodwill. Of course, the costs involved in other compromises are even greater. For example, if a divorced couple haggles over custody in a way that leaves them bitter and emotionally scars their children, it's hard to say that anybody has won no matter what the outcome.

Some compromises do leave everyone satisfied. You and the seller might settle on a price for a used car that is between what the seller was asking and what you wanted to pay. While neither of you got everything you wanted, the outcome would still leave both of you satisfied. Likewise, you and your companion might agree to see a film that is the second choice for both of you in order to spend an evening together. As long as everyone is at least somewhat satisfied with an outcome, compromise can be an effective way to resolve conflicts. Catherine Sanderson and Kim Karetsky (2002) found that college students with a strong focus on intimacy goals were likely to engage in open discussion and compromise, show concern for their partner, and seek social support—and importantly, they were likely to successfully resolve the conflict. When compromises are satisfying and successful, it might be more accurate to categorize them as the final style we'll discuss: collaboration.

COLLABORATION (WIN-WIN)

Collaboration seeks win-win solutions to conflict. It involves a high degree of concern for both self and others, with the goal of solving problems not "my way" or "your way" but "our way." In the best case, collaborating can lead to a *win-win* outcome, where each person gets what she or he wants (Lewis, 2006).

If Chris and Pat were to collaborate, they might determine that the best way for both of them to get what they want is to buy a second television—and then work together to raise the money. Or they might realize that they don't

SELF-ASSESSMENT

Your Method of Conflict Resolution

Think of a relationship with someone with whom you interact regularly and with whom you engage in conflict (for example, a parent, sibling, roommate, close friend, spouse, partner, or lover). How do you usually respond to your conflict with this person? In each pair below, circle the **A** or **B** statement that is *most characteristic* of your behavior. In some cases, neither answer may be very typical of your behavior. If this happens, select the response that you would be *more likely* to use.

1. A. There are times when I let the other person take responsibility for solving the problem.
B. It's important to me that others are happy, even if it comes at my expense.
2. A. I try to find a compromise solution.
B. I attempt to deal with all of the other person's and my concerns.
3. A. I am usually firm in pursuing my goals.
B. I might try to soothe the other's feelings and preserve our relationship.
4. A. I try to find a compromise solution.
B. I sometimes sacrifice my own wishes for the wishes of the other person.
5. A. I consistently seek the other's help in working out a solution.
B. I don't worry about my own concerns if satisfying them means damaging the relationship.
6. A. I try to avoid creating unpleasantness for myself.
B. I try to win my position.
7. A. I try to postpone the issue until I have had some time to think it over.
B. I give up some points in exchange for others.
8. A. I am usually firm in pursuing my goals.
B. I attempt to get all concerns and issues immediately out in the open.
9. A. I feel that differences are not always worth worrying about.
B. I try to integrate my concerns with the other person's concerns.
10. A. I am firm in pursuing my goals.
B. I try to find a compromise solution.
11. A. I attempt to get all concerns and issues immediately out in the open.
B. I might try to soothe the other's feelings and preserve our relationship.
12. A. I sometimes avoid taking positions that would create controversy.
B. I will let the other person have some of what she or he wants if she or he lets me have some of what I want.

have to both watch television at home, and that one (or both) of them might even have more fun watching favorite shows with like-minded friends.

In **win-win problem solving**, the goal is to find a solution that satisfies the needs of everyone involved. Not only do the partners avoid trying to win at each other's expense, but there's also a belief that working together can provide a solution in which all reach their goals without needing to compromise.

13. A. I propose a middle ground.
B. I press to get my points made.

14. A. I tell the other person my ideas and ask for his or hers.
B. I try to show the other person the logic and benefits of my position.

15. A. I might try to soothe the other's feelings and preserve our relationship.
B. I try to do what is necessary to avoid tensions.

SCORING:

For question 1, circle the **A** or **B** below according to your answer; for question 2, circle the **A** or **B** below, according to your answer. Repeat the process for all 15 questions.

	CT	CL	C	A	AC
1.				A	B
2.		B	A		
3.	A				B
4.			A		B
5.		A			B
6.	B			A	
7.			B	A	
8.	A	B			
9.		B		A	
10.	A		B		
11.		A			B
12.			B	A	
13.	B		A		
14.	B	A			
15.				B	A

Number of **A**s and **B**s circled in column CT (**C**ompe**T**ition) ______
Number of **A**s and **B**s circled in column CL (**C**o**L**laboration) ______
Number of **A**s and **B**s circled in column C (**C**ompromise) ______
Number of **A**s and **B**s circled in column A (**A**voidance) ______
Number of **A**s and **B**s circled in column AC (**AC**commodation) ______

How do your five scores compare? Which is your highest, your most-likely method of conflict resolution, and which is your lowest, your least-likely method?

Adapted from Thomas, K. W., & Kilmann, R. (1978). Comparison of four instruments measuring conflict behavior. *Psychological Report, 42,* 1139–1145.

A few examples show how collaboration can lead to win-win outcomes:

- A boss and her employees get into a conflict over scheduling. The employees often want to shift the hours they're scheduled to work so that they can accommodate personal needs, whereas the boss needs to be sure that the operation is fully staffed at all times. After some discussion they arrive at a solution that satisfies everyone: The boss works up a monthly master schedule indicating the hours during which each employee is responsible for being on the job. Employees are free to trade hours among themselves, as long as the operation is fully staffed at all times.

- A conflict about testing arises in a college class. Due to sickness and other reasons, a certain number of students need to take exams on a makeup basis. The instructor doesn't want to give these students any advantage over their peers and also doesn't want to go through the task of making up a brand-new test for just a few people. After working on the problem together, instructor and students arrive at a win-win solution. The instructor will hand out a list of 20 possible exam questions in advance of the test day. At examination time, 5 of these questions are randomly drawn for the class to answer. Students who take makeup exams will draw from the same pool of questions at the time of their test. In this way, makeup students are taking a fresh test without the instructor having to create a new exam.
- A newly married husband and wife find themselves arguing frequently over their budget. The husband enjoys buying impractical and enjoyable items for himself and for the house, whereas the wife fears that such purchases will ruin their carefully constructed budget. Their solution is to set aside a small amount of money each month for "fun" purchases. The amount is small enough to be affordable yet gives the husband a chance to escape from their Spartan lifestyle. The wife is satisfied with the arrangement because the luxury money is now a budget category by itself, which gets rid of the "out of control" feeling that comes when her husband makes unexpected purchases. The plan works so well that the couple continues to use it even after their income rises, by increasing the amount devoted to luxuries.

Although such solutions might seem obvious when you read them here, a moment's reflection will show you that such cooperative problem solving is all too rare. People faced with these types of conflicts often resort to such styles as avoiding, accommodating, or competing, and they wind up handling the issues in a manner that results in either a win-lose or lose-lose outcome. As we pointed out earlier, it's a shame to see one or both partners in a conflict come away unsatisfied when they could both get what they're seeking by communicating in a win-win manner. Later in this chapter, you'll learn a specific process for arriving at collaborative solutions to problems.

Although a win-win approach sounds ideal, it is not always possible, or even appropriate (Budescu et al., 1999). Collaborative problem solving can be quite time consuming, and some conflict decisions need to be made quickly. Moreover, many conflicts are about relatively minor issues that don't call for a great deal of creativity and brainstorming. As you'll see in the following section, there will certainly be times when compromising is the most sensible approach. You will even encounter instances when pushing for your own solution is reasonable. Even more surprisingly, you will probably discover that there are times when it makes sense to willingly accept the loser's role. Much

TABLE 11.1 ***Choosing the Most Appropriate Conflict Style***

AVOIDANCE (LOSE-LOSE)	ACCOMMODATION (LOSE-WIN)	COMPETITION (WIN-LOSE)	COMPROMISE (NEGOTIATED LOSE-LOSE)	COLLABORATION (WIN-WIN)
When the issue is of little importance	When the issue is more important to the other person than it is to you	When the issue is not important enough to negotiate at length	When the issue is moderately important but not enough for a stalemate	When the issue is too important for a compromise
To cool down and gain perspective	When you discover you are wrong	When you are convinced that your position is right and necessary	When opponents are strongly committed to mutually exclusive goals	To merge insights with someone who has a different perspective on the problem
When the costs of confrontation outweigh the benefits	When the long-term cost of winning may not be worth the short-term gain	When there is not enough time to seek a win-win outcome	To achieve quick, temporary solutions to complex problems	To come up with creative and unique solutions to problems
	To build up credits for later conflicts	When the other person is not willing to seek a win-win outcome	As a backup mode when collaboration doesn't work	To develop a relationship by showing commitment to the concerns of both parties
	To let others learn by making their own mistakes	To protect yourself against a person who takes advantage of noncompetitive people		When a long-term relationship between you and the other person is important

Adapted from Wilmot, W. W., & Hocker, J. L. (2007). *Interpersonal conflict* (7th ed.), New York: McGraw-Hill.

of the time, however, good intentions and creative thinking can lead to outcomes that satisfy everyone's needs.

WHICH STYLE TO USE?

Although collaborative problem solving might seem like the most attractive alternative to the other styles described in this chapter, it's an oversimplification to imagine that there is a single "best" way to respond to conflicts (Canary & Spitzberg, 1987). Generally speaking, win-win approaches are preferable to win-lose and lose-lose solutions. But we've already seen that there are times when avoidance, accommodation, competition, and compromise are appropriate. Table 11.1 lists some of the factors to consider when deciding which style to use when facing a conflict.

A personal conflict style isn't necessarily a personality "trait" that carries across all situations. Wilmot and Hocker (2007) suggest that roughly 50 percent of the population change their style from one situation to another. As you learned in Chapter 1, this sort of behavioral flexibility is a characteristic of competent communicators. Several factors govern which style to use.

The Situation When someone clearly has more power than you, accommodation may be the best approach. If the boss tells you to "fill that order *now!*" you probably ought to do it without comment. A more competitive response ("Why don't you ask Karen to do it? She has less work than I do.") might state your true feelings, but it could also cost you your job.

The Other Person Although win-win is a fine ideal, sometimes the other person isn't interested in (or good at) collaborating. You probably know communicators who are so competitive that they put winning on even minor issues ahead of the well-being of your relationship. In such cases, your efforts to collaborate may have a low chance of success. Table 11.1 summarizes the pros and cons of each approach, taking into account the attitudes of the other person.

Your Goals When you want to solve a problem, it's generally good to be assertive (see Chapter 5 for information on creating assertive "I" messages). But there are other reasons for communicating in a conflict. Sometimes your overriding concern is to calm down an enraged or upset communicator. For example, tolerating an outburst from your crotchety and sick neighbor is probably better than standing up for yourself and triggering a stroke. Likewise, you might choose to sit quietly through the nagging of a family member rather than ruin Thanksgiving dinner. In other cases, your moral principles might compel an aggressive statement, even though it might not get you what you originally sought: "I've had enough of your racist jokes. I've tried to explain why they're so offensive, but you obviously haven't listened. I'm leaving!" Or your goal may be to be seen in a favorable way, in which case you may want to avoid being aggressive.

Conflict in Relational Systems

So far, we have been describing individual conflict styles. Even though the style you choose in a conflict is important, your approach isn't the only factor that will determine how a conflict unfolds. In reality, conflict is *relational*: Its character is usually determined by the way the people involved interact (Knapp et al., 1988; Wilmot & Hocker, 2007). For example, you might be determined to handle a conflict with your neighbors collaboratively, only to be driven to competition by their uncooperative nature or even to avoidance by their physical threats. Likewise, you might plan to hint to a professor that you are bothered by his apparent indifference but wind up discussing the matter in an open, assertive way in reaction to his constructive suggestion. Examples like these indicate that conflict isn't just a matter of individual choice. Rather, it depends on how the partners interact.

When two or more people are in a long-term relationship, they develop their own **relational conflict style**—a pattern of managing disagreements that repeats itself over time. The mutual influence parties have on one another is so powerful that it can overcome our disposition to handle conflicts in the manner that comes most easily to one or the other (Burggraf & Sillars, 1987). As we will soon see, some relational conflict styles are constructive, while others can make life miserable and threaten relationships.

COMPLEMENTARY, SYMMETRICAL, AND PARALLEL STYLES

Partners in interpersonal relationships—and impersonal ones, too—can use one of three styles to manage their conflicts. In relationships with a **complementary conflict style**, the partners use different but mutually reinforcing behaviors. As Table 11.2 illustrates, some complementary styles are destructive, while others are constructive. In a **symmetrical conflict style**, both people use the same tactics. Some relationships are characterized by a **parallel conflict style**, which shifts between complementary and symmetrical patterns from one issue to another. Table 11.2 illustrates how the same conflict can unfold in very different ways, depending on whether the partners' communication is symmetrical or complementary. A parallel style would alternate between these two forms, depending on the situation.

Research shows that a complementary "fight-flight" style is common in many unhappy marriages. One partner—most commonly the wife—addresses the conflict directly, while the other—usually the husband—withdraws (Krokoff, 1990; Sillars et al., 1984). As discussed in Chapter 4, it's easy to see how this pattern can lead to a cycle of increasing hostility and isolation, since each partner punctuates the conflict differently, blaming the other for making matters worse. "I withdraw because she's so critical," a husband might say. However, the wife wouldn't organize the sequence in the same way. "I criticize because he withdraws" would be her perception.

Complementary styles aren't the only ones that can lead to problems. Some distressed relationships suffer from destructively symmetrical communication. If both partners treat one another with matching hostility, one threat and insult leads to another in an **escalatory spiral**. If the partners both withdraw from one another instead of facing their problems, a complementary **de-escalatory spiral** results, in which the satisfaction and vitality ebb from the relationship, leaving it a shell of its former self.

As Table 11.2 shows, both complementary and symmetrical behavior can produce "good" results as well as "bad" ones. If the complementary behaviors are positive, then a positive spiral results, and the conflict stands a good chance of being resolved. This is the case in the second example in Table 11.2, in which the boss is open to hearing the employee's concerns, listening willingly as the employee talks. Here, a complementary talk-listen pattern works well.

Symmetrical styles also can be beneficial, as another look at the boss-employee example shows. The clearest example of constructive symmetry occurs when both people communicate assertively, listening to one another's concerns and working together to resolve them (Ridley et al., 2001, found these couples appraised their marriage more positively than any other type of couple). The potential for this sort of solution occurs in the parent-teenager conflict in Table 11.2. With enough mutual respect and careful listening, both

TABLE 11.2 ***Complementary and Symmetrical Conflict Styles***

SITUATION	COMPLEMENTARY STYLES	SYMMETRICAL STYLES
Wife is upset because husband is spending little time at home.	Wife complains; husband withdraws, spending even less time at home. (Destructive complementarity)	Wife raises concern clearly and assertively, without aggression. Husband responds by explaining his concerns in the same manner. (Constructive symmetry)
Boss makes fun of employee in front of other workers.	Employee seeks out boss for private conversation, explaining why being the butt of public joking was embarrassing. (Constructive complementarity)	Employee maliciously "jokes" about boss at company party. (Destructive symmetry)
Parents are uncomfortable about teenager's new friends.	Parents express concerns. Teen dismisses them, saying "There's nothing to worry about." (Destructive complementarity)	Teen expresses concern that parents are being too protective. Parents and teen negotiate a mutually agreeable solution. (Constructive symmetry)

the parents and their teenager can understand one another's concerns and possibly find a way to give all three people what they want.

INTIMATE AND AGGRESSIVE STYLES

Another way to look at conflict styles is to examine the interaction between emotional closeness and aggression. The following scheme was originally used to describe communication between couples, but it also works well for other types of relationships.

- *Nonintimate-Aggressive:* Partners dispute issues but without dealing with one another on an emotional level. In some relationships, aggression is expressed directly: "Forget it. I'm not going to another stupid party with your friends. All they do is gossip and eat." In other relationships, indirect aggression is the norm: (*sarcastically*) "Sure, I'd love to go to another party with your friends." Neither of these approaches is satisfying, since there are few rewards to justify the costs of the unpleasantness.
- *Nonintimate-Nonaggressive:* The partners avoid conflicts—and one another—instead of facing issues head-on: "You won't be coming home for the holidays? Oh well, I guess that's OK. . . ." Relationships of this sort can be quite stable, but because this pattern of communication doesn't confront and resolve problems, the vitality and satisfaction can decline over time.
- *Intimate-Aggressive:* This pattern combines aggression and intimacy in a manner that might seem upsetting to outsiders, but it can work well in some relationships. Lovers may fight like cats and dogs but then make up just as intensely. Coworkers might argue about how to get the job done but cherish their association.

- *Intimate-Nonaggressive:* This sort of relationship has a low amount of attacking or blaming. Partners may confront one another directly or indirectly, but one way or another they manage to prevent issues from interfering with their relationship.

The pattern partners choose may reveal a great deal about the kind of relationship they have chosen. Mary Ann Fitzpatrick (1977, 1988; Kelley, 1999) identified three types of couples: Separates, Independents, and Traditionals. (Chapter 12 discusses the three types in more detail.) Further research revealed that partners in each type of relationship approached conflict in a different manner (Fitzpatrick, 1988; Fitzpatrick et al., 1982), most likely because they thought about conflict differently (Gendrin & Werner, 1996). Separates took a nonintimate-nonaggressive approach (and were the least satisfied of all subjects studied). They maintained a neutral emotional climate and kept their discussion of conflict to a minimum. Successful independents were best described as intimate-aggressive. They expressed negative emotions frequently, but also sought and revealed a large amount of personal information. Satisfied traditional couples fit the intimate-nonaggressive pattern, communicating more positive and less negative information than did independents.

Information like this suggests that there's no single "best" relational conflict style (Gottman, 2003). Some families or couples may fight intensely but love one another just as strongly. Others might handle issues more rationally and calmly. Even a nonintimate style can work well when there's no desire to have an interpersonal relationship. For example, you might be willing to accommodate the demands of an eccentric professor for a semester, since rolling with the punches gets you the education you are seeking, without provoking a confrontation that could be upsetting and costly.

CONFLICT RITUALS

When people have been in a relationship for some time, their communication often develops into **conflict rituals**—unacknowledged but very real repeating patterns of interlocking behavior (Wilmot & Hocker, 2007). Consider a few common rituals:

A young child interrupts his parents, demanding to be included in their conversation. At first the parents tell the child to wait, but he whines and cries until the parents find it easier to listen than to ignore the fussing.

FOCUS ON RESEARCH

Ongoing Arguments and Stress

research

Many of the conflict examples in this chapter are about one-time episodes that get resolved in specific ways. Of course, not all conflicts end so neatly. Communication scholars Rachel Malis and Michael Roloff have studied *serial arguing*—repeated argumentative episodes about the same issue—to understand better its effects on the parties involved.

In one study, more than 200 college students described a serial argument they had in a dating relationship. On average, they reported having 11 argument episodes about the same issue with their dating partner. As predicted, serial arguing led to personal and relational stress. Here are some specific findings:

- The most stress-provoking strategy for coping with serial arguing is *resignation*—passively enduring the ongoing argument with no hope for resolving it.
- Better strategies for reducing stress include *selective ignoring* (focusing on positives rather than negatives in the relationship) and *optimistic comparisons* (noting that other couples have worse serial arguments than yours).
- The best stress-reducer for serial arguers is *resolvability*—a belief that progress is being made toward bringing the argument to an end.

Most couples can easily identify at least one serial argument in their relationship. The issue then is not whether serial arguments will occur, but how they're managed.

Malis, R. S., & Roloff, M. E. (2006). Features of serial arguing and coping strategies: Links with stress and well-being. In B. A. LePoire (Ed.), *Applied interpersonal communication matters* (pp. 39–65). New York: Peter Lang.

A couple fights. One partner leaves. The other accepts blame for the problem and begs forgiveness. The first partner returns, and a happy reunion takes place. Soon they fight again.

One friend is unhappy with the other. The unhappy person withdraws until the other asks what's wrong. "Nothing," the first replies. The questioning persists until the problem is finally out in the open. The friends then solve the issue and continue happily until the next problem arises, when the pattern repeats itself.

There's nothing inherently wrong with the interaction in many rituals (Olson, 2002a). Consider the preceding examples. In the first, the child's whining may be the only way he can get the parent's attention. In the second, both partners might use the fighting as a way to blow off steam, and both might find that the joy of a reunion is worth the grief of the separation. The third ritual might work well when one friend is more assertive than the other.

Rituals can cause problems, though, when they become the *only* way relational partners handle their conflicts. As you learned in Chapter 1, competent communicators have a large repertoire of behaviors, and they are able to choose the most effective response for a given situation. Relying on one pattern to handle all conflicts is no more effective than using a screwdriver to handle every home repair, or putting the same seasoning in every dish you cook: What works in one situation isn't likely to succeed in many others. Conflict rituals may be familiar and comfortable, but they aren't the best way to solve the variety of conflicts that are part of any relationship.

Variables in Conflict Styles

By now you can see that every relational system is unique. The communication patterns in one family, business, or classroom are likely to be very different from any other. But along with the differences that arise in individual relationships, there are two powerful variables that affect the way people manage conflict: gender and culture. We will now take a brief look at each of these factors and see how they affect the ways that conflict is managed.

GENDER

Some research suggests that men and women often approach conflicts differently (e.g., Archer, 2002; Gayle et al., 2002). Even in childhood, there is evidence that boys are (on average, of course) more likely to be aggressive, demanding, and competitive, while girls are more cooperative and accommodating. Studies of children from preschool to early adolescence have shown that boys try to get their way by ordering one another around: "Lie down." "Get off my steps." "Gimme your arm." By contrast, girls are more likely to make proposals for action that begin with the word *let's:* "Let's go find some." "Let's ask her if she has any bottles." "Let's move *these* out *first*" (Tannen, 1990). Whereas boys tell each other what role to take in pretend play ("Come on, be a doctor"), girls more commonly ask each other what role they want ("Will you be the patient for a few minutes?") or make a joint proposal ("We can both be doctors"). Furthermore, boys often make demands without offering an explanation ("Look, man, I want the Game Cube right now"). In contrast, girls often give reasons for their suggestions ("We gotta clean 'em first 'cause they got germs").

Adolescent girls use aggression in conflicts, but their methods are usually more indirect than those of boys. Whereas teenage boys often engage in verbal showdowns and may even engage in physical fights,

"Norman won't collaborate."

teenage girls typically use gossip, backbiting, and social exclusion (Hess & Hagan, 2006; Underwood, 2003). This is not to suggest that girls' aggression is any less destructive than boys'. The movie *Mean Girls* (based on Rosalind Wiseman's book *Queen Bees and Wannabes*, 2003) offers a vivid depiction of just how injurious these indirect assaults can be on the self-concepts and relationships of young women.

Gender differences in dealing with conflict often persist into adulthood. Esin Tezer and Ayhan Demir (2001) studied the conflict behaviors late adolescents use with same-sex and opposite-sex peers. They found that compared to females, males use more competing behaviors with same-sex peers and more avoiding behaviors with opposite-sex peers—however, they were also more likely to accommodate with others regardless of their sex. On the other hand, regardless of culture or the sex of the person with whom they are interacting, females are more likely than males to compromise (Holt & DeVore, 2005).

Another survey of college students reinforced stereotypes about the influence of gender in conflicts (Collier, 1991). Regardless of their cultural background, female students described men as being concerned with power and more interested in content than in relational issues. Sentences used to describe male conflict styles included: "The most important thing to males in conflict is their egos," "Men don't worry about feelings," and "Men are more direct." In contrast, women were described as being more concerned with maintaining the relationship during a conflict. Sentences used to describe female conflict styles included: "Women are better listeners," "Women try to solve problems without controlling the other person," and "Females are more concerned with others' feelings."

In contrast with the "Men Are from Mars, Women Are from Venus" view of conflict, another body of research suggests that the differences in how the two sexes handle conflict are rather small, and not at all representative of the stereotypical picture of aggressive men and passive women (Gayle et al., 1998; Samter & Cupach, 1998). Where differences between the sexes do occur, they can sometimes be exactly the opposite of sex-role stereotypes of aggressive men and accommodating women. For example, when the actual conflict behaviors of couples are observed, women turn out to be more assertive than men about expressing their ideas and feelings, and men are more likely to withdraw from discussing issues (Canary et al., 1995).

In other cases, people may *think* that there are greater differences in male and female ways of handling conflicts than actually exist (Allen, 1998). People who assume that men are aggressive and women accommodating may notice behavior that fits these stereotypes ("See how much he bosses her around? A typical man!"). On the other hand, behavior that doesn't fit these preconceived ideas (accommodating men, pushy women) goes unnoticed.

What, then, can we conclude about the influence of gender on conflict? Research has demonstrated that there are, indeed, some small but measurable differences in the two sexes. But, while men and women may have characteristically different conflict styles, the individual style of each communicator is more important than his or her sex in shaping the way he or she handles conflict.

CULTURE

People from most cultures prefer mutually beneficial resolutions to disagreements whenever possible (Cai & Fink, 2002). Nonetheless, the ways in which people communicate during conflicts do vary from one culture to another.

As you read in Chapter 2, the kind of straight-talking, assertive approach that characterizes many North Americans and Western Europeans is not the norm in other parts of the world. Assertiveness that might seem perfectly appropriate to a native of the United States or Canada would be rude and insensitive in many Asian countries (Gudykunst & Ting-Toomey, 1988; Samovar & Porter, 2004). Perhaps not surprisingly, members of individualistic cultures choose competing as a conflict style more than those in collectivistic cultures, whereas members of collectivistic cultures prefer the styles of accommodating, compromising, and problem solving (Holt & DeVore, 2005).

Cultures like Japanese and Chinese value self-restraint, avoid confrontation, and place a premium on preserving and honoring the "face" of the other person. For this reason, what seems like "beating around the bush" to an American would be polite to an Asian. In Japan, for example, even a simple request like "close the door" would be too straightforward (Okabe, 1987). A more indirect statement, such as "It is somewhat cold today," would be more appropriate. To take a more important example, Japanese are reluctant to say "no" to a request. A more likely answer would be "let me think about it for a while," which anyone familiar with Japanese culture would recognize as a refusal.

The Japanese notion of self-restraint is reflected in the important concept of *wa*, or harmony. This aversion to conflict is even manifested in the Japanese legal system. Estimates are that the Japanese only have one lawyer for every 10,000 people, while in the United States, a culture that values assertive behavior, there is one lawyer for every 50 people (Samovar & Porter, 2004).

The same attitude toward conflict prevails in China, where one proverb states, "The first person to raise his voice loses the argument." Among Chinese college students (in both the People's Republic and Taiwan), the three most common methods of persuasion used are "hinting," "setting an example by one's own actions," and "strategically agreeing to whatever pleases others" (Ma & Chuang, 2001). However, young adults in China favor collaborative problem solving more than do their elders, who prefer accommodating styles (Zhang et al., 2005).

It isn't necessary to look at Asia to encounter cultural differences in conflict. The style of some other familiar cultures differs in important ways from the Northern European and North American norm. These cultures see verbal disputes as a form of intimacy and even a game. For example, Americans visiting Greece often think they are witnessing an argument when they are overhearing a friendly conversation (Tannen, 1990). Likewise, both French and Arab men (but not women) find argument stimulating (Copeland & Griggs, 1985). A comparative study of American and Italian nursery school children showed that one of the Italian children's favorite pastimes was a kind of heated debating that Italians call *discussione* but that Americans would regard as arguing. Likewise, research has shown that in the conversations of working-class Jewish speakers of Eastern European origin, arguments are used as a means of being sociable.

Within the United States, the ethnic background of communicators also plays a role in their ideas about conflict. When a group of Mexican American and European American college students were asked about their views regarding conflict, some important differences emerged (Collier, 1991). For example, European Americans seem more willing to accept conflict as a natural part of relationships, while Mexican Americans describe the short- and long-term dangers of disagreeing. European Americans' willingness to experience conflicts may be part of their individualistic, low-context communication style of speaking directly and avoiding uncertainty. It's not surprising that people from cultures that emphasize harmony among people with close relationships tend to handle conflicts in less direct ways. With differences like these, it's easy to imagine how two friends, lovers, or fellow workers from different cultural backgrounds might have trouble finding a conflict style that is comfortable for both of them.

Despite these differences, it's important to realize that culture isn't the only factor that influences the way people think about conflict or how they behave when they disagree. Some research (e.g., Beatty & McCroskey, 1997) suggests that our approach to conflict may be part of our biological makeup. Furthermore, scholarship suggests a person's self-concept is more powerful than his or her culture in determining conflict style (Oetzel et al., 2001; Ting-Tomey et al., 2001). For example, African Americans, Asian Americans, European Americans, and Latin Americans who view themselves as mostly independent of others are likely to use a direct, solution-oriented conflict style, regard-

Culture and Conflict: *The Joy Luck Club*

The Joy Luck Club is not one story but many, told in film through flashbacks, narratives, and gripping portrayals. The primary stories involve four Chinese women and their daughters. The mothers all flee difficult situations in China to start new lives in the United States, where they raise their daughters with a mixture of Chinese and American styles. Many of the movie's conflicts are rooted in cultural value clashes.

The mothers were raised in the high-context, collectivistic environment of China, where open conflict is discouraged and individual needs (particularly of women) are submerged for the larger good. To achieve their goals, the mothers use a variety of indirect and passive-aggressive methods. Their daughters, raised in the United States, adopt a more low-context, direct form of communication. They are also more assertive and aggressive in their conflict styles, particularly when dealing with their mothers.

The daughters have a harder time dealing with the men in their lives. For example, Rose (Rosalind Chao) begins her relationship with Ted (Andrew McCarthy) very assertively, telling him candidly what she thinks and how she feels about him (he is charmed by her directness). They marry and she becomes an accommodator, constantly submerging her needs for his. Rather than liking Rose's accommodating, Ted comes to despise it. He exhorts her to be more assertive: "Once in awhile, I would like to hear what you want. I'd like to hear your voice, even if we disagree." He then suggests that they separate.

Several of the stories have happy endings. In Rose's case, she fights for her rights with Ted—and ultimately they reconcile. In fact, each woman in the movie takes a stand on an important issue in her life, and most of the outcomes are positive.

The women in *The Joy Luck Club* learn to both embrace and reject aspects of their cultural heritage as they attempt to manage their conflicts effectively.

less of their cultural heritage. Those who see themselves as mostly interdependent are likely to use a style that avoids direct confrontation. And those who see themselves as both independent and interdependent are likely to have the widest variety of conflict behaviors on which to draw.

Other personality variables play an important role in predicting a person's conflict style. Valerie Wood and Paul Bell (2008) found that agreeable communicators tend to use a collaborative conflict style, while those who are both agreeable and introverted tend to accommodate. Communicators who are introverted tend to avoid conflict, while those who are extroverted and disagreeable tend to use a competitive conflict style.

Beyond individual temperament and self-concept, the environment in which we are raised can shape the way we approach conflict. Parental conflict style plays a role. Some research has revealed a significant relationship between the way a mother handles conflict and the style used by her adult children (Martin et al., 1997). Elizabeth Turner (2008) found that each parent's conflict style influenced the children's conflict behavior. For example, when fathers use a competitive conflict style, their children are more likely to use destructive conflict strategies, although they tend to engage in fewer conflicts.

Along with family influences, the "culture" of each relationship can shape how we behave (Messman & Canary, 1998). You might handle disagreements calmly in a job where rationality and civility are the norm, but shriek like a banshee at home if that's the way you and a relational partner handle disputes.

Conflict Management in Practice

The collaborative conflict management style described earlier in this chapter may be unfamiliar to those who are used to handling conflict in other ways. As a result, collaboration sometimes requires more specific guidelines to put into practice. Win-win problem solving works best when it follows a seven-step approach that is based on plans developed by Deborah Weider-Hatfield (1981) and Ellen Raider and her colleagues (2006). Notice how many of the skills that have been discussed throughout this book are incorporated in this process.

1. Define your needs. Begin by deciding what you want or need. Sometimes the answer is obvious, as in our earlier example of the neighbor whose loud music kept others awake. In other instances, however, the apparent problem masks a more fundamental one. Consider an example: After dating for a few months, Elizabeth started to call Jim after they parted for the evening—a "goodnight call." Although the calling was fine with Jim at the beginning, he began to find it irritating after several weeks.

At first, Jim thought his aggravation focused on the nuisance of talking late at night when he was ready for sleep. More self-examination showed that his irritation centered on the relational message he thought Elizabeth's calls implied: that she was either snooping on Jim or was so insecure she needed constant assurances of his love. Once Jim recognized the true sources of his irritation, his needs became clear: (1) to have Elizabeth's trust and (2) to be free of her insecurities.

Because your needs won't always be clear, it's often necessary to think about a problem alone, before approaching the other person involved. Talking to a third person can sometimes help you sort out your thoughts. In either case, you should explore both the apparent content of your dissatisfaction and the relational issues that may lurk behind it.

REFLECTION

Win-Win Solution Reduces Friction

After 4 months of living together, my two neat roommates were fed up with cleaning up after me and the other messy member of our little household, and the two of us were tired of hearing the neat freaks complain about our habits.

Last week we had a meeting (again) about the dishes and glasses. But this time we didn't argue about who was right or wrong. Instead, we looked for a win-win solution. And once we started looking, we found it: Each of us gets his own dishes, glasses, and silverware—two of each item per person. We are responsible for cleaning only our own things. Now if you look in our kitchen cabinets, you only find eight glasses, eight plates, and so on. There isn't enough stuff to make a mess, and each of us has to wash his own things if he wants to eat. Everybody is happy. Some people might think our solution is silly, but it has certainly worked well for us—and that's all that matters.

2. Share your needs with the other person. Once you've defined your needs, it's time to share them with your partner. Two guidelines are important here: First, be sure to choose a time and place that is suitable. Unloading on a tired or busy partner lowers the odds that your concerns will be well received. Likewise, be sure you are at your best: Don't bring an issue up when your anger may cause you to say things you'll later regret, when your discouragement blows the problem out of proportion, or when you're distracted by other business. Making a date to discuss the problem—after dinner, over a cup of coffee, or even a day in advance—often can boost the odds of a successful outcome.

The second guideline for sharing a problem is to use the descriptive "I" language outlined in Chapter 5. Rather than implying blame, messages worded in this way convey how your partner's behavior affects you. Notice how Jim's use of the assertive message format conveys a descriptive, nonjudgmental attitude as he shares his concerns with Elizabeth: "When you call me after every date [sense data], I begin to wonder whether you're checking up on me [interpretation of Elizabeth's behavior]. I've also started to think that you're feeling insecure about whether I care about you and that you need lots of reassurance [more interpretation]. I'm starting to feel closed in by the calls [feeling], and I feel myself pulling back from you [consequence]. I don't like the way we're headed, and I don't think it's necessary. I'd like to know whether you are feeling insecure and to find a way that we can feel sure about each other's feelings without needing so much reassurance [intentions]."

In a tense situation, it may not be easy to start sharing your needs. Raider et al. (2006) recommend beginning with what they call *ritual sharing*, which is preliminary, casual conversation. The goal is to build rapport and establish common ground and, perhaps, to pick up information.

3. Listen to the other person's needs. Once your own wants and needs are clear, it's time to find out what the other person wants and needs. (Now the listening skills described in Chapter 7 and the supportive behaviors described in Chapter 10 become most important.) When Jim began to talk to Elizabeth about her telephoning, he learned some interesting things. In his haste to hang up the phone the first few times she called, he had given her the impression that he didn't care about her once the date was over. Feeling insecure about his love, she called as a way of getting attention and expressions of love from him.

Once Jim realized this fact, it became clear that he needed to find a solution that would leave Elizabeth feeling secure and at the same time relieve him of feeling pressured.

Arriving at a shared definition of the problem requires skills associated with creating a supportive and confirming climate. The ability to be nonjudgmental, descriptive, and empathic is an important, support-producing skill. Both Jim and Elizabeth needed to engage in paraphrasing to discover all the details of the conflict.

When they're really communicating effectively, partners can help each other clarify what they're seeking. Truly believing that their happiness depends on each other's satisfaction, they actively try to analyze what obstacles need to be overcome.

4. Generate possible solutions. In the next step, the partners try to think of as many ways to satisfy both of their needs as possible. They can best do so by "brainstorming"—inventing as many potential solutions as they can. The key to success in brainstorming is to seek quantity without worrying about quality. The rule is to prohibit criticism of all ideas, no matter how outlandish they may sound. An idea that seems farfetched can sometimes lead to a more workable one. Another rule of brainstorming is that ideas aren't personal property. If one person makes a suggestion, the other should feel free to suggest another solution that builds upon or modifies the original one. The original suggestion and its offshoots are all potential solutions that will be considered later. Once partners get over their possessiveness about ideas, the level of defensiveness drops and both people can work together to find the best solution without worrying about whose idea it is.

All of the supportive and confirming behaviors discussed in Chapter 10 are important during this step. However, two of them stand out as crucial: the ability to communicate provisionalism rather than certainty, and the ability to refrain from premature evaluations of any solution. The aim of this step is to generate *all* the possible solutions—whether they are immediately reasonable or not. By the partners' behaving provisionally and avoiding any evaluation until all the solutions are generated, creative and spontaneous behavior is encouraged. The result is a long list of solutions that most likely contains the best solution, one that might not have been expressed if the communication climate were defensive.

Jim and Elizabeth used brainstorming to generate solutions to their telephone problem. Their list consisted of continuing the calling but limiting the time spent on the phone, limiting the calls to a "once in a while" basis, Elizabeth's keeping a journal that could serve as a substitute for calling, Jim's calling Elizabeth on a "once in a while" basis, cutting out all calling, moving in together to eliminate the necessity for calling, getting married, and breaking up. Although some of these solutions were clearly unacceptable to both partners, they listed all the ideas they could think of, preparing themselves for the next step in win-win problem solving.

5. Evaluate the possible solutions and choose the best one. The time to evaluate the solutions is after they all have been generated, after the partners feel they have exhausted all the possibilities. In this step, the possible solutions generated during the previous step are evaluated for their ability to satisfy everyone's important goals. How does each solution stand up against the individual and mutual goals? Which solution satisfies the most goals? Partners need to work cooperatively in examining each solution and in finally selecting the best one.

It is important during this step to react spontaneously rather than strategically. Selecting a particular solution because the other person finds it satisfactory (an accommodation strategy), while seemingly a "nice" thing to do, is as manipulative a strategy as getting the other person to accept a solution satisfactory only to you (a win-lose strategy). Respond as you feel as solutions are evaluated, and encourage your partner to do the same. Any solution agreed upon as "best" has little chance of satisfying both partners' needs if it was strategically manipulated to the top of the list.

The solution Elizabeth and Jim selected as satisfying her need to feel secure, his need to be undisturbed before turning in, and their mutual goal of maintaining their relationship at a highly intimate level was to limit both the frequency and length of the calls. Also, Jim agreed to share in the calling.

6. Implement the solution. Now the time comes to try out the idea selected to see if it does, indeed, satisfy everyone's needs. The key questions to answer are *who* does *what* to *whom,* and *when*?

Before Jim and Elizabeth tried out their solution, they went over the agreement to make sure it was clear. This step proved to be important, for a potential misunderstanding existed. When will the solution be implemented? Should Elizabeth wait a few weeks before calling? Should Jim begin the calling? They agreed that Jim would call after their next date.

Another problem concerned their different definitions of length. How long is too long? They decided that more than a few minutes would be too long.

The solution was implemented after they discussed the solution and came to mutual agreement about its particulars. This process may seem awkward and time-consuming, but both Elizabeth and Jim decided that without a clear understanding of the solution, they were opening the door to future conflicts.

Interestingly, the discussion concerning their mutual needs and how the solution satisfied them was an important part of their relationship's development. Jim learned that Elizabeth did, sometimes, feel insecure about his love; Elizabeth learned that Jim needed time to himself and that this need did not reflect on his love for her. Soon after implementing the solution, they found that the problem ceased to exist. Jim no longer felt the calls were invading his privacy, and Elizabeth, after talks with Jim, felt more secure about his love.

7. Follow up the solution. To stop after selecting and implementing a particular solution assumes any solution is forever, that time does not change things, that people remain constant, and that events never alter circumstances.

Of course, this assumption is not the case: As people and circumstances change, a particular solution may lose or increase its effectiveness. Regardless, a follow-up evaluation needs to take place.

After you've tested your solution for a short time, it's a good idea to plan a meeting to talk about how things are going. You may find that you need to make some changes or even rethink the whole problem.

Reviewing the effects of your solution does not mean that something is wrong and must be corrected. Indeed, everything may point to the conclusion that the solution is still working to satisfy your needs and the mutually shared goal, and that the mutually shared goal is still important to both of you.

It is important at this stage in the win-win problem-solving process to be honest with yourself as well as with the other person. It may be difficult for you to say "We need to talk about this again," yet it could be essential if the problem is to remain resolved. Planning a follow-up talk when the solution is first implemented is important.

Elizabeth and Jim decided to wait one month before discussing the effects of their solution. Their talk was short, because both felt the problem no longer existed. Also, their discussions helped their relationship grow: They learned more about each other, felt closer, and developed a way to handle their conflicts constructively.

Summary

Despite wishes and cultural myths to the contrary, conflict is a natural and unavoidable part of any relationship. Since conflict can't be escaped, the challenge is how to deal with it effectively so that it strengthens a relationship rather than weakens it.

All conflicts possess the same characteristics: expressed struggle, perceived incompatible goals, perceived scarce resources, interdependence, and inevitability. Functional conflicts cope with these characteristics in very different ways from dysfunctional ones. Partners view one another as an integrated unit and not as opponents. They treat one another with respect, strive to cooperate instead of compete, and work to de-escalate the intensity of their conflict. They focus on rather than avoid the issues in dispute and seek positive, long-term solutions that meet each other's needs.

Communicators can respond to conflicts in a variety of ways: avoidance, accommodation, competition, compromise, or collaboration. Each of these approaches can be justified in certain circumstances. The way a conflict is handled isn't always the choice of a single person, since the interact ants influence one another as they develop a relational conflict style. This style is also influenced by the partners' genders and the influences of their cultural backgrounds.

In most circumstances a collaborative, win-win outcome is the ideal, and it can be achieved by following the guidelines outlined in the last section of this chapter.

Activities

1. Invitation to Insight

Even the best relationships have conflicts. Using the characteristics on pages 350–353, describe at least five conflicts in one of your important relationships. Then answer the following questions:

a. Which conflicts involve primarily content issues? Which involve primarily relational issues?
b. Which conflicts were one-time affairs, and which recur?

2. Invitation to Insight

From your recent experiences recall two conflict incidents, one functional and one dysfunctional. Then answer the following questions:

a. What distinguished these two conflicts?
b. What were the consequences of each?
c. How might the dysfunctional conflict have turned out differently if it had been handled in a more functional manner?
d. How could you have communicated differently to make the dysfunctional conflict more functional?

3. Skill Builder

Review the hypothetical conflict between Chris and Pat (p. 358) and come up with examples (other than the ones mentioned in the text) of how they might use each of these conflict styles in their situation:

a. Avoidance
b. Accommodation
c. Competition
d. Compromise
e. Collaboration

In particular, see if you can come up with several collaborative, win-win solutions to their problem.

4. Invitation to Insight

Interview someone who knows you well. Ask your informant which personal conflict styles (avoidance, accommodation, etc.) you use most often and the effect each of these styles has on your relationship with this person. Based on your findings, discuss whether different behavior might produce more productive results.

5. Invitation to Insight

This activity will be most productive if you consult with several people with whom you share an interpersonal relationship as you answer the following questions:

a. Is your relational style of handling conflict complementary, symmetrical, or parallel? What are the consequences of this style?
b. What combination of intimacy and aggressiveness characterizes your approach to conflict? Are you satisfied with this approach?

c. What conflict rituals do you follow in this relationship? Are these rituals functional or dysfunctional? What might be better alternatives?

6. Skill Builder

To explore how the win-win approach might work in your life, try one of the following alternatives:

a. Use the steps on pages 377–381 to describe how you could manage a conflict by following the win-win approach. How could you try this approach in your personal life? What difference might such an approach make?
b. Try the win-win approach with a relational partner. What parts prove most helpful? Which are most difficult? How can you improve your relationship by using some or all of the win-win approach in future conflicts?

CHAPTER

12 Communication in Families and at Work

CHAPTER OUTLINE

After studying the material in this chapter . . .

YOU SHOULD UNDERSTAND:

1. The defining characteristics of a family and the elements of family communication.
2. The nature of cohesion, adaptability, boundaries, and conflict in functional and dysfunctional families.
3. The value of personal networking and interviewing skills in career advancement.
4. Various communication types and channels in organizations, and how they operate within personal relationships and organizational cultures.
5. The types of power individual group members can possess.

YOU SHOULD BE ABLE TO:

1. Describe the defining characteristics of families to which you belong and the roles, narratives, models, and rules of your family systems.
2. Identify your family's cohesion, adaptability, boundaries, and conflict management styles.
3. Describe how you can cultivate and use personal networks to enhance your career success.
4. Plan, participate in, and follow up on an employment interview in a way that creates a positive relationship with a potential employer.
5. Define the type of interaction (face-to-face or mediated) that can maximize your on-the-job effectiveness.
6. Diagnose the culture of an organization and determine how well it fits with your personal communication style.
7. Identify the types of power you possess in a given group and describe how you can use them to help the group operate effectively.

KEY TERMS

- Boundaries (396)
- Chaotic family (398)
- Conformity orientation (395)
- Conversation orientation (395)
- Designated leader (413)
- Disengaged family (396)
- Downward communication (408)
- Enmeshed family (396)
- Family (386)
- Family of origin (392)
- Formal communication (408)
- Horizontal communication (408)
- Informal communication (409)
- Organizational cultures (413)
- Networking (401)
- Power (414)
- Rigid family (398)
- System (390)
- Upward communication (408)
- Virtual teams (410t)

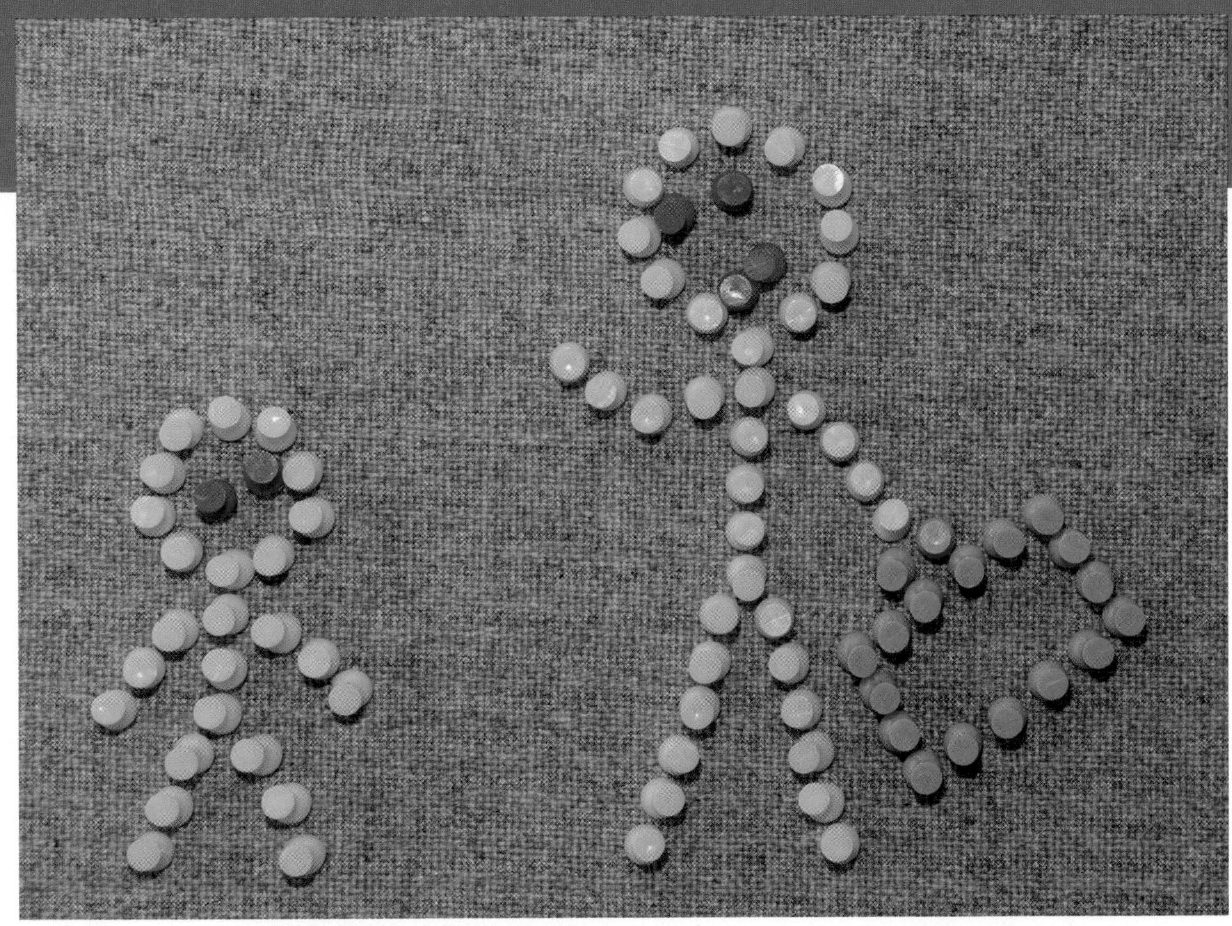

Many of the examples throughout this book are taken from two settings: the family and the workplace. This is because family and work relationships, no matter where they fall on the impersonal-interpersonal spectrum, no matter whether they provide our greatest happiness or misery, are among the most important influences on how we communicate.

Communication in Families

WHAT IS A FAMILY?

A few generations ago, this was an easy question for most people to answer. Common notions of a family in the Western world typically stressed shared residence, reproduction or adoption of children by different-sexed adults, and a "socially approved sexual relationship" (Murdock, 1965, p. 1). In recent years, social scientists, lawyers, judges, and theologians have grappled with much broader definitions as they considered questions such as deciding who the parents are when there is an egg or sperm donor, determining the rights of adoptive parents and adopted children, and deciding whether homosexual couples can adopt a child.

After reviewing various definitions over the last century, Kathleen Galvin and her colleagues (2007) define **family** broadly enough to include many types of relationships: A family is a system with two or more interdependent people who have a common history and a present reality, and who expect to influence each other in the future. This definition includes the following different family arrangements:

- Two parents (of different or same sex) and their children (biological or adopted)
- A couple (married or not, heterosexual or not) who live together over time and have a committed, binding relationship
- A single parent (married, never married, or divorced) who lives with his or her biological or adopted child

"I guess we'd be considered a family. We're living together, we love each other, and we haven't eaten the children yet."

- Two adults and their children, all, some, or none of whom may be the offspring from their union
- Groups of relatives who have blood or legal ties and who live with or near each other.

Whether or not you consider all of these arrangements as legitimate families, you'll soon see that they all share important characteristics that make communication among members different from that in other sorts of relationships.

TYPES OF FAMILY COMMUNICATION

Within families, communications between different family members each have their own characteristics. In this section we'll take a brief look at some of these relationships.

Spouses/Partners The way spouses or partners communicate with one another reflects both their personal style and their thinking about what their relationship should be like. There are many ways to examine communication patterns between partners. We will describe two of them.

Perhaps the best-known typology of couples' communication was developed by Mary Ann Fitzpatrick (1988), who identified three basic couple types: *Independents, Separates,* and *Traditionals.*

Traditional couples strive to maintain stability by upholding a conventional belief system that values traditional sex roles, a great degree of interdependence (i.e., little psychological or physical distance), and an inclination to avoid conflict. Compared with other couple types, Traditionals tend to have high marital satisfaction (the highest of all the couple types) and a moderately high expression of affection.

Independent couples avoid adhering to traditional sex roles. While they may be physically close, they maintain their psychological distance. Unlike Traditionals, they don't avoid conflict. Independent couples tend to have low marital satisfaction and a low expression of affection.

Separate couples place a higher value on their individual freedom than on their relationship. They are more conflict-avoidant than Independents, have greater space needs, and share less. Like Independent couples, Separates tend to have low expression of affection and marital satisfaction.

Fitzpatrick found that 20 percent of couples are Traditionals, 17 percent are Separates, and 22 percent are Independents. The remaining 40 percent are mixed couples in which each partner favors a different style: Traditional-Independent, Independent-Separate, and so on. Couples with two traditional partners tend to have the highest marital satisfaction, perhaps because they have greater fulfillment of their expectations than do other couple types (Kelley, 1999). Mixed couples tend to have a moderately high expression of affection and moderately high marital satisfaction—higher than Independents and Separates, but lower than Traditionals. Their beliefs regarding sex roles and the extent to which they are likely to be close to each other depend on the type of mixed relationship they have. For example, couples consisting of Separate and Traditional partners tend to have moderately high marital satisfaction and closeness, and a high expression of affection, whereas other mixed types tend to be less close and have a lower expression of affection.

Gender roles offer another way to look at communication between partners. As Chapter 4 explained, gender-related communication can be broken into four categories: Stereotypically *masculine* communication emphasizes instrumental, task-related topics and is low in expressive, emotional content. By contrast, stereotypically *feminine* communication is high in expressiveness and low in instrumentality. *Androgynous* communication is high in both emotional and instrumental messages, while *undifferentiated* communication is low in both instrumentality and expressiveness.

A three-year study of almost 200 couples (married an average of 17 years) revealed that communication in about 38 percent of the relationships fit stereotypical gender roles: Wives focused more on emotional expressiveness, while husbands' messages were typically focused on task-related, instrumental topics (Helms, 2006). Communication among the remaining couples didn't follow gender stereotypes. About 37 percent of all the couples studied fit the undifferentiated category—low in both content and emotional expression. About a quarter of the sample fit the androgynous pattern, with communication high in both instrumentality and expressivity.

Is there a relationship between gender-type communication and the satisfaction of a couple? The Helms research suggests the answer is "yes." Gender-typed pairs reported lower levels of satisfaction than androgynous pairs, with the lowest level of love and satisfaction reported for stereotypically feminine wives married to extremely masculine husbands.

Although androgynous couples fared best overall, the researchers also found that similarity was important. (Recall the discussion in Chapter 9 about similarity as a basis for attraction.) Couples with similar expressive and instrumental scores, such as found in undifferentiated couples, were about as satisfied as androgynous couples. By contrast, spouses with different expressive scores in a gender-typed couple feel less in love and less understood and have overall lower marital quality.

Parent-Child Family communication becomes more complex—and arguably more interesting and challenging—when children arrive on the scene. One study shows that the number of daily tasks in the average household jumps from 6 to 36 after the birth of a child (Huston & Vangelisti, 1995). In other words, children give parents much more to do and to talk about. Describing parent-child communication in detail would take an entire book, but in the following pages we'll preview some especially important dimensions.

PATTERNS OF INTERACTION With the arrival of the first child, communication within the family becomes more complicated. Along with being a threesome, the members can form three very different dyads: Parent A and Parent B, Parent A and the child, and Parent B and the child. It's easy to see how any or all of these dyads can form coalitions that both enrich and complicate family communication.

The combinations are even more numerous when more children come along, and they can grow even more complex in nontraditional families (McBride, 2007; Murray, 2002). Consider a few examples: If a single parent is dating, how does that affect the way parent and child communicate? How does the parent's dating partner communicate with the child? In *blended families* (in which people who marry have children from a prior marriage), how do siblings who are blood-related interact with siblings who are not? How does age affect interaction, given that the family may now have children who are the same age? Do the parents interact with their blood-related children differently than with the other children? And what happens to family interaction when the parents in the blended family have a child of their own and a child who is blood-related to both of them?

MANAGING THE CONNECTION-AUTONOMY DIALECTIC In Chapter 9 you read about the connection-autonomy dialectic, in which we struggle in every important relationship to meet the incompatible goals of closeness on one hand and independence on the other.

In his book *Intimate Behavior,* Desmond Morris suggests that each of us repeatedly goes through three stages: "Hold me tight," "Put me down," and "Leave me alone" (Morris, 1973). This cycle becomes apparent in the first years of life, when children move from the "hold me tight" phase that characterizes infancy into a new "put me down" stage of exploring the world by crawling, walking, touching, and tasting. This move for independence isn't all in one direction: The same 3-year-old who insists "I can do it myself" in August may cling to parents on the first day of preschool in September.

As children grow into adolescents, the "leave me alone" orientation becomes apparent. Teenagers who used to happily spend time with their parents now may groan at the thought of a family vacation, or even the notion of sitting down at the dinner table each evening. More time is spent alone or with friends. Often, answering the question "Who am I?" requires challenging family rules and beliefs, establishing powerful nonfamily relationships, and weakening family bonds. Through conflict, hopefully, an answer emerges; then, the adolescent can turn around and reestablish good relationships with family members.

Families who are most successful at negotiating this difficult period tend to be those with high flexibility who, for example, can change how they discipline and how they determine family roles. Adolescents are most likely to be healthy and well-adjusted when rules and roles can be discussed adult-to-adult with their parents, when they can explore alternative identities without excessive criticism, when their caring family relationships do not give way to conflict and abuse, and when they are encouraged to take responsibility for their lives. "The quality of the communication between parents and adolescents is a critical feature of all these tasks" (Noller, 1995, p. 106).

In families in the United States, it is common for children to leave the family—to be "launched"—when they are in their late teens or early 20s. Communication between parent and adolescent changes as the family adjusts to the dramatic alteration in family life. During this stage, the launched member needs to consider how to stay connected to the family: for example, how often to call home, whether to go home or not during vacations, and how to maintain open lines of communication with both parents.

With the launching of one of the children in the family, there are tasks for those "left behind." For example, the parents need to renegotiate their coupleness, and both the parents and the remaining children need to negotiate who takes on the roles filled by the launched family member. (If the launched member helped resolve conflicts among other people in the family, how will that happen now?)

Finally, communication between elderly parents and their adult children provides its own set of challenges. For example, more parent-child contact is likely when the child is a daughter, who often has a partner and children that also have a claim on her time and energy. In many families, interaction comes full circle, as the children now provide for their frail, elderly parents, with the care they once received, while simultaneously meeting the obligations of their jobs and their own immediate families (Kees et al., 2007; Merrill, 1997).

Siblings Like couples, siblings have identifiable communication strategies for maintaining their relationship. One study (Myers & Weber, 2004) revealed several categories of behaviors including *confirmation* (see Chapter 10 of this book); *humor*; *social support*, and *escape.* Sibling intimacy begins in early childhood, and the more positive the childhood, the closer siblings feel—although siblings generally remain involved with each other even if their early relationship was marked by family conflict.

Sibling relationships may be complex, but three dimensions of interaction explain a great deal of sibling-to-sibling communication: affection, hostility, and rivalry (Myers & Bryant, 2008; Tseung & Schott, 2004). Clare Stocker and Susan McHale (1992) found that siblings' indications of affection were positively related: If one had a great deal of affection for the other, the odds are the other returned the same feelings. Unlike affection, however, rivalry and hostility were unrelated to each other—one could be hostile or consider the other a rival, and the feelings may not be reciprocated. Interestingly, sibling relationships in a single-parent family—after separation and divorce—are more likely to be higher in both affection *and* hostility than in two-parent families (Noller, 2005).

Think about your interaction with your siblings over the years and you can probably identify many roles you played in each others' lives: playmate, confidant, friend, counselor, role model, and perhaps adversary. Research shows that sibling relationships can offer vital support throughout our lives (Goetting, 1986; Rittenour et al., 2007), and thus it is important to maintain them through behaviors such as sharing tasks, expressing positivity, and offering assurances (Myers, 2003). Another way older siblings can nurture their relationships is by talking about their family: reminiscing about their childhood, crazy family events, and wild relatives. Sharing these stories holds the siblings together, as well as helps them clarify family events and validate their feelings and life choices (McGoldrick et al., 1999).

ELEMENTS OF FAMILY COMMUNICATION

Whatever form families take, the communication that occurs within them shares some important characteristics, which we will examine now.

Families as Communication Systems Every family has its own unique ways of communicating. Despite these differences, all families are **systems** whose members interact with one another to form a whole. Families, like all systems, possess a number of characteristics that shape the way members communicate (Galvin et al., 2006; Lerner et al., 2002).

FAMILY MEMBERS ARE INTERDEPENDENT If you touch one piece of a mobile, all the other parts will move in response. In the same way, one family member's feelings and behaviors affect all the other members. If, for example, one family member leaves home to marry, or a parent loses a job, or two brothers get angry with each other and decide to stop talking, or a member wins the lottery, the system is no longer the same. Each event is a reaction to the family's history, and each event shapes future interaction.

A FAMILY IS MORE THAN THE SUM OF ITS PARTS Even if you knew each member of a family separately, you still wouldn't know the family in its entirety. This means that, to understand a family, you must see it as a whole.

FAMILIES HAVE SYSTEMS WITHIN THE LARGER SYSTEM Like boxes within boxes, families have subsystems (systems within the family). For example, a traditional family of four can have six communication subsystems with two people: mother and father, mother and son, mother and daughter, father and son, father and daughter, and daughter and son. If you add three-person subsystems to these six (e.g., mother, father, and daughter), the number of combinations is even greater. The nuclear family itself is a subsystem of larger suprasystems (systems of which the family is a part) that include aunts and uncles, cousins, grandparents, in-laws, and so on.

FAMILY SYSTEMS ARE AFFECTED BY THEIR ENVIRONMENT As "open systems," families are influenced by the world in which they are situated. Some environmental influences are personal. If, for example, one member has a bad (or good) day at work or school, her experiences will probably shape the way she interacts at home. Other environmental influences involve social forces. For example, a family that wants to maintain traditional values will be challenged by media images that present very different depictions of how to behave.

A Unique Family System: *Little Miss Sunshine*

At first glance, the Hoovers appear to be a dysfunctional family. Dad Richard (Greg Kinnear) is a motivational speaker who spouts clichés about success, although he can't get any work. Teenage brother Dwayne (Paul Dana) hasn't spoken a word in nine months. Grandpa Edwin (Alan Arkin) has a fondness for drugs. Suicidal Uncle Frank (Steve Carell) is nursing the pain of being spurned by his former boyfriend. Even the stalwart mom Sheryl (Toni Collette) has her quirks. Given these idiosyncrasies, it's no surprise that the Hoovers experience many ups and downs on their road trip to deliver loveable 7-year-old Olive (Abigail Breslin) to the "Little Miss Sunshine" beauty competition in California.

For all their foibles, the Hoovers exhibit the qualities of a family system. Within the larger family, subsystems exist: Olive and her grandfather, father Richard and mother Sheryl, and Dwayne and Frank. The Hoovers' fate is linked to the outside environment: the market for motivational speakers and the craziness of the beauty pageant system, for example. Perhaps most importantly, the Hoovers are interdependent: Each member's life is affected by the deeds of the others.

The Hoover's ramshackle Volkswagen van serves as a humorous metaphor for the family. It isn't pretty, and it's full of malfunctioning parts; but it goes to new places due to the unique contributions of every family member.

REFLECTION

Family Roles Resist Change

Growing up, my older brother was always the smart, serious kid who had his life planned out for the next 50 years. I, on the other hand, was the funny one who never really cared about grades or planned for the future.

During my freshman year at college, I got really involved in my studies and became much more responsible. I was really proud of the changes I'd made in my life. When I came home for Thanksgiving break I was excited to show my family how much I had matured.

However, the moment we were all together my parents started asking my brother about stock investments. They only asked me whether I was having fun at parties and whether or not I'd spent all of my money at the mall.

I was very upset they didn't see the person I had become. When I asked my family why they didn't ask me about serious stuff, they said, "That's just not who you are." I guess old patterns don't change easily.

Roles Although they are rarely discussed, the roles family members play shape the way members communicate. The most obvious roles are based on *kinship*: father, sister, uncle, cousin, and so on. Various cultures—and even families within them—may have different notions of what each kinship role means. Along with kinship roles, *functional roles* dictate who does what within a family: income earner, chore-performer, child care provider, and so on. *Social roles* are less obvious, but they play an equally important role in managing relationships: harmonizer, problem solver, tension reliever, helpless victim, and so on.

A bit of reflection may reveal some of the roles in your family. Perhaps one child is the athletic one, while another is the academic star. One parent may be the emotional person, while the other is the voice of reason. One sibling may be responsible, while another may be the one with a reputation for messing up. (See the Reflection on this page for an example.)

Regardless of the particulars, one of the most powerful ways that role expectations are conveyed is through communication (Whitchurch & Dickson, 1999). We learn what others expect of us by receiving messages from others—both within our family and beyond. And we carve out our own identity through our own words and actions. As with every aspect of relationships, meanings are negotiated through communication—and often through narratives, as we'll now discuss.

Family Narratives Chapter 4 described how shared narratives provide a story line that keeps relationships operating harmoniously. Narratives are especially important in families, where they serve a variety of functions (Galvin et al., 2007), for example, reaffirming the family's identity by reinforcing shared goals, teaching moral values, and stressing family concerns. The Focus on Research box on page 393 describes the most common kinds of family narratives. Family stories connect the generations, as when grandparents tell grandchildren stories about the family's history. Stories, too, are often funny and fun to tell, giving family members a chance to laugh together.

Narratives may reflect a family's view of how members relate to one another: "We help each other a lot" or "We are proud of our heritage." Others reflect values about how to operate in the world: "It's impossible to be successful without a good education," or "It's our responsibility to help others less fortunate than ourselves." Even dysfunctional families can be united by a shared narrative: "What a hopeless bunch! We can never get along." With a bit of thought, you can probably come up with several phrases that capture your family's narratives.

Models for Other Relationships Experiences in our **family of origin**—the family in which we grow up—shape the way we communicate throughout life. They teach us important lessons—sometimes positive, sometimes negative—about future relationships. Perhaps most important, families of origin provide the primary model for how we will create our own families. Should family members share personal information or keep it to themselves? How is power distributed among the members? How much time should members spend together and apart? How are conflict and closeness managed among family members? We form our answers to these questions in large measure by observing our family of origin (Huang, 1999; VanLear, 1992). For example, Sarah Whitton and her colleagues (2008) found that levels of both hostility and positive engagement expressed by parents and adolescents during family interactions when the child is 14 are linked with levels of hostility and positive engagement expressed by offspring and their spouses during marital interactions 17 years later.

Unfortunately, some types of family dysfunction are passed from one generation to another. Adolescents in homes where there is spousal abuse, for example, are particularly at risk of being physically abused themselves (Tajima, 2002), and a son's exposure to parental physical and/or verbal aggression is a good predictor of his perpetrating violence on a female partner (Schumacher et al., 2001; Shook et al., 2000).

Along with our personal experiences, each culture's model for appropriate family interaction shapes our notion of how to communicate (Hines et al., 1999; Sherman & Dumlao, 2008). In the dominant culture of North America, for example, children often have an image of their family that describes emotional support and loyalty coming from a limited number of people; in general, the family is isolated from other families (Moghaddam et al., 1993). In these types of families

FOCUS ON RESEARCH

Family Stories: Constructing a Collective Identity through Communication

Think of a familiar story about your family—one of the tales that you and yours have told over and over. What does that narrative reveal about your family? Communication researcher Jody Koenig Kellas asked 58 families to tell her their stories. An analysis of those narratives offered insights into each family's communication patterns, sense of identity, and relational satisfaction.

Kellas had each family select a story from its history that best captured what that family was all about. She then asked each family to tell her its chosen story, with all members participating in recounting the tale. Some of the stories were about family accomplishments and togetherness. Others were about fun and mischief. More serious stories focused on family traditions and culture and even on feelings of separation and stress.

In addition to analyzing the stories, Kellas ran several surveys with the families and found some interesting correlations. For instance, families who told stories about their accomplishments scored significantly higher in successful functioning and cohesion than families who told stories about stressful events. The ways in which the families told their stories was also revealing: Those who were most engaged in storytelling, turn-taking, and use of "we" language had the highest levels of family satisfaction.

The next time you're telling stories with family members, be mindful that you are doing much more than sharing recollections: The tales you tell both reflect and construct who you are as a family.

Kellas, J. K. (2005). Family ties: Communicating identity through jointly told family stories. *Communication Monographs, 72,* 365–389.

children quickly learn to be independent and self-reliant. In many other cultures the image of the family is very different. In the extended families typical of Mexico, Latin America, Africa, parts of Europe, the Middle East, and Asia, support and loyalty extend beyond the immediate family of parents and siblings to include grandparents, cousins, aunts, uncles, great aunts and uncles, and even godparents.

Communication Rules Despite their similar properties, not all families communicate in the same way. As unique cultures, families have their own sets of rules about a variety of communication practices. Some communication rules are explicit: "If you're going to be more than a half hour late, phone home." Other rules aren't ever discussed, but they are just as important: "If Mom slams the door after coming home from work, wait until she's had time to relax before speaking to her."

Families have many rules governing communication among members and also with outsiders. There are rules concerning *who may speak with or to whom.* For example, in some families during dinner conversation parents may direct comments to the children but the children may be expected to "be seen and not heard" or to participate only when invited to participate. In other families, rules guiding the give-and-take at the dinner table may allow any family member to address any other member.

Along with rules about who to speak with, families have rules about *how you may speak.* For example, you may use one vocabulary with Dad and another with Mom, or you may argue with Mom and raise your voice, but not with Dad. Sometimes the rules about "to whom" and "about what" and "how" combine: talk directly and openly with Mom when you want advice about what to wear, and speak with Dad circumspectly and in your "superpolite voice" when you want to talk about finances.

Rules for communicating with people outside the family are often explicit. Parents may tell a young child "It's OK to talk with people you know, but don't talk to strangers when we're not around." Use of the Internet, which means access to people and ideas outside the home, also is regulated by a host of rules (Papadakis, 2003). For example, parents can restrict the areas that can be visited online, as well as when (such as after homework is done) and how long the Internet can be accessed.

Families also have rules—sometimes explicit, but often unstated—about *topics of conversation* (Caughlin & Petronio, 2004). Adolescents, for example, tend to avoid discussing dating with their parents but not their siblings (Guerrero & Afifi, 1995). Culture has a powerful influence on what family topics are off limits: Topics related to sexuality, romantic relationships, and parental authority remain taboo for many generations of Chinese and Chinese Americans, while they are more acceptable in many European American families (Tanarugsachock, 1994).

Managing the openness-closedness dialectic can be especially challenging in stepfamilies. Tamara Golish (2000) interviewed 115 adolescents and young adults in stepfamilies to learn about topics they tend to avoid with their parents and stepparents. Stepchildren reported more topic avoidance with their stepparents than with their parents. In particular, stepchildren say they often avoid "deep conversations" or talking about money and family issues with their stepparents. One factor affecting the comfort level in stepfamily communication is the type of parenting style used by the stepparents. Stepchildren feel more dissatisfied and avoid more topics with stepparents who are highly authoritarian (i.e., demanding and rigid). Interestingly, stepchildren also say they are dissatisfied with highly permissive stepparents.

Ascan Koerner and Mary Ann Fitzpatrick (2002, 2006a) have identified two categories of rules about communication in the family: conversation and conformity. **Conversation orientation** involves the degree to which families favor an open climate of discussion of a wide array of topics. Families with a high conversation orientation interact freely, frequently, and spontaneously, without many limitations regarding topic or time spent interacting. They believe that this interaction is important in order to have an enjoyable and rewarding family life—conversation-oriented families communicate with their children for relationally oriented motives, such as affection, pleasure, and relaxation (Barbato et al., 2003), and conflict is characterized by integrating and compromising strategies (Sherman & Dumlao, 2008). On the other hand, members of families with a low conversation orientation interact less, and there is less exchange of private thoughts. It's no surprise that families with a strong conversation orientation regard communication as rewarding (Avtgis, 1999), and that children who grow up in conversation-oriented families have a greater number of interpersonal skills in their later relationships (Koesten, 2004).

Conformity orientation refers to the degree to which family communication stresses uniformity of attitudes, values, and beliefs. High-conformity families seek harmony, conflict avoidance, interdependence, and obedience. They are often hierarchical, with a clear sense that some members have more authority than others—so it's not surprising that conflict in these families is characterized by avoiding and obliging strategies (Sherman & Dumlao, 2008). Conformity-oriented families communicate with their children for personal-influence motives (control and escape) and to show affection (Barbato et al., 2003). By contrast, communication in families with a low conformity orientation is characterized by individuality, independence, and equality. The belief in such families is that individual growth should be encouraged, and that family interests should be subordinated to individual interests. Figure 12.1 displays the four types of families that result from crossing conversation orientation and conformity orientation.

Families high in both conversation orientation and conformity orientation are *consensual:* communication in these families reflects the tension between the pressure to agree and preserve the hierarchy, and an interest in open communication and exploration.

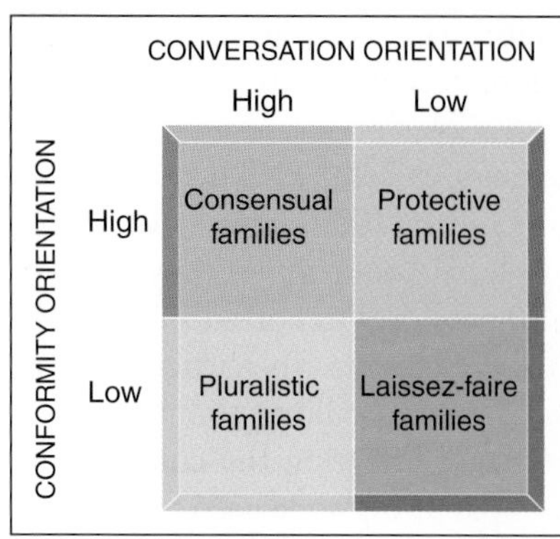

FIGURE 12.1 Conversation and Conformity Orientations in Families

Families high in conversation orientation and low in conformity orientation are *pluralistic:* Communication in these families is open and unrestrained, with all family members' contributions evaluated on their own merits.

Families low in conversation orientation and high in conformity orientation are *protective:* Communication in these families emphasizes obedience to authority and the reluctance to share thoughts and feelings.

Families low in both conversation orientation and conformity orientation are *laissez-faire:* Communication in these families reflects family members' lack of involvement with each other, the fact that they are emotionally divorced, and that decision making is individual.

Which of these styles best represents your family? Which style would you *like* to be true of your family?

EFFECTIVE COMMUNICATION IN FAMILIES

It's impossible to cover every aspect of effective family communication in just a few pages. Still, the following points can offer guidelines to make any family's interaction more satisfying and rewarding.

Strive for Closeness While Respecting Boundaries Chapter 9 described the conflicting needs we all have for both integration and separation in our relationships, as well as for both expression and privacy. Nowhere are these opposing drives stronger than in families. We all know the importance of keeping close ties with our kin, although too much cohesion can be a problem. When cohesion is too high, a family may be **enmeshed**, that is, suffer from too much consensus, too little independence, and a very high demand for loyalty—all of which may feel stifling. At the other extreme, of course, members of families with too little cohesion may be **disengaged**—disconnected, with limited attachment or commitment to one another (Olson, 2000).

Families cope with these dialectical tensions by creating **boundaries**—limits a family sets on its members' actions. Communication researchers have devoted a good deal of attention to the importance of boundary management in interpersonal and family relationships (Petronio, 2000). The most obvious

SELF-ASSESSMENT

How Cohesive and Adaptable Is Your Family?

With either your current family or family of origin in mind, respond to each item, adapted from Olson's Family Adaptability and Cohesion Evaluation Scale (FACES III). How true of your family is each item? Use the numbers 1 through 5 according to the following scale:

NEVER TRUE **0 1 2 3 4 5 6 7** ALWAYS TRUE

1. **Family members feel closer to people inside the family than outside the family.**
2. **Family members are not afraid to say what is on their minds.**
3. **Our family does things together.**
4. **Each family member has input in major family decisions.**
5. **Family members know each other's close friends.**
6. **In our family, everyone shares responsibilities.**
7. **Family members feel very close to each other.**
8. **Our family tries new ways of dealing with problems.**
9. **Family members share interests and hobbies with each other.**
10. **We shift household responsibilities from person to person.**

Total your scores for item 1, 3, 5, 7, and 9. This is your *cohesion* score.
Total your scores for item 2, 4, 6, 8, and 10. This is your *adaptability* score.

Scores of 20 and higher on the cohesion scale are high, scores of 10 and lower are low, and scores between 10 and 20 indicate moderate levels of cohesion. Scores of 17 and higher on the adaptability scale are high, scores of 10 and lower are low, and scores between 10 and 17 indicate moderate levels of adaptability. Give some thought to whether you're satisfied with your family's levels of cohesion and adaptability—and if you're not, consider ways that you might help bring about change.

Olson, D. H. (1986). Circumplex Model VII: Validation studies and Faces III. *Family Processes, 25,* 337–351.

boundaries are physical (e.g., don't enter a bedroom without knocking if the door is closed; stay out of the garage when Dad is tinkering with the car). Other boundaries involve conversational topics, as discussed in the previous section. In some families, discussion of finances is off limits. In others, expression of certain emotions is restricted. Sex is one of the most-avoided topics with parents and stepparents (Golish & Caughlin, 2002).

In addition to governing what to talk about, boundaries can also dictate how topics are handled. In some families it is fine to persist if the first overture to discussion is rebuffed ("Come on, what's on your mind?"). In other families, privacy rules discourage this kind of persistence. While the particulars may differ, every family has communication boundaries—and newcomers would be wise to learn and heed those boundaries (consider the many television shows and movies that poke fun at in-laws violating each other's family rules).

The challenge families face is to define boundaries that include important kinds of relational communication while allowing members to have the privacy and freedom that everyone desires. Sometimes these boundaries need to be openly negotiated. At other times they are established through trial and error. In either case, healthy boundaries allow us to balance the opposing and equally important needs for connection and autonomy, for openness and closedness.

Strive for a Moderate Level of Adaptability A family experiences stress both from within (e.g., children get older and their needs change) and without (e.g., Mom loses her job). In the face of stresses like these, a healthy family needs to adapt the way it functions and how members deal with one another. To see how adaptability can help a family function, consider the stress a family experiences when a child reaches adolescence. To adapt to this change, parents can begin to share control with their teenager as they negotiate issues like schedules, responsibilities, and rules.

When adaptability is too high, the result may be a **chaotic family:** one that has erratic leadership or no leadership at all, dramatic shifts in roles, unclear roles, and impulsive decision making. When adaptability is too low, the result may be a **rigid family** with authoritarian leadership (usually in the hands of one person, the mother or father), strict discipline, roles that are inflexible, and unchanging rules. The extent to which a family is able to avoid these extremes in adaptability determines, to a large extent, how functional it is (Olson, 2000). Inasmuch as change is an inevitable fact of family life, it is important for healthy families to roll—at an appropriate level—with the changes that come their way.

Just as families cope with tensions related to cohesion by creating boundaries, families also create boundaries that regulate adaptability. For example, a rigid family might have strong topic boundaries and a lot of rules to make sure that who speaks to whom about what is carefully regulated. The goal is to make sure that the family hierarchy is maintained and lines of authority are clear. By contrast, a chaotic family is likely to have few if any rules in this area of family life. Similarly, a rigid family is likely to have many rules and clear boundaries regarding appropriate sex-role behavior, such as "the son mows the lawn" and "the daughter does the dishes," whereas in a chaotic family there may be no rules regarding who mows and who does the dishes.

Families generally function better if their levels of cohesion, conformity, and adaptability are moderate, rather than being extremely high or low (Olson & Lavee, 1989; Schrodt, 2005). It's easy to understand how too much cohesion, conformity, and adaptability could become stifling, and how too little could result in members drifting apart.

Encourage Confirming Messages Chapter 10 introduced the importance of confirming messages—ones that show in one way or another that we value the other person. Confirming messages from parents help satisfy a great many of their children's needs, such as the need for nurturance and respect. Kathleen Ellis

(2002) looked at the different ways mothers and fathers communicate valuing and support to their children. She found that two highly confirming behaviors parents offer are (1) telling their children that they are unique and valuable as human beings, and (2) genuinely listening to their children when being told something of importance. Two highly disconfirming behaviors are (1) belittling their children, and (2) making statements that communicate that their ideas don't count: "Nobody asked for your opinion" or "What do you know about this anyway?" Confirming messages are just as important for teenagers as for young children. One study found a strong relationship between the amount of confirmation adolescents feel and the openness they exhibit in communication with their parents (Dailey, 2006).

Confirming communication is also important to successful marriages. Marital researcher John Gottman (2003) acknowledges that most couples aren't confirming in all of their communication—that would be unrealistic. The key, says Gottman, is having an appropriate ratio of positive-to-negative messages. His studies show that satisfied couples—and these include couples who fight with each other—consistently have a 5:1 ratio of positive-to-negative communication, with positive messages including features such as humor, empathizing, and expressions of affection.

Deal Constructively with Conflict As you read in Chapter 11, conflict is natural and inevitable. Conflict in families, however, is special because it occurs more often and may be more violent than in other relationships, whether between spouses/partners, parents and children, or between siblings (Koerner & Fitzpatrick, 2006b). In families, as in other relationships, the question isn't how to avoid conflict—that's impossible. Rather, the challenge is to resolve conflicts in a way that makes relationships stronger rather than weaker.

Sometimes families handle their conflicts in destructive ways. For instance, physical and verbal aggression are inappropriate responses to conflict; however, the other extreme, ignoring a conflict, may be just as destructive to the family. For example, both husbands and wives feel less understood, and less satisfied with their marriages, when their partners respond to a conflict by withdrawing (Weger & Metts, 2005).

Families can improve their communication by recognizing that family conflict should be dealt with. Placing conflict on the back burner, attempting to ignore it, smoothing it over, or denying that it exists creates tensions. The key to resolution lies in how the conflict is dealt with. There are several general principles of conflict management in the family.

DON'T SWEAT THE SMALL STUFF There will always be differences of opinion and style in families. Many need attention, but others simply aren't worth bothering about. If it's not a big issue, it might be best to let it slide. (Of course, what constitutes a "big issue" is often a matter of perception.)

FOCUS ON MANAGEABLE ISSUES Many big issues can be broken down into smaller, more manageable parts. For example, rather than arguing about a family member's "controlling personality," consider addressing specific problems: differing opinions about household neatness, the need to be informed about family plans, interference with your personal decisions, and so on.

SHARE APPRECIATIONS AS WELL AS GRIPES Along with addressing differences, let family members know that you appreciate them. As you read in Chapter 10, hearing an abundance of confirming messages makes it easier for us to hear negative information without feeling defensive and unappreciated.

SEEK WIN-WIN SOLUTIONS Strong feelings that are not resolved in one conflict will probably resurface later in another. The guidelines for win-win problem-solving in Chapter 11 can work especially well with family conflicts, especially when members realize that when one person is unhappy, all the others are likely to suffer. On the other hand, when all members contribute to and are satisfied with a solution to a family problem, it builds cohesion, trust, and good will.

Not all conflicts are resolvable, but just because a conflict is not resolvable does not mean that it needs to be a constant source of stress in the family. Conflicts regarding religious differences, in-laws, and even food preferences might never be resolved, but so long as the people with the problem engage in confirming as opposed to disconfirming behavior and fight fairly, the conflict does not have to reduce family commitment or satisfaction.

Based on his own research and a review of the literature on "excellent family communication," John Caughlin (2003) offers a list of standards college students have about what constitutes effective family communication. Several of these standards highlight the points discussed earlier and are good predictors of family satisfaction: Family members who communicate well provide each other with emotional support, express affection verbally and nonverbally, are polite to one another, and base discipline on clear rules.

Interpersonal Communication at Work

Interpersonal effectiveness is just as important on the job as it is in families and other personal relationships. One survey asked almost 400 human resources managers from organizations across the U.S. to identify the skills most necessary for successful job performance (Winsor et al., 1997). "Interpersonal/human relations" was at the top of the list. Respondents also were asked to list skills the ideal manger should possess. The top three items were to listen effectively and counsel, work well with others one-on-one, and work well in small groups. Across the board, communication skills were ranked higher than factors such as grade-point average, specific degree held, and technical skills. A report published by the Public Forum Institute (2002) underscores this same point. More than 1000 people in forums across the country were asked, "What job skills do you most look for in an applicant?" Here is what the report says:

> Participants responded that soft skills, such as interpersonal relations, critical thinking and problem solving, were more sought after in candidates than were hard skills, such as computer literacy, writing, and technical skills. (p. 6)

This quote underlines the point that communication skills are important in virtually every career, not just those that are traditionally regarded as people-oriented. For example, one study revealed that practitioners in accounting firms spent 80 percent of their work time communicating with others, individually and in groups (Nellermoe et al., 1999). The need for communication skills is just as important in high-tech fields (Darling & Dannels, 2003). Writing in *The Scientist,* author Jim Richman (2002) made the point emphatically: "If I give any advice, it is that you can never do enough training around your overall communication skills" (p. 42). The verdict seems clear: Successful employees need to bring strong communication skills to the workplace.

The following pages will cover some of the most common and important dimensions of interpersonal communication on the job. This information is no substitute for a full course in organizational or business and professional communication, but it will give you an appreciation of how competent communication on the job can lead to greater effectiveness and satisfaction.

ADVANCING YOUR CAREER

The first steps in a successful career are identifying the type of work you will enjoy and do well at and then securing employment. Not surprisingly, interpersonal communication skills can help you do just that.

Networking When it comes to getting a job and advancing within an organization, *who* you know—personal relationships, in other words—can be just as critical as *what* you know. The vast majority of people don't find new positions from formal sources like advertisements, headhunters, or websites (Bolles, 2008; Granovetter, 1995). Instead most successful job-seekers find employment opportunites through personal contacts. The reverse is also true: Most employers find good employees through their personal networks (Baker, 2000).

Networking is the process of deliberately meeting people and maintaining contacts to get career information, advice, and leads. As such, it satisfies one of the "practical needs" outlined in Chapter 1 of this book. Sometimes networking can find you a rewarding job. Just as important, networking contacts can provide advice about how best to do your current job and how to plan your career.

IDENTIFYING YOUR NETWORKS Most of us are members of many networks, including family, friends, and neighborhood, school, recreational, and religious groups. Your communication in some networks is mostly face to face, while the communication in others may be mostly mediated. Social networking sites like Facebook, Friendster, and MySpace fall into this category.

While these immediate contacts can be useful sources for job leads, distant connections can be even better: old schoolmates, colleagues from past jobs, professionals whose services you have used, relatives of your friends, and so on (Granovetter, 1973). Each of those distant contacts has his or her own network that may include someone in a position to offer you a career opportunity. Somewhere in their networks may be people who can help you advance in your career.

You can even join networks of strangers to seek job leads. Some of these groups meet in person in local communities; others operate online. (For a list of career networking websites, see www.rileyguide.com or www.quintcareers.com).

CULTIVATING YOUR NETWORKS As you consider cultivating a network for career advancement, several guidelines can be helpful (Adler & Elmhorst, 2008). First, view everyone you meet as a networking prospect. Almost everyone you meet has the potential to be a source of useful information. The stranger seated next to you on a plane or bus might know people who can help you. The neighbor with whom you chat at a block party might have the knowledge or skill to help you solve a problem. A helpful professor might have insights or contacts that could change your life.

A second tip is to seek rererrals to secondary sources from people you know. If you ask 10 personal acquaintences for referrals and each of them knows 10 others who might be able to help, you have the potential of support from 100 information givers.

Beyond mining your multifaceted personal relationships for contacts, you can benefit greatly from seeking a mentor who will focus on helping you succeed in your career. A *mentor* is a person who acts as a guide, trainer, coach, and counselor; who teaches you the informal rules of an organization or a field; and who imparts the kinds of wisdom that come from firsthand experience. Many organizations have formal programs that match new employees with experienced ones. Other mentor–protégé relationships develop informally and unofficially. However you find one, a mentor can be invaluable. This is especially true for women, minorities, and people trying to break into nontraditional fields where "good old boy" networks can be hard to penetrate.

Don't imagine that networking requires you to be dishonest or exploitive. As long as you express a genuine desire for information openly, there's no reason to feel apologetic. Furthermore, seeking information doesn't mean you have to stop enjoying others' company for social reasons.

Interviewing for Employment Few conversations have more potential for both stress and promise than employment interviews. Unless you are already known by a prospective employer, the interview process is a chance to explore the fit between yourself and the organization where you are likely to spend the majority of your waking hours.

An employment interview is a conversation, but one unlike the kinds of social chats that occur in other settings (Stewart & Cash, 2006). They are much more *purposeful,* for both the interviewer and the prospective employee have clear goals. A second characteristic that distinguishes interviews is *structure.* In a typical conversation, neither person knows or cares when the exchange will end or exactly what topics will be covered. By contrast, any good interview has a distinct opening, body, and conclusion. A third feature of interviews is *control.* Whereas conversations don't require any guidance from one of the parties, an interviewer's job is to keep the exchange moving toward the preset purpose. Finally, interviews usually have a unique *balance of participation.* Though most conversations involve roughly the same amount of input from each person, participation in an interview ought to be in the 70:30 percent ratio, with the interviewee doing most of the talking.

To make an interview successful, both the interviewer and interviewee have responsibilities before, during, and after they meet. As an interviewee, you can make the experience pay off by following the guidelines in the rest of this section.

BEFORE THE INTERVIEW A good interview begins before the people sit down to talk. You can make your interviews more successful through careful planning (*Before the Interview,* 1999; Safro, 2001).

1. **Clarify the Interviewer's Goals**. Imagine you are preparing for an employment interview. You know that the company is looking for the best applicant to fill the job. But just what kinds of qualities are they seeking? Are education and training most important? Experience? Initiative? Knowing these criteria in advance will boost your chances of doing well in the interview.

   There will be times when an interviewer has hidden goals, which you should do your best to discover. For instance, your prospective boss's questions about your daily job routine might really be a way of exploring your work practices. As this example shows, not all hidden goals are malicious, but in any case you'll feel more comfortable and behave more effectively when you know what the interviewer wants from you.

2. **Come Prepared**. A good interviewee doesn't come to an interview empty-handed. You'll want to bring materials that will help the employer learn more about why you are ready, willing, and able to do the job. For instance, bring extra copies of your resume—because more than one person might interview you that day. Come prepared to take notes: You'll need something to write on and a pen or pencil. If appropriate, bring copies of your past work: reports you've helped prepare, performance reviews by former employers, drawings or designs you have created in work or school, letters of recommendation, and so on. Besides demonstrating your qualifications, items like these show that you know how to sell yourself. Bring along the names, addresses, and phone numbers of any references you haven't listed in your resume.

   Besides coming with the basic materials, you can impress the interviewer and serve yourself well by doing advance research on the organization. What products or services does it provide? What is its position in the marketplace and the community? What challenges and trends does the organization face? What makes this organization unique among its competitors? Showing your awareness of this information will distinguish you as a serious candidate.

DURING THE INTERVIEW Once you are in the interview itself, there are several important points to keep in mind. These guidelines both show your competence and help you build a good relationship with your interviewer.

1. **Make a Good First Impression**. First impressions can make or break an interview. Typically, the first impression you make will be based on your cover letter and resume, which is why it's important for them to be well constructed and error free (many books offer tips on developing these important documents: e.g., Brown, 2002, and Parker, 2003). In addition, your punctuality (or lack thereof) will make a statement about how you manage time. Plan to arrive 10–15 minutes early to leave room for any unexpected delays. If you're unsure about the company's location, make a test run the day before.

   Just as the first stages of a date will generally shape what comes later, the success or failure of an interview is often determined in the first exchange (Jorgenson, 1992). Research shows that many interviewers form their opinions about candidates within the first 4 minutes of conversation (Avery & Campion, 1982). Physical attractiveness is a major influence on how applicants are rated, so it makes sense to do everything possible to look your best. The proper style of clothing can vary from one type of job or organization to another. When in doubt, it's best to dress formally and conservatively. It's unlikely an employer will think less of you for being overdressed, but looking too casual can be taken as a sign that you don't take the job or the interview seriously.

2. **Get Off to a Good Start**. The usual format for an opening begins with some sort of greeting, which includes any introductions that are necessary. A period of informal conversation often follows, in which the interviewer and applicant talk about subjects of mutual interest not necessarily related to the interview topic. This period gives both people a chance to get settled and acquainted before getting down to business. The idea is to establish some common ground between interviewer and applicant. One way to do so is to look around the interviewer's office for information about that person's interests and hobbies. A prominent plaque, a sports pennant, a wall photo, or a piece of art can all be topics for conversation.
3. **Give Clear, Detailed Answers**. Put yourself in the interviewer's shoes and be as specific and helpful as you hope others would be for you. A good answer provides a general theme and then offers specifics. For example, suppose a potential employer asks, "What did you learn in your interpersonal communication course that will help you in this job?" You could follow this theme-specific format with an answer like this: "I learned how to build and maintain positive relationships, and that can help me with people in the company and with customers. For example, we learned how to listen well, negotiate win-win solutions, raise difficult issues skillfully, and handle criticism without getting defensive." Be prepared: A good interviewer will probably ask a follow-up question such as "Give me an example of a time when you've used those skills." It's a good idea to come to an interview with several brief stories, illustrations, and examples that provide evidence of your abilities and skills.
4. **Keep Your Answers Focused**. It's easy to rattle on in an interview, either out of enthusiasm, a desire to show off your knowledge, or nervousness, but in most cases long answers are not a good idea. The interviewer probably has lots of ground to cover, and long-winded answers won't help this task. As a rule of thumb, your answers shouldn't run much over a minute or two without inviting the interviewer to either follow up or move on to the next question. Of course, you'll want to give clear, detailed answers with examples, as described in the preceding guideline. Keep in mind, though, that an interview is a conversation—and as is true of any conversation, turn-taking dialogue is better than a long monologue.
5. **Follow the Interviewer's Lead**. Let the interviewer set the emotional tone of the session. If he or she is informal, you can loosen up a bit, but if the approach is formal and proper, you should act the same way. A great deal depends on the personal interaction between interviewer and candidate, so try to match the interviewer's style without becoming phony. If the tone of the interview doesn't fit well with you, this may be a signal that you won't feel comfortable with this organization. It may be smart to see whether the interviewer's approach represents the whole company, either by asking for a

tour or speaking with other employees on your own. This desire to learn about the company shows that you are a thinking person who takes the job seriously, so your curiosity isn't likely to offend the interviewer.

6. **Come Prepared to Answer the Interviewer's Questions**. This principle is especially important in interviews where you are seeking a job. Whatever specific questions you might be asked, the employer is always asking "How can you help us?" If you remember this, you can respond in ways that show how you can meet the employer's needs. If you've spent time learning about your potential employer, you'll be in a good position to talk about that company's concerns and how you can satisfy them. Knowing that you can, indeed, help the company can boost your self-confidence and lead you to feel more comfortable when facing a potential employer (Linden et al., 1993). Table 12.1 provides suggestions for answering common questions employers ask.
7. **Come Prepared to Ask the Interviewer Questions** Near the end of an employment interview, it is typical for an interviewer to ask the applicant, "Do you have any questions?" An ineffective response would be "No, I can't think of any," which suggests a lack of initiative and inquisitiveness. Instead, come prepared with a list of questions about the company and the position for which you're applying (Fry, 2003). Don't forget: You're trying to determine if this job is a good match for you, so you are interviewing the company as much as they are interviewing you.

   Good questions will allow you to demonstrate the homework you've done on the organization: "I saw on your website that the company is developing new training programs. How might these programs assist me in my position?" Questions to avoid include queries about salary or benefits—at least in an initial interview. Such questions focus on what the company will do for you, while your goal is to show what you can do for the company.

AFTER THE INTERVIEW Follow up your meeting with a note of thanks to the interviewer. Most candidates don't take this step, which will make your response especially impressive. Express your appreciation for the chance to get acquainted with the company, and let the interviewer know that the session left you excited about the chance of becoming associated with it. It's also a good idea to identify specific information you learned about the company during the interview: "I enjoyed hearing about the new software program your company is using to facilitate performance reviews." Whenever possible, show how the things you learned make you a good match for the job: "My familiarity with a variety of computer programs should help me learn your new system quickly, and my training in communication will assist me in conducting performance reviews." Finally, your note can confirm the next steps in the interviewing process: "You explained that I should be hearing from the company within the next week. I'll be looking forward to a phone call."

TABLE 12.1 ***Common Employment Interview Questions***

1. Tell me something about yourself.
This broad opening question gives you a chance to describe what qualities you possess that can help the employer. Remember that your response should be *job-related*—this is not the time to talk about where you grew up or your hobbies.

2. What makes you think you're qualified to work for this company?
This question may sound like an attack, but it really is another way of asking "How can you help us?" It gives you another chance to show how your skills and interests fit with the company's goals.

3. What accomplishments have given you the most satisfaction?
The accomplishments you choose needn't be directly related to former employment; however, they should demonstrate qualities that would help you be successful in the job for which you're interviewing. Your accomplishments might demonstrate creativity, perseverance in the face of obstacles, self-control, or dependability.

4. Why do you want to work for us?
Employers are impressed by candidates who have done their homework about the organization. This question offers the chance to demonstrate your knowledge of the employer's organization, and to show how your talents fit with its goals.

5. What college subjects did you like best and least?
Whatever your answer, show how your preferences about schoolwork relate to the job for which you are applying. When necessary, show how apparently unrelated subjects do illustrate your readiness for a job. For example, you might say, "I really enjoyed cultural anthropology courses because they showed me the importance of understanding different cultures. I think those courses would help me a lot in relating to our overseas customers and suppliers."

6. Where do you see yourself in 5 years?
This familiar question is really asking "How ambitious are you?" "How well do your plans fit with this company's goals?" "How realistic are you?" If you have studied the industry and the company, your answer will reflect an understanding of the workplace realities and a sense of personal planning that should impress an employer.

7. What major problems have you faced, and how have you dealt with them?
The specific problem isn't as important as the way you responded to it. What (admirable) qualities did you demonstrate as you grappled with the problem you have chosen to describe? Perseverance? Calmness? Creativity? You may even choose to describe a problem you didn't handle well, and show what you learned from the experience that can help you in the future.

8. What are your greatest strengths?
The "strength" question offers another chance to sell yourself. Emphasize qualities that apply to employment. "I'm a pretty good athlete" isn't a persuasive answer *unless* you can show how your skill is job-related. For instance, you might talk about being a team player, your competitive drive, or your ability to work hard and not quit in the face of adversity.

9. What are your greatest weaknesses?
Whatever answer you give to the "weakness" question, try to show how your awareness of your flaws makes you a desirable person to hire. There are four ways to respond to this question.

- You can discuss a weakness that also can be viewed as a strength: "When I'm involved in a big project I tend to work too hard, and I can wear myself out."
- You can discuss a weakness that is not related to the job at hand, and end your answer with a strength that is related to the job. For a job in sales: "I'm not very interested in accounting. I'd much rather work with people selling a product I believe in."
- You can discuss a weakness the interviewer already knows about from your resume, application, or the interview. "I don't have a lot of experience in multimedia design at this early stage of my career. But my experience in other kinds of computer programming and my internship in graphic arts have convinced me that I can learn quickly."
- You can discuss a weakness you have been working to remedy. "I know being bilingual is important for this job. That's why I've enrolled in a Spanish course."

Adapted from Adler, R. B., & Rodman, G. (2009). *Understanding human communication* (10th ed.). New York: Oxford University Press, pp. A-16–A-19, and Locker, K. O. (2000). *Business and administrative communication* (5th ed.). Homewood, IL: Irwin, pp. 574–575.

COMMUNICATING IN ORGANIZATIONS

Once you've joined an organization, a new set of challenges arise, and new communication skills are needed to supplement the ones you have learned so far.

Formal and Informal Relationships In most work settings, people are identified by titles and roles: accounting supervisor, management trainee, service representative, and so on. These roles combine to create **formal communication**—interaction that follows officially established channels. There are three types of formal communication within all but the very smallest organizations (Adler & Elmhorst, 2008; Sanchez, 1999). In **upward communication**, subordinates communicate with their bosses—sometimes in a way that distorts negative information and puts it in a positive light (Dansereau & Markham, 1987). Upward communication can cover a variety of topics, although some are perceived as more appropriate than others (Kassing, 2005):

What Subordinates Are Doing
"We'll certainly have that job finished by closing time today."

Unsolved Work Problems
"We're still having trouble with our online connection."

Suggestions for Improvement
"I think we've figured out a way to give everybody the vacation schedules they requested."

How Subordinates Are Feeling
"I've been promised a promotion for 6 months, and it still hasn't happened."

In **downward communication**, managers address messages to subordinates. Downward messages often include:

Job Instructions
"Here's the way to do it. . . ."

Job Rationale
"We back up the files every night in case the hard drive crashes."

Feedback
"Great job! Just one suggestion . . ."

Horizontal communication occurs between people who don't have direct supervisor-subordinate relationships. These types of messages may include:

Task Coordination
"If you can get me the job tomorrow, I'll have it finished by Thursday."

Sharing Information
Sales rep to engineer: "The customers are asking for longer battery life. Is that possible?"

Conflict Resolution
"I was really unhappy when you criticized me in front of the boss. Can we talk about it?"

FOCUS ON RESEARCH

Socializing New Employees through Memorable Messages

research

The first few weeks on a job can be challenging and even intimidating for new employees. Communication researchers Kevin Barge and David Schleuter found that certain "memorable messages" can make a big difference in helping newcomers feel welcomed to and oriented about their companies.

The researchers surveyed more than 100 employees who had been at their current jobs less than two years. The participants were asked to describe a single memorable message that made an impact on their work life when they first entered their organization. In addition, the respondents supplied information about when, where, how, and by whom the message was said as well as the effect it had on them. Here are a few of the findings.

- More than two-thirds of the respondents said the memorable message was delivered within their first week on the job—some on the first day.
- Many of the messages were about professional behavior and office rules ("It's crucial to be punctual"; "Be careful when you challenge the boss"). Office politics also came into play ("Always be nice to the secretary Nadine because she's the gateway to the supervisor").
- Not all the messages were warnings; some were warm and welcoming ("It's one big family here"; "We're glad they hired you").
- Virtually all of the messages were perceived as positive, supportive, and designed to help the recipient, the company, or both.

Perhaps most interesting was how the messages were delivered. Most came during informal conversations, and over 90 percent happened in face-to-face settings. It would appear that while orientation sessions, handbooks, e-mails, and memos can supply important information for new employees, the most useful messages for socializing newcomers may come during informal chats in the hallway.

Barge, J. K., & Schlueter, D. W. (2004). Memorable messages and newcomer socialization. *Western Journal of Communication, 68*, 233–256.

These examples suggest the importance of keeping formal channels open and operating: Imagine the likely consequences if any one of these messages wasn't delivered.

Formal relationships are important, but they aren't the only kinds that operate at work. **Informal communication** is based on friendships, shared personal or career interests, and proximity. Coworkers may have children in the same school, shared loyalty to a sports team, membership in the same church, or mutual friends. They may carpool to share commuting expenses or work out together at the gym during lunch hour. They may develop a close friendship through self-disclosure and more frequent interaction, both on and away from the job (Sias & Cahill, 1998). They may even be romantic partners, although this is likely to pose problems for on-the-job interaction (Riach & Wilson, 2007).

Informal messages can supplement more formal ones in a variety of ways. Sometimes they *confirm* formal messages: "This time they're really serious about our not using e-mail for personal messages." At other times they can *contradict* formal ones: "They say the deadline is Friday, but first thing Monday morning is OK." Some informal messages can *expand* on official information: "Khakis are fine. When they say 'no casual attire,' they mean no jeans and T-shirts." Informal communication can help you *circumvent* formal channels: "If you call Sharon in accounting, she can get you reimbursed quickly without all that paperwork."

Informal relationships are often more efficient and accurate than formal networks (Hellweg, 1987). An observation in the *Harvard Business Review* captured the relationship between formal and informal networks: "If the formal organization is the skeleton of a company, the informal is the central nervous system" (Krackhardt & Hanson, 1993, p. 104).

It's important to note that communication in the workplace doesn't always fall into neat and simple categories (Reamer, 2002). Often, we must move between formal and informal communication within a particular relationship. For instance, your boss might drop by your cubicle to share some office gossip with you—and a few minutes later take you to task about an assignment you neglected. Romantic partners who work together may have difficulty negotiating where their personal relationship ends and their professional relationship begins. And many employees feel awkward when a coworker is promoted to supervisor because it changes the rules of their communication. As these examples suggest, the characteristics of competent communication discussed in Chapter 1—such as adaptability, self-monitoring, and a large repertoire of skills—are as important in the workplace as they are in other contexts.

DARK SIDE OF COMMUNICATION

Micromanaging: Workplace Leadership Gone Awry

Most employees want to work for a supervisor who gives them direction, leadership, and advice—up to a point. Management consultant Harry Chambers identifies *micromanagers* as bosses who take legitimate managerial behaviors to such an extreme that they become disruptive and actually interfere with people's ability to do their jobs.

The traits of a micromanager are probably familiar to those who have been victims: Double-checking employees' work and constantly finding fault; nitpicking about insignificant details; redoing work that's been delegated to others; and a general lack of trust, praise, and endorsement. Many of the defense-producing behaviors discussed in Chapter 10—evaluation, control, and superiority—are hallmarks of a micromanager.

Chambers offers several tips for workers unlucky enough to have micromanaging bosses. One strategy is to find out what issues are really important to the boss and to raise them before he or she does. Another is to identify other people whom the boss seems to treat better than you, and adopt the approach that works for them. Chambers points out that it's almost never possible to "fix" an overcontrolling manager. Instead, the best approach is to anticipate and defuse the boss's worst moves.

Chambers, H. E. (2005). Surviving the micromanager: How to succeed with a "my way" boss. *Canadian Manager, 30*, 24–25.

Face-to-Face and Mediated Relationships As in personal settings, people in working relationships can communicate either face to face or through a variety of electronic media. Telephone and e-mail are the most common types of mediated communication channels, although not the only ones. Faxes, teleconferencing, and instant messaging are other ways to keep in touch.

Face-to-face interaction is still the most common type of communication at work ("Business Meeting Is Alive and Well," 1997), but mediated relation-

ships are common and essential. Many businesses operate almost exclusively with customers via phone and e-mail, and employees within organizations often create effective working and personal relationships without spending much, if any, time together in person.

Virtual teams, whose memberships transcend the boundaries of location and time, can be a very effective and satisfying way to conduct business (Larsen & McInerney, 2002; Timmerman & Scott, 2006). Groups that operate electronically can communicate in ways that otherwise wouldn't be possible. They can use the phone and Internet to tackle jobs much more quickly than a similar group that would have to assemble physically. They can use different working schedules to their advantage. For example, a person on the East Coast of the United States—or even in Europe—can hand off work at the end of the day to a colleague in California, who can process and return it in time for the next morning.

The book you are reading is a perfect example of how relationships can prosper in virtual teams. The authors live thousands of miles apart—in California, North Carolina, and Kentucky. We have worked together for more than a dozen years, and during that time the three of us have only been together in person on a few occasions. Virtually all of our professional contact while working on several editions of this book has been through the exchange of e-mails. This arrangement probably sounds impersonal, but in fact our relationship has grown from a professional partnership into very satisfying friendships. In the course of our almost daily e-mails, we have exchanged stories about our families, swapped jokes, and shared our achievements and sorrows. We marvel at the fact that it's possible to have a solid friendship—let alone write a book about interpersonal communication—with very little face-to-face interaction.

As Table 1.1 (page 26) shows, each communication medium has its own advantages and drawbacks. And there are occasions where even the best technology is no substitute for "face time." Still, both face-to-face and mediated working relationships can clearly be interpersonal in every sense of the word.

RELATIONSHIPS IN WORK GROUPS

Working in teams is an essential part of almost every job (Devine et al., 1999). And anyone with group experience knows that good personal relationships are essential in a well-functioning team. Communication researchers Carl Larson and Frank LaFasto (1989) studied over 75 top-notch work teams from a diverse range of settings that included two championship football teams, the scientists who developed the IBM personal computer, a Mount Everest expedition, and a cardiac surgery team. Among the qualities that distinguish winning teams is a collaborative climate in which members trust and support one another. The following pages will introduce some communication skills that can help build this sort of collaborative, confirming climate.

Personal Skills in Work Groups Effective team members must, of course, have the task-related skills to tackle the job at hand. But relational skills are just as important. Over 60 years ago, Kenneth Benne and Paul Sheats (1948) identified a list of relational roles that need to be filled at one time or another in every group's life. These roles include

- encouraging participation
- harmonizing
- relieving tension
- evaluating the group's emotional climate
- giving praise
- listening thoughtfully to the concerns of others

If a group isn't operating efficiently, one place to look for remedies is at the communication climate among members. Ask yourself if any of these relational functions needs filling.

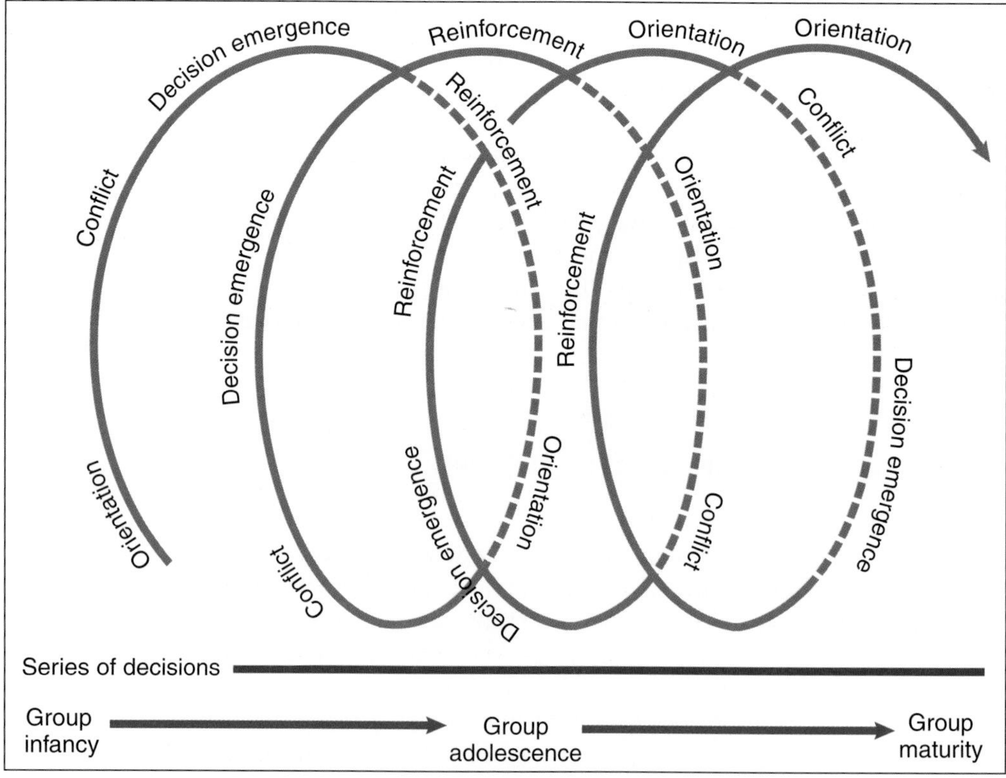

FIGURE 12.2 Cyclical Stages in an Ongoing Group

From Brilhart, J. K., Galanes, G. J., & Adams, K. (2001). *Effective group discussion* (10th ed.). New York: McGraw-Hill, p. 289. Reproduced with permission of the McGraw-Hill Companies.

Don't get the idea that an effective group will be free of conflicts. Even the best team will experience struggles on the path to consensus. In fact, most groups go through a predictable series of stages as they work together (Brilhart et al., 2001; McNamara, 2008). Figure 12.2 illustrates this pattern. Politeness and harmony are the norm during the *orientation* stage when a team first tackles a job. But as time goes on and differences emerge, the group enters a period of *conflict.* Disagreement doesn't necessarily involve hostility, but even civil and reasoned differences can require you to use the listening skills described in Chapter 7, the climate-building approaches in Chapter 10, and the conflict management guidelines in Chapter 11. Once a group has worked through the conflict stage, it typically enters an *emergence* stage where members accept—sometimes enthusiastically and sometimes reluctantly—the team's decision. Members recognize that this is a time to seek harmony. A fourth stage in group decision making is *reinforcement.* This is when members not only accept the decision but endorse it.

This process typically repeats itself in a cyclical fashion—and different stages are likely to overlap somewhat—as a group faces each new challenge. Just like dyadic relationships, groups have their ups and downs. Knowing that each step—especially conflict—is a natural part of working together can be reassuring.

Group Cultures In Chapter 2 you read about cultures rooted in nationality, ethnicity, age, and geographic region. Working groups—entire organizations and smaller groups within them—have their own **organizational culture** too—relatively stable, shared rules about how to behave and a set of values about what is important. In everyday language, culture is the insiders' view of "the way things are around here" (Ashkanasy et al., 2000; Deal & Kennedy, 1983).

You can prove this for yourself by thinking about different classes you have attended during your life as a student. Even though the basic process of learning is the same from one discipline and school to another, you probably can recognize that each class had its own culture—its unique style of handling behavior. The cultures of working groups involve many dimensions of communication such as *sociability* (friendly or aloof), *distribution of power* (controlled by authority figures or shared among members), *tolerance for new ideas* (welcomed or resisted), *ways of managing conflict* (direct or indirect), and *emotional support* (more or less plentiful).

Perhaps the most important insight about cultures in working groups is that they can make the difference between satisfaction and misery. If you're lucky enough to belong to a group that has a healthy culture—for example, one that is friendly, has shared power, welcomes new ideas, manages conflict directly, and provides emotional support—working on even the toughest jobs can be rewarding. On the other hand, if you are stuck in a group with an unsatisfying culture, great pay and plush working conditions won't prevent you from feeling miserable.

You may not be able to exert much influence on the culture of large organizations, whether they are a university you're attending or a corporation for which you work. What you can do, though, is think about the culture of the organization before you decide to join it. After you are on the job, you can shape the culture of smaller groups to which you belong. The way you and your fellow workers treat one another, as well as your attitudes toward work, can make a tremendous difference in the quality of the many hours you spend on the job.

Bad Day(s) at Work: *Office Space*

Peter Gibbons (Ron Livingston) hates his job—with good reason. He works for a computer firm that treats its employees like cogs in a machine. The company is top-heavy with impersonal managers who bombard their supervisees with memos and pounce on the smallest infractions of office policy. As a result, the employees lack motivation and feel little commitment to the organization.

Peter's boss is Bill Lumbergh (Gary Cole), who on the surface talks a good game. He doesn't raise his voice or use abusive language when correcting Peter; in fact, he offers suggestions in positive terms ("If you could go ahead and make sure to do that from now on, that would be great"). Unfortunately, he delivers these messages in a syrupy tone of voice that reeks of condescension. Moreover, Lumbergh doesn't listen or respond to his employees, nor does he ask for their input or participation. He simply delivers monologues and walks away.

In a humorous turn of events, Peter visits a hypnotherapist who releases him from his inhibitions. Peter begins coming to work late, doing as he pleases in his office cubicle, and ignoring Lumbergh. When consultants are brought in to downsize the company, Peter levels with them about all of the organization's problems. As only happens in a Hollywood comedy, Peter is promoted for his candor. In real life he would have been fired—but that's what makes the story both funny and satisfying for anyone who longs to "tell it like it is" in the workplace.

Office Space is a good example of a bad organizational culture. For anyone who has had the misfortune of working in a dysfunctional organization, the movie will probably elicit a chuckle—because the office communication will look and sound all too familiar.

Leadership, Power, and Influence in Working Groups When most people think about influence in groups, they focus on the **designated leader**—the person (or people) with official titles that indicate authority: manager, chairperson, and so on. There's no doubt that designated leaders play an important role in making things happen. But you don't have to be a designated leader to influence the effectiveness of a group. Every member of a working team has at least one resource of **power** that can affect what happens in a group (Andrews & Baird, 2000; French & Raven, 1968). Consider, for example, *expert power.* Designated leaders often aren't the best or only experts: Individual members often have a special kind of knowledge or talent—the ability to use a type of software, experience in the topic at hand, and so on.

Some types of power involve interpersonal relationships. *Reward power* is a good example. Rewards obviously include the designated leader's ability to hire and pay workers. But members can bestow their own rewards: Helping one another is a kind of reward that can help the group solve the job at hand. It also builds goodwill that serves both the reward-giver and the team well. Along with rewarding one another, group members can use *coercive power* to get what they want by using unpleasant consequences, or the threat of them, to punish one another. You don't have to be a designated leader to punish. Complaining, withholding help, and blocking progress are examples of ways members can punish one another and their boss.

The clearest type of interpersonal influence is *referent power*—the influence that comes from members' liking and respect for one another. Members with good interpersonal skills are likely to have high referent power that enables them to shape the way the group operates. Referent power is the area in which the greatest difference between designated leaders and influential group members can exist. An unpopular manager might have to use the rewards and punishments that come with the job title to get members to gain compliance. But a popular member with no formal title can get others to cooperate based on the influence that comes with high regard from other members (Pescosolido, 2001).

Summary

Contemporary families have a variety of traditional and nontraditional arrangements. Family relationships often include spouses/partners, parents and children, and siblings—each with unique characteristics. Over time, families develop into systems, as members interact with one another to form a whole. Family members also adopt particular roles, share and live out narratives, and create rules for interaction. Families of origin often serve as models for other relationships in our lives.

Effective communication in families requires that members establish and maintain a moderate level of cohesion, and they do this by establishing appropriate boundaries. In addition, functional families are adaptable, managing change without too much rigidity or acquiescence. Members of healthy families encourage each other with confirming messages and strive for win-win solutions to their conflicts.

Interpersonal effectiveness is as important in your career as it is in personal and family relationships. Career-related communication begins before you find employment. Networking with both immediate and more distant contacts can provide job leads and information that can help you find the right work setting. Once you have identified a prospective employer, your behavior in an employment interview can boost your chances of making sure there is a good fit between you and the organization and also increasing your chances of receiving a job offer.

Communication skills are critical once you are hired. Relationships in the workplace include both formal and informal networks as well as employing upward, downward, and horizontal communication. On-the-job communication often occurs in work groups, which may meet in person or in virtual teams. Work groups go through predictable stages, create their own cultures, and provide opportunities for leadership, power, and influence.

Activities

1. Invitation to Insight

Explore the following types of roles in either your current family or your family of origin. Describe the three most important roles in each category, who fills each of these roles, and the kinds of communication that typically occur in role fulfillment.

a. Kinship roles
b. Functional roles
c. Social roles

2. Invitation to Insight

Understand your own family system better by giving examples of each of the characteristics described on page 391:

a. Interdependence of members
b. How the family is more than the sum of its parts
c. Family subsystems and suprasystems
d. How environmental influences affect the family

3. Invitation to Insight

Describe an ongoing narrative in either your current family or your family of origin. Explain:

a. The narrative
b. When and how it is retold
c. The way this narrative portrays your family
d. The function the narrative serves

4. Skill Builder

Explore the power of networking by following these steps:

a. Identify a career goal that appeals to you.
b. Brainstorm the names of people in both your immediate networks and distant contacts who might be able to help you move closer to achieving your goal. Imagine how you might ask those people for referrals to members of their networks who could help you achieve your goals.
c. Based on the list of potential contacts, devise a plan for using networks to achieve the career goal you have identified.

5. Invitation to Insight

Describe the type of organizational culture that suits you best. Next, identify an organization where you might want to work, and explore how well its culture fits the preferences you identified. To formulate your answer, use information about the organization you have read about or observed. If you are seriously interested in the organization, consider using this activity as a reason for making contact with a representative of the organization and interviewing that person.

6. Skill Builder

Improve your ability to choose the most effective way of communicating in organizations by following these steps:

a. Choose an environment in which you work. (You may use school for the following analysis.)
b. Identify all the communication media used to convey messages in a one-week period: face-to-face, print, telephone, e-mail, website, instant messaging, text messaging, fax, and so on.
c. Analyze each situation to determine whether the medium chosen was most effective. If not, suggest a better alternative.
d. Based on your observations, identify situations in which it is best to use each type of communication available to you.

7. Ethical Challenge

Imagine yourself interviewing for a job you really want. Consider how you will represent yourself in a way that maximizes the chances of your receiving an offer of employment. To what degree is the narrative you would create in presenting yourself accurate, and to what degree is it less than totally honest? Could you justify the approach you would take as ethical?

Glossary

Abstraction ladder A range of more abstract to less abstract terms describing an event or object.

Accommodation A lose-win conflict style in which one person defers to the other.

Achievement culture A culture that places a high value on the achievement of material success and a focus on the task at hand. Also termed "masculine" culture.

Advising (response) A listening response in which the receiver offers suggestions about how the speaker should deal with a problem.

Aggressiveness Verbal attacks that demean others' self-concept and inflict psychological pain.

Ambiguous language Language consisting of words and phrases that have more than one commonly accepted definition.

Ambiguous response A response with more than one meaning, leaving the other person unsure of the responder's position.

Ambushing A style in which the receiver listens carefully in order to gather information to use in an attack on the speaker.

Analyzing (response) A listening response in which the listener offers an interpretation of a speaker's message.

Androgynous Possessing both masculine and feminine traits.

Argumentativeness Presenting and defending positions on issues while attacking positions taken by others.

Attending A phase of the listening process in which the communicator focuses on a message, excluding other messages.

Attribution The process of attaching meaning to another person's behavior.

Avoidance A lose-lose conflict style in which people nonassertively ignore or stay away from conflict.

Avoiding A relational stage immediately prior to terminating in which the partners minimize contact with one another.

Benevolent lie A lie that is not considered malicious by the person who tells it.

Bonding A stage of relational development in which the partners make symbolic public gestures to show that their relationship exists.

Boundaries Limits that a family sets on its members' actions, such as what topics are permissible to discuss, how to discuss certain topics, and with whom family members may interact outside the family.

"But" statement A statement in which the second half cancels the meaning of the first, for example, "I'd like to help you, *but* I have to go or I'll miss my bus."

Certainty Dogmatically stating or implying that one's position is correct and others' ideas are not worth considering. Likely to arouse defensiveness, according to Gibb.

Channel The medium through which a message passes from sender to receiver.

Chaotic family A family that has erratic leadership or no leadership at all, dramatic shifts in roles, unclear roles, and impulsive decision making.

Chronemics The study of how people use and structure time.

Circumscribing A relational stage in which partners begin to reduce the scope of their contact and commitment to one another.

Closed questions Questions that limit the range of possible responses, such as questions that seek a yes-or-no answer.

Co-culture A group within an encompassing culture with a perceived identity.

Cognitive complexity The ability to construct a variety of frameworks for viewing an issue.

Cognitive conservatism The tendency to seek out information that conforms to an existing self-concept and to ignore information that contradicts it.

Collaboration A win-win conflict style in which both people get what they want.

Collectivistic culture A culture whose members feel loyalties and obligations to an in-group, such as an extended family, a community, and even a work organization.

Communication apprehension Feelings of anxiety that plague some people at the prospect of communicating in an unfamiliar or difficult context.

Communication climate The emotional tone of a relationship between two or more individuals.

Communication competence The ability to achieve one's goals in a manner that is personally acceptable and, ideally, acceptable to others.

Comparison level (CL) The minimum standard of what behavior is acceptable from a relationship partner.

Comparison level of alternatives (CL_{alt}) A comparison between the rewards one is receiving in a present situation and those one could expect to receive in others.

Competition A win-lose conflict style in which one person wins at the other person's expense.

Complaining A disagreeing message that directly or indirectly communicates dissatisfaction with another person.

Complementary conflict style When partners in a conflict use different but mutually reinforcing behaviors.

Compliance-gaining strategy A tactic or plan used to persuade others to think or behave in a desired way.

Compromise A conflict style in which both people get only part of what they want because they sacrifice some of their goals.

Computer-mediated communication (CMC) Communication that occurs via computerized channels (e.g., e-mail, instant messaging, computer conferencing).

Confirmation bias The tendency to seek out and organize data that supports already existing opinions.

Confirming communication A message that expresses caring or respect for another person; the person is valued by the speaker.

Conflict ritual Repeating pattern of interlocking conflict behaviors.

Conflict An expressed struggle between at least two interdependent people who perceive incompatible goals, scarce rewards, and interference from the other person in achieving her or his goals.

Conformity orientation The degree to which family communication stresses uniformity of attitudes, values, and beliefs.

Connection-autonomy dialectic The tension between the need for integration and the need for independence in a relationship.

Content dimension The dimension of a message that communicates information about the subject being discussed. See *Relational dimension.*

Controlling communication According to Gibb, messages that attempt to impose some sort of outcome on another person, resulting in a defensive response.

Conventionality-uniqueness dialectic The tension between the need to behave in ways that conform to others' expectations and the need to assert one's individuality by behaving in ways that violate others' expectations.

Convergence The process of adapting one's speech style to match that of others with whom one wants to identify. See also *Divergence.*

Conversation orientation The degree to which families favor an open climate of discussion of a wide array of topics.

Counterfeit questions Questions that are disguised attempts to send a message rather than elicit information.

Culture According to Samovar and Porter, "the language, values, beliefs, traditions, and customs people share and learn."

Debilitative emotions Emotions of high intensity and long duration that prevent a person from functioning effectively.

De-escalatory spiral A reciprocal communication pattern in which one person's nonthreatening behavior leads to reduced hostility by the other, with the level of hostility steadily decreasing. Opposite of *Escalatory spiral.*

Defensive listening A response style in which the receiver perceives a speaker's comments as an attack.

Defensiveness The attempt to protect a presenting image a person believes is being attacked.

Description Messages that describe a speaker's position without evaluating others.

Designated leader The person (or people) with official titles that indicate authority, for example, "manager."

Dialectical tensions Relational tensions that arise when two opposing or incompatible forces exist simultaneously.

Differentiating A relational stage in which the partners reestablish their individual identities after having bonded.

Direct aggression An expression of the sender's thoughts and/or feelings that attacks the position and dignity of the receiver.

Direct request A compliance-gaining strategy in which the communicator directly asks another person to meet his or her needs.

Disagreeing message A message that essentially communicates to another person, "You are wrong," and includes argumentativeness, complaining, and aggressiveness.

Disconfirming communication A message that expresses a lack of caring or respect for another person; the person is not valued by the speaker.

Disengaged family Families with too little cohesion, in which members have limited attachment or commitment to one another.

Disfluencies Nonlinguistic verbalizations, for example, *um, er, ah.*

Disinhibition Expressing messages without considering the consequences of doing so.

Divergence Speaking in a way that emphasizes difference from others. See also *Convergence.*

Downward communication Communication from managers to subordinates.

Dyad Two communicators who interact with one another.

Dysfunctional conflict Harmful conflict characterized by communication that is coercive, uncooperative, and unfocused, which often results in a win-lose outcome and a damaged relationship.

Emblems Deliberate nonverbal behaviors with precise meanings, known to virtually all members of a cultural group.

Emotional contagion The process by which emotions are transferred from one person to another.

Emotive language Language that conveys the sender's attitude rather than simply offering an objective description.

Empathizing (response) A listening response that conveys identification with a speaker's perceptions and emotions.

Empathy The ability to project oneself into another person's point of view in an attempt to experience the other's thoughts and feelings.

Enmeshed family Families with too much consensus, too little independence, and a very high demand for loyalty.

Environment Both the physical setting in which communication occurs and the personal perspectives of the people involved.

Equality A type of supportive communication described by Gibb, which suggests that the sender regards the receiver with respect.

Equivocal language Ambiguous language that has two or more equally plausible meanings.

Escalatory spiral A reciprocal communication pattern in which one person's attack leads to a counterattack by the other, with the level of hostility steadily increasing. Opposite of *De-escalatory spiral.*

Ethnocentrism An attitude that one's own culture is superior to that of others.

Euphemism A pleasant term substituted for a blunt one in order to soften the impact of unpleasant information.

Evaluating (response) A listening response that appraises a sender's thoughts or behaviors and implies that the person evaluating is qualified to pass judgment on the other.

Evaluation A message in which a sender judges a receiver in some way, usually resulting in a defensive response.

Experimenting An early stage in relational development, consisting of a search for common ground. If the experimentation is successful, the relationship progresses to intensifying. If not, it may go no further.

Expression-privacy dialectic The tension between the desire to be open and disclosive and the desire to be closed and private.

Face The image an individual wants to project to the world. See *Presenting self.*

Face-maintenance strategies Strategies that lead others to act in ways that reinforce the communicator's presenting self.

Face-threatening acts Behavior by another that is perceived as attacking an individual's presenting image, or face.

Facework Actions people take to preserve their own and others' presenting images.

Facilitative emotions Emotions that contribute to effective functioning.

Factual statement A statement that can be verified as true or false. See also *Inferential statement; Opinion statement.*

Fallacy of approval The irrational belief that it is vital to win the approval of virtually every person with whom a communicator interacts.

Fallacy of catastrophic expectations The irrational belief that the worst possible outcome will probably occur.
Fallacy of causation The irrational belief that emotions are caused by others and not by the person who has them.
Fallacy of helplessness The irrational belief that satisfaction in life is determined by forces beyond one's control.
Fallacy of overgeneralization Irrational beliefs in which (1) conclusions (usually negative) are based on limited evidence or (2) communicators exaggerate their shortcomings.
Fallacy of perfection The irrational belief that a worthwhile communicator should be able to handle every situation with complete confidence and skill.
Fallacy of should The irrational belief that people should behave in the most desirable way.
Family A system with two or more interdependent people who have a common past history and a present reality and who expect to influence each other in the future.
Family of origin The family in which a person grows up.
Feedback A discernable response of a receiver to a sender's message. See Chapter 1 for a discussion of this concept's history and potential limitations.
Filling in gaps A listening habit that involves adding details never mentioned by a speaker to complete a message.
First-order reality The physically observable qualities of a thing or situation.
Formal communication Interaction that follows officially established channels in an organization.
Functional conflict Beneficial conflict characterized by communication that is respectful, cooperative, and focused, which results in the resolution of a problem and the strengthening of a relationship.
Gender Psychological sex-type.
Halo effect The tendency to form an overall positive impression of a person on the basis of one positive characteristic.
Haptics The study of touch in human communication.
Hearing The first stage in the listening process, in which sound waves are received by a communicator.
High-context culture A culture that relies heavily on verbal and nonverbal cues to maintain social harmony.
Horizontal communication Communication between people who do not have direct supervisor-subordinate relationships.
"I" language A statement that describes the speaker's reaction to another person's behavior without making judgments about its worth. See also *"You" language.*
Identity management The communication strategies people use to influence how others view them.
Impersonal response A disconfirming response that is superficial or trite.
Impervious response A disconfirming response that ignores another person's attempt to communicate.
Inclusion-seclusion dialectic The tension between a couple's desire for involvement with the "outside world" and their desire to live their own lives, free of what can feel like interference from others.
Incongruous response A disconfirming response in which two messages, one of which is usually nonverbal, contradict one another.

Indirect appeal A compliance-gaining strategy based on the hope that the other person will infer or assume the communicator's unexpressed intent.

Individualistic culture A culture in which people view their primary responsibility as helping themselves.

Inferential statement A statement based on an interpretation of evidence. See also *Factual statement; Opinion statement.*

Informal communication Communication based on friendship, shared personal or career interests, and proximity.

In-group A group with which an individual identifies herself or himself.

Initiating The first stage in relational development, in which the interactants express interest in one another.

Insulated listening A style in which the receiver ignores undesirable information.

Integrating A relational stage in which the interactants begin to take on a single identity.

Integration-separation dialectic The tension between the desire for connection with others and the desire for independence.

Intensifying A relational stage following experimenting, in which the interactants move toward integration by increasing their amount of contact and the breadth and depth of their self-disclosure.

Intercultural communication Communication that occurs when members of two or more cultures or other groups exchange messages in a manner that is influenced by their different cultural perceptions and symbol systems.

Interpersonal communication, qualitative Communication in which people treat each other as unique individuals as opposed to objects.

Interpersonal communication, quantitative Communication between two people.

Interpretation The process of attaching meaning to sense data. Synonymous with decoding.

Interrupting response A disconfirming response in which one communicator interrupts another.

Intimacy A state achieved via intellectual, emotional, and/or physical closeness as well as via shared activities.

Intimate distance One of Hall's four distance zones, ranging from skin contact to 18 inches.

Irrelevant response A disconfirming response in which one communicator's comments bear no relationship to the previous speaker's ideas.

"It" statement A statement in which "it" replaces the personal pronoun "I," making the statement less direct and more evasive.

Johari Window A model that describes the relationship between self-disclosure and self-awareness.

Kinesics The study of body movements.

Lie A deliberate act of deception.

Linguistic relativism The notion that the language individuals use exerts a strong influence on their perceptions.

Listening The process of hearing, attending, understanding, remembering, and responding to messages.

Listening fidelity The degree of congruence between what a listener understands and what the message-sender was attempting to communicate.

Low-context culture A culture that uses language primarily to express thoughts, feelings, and ideas as clearly and logically as possible.

Manipulators Movements in which one part of the body grooms, massages, rubs, holds, fidgets with, pinches, picks, or otherwise manipulates another part.

Metacommunication Messages (usually relational) that refer to other messages; communication about communication.

Mindful listening Careful and thoughtful attention and responses to others' messages.

Mindless listening Reacting to others' messages automatically and routinely, without much mental involvement.

Narrative The stories we use to describe our personal worlds.

Negotiation A process in which two or more people discuss specific proposals in order to find a mutually acceptable agreement.

Networking The process of deliberately meeting people and maintaining contacts to get career information, advice, and leads.

Neutrality A defense-arousing behavior described by Gibb in which the sender expresses indifference toward a receiver.

Noise External, physiological, and psychological distractions that interfere with the accurate transmission and reception of a message.

Nonverbal communication Messages expressed by other than linguistic means.

Norm of reciprocity A social convention that obligates a communicator to return the favors extended by others.

Nurturing culture A culture that regards the support of relationships as an especially important goal. Also termed "feminine" culture.

Oculesics The study of how the eyes can communicate.

Open questions Questions that allow for a variety of extended responses.

Openness-closedness dialectic The tension between the desire to be honest and open and the desire for privacy.

Opinion statement A statement based on a speaker's beliefs. See also *Factual statement; Inferential statement.*

Organization The stage in the perception process that involves arranging data in a meaningful way.

Out-group A group that an individual sees as different from herself or himself.

Paralanguage Nonlinguistic means of vocal expression, for example, rate, pitch, and tone.

Parallel conflict style When partners in a conflict shift from complementary to symmetrical patterns from one conflict issue to another.

Paraphrasing Restating a speaker's thoughts and feelings in the listener's own words.

Passive aggression An indirect expression of aggression, delivered in a way that allows the sender to maintain a facade of kindness.

Perceived self The person we believe ourselves to be in moments of candor. It may be identical with or different from the presenting and desired selves.

Perception checking A three-part method for verifying the accuracy of interpretations, including a description of the sense data, two possible interpretations, and a request for confirmation of the interpretations.

Personal distance One of Hall's four distance zones, ranging from 18 inches to 4 feet.

Personal space The distance we put between ourselves and others.

Phonological rules Rules governing the way in which sounds are pronounced in a language.

Power distance The degree to which members of a society accept the unequal distribution of power among members.

Power A source of influence, such as expert power.

Powerless speech mannerisms Forms of speech that communicate to others a lack of power in the speaker: hedges, hesitations, intensifiers, and so on.

Pragmatic rules Rules that govern interpretation of language in terms of its social context. See also *Semantic rules; Syntactic rules.*

Predictability-novelty dialectic Within a relationship, the tension between the need for a predictable relational partner and one who is more spontaneous and less predictable.

Prejudice An unfairly biased and intolerant attitude toward others who belong to an out-group.

Presenting self The image a person presents to others. It may be identical with or different from the perceived and desired selves.

Problem orientation A supportive style of communication described by Gibb in which the communicators focus on working together to solve their problems instead of trying to impose their own solutions on one another.

Provisionalism A supportive style of communication described by Gibb in which a sender expresses open-mindedness to others' ideas and opinions.

Proxemics The study of how people and animals use space.

Pseudolistening An imitation of true listening in which the receiver's mind is elsewhere.

Psychological sex-type When a person, regardless of her or his biological sex, can act in a masculine manner or a feminine manner or can exhibit strongly both types of characteristics (androgynous) or neither (undifferentiated); the word *gender* is a short-hand term for psychological sex-type.

Public distance One of Hall's four distance zones, extending outward from 12 feet.

Punctuation The process of determining the causal order of events.

Qualitative interpersonal communication Communication in which people treat each other as unique individuals as opposed to objects.

Quantitative interpersonal communication Any interaction between two people.

Questioning (response) A listening response in which the receiver seeks additional information from the sender.

Racist language Language that classifies members of one racial group as superior and others as inferior.

Reference groups Groups against which we compare ourselves, thereby influencing our self-concept and self-esteem.

Reflected appraisal The theory that a person's self-concept matches the way the person believes others regard him or her.

Regulators Nonverbal cues that help control verbal interaction.

Relational appeal Compliance-gaining strategy that relies on the target's relationship with the person making the request (e.g., "Help me because you're my friend").

Relational commitment A promise, explicit or implied, to remain in a relationship and to make that relationship successful.

Relational conflict style A pattern of managing disagreements that repeats itself over time.

Relational dimension The dimension of a message that expresses the social relationship between two or more individuals. See *Content dimension.*

Relational maintenance Communication aimed at keeping relationships operating smoothly and satisfactorily (e.g., behaving in a positive way, being open, and assuring your partner that you're committed to the relationship).
Relative language Words that gain their meaning by comparison.
Remembering A phase of the listening process in which a message is recalled.
Responding A phase of the listening process in which feedback occurs, offering evidence that the message has been received.
Revelation-concealment dialectic The tension between a couple's desire to be open and honest with the "outside world" and their desire to keep things to themselves.
Richness The quantity of nonverbal cues that accompany spoken messages.
Rigid family Families with authoritarian leadership, strict discipline, roles that are inflexible, and unchanging rules.
Rumination Recurrent thoughts not demanded by the immediate environment.
Salience The significance attached to a particular person or phenomenon.
"Sandwich" method Embedding an expression of concern between two positive comments.
Sapir-Whorf hypothesis The best-known declaration of linguistic relativism, formulated by Benjamin Whorf and Edward Sapir.
Second-order realities Perceptions that arise from attaching meaning to first-order things or situations. See *First-order realities.*
Selection A phase of the perception process in which a communicator attends to a stimulus from the environment. Also, a way communicators manage dialectical tensions by responding to one end of the dialectical spectrum and ignoring the other.
Selective listening A listening style in which the receiver responds only to messages that interest her or him.
Self-concept The relatively stable set of perceptions each individual holds of herself or himself. See also *Self-esteem.*
Self-disclosure The process of deliberately revealing information about oneself that is significant and that would not normally be known by others.
Self-esteem The part of the self-concept that involves evaluations of self-worth. See *Self-concept.*
Self-fulfilling prophecy The causal relationship that occurs when a person's expectations of an event and her or his subsequent behavior based on those expectations make the outcome more likely to occur than would otherwise have been true.
Self-monitoring The process of attending to one's behavior and using these observations to shape the way one behaves.
Self-serving bias The tendency to judge oneself in the most generous terms possible while being more critical of others.
Self-talk The nonvocal, internal monologue that is our process of thinking.
Semantic rules Rules that govern the meaning of language, as opposed to its structure. See *Syntactic rules; Pragmatic rules.*
Sexist language Words, phrases, and expressions that unnecessarily differentiate between females and males or exclude, trivialize, or diminish either sex.
Significant other A person whose opinion is important enough to affect one's self-concept strongly.

Silent listening Staying attentive and nonverbally responsive without offering verbal feedback.
Sincere questions Genuine attempts to elicit information from others.
Social comparison Evaluating oneself in terms of or by comparison to others.
Social distance One of Hall's four distance zones, ranging from 4 to 12 feet.
Social identity The part of the self-concept that is based on membership in groups.
Social penetration model A model that describes relationships in terms of their breadth and depth.
Spiral A reciprocal communication pattern in which messages reinforce one another. See *Escalatory spiral; De-escalatory spiral.*
Spontaneity A supportive communication behavior described by Gibb in which the sender expresses a message without any attempt to manipulate the receiver.
Stability-change dialectic The tension between the desire to keep a relationship predictable and stable and the desire for novelty and change.
Stage hogging A listening style in which the receiver is more concerned with making his or her own point than in understanding the speaker.
Stagnating A relational stage characterized by declining enthusiasm and standardized forms of behavior.
Standpoint theory A body of scholarship that explores how one's position in a society shapes one's view of society in general and of specific individuals.
Static evaluation Treating people or objects as if they were unchanging.
Stereotyping Exaggerated beliefs associated with a categorizing system.
Strategy A defense-arousing style of communication described by Gibb in which a sender tries to manipulate or deceive a receiver.
Superiority A defense-arousing style of communication described by Gibb in which the sender states or implies that the receiver is not worthy of respect.
Supporting (response) A listening response in which the receiver reveals her or his solidarity with the speaker's situation.
Symmetrical conflict style Partners in a conflict use the same tactics.
Sympathy Feeling compassion for another person's emotions; entails less identification than *empathy.*
Syntactic rules Rules that govern the ways symbols can be arranged, as opposed to the meanings of those symbols. See *Semantic rules; Pragmatic rules.*
System A group, such as a family, whose members interact with one another to form a whole.
Tangential response A disconfirming response that uses the speaker's remark as a starting point for a shift to a new topic.
Terminating The conclusion of a relationship, characterized by the acknowledgment of one or both partners that the relationship is over.
Territory A stationary area claimed by a person or animal.
Transactional The dynamic process in which communicators create meaning together through interaction.
Uncertainty avoidance The tendency of a culture's members to feel threatened by ambiguous situations, and how much they try to avoid them.
Understanding A stage in the listening process in which the receiver attaches meaning to a message.

Upward communication Communication from subordinates to their bosses.

Virtual teams Teams whose membership transcends the boundaries of location and time.

"We" language The use of first-person-plural pronouns to include others, either appropriately or inappropriately. Language implying that the issue being discussed is the concern and responsibility of both the speaker and the receiver of a message. See *"I" language; "You" language.*

Win-win problem solving An approach to conflict resolution in which people work together to satisfy all their goals.

"You" language A statement that expresses or implies a judgment of the other person. See *Evaluation; "I" language.*

References

5.2 million young Americans may have hearing problems. (2001, July 4). *New York Times*, p. A11.

Aboud, F. E., & Mendelson, M. J. (1998). Determinants of friendship selection and quality: Developmental perspectives. In W. M. Bukowski & A. F. Newcomb (Eds.), *The company they keep: Friendship in childhood and adolescence* (pp. 87–112). New York: Cambridge University Press.

Adamopoulos, J. (1991). The emergence of interpersonal behavior: Diachronic and cross-cultural processes in the evolution of intimacy. In S. Ting-Toomey & F. Korzenny (Eds.), *Cross-cultural interpersonal communication* (pp. 155–170). Newbury Park, CA: Sage.

Adams, G., Anderson, S. L., & Adonu, J. K. (2004). The cultural grounding of closeness and intimacy. In D. Mashek & A. Aron (Eds.), *The handbook of closeness and intimacy* (pp. 321–339). Mahwah, NJ: Erlbaum.

Adler, R. B., & Elmhorst, J. M. (2008). *Communicating at work: Principles and practices for business and the professions* (9th ed.). New York: McGraw-Hill.

Adler, R. B., & Rodman, G. (2009). *Understanding human communication* (10th ed.). New York: Oxford University Press.

Adler, T. (1992, October). Personality, like plaster, is pretty stable over time. *APA Monitor,* p. 18.

Adler, T. (1993, February). Congressional staffers witness miracle of touch. *APA Monitor,* pp. 12–13.

Afifi, W. A., & Caughlin, J. P. (2007). A close look at revealing secrets and some consequences that follow. *Communication Research, 33,* 467–488.

Afifi, W. A., & Johnson, M. L. (1999). The use and interpretation of tie signs in a public setting: Relationship and sex differences. *Journal of Social and Personal Relationships, 16,* 9–38.

Agne, R., Thompson, T. L., & Cusella, L. P. (2000). Stigma in the line of face: Self-disclosure of patients' HIV status to health care providers. *Journal of Applied Communication Research, 28,* 235–261.

Akehurst, L., Bull, R., Vrij, A., & Köhnken, G. (2004). The effects of training professional groups and lay persons to use criteria-based content analysis to detect deception. *Applied Cognitive Psychology, 18,* 877–891.

Alaimo, K., Olson, C. M., & Frongillo, E. A. (2001). Food insufficiency and American school-aged children's cognitive, academic, and psychosocial development. *Pediatrics, 108,* 44–53.

Albada, K. F., Knapp, M. L., & Theune, K. E. (2002). Interaction Appearance Theory: Changing perceptions of physical attractiveness through social interaction. *Communication Theory, 12,* 8–40.

Alberts, J. K. (1988). An analysis of couples' conversational complaints. *Communication Monographs, 55,* 184–197.

Alberts, J. K. (1990). Perceived effectiveness of couples' conversational complaints. *Communication Studies, 40,* 280–291.

Alberts, J. K., & Driscoll, G. (1992). Containment versus escalation: The trajectory of couples' conversational complaints. *Western Journal of Communication, 56,* 394–412.

Alberts, J. K., Kellar-Guenther, U., & Corman, S. R. (1996). That's not funny: Understanding recipients' responses to teasing. *Western Journal of Communication, 60,* 337–357.

Alberts, J. K., Yoshimura, C. G., Rabby, M., & Loschiavo, R. (2005). Mapping the topography of couples' daily conversation. *Journal of Social and Personal Relationships, 22,* 299–322.

Albrecht, T. L., & Adelman, M. B. (1987). Communicating social support: A theoretical perspective. In T. L. Albrecht & M. B. Adelman (Eds.), *Communicating social support* (pp. 18–39). Newbury Park, CA: Sage.

Aleman, M. W. (2005). Embracing and resisting romantic fantasies as the rhetorical vision on a SeniorNet discussion board. *Journal of Communication, 55*(1), 5–21.

Allan, J., Fairtlough, G., & Heinzen, B. (2002). *The power of the tale: Using narratives for organisational success.* Chichester, England: Wiley.

Allen, B., (1995). "Diversity" and organizational communication. *Journal of Applied Communication Research, 23,* 143–155.

Allen, M. (1998). Methodological considerations when examining a gendered world. In D. J. Canary & K. Dindia (Eds.), *Handbook of sex differences and similarities in communication* (pp. 427–444). Mahwah, NJ: Erlbaum.

Almaney, A., & Alwan, A. (1982). *Communicating with the Arabs.* Prospect Heights, IL: Waveland.

Altman, I., & Taylor, D. A. (1973). *Social penetration: The development of interpersonal relationships.* New York: Holt, Rinehart & Winston.

Ambady, N., Koo, J., Lee, F., & Rosenthal, R. (1996). More than words: Linguistic and nonlinguistic politeness in two cultures. *Journal of Personality and Social Psychology, 70,* 996–1011.

Ambady, N. LaPlante, D., Nguyen, T., Rosenthal, R., Chaumeton, N. &, Levinson, W. (2002). Surgeons' tone of voice: A clue to malpractice history. *Surgery, 132,* 5–9.

Ambady, N., & Rosenthal, R. (1993). Half a minute: Predicting teacher evaluations from thin slices of nonverbal behavior and physical attractiveness. *Journal of Personality and Social Psychology, 64,* 431–441.

Amichai-Hamburger, Y., & Ben-Artzi, E. (2003). Loneliness and Internet use. *Computers in Human Behavior, 19*(1), 71–80.

Amodio, D. M., & Showers, C. J. (2005). "Similarity breeds liking" revisited: The moderating role of commitment. *Journal of Social and Personal Relationships, 22,* 817–836.

Andersen, P. A. (1992). Nonverbal communication in the small group. In R. S. Cathcart & L. A. Samovar (Eds.), *Small group communication: A reader* (6th ed., pp. 272–286). Dubuque, IA: William C Brown.

Andersen, P. A. (1999). *Nonverbal communication: Forms and functions.* Palo Alto, CA: Mayfield.

Andersen, P. A., Lustig, M. W., & Andersen, J. F. (1987a). *Changes in latitude, changes in attitude: The relationship between climate, latitude, and interpersonal communication predispositions.* Paper presented at the annual convention of the Speech Communication Association, Boston.

Andersen, P. A., Lustig, M. W., & Andersen, J. F. (1987b). Regional patterns of communication in the United States: A theoretical perspective. *Communication Monographs, 54,* 128–144.

Anderson, R. A., Corazzini, K. N., & McDaniel, R. R., Jr. (2004). Complexity science and the dynamics of climate and communication: Reducing nursing home turnover. *Gerontologist, 44,* 378–388.

Andrews, P. H., & Baird, J. E. (2000). *Communication for business and the professions* (7th ed.). New York: McGraw-Hill.

Anglin, D. M., & Whaley, A. L. (2006). Racial/ethnic self-labeling in relation to group socialization and identity in African-descended individuals. *Journal of Language & Social Psychology, 25,* 457–463.

Antioch College. (2006). *The Antioch College sexual offense prevention policy.* Available at: http://www.antioch-college.edu/Campus/sopp/SOPP2006%20.pdf

Applegate, J. (1990). Constructs and communication: A pragmatic integration. In G. J. Neimeyer & R. A. Neimeyer (Eds.), *Advances in personal construct psychology* (pp. 203–230). Stamford, CT: JAI Press.

Arasaratnam, L. A. (2006). Further testing of a new model of intercultural communication competence. *Communication Research Reports, 23,* 93–99.

Arasaratnam, L. A. (2007). Research in intercultural communication competence. *Journal of International Communication, 13*(2), 66–73.

Archer, J. (2002). Sex differences in physically aggressive acts between heterosexual partners: A meta-analytic review. *Aggression and Violent Behavior, 7,* 313–351.

Archer, R., & Berg, J. (1978, November). To encourage intimacy, don't force it. *Psychology Today, 12,* 39–40.

Argyle, M., & Henderson, M. (1985). The rules of relationships. In S. Duck & D. Perlman (Eds.), *Understanding personal relationships: An interdisciplinary approach* (pp. 63–84). Beverly Hills, CA: Sage.

Armstrong, G. B., Boiarsky, G. A., & Mares, M. L. (1991). Background television and reading performance. *Communication Monographs, 58,* 235–253.

Aronson, E., Willerman, B., & Floyd, J. (1966). The effect of a pratfall on increasing interpersonal attractiveness. *Psychonomic Science, 4,* 227–228.

Arsenault, A. (2007, May). *Too much information?: Gatekeeping and information dissemination in a networked world.* Paper presented at the annual meeting of the International Communication Association, San Francisco.

Asante, M. K. (2002). Language and agency in the transformation of American identity. In W. F. Eadie & P. E. Nelson (Eds.), *The changing conversation in America: Lectures from the Smithsonian* (pp. 77–89). Thousand Oaks, CA: Sage.

Ashkanasy, N. M., Wilderom, C., & Peterson, M. F. (Eds.). (2000). *Handbook of organizational culture and climate.* Thousand Oaks, CA: Sage.

Atheunis, M. L., Valkenburg, P. M., & Peter, J. (2007). Computer-mediated communication and interpersonal attraction: An experimental test of two explanatory hypotheses. *CyberPsychology & Behavior, 10,* 831–835.

Atkin, C. K., Smith, S. W., Roberto, A. J., Fediuk, T., & Wagner, T. (2002). Correlates of verbally aggressive communication in adolescents. *Journal of Applied Communication Research, 30,* 251–268.

Atkinson, E. (2001). Deconstructing boundaries: Out on the inside? *Qualitative Studies in Education, 14,* 307–316.

Attacks on U.S. soil. (2001, September 12). *Washington Post.* Retrieved from http://discuss.washingtonpost.com/wp-srv/zforum/01/nation_weaver091201.htm

Attardo, S., Eisterhold, J., Hay, J., & Poggi, I. (2003). Multimodal markers of irony and sarcasm. *Humor: International Journal of Humor Research, 16,* 243–260.

Aune, R. K., & Kikuchi, T. (1993). Effects of language intensity similarity on perceptions of credibility, relational attributions, and persuasion. *Journal of Language and Social Psychology, 12,* 224–238.

Avery, R. D., & Campion, J. E. (1982). The employment interview: A summary and review of recent research. *Personnel Psychology, 35,* 284–308.

Avtgis, T. A. (1999). The relationship between unwillingness to communicate and family communication patterns. *Communication Research Reports, 16,* 333–338.

Avtgis, T. A., West, D. V., & Anderson, T. L. (1998). Relationship stages: An inductive analysis identifying cognitive, affective, and behavioral dimensions of Knapp's relational stages model. *Communication Research Reports, 15,* 280–287.

Aylor, B., & Dainton, M. (2004). Biological sex and psychological gender as predictors of routine and strategic relational maintenance. *Sex Roles, 50,* 689–697.

Ayres, J., & Crosby, S. (1995). Two studies concerning the predictive validity of the personal report of communication apprehension in employment interviews. *Communication Research Reports, 12,* 145–151.

Ayres, J., & Hopf, T. (1993). *Coping with speech anxiety.* Norwood, NJ: Ablex.

Bach, G. R., & Wyden, P. (1968). *The intimate enemy.* New York: Avon.

Bachman, G. F., & Guerrero, L. K. (2006). Forgiveness, apology, and communicative responses to hurtful event. *Communication Reports, 19,* 45–56.

Back, M. D., Schmukle, S. C., & Egloff, B. (2008). Becoming friends by chance. *Psychological Science, 19,* 439–440.

Bailey, R.W. (2003). Ideologies, attitudes, and perceptions. *American Speech, 88,* 115–142.

Baker, W. (2000). *Achieving success through social capital.* San Francisco: Jossey-Bass.
Bakker, A. B. (2005). Flow among music teachers and their students: The crossover of peak experiences. *Journal of Vocational Behavior, 66,* 26–44.
Baldwin, M. W., & Keelan, J. P. R. (1999). Interpersonal expectations as a function of self-esteem and sex. *Journal of Social and Personal Relationships, 16,* 822–833.
Balswick, J. O. (1988). *The inexpressive male: A tragedy of American society.* Lexington, MA: Lexington Books.
Bank, S. P. (1995). Before the last leaves fall: Sibling connections among the elderly. *Journal of Geriatric Psychiatry, 28,* 183–195.
Banks, S. P. (1987). Achieving "unmarkedness" in organizational discourse: A praxis perspective in ethnolinguistic identity. *Journal of Language and Social Psychology, 6,* 171–190.
Barak, A., & Gluck-Ofri, O. (2007). Degree and reciprocity of self-disclosure in online forums. *CyberPsychology & Behavior, 10,* 407–417.
Barbato, C. A., Graham, E. E., & Perse, E. M. (2003). Communicating in the family: An examination of the relationship of family communication climate and interpersonal communication motives. *Journal of Family Communication, 3*(3), 123–148.
Barbee, P. P., Gulley, M. R., & Cunningham, M. R. (1990). Support seeking in personal relationships. *Journal of Social and Personal Relationships, 7,* 531–540.
Barge, J. K., & Schlueter, D. W. (2004). Memorable messages and newcomer socialization. *Western Journal of Communication, 68,* 233–256.
Bargh, J. A. (1988). Automatic information processing: Implications for communication and affect. In L. Donohew & H. E. Sypher (Eds.), *Communication, social cognition, and affect* (pp. 9–32). Hillsdale, NJ: Erlbaum.
Barker, L. L. (1971). *Listening behavior.* Englewood Cliffs, NJ: Prentice-Hall.
Barker, L. L., Edwards, R., Gaines, C., Gladney, K., & Holley, F. (1981). An investigation of proportional time spent in various communication activities by college students. *Journal of Applied Communication Research, 8,* 101–109.
Barnes, S. B. (2003). *Computer-mediated communication: Human-to-human communication across the Internet.* Boston: Allyn & Bacon.
Barrett, L. F., Gross, J., Christensen, T., & Benvenuto, M. (2001). Knowing what you're feeling and knowing what to do about it: Mapping the relation between emotion differentiation and emotion regulation. *Cognition and Emotion, 15,* 713–724.
Barrick, M. R., Bradley, B. H., Kristof-Brown, A, L., & Colbert, A. E. (2007). The moderating role of top management team interdependence: Implications for real teams and working groups. *Academy of Management Journal, 50,* 544–557.
Barry, D. (1990). *Dave Barry turns 40.* New York: Fawcett Columbine.
Bartels, J., Pruyn, A., De Jong, M., & Joustra, I. (2008). Multiple organizational identification levels and the impact of perceived external prestige and communication climate. *Journal of Organizational Behavior, 28*, 173–190.
Baruch, Y., & Jenkins, S. (2006). Swearing at work and permissive leadership culture: When anti-social becomes social and incivility is acceptable. *Leadership & Organization Development Journal, 28,* 492–507.
Basso, K. (1970). To give up on words: Silence in Western Apache culture. *Southern Journal of Anthropology, 26,* 213–230.
Bateson, G., & Jackson, D. D. (1964). Some varieties of pathogenic organization. *Disorders of Communication* [Research Publications: Association for Research in Nervous and Mental Disease], *42,* 270–283.
Battaglia, D. M., Richard, F. D., Datteri, D. L., & Lord, C. G. (1998). Breaking up is (relatively) easy to do: A script for the dissolution of close relationships. *Journal of Social and Personal Relationships, 15,* 829–845.
Baumeister, R. F. (2005). *The cultural animal: Human nature, meaning, and social life.* New York: Oxford University Press.
Baumeister, R. F., Bratslavsky, E., Finkenauer, C., & Vohs, K. D. (2001). Bad is stronger than good. *Review of General Psychology, 5,* 323–370.

Baumeister, R. F., Campbell, J. D., Krueger, J. I., & Vohs, K. D. (2003). Does high self-esteem cause better performance, interpersonal success, happiness, or healthier lifestyles? *Psychological Science in the Public Interest, 4,* 1–44.

Baumeister, R. F., & Leary, M. R. (1995). The need to belong: Desire for interpersonal attachments as a fundamental human motivation. *Psychological Bulletin, 117,* 497–529.

Bavelas, J. B., Black, A., Chovil, N., & Mullett, J. (1990). *Equivocal communication.* Newbury Park, CA: Sage.

Bavelas, J. B., Coates, L., & Johnson, T. (2002). Listener responses as a collaborative process: The role of gaze. *Journal of Communication, 52,* 566–580.

Baxter, L. A. (1987). Symbols of relationship identity in relationship culture. *Journal of Social and Personal Relationships, 4,* 261–280.

Baxter, L. A. (1992). Forms and functions of intimate play in personal relationships. *Human Communication Research, 18,* 336–363.

Baxter, L. A. (1994). A dialogic approach to relationship maintenance. In D. J. Canary & L. Stafford (Eds.), *Communication and relational maintenance* (pp. 233–254). San Diego: Academic Press.

Baxter, L. A., & Braithwaite, D. O. (2006). Social dialectics: The contradictions of relating. In B. Whaley & W. Samter (Eds.), *Contemporary communication theories and exemplars.* Mahwah, NJ: Erlbaum.

Baxter, L. A., Braithwaite, D. O., Golish, T. D., & Olson, L. N. (2002). Contradictions of interaction for wives of elderly husbands with adult dementia. *Journal of Applied Communication Research, 30,* 1–20.

Baxter, L. A., & Erbert, L. A. (1999). Perceptions of dialectical contradictions in turning points of development in heterosexual romantic relationships. *Journal of Social and Personal Relationships, 16,* 547–569.

Baxter, L. A., & Montgomery, B. M. (1996). *Relating: Dialogues and dialectics.* New York: Guilford Press.

Baxter, L. A., & Pittman, G. (2001). Communicatively remembering turning points of relational development in heterosexual romantic relationships. *Communication Reports, 14,* 1–17.

Baxter, L. A., & Wilmot, W. W. (1985). Taboo topics in close relationships. *Journal of Social and Personal Relationships, 2,* 253–269.

Bazil, L. G. D. (1999). The effects of social behavior on fourth- and fifth-grade girls' perceptions of physically attractive and unattractive peers. *Dissertation Abstracts International, 59,* 4533B.

Beatty, M. J., Burant, P. A., Dobos, J. A., & Rudd, J. E. (1996). Trait verbal aggressiveness and the appropriateness and effectiveness of fathers' interaction plans. *Communication Quarterly, 44,* 1–15.

Beatty, M. J., Marshall, L. A., & Rudd, J. E. (2001). A twins study of communicative adaptability: Heritability of individual differences. *Quarterly Journal of Speech, 87,* 366–377.

Beatty, M. J., & McCroskey, J. C. (1997). It's in our nature: Verbal aggressiveness as temperamental expression. *Communication Quarterly, 45,* 446–460.

Beatty, M. J., McCroskey, J. C., & Heisel, A. D. (1998). Communication apprehension as temperamental expression: A communibiological paradigm. *Communication Monographs, 65,* 197–219.

Beaulieu, C. M. (2004). Intercultural study of personal space: A case study. *Journal of Applied Social Psychology, 34,* 794–805.

Beck, C. E., & Beck, E. A. (1996). The manager's open door and the communication climate. In K. M. Galvin & P. Cooper (Eds.), *Making connections: Readings in relational communication* (pp. 286–290). Los Angeles: Roxbury.

Becker, J. A. H., Ellevold, B., & Stamp, G. H. (2008) The creation of defensiveness in social interaction II: A model of defensive communication among romantic couples. *Communication Monographs, 75,* 86–110.

Before the interview. (1999). Washington, DC: U.S. Department of the Interior.

Belkin, L. Y. (2008). Emotional contagion in the electronic communication context in organizations. *DAI, 68*(9-A), 3940.

Bell, B. S., & Kozlowski, S. W. J. (2002). A typology of virtual teams: Implications for effective leadership. *Group and Organization Management, 27*(1), 14–49.

Bell, R. A., Buerkel-Rothfuss, N. L., & Gore, K. E. (1987). Did you bring the yarmulke for the Cabbage Patch Kid?: The idiomatic communication of young lovers. *Human Communication Research, 14,* 47–67.

Bell, R. A., & Healey, J. G. (1992). Idiomatic communication and interpersonal solidarity in friends' relational cultures. *Human Communication Research, 18,* 307–335.

Bellah, R. N., Madsen, R., Sullivan, W. M., Swidler, A., & Tipton, S. M. (1985). *Habits of the heart: Individualism and commitment in American life.* Berkeley: University of California Press.

Bello, R., & Edwards, R. (2005). Interpretations of messages: The influence of various forms of equivocation, face concerns, and sex differences. *Journal of Language and Social Psychology, 24,* 160–181.

Bem, S. L. (1974). The measurement of psychological androgyny. *Journal of Consulting and Clinical Psychology, 42,* 155–162.

Bender, S. L., & Messner, E. (2003). *Becoming a therapist: What do I say, and why?* New York: Guilford Press.

Benenson, J. F., Gordon, A. J., & Roy, R. (2000). Children's evaluative appraisals of competition in tetrads versus dyads. *Small Group Research, 31,* 635–652.

Benne, K. D., & Sheats, P. (1948). Functional roles of group members. *Journal of Social Issues, 4,* 41–49.

Bennehum, D. S. (2005, July). Old emails never die. Wired. Retrieved from http://www.wired.com/wired/archive/7.05/email_pr.html

Benoit, W. L., & Benoit, P. J. (1987). Everyday argument practices of naive social actors. In J. Wenzel (Ed.), *Argument and critical practice.* Annandale, VA: Speech Communication Association.

Ben-Ze'ev, A. (2003). Privacy, emotional closeness, and openness in cyberspace. *Computers in Human Behavior, 19,* 451–467.

Berger, C. R. (1979). Beyond initial interactions: Uncertainty, understanding, and the development of interpersonal relationships. In H. Giles & R. St. Clair (Eds.), *Language and social psychology* (pp. 122–144). Oxford, England: Blackwell.

Berger, C. R. (1987). Communicating under uncertainty. In M. Roloff & G. Miller (Eds.), *Interpersonal processes: New directions in communication research* (pp. 39–62). Newbury Park, CA: Sage.

Berger, C. R. (1988). Uncertainty and information exchange in developing relationships. In S. Duck & D. F. Hay (Eds.), *Handbook of personal relationships: Theory, research and interventions* (pp. 239–255). New York: Wiley.

Berger, C. R., & diBattista, P. (1993). Communication failure and plan adaptation: If at first you don't succeed, say it louder and slower. *Communication Monographs, 60,* 220–238.

Berger, C. R., & Kellermann, K. (1994). Acquiring social information. In J. M. Wiemann & J. A. Daly (Eds.), *Communicating strategically* (pp. 1–31). Hillsdale, NJ: Erlbaum.

Bergman, M. E., Watrous-Rodriguez, K. M., & Chalkley, K. M. (2008). Identity and language: Contributions to and consequences of speaking Spanish in the workplace. *Hispanic Journal of Behavioral Sciences, 30*(1), 40–68.

Bergner, R. M., & Holmes, J. R. (2000). Self-concepts and self-concept change: A status dynamic approach. *Psychotherapy: Theory, Research, Practice, Training, 37,* 36–44.

Berscheid, E., & Ammazzalorso, H. (2001). Emotional experience in close relationships. In G. J. O. Fletcher & M. S. Clark (Eds.), *Blackwell handbook of social psychology: Interpersonal processes* (pp. 308–330). Oxford, England: Blackwell.

Berscheid, E., Schneider, M., & Omoto, A. M. (1989). Issues in studying close relationships: Conceptualizing and measuring closeness. In C. Hendrick (Ed.), *Close relationships* (pp. 63–91). Newbury Park, CA: Sage.

Berscheid, E., & Walster, E. H. (1978). *Interpersonal attraction* (2nd ed.). Reading, MA: Addison-Wesley.

Bharti, A. (1985). The self in Hindu thought and action. In A. J. Marsella, G. DeVos, & F. L. K. Hsu (Eds.), *Culture and self: Asian and Western perspectives.* New York: Tavistock.

Bingham, S. G., & Battey, K. M. (2005). Communication of social support to sexual harassment victims: Professors' responses to a student's narrative of unwanted sexual attention. *Communication Studies, 56,* 131–155.

Bippus, A. M. (2001). Recipients' criteria for evaluating the skillfulness of comforting communication and the outcomes of comforting interactions. *Communication Monographs, 68,* 301–313.

Bippus, A. M., & Young, S. L. (2005). Owning your emotions: Reactions to expressions of self- versus other-attributed positive and negative emotions. *Journal of Applied Communication Research, 33,* 26–45.

Birdwhistell, R. L. (1970). *Kinesics and context.* Philadelphia: University of Pennsylvania Press.

Bischoping, K. (1993). Gender differences in conversation topic, 1922–1990. *Sex Roles, 28,* 1–18.

Bisson, M. A., & Levine, T. R. (2007) Negotiating a friends with benefits relationship. *Archives of Sexual Behavior.* Available at: http://www.springerlink.com/content/t22037j0215j4367/fulltext.pdf.

Bjorklund, D. F., Cassel, W. S., Bjorklund, B. R., Brown, R. D., Park, C. L., & Ernst, K. (2000). Social demand characteristics in children's and adults' eyewitness memory and suggestibility: The effect of different interviewers on free recall and recognition. *Applied Cognitive Psychology, 14,* 421–433.

Blacker, L. (1999). The launching phase of the life cycle. In B. Carter & M. McGoldrick (Eds.), *The expanded family life cycle: Individual, family, and social perspectives* (3rd ed., pp. 287–306). Boston: Allyn & Bacon.

Blake, R. R., & Mouton, J. S. (1964). *The managerial grid.* Houston: Gulf Publishing.

Blank, P. D. (Ed.). (1993). *Interpersonal expectations: Theory, research, and applications.* Cambridge, England: Cambridge University Press.

Boase, J., Horrigan, J. B., Wellman, B., & Rainie, L. (2006). The strength of Internet ties. *Pew Internet & American Life Project.* Available at: http://www.pewinternet.org/pdfs/PIP_Internet_ties.pdf.

Bodary, D. L. (2000). Hemispheric style and social interaction preferences: An exploratory investigation. *Dissertation Abstracts International, 61,* 25.

Bok, S. (1978). *Lying: Moral choice in public and private life.* New York: Pantheon.

Bolles, R. N. (2008). *What color is your parachute? A practical manual for job-hunters and career-changers.* Berkeley, CA: Ten Speed Press.

Bonvicini, K. A. (2008). Physician empathy: Impact of communication training on physician behavior and patient perceptions. *DAI, 68*(8-B), 5107.

Booth-Butterfield, M., & Booth-Butterfield, S. (1998). Emotionality and affective orientation. In J. C. McCroskey, J. A. Daly, M. M. Martin, & M. J. Beatty (Eds.), *Communication and personality: Trait perspectives* (pp. 171–190). Cresskill, NJ: Hampton.

Booth-Butterfield, M., & Jordan, F. (1989). Communication adaptation among racially homogeneous and heterogeneous groups. *Southern Communication Journal, 54,* 253–272.

Bostrom, R. N. (1996). Aspects of listening behavior. In O. Hargie (Ed.), *Handbook of communication skills* (2nd ed., pp 236–259). London: Routledge.

Bostrom, R. N., & Waldhart, E. S. (1980). Components in listening behavior: The role of short-term memory. *Human Communication Research, 6,* 221–227.

Bourhis, J., & Allen, M. (1992). Meta-analysis of the relationship between communication apprehension and cognitive performance. *Communication Education, 41,* 68–76.

Bower, B. (1998, September 12). Social disconnections on-line. *Science News, 154,* 168.

Brackett, M. A., Warner, R. M., & Bosco, J. S. (2005). Emotional intelligence and relationship quality among couples. *Personal Relationships, 12,* 197–212.

Bradbury, T. N., & Fincham, F. D. (1990). Attributions in marriage: Review and critique. *Psychological Bulletin, 107,* 3–33.

Braithwaite, D. O., Baxter, L. A., & Harper, A. M. (1998). The role of rituals in the management of the dialectical tension of "old" and "new" in blended families. *Communication Studies, 49,* 101–120.

Braithwaite, D. O., & Eckstein, N. (2003). Reconceptualizing supportive interactions: How persons with disabilities communicatively manage assistance. *Journal of Applied Communication Research, 31,* 1–26.

Braithwaite, D. O., Olson, L. N., Golish, T. D., Soukup, C., & Turman, P. (2001). "Becoming a family": Developmental processes represented in blended family discourse. *Journal of Applied Communication Research, 29*, 221–247.

Brantley, A., Knox, D., & Zusman, M. E. (2002). When and why gender differences in saying "I love you" among college students. *College Student Journal, 36,* 614–615.

Brashers, D. E., & Jackson, S. (1999). Changing conceptions of "message effect": A 24-year overview. *Human Communication Research, 25,* 457–477.

Brescoll, V. L., & Uhlmann, E. L. (2008). Can an angry woman get ahead? Status conferral, gender, and expression of emotion in the workplace. *Psychological Science, 19,* 268–275.

Brightman, V., Segal, A., Werther, P., & Steiner, J. (1975). Ethological study of facial expression in response to taste stimuli. *Journal of Dental Research, 54,* 141.

Brilhart, J. K., Galanes, G. J., & Adams, K. (2001). *Effective group discussion* (10th ed.). New York: McGraw-Hill.

Broome, B. J. (1991). Building shared meaning: Implications of a relational approach to empathy for teaching intercultural communication. *Communication Education, 40,* 235–249.

Brown, D. (1991). *Human universals.* New York: McGraw-Hill.

Brown, J. D., & Mankowski, T. A. (1993). Self-esteem, mood, and self-evaluation: Changes in mood and the way you see you. *Journal of Personality and Social Psychology, 64,* 421–430.

Brown, J. R. (2004). Conflict, emotions and appreciation of differences. *Gestalt Review, 8,* 323–335.

Brown, L. (1982). *Communicating facts and ideas in business.* Englewood Cliffs, NJ: Prentice-Hall.

Brown, L. (2002). *Resume writing made easy* (7th ed.). Upper Saddle River, NJ: Prentice-Hall PTR.

Brownell, J. (1990). Perceptions of effective listeners: A management study. *Journal of Business Communication, 27,* 401–415.

Bruess, C. J. S., & Pearson, J. C. (1997). Interpersonal rituals in marriage and adult friendship. *Communication Monographs, 64,* 25–46.

Buck, R., & VanLear, C. A. (2002). Verbal and nonverbal communication: Distinguishing symbolic, spontaneous and pseudo-spontaneous nonverbal behavior. *Journal of Communication, 52,* 522–541.

Budescu, D. V., Erev, I., & Zwick, R. (Eds.). (1999). *Games and human behavior: Essays in honor of Amnon Rapoport.* Mahwah, NJ: Erlbaum.

Buller, D. B., & Aune, K. (1988). The effects of vocalics and nonverbal sensitivity on compliance: A speech accommodation theory explanation. *Human Communication Research, 14,* 301–332.

Buller, D. B., & Aune, K. (1992). The effects of speech rate similarity on compliance application of communication accommodation theory. *Western Journal of Communication, 56,* 37–53.

Buller, D. B., & Burgoon, J. K. (1994). Deception: Strategic and nonstrategic communication. In J. A. Daly & J. M. Wiemann (Eds.), *Strategic interpersonal communication* (pp. 191–223). Hillsdale, NJ: Erlbaum.

Buller, D. B., & Burgoon, J. K. (1996). Interpersonal deception theory. *Communication Theory, 6,* 203–242.

Burggraf, C. S., & Sillars, A. L. (1987). A critical examination of sex differences in marital communication. *Communication Monographs, 54,* 276–294.

Burgoon, J. K., & Bacue, A. E. (2003). Nonverbal communication skills. In B. Burleson & J. O. Greene (Eds.), *Handbook of communication and social interaction skills* (pp. 179–219). Mahwah, NJ: Erlbaum.

Burgoon, J. K., Berger, C. R., & Waldron, V. R. (2000). Mindfulness and interpersonal communication. *Journal of Social Issues, 56,* 105–127.

Burgoon, J. K., Birk, T., & Pfau, M. (1990). Nonverbal behaviors, persuasion, and credibility. *Human Communication Research, 17,* 140–169.

Burgoon, J. K., Buller, D. B., & Guerrero, L. K. (1995). Interpersonal deception: IX. Effects of social skill and nonverbal communication on deception success and detection accuracy. *Journal of Language and Social Psychology, 14,* 289–311.

Burgoon, J. K., Buller, D. B., Guerrero, L. K., & Feldman, C. M. (1994). Interpersonal deception: VI. Effects of preinteractional and interactional factors on deceiver and observer perceptions of deception success. *Communication Studies, 45,* 263–280.

Burgoon, J. K., & Burgoon, M. (2001). Expectancy theories. In P. Robinson & H. Giles (Eds.), *The new handbook of language and social psychology* (2nd ed.). Sussex, England: Wiley.

Burgoon, J. K., & Le Poire, B. A. (1999). Nonverbal cues and interpersonal judgments: Participant and observer perceptions of intimacy, dominance, and composure. *Communication Monographs, 66,* 105–124.

Burgoon, J. K., Parrott, R., Le Poire, B. A., Kelley, D. L., Walther, J. B., & Perry, D. (1989). Maintaining and restoring privacy through different types of relationships. *Journal of Social and Personal Relationships, 6,* 131–158.

Burgoon, J. K., Walther, J., & Baesler, E. (1992). Interpretations, evaluations, and consequences of interpersonal touch. *Human Communication Research, 19,* 237–263.

Burkitt, I. (1992). *Social selves: Theories of the social formation of personality.* Newbury Park, CA: Sage.

Burleson, B. R. (1982). The development of comforting communication skills in childhood and adolescence. *Child Development, 53,* 1578–1588.

Burleson, B. R. (1984). Comforting communication. In H. Sypher & J. Applegate (Eds.), *Communication by children and adults: Social cognitive and strategic processes* (pp. 63–104). Beverly Hills, CA: Sage.

Burleson, B. R. (1994). Comforting messages: Features, functions and outcomes. In J. A. Daly & J. M. Wiemann (Eds.), *Strategic interpersonal communication* (pp. 135–161). Hillsdale, NJ: Erlbaum.

Burleson, B. R. (2003). Emotional support skill. In J. O. Greene & B. R. Burleson (Eds.), *Handbook of communication and social interaction skills* (pp. 551–594). Mahwah, NJ: Erlbaum.

Burleson, B. R. (2007). Constructivism: A general theory of communication skill. In B. B. Whaley & W. Samter (Eds.), *Explaining communication: Contemporary theories and exemplars* (pp. 105–128). Mahwah, NJ: Erlbaum.

Burleson, B. R., & Caplan, S. E. (1998). Cognitive complexity. In J. C. McCroskey, J. A. Daly, M. M. Martin, & M. J. Beatty (Eds.), *Communication and personality: Trait perspectives* (pp. 233–286). Cresskill, NJ: Hampton Press.

Burleson, B. R., Holmstrom, A. J., & Gilstrap, C. M. (2005). "Guys can't say that to guys": Four experiments assessing the normative motivation account for deficiencies in the emotional support provided by men. *Communication Monographs, 72,* 468–501.

Burleson, B. R., Kunkel, A. W., Samter, W., & Werking, K. J. (1996). Men's and women's evaluations of communication skills in personal relationships: When sex differences make a difference—and when they don't. *Journal of Social and Personal Relationships, 13,* 201–224.

Burleson, B. R., & Samter, W. (1985). Individual differences in the perception of comforting messages: An exploratory investigation. *Central States Speech Journal, 36,* 39–50.

Burleson, B. R., & Samter, W. (1994). A social skills approach to relationship maintenance. In D. J. Canary & L. Stafford (Eds.), *Communication and relationship maintenance: How individual differences in communication skills affect the achievement of relationship functions* (pp. 61–90). San Diego: Academic Press.

Burleson, B. R., & Samter, W. (1996). Similarity in the communication skills of young adults: Foundations of attraction, friendship, and relationship satisfaction. *Communication Reports, 9,* 127–139.

Burns, K. L., & Beier, E. G. (1973). Significance of vocal and visual channels for the decoding of emotional meaning. *Journal of Communication, 23,* 118–130.

Burton, C. M., & King, L. A. (2008). Effects of (very) brief writing on health: The two-minute miracle. *British Journal of Health Psychology, 13,* 9–14.

Bushman, B. J. (1988). The effects of apparel on compliance: A field experiment with a female authority figure. *Personality and Social Psychology Bulletin, 14,* 459–467.

Bushman, B. J., Baumeister, R. F., & Stack, A. D. (1999). Catharsis, aggression, and persuasive influence: Self-fulfilling or self-defeating prophecies? *Journal of Personality and Social Psychology, 76,* 367–376.

Business meeting is alive and well . . . for now, The. (1997, September). *Risk Management, 44,* 6.

Buss, D. M. (1985, January-February). Human mate selection. *American Scientist, 73,* 47–51.

Butler, M. M. (2005). Communication apprehension and its impact on individuals in the work place. *Dissertation Abstracts International, 65,* 3215.

Buttny, R. (1997). Reported speech in talking race on campus. *Human Communication Research, 23,* 477–506.

Button, S. B. (2004). Identity management strategies utilized by lesbian and gay employees: A quantitative investigation. *Group and Organizational Management, 29,* 470–494.

Buunk, A. P. (2005). How do people respond to others with high commitment or autonomy in their relationships? *Journal of Social and Personal Relationships, 22,* 653–672.

Buzzanell, P. M. (1999). Tensions and burdens in employment interviewing processes: Perspectives of non-dominant group members. *Journal of Business Communication, 36,* 143–162.

Byrne, D. (1997). An overview (and underview) of research and theory within the attraction paradigm. *Journal of Social and Personal Relationships, 14,* 417–431.

Byron, K. (2008). Carrying too heavy a load? The communication and miscommunication of emotion by email. *Academy of Management Review, 33,* 309–327.

Cahn, D. D. (1992). *Conflict in intimate relationships.* New York: Guilford Press.

Cai, D. A., & Fink, E. L. (2002). Conflict style differences between individualists and collectivists. *Communication Monographs, 69,* 67–87.

Camden, C., Motley, M. T., & Wilson, A. (1984). White lies in interpersonal communication: A taxonomy and preliminary investigation of social motivations. *Western Journal of Speech Communication, 48,* 309–325.

Campbell, S. (2006). Perceptions of mobile phones in college classrooms: Ringing, cheating, and classroom policies. *Communication Education, 55,* 280–294.

Campbell, S. W., & Russo, T. C. (2003). The social construction of mobile telephony: An application of the social influence model to perceptions and uses of mobile phones within personal communication networks. *Communication Monographs, 70,* 317–334.

Canary, D. (2003). Managing interpersonal conflict: A model of events related to strategic choices. In J. O. Greene & B. R. Burleson (Eds.), *Handbook of communication and social interaction skills* (pp. 515–549). Mahwah, NJ: Erlbaum.

Canary, D. J., Cupach, W. R., & Messman, S. J. (1995). *Relationship conflict.* Newbury Park, CA: Sage.

Canary, D. J., & Emmers-Sommer, T. M. (1997). *Sex and gender differences in personal relationships.* New York: Guilford Press.

Canary, D. J., & Hause, K. (1993). Is there any reason to research sex differences in communication? *Communication Quarterly, 41,* 482–517.

Canary, D. J., & Messman, S. J. (2000). Relationship conflict. In C. Hendrick & S. S. Hendrick (Eds.), *Close relationships: A sourcebook* (pp. 261–270). Thousand Oaks, CA: Sage.

Canary, D. J., & Spitzberg, B. H. (1987). Appropriateness and effectiveness perceptions of conflict strategies. *Human Communication Research, 15,* 93–118.

Canary, D. J., & Stafford, L. (1992). Relational maintenance strategies and equity in marriage. *Communication Monographs, 59,* 243–267.

Canary, D. J., & Stafford, L. (2001). Equity in maintaining personal relationships. In J. H. Harvey & A. E. Wenzel (Eds.), *Close romantic relationships: Maintenance and enhancement* (pp. 133–150). Mahwah, NJ: Erlbaum.

Canary, D. J., & Wahba, J. (2006). Do women work harder than men at maintaining relationships? In K. Dindia & D. J. Canary (Eds.), *Sex differences and similarities in communication* (2nd ed.). Mahwah, NJ: Erlbaum.

Canary, D. J., Weger, H., Jr., & Stafford, L. (1991). Couples' argument sequences and their associations with relational characteristics. *Western Journal of Speech Communication, 55,* 159–179.

Canli, T., Desmond, J. E., Zhao, Z., & Gabrieli, J. D. E. (2002). Sex differences in the neural basis of emotional memories. *Proceedings of the National Academy of Sciences, 10,* 10789–10794.

Canli, T., Zhao, Z., Desmond, J.E., Kang, E., Gross, J., & Gabrieli, J. D. E. (2001). An fMRI study of personality influences on brain reactivity to emotional stimuli. *Behavioral Neuroscience, 115,* 33–42.

Carrell, L. J. (1997). Diversity in the communication curriculum: Impact on student empathy. *Communication Education, 46,* 234–244.

Carrell, L. J., & Willmington, S. C. (1996). A comparison of self-report and performance data in assessing speaking and listening competence. *Communication Reports, 9,* 185–191.

Carroll, J. M., & Russell, J. A. (1996). Do facial expressions signal specific emotions? Judging emotion from the face in context. *Journal of Personality and Social Psychology, 70,* 205–218.

Carson, C. L., & Cupach, W. R. (2000a). Facing corrections in the workplace: The influence of perceived face threat on the consequences of managerial reproaches. *Journal of Applied Communication Research, 28,* 215–234.

Carson, C. L., & Cupach, W. R. (2000b). Fueling the flames of the green-eyed monster: The role of ruminative thought in reaction to romantic jealousy. *Western Journal of Communication, 64,* 308–329.

Casmir, F. L. (1991). Culture, communication, and education. *Communication Education, 40,* 229–234.

Cassell, J., & Tversky, D. (2005). The language of online intercultural community formation. *Journal of Computer-Mediated Communication, 10*(2). Available at: http://www.blackwell-synergy.com/doi/full/10.1111/j.1083-6101.2005.tb00239.x

Castelan-Cargile, A., & Bradac, J. J. (2001). Attitudes towards language: A review of speaker-evaluation research and a general process model. In W. B. Gudykunst (Ed.), *Communication yearbook 25* (pp. 347–382). Thousand Oaks, CA: Sage.

Caughlin, J. P. (2003). Family communication standards: What counts as excellent family communication and how are such standards associated with family satisfaction? *Human Communication Research, 29,* 5–40.

Caughlin, J. P., Afifi, W. A., Carpenter-Theune, K. E., & Miller, L. E. (2005). Reasons for, and consequences of, revealing personal secrets in close relationships: A longitudinal study. *Personal Relationships, 12,* 43–59.

Caughlin, J. P., & Arr, T. D. (2004). When is topic avoidance unsatisfying? Examining moderators of the association between avoidance and dissatisfaction. *Human Communication Research, 30,* 479–513.

Caughlin, J. P., & Golish, T. D. (2002). An analysis of the association between topic avoidance and dissatisfaction: Comparing perceptual and interpersonal explanations. *Communication Monographs, 69,* 275–295.

Caughlin, J. P., & Huston, T. L. (2002). A contextual analysis of the association between demand/withdraw and marital satisfaction. *Personal Relationships, 9,* 95–119.

Caughlin, J. P., & Petronio, S. (2004). Privacy in families. In A. L. Vangelisti (Ed.), *Handbook of family communication* (pp. 379–412). Mahwah, NJ: Erlbaum.

Cavaliere, F. (1995, July). Society appears more open to gay parenting. *American Psychological Association Monitor,* p. 51.

Cegala, D. J., Savage, G. T., Brunner, C. C., & Conrad, A. B. (1982). An elaboration of the meaning of interaction involvement: Toward the development of a theoretical concept. *Communication Monographs, 49,* 229–248.

Cesario, J., & Higgins, E. T. (2008). Making message recipients "feel right": How nonverbal cues can increase persuasion. *Psychological Science, 19,* 415–420.

Chaiken, S., & Trope, Y. (Eds.). (1999). *Dual-process theories in social psychology.* New York: Guilford Press.

Chambers, H. E. (2005). Surviving the micromanager: How to succeed with a "my way" boss. *Canadian Manager, 30,* 24–25.

Chan, Y. K. (1999). Density, crowding, and factors intervening in their relationship: Evidence from a hyper-dense metropolis. *Social Indicators Research, 48,* 103–124.

Chandler, D. (1998). *Personal home pages and the construction of identities on the web.* Retrieved from http://www.aber.ac.uk/dgc/webident.html

Chang, S., & Tharenou, P. (2004). Competencies needed for managing a multicultural workgroup. *Asia Pacific Journal of Human-Resources, 42,* 57–74.

Chen, G. M., & Starosta, W. J. (1996). Intercultural communication competence: A synthesis. In B. R. Burleson & A. W. Kunkel, (Eds.), *Communication yearbook 19* (pp. 353–383). Thousand Oaks, CA: Sage.

Chen, G. M., & Starosta, W. J. (2000). The development and validation of the Intercultural Sensitivity Scale. *Human Communication, 3,* 1–14.

Chen, L. (1997). Verbal adaptive strategies in U.S. American dyadic interactions with U.S. American or East-Asian partners. *Communication Monographs, 64,* 302–323.

Cherniss, G., Extein, M. Goleman, D., & Weissberg, R. P. (2006). Emotional Intelligence: What does the research really indicate? *Educational Psychologist, 41*(4), 239–245.

Cheung, C. (2000). A home on the web: Presentations of self in personal homepages. In D. Gauntlett (Ed.), *Web studies* (pp. 43–51). London: Arnold.

Cheung, C. (2005). Identity construction and self-presentation on personal homepages. In J. O'Brien (Ed.), *The production of reality* (4th ed.). Thousand Oaks, CA: Sage.

Chiang, Y. S. D., & Schmida, M. (2002). Language identity and language ownership: Linguistic conflicts of first-year university writing students. In V. Zamel & R. Spack (Eds.), *Enriching ESOL pedagogy: Readings and activities for engagement, reflection, and inquiry* (pp. 393–409). Mahwah, NJ: Erlbaum.

Choi, Y. S., Gray, H. M., & Ambady, N. (2005). The glimpsed world: Unintended communication and unintended perception. In R. R. Hassin, J. S. Uleman, & J. A. Bargh (Eds.), *The new unconscious* (pp. 309–333). New York: Oxford University Press.

Chovil, N. (1991). Social determinants of facial displays. *Journal of Nonverbal Behavior, 15,* 141–154.

Christenfeld, N., & Larsen, B. (2008). The name game. *The Psychologist, 21,* 210–213.

Christensen, A. J. (2004). *Patient adherence to medical treatment regimens: Bridging the gap between behavioral science and biomedicine.* New Haven, CT: Yale University Press.

Christian, A. (2005). Contesting the myth of the "wicked stepmother": Narrative analysis of an online stepfamily support group. *Western Journal of Communication, 69,* 27–48.

Cissna, K. N., & Sieberg, E. (1999). Patterns of interactional confirmation and disconfirmation. In J. Stewart (Ed.), *Bridges not walls* (7th ed., pp. 336–346). New York: McGraw-Hill.

Clark, A. (2000). *A theory of sentience.* New York: Oxford University Press.

Clark, M. S., & Finkel, E. J. (2005). Willingness to express emotion: The impact of relationship type, communal orientation, and their interaction. *Personal Relationships, 12,* 169–180.

Clark, R. A., & Delia, J. G. (1997). Individuals' preferences for friends' approaches to providing support in distressing situations. *Communication Reports, 10,* 115–121.

Clark, R. A., MacGeorge, E. L., & Robinson, L. (2008). Evaluation of peer comforting strategies by children and adolescents. *Human Communication Research, 34,* 319–345.

Clark, R. A., Pierce, A. J., Finn, K., Hsu, K., Toosley, A., & Williams, L. (1998). The impact of alternative approaches to comforting, closeness of relationship, and gender on multiple measures of effectiveness. *Communication Studies, 49,* 224–239.

Clarke, F. P. (1973). *Interpersonal communication variables as predictors of marital satisfaction-dissatisfaction.* Unpublished doctoral dissertation, University of Denver.

Clasen, P. (2004). Antz in the communication classroom. *Communication Teacher,* 13, 49–52.

Clevenger, T. (1991). Can one not communicate? A conflict of models. *Communication Studies, 42,* 340–353.

Cline, R. J., & McKenzie, N. J. (2000). Interpersonal roulette and HIV/AIDS as disability: Stigma and social support in tension. In D. O. Braithwaite & T. L. Thompson (Eds.), *Handbook of communication and people with disabilities: Research and application* (pp. 467–483). Mahwah, NJ: Erlbaum.

Cloven, D. H., & Roloff, M. E. (1991). Sense-making activities and interpersonal conflict: Communicative cures for the mulling blues. *Western Journal of Speech Communication, 55,* 134–158.

Coates, J. (1986). *Women, men and language.* London: Longman.

Cohen, A. (2007). One nation, many cultures: A cross-cultural study of the relationship between personal cultural values and commitment in the workplace to in-role performance and organizational citizenship behavior. *Cross-Cultural Research: The Journal of Comparative Social Science, 41,* 273–300.

Cohen, E. D. (2007). *The new rational therapy: Thinking your way to serenity, success, and profound happiness.* Lanham, MD: Rowman & Littlefield.

Cole, P. M., Bruschi, C. J., & Tamang, B. L. (2002). Cultural differences in children's emotional reactions to difficult situations. *Child Development, 73,* 983–996.

Cole, S. W., Hawkley, L. C., Arevalo, J. M., Sung, C. Y., Rose, R. M., & Cacioppo, J. T. (2007). Social regulation of gene expression in human leukocytes. *Genome Biology, 8,* 189–201.

Cole, T. (2001). Lying to the one you love: The use of deception in romantic relationships. *Journal of Social and Personal Relationships, 18,* 107–129.

Coleman, L. M., & DePaulo, B. M. (1991). Uncovering the human spirit: Moving beyond disability and "missed" communications. In N. Coupland, H. Giles, & J. M. Wiemann (Eds.), *"Miscommunication" and problematic talk* (pp. 61–84). Newbury Park, CA: Sage.

Collier, M. J. (1991). Conflict competence within African, Mexican, and Anglo American friendships. In S. Ting-Toomey & F. Korzenny (Eds.), *Cross-cultural interpersonal communication* (pp. 132–154). Newbury Park, CA: Sage.

Collier, M. J. (1996). Communication competence problematics in ethnic relationships. *Communication Monographs, 63,* 314–336.

Conlan, S. K. (2008). Romantic relationship termination. *DAI, 68*(7-B), 4884.

Conlee, C., Olvera, J., & Vagim, N. (1993). The relationships among physician nonverbal immediacy and measures of patient satisfaction with physician care. *Communication Reports, 6,* 25–33.

Consedine, N. S., Magai, C., & Bonanno, G. A. (2002). Moderators of the emotion inhibition–health relationship: A review and research agenda. *Review of General Psychology, 6,* 204–228.

Cooks, L. (2000). Family secrets and the lie of identity. In S. Petronio (Ed.), *Balancing the secrets of private disclosures* (pp. 197–211). Mahwah, NJ: Erlbaum.

Coon, D. (2009). *Psychology: A modular approach to mind and behavior* (11th ed.). Boston: Cengage.

Cooper, J., & Jones, E. E. (1969). Opinion divergence as a strategy to avoid being miscast. *Journal of Personality and Social Psychology, 13,* 23–30.

Cooper, L. O., Seibold, D. R., & Suchner, R. (1997). Listening in organizations: An analysis of error structures in models of listening competency. *Communication Research Reports, 14,* 312–320.

Copeland, L., & Griggs, L. (1985). *Going international.* New York: Random House.

Corballis, M. C. (2002). *From hand to mouth: The origins of language.* Princeton, NJ: Princeton University Press.

Cory, C. T. (1980, May). Bafflegab pays. *Psychology Today, 13,* 12.

Cotterill, J. (2004). Collocation, connotation, and courtroom semantics: Lawyers' control of witness testimony through lexical negotiation. *Applied Linguistics, 25,* 513–537.

Cowan, G., & Mills, R. D. (2004). Personal inadequacy and intimacy predictors of men's hostility toward women. *Sex Roles, 51,* 67–78.

Cowan, N., & AuBuchon, A. M. (2008). Short-term memory loss over time without retroactive stimulus interference. *Psychonomic Bulletin & Review, 15,* 230–235.

Cox, S. A. (1999). Group communication and employee turnover: How coworkers encourage peers to voluntarily exit. *Southern Communication Journal, 64,* 181–192.

Cozby, P. C. (1973). Self-disclosure: A literature review. *Psychological Bulletin, 79,* 73–91.

Crane, D. R. (1987). Diagnosing relationships with spatial distance: An empirical test of a clinical principle. *Journal of Marital and Family Therapy, 13,* 307–310.

Crohan, S. E. (1992). Marital happiness and spousal consensus on beliefs about marital conflict: A longitudinal investigation. *Journal of Social and Personal Relationships, 9,* 89–102.

Cronen, V. E., & Chetro-Szivos, J. (2001). Pragmatism as a way of inquiring with special reference to a theory of communication and the general form of pragmatic social theory. In D. K. Perry (Ed.), *American pragmatism and communication research* (pp. 27–65). Mahwah, NJ: Erlbaum.

Cronkhite, G. (1976). *Communication and awareness.* Menlo Park, CA: Cummings.

Cross, S. E., & Madson, L. (1997). Models of the self: Self-construals and gender. *Psychological Bulletin, 122,* 5–37.

Crowther, C. E., & Stone, G. (1986). *Intimacy: Strategies for successful relationships.* Santa Barbara, CA: Capra Press.

Crusco, A. H., & Wetzel, G. G. (1984). The Midas Touch: Effects of interpersonal touch on restaurant tipping. *Personality and Social Psychology Bulletin, 10,* 512–517.

Cunningham, M. R., & Barbee, A. P. (2000). Social support. In C. Hendrick & S. S. Hendrick (Eds.), *Close relationships: A sourcebook* (pp. 273–285). Thousand Oaks, CA: Sage.

Cunningham, M. R., Shamblen, S. R., Barbee, A. P., & Ault, L. K. (2005). Social allergies in romantic relationships: Behavioral repetition, emotional sensitization, and dissatisfaction in dating couples. *Personal Relationships, 12,* 273–295.

Cupach, W. R., & Messman, S. J. (1999). Face predilections and friendship solidarity. *Communication Reports, 12,* 117–124.

Cupach, W. R., & Metts, S. (1986). Accounts of relational dissolution: A comparison of marital and non-marital relationships. *Communication Monographs, 53,* 311–334.

Czech, K. (2007). Communication and leadership: Faculty perceptions of the department chair. *DAI, 68*(5-A), 1741.

Dailey, R. M. (2006). Confirmation in parent–adolescent relationships and adolescent openness: Toward extending confirmation theory. *Communication Monographs, 73,* 434–458.

Dainton, M. (2000). Maintenance behaviors, expectations for maintenance, and satisfaction: Linking comparison levels to relational maintenance strategies. *Journal of Social and Personal Relationships, 17,* 827–842.

Damnet, A., & Borland, H. (2007). Acquiring nonverbal competence in English language contexts: The case of Thai learners of English viewing American and Australian films. *Journal of Asian Pacific Communication, 17,* 127–148.

Dansereau, F., & Markham, S. E. (1987). Superior-subordinate communication: Multiple levels of analysis. In F. M. Jablin, L. L. Putnam, K. H. Roberts, & L. W. Porter (Eds.), *Handbook of organizational communication* (pp. 343–388). Newbury Park, CA: Sage.

Darling, A. L., & Dannels, D. P. (2003). Practicing engineers talk about the importance of talk: A report on the role of oral communication in the workplace. *Communication Education, 52,* 1–16.

Davidowitz, M., & Myrick, R. (1984). Responding to the bereaved: An analysis of "helping" styles. *Death Education, 8,* 1–10.

Davis, S. F., & Kieffer, J. C. (1998). Restaurant servers influence tipping behavior. *Psychological Reports, 83,* 223–226.

Deal, T. E., & Kennedy, A. A. (1983). Culture: A new look through old lenses. *Journal of Applied Behavioral Science, 19,* 498–505.

DeAngelis, T. (1992, October). The "who am I" question wears a cloak of culture. *APA Monitor,* pp. 22–23.

DeCapua, A. (2007). The use of language to create realities: The example of Good Bye, Lenin! *Semiotica, 166*(1–4), 69–79.

Deaux, K. (1972). To err is humanizing: But sex makes a difference. *Representative Research in Social Psychology, 3,* 20–28.

DeMaris, A. (2007). The role of relationship inequity in marital disruption. *Journal of Social and Personal Relationships, 24,* 177–195.

Dennis, A. R., Kinney, S. T., & Hung, Y. T. (1999). Gender differences in the effects of media richness. *Small Group Research, 30,* 405–437.

DePaulo, B. M. (1992). Nonverbal behavior and self-presentation. *Psychological Bulletin, 3,* 203–243.

DePaulo, B. M. (1994). Spotting lies: Can humans learn to do better? *Current Directions in Psychological Science, 3,* 83–86.

DePaulo, B. M., & Kashy, D. A. (1998). Everyday lies in close and casual relationships. *Journal of Personality and Social Psychology, 74,* 63–79.

DePaulo, B. M., Kashy, D. A., Kirkendol, S. E., & Wyer, M. M. (1996). Lying in everyday life. *Journal of Personality and Social Psychology, 70,* 779–795.

Derlega, V. J., Barbee, A. P., & Winstead, B. A. (1994). Friendship, gender, and social support: Laboratory studies of supportive interactions. In B. R. Burleson, T. L. Albrecht, & I. G. Sarson (Eds.), *Communication of social support: Message, interactions, relationships, and community* (pp. 136–151). Newbury Park, CA: Sage.

Derlega, V. J., Lewis, R. J., Harrison, S., Winstead, B. A., & Costanza, R. (1989). Gender differences in the initiation and attribution of tactile intimacy. *Journal of Nonverbal Behavior, 13,* 83–96.

Derlega, V. J., Metts, S., Petronio, S., & Margulis, S. T. (1993). *Self-disclosure.* Newbury Park, CA: Sage.

Derlega, V. J., Winstead, B. A., & Folk-Barron, L. (2000). Reasons for and against disclosing HIV-seropositive test results to an intimate partner: A functional perspective. In S. Petronio (Ed.), *Balancing the secrets of private disclosures* (pp. 71–82). Mahwah, NJ: Erlbaum.

deTurck, M. A., & Miller, G. R. (1990). Training observers to detect deception: Effects of self-monitoring and rehearsal. *Human Communication Research, 16,* 603–620.

DeTurk, S. (2001). Intercultural empathy: Myth, competency, or possibility for alliance building? *Communication Education, 50,* 374–384.

Deutsch, M. (2006). Cooperation and competition. In M. Deutsch, P. T. Coleman, & E. C. Marcus, *The handbook of conflict resolution: Theory and practice* (2nd ed., pp. 23–42). Hoboken, NJ: Wiley.

Devine, D. J., Clayton, L. D., Phillips, J. L., Dunford, B. B., & Melner, S. B. (1999). Teams in organizations: Prevalence, characteristics, and effectiveness. *Small Group Research, 30,* 678–711.

de Waal, F. B. M. (2008). Putting the altruism back into altruism: The evolution of empathy. *Annual Review of Psychology, 59,* 279–300.

Dickson, F. C., & Walker, K. L. (2001). The expression of emotion in later-life married men. *Qualitative Research Reports in Communication, 2,* 66–71.

Dieckmann, L. E. (2000). Private secrets and public disclosures: The case of battered women. In S. Petronio (Ed.), *Balancing the secrets of private disclosures* (pp. 275–286). Mahwah, NJ: Erlbaum.

Diekman, A. B., & Eagly, A. H. (2000). Stereotypes as dynamic constructs: Women and men of the past, present, and future. *Personality and Social Psychology Bulletin, 26,* 1171–1188.

Dillard, J. P., Solomon, D. H., & Palmer, M. T. (1999). Structuring the concept of relational communication. *Communication Monographs, 66,* 49–65.

Dindia, K. (2000a). Self-disclosure research: Advances through meta-analysis. In M. A. Allen, R. W. Preiss, B. M. Gayle, & N. Burrell (Eds.), *Interpersonal communication: Advances through meta-analysis.* Mahwah, NJ: Erlbaum.

Dindia, K. (2000b). Sex differences in self-disclosure, reciprocity of self-disclosure, and self-disclosure and liking: Three meta-analyses reviewed. In S. Petronio (Ed.), *Balancing the secrets of private disclosures* (pp. 21–35). Mahwah, NJ: Erlbaum.

Dindia, K. (2002). Self-disclosure research: Knowledge through meta-analysis. In M. Allen & R. W. Preiss (Eds.), *Interpersonal communication research: Advances through meta-analysis* (pp. 169–185). Mahwah, NJ: Erlbaum.

Dindia, K. (2006). Men are from North Dakota, women are from South Dakota. In K. Dindia & D. J. Canary (Eds.), *Sex differences and similarities in communication* (2nd ed.). Mahwah, NJ: Erlbaum.

Dindia, K., & Allen, M. (1992). Sex differences in self-disclosure: A meta-analysis. *Psychological Bulletin, 112,* 106–124.

Dindia, K., & Baxter, L. A. (1987). Strategies for maintaining and repairing marital relationships. *Journal of Social and Personal Relationships, 4,* 143–158.

Dindia, K., Fitzpatrick, M. A., & Kenny, D. A. (1997). Self-disclosure in spouse and stranger dyads: A social relations analysis. *Human Communication Research, 23,* 388–412.

Dion, K. K. (1973). Young children's stereotyping of facial attractiveness. *Developmental Psychology, 9,* 183–188.

Dion, K., Berscheid, E., & Walster, E. (1972). What is beautiful is good. *Journal of Personality and Social Psychology, 24,* 285–290.

Doherty, R. W. (1997). The emotional contagion scale: A measure of individual differences. *Journal of Nonverbal Behavior, 21,* 131–154.

Domenici, K., & Littlejohn, S. W. (2006). *Facework: Bridging theory and practice.* Thousand Oaks, CA: Sage.

Doss, B. D., Mitchell, A. E., & De la Garza-Mercer, F. (2008). Marital distress. In M. Hersen & J. Rosqvist (Eds.), *Handbook of psychological assessment, case conceptualization, and treatment, Vol. 1: Adults* (pp. 563–589). Hoboken, NJ: John Wiley & Sons, 2008.

Dougherty, D. S. (2001). Sexual harassment as [dys]functional process: A feminist standpoint analysis. *Journal of Applied Communication Research, 29,* 372–402.

Dougherty, T., Turban, D., & Collander, J. (1994). Conforming first impressions in the employment interview. *Journal of Applied Psychology, 79,* 659–665.

Dovidio, J. F., Hebl, M., Richeson, J. A., & Shelton, J. N. (2006). Nonverbal communication, race, and intergroup interaction. In V. Manusov & M. L. Patterson (Eds.), *The Sage handbook of nonverbal communication* (pp. 481–500). Thousand Oaks, CA: Sage.

Downs, V. G. (1988). Grandparents and grandchildren: The relationship between self-disclosure and solidarity in an intergenerational relationship. *Communication Research Reports, 5,* 173–179.

Drigotas, S. M. (2002). The Michelangelo phenomenon and personal well-being. *Journal of Personality, 70,* 59–79.

Driscoll, M. S., Newman, D. L., & Seal, J. M. (1988). The effect of touch on the perception of counselors. *Counselor Education and Supervision, 27,* 344–354.

Droogsma, R. A. (2007). Redefining hijab: American Muslim women's standpoints on veiling. *Journal of Applied Communication Research, 35,* 294–319.

Druckmann, D., Rozelle, R. M., & Baxter, J. C. (1982). *Nonverbal communication: Survey, theory, and research.* Beverly Hills, CA: Sage.

Drullman, R., & Smoorenburg, G. F. (1997). Audio-visual perception of compressed speech by profoundly hearing-impaired subjects. *Audiology, 36*(3), 165–177.

Drummond, K., & Hopper, R. (1993). Acknowledgment tokens in series. *Communication Reports, 6,* 47–53.

Dubowitz, H., Newton, R. R., Litrownik, A. J., Lewis, T., Briggs, E. C., Thompson, R., English, D., Lee, L. C., & Feerick, M. M. (2005). Examination of a conceptual model of child neglect. *Child Maltreatment: Journal of the American Professional Society on the Abuse of Children, 10,* 173–189.

Duck, S. (1987). How to lose friends without influencing people. In M. E. Roloff & G. R. Miller (Eds.), *Interpersonal processes: New directions in communication research* (pp. 278–298). Beverly Hills, CA: Sage.

Duck, S. (1991). Some evident truths about conversations in everyday relationships: All communications are not created equal. *Human Communication Research, 18,* 228–267.

Duck, S. (1992). Social emotions: Showing our feelings about other people. In *Human Relationships* (pp. 1–34). Newbury Park, CA: Sage.

Duck, S. (1994). Maintenance as a shared meaning system. In D. J. Canary & L. Stafford (Eds.), *Communication and relationship maintenance: How individual differences in communication skills affect the achievement of relationship functions* (pp. 45–60). San Diego: Academic Press.

Duck, S. (1998). *Human relationships* (3rd ed.). London: Sage.

Duck, S., & Barnes, M. K. (1992). Disagreeing about agreement: Reconciling differences about similarity. *Communication Monographs, 59,* 199–208.

Duck, S., & Miell, D. E. (1986). Charting the development of personal relationships. In R. Gilmour & S. Duck (Eds.), *The emerging field of personal relationships.* Hillsdale, NJ: Erlbaum.

Duck, S., & Pittman, G. (1994). Social and personal relationships. In M. L. Knapp & G. R. Miller (Eds.), *Handbook of interpersonal communication* (2nd ed.). Newbury Park, CA: Sage.

Dunlap, L. L. (2002). *What all children need: Theory and application.* Lanham, MD: University Press of America.

Dwyer, K. K. (2000). The multidimensional model: Teaching students to self-manage high communication apprehension by self-selecting treatments. *Communication Education, 49,* 72–81.

Eagly, A.H., & Wood, W. (1999). The origins of sex differences in human behavior: Evolved dispositions versus social roles. *American Psychologist, 54,* 408–423.

Eaton, J., & Struthers, C. W. (2006). The reduction of psychological aggression across varied interpersonal contexts through repentance and forgiveness. *Aggressive Behavior, 32,* 195–206.

Ebeling-Witte, S., Frank, M. L., & Lester, D. (2007). Shyness, Internet use, and personality. *CyberPsychology & Behavior, 10,* 713–716.

Ebesu-Hubbard, A. S. (2001). Conflict between relationally uncertain romantic partners: The influence of relational responsiveness and empathy. *Communication Monographs, 68,* 400–414.

Edwards, C., Edwards, A., Qingmei Q., & Wahl, S. T. (2007). The influence of computer-mediated word-of-mouth communication on student perceptions of instructors and attitudes toward learning course content. *Communication Education, 56,* 255–277.

Edwards, R., & Bello, R. (2001). Interpretations of messages: The influence of equivocation, face concerns, and ego involvement. *Human Communication Research, 27,* 597–691.

Edwards, R., & Hamilton, M. A. (2004). You need to understand my gender role: An empirical test of Tannen's model of gender and communication. *Sex Roles, 50,* 491–504.

Eibl-Eibesfeldt, I. (1972). Similarities and differences between cultures in expressive movements. In R. A. Hinde (Ed.), *Non-verbal communication.* Oxford, England: Cambridge University Press.

Eisenberg, E. M. (1984). Ambiguity as strategy in organizational communication. *Communication Monographs, 51,* 227–242.

Eisenberg, E. M. (1990). Jamming: Transcendence through organizing. *Communication Research, 17,* 139–164.

Eisenberg, E. M. (Ed.). (2007). *Strategic ambiguities: Essays on communication, organization and identity.* Thousand Oaks, CA: Sage.

Eisenberg, E. M., & Goodall Jr., H. (2001). *Organizational communication* (3rd ed.). New York: Bedfort/St. Martin's.

Eisenberg, E. M., & Witten, M. G. (1987). Reconsidering openness in organizational communication. *Academy of Management Review, 12,* 418–426.

Ekman P, (1981). Mistakes when deceiving. In T. A. Sebeok & R. Rosenthal (Eds.), *The Clever Hans phenomenon: Communication with horses, whales, apes, and people* (pp. 269–278). New York: New York Academy of Sciences.

Ekman, P. (1985). *Telling lies: Clues to deceit in the marketplace, politics, and marriage.* New York: Norton.

Ekman, P. (1999). Basic emotions. In T. Dalgleish & T. Power (Eds.), *The handbook of cognition and emotion* (pp. 45–60). Sussex, England: Wiley.

Ekman, P., & Friesen, W. V. (1974a). Detecting deception from the body or face. *Journal of Personality and Social Psychology, 29,* 288–298.

Ekman, P., & Friesen, W. V. (1974b). Nonverbal behavior and psychopathology. In R. J. Friedman & M. N. Katz (Eds.), *The psychology of depression: Contemporary theory and research.* Washington, DC: J. Winston.

Ekman, P., & Friesen, W. V. (1975). *Unmasking the face: A guide to recognizing emotions from facial clues.* Englewood Cliffs, NJ: Prentice-Hall.

Ekman, P., Levenson, R. W., & Friesen, W. V. (1983, September). Autonomic nervous system activity distinguishes among emotions. *Science, 221,* 1208–1210.

Ekman, P., Sorenson, E. R., & Friesen, W. V. (1969, April). Pan-cultural elements in facial displays of emotions. *Science, 164,* 86–88.

El-Alayli, A., Myers, C. J., Petersen, T. L., & Lystad, A. L. (2008). "I don't mean to sound arrogant, but..." The effects of using disclaimers on person perception. *Personality and Social Psychology Bulletin, 34,* 130–143.

Eldridge, K. A., & Christensen, A. (2002). Demand-withdraw communication during couple conflict: A review and analysis. In P. Noller & J. A. Feeney (Eds.), *Under-*

standing marriage: Developments in the study of couple interaction (pp. 289–322). New York: Cambridge University Press.

Elfenbein, H. A., & Ambady, N. (2002). On the universality and cultural specificity of emotion recognition: A meta-analysis. *Psychological Bulletin, 128,* 203–235.

Elias, F. G., Johnson, M. E., & Fortman, J. B. (1989). Task-focused self-disclosure: Effects on group cohesiveness, commitment to task, and productivity. *Small Group Behavior, 20,* 87–96.

Ellis, A. (2001). *Overcoming destructive beliefs, feeling and behaving: New directions for rational emotive behavior therapy.* Amherst, NY: Prometheus Books.

Ellis, A. (2004). Expanding the ABCs of rational emotive behavior therapy. In M. J. Mahoney, P. DeVito, D. Martin, & A. Freeman (Eds.), *Cognition and psychotherapy* (2nd ed., pp. 185–196). New York: Springer.

Ellis, A., & Dryden, W. (1997). The practice of rational emotive behavior therapy (2nd ed.). New York: Springer.

Ellis, D. G., & McCallister, L. (1980). Relational control sequences in sex-typed and androgynous groups. *Western Journal of Speech Communication, 44,* 35–49.

Ellis, K. (2002). Perceived parental confirmation: Development and validation of an instrument. *Southern Communication Journal, 67,* 319–334.

Ellison, N., Heino, R., & Gibbs, J. (2006). Managing impressions online: Self-presentation processes in the online dating environment. *Journal of Computer-Mediated Communication, 11*(2), article 2. http://jcmc.indiana.edu/vol11/issue2/ellison.html

Emanuel, R., Adams, J., Baker, K., Daufin, E. K., Ellington, C., Fitts, E., Himsel, J., Holladay, L., & Okeowo, D. (2008). How college students spend their time communicating. *International Journal of Listening, 22,* 13–28.

Emmers-Sommer, T. M. (2003). When partners falter: Repair after a transgression. In D. J. Canary & M. Dainton (Eds.), *Maintaining relationships through communication* (pp. 185–205). Mahwah, NJ: Erlbaum.

Ennis, E., Vrij, A., & Chance, C. (2008). Individual differences and lying in everyday life. *Journal of Social and Personal Relationships, 25,* 105–118.

Epley, N., Savitsky, K., & Gilovich, T. (2002). Empathy neglect: Reconciling the spotlight effect and the correspondence bias. *Journal of Personality and Social Psychology, 83,* 300–312.

Erbert, L. A. (2000). Conflict and dialectics: Perceptions of dialectical contradictions in marital conflict. *Journal of Social and Personal Relationships, 17,* 638–659.

Erbert, L. A., & Floyd, K. (2004). Affectionate expressions as face-threatening acts: Receiver assessments. *Communication Studies, 55,* 230–246.

Eskritt, M., & Lee, K. (2003). Do actions speak louder than words? Preschool children's use of the verbal-nonverbal consistency principle during inconsistent communications. *Journal of Nonverbal Behavior, 27,* 25–41.

Evans, G. W., & Wener, R. E. (2007). Crowding and personal space invasion on the train: Please don't make me sit in the middle. *Journal of Environmental Psychology, 27*(1), 90–94.

Exline, J. J., Baumeister, R. F., & Zell, L (2008). Not so innocent: Does seeing one's own capability for wrongdoing predict forgiveness? *Journal of Personality and Social Psychology, 94,* 495–515.

Exline, J. J., Deshea, L., & Holeman, V. T. (2007). Is apology worth the risk? Predictors, outcomes, and ways to avoid regret. *Journal of Social & Clinical Psychology, 26,* 479–504.

Fadiman, A. (1997). *The spirit catches you and you fall down.* New York: Farrar, Straus & Giroux.

Farah, A., & Atoum, A. (2002). Personality traits as self-evaluated and as judged by others. *Social Behavior and Personality, 30,* 149–156.

Faul, S. (1994). *The xenophobe's guide to the Americans.* Horsham, England: Ravette.

Feeney, J. A. (1999). Issues of closeness and distance in dating relationships: Effects of sex and attachment style. *Journal of Social and Personal Relationships, 16,* 571–590.

Feeney, J. A. (2005). Hurt feelings in couple relationships: Exploring the role of attachment and perceptions of personal injury. *Personal Relationships, 12,* 253–271.

Fehr, B. (1996). *Friendship processes.* Thousand Oaks, CA: Sage.

Fehr, B., & Broughton, R. (2001). Gender and personality differences in conceptions of love: An interpersonal theory analysis. *Personal Relationships, 8,* 115–136.

Fehr, B., & Harasymchuk, C. (2005). The experience of emotions in close relationships: Toward an integration of the emotion-in-relationships and interpersonal script models. *Personal Relationships, 12,* 181–196.

Feldstein, S., Dohm, F. A., & Crown, C. L. (2001). Gender and speech rate in the perception of competence and social attractiveness. *Journal of Social Psychology, 141,* 785–806.

Felmlee, D. H. (2001). From appealing to appalling: Disenchantment with a romantic partner. *Sociological Perspectives, 44,* 263–280.

Felson, R. B. (1985). Reflected appraisal and the development of self. *Social Psychology Quarterly, 48,* 71–78.

Ferguson, G. M., & Cramer, P. (2007). Self-esteem among Jamaican children: Exploring the impact of *skin color* and rural/urban residence. *Journal of Applied Developmental Psychology, 28*, 345–359.

Fernald, A. (2001). Hearing, listening, and understanding: Auditory development in infancy. In G. Bremner & A. Fogel (Eds.), *Blackwell handbook of infant development* (pp. 35–70). Malden, MA: Blackwell.

Ferrari, M., & Koyama, E. (2002). Meta-emotions about anger and amae: A cross-cultural comparison. *Consciousness and Emotion, 3,* 197–211.

Field, T. (2003). *Touch.* Cambridge, MA: MIT Press.

Figley, C. R. (1995). Compassion fatigue as secondary traumatic stress disorder: An overview. In C. R. Figley (Ed.), *Compassion fatigue: Coping with secondary traumatic stress disorder in those who treat the traumatized* (pp. 1–20). New York: Brunner/Mazel.

Filley, A. C. (1975). *Interpersonal conflict resolution.* Glenview, IL: Scott, Foresman.

Fine, G. A., & Beim, A. (2007). Introduction: Interactionist approaches to collective memory. *Symbolic Interaction, 30,* 1–5.

Fisher, D. V. (1986). Decision-making and self-disclosure. *Journal of Social and Personal Relationships, 3,* 323–336.

Fisher, H. (2007, May/June). The laws of chemistry. *Psychology Today, 40,* 76–81.

Fitch-Hauser, M., Powers, W. G., O'Brien, K., & Hanson, S. (2007). Extending the conceptualization of listening fidelity. *International Journal of Listening, 21,* 81–91.

Fitts, W. H. (1971). *The self-concept and self-actualization.* Nashville, TN: Counselor Recordings and Tests.

Fitzpatrick, J., & Sollie, D. L. (1999). Influence of individual and interpersonal factors on satisfaction and stability in romantic relationships. *Personal Relationships, 6,* 337–350.

Fitzpatrick, M. A. (1977). A typological approach to communication in relationships. In B. Rubin (Ed.), *Communication yearbook 1* (pp. 263–275). New Brunswick, NJ: Transaction Books.

Fitzpatrick, M. A. (1988). *Between husbands and wives: Communication in marriage.* Newbury Park, CA: Sage.

Fitzpatrick, M. A., Fallis, S., & Vance, L. (1982). Multifunctional coding of conflict resolution strategies in marital dyads. *Family Relations, 21,* 61–71.

Fitzpatrick, M. A., & Vangelisti, A. L. (2001). Communication, relationships, and health. In W. P. Robinson & H. Giles (Eds.), *The new handbook of language and social psychology* (2nd ed., pp. 505–530). New York: Wiley.

Fitzpatrick, T. R., Gitelson, R. J., Andereck, K. L., & Mesbur, E. S. (2005). Social support factors and health among a senior center population in Southern Ontario, Canada. *Social Work in Health Care, 40*(3), 15–38.

Flanagin, A. J., Tiyaamornwong, V., O'Connor, J., & Seibold, D. R. (2002). Computer-mediated group work: The interaction of member sex and anonymity. *Communication Research, 29,* 66–93.

Fletcher, G. J. O., Fincham, F. D., Cramer, L., & Heron, N. (1987). The role of attributions in the development of dating relationships. *Journal of Personality and Social Psychology, 53,* 481–489.

Flora, C. (2004, May-June). The once-over can you trust first impressions? *Psychology Today, 37*(3), 60–64.

Flora, C. (2005, Jan-Feb). Close quarters. *Psychology Today, 37,* 15–16.

Flora, J., & Segrin, C. (2000). Relationship development in dating couples: Implications for relational satisfaction and loneliness. *Journal of Social and Personal Relationships, 17,* 811–825.

Floyd, J. J. (1985). *Listening: A practical approach.* Glenview, IL: Scott, Foresman.

Floyd, K. (1996). Communicating closeness among siblings: An application of the gendered closeness perspective. *Communication Research Reports, 13,* 27–34.

Floyd, K. (1997). Communication affection in dyadic relationships: An assessment of behavior and expectancies. *Communication Quarterly, 45,* 68–80.

Floyd, K. (2000). Attributions for nonverbal expressions of liking and disliking: The extended self-serving bias. *Western Journal of Communication, 64,* 385–404.

Floyd, K., Mikkelson, A. C., Hesse, C., & Pauley, P. M. (2007). Affectionate writing reduces total cholesterol: Two randomized, controlled trials. *Human Communication* Research, 33, 119–142.

Floyd, K., & Morman, M. T. (2000). Reacting to the verbal expression of affection in same-sex interaction. *Southern Communication Journal, 65,* 287–299.

Fogel, A., & Branco, A. U. (1997). Metacommunication as a source of indeterminism in relationship development. In A. Fogel, M. C. D. P. Lyra, & J. Valsiner (Eds.), *Dynamics and indeterminism in developmental and social processes* (pp. 65–92). Hillsdale, NJ: Erlbaum.

Fogel, A., de Koeyer, I., Bellagamba, F., & Bell, H. (2002). The dialogical self in the first two years of life: Embarking on a journey of discovery. *Theory and Psychology, 12,* 191–205.

Ford, W. S. Z. (2001). Customer expectations for interactions with service providers: Relationship versus encounter orientation and personalized service communication. *Journal of Applied Communication Research, 29,* 1–29.

Forgas, J. P., & Bower, G. H. (2001). Mood effects on person-perception judgments. In W. G. Parrott (Ed.), *Emotions in social psychology: Essential readings* (pp. 204–215). New York: Psychology Press.

Fortenberry, J. H., Maclean, J., Morris, P., & O'Connell, M. (1978). Mode of dress as a perceptual cue to deference. *Journal of Social Psychology, 104,* 131–139.

Fortney, S. D., Johnson, D. I., & Long, K. M. (2001). The impact of compulsive communicators on the self-perceived competence of classroom peers: An investigation and test of instructional strategies. *Communication Education, 50,* 357–373.

Foss, K. A., & Edson, B. A. (1989). What's in a name? Accounts of married women's name choices. *Western Journal of Speech Communication, 53,* 356–373.

Foss, S. K., & Foss, K. A. (2003). *Inviting transformation: Presentational speaking for a changing world* (2nd ed.). Long Grove, IL: Waveland.

Foss, S. K., & Griffin, C. L. (1995). Beyond persuasion: A proposal for an invitational rhetoric. *Communication Monographs, 62,* 2–18.

Foster, E. (2008). Commitment, communication, and contending with heteronormativity: An invitation to greater reflexivity in interpersonal research. *Southern Communication Journal, 73,* 84–101.

Fox, A. B., Bukatko, D., Hallahan, M., & Crawford, M. (2007). The medium makes a difference: Gender similarities and differences in instant messaging. *Journal of Language and Social Psychology, 26,* 389–397.

Francis, J., & Wales, R. (1994). Speech a la mode: Prosodic cues, message interpretation, and impression formation. *Journal of Language and Social Psychology, 13,* 34–44.

Francis, L. E. (2003). Feeling good, feeling well: Identity, emotion, and health. In T. J. Owens & P. J. Burke (Eds.), *Advances in identity theory and research* (pp. 123–134). New York: Kluwer Academic/Plenum Publishers.

Frawley, T. (2008). Gender schema and prejudicial recall: How children misremember, fabricate, and distort gendered picture book information. *Journal of Research in Childhood Education, 22,* 291–303.

Fredrickson, B. L. (2003, July-August). The value of positive emotions: The emerging science of positive psychology is coming to understand why it's good to feel good. *American Scientist, 91,* 330–335.

Fredrickson, B. L., & Branigan, C. (2005). Positive emotions broaden the scope of attention and thought-action repertoires. *Cognition and Emotion, 19,* 313–332.

French, J. R., & Raven, B. (1968). The bases of social power. In D. Cartwright & A. Zander (Eds.), *Group dynamics: Research and theory* (pp. 259–269). New York: Harper & Row.

Frith, H. (2004). The best of friends: The politics of girls' friendships. *Feminism and Psychology, 14,* 357–360.

Fromme, D. K., Jaynes, W. E., Taylor, D. K., Hanold, E. G., Daniell, J., Rountree, J. R., & Fromme, M. (1989). Nonverbal behavior and attitudes toward touch. *Journal of Nonverbal Behavior, 13,* 3–14.

Frumkin, L. A. (2001). The effect of eyewitnesses' accent, nationality, and authority on the perceived favorability of their testimony. *Dissertation Abstracts International, 61,* 4474.

Frumkin, L. (2007). Influences of accent and ethnic background on perceptions of eyewitness testimony. *Psychology, Crime & Law, 13,* 317–331.

Fry, R. W. (2003). *101 smart questions to ask on your interview.* Franklin Lakes, NJ: Career Press.

Fryer, R. G., & Levitt, S. D. (2004). The causes and consequences of distinctively black names. *Quarterly Journal of Economics, 119,* 767–805.

Fulmer, R. (1999). Becoming an adult: Leaving home and staying connected. In B. Carter & M. McGoldrick (Eds.), *The expanded family life cycle: Individual, family, and social perspectives* (3rd ed., pp. 215–230). Boston: Allyn & Bacon.

Fussell, S. R. (Ed.). (2002). *The verbal communication of emotions: Interdisciplinary perspectives.* Mahwah, NJ: Erlbaum.

Futch, A., & Edwards, R. (1999). The effects of sense of humor, defensiveness, and gender on the interpretation of ambiguous messages. *Communication Quarterly, 47,* 80–97.

Gabric, D., & McFadden, K. L. (2001). Student and employer perceptions of desirable entry-level operations management skills. *Mid-American Journal of Business, 16,* 51–59.

Gadlin, H. (1977). Private lives and public order: A critical view of the history of intimate relations in the United States. In G. Levinger & H. L. Raush (Eds.), *Close relationships: Perspectives on the meaning of intimacy* (pp. 33–72). Amherst, MA: University of Massachusetts Press.

Galanxhi, H., & Nah, F. F.-H. (2007). Deception in cyberspace: A comparison of text-only vs., avatar-supported medium. *International Journal of Human–Computer Studies, 65,* 770–783.

Gallois, C. (1993). The language and communication of emotion: Universal, interpersonal, or intergroup? *American Behavioral Scientist, 36,* 309–338.

Galvin, K. M., Bylund, C. L., & Brommel, B. J. (2007). *Family communication: Cohesion and change* (7th ed.). Boston, MA: Allyn & Bacon.

Galvin, K. M., Dickson, F. C., & Marrow, S. R. (2006). Systems theory: Patterns and w(holes) in family communication. In D. O. Braithwaite & L. A. Baxter (Eds.),

Engaging theories in family communication: Multiple perspectives (pp. 309–324). Thousand Oaks, CA: Sage.

Gara, M. A., Woolfolk, R. L., Cohen, B. D., Gioldston, R. B., & Allen, L. A. (1993). Perception of self and other in major depression. *Journal of Abnormal Psychology, 102,* 93–100.

Gayle, B. M., & Preiss, R. W. (1999). Language intensity plus: A methodological approach to validate emotions in conflicts. *Communication Reports, 12,* 43–50.

Gayle, B. M., Preiss, R. W., & Allen, M. A. (1998). Embedded gender expectations: A covariate analysis of conflict situations and issues. *Communication Research Reports, 15,* 379–387.

Gayle, B. M., Preiss, R. W., & Allen, M. A. (2002). A meta-analytic interpretation of intimate and nonintimate interpersonal conflict. In M. Allen, R. W. Preiss, B. M. Gayle, & N. Burrell (Eds.), *Interpersonal communication research: Advances through meta-analysis* (pp. 345–368). Mahwah, NJ: Erlbaum.

Geddes, D. (1992). Sex-roles in management: The impact of varying power of speech style on union members' perception of satisfaction and effectiveness. *Journal of Psychology, 126,* 589–607.

Gendrin, D. M., & Werner, B. L. (1996). Internal dialogues about conflict: Implications for managing marital discord. *Imagination, Cognition and Personality, 16*(2), 125–138.

Genov, A. B. (2001). Autonomic and situational determinants of the subjective experience of emotion: An individual differences approach. *Dissertation Abstracts International, 61,* 5043.

Gentile, J. S. (2004). Telling the untold tales: Memory's caretaker. *Text and Performance Quarterly, 24,* 201–204.

Georgakopoulos, A. (2004). The role of silence and avoidance in interpersonal conflict. *Peace and Conflict Studies, 11,* 85–95.

Gergen, K. J. (1971). *The concept of self.* New York: Holt, Rinehart & Winston.

Gergen, K. J. (1991). *The saturated self: Dilemmas of identity in contemporary life.* New York: Basic Books.

Gibb, J. R. (1961). Defensive communication. *Journal of Communication, 11,* 141–148.

Giles, H. (1971). Evaluation of personality content from accented speech as a function of listeners' social attitudes. *Perceptual and Motor Skills, 34,* 168–170.

Giles, H., Coupland, N., & Wiemann, J. M. (1992a). "Talk is cheap . . ." but "my word is my bond": Beliefs about talk. In K. Bolton & H. Kwok (Eds.), *Sociolinguistics today: International perspectives* (pp. 218–243). London: Routledge & Kegan Paul.

Giles, H., & Franklyn-Stokes, A. (1989). Communicator characteristics. In M. K. Asante & W. B. Gudykunst (Eds.), *Handbook of international and intercultural communication* (pp. 117–144). Newbury Park, CA: Sage.

Giles, H., Henwood, K., Coupland, N., Harriman, J., & Coupland, J. (1992b). Language attitudes and cognitive mediation. *Human Communication Research, 18,* 500–527.

Giles, H., Mulac, A., Bradac, J. J., & Smith, P. J. (1992c). Speech accommodation. In W. B. Gudykunst & Y. Y. Kim (Eds.), *Readings on communicating with strangers.* New York: McGraw-Hill.

Gilovitch, T., & Savitsky, K. (1999). The spotlight effect and the illusion of transparency: Egocentric assessments of how we are seen by others. *Current Directions in Psychological Science, 8,* 165–168.

Ginsburg, D. (1999). *ATM: Solutions for enterprise internetworking* (2nd ed.). Boston: Addison-Wesley.

Gladwell, M. (2004). *Blink: The power of thinking without thinking.* Boston: Little, Brown.

Glanz, B. A. (2007). *What can I do? Ideas to help those who have experienced loss.* Minneapolis: Augsburg Fortress.

Gleason, J. B., & Greif, E. B. (1983). Men's speech to young children. In B. Thorne, C. Kramarae, & N. Henley (Eds.), *Language, gender, and society* (pp. 140–150). Rowley, MA: Newbury House.

Goetting, A. (1986). The developmental tasks of siblingship over the life cycle. *Journal of Marriage and the Family, 48,* 703–714.

Goffman, E. (1959). *The presentation of self in everyday life.* Garden City, NY: Doubleday.

Goffman, E. (1971). *Relations in public.* New York: Basic Books.

Golash-Boza, T., & Darity, W. (2008). Latino racial choices: The effects of skin colour and discrimination on Latinos' and Latinas' racial self-identifications. *Ethnic & Racial Studies, 31*, 899–934.

Goldin, C., & Shim, M. (2004). Making a name: Women's surnames at marriage and beyond. *Journal of Economic Perspectives, 18*, 143–160.

Goldschmidt, M. M. (2004). Good person stories: The favor narrative as a self-presentation strategy. *Qualitative Research Reports in Communication, 5,* 28–33.

Goldschmidt, W. (1990). *The human career.* Cambridge, MA: Basil Blackman.

Goldsmith, D. J. (2000). Soliciting advice: The role of sequential placement in mitigating face threat. *Communication Monographs, 67,* 1–19.

Goldsmith, D. J., & Fitch, K. (1997). The normative context of advice as social support. *Human Communication Research, 23,* 454–476.

Goldsmith, D. J., & Fulfs, P. A. (1999). "You just don't have the evidence": An analysis of claims and evidence in Deborah Tannen's *You just don't understand.* In M. E. Roloff (Ed.), *Communication yearbook 22* (pp. 1–49). Thousand Oaks, CA: Sage.

Goldsmith, D. J., & MacGeorge, E. L. (2000). The impact of politeness and relationship on perceived quality of advice about a problem. *Human Communication Research, 26,* 234–263.

Goldstein, S. (2008). Current literature in ADHD. *Journal of Attention Disorders, 11,* 614–616.

Goleman, D. (1995). *Emotional intelligence: Why it can matter more than I.Q.* New York: Bantam.

Golen, S. (1990). A factor analysis of barriers to effective listening. *Journal of Business Communication, 27,* 25–36.

Golish, T. D. (2000). Is openness always better? Exploring the role of topic avoidance, satisfaction, and parenting styles of stepparents. *Communication Quarterly, 48,* 137–158.

Golish, T. D., & Caughlin, J. P. (2002). "I'd rather not talk about it": Adolescents' and young adults' use of topic avoidance in stepfamilies. *Journal of Applied Communication Research, 30,* 78–106.

Good, G. E., Porter, M. J., & Dillon, M. G. (2002). When men divulge: Men's self-disclosure on prime time situation comedies. *Sex Roles, 46,* 419–427.

Goodboy, A. K., & Myers, S. A. (2008). The effect of teacher confirmation on student communication and learning outcomes. *Communication Education, 57,* 153–179.

Goodman, C. R., & Shippy, R. A. (2002). Is it contagious? Affect similarity among spouses. *Aging and Mental Health, 6,* 266–274.

Goodman, G., & Esterly, G. (1990). Questions—The most popular piece of language. In J. Stewart (Ed.), *Bridges not walls* (5th ed., pp. 69–77). New York: McGraw-Hill.

Gordon, T. (1970). *P.E.T.: Parent effectiveness training.* New York: Wyden.

Gorham, J. (1988). The relationship between verbal teacher immediacy behaviors and student learning. *Communication Education, 37,* 40–53.

Gottman, J. M. (1994). *Why marriages succeed or fail.* New York: Simon & Schuster.

Gottman, J. (2000, September). Welcome to the love lab. *Psychology Today Online.* Available: http://www.findarticles.com/m1175/5_33/66380417/p1/article.jhtml

Gottman, J. (2003). Why marriages fail. In K. M. Galvin & P. J. Cooper (Eds.), *Making connections: Readings in relational communication* (pp. 258–266). Los Angeles: Roxbury.

Gottman, J. M., Katz, L. F., & Hooven, C. (1997). *Meta-emotion: How families communicate emotionally.* Mahwah, NJ: Erlbaum.

Gottman, J. M., & Levenson, R.W. (1999). Rebound for marital conflict and divorce prediction. *Family Process, 38,* 287–292.

Gottman, J. M., & Silver, N. (1999). *The seven principles for making marriages work.* New York: Three Rivers Press.

Graham, S. M., Huang, J. Y., Clark, M. S., & Helgeson, V. S. (2008). The positives of negative emotions: Willingness to express negative emotions promotes relationships. *Personality and Social Psychology Bulletin, 34,* 394–406.

Granovetter, M. S. (1973). The strength of weak ties. *American Journal of Sociology, 78,* 1360–1380.

Granovetter, M. S. (1995). G*etting a job: A study of contacts and careers* (2nd ed.). Chicago: University of Chicago Press.

Grant, C. H., III, Cissna, K. N., & Rosenfeld, L. B. (2000). Patients' perceptions of physicians' communication and outcomes of the accrual to trial process. *Health Communication, 12*(1), 23–39.

Gray, J. (1992). *Men are from Mars; women are from Venus: A practical guide for improving communication and getting what you want in your relationship.* New York: HarperCollins.

Greenberg, L. S., & Goldman, R. N. (2008). Fear in couples therapy. In L. S. Greenberg & R. N. Goldman (Eds.), *Emotion-focused couples therapy: The dynamics of emotion, love, and power* (pp. 283–313). Washington, DC: American Psychological Association.

Greene, K., Derlega, V. J., & Mathews, A. (2006). Self-disclosure in personal relationships. In A. Vangelisti & D. Perlman (Eds.), *The Cambridge handbook of personal relationships.* New York: Cambridge University Press.

Greenlees, I., Bradley, A., Holder, T., & Thelwell, R. (2005). The impact of opponents' non-verbal behaviour on the first impressions and outcome expectations of table-tennis players. *Psychology of Sport and Exercise*, 6, 103–115.

Greenwald, A. G. (1995). Getting (my) self into social psychology. In G. G. Brannigan & M. R. Merrens (Eds.), *The social psychologists: Research adventures* (pp. 3–16). New York: McGraw-Hill.

Grewal, D., & Salovey, P. (2005). Feeling smart: The science of emotional intelligence. *American Scientist, 93,* 330–339.

Griffin, E. A. (2006). *A first look at communication theory with conversations with communication theorists* (6th ed.). New York: McGraw-Hill.

Grob, L. M., Meyers, R. A., & Schuh, R. (1997). Powerful/powerless language use in group interactions: Sex differences or similarities? *Communication Quarterly, 45,* 282–303.

Gross, J. J., Sutton, S. K., & Ketelaar, T. V. (1998). Relations between affect and personality: Support for the affect-level and affective-reactivity views. *Personality and Social Psychology Bulletin, 24,* 279–288.

Gross, M. A., Guerrero, L. K., & Alberts, J. K. (2004). Perceptions of conflict strategies and communication competence in task-oriented dyads. *Journal of Applied Communication Research, 32,* 249–270.

Gudykunst, W. B. (1993a). *Communication in Japan and the United States.* Albany: State University of New York Press.

Gudykunst, W. B. (1993b). Toward a theory of effective interpersonal and intergroup communication: An anxiety/uncertainty management (AUM) perspective. In J. Koester & R. L. Wiseman (Eds.), *Intercultural communication competence* (pp. 33–71). Thousand Oaks, CA: Sage.

Gudykunst, W. B., & Kim, Y. Y. (2002). *Communicating with strangers: An approach to intercultural communication* (4th ed.). New York: McGraw-Hill.

Gudykunst, W. B., & Matsumoto, Y. (1996). Cross-cultural variability of communication in personal relationships. In W. B. Gudykunst, S. Ting-Toomey, & T. Nishida (Eds.), *Communication in personal relationships across cultures* (pp. 19–56). Newbury Park, CA: Sage.

Gudykunst, W. B., & Ting-Toomey, S. (1988). *Culture and interpersonal communication.* Newbury Park, CA: Sage.

Guéguen, N., & Fischer-Lokou, J. (2002). An evaluation of touch on a large request: A field setting. *Psychological Reports, 90,* 267–269.

Guéguen, N., & Jacob, C. (2005). The effect of touch on tipping: An evaluation in a French bar. *International Journal of Hospitality Management, 24,* 295–299.

Guéguen, N., Jacob, C., & Boulbry, G. (2007). The effect of touch on compliance with a restaurant's employee suggestion. *International Journal of Hospitality Management, 26,* 1019–1023.

Guerin, B. (2003). Combating prejudice and racism: New interventions from a functional analysis of racist language. *Journal of Community and Applied Social Psychology, 13,* 29–45.

Guerrero, L. K., & Afifi, W. A. (1995). Some things are better left unsaid: Topic avoidance in family relationships. *Communication Quarterly, 43,* 276–296.

Guerrero, L. K., Anderson, P. A., & Afifi, W. A. (2007). *Close encounters: Communication in relationships* (2nd ed.). Thousand Oaks, CA: Sage.

Guerrero, L. K., Jones, S. M., & Boburka, R. R. (2006). Sex differences in emotional communication. In K. Dindia & D. J. Canary (Eds.), *Sex differences and similarities in communication* (2nd ed.). Mahwah, NJ: Erlbaum.

Guynn, J. (2008, March 31). Silicon Valley meetings go "topless." *Los Angeles Times.* Available at: http://www.latimes.com/business/la-fi-nolaptops31mar31,0,7194079.story

Hackman, M., & Walker, K. (1990). Instructional communication in the televised classroom: The effects of system design and teacher immediacy. *Communication Education, 39,* 196–206.

Haidt, J., & Keltner, D. (1999). Culture and facial expression: Open-ended methods find more expressions and a gradient of recognition. *Cognition and Emotion, 13,* 225–266.

Hajek, C., & Giles, H. (2003). New directions in intercultural communication competence: The process model. In B. R. Burleson & J. O. Greene (Eds.), *Handbook of communication and social interaction skills* (pp. 935–957). Mahwah, NJ: Erlbaum.

Hale, J. L., Tighe, M. R., & Mongeau, P. A. (1997). Effects of event type and sex on comforting messages. *Communication Research Reports, 14,* 214–220.

Hall, E. T. (1959). *Beyond culture.* New York: Doubleday.

Hall, E. T. (1969). *The hidden dimension.* Garden City, NY: Anchor.

Hall, J. A., & Matsumoto, D. (2004). Gender differences in judgments of multiple emotions from facial expressions. *Emotion, 4,* 201–206.

Halone, K. K., & Pecchioni, L. L. (2001). Relational listening: A grounded theoretical model. *Communication Reports, 14,* 59–65.

Hamachek, D. E. (1982). *Encounters with others: Interpersonal relationships and you.* New York: Holt, Rinehart & Winston.

Hamachek, D. E. (1992). *Encounters with the self* (3rd ed.). Fort Worth, TX: Harcourt Brace.

Hample, D. (1980). Purposes and effects of lying. *Southern Speech Communication Journal, 46,* 33–47.

Hample, D. (2006). Anti-comforting messages. In K. M. Galvin & P. J. Cooper (Eds.), *Making connections: Readings in relational communication* (4th ed., pp. 222–227). Los Angeles: Roxbury.

Hample, D., & Dallinger, J. M. (2000). The effects of situation on the use or suppression of possible compliance gaining appeals. In M. A. Allen, R. W. Preiss, B. M. Gayle, & N. Burrell (Eds.), *Interpersonal communication: Advances through meta-analysis* (pp. 187–209). Mahwah, NJ: Erlbaum.

Hample, D., Warner, B., & Norton, H. (2007). *The effects of arguing expectations and predispositions on perceptions of argument quality and playfulness.* Paper presented at the annual meeting of the International Communication Association, San Francisco.

Hampson, E., van Anders, S. M., & Mullin, L. I. (2006). A female advantage in the recognition of emotional facial expressions: Test of an evolutionary hypothesis. *Evolution and Human Behavior, 27*, 401–416.

Han, M. (2003). Body image dissatisfaction and eating disturbance among Korean college female students: Relationships to media exposure, upward comparison, and perceived reality. *Communication Studies, 34,* 65–78.

Han, S. (2001). Gay identity disclosure to parents by Asian American gay men. *Dissertation Abstracts International, 62,* 329.

Hancock, J. T., & Dunham, P. J. (2001). Impression formation in computer-mediated communication revisited: An analysis of the breadth and intensity of impressions. *Communication Research, 28,* 325–347.

Hansen, J. (2007). *24/7: How cell phones and the internet change the way we live, work, and play.* New York: Praeger.

Hansson, G. (1996). Emotions in poetry: Where are they and how do we find them? In R. J. Kreuz & M. S. MacNealy (Eds.), *Empirical approaches to literature and aesthetics. Advances in discourse processes* (Vol. 52, pp. 275–288). Norwood, NJ: Ablex.

Hanzal, A., Segrin, C., & Dorros, S. M. (2008). The role of marital status and age on men's and women's reactions to touch from a relational partner. *Journal of Nonverbal Behavior, 32,* 21–35.

Harrell, A. (2005, March 11). *Physical attractiveness of children and parental supervision in grocery stores: An evolutionary explanation of the neglect of ugly kids.* Paper presented at the Warren E. Kalbach Population Conference, Edmonton, Alberta.

Harrison, K., & Cantor, J. (1997). The relationship between media consumption and eating disorders. *Journal of Communication, 47,* 40–67.

Harwood, J. (2005). Communication as social identity. In G. J. Shepherd, J. St. John, & T. Striphas (Eds.), *Communication as . . . : Perspectives on theory.* Thousand Oaks, CA: Sage.

Harwood, J., Bouchard, E., Giles, H., & Tyoski, S. (1997). Evaluations of patronizing speech and three response styles in a non-service-providing context. *Journal of Applied Communication Research, 25,* 170–195.

Harwood, J., & Giles, H. (1996). Reactions to older people being patronized: The roles of response strategies and attributed thoughts. *Journal of Language and Social Psychology, 15,* 395–421.

Hatchett, G. T., & Park, H. L. (2004). Relationships among optimism, coping styles, psychopathology, and counseling outcome. *Personality and Individual Differences, 36,* 1755–1769.

Hatfield, E., Cacioppo, J. T., Rapson, R. L., & Oatley, K. (1984). *Emotional contagion.* Cambridge, England: Cambridge University Press.

Hatfield, E., & Rapson, R. L. (2006). Passionate love, sexual desire, and mate selection: Cross-cultural and historical perspectives. In P. Noller & J. A. Feeney (Eds.), *Close relationships: Functions, forms and processes* (pp. 227–243). Hove, England: Psychology Press/Taylor & Francis.

Hatfield, E., & Sprecher, S. (1986). *Mirror, mirror: The importance of looks in everyday life.* Albany: State University of New York Press.

Hawken, L., Duran, R. L., & Kelly, L. (1991). The relationship of interpersonal communication variables to academic success and persistence in college. *Communication Quarterly, 39,* 297–308.

Hayes, H. (2006). "Don't worry about a thing, dear": Why women need financial intimacy. San Mateo, CA: Primelife.

Heard, H. E. (2007). The family structure trajectory and adolescent school performance: Differential effects by race and ethnicity. *Journal of Family Issues, 28,* 319–354.

Hecht, M. L., Collier, M. J., & Ribeau, S. A. (1993). *African American communication: Perspectives, principles, and pragmatics.* Hillsdale, NJ: Erlbaum.

Hegelson, V. S., & Gottlieb, B. H. (2000). Support groups. In S. Cohen, L. G. Underwood, & B. H. Gottlieb (Eds.), *Social support measurement and intervention* (pp. 221–245). New York: Oxford University Press.

Hegstrom, T. G. (1979). Message impact: What percentage is nonverbal? *Western Journal of Speech Communication, 43,* 134–142.

Hellweg, S. (1987). Organizational grapevines: A state of the art review. In B. Dervin & M. Boight (Eds.), *Progress in the communication sciences, 8.* Norwood, NJ: Ablex.

Helmreich, R., Aronson, E., & Lefan, J. (1970). To err is humanizing—sometimes: Effects of self-esteem, competence, and a pratfall on interpersonal attraction. *Journal of Personality and Social Psychology, 16,* 259–264.

Helms, H. M., Proulx, C. M., Klute, M. M., McHale, S. M., & Crouter, A. C. (2006). Spouses' gender-typed attributes and their links with marital quality: A pattern analytic approach. *Journal of Social and Personal Relationships, 23,* 843–864.

Helweg, L. M., Cunningham, S. J., Carrico, A., & Pergram, A. M. (2004). To nod or not to nod: An observational study of nonverbal communication and status in female and male college students. *Psychology of Women Quarterly,* 28, 358–361.

Henderson, S., & Gilding, M. (2004). "I've never clicked this much with anyone in my life": Trust and hyperpersonal communication in online friendships. *New Media & Society, 6,* 487–506.

Hendrick, C., Hendrick, S. S., & Dicke, A. (1998). The love attitudes scale: Short form. *Journal of Social and Personal Relationships, 15,* 147–159.

Hergovitch, A., Sirsch, U., & Felinger, M. (2002). Self-appraisals, actual appraisals and reflected appraisals of preadolescent children. *Social Behavior and Personality, 30,* 603–612.

Hess, J. A. (2000). Maintaining nonvoluntary relationships with disliked partners: An investigation into the use of distancing behaviors. *Human Communication Research, 26,* 458–488.

Hess, N. H., & Hagen, E. H. (2006). Sex differences in indirect aggression: Psychological evidence from young adults. *Evolution and Human Behavior, 27,* 231–245.

Hett, A. M. (1993). Language of silence: An ethnographic case study of the expressive language skills of preschool Native American girls. *Dissertation Abstracts International, 53,* 3062.

Heydenberk, W., & Heydenberk, R. (2007). More than manners: Conflict resolution in primary level classrooms. *Early Childhood Education Journal, 35,* 119–126.

Hian, L. B., Chuan, S. L., Trevor, T. M. K., & Detenber, B. H. (2004). Getting to know you: Exploring the development of relational intimacy in computer-mediated communication. *Journal of Computer-Mediated Communication, 9*(3). Available at: http://jcmc.indiana.edu/vol9/issue3/detenber.html.

Hicks, C. B., & Tharpe, A. M. (2002). Listening effort and fatigue in school-age children with and without hearing loss. *Journal of Speech, Language, and Hearing Research, 45,* 573–584.

Hidalgo, M. C., & Hernandez, B. (2001). Place attachment: Conceptual and empirical questions. *Journal of Environmental Psychology, 21,* 273–281.

Hinde, R. A., Finkenauer, C., & Auhagen, A. E. (2001). Relationships and the self-concept. *Personal Relationships, 8,* 187–204.

Hines, P. M., Preto, N. G., McGoldrick, M., Almeida, R., & Weltman, S. (1999). Culture and the family life cycle. In B. Carter & M. McGoldrick (Eds.), *The expanded family life cycle: Individual, family, and social perspectives* (3rd ed., pp. 69–87). Needham Heights, MA: Allyn & Bacon.

Hochberg, J. (Ed.). (1998). Perception and cognition at century's end. *Handbook of perception and cognition* (2nd ed.). San Diego, CA: Academic Press.

Hocker, J. L., & Wilmot, W. W. (1997). *Interpersonal conflict* (5th ed.). New York: McGraw-Hill.

Hoffman, M. L. (1991). Empathy, social cognition, and moral action. In W. Kurtines & J. Gerwirtz (Eds.), *Moral behavior and development: Theory, research, and applications* (Vol. 1, pp. 275–301). Hillsdale, NJ: Erlbaum.

Hofstede, G. (1984). *Culture's consequences.* Newbury Park, CA: Sage.

Hofstede, G. (2003). *Culture's consequences: Comparing values, behaviors, institutions, and organizations across nations* (2nd ed.). Thousand Oaks, CA: Sage.

Hoijer, H. (1994). The Sapir–Whorf hypothesis. In L. A. Samovar & R. E. Porter (Eds.), *Intercultural communication: A reader* (7th ed.). Belmont, CA: Wadsworth.

Holt, J. L., & DeVore, C. J. (2005). Culture, gender, organizational role, and styles of conflict resolution: A meta-analysis. *International Journal of Intercultural Relations, 29,* 165–196.

Holte, A., & Wichstrom, L. (1990). Disconfirmatory feedback in families of schizophrenics. *Scandinavian Journal of Psychology, 31,* 198–211.

Homans, G. C. (1961). *Social behavior: Its elementary form.* New York: Harcourt Brace.

Homburg, C., & Fürst, A. (2007). See no evil, hear no evil, speak no evil: A study of defensive organizational behavior towards customer complaints. *Journal of the Academy of Marketing Science, 35,* 523–536.

Honeycutt, J. M. (1999). Typological differences in predicting marital happiness from oral history behaviors and imagined interactions. *Communication Monographs, 66,* 276–291.

Hornsey, M. J., Oppes, T., & Svensson, A. (2002). "It's ok if we say it, but you can't": Responses to intergroup and intragroup criticism. *European Journal of Social Psychology, 32,* 293–307.

Hornsey, M. J., Robson, E., Smith, J., Esposo, S., & Sutton, R. M. (2008). Sugaring the pill: Assessing rhetorical strategies designed to minimize defensive reactions to group criticism. *Human Communication Research, 34,* 70–98.

Horrigan, J. B., Rainie, L., & Fox, S. (2001, October 31). *Online communities: Networks that nurture long-distance relationships and local ties.* Pew Internet and American Life Project. Retrieved from http://www.pewinternet.org/reports/pdfs/PIP_Communities_Report.pdf

Hosman, L. A. (1989). The evaluative consequences of hedges, hesitations, and intensifiers: Powerful and powerless speech styles. *Human Communication Research, 15,* 383–406.

Hosman, L. A., & Siltanen, S. A. (2006). Powerful and powerless language forms: Their consequences for impression formation, attributions of control of self and control of others, cognitive responses, and message memory. *Journal of Language & Social Psychology, 25,* 33–46.

Houghton, T. J. (2001). A study of communication among supervisors: The influence of supervisor/supervisee verbal aggressiveness on communication climate and organizational commitment. *Dissertation Abstracts International, 61,* 3826.

Hu, Y., Wood, J. F., Smith, V., & Westbrook, N. (2004). Friendships through IM: Examining the relationship between instant messaging and intimacy. *Journal of Computer-Mediated Communication 10*(1). Available at: http://jcmc.indiana.edu/vol10/issue1/hu.html

Huang, L. (1999). Family communication patterns and personality characteristics. *Communication Quarterly, 47,* 230–243.

Hubbell, A. P. (1999, November). *"I love your family—they are just like you": Lies we tell to lovers and perceptions of their honesty and appropriateness.* Paper delivered at the annual meeting of the International Communication Association, San Francisco.

Hudson, H. E. (2006). *From rural village to global village: Telecommunications for development in the information age.* Mawah, NJ: Erlbaum.

Hughes, P. C., & Baldwin, J. R. (2002). Communication and stereotypical impressions. *Howard Journal of Communications, 13,* 113–128.

Hulbert, J. E. (1989). Barriers to effective listening. *Bulletin for the Association for Business Communication, 52,* 3–5.

Hummert, M. L., Garstka, T. A., Ryan, E. B., & Bonnesen, J. L. (2004). The role of age stereotypes in interpersonal communication. In Pennsylvania State University Department of Communication Arts and Sciences (Ed.), *Handbook of communication and aging research* (2nd ed., pp. 91–114). Mahwah, NJ: Erlbaum.

Huston, T. L., & Vangelisti, A. L. (1995). How parenthood affects marriage. In M. A. Fitzpatrick & A. L. Vangelisti (Eds.), *Explaining family interactions* (pp. 147–176). Thousand Oaks, CA: Sage.

Hyde, R. B. (1993). Council: Using a talking stick to teach listening. *Communication Teacher, 7*(2), 1–2.

Iannone, N. F., & Iannone, M. P. (2000). *Supervision of police personnel* (6th ed.). New York: Prentice Hall.

Ifert, D. E., & Roloff, M. E. (1998). Understanding obstacles preventing compliance: Conceptualization and classification. *Communication Research, 25,* 131–153.

Imhof, M. (2003). The social construction of the listener: Listening behavior across situations, perceived listening status, and cultures. *Communication Research Reports, 20,* 357–366.

Impett, E. A., & Peplau, L. A. (2006). "His" and "her" relationships? A review of the empirical evidence. In A. Vangelisti & D. Perlman (Eds.), *The Cambridge handbook of personal relationships.* New York: Cambridge University Press.

Infante, D. A. (1987). Aggressiveness. In J. C. McCroskey & J. A. Daly (Eds.), *Personality and interpersonal communication* (pp. 157–192). Newbury Park, CA: Sage.

Infante, D. A. (1988). *Arguing constructively.* Prospect Heights, IL: Waveland Press.

Infante, D. A., Chandler, T. A., & Rudd, J. E. (1989). Test of an argumentative skill deficiency model of interspousal violence. *Communication Monographs,* 56, 163–177.

Infante, D. A., & Gorden, W. I. (1985). Superiors' argumentativeness and verbal aggressiveness as predictors of subordinates' satisfaction. *Human Communication Research, 12,* 117–125.

Infante, D. A., & Gorden, W. I. (1987). Superior and subordinate communication profiles: Implications for independent-mindedness and upward effectiveness. *Central States Speech Journal, 38,* 73–80.

Infante, D. A., & Gorden, W. I. (1989). Argumentativeness and affirming communicator style as predictors of satisfaction/dissatisfaction with subordinates. *Communication Quarterly, 37,* 81–90.

Infante, D. A., & Rancer, A. S. (1982). A conceptualization and measure of argumentativeness. *Journal of Personality Assessment, 46,* 72–80.

Infante, D. A., & Rancer, A. S. (1996). Argumentativeness and verbal aggressiveness: A review of recent theory and research. *Communication Yearbook, 19,* 320–351.

Infante, D. A., Riddle, B. L., Horvath, C. L., & Tumlin, S. A. (1992). Verbal aggressiveness: Messages and reasons. *Communication Quarterly, 40,* 116–126.

Infante, D. A., & Wigley, C. J., III. (1986). Verbal aggressiveness: An interpersonal model and measure. *Communication Monographs, 53,* 61–69.

Inman, C. (1996). Friendships among men: Closeness in the doing. In J. T. Wood (Ed.), *Gendered relationships* (pp. 95–110). Mountain View, CA: Mayfield Publishing.

Irizarry, C. A. (2004). Face and the female professional: A thematic analysis of face-threatening communication in the workplace. *Qualitative Research Reports in Communication, 5,* 15–21.

Ishikawa, H., & Yamazaki, Y. (2005). How applicable are Western models of patient–physician relationship in Asia?: Changing patient–physician relationship in contemporary Japan. *International Journal of Japanese Sociology, 14*(1), 84–93.

IT Facts (2008). 56% of Internet users send e-mail every day. Retrieved from http://www.itfacts.biz/56-of-internet-users-send-e-mail-every-day/9964

Iverson, J. M. (1999). How to get to the cafeteria: Gesture and speech in blind and sighted children's spatial descriptions. *Developmental Psychology, 35,* 1132–1142.

Iverson, J. M., & Goldin-Meadow, S. (1997). What's communication got to do with it? Gesture in children blind from birth. *Developmental Psychology, 33,* 453–467.

Iyer, P. (1990). *The lady and the monk: Four seasons in Kyoto.* New York: Vintage.

Izard, C. E. (1971). *The face of emotion.* New York: Appleton-Century-Crofts.

Jackson, W. C. (1978, September 7). *Wisconsin State Journal,* UPI.

Jaksa, J. A., & Pritchard, M. (1994). *Communication ethics: Methods of analysis* (2nd ed.). Belmont, CA: Wadsworth.

Janas, M. (2001). Getting a clear view. *Journal of Staff Development, 22*(2), 32–34.

Jandt, F. (2007). *An introduction to intercultural communication: Identities in a global community.* Thousand Oaks, CA: Sage.

Jaret, C., Reitzes, D., & Shapkina, N. (2005). Reflected appraisals and self-esteem. *Sociological Perspectives, 48,* 403–419.

Jeffries, V. (2002). The structure and dynamics of love: Toward a theory of marital quality and stability. *Humboldt Journal of Social Relations, 27*(1), 42–72.

Jerome, E. M., & Liss, M. (2005). Relationships between sensory processing style, adult attachment, and coping. *Personality and Individual Differences, 38,* 1341–1352.

Job Outlook 2007. (2006). National Association of Colleges and Employers [Online]. Retrieved January 27, 2008, from http://www.unr.edu/career/docs/outlook_student.pdf

Johnson, A. J., Haigh, M. M., Becker, J. A. H., Craig, E. A., & Wigley, S. (2008). College students' use of relational management strategies in email in long-distance and geographically close relationships. *Journal of Computer-Mediated Communication, 13,* 381–404.

Johnson, A. J., Wittenberg, E., Haigh, M., Wigley, S., Becker, J., Brown, K., & Craig, E. (2004). The process of relationship development and deterioration: Turning points in friendships that have terminated. *Communication Quarterly, 52,* 54–67.

Johnson, H. M. (1998). *How do I love me?* (3rd ed.) Salem, WI: Sheffield.

Johnson, K. L., & Edwards, R. (1991). The effects of gender and type of romantic touch on perceptions of relations commitment. *Journal of Nonverbal Behavior, 15,* 43–55.

Johnson, P., Lindsey, A. E., & Zakahi, W. R. (2001). Anglo American, Hispanic American, Chilean, Mexican and Spanish perceptions of competent communication in initial interaction. *Communication Research Reports, 18,* 36–43.

Johnson, S. (1987). *Going out of our minds: The metaphysics of liberation.* Freedom, CA: Crossing.

Johnson, S., & Bechler, C. (1998). Examining the relationship between listening effectiveness and leadership emergence: Perceptions, behaviors, and recall. *Small Group Research, 29,* 452–471.

Jones, C., Berry, L., & Stevens, C. (2007). Synthesized speech intelligibility and persuasion: Speech rate and non-native listeners. *Computer Speech & Language, 21,* 641–651.

Jones, J. T., Pelham, B. W., & Carvallo, M. (2004). How do I love thee? Let me count the Js: Implicit egotism and interpersonal attraction. *Journal of Personality and Social Psychology, 87,* 665–683.

Jones, S. E. (1986). Sex differences in touch behavior. *Western Journal of Speech Communication, 50,* 227–241.

Jones, S. M., & Burleson, B. R. (2003). Effects of helper and recipient sex on the experience and outcomes of comforting messages: An experimental investigation. *Sex Roles, 48,* 1–19.

Jones, S. M., & Wirtz, J. G. (2006). How does the comforting process work? An empirical test of an appraisal-based model of comforting. *Human Communication Research, 32,* 217–243.

Jorgenson, J. (1992). Communication, rapport, and the interview: A social perspective. *Communication Theory, 2,* 148–157.

Kahn, A. S., & Yoder, J. D. (1989). The psychology of women and conservatism: Rediscovering social change. *Psychology of Women Quarterly, 13,* 417–432.

Kahneman, D., Krueger, A. B., Schkade, D. A., Schwarz, N., & Stone, A. A. (2004). A daily measure. *Science,* 306, 1645.

Kanaga, K. R., & Flynn, M. (1981). The relationship between invasion of personal space and stress. *Human Relations, 34,* 239–248.

Kanten, A. B., & Teigen, K. H. (2008). Better than average and better with time: Relative evaluations of self and others in the past, present, and future. *European Journal of Social Psychology, 38,* 343–353.

Kashy, D. A., & DePaulo, B. M. (1996). Who lies? *Journal of Personality and Social Psychology, 70,* 1037–1051.

Kassing, J. W. (1997). Development of the Intercultural Willingness to Communicate Scale. *Communication Research Reports, 14,* 399–407.

Kassing, J. W. (2005). Speaking up competently: A comparison of perceived competence in upward dissent strategies. *Communication Research Reports, 22,* 227–234.

Katriel, T., & Philipsen, G. (1981). "What we need is communication": "Communication" as a cultural category in some American speech. *Communication Monographs, 48,* 301–317.

Katz, J. E., Rice, E. E., & Aspden, P. (2001). The Internet, 1995–2000: Access, civic involvement, and social interaction. *American Behavioral Scientist, 45,* 404–419.

Kaufman, D., & Mahoney, J. M. (1999). The effect of waitresses' touch on alcohol consumption in dyads. *Journal of Social Psychology, 139,* 261–267.

Kaufmann, P. J. (1993). *Sensible listening: The key to responsive interaction* (2nd ed.). Dubuque, IA: Kendall/Hunt.

Kees, N. L., Aberle, J. T., & Fruhauf, C. A. (2007). Aging parents and end-of-life decisions: Helping families negotiate difficult conversations. In D. Linville & K. M. Hertlein (Eds.), *The therapist's notebook for family health care: Homework, handouts, and activities for individuals, couples, and families coping with illness, loss, and disability* (pp. 211–216). New York: Haworth Press.

Kellas, J. K. (2005). Family ties: Communicating identity through jointly told family stories. *Communication Monographs, 72,* 365–389.

Keller, H. (2005). *The story of my life.* New York: Simon & Schuster.

Kellermann, K. (1989). The negativity effect in interaction: It's all in your point of view. *Human Communication Research, 16,* 147–183.

Kellermann, K., Reynolds, R., & Chen, J. B. (1991). Strategies of conversational retreat: When parting is not sweet sorrow. *Communication Monographs, 58,* 362–383.

Kelley, D. (1998). The communication of forgiveness. *Communication Studies,* 49, 255–272.

Kelley, D. L. (1999). Relational expectancy fulfillment as an explanatory variable for distinguishing couple types. *Human Communication Research, 25,* 420–442.

Kelley, D. L. & Waldron, V. R. (2005). An investigation of forgiveness-seeking communication and relational outcomes. *Communication Quarterly, 53,* 339–358.

Kelly, A. E. (1999). Revealing personal secrets. *Current Directions in Psychological Science, 8*(4), 105–108.

Kelly, L., Duran, R. L., & Zolten, J. J. (2001). The effect of reticence on college students' use of electronic mail to communicate with faculty. *Communication Education, 50,* 170–176.

Kelly, L., & Watson, A. K. (1986). *Speaking with confidence and skill.* Lanham, MD: University Press of America.

Kennedy-Moore, E., & Watson, J. C. (1999). *Expressing emotion: Myths, realities, and therapeutic strategies.* New York: Guilford Press.

Kerem, E., Fishman, N., & Josselson, R. (2001). The experience of empathy in everyday relationships: Cognitive and affective elements. *Journal of Social and Personal Relationships, 18,* 709–729.

Keyser, B., & Henley, A. S. (2002). Speakers' overestimation of their effectiveness. *Psychological Science, 13,* 207–212.

Khuri, F. I. (2001). *The body in Islamic culture.* London: Saqi Books.

Kihlstrom, J. F., & Klein, S. B. (1994). The self as a knowledge structure. In R. S. Wyer & T. K. Srull (Eds.), *Handbook of social cognition, Volume 1: Basic processes* (2nd ed., pp. 153–208). Hillsdale, NJ: Erlbaum.

Kim, E. J., & Buschmann, M. T. (1999). The effect of expressive physical touch on patients with dementia. *International Journal of Nursing Studies, 36,* 235–243.

Kim, M. S., Hunter, J. E., Miyahara, A., Horvath, A. M., Bresnahan, M., & Yoon, H. (1996). Individual- vs. culture-level dimensions of individualism and collectivism: Effects on preferred conversational styles. *Communication Monographs, 63,* 28–49.

Kim, M. S., Lee, H., Kim, I. D., & Hunter, J. E. (2004). A test of a cultural model of conflict styles. *Journal of Asian Pacific Communication, 14,* 197–222.

Kim, M. S., Shin, H. C., & Cai, D. (1998). Cultural influences on the preferred forms of requesting and re-requesting. *Communication Monographs, 65,* 47–66.

Kimmel, M. S. (2008) *The gendered society* (3rd ed.). New York: Oxford University Press.

Kim-Prieto, C., & Eid, M. (2004). Norms for experiencing emotions in Sub-Saharan Africa. *Journal of Happiness Studies, 5,* 241–268.

Kirchler, E. (1988). Marital happiness and interaction in everyday surroundings: A time-sample diary approach for couples. *Journal of Social and Personal Relationships, 5,* 375–382.

Kirkland, S. L., Greenberg, J., & Pysczynski, T. (1987). Further evidence of the deleterious effects of overheard derogatory ethnic labels: Derogation beyond the target. *Personality and Social Psychology Bulletin, 12,* 216–227.

Kirkpatrick, D. (1992, March 23). Here comes the payoff from PCs. *Fortune,* 93–102.

Kissling, E. A. (1996). "That's just a basic teen-age rule": Girls' linguistic strategies for managing the menstrual communication taboo. *Journal of Applied Communication Research, 24,* 292–309.

Kleinke, C. L., Peterson, T. R., & Rutledge, T. R. (1998). Effects of self-generated facial expressions on mood. *Journal of Personality and Social Psychology, 74,* 272–279.

Kleinke, C. R. (1977). Compliance to requests made by gazing and touching experimenters in field settings. *Journal of Experimental Social Psychology, 13,* 218–223.

Kline, S. L., & Chatani, K. (2001). Social perception and message awareness as correlates of person-centered regulative messages. *Communication Research Reports, 18,* 274–284.

Klohnen, E. C., & Luo, S. (2003). Interpersonal attraction and personality: What is attractive—self similarity, ideal similarity, complementarity or attachment security? *Journal of Personality and Social Psychology, 85,* 709–722.

Klopf, D. (1984). Cross-cultural apprehension research: A summary of Pacific Basin studies. In J. Daly & J. McCroskey (Eds.), *Avoiding communication: Shyness, reticence, and communication apprehension* (pp. 157–169). Beverly Hills, CA: Sage.

Knapp, M. L. (2006). Lying and deception in close relationships. In A. Vangelisti & D. Perlman (Eds.), *The Cambridge handbook of personal relationships.* New York: Cambridge University Press.

Knapp, M. L., & Hall, J. A. (2006). *Nonverbal communication in human interaction* (6th ed.). Belmont, CA: Wadsworth.

Knapp, M. L., Putnam, L. L., & Davis, L. J. (1988). Measuring interpersonal conflict in organizations: Where do we go from here? *Management Communication Quarterly, 1,* 414–429.

Knapp, M. L., & Vangelisti, A. (2006). *Interpersonal communication and human relationships* (6th ed.). Boston: Allyn & Bacon.

Kniffin, K. M., & Wilson, D. S. (2004). The effect of nonphysical traits on the perception of physical attractiveness: Three naturalistic studies. *Evolution and Human Behavior, 25*(2), 88–101.

Knobloch, L. K., Miller, L. E., Bond, B. J., & Mannone, S. E. (2007). Relational uncertainty and message processing in marriage. *Communication Monographs, 74,* 154–180.

Knobloch, L. K., & Solomon, D. H. (2002). Information seeking beyond initial interaction: Negotiating relational uncertainty within close relationships. *Human Communication Research, 28,* 243–257.

Knobloch, L. K., & Solomon, D. H. (2003). Manifestations of relationship conception in conversation. *Human Communication Research, 29,* 482–515.

Knobloch-Westerwick, S., & Alter, S. (2006). Mood adjustment to social situations through mass media use: How men ruminate and women dissipate angry moods. *Human Communication* Research, 32, 58–73.

Koerner, A. F., & Fitzpatrick, M. A. (2002). Toward a theory of family communication. *Communication Theory, 12,* 70–91.

Koerner, A. F., & Fitzpatrick, M. A. (2006a). Family communications patterns theory: A social cognitive approach. In D. O. Braithwaite & L. A. Baxter (Eds.), *Engaging theories in family communication: Multiple perspectives.* Thousand Oaks, CA: Sage.

Koerner, A. F., & Fitzpatrick, M. A. (2006b). Family conflict communication. In J. Oetzel & S. Ting-Toomey (Eds.), *Handbook of conflict communication.* Thousand Oaks, CA: Sage.

Koesten, J. (2004). Family communication patterns, sex of subject, and communication competence. *Communication Monographs, 71,* 226–244.

Kohn, S. E., & O'Connell, V. D. (2005). *Six habits of highly effective bosses.* Franklin Lakes, NJ: Career Press.

Kolb, J. A. (1998). The relationship between self-monitoring and leadership in student project groups. *Journal of Business Communication, 35,* 264–282.

Kolligan, J., Jr. (1990). Perceived fraudulence as a dimension of perceived incompetence. In R. J. Sternberg & J. Kolligan, Jr. (Eds.), *Competence considered* (pp. 261–285). New Haven, CT: Yale University Press.

Kopacz, M. A. (2006). Nonverbal communication as a persuasion tool: Current status and future directions. *Rocky Mountain Communication Review, 3*(1), 1–19.

Kopp, J. (1988). Self-monitoring: A literature review of research and practice. *Social Work Research and Abstracts, 24*(4), 8–20.

Korabik, K., & McCreary, D. R. (2000). Testing a model of socially desirable and undesirable gender-role attributes. *Sex Roles, 43,* 665–685.

Korzybski, A. (1933). *Science and sanity.* Lancaster, PA: Science Press.

Koukounas, E., & Letch, N. M. (2001). Psychological correlates of perception of sexual intent in women. *Journal of Social Psychology, 141,* 443–456.

Kowner, R., & Wiseman, R. (2003). Culture and status-related behavior: Japanese and American perceptions of interaction in asymmetric dyads. *Cross Cultural Research: The Journal of Comparative Social Science, 37,* 178–210.

Krackhardt , D., & Hanson, J. R. (1993). Informal networks: The company behind the chart. *Harvard Business Review, 71,* 104–111.

Kramer, M. W., & Hess, J. A. (2002). Communication rules for the display of emotions in organizational settings. *Management Communication Quarterly, 16,* 66–80.

Krauss, R. M., Morrel-Samuels, P., & Colasante, C. (1991). Do conversational hand gestures communicate? *Journal of Personality and Social Psychology, 61,* 743–754.

Kroeber, A. L., & Kluckholn, C. (1952). *Culture: A critical review of concepts and definitions* (Harvard University, Peabody Museum of American Archeology and Ethnology Papers 47).

Krokoff, L. J. (1990). Hidden agendas in marriage: Affective and longitudinal dimensions. *Communication Research, 17,* 483–499.

Kubany, E. S., Richard, D. C., Bauer, G. B., & Muraoka, M. Y. (1992). Impact of assertive and accusatory communication of distress and anger: A verbal component analysis. *Aggressive Behavior, 18,* 337–347.

Kubic, K. N., & Chory, R. M. (2007). Exposure to television makeover programs and perceptions of self. *Communication Research Reports, 24,* 283–291.

Kuo, F. E., & Sullivan, W. C. (2001a). Aggression and violence in the inner city: Effects of environment via mental fatigue. *Environment and Behavior, 33,* 543–571.

Kuo, F. E., & Sullivan, W. C. (2001b). Environment and crime in the inner city: Does vegetation reduce crime? *Environment and Behavior, 33,* 343–367.

Kurzban, R., & Weeden, J. (2005). HurryDate: Mate preferences in action. *Evolution and Human Behavior, 26,* 227–244.

Laing, R. D. (1961). *The self and others: Further studies in sanity and madness.* London: Tavistock.

Lakin, J. L. (2006). Automatic cognitive processes and nonverbal communication. In V. Manusov & M. L. Patterson (Eds.), *The Sage handbook of nonverbal communication* (pp. 59–77). Thousand Oaks, CA: Sage.

Landrum, R. E., & Harrold, R. (2003). What employers want from psychology graduates. *Teaching of Psychology, 30,* 131–133.

Lane, K., Balleweg, B. J., Suler, J. R., Fernald, P. S., & Goldstein, G. S. (2000). Acquiring skills—Undergraduate students. In M. E. Ware & D. E. Johnson (Eds.), *Handbook of demonstrations and activities in the teaching of psychology: Vol. 3. Personality, abnormal, clinical-counseling, and social* (2nd ed., pp. 109–124). Mahwah, NJ: Erlbaum.

Langer, E. (1990). *Mindfulness.* Reading, MA: Addison-Wesley.

Langlois, J. H., & Roggman, L. A. (1990). Attractive faces are only average. *Psychological Science, 1,* 115–121.

Lapakko, D. (1997). Three cheers for language: A closer examination of a widely cited study of nonverbal communication. *Communication Education, 46,* 63–67.

Larkey, L. K., Hecht, M. L., & Martin, J. (1993). What's in a name? African American ethnic identity terms and self-determination. *Journal of Language and Social Psychology, 12,* 302–317.

Larsen, K. R. T., & McInerney, C. R. (2002). Preparing to work in the virtual organization. *Information & Management, 39,* 445–456.

Larson, C. E., & LaFasto, F. M. (1989). *TeamWork: What must go right/What can go wrong.* Newbury Park, CA: Sage.

Larson, J. H., Crane, D. R., & Smith, C. W. (1991). Morning and night couples: The effect of wake and sleep patterns on marital adjustment. *Journal of Marital and Family Therapy, 17,* 53–65.

Laurenceau, J. P., & Kleinman, B. M. (2006). Intimacy in personal relationships. In A. Vangelisti & D. Perlman (Eds.), *The Cambridge handbook of personal relationships.* New York: Cambridge University Press.

Lawler, K. A., Younger, J. W., Piferi, R. L., Billington, E., Jobe, R., Edmondson, K., & Jones, W. H. (2003). A change of heart: Cardiovascular correlates of forgiveness in response to interpersonal conflict. *Journal of Behavioral Medicine, 26,* 373–393.

Le Blanc, P. M., Bakker, A. B., Peeters, M. C. W., van Heesch, N. C. A., & Schaufeli, W. B. (2001). Emotional job demands and burnout among oncology care providers. *Anxiety, Stress and Coping: An International Journal, 14,* 243–263.

Le Poire, B. A., & Yoshimura, S. M. (1999). The effects of expectancies and actual communication on nonverbal adaptation and communication outcomes: A test of interaction adaptation theory. *Communication Monographs, 66,* 1–30.

Leary, M. R., & Kowalski, R. M. (1990). Impression management: A literature review and two-component model. *Psychological Bulletin, 107,* 34–47.

Leathers, D. G. (1992). *Successful nonverbal communication: Principles and applications* (2nd ed.). New York: Macmillan.

Lebula, C., & Lucas, C. (1945). The effects of attitudes on descriptions of pictures. *Journal of Experimental Psychology, 35,* 517–524.

Lee, J. (1998). Effective maintenance communication in superior-subordinate relationships. *Western Journal of Communication, 62,* 181–208.

Lee, J. A. (1973). *The colors of love: Exploration of the ways of loving.* Don Mills, Ontario: New Press.

Leets, L. (2001). Explaining perceptions of racist speech. *Communication Research, 28,* 676–706.

Leets, L. (2003). Disentangling perceptions of subtle racist speech: A cultural perspective. *Journal of Language and Social Psychology. 22,* 1–24.

Lenhart, A., Madden, M., Cacgill, A.R., & Smith, A. (2007). *Teens and social media.* Washington, DC: Pew Internet & American Life Project.

Lenhart, A., Rainie, L., & Lewis, O. (2001). *Teenage life online.* Pew Internet and American Life Project. Retrieved from http://www.pewinternet.org/reports/toc.asp?Report536

Lerner, R. M., Rothbaum, F., Boulos, S., & Castellino, D. R. (2002). Developmental systems perspective on parenting. In M. Bornstein (Ed.), *Handbook of parenting: Vol. 2. Biology and ecology of parenting* (2nd ed., pp. 315–344). Mahwah, NJ: Erlbaum.

Levenson, R. W., Ekman, P., & Friesen, W. V. (1990). Voluntary facial action generates emotion-specific autonomic nervous system activity. *Psychophysiology, 27,* 363–384.

Levesque, M. J., & Kenny, D. A. (1993). Accuracy of behavioral predictions at zero acquaintance: A social relations analysis. *Journal of Personality and Social Psychology, 65,* 1178–1187.

Levine, D. (2000). Virtual attraction: What rocks your boat. *CyberPsychology and Behavior, 3,* 565–573.

Levine, R. V. (1988). The pace of life across cultures. In J. E. McGrath (Ed.), *The social psychology of time* (pp. 39–60). Newbury Park, CA: Sage.

Levine, R. V., & Norenzayan, A. (1999). The pace of life in 31 countries. *Journal of Cross-Cultural Psychology, 30,* 178–205.

Levine, T. R., Asada, K. J. K., & Park, H. S. (2006). The lying chicken and the gaze avoidant egg: Eye contact, deception, and causal order. *Southern Communication Journal, 71,* 401–411.

Levitt, S. D., & Dubner, S. J. (2005). *Freakonomics: A rogue economist explores the hidden side of everything.* New York: William Morrow.

Lewis, L. K. (2006). Collaborative interaction: Review of communication scholarship and a research agenda. *Communication Yearbook, 30,* 197–247.

Lewis, M. H., & Reinsch, N. L., Jr. (1988). Listening in organizational environments. *Journal of Business Communication, 25,* 49–67.

Li, Q. (2007). New *bottle* but old wine: A research of cyberbullying in schools. *Computers in Human Behavior, 23,* 1777–1791.

Lieberson, S. (2000). *A matter of taste: How names, fashions, and culture change.* New Haven, CT: Yale University Press.

Lillian, D. L. (2007). A thorn by any other name: Sexist discourse as hate speech. *Discourse & Society, 18,* 719–740.

Lim, G. Y., & Roloff, M. E. (1999). Attributing sexual consent. *Journal of Applied Communication Research, 27,* 1–23.

Limon, M. S., & LaFrance, B. H. (2005). Communication traits and leadership emergence: Examining the impact of argumentativeness, communication apprehension, and verbal aggressiveness in work groups. *Southern Communication Journal, 70,* 123–133.

Linden, R. B., Martin, C. L., & Parsons, C. K. (1993). Interviewer and applicant behaviors in employment interviews. *Academy of Management Journal, 36,* 372–386.

Lindsey, A. E., & Vigil, V. (1999). The interpretation and evaluation of winking in stranger dyads. *Communication Research Reports, 16,* 256–265.

Lippard, P. V. (1988). Ask me no questions, I'll tell you no lies: Situational exigencies for interpersonal deception. *Western Journal of Speech Communication, 52,* 91–103.

Lippert, T., & Prager, K. J. (2001). Daily experiences of intimacy: A study of couples. *Personal Relationships, 8,* 283–298.

Listen to this: Hearing problems can stress relationships. (2008). Available at: http://www.energizer.com/livehealthy/#listentothis

Littlejohn, S. W. (2008). *Theories of human communication* (9th ed.). Boston: Cengage.

Litwin, A. H., & Hallstein, L. O. (2007). Shadows and silences: How women's positioning and unspoken friendship rules in organizational settings cultivate difficulties among some women at work. *Women's Studies in Communication, 30*(1), 111–142.

Lobchuk, M. M. (2006). Concept analysis of perspective-taking: Meeting informal caregiver needs for communication competence and accurate perception. *Journal of Advanced Nursing, 54,* 330–341.

Lock, C. (2004, July 31). Deception detection: Psychologists try to learn how to spot a liar. *Science News, 16,* 72.

Locker, K. O. (2000). *Business and administrative communication* (5th ed.). Homewood, IL: Irwin.

Long, E. C. J., Angera, J. J., Carter, S. J., Nakamoto, M., & Kalso, M. (1999). Understanding the one you love: A longitudinal assessment of an empathy training program for couples in romantic relationships. *Family Relations: Interdisciplinary Journal of Applied Family Studies, 48,* 235–242.

Lourenco, O., & Machado, A. (1996). In defense of Piaget's theory: A reply to 10 common criticisms. *Psychological Review, 103,* 143–164.

Lucas, R. E., Le, K., & Dyrenforth, P. S. (2008). Explaining the extraversion/positive affect relation: Sociability cannot account for extraverts' greater happiness. *Journal of Personality, 76,* 385–414.

Luft, J. (1969). *Of human interaction.* Palo Alto, CA: National Press Books.

Lundqvist, L.-O. (2008). The relationship between the biosocial model of personality and susceptibility to emotional contagion: A structural equation modeling approach. *Personality and Individual Differences, 45,* 89–95.

Lunkenheimer, E. S., Shields, A. M., & Cortina, K. S. (2007). Parental emotion coaching and dismissing in family interaction. *Social Development, 16,* 232–248.

Luo, S., & Klohnen, E. (2005). Assortive mating and marital quality in newlyweds; A couple-centered approach. *Journal of Personality and Social Psychology, 88,* 304–326.

Lustig, M. W., & Koester, J. (1999). *Intercultural competence: Interpersonal communication across cultures* (3rd ed.). New York: Longman.

Lustig, M. W., & Koester, J. (2005). *Intercultural competence: Interpersonal communication across cultures* (4th ed.). Upper Saddle River, NJ: Allyn & Bacon.

Ma, R., & Chuang, R. (2001). Persuasion strategies of Chinese college students in interpersonal contexts. *Southern Communication Journal, 66*, 267–278.

MacGeorge, E. L., Lichtman, R. M., & Pressey, L. C. (2002). The evaluation of advice in supportive interactions: Facework and contextual factors. *Human Communication Research, 28,* 451–463.

MacIntyre, P. D., & Thivierge, K. A. (1995). The effects of speaker personality on anticipated reactions to public speaking. *Communication Research Reports, 12,* 125–133.

Macrae, C. N., & Bodenhausen, G. V. (2001). Social cognition: Categorical person perception. *British Journal of Psychology, 92,* 239–256.

Magnusson, A. (2006). Nonverbal conversation-regulating signals of the blind adult. *Communication Studies*, 57, 421–433.

Maguire, M. (2005). Biological cycles and cognitive performance. In A. Esgate, D. Groome K. Baker, D. Heathcote, R. Kemp, M. Maguire, & C. Reed (Eds.), *An introduction to applied cognitive psychology* (pp. 137–161). New York: Psychology Press.

Makin, V. S. (2004). Face management and the role of interpersonal politeness variables in euphemism production and comprehension. *Dissertation Abstracts International, 64,* 4077.

Malis, R. S., & Roloff, M. E. (2006). Features of serial arguing and coping strategies: Links with stress and well-being. In B. A. LePoire (Ed.), *Applied interpersonal communication matters* (pp. 39–65). New York: Peter Lang.

Malis, R. S., & Roloff, M. (2007, May). *Communication during serial arguments: Connections with individuals' mental and physical well-being.* Paper presented at the annual conference of the International Communication Association, San Francisco.

Mallalieu, S. D., Hanton, S., & Jones, G. (2003). Emotional labeling and competitive anxiety in preparation and competition. *The Sport Psychologist, 17,* 157–174.

Malle, B. F., & Hodges, S. D. (Eds.). (2005). *Other minds: How humans bridge the divide between self and others.* New York: Guilford Press.

Malouf, D. (2003, November). Made in England: Australia's British inheritance. *Quarterly Essay, 12.*

Maltz, D., & Borker, R. (1982). A cultural approach to male-female miscommunication. In J. J. Gumpertz (Ed.), *Language and social identity* (pp. 196–216). Cambridge: Cambridge University Press.

Manusov, V. (1993). It depends on your perspective: Effects of stance and beliefs about intent on person perception. *Western Journal of Communication, 57,* 27–41.

Manusov, V., Winchatz, M. R., & Manning, L. M. (1997). Acting out our minds: Incorporating behavior into models of stereotype-based expectancies for cross-cultural interactions. *Communication Monographs, 64,* 119–139.

Marangoni, C., & Ickes, W. (1989). Loneliness: A theoretical review with implications for measurement. *Journal of Social and Personal Relationships, 6,* 93–128.

Marchant, V. (1999, June 28). Listen up! *Time, 153,* 74.

Marcus, M. G. (1976, October). The power of a name. *Psychology Today, 9,* 75–77, 106.

Marek, C. I., Wanzer, M. B., & Knapp, J. L. (2004). An exploratory investigation of the relationship between roommates' first impressions and subsequent communication patterns. *Communication Research Reports, 21,* 210–220.

Mares, M.-L. (1995). The aging family. In M. A. Fitzpatrick & A. L. Vangelisti (Eds.), *Explaining family interactions* (pp. 344–374). Thousand Oaks, CA: Sage.

Markus, H. R., & Kitayama, S. (1991). Culture and the self: Implications for cognition, emotion, and motivation. *Psychological Review, 98,* 224–253.

Marriott, M. (1998, July 2). The blossoming of Internet chat [online]. *New York Times.* Retrieved from http://www.nytimes.com/library/tech/98/07/circuits/articles/02/chat.html

Marsh, A. A., Elfenbein, H. A., & Ambady, N. (2003). Nonverbal "accents": Cultural differences in facial expressions of emotion. *Psychological Science, 14,* 373–376.

Marshall, T. C. (2008). Cultural differences in intimacy: The influence of gender-role ideology and individualism-collectivism. *Journal of Social and Personal Relationships, 25,* 143–168.

Martin, M. M., Anderson, C. M., Burant, P. A., & Weber, K. (1997). Verbal aggression in sibling relationships. *Communication Quarterly, 45,* 304–317.

Martin, M. M., Anderson, C. M., & Hovarth, C. L. (1996). Feelings about verbal aggression: Justifications for sending and hurt from receiving verbally aggressive messages. *Communication Research Reports, 13,* 19–26.

Martin, M. M., Anderson, C. M., & Mottet, T. P. (1999). Perceived understanding and self-disclosure in the stepparent-stepchild relationship. *Journal of Psychology, 133,* 281–290.

Martz, J. M., Verette, J., Arriaga, X. B., Slovik, L. F., Cox, C. L., & Rusbult, C. E. (1998). Positive illusion in close relationships. *Personal Relationships, 5,* 159–181.

Mashek, D., & Sherman, M. (2004). Desiring less closeness with intimate others. In D. Mashek & A. Aron (Eds.), *The handbook of closeness and intimacy* (pp. 343–356). Mahwah, NJ: Erlbaum.

Maslow, A. H. (1968). *Toward a psychology of being.* New York: Van Nostrand Reinhold.

Maslow, A. H., & Mintz, N. L. (1956). Effects of aesthetic surroundings: I. Initial effects of those aesthetic surroundings upon perceiving "energy" and "well-being" in faces. *Journal of Psychology, 41,* 247–254.

Mast, M. S., & Hall, J. A. (2004). Who is the boss and who is not? Accuracy of judging status. *Journal of Nonverbal Behavior, 28,* 145–165.

Matsumoto, D. (1991). Cultural influences on facial expressions of emotion. *Southern Communication Journal, 56,* 128–137.

Matsumoto, D. (1993). Ethnic differences in affect intensity, emotion judgments, display rule attitudes, and self-reported emotional expression in an American sample. *Motivation and Emotion, 17,* 107–123.

Matsumoto, D. (2006). Culture and nonverbal behavior. In V. Manusov & M. L. Patterson (Eds.), *The Sage handbook of nonverbal communication* (pp. 219–235). Thousand Oaks, CA: Sage.

Matsumoto, D., & Yoo, S. H. (2005). Culture and applied nonverbal communication. In R. S. Feldman & R. E. Riggio (Eds.), *Applications of nonverbal communication* (pp. 255–277). Mahwah, NJ: Erlbaum.

Matveev, A. V. (2004). Describing intercultural communication competence: In-depth interviews with American and Russian managers. *Qualitative Research Reports in Communication, 5,* 55–62.

Mayne, T. J. (1999). Negative affect and health: The importance of being earnest. *Cognition and Emotion, 13,* 601–635.

McBride, J. L. (2007). The family. In O. J. Z. Sahler & J. E. Carr (Eds.), *The behavioral sciences and health care* (2nd ed. rev. and updated, pp. 147–156). Ashland, OH: Hogrefe & Huber.

McCain, J. (1999). *Faith of my fathers.* New York: Random House.

McCornack, S. A. (1992). Information manipulation theory. *Communication Monographs, 59,* 1–16.

McCornack, S. A., & Levine, T. R. (1990). When lies are uncovered: Emotional and relational outcomes of discovered deception. *Communication Monographs, 57,* 119–138.

McCroskey, J. C., & Richmond, V. P. (1995). Correlates of compulsive communication: Quantitative and qualitative characteristics. *Communication Quarterly, 43,* 39–52.

McCroskey, J. C., & Richmond, V. P. (1996). *Fundamentals of human communication: An interpersonal perspective.* Prospect Heights, IL: Waveland.

McCroskey, J. C., Richmond, V. P., Heisel, A. D., & Hayhurst, J. L. (2004). Eysenck's Big Three and communication traits: Communication traits as manifestations of temperament. *Communication Research Reports, 21,* 404–410.

McCroskey, J. C., & Wheeless, L. (1976). *Introduction to human communication.* Boston: Allyn & Bacon.

McDaniel, S. H., Beckman, H. B., Morse, D. S., Silberman, J., Seaburn, D. B., & Epstein, R. M. (2007). Physician self-disclosure in primary care visits: Enough about you, what about me? *Archives of Internal Medicine*, 167, 1321–1326.

McGinty, K., Knox, D., and Zusman, M. E. (2007). Friends with benefits: Women want "friends," men want "benefits." *College Student Journal, 41,* 1128–1131.

McGee, D. S., & Cegala, D. J. (1998). Patient communication skills training for improved competence in the primary care medical consultation. *Journal of Applied Communication Research, 26,* 412–430.

McGlone, M. S., & Batchelor, J. A. (2003). Looking out for number one: Euphemism and face. *Journal of Communication, 53,* 251–264.

McGlone, M. S., Beck, G., & Pfiester, A. (2006). Contamination and camouflage in euphemisms. *Communication Monographs, 73*, 261–282.

McGoldrick, M., Watson, M., & Benton, W. (1999). Siblings through the life cycle. In B. Carter & M. McGoldrick (Eds.), *The expanded family life cycle: Individual, family, and social perspectives* (3rd ed., pp. 153–168). Needham Heights, MA: Allyn & Bacon.

McGrath, C. (2006). The ideal lobbyist: Personal characteristics of effective lobbyists. *Journal of Communication Management, 10*(2), 67–79.

McGregor, D. (1960). *The human side of enterprise.* New York: McGraw-Hill.

McIntire, R. (1999). *Raising good kids in tough times: 7 crucial habits for parent success.* Berkeley Springs, WV: Summit Crossroads Press.

McKenzie, J. (2008). Autism breakthrough: Girl's writings explain her behavior and feelings. Available at: http://abcnews.go.com/Health/story?id=4311223

McLuhan, M. (1964). *Understanding media: The extensions of man.* New York: McGraw-Hill.

McMullen, R. C., Shippen, M. E., & Dangel, H. L. (2007). Middle school teachers' expectations of organizational behaviors of students with learning disabilities. *Journal of Instructional Psychology, 34*(2), 75–80.

McNamara, C. (2008). *Group dynamics: Basic nature of groups and how they develop.* Available at: http://www.managementhelp.org/grp_skll/theory/theory.htm

McNaughton, D., Hamlin, D., McCarthy, J., Head-Reeves, D., & Schreiner, M. (2008). Learning to listen: Teaching an active listening strategy to preservice education professionals. *Topics in Early Childhood Special Education, 27*, 223–231.

McPherson, M. B., & Liang, Y. (2007). Students' reactions to teachers' management of compulsive communicators. *Communication Education, 56*, 18–33.

Meaux, J. B. (2002). Time perception, behavioral inhibition, and ADHD. *Dissertation Abstracts International, 62*, 3556.

Mehl, M. R., Vazire, S., Ramírez-Esparza, N., Slatcher, R. B., & Pennebaker, J. W. (2007). Are women really more talkative than men? *Science, 317*, 82.

Mehrabian, A. (1972). *Nonverbal communication.* Chicago: Aldine-Atherton.

Mehrabian, A. (2001). Characteristics attributed to individuals on the basis of their first names. *Genetic, Social, and General Psychology Monographs, 127*, 59–88.

Mehrabian, A., & Blum, J. S. (2003). Physical appearance, attractiveness, and the mediating role of emotions. In N. J. Pallone (Ed.), *Love, romance, sexual interaction: Research perspectives from current psychology* (pp. 1–29). New Brunswick, NJ: Transaction.

Mehrabian, A., & Weiner, M. (1967). Decoding of inconsistent communications. *Journal of Personality and Social Psychology, 6*, 109–114.

Mendes de Leon, C. F. (2005). Why do friendships matter for survival? *Journal of Epidemiology and Community Health, 59*: 538–539.

Merolla, A. J. (2008). Communicating forgiveness in friendships and dating relationships. *Communication Studies, 59*, 114–131.

Merolla, A. J., Weber, K. D., Myers, S. A., & Booth-Butterfield, M. (2004). The impact of past dating relationship solidarity on commitment, satisfaction, and investment in current relationships. *Communication Quarterly, 52*, 251–264.

Merrill, D. M. (1997). *Caring for elderly parents: Juggling work, family, and caregiving in middle and working class families.* Westport, CT: Auburn House/Greenwood.

Messman, S. J., & Canary, D. J. (1998). Patterns of conflict in personal relationships. In B. H. Spitzberg & W. R. Cupach (Eds.), *The dark side of close relationships* (pp. 121–152). Mahwah, NJ: Erlbaum.

Messman, S. J., & Mikesell, R. L. (2000). Competition and interpersonal conflict in dating relationships. *Communication Reports, 13*, 21–34.

Metts, S. (1989). An exploratory investigation of deception in close relationships. *Journal of Social and Personal Relationships, 6*, 159–179.

Metts, S., & Cupach, W. R. (1990). The influence of relationship beliefs and problem-solving relationships on satisfaction in romantic relationships. *Human Communication Research, 17*, 170–185.

Metts, S., Cupach, W. R., & Bejllovec, R. A. (1989). "I love you too much to ever start liking you": Redefining romantic relationships. *Journal of Social and Personal Relationships, 6*, 259–274.

Metts, S., Cupach, W. R., & Imahori, T. T. (1992). Perceptions of sexual compliance-resisting messages in three types of cross-sex relationships. *Western Journal of Communication, 56*, 1–17.

Metts, S., & Grohskopf, E. (2003). Impression management: Goals, strategies, and skills. In B. Burleson & J. O. Greene (Eds.), *Handbook of communication and social interaction skills* (pp. 357–399). Mahwah, NJ: Erlbaum.

Mignault, A., & Chaudhuri, A. (2003). The many faces of a neutral face: Head tilt and perception of dominance and emotion. *Journal of Nonverbal Behavior, 27*, 111–132.

Miller, G. F. (1998). How mate choice shaped human nature: A review of sexual selection and human evolution. In C. B. Crawford & D. L. Krebs, *Handbook of evolutionary psychology: Ideas, issues, and applications* (pp. 87–129). Mahwah, NJ: Erlbaum.

Miller, G. R., & Steinberg, M. (1975). *Between people: A new analysis of interpersonal communication.* Chicago: SRA.

Miller, K., Joseph, L., & Apker, J. (2000). Strategic ambiguity in the role development process. *Journal of Applied Communication Research, 28,* 193–214.

Miller, K. I., & Birkholt, M. (1995). Empathy and burnout in human service work: An extension of a communication model. *Communication Research, 22,* 123–147.

Miller, L. C., Cooke, L. L., Tsang, J., & Morgan, F. (1992). Should I brag? Nature and impact of positive and boastful disclosures for women and men. *Human Communication Research, 18,* 364–399.

Miller, P., Niehuis, S., & Huston, T. L. (2006). Positive illusions in marital relationships: A 13-year longitudinal study. *Personality and Social Psychology Bulletin, 32,* 1579–1594.

Miller, S., Nunnally, E. W., & Wackman, D. B. (1975). *Alive and aware: How to improve your relationships through better communication.* Minneapolis, MN: Interpersonal Communication Programs.

Millikan, R. G. (2001). The language-thought partnership: A bird's eye view. *Language and Communication, 21,* 157–166.

Miró, E., Cano, M. C., Espinoza-Fernández, L., & Beula-Casal, G. (2003). Time estimation during prolonged sleep deprivation and its relation to activation measures. *Human Factors, 45,* 148–159.

Moberg, P. J. (2001). Linking conflict strategy to the five-factor model: Theoretical and empirical foundations. *International Journal of Conflict Management, 12,* 47–68.

Moffat, M., Cleland, J., van der Molen, T., & Price, D. (2007). Poor communication may impair optimal asthma care: A qualitative study. *Family Practice, 24*(1), 65–70.

Moghaddam, F. M., Taylor, D. M., & Wright, S. C. (1993). *Social-psychology in cross-cultural perspective.* New York: Freeman.

Mohd Salleh, L. (2008). Communication competence of Malaysian leaders as a function of emotional intelligence and cognitive complexity. *DAI, 68*(7-A), 2727.

Moody, E. J. (2001). Internet use and its relationship to loneliness. *Cyber Psychology and Behavior, 4,* 393–401.

Morman, M. T., & Floyd, K. (1999). Affectionate communication between fathers and young adult sons: Individual- and relational-level correlates. *Communication Studies, 50,* 294–309.

Morman, M. T., & Floyd, K. (2002). A "changing culture of fatherhood": Effects of affectionate communication, closeness, and satisfaction in men's relationships with their fathers and their sons. *Western Journal of Communication, 66,* 395–411.

Morreale, S. P., & Pearson, J. C. (2008). Why communication education is important: The centrality of the discipline in the 21st century. *Communication Education, 57*(2), 224–240.

Morris, D. (1973). *Intimate behavior.* New York: Bantam.

Morris, T. L., Gorham, J., Cohen, S. H., & Huffman, D. (1996). Fashion in the classroom: Effects of attire on student perceptions of instructors in college classes. *Communication Education, 45,* 135–148.

Morton, J. B., & Trehub, S. E. (2001). Children's understanding of emotion in speech. *Child Development, 72,* 834–843.

Moss, G., Kubacki, K., Hersh, M., & Gunn, R. (2007). Knowledge management in higher education: A comparison of individualistic and collectivist cultures. *European Journal of Education, 42,* 377–394.

Motley, M. T. (1990). On whether one can(not) communicate: An examination via traditional communication postulates. *Western Journal of Speech Communication, 54,* 1–20.

Motley, M. T. (1992). Mindfulness in solving communicators' dilemmas. *Communication Monographs, 59,* 306–314.

Motley, M. T. (1993). Facial affect and verbal context in conversation: Facial expression as interjection. *Human Communication Research, 20,* 3–40.

Mulac, A. (2006). The gender-linked language effect: Do language differences really make a difference? In K. Dindia & D. J. Canary (Eds.), *Sex differences and similarities in communication* (2nd ed.). Mahwah, NJ: Erlbaum.

Mulac, A., Bradac, J. J., & Gibbons, P. (2001). Empirical support for the gender-as-culture hypothesis: An intercultural analysis of male/female language differences. *Human Communication Research, 27,* 121–152.

Mulac, A., Wiemann, J. M., Widenmann, S. J., & Gibson, T. W. (1988). Male/female language differences and effects in same-sex and mixed-sex dyads: The gender-linked language effect. *Communication Monographs, 55,* 315–335.

Muñoz-Rivas, M. J., Graña, J. L., O'Leary, K. D., & González, M. P. (2007). Aggression in adolescent dating relationships: Prevalence, justification, and health consequences. *Journal of Adolescent Health, 40,* 298–304.

Murdock, G. P. (1965). *Social structure.* New York: Free Press.

Murray, J. E., Jr. (2002). *The current state of marriage and family.* Pittsburgh, PA: Duquesne University Family Institute. Retrieved July 22, 2005 from http://www2.duq.edu/familyinstitute/templates/features/csmf/children.html

Murray, S. L., Holmes, J. G., & Griffin, D. W. (1996). The benefits of positive illusions: Idealization and the construction of satisfaction in close relationships. *Journal of Personality and Social Psychology, 70,* 79–98.

Mwakalyelye, N., & DeAngelis, T. (1995, October). The power of touch helps vulnerable babies thrive. *APA Monitor,* p. 25.

Myers, D. (1980, May). The inflated self. *Psychology Today, 14,* 16.

Myers, P. N., & Biocca, F. A. (1992). The elasticc body image: The effect of television advertising and programming on body image distortions in young women. *Journal of Communication, 42,* 108–134.

Myers, S. A. (1998). Students' self-disclosure in the college classroom. *Psychological Reports, 83*(3, Pt 1), 1067–1070.

Myers, S. (2000). Empathic listening: Reports on the experience of being heard. *Journal of Humanistic Psychology, 40,* 148–173.

Myers, S. A. (2002). Perceived aggressive instructor communication and student state motivation, learning, and satisfaction. *Communication Reports, 15,* 113–121.

Myers, S. A. (2003). Sibling use of relational maintenance behaviors. In K. M. Galvin & P. J. Cooper (Eds.), *Making connections: Readings in relational communication* (pp. 300–308). Los Angeles: Roxbury.

Myers, S. A., & Bryant, L. E. (2008). The use of behavioral indicators of sibling commitment among emerging adults. *Journal of Family Communication, 8,* 101–125.

Myers, S. A., Edwards, C., Wahl, S. T., & Martin, M. M. (2007). The relationship between perceived instructor aggressive communication and college student involvement. *Communication Education, 56,* 495–508.

Myers, S. A., & Rocca, K. A. (2001). Perceived instructor argumentativeness and verbal aggressiveness in the college classroom: Effects on student perceptions of climate, apprehension, and state motivation. *Western Journal of Communication, 65,* 113–137.

Myers, S. A., & Weber, K. D. (2004). Preliminary development of a measure of sibling relational maintenance behavior: Scale development and initial findings. *Communication Quarterly, 52,* 334–346.

Myers-Scotton, C. (2000). What matters: The out of sight in mixed languages. *Bilingualism: Language and Cognition, 3,* 119–121.

National Communication Association. (1999). *How Americans communicate* [online]. Retrieved from http://www.natcom.org/research/Roper/how_americans_communicate.htm

National Institute of Mental Health. (2008, April 3). *Attention deficit hyperactivity disorder.* Available at: http://www.nimh.nih.gov/health/publications/adhd/complete-publication .shtml

National Youth Violence Prevention Resource Center. (2007, December 20). *Gangs fact sheet.* Available at: http://www.safeyouth.org/scripts/facts/gangs.asp

Neidenthal, P. M., Brauer, M., Halberstadt, J. B., & Innes-Ker, A. H. (2001). When did her smile drop? Facial mimicry and the influences of emotional state on the detection of change in emotional expression. *Cognition and Emotion, 15,* 853–864.

Nellermoe, D. A., Weirich, T. R., & Reinstein, A. (1999). Using practitioners' viewpoints to improve accounting students' communications skills. *Business Communication Quarterly, 62*(2), 41–60.

Nelson, J. E., & Beggan, J. K. (2004). Self-serving judgments about winning the lottery. *Journal of Psychology: Interdisciplinary and Applied, 138,* 253–264.

Nelson, T. D. (2005). Ageism: Prejudice against our featured future self. *Journal of Social Issues, 61,* 207–221.

Nelton, S. (1996, February). Emotions in the workplace. *Nation's Business,* pp. 25–30.

Neuliep, J. W. (1996). The influence of theory X and Y management style on the perception of ethical behavior in organizations. *Journal of Social Behavior and Personality, 11,* 301–311.

Nemati, A., & Bayer, J. M. (2007). AddedGender differences in the use of linguistic forms in the speech of men and women: A comparative study of Persian and English. *Language in India, 7,* 1–12. Available at: http://www.languageinindia.com/sep2007/ genderstudy.pdf

Neuliep, J. W., & Grohskopf, E. L. (2000). Uncertainty reduction and communication satisfaction during initial interaction: An initial test and replication of a new axiom. *Communication Reports, 13,* 67–77.

Newton, D. A., & Burgoon, J. K. (1990). The use and consequences of verbal influence strategies during interpersonal disagreements. *Human Communication Research, 16,* 477–518.

Ng, S. H., & Bradac, J. J. (1993). *Power in language: Verbal communication and social influence.* Newbury Park, CA: Sage.

Nichols, R. G. (1948). Factors in listening comprehension. *Speech Monographs, 1,* 154–163.

Nie, N. H. (2001). Sociability, interpersonal relations, and the Internet. *American Behavioral Scientist, 45,* 420–435.

Nie, N. H., & Erbring, L. (2000, February 17). *Internet and society: A preliminary report.* Stanford, CA: Stanford Institute for the Quantitative Study of Society (SIQSS). Retrieved from http://www.stanford.edu/group/siqss/Press_Release/Preliminary _Report.pdf

Niven, D., & Zilber, J. (2000). Elite use of racial labels: Ideology and preference for African American or Black. *Howard Journal of Communications, 11,* 267–277.

Noller, P. (1995). Parent-adolescent relationships. In M. A. Fitzpatrick & A. L. Vangelisti (Eds.), *Explaining family interactions* (pp. 77–111). Thousand Oaks, CA: Sage.

Noller, P. (2005). Sibling relationships in adolescence: Learning and growing together. *Personal Relationships, 12,* 1–22.

Noller, P., & Fitzpatrick, M. A. (1993). *Communication in family relationships.* Englewood Cliffs, NJ: Prentice-Hall.

Notarius, C. I., & Herrick, L. R. (1988). Listener response strategies to a distressed other. *Journal of Social and Personal Relationships, 5,* 97–108.

Nowicki, S., & Manheim, S. (1991). Interpersonal complementarity and time of interaction in female relationships. *Journal of Research in Personality, 25,* 322–333.

O'Barr, W. M. (1982). *Linguistic evidence: Language, power, and strategy in the courtroom.* New York: Academic Press.

O'Brien, J. (2005). What is real? In J. O'Brien (Ed.), *The production of reality: Essays and readings on social interaction* (4th ed.). Thousand Oaks, CA: Pine Forge Press.

O'Hair, D., & Cody, M. J. (1993). Interpersonal deception: The dark side of interpersonal communication? In B. H. Spitzberg & W. R. Cupach (Eds.), *The dark side of interpersonal communication* (pp. 181–214). Hillsdale, NJ: Erlbaum.

O'Keefe, D. J. (2002). *Persuasion: Theory and research* (2nd ed.). Newbury Park, CA: Sage.

O'Sullivan, P. B. (2000). What you don't know won't hurt me: Impression management functions of communication channels in relationships. *Human Communication Research, 26,* 403–431.

O'Sullivan, P. B., & Flanagin, A. J. (2003). Reconceptualizing "flaming" and other problematic messages. *New Media and Society, 5,* 69–94.

Oatley, K., & Duncan, E. (1992). Incidents of emotion in daily life. In K. T. Strongman (Ed.), *International review of studies on emotion* (Vol. 2, pp. 249–293). Chichester, England: Wiley.

Odden, C. M., & Sias, P. M. (1997). Peer communication relationships and psychological climate. *Communication Quarterly, 45,* 153–166.

Oduro-Frimpong, J. (2007). Semiotic silence: Its use as a conflict-management strategy in intimate relationships. *Semiotica, 167,* 283–308.

Oetzel, J. G. (1998). The effects of self-construals and ethnicity on self-reported conflict styles. *Communication Reports, 11,* 133–144.

Oetzel, J. G., & Ting-Toomey, S. (2003). Face concerns in interpersonal conflict: A cross-cultural empirical test of the face negotiation theory. *Communication Research, 30,* 599–625.

Oetzel, J., Ting-Toomey, S., Masumoto, T., Yokochi, Y., Pan, X., Takai, J., & Wilcox, R. (2001). Face and facework in conflict: A cross-cultural comparison of China, Germany, Japan, and the United States. *Communication Monographs, 68,* 235–258.

Officer, S. A., & Rosenfeld, L. B. (1985). Self-disclosure to male and female coaches by high school female athletes. *Journal of Sport Psychology, 7,* 360–370.

Ogden, C. K., & Richards, I. A. (1923). *The meaning of meaning.* New York: Harcourt Brace.

Okabe, K. (1987). Indirect speech acts of the Japanese. In D. L. Kincaid (Ed.), *Communication theory: Eastern and Western perspectives* (pp. 127–136). San Diego: Academic Press.

Olaniran, B. (2004). Computer-mediated communication in cross-cultural virtual teams. *International and Intercultural Communication Annual, 27,* 142–166.

Olson, D. H. (1986). Circumplex Model VII: Validation studies and Faces III. *Family Processes, 25,* 337–351.

Olson, D. H. (2000). Circumplex model of marital and family systems. *Journal of Family Therapy, 22*(2), 144–167.

Olson, D. H., & Lavee, Y. (1989). Family systems and family stress: A family life cycle perspective. In K. Kreppner & R. M. Lerner (Eds.), *Family systems and life-span development* (pp. 165–195). Hillsdale, NJ: Erlbaum.

Olson, L. N. (2002). "As ugly and painful as it was, it was effective." Individuals' unique assessment of communication competence during aggressive conflict episodes. *Communication Studies, 53,* 171–188.

Olson, L. N. (2003). "From lace teddies to flannel PJ's": An analysis of males' experience and expressions of love. *Qualitative Research Reports in Communication, 4,* 38–44.

Olson, L. N., & Braithwaite, D. O. (2004). "If you hit me again, I'll hit you back": Conflict management strategies of individuals experiencing aggression during conflicts. *Communication Studies, 55,* 271–285.

Onyekwere, E. O., Rubin, R. B., & Infante, D. A. (1991). Interpersonal perception and communication satisfaction as a function of argumentativeness and ego-involvement. *Communication Quarterly, 39,* 35–47.

Orbe, M. P. (1998). From the standpoint(s) of traditionally muted groups: Explicating a co-cultural communication theoretical model. *Communication Theory, 8,* 1–26.

Orbe, M. P., & Groscurth, C. R. (2004). A co-cultural theoretical analysis of communicating on campus and at home: Exploring the negotiation strategies of first generation college (FGC) students. *Qualitative Research Reports in Communication, 5,* 41–47.

Orbe, M. P., & Spellers, R. E. (2005). From the margins to the center: Utilizing co-cultural theory in diverse contexts. In W. B. Gudykunst (Ed.), *Theorizing about intercultural communication* (pp. 173–192). Thousand Oaks, CA: Sage.

Orcutt, H. K. (2006). The prospective relationship of interpersonal forgiveness and psychological distress symptoms among college women. *Journal of Counseling Psychology, 53,* 350–361.

Orman, S. (2005). *The money book for the young, fabulous, and broke.* New York: Riverhead.

Ortony, A., & Turner, T. J. (1990). What's basic about basic emotions? *Psychological Review, 97,* 315–331.

Osterman, K. (2001). Students' need for belonging in the school community. *Review of Educational Research, 70,* 323–367.

Overall, N. C., & Sibley, C. G. (2008). Attachment and attraction toward romantic partners versus relevant alternatives within daily interactions. *Personality and Individual Differences, 44,* 1126–1137.

Owen, W. F. (1987). The verbal expression of love by women and men as a critical communication event in personal relationships. *Women's Studies in Communication, 10,* 15–24.

Padden, C., & Humphries, T. (1988). *Deaf in America: Voices from a culture.* Cambridge, MA: Harvard University Press.

Pahl, S., & Eiser, J. R. (2007). How malleable is comparative self-positivity? The effects of manipulating judgmental focus and accessibility. *European Journal of Social Psychology, 37,* 617–627.

Pal, G. C. (2007). Is there a universal self-serving attribution bias? *Psychological Studies, 52,* 85–89.

Palmer, M. T., & Simmons, K. B. (1995). Communicating intentions through nonverbal behaviors: Conscious and nonconscious encoding of liking. *Human Communication Research, 22,* 128–160.

Palomares, N. A. (2008). Explaining gender-based language use: Effects of gender identity salience on references to emotion and tentative language in intra- and intergroup contexts. *Human Communication Research, 34,* 263–286.

Palombo, J. (2006). *Nonverbal learning disabilities: A clinical perspective.* New York: W.W. Norton.

Pam, A., & Pearson, J. (1998). *Splitting up: Enmeshment and estrangement in the process of divorce.* New York: Guilford Press.

Panksepp, J. (2007). Criteria for basic emotions: Is DISGUST a primary "emotion"? *Cognition & Emotion, 21,* 1819–1828.

Papa, M. J., & Natalle, E. J. (1989). Gender, strategy selection, and discussion satisfaction in interpersonal conflict. *Western Journal of Speech Communication, 52,* 260–272.

Papadakis, M. (2003). Data on family and the Internet: What do we know and how do we know it. In J. Turow & A. L. Kavanaugh (Eds.), *The wired homestead* (pp. 121–140). Cambridge, MA: MIT Press.

Parisse, C. (2005). New perspectives on language development and the innateness of grammatical knowledge. *Language Sciences, 27,* 383–401.

Park, H. S., Levine, T. R., McCornack, S. A., Morrison, K., & Ferrara, M. (2002). How people really detect lies. *Communication Monographs, 69,* 144–157.

Parker, Y. (2003). *Damn good resume guide: A crash course in resume writing* (4th ed.). Berkeley, CA: Ten Speed Press.

Parks, J. B., & Robertson, M. A. (2000). Development and validation of an instrument to measure attitudes toward sexist/nonsexist language. *Sex Roles, 42,* 415–438.

Parks, M. R. (1982). Ideology in interpersonal communication: Off the couch and into the world. In M. Burgoon (Ed.), *Communication yearbook 5* (pp. 79–107). New Brunswick, NJ: Transaction.

Parton, S., Siltanen, S. A., Hosman, L. A., & Langenderfer, J. (2002). Employment interviews outcomes and speech style effects. *Journal of Language and Social Psychology, 21,* 144–161.

Pasupathi, M., Stallworth, L. M., & Murdoch, K. (1998). How what we tell becomes what we know: Listener effects on speakers' long-term memory for events. *Discourse Processes, 26,* 1–25.

Patterson, M. L., & Ritts, V. (1997). Social and communicative anxiety: A review and meta-analysis. In B. R. Burleson (Ed.), *Communication yearbook 20* (pp. 263–303). Thousand Oaks, CA: Sage.

Pawlowski, D. R. (1998). Dialectical tensions in marital partners' accounts of their relationships. *Communication Quarterly, 46,* 396–416.

Pearce, W. B. (2005). The Coordinated Management of Meaning (CMM). In W. B. Gudykunst (Ed.), *Theorizing about intercultural communication* (pp. 35–54). London: Sage.

Pearce, W. B., & Cronen, V. (1980). Communication, action, and meaning. New York: Praeger.

Pearce, W. B., & Sharp, S. M. (1973). Self-disclosing communication. *Journal of Communication, 23,* 409–425.

Pearson, J. C. (2000). Positive distortion: "The most beautiful woman in the world." In K. M. Galvin & P. J. Cooper (Eds.), *Making connections: Readings in relational communication* (2nd ed., pp. 184–190). Los Angeles: Roxbury.

Pennebaker, J. W. (1997). *Opening up: The healing power of expressing emotions* (Rev. ed.). New York: Guilford Press.

Pennebaker, J. (2004). *Writing to heal: A guided journal for recovering from trauma and emotional upheaval.* Oakland, CA: New Harbinger.

Pennebaker, J. W., Rime, B., & Blankenship, V. E. (1996). Stereotypes of emotional expressiveness of northerners and southerners: A cross-cultural test of Montesquieu's hypotheses. *Journal of Personality and Social Psychology, 70,* 372–380.

Pentok-Voak, I. S., Cahill, S., Pound, N., Kempe, V., Schaeffler, S., & Schaeffler, F. (2007). Male facial attractiveness, perceived personality, and child-directed speech. *Evolution and Human Behavior, 28*(4), 253–259.

Peper, M. (2000). Awareness of emotions: A neuropsychological perspective. In R. D. Ellis & N. Newton (Eds.), *The caldron of consciousness: Motivation, affect and self-organization—An anthology* (pp. 243–269). Philadelphia: John Benjamins.

Pescosolido, A. T. (2001). Informal leaders and the development of group efficacy. *Small Group Research, 32,* 74–93.

Peterson, C. (2006). *A primer in positive psychology.* New York: Oxford University Press.

Peterson, M. S. (1997). Personnel interviewers' perceptions of the importance and adequacy of applicants' communication skills. *Communication Education, 46,* 287–291.

Petronio. S. (2000). The boundaries of privacy: Praxis of everyday life. In S. Petronio (Ed.), *Balancing the secrets of private disclosures* (pp. 37–49). Mahwah, NJ: Erlbaum.

Piaget, J. (1952). *The origins of intelligence in children.* New York: International Universities Press.

Planalp, S. (1998). Communicating emotion in everyday life: Cues, channels, and processes. In P. A. Anderson & L. A. Guerrero (Eds.), *Handbook of communication and emotion: Research, theory, applications, and contexts* (pp. 29–48). San Diego, CA: Academic Press.

Planalp, S. (1999). *Communicating emotion: Social, moral, and cultural processes.* New York: Cambridge University Press.

Planalp, S., Fitness, J., & Fehr, B. (2006). Emotion in theories of close relationships. In A. L. Vangelisti & D. Perlman (Eds.), *The Cambridge handbook of personal relationships* (pp. 369–384). New York: Cambridge University Press.

Plax, T. G., & Rosenfeld, L. B. (1979). Receiver differences and the comprehension of spoken messages. *Journal of Experimental Education, 48,* 23–28.

Plutchik, R. (1984). Emotions: A general psychoevolutionary theory. In K. R. Scherer & P. Ekman (Eds.), *Approaches to emotion* (pp. 197–219). Hillsdale, NJ: Erlbaum.

Pollack, W. (1999). *Real boys: Rescuing our sons from the myths of boyhood.* New York: Owl Books.

Postman, N., & Weingartner, C. (1969). *Teaching as a subversive activity.* New York: Delacorte.

Powell, J. (1969). *Why am I afraid to tell you who I am?* Niles, IL: Argus Communications.

Powers, W. G., & Bodie, G. D. (2003). Listening fidelity: Seeking congruence between cognitions of the listener and the sender. *International Journal of Listening, 17,* 19–31.

Prager, K. J., & Buhrmester, D. (1998). Intimacy and need fulfillment in couple relationships. *Journal of Social and Personal Relationships, 15,* 435–469.

Pratt, L., Wiseman, R. L., Cody, M. J., & Wendt, P. F. (1999). Interrogative strategies and information exchange in computer-mediated communication. *Communication Quarterly, 47,* 46–66.

Precht, K. (2008). Sex similarities and differences in stance in informal American conversation. *Journal of Sociolinguistics, 12,* 89–111.

Prentice, W. E. (2005). *Therapeutic modalities in rehabilitation.* New York: McGraw-Hill.

Priest, P. J., & Dominick, J. R. (1994). Pulp pulpits: Self-disclosure on "Donahue." *Journal of Communication, 44,* 74–97.

Proctor, R. F. (1989). Responsibility or egocentrism? The paradox of owned messages. *Speech Association of Minnesota Journal, 26,* 57–69.

Proctor, R. F., & Wilcox, J. R. (1993). An exploratory analysis of responses to owned messages in interpersonal communication. *ETC: A Review of General Semantics, 50,* 201–220.

Public Forum Institute (Washington, DC). (2002, January). *Help wanted: Workforce development and the new economy.* Retrieved from http://www.publicforuminstitute.org/publications/reports/workforce02.pdf

Putnam, R. D. (2000). *Bowling alone.* New York: Touchstone.

Quinto-Pozos, D. (2008). Sign language contact and interference: ASL and LSM. *Language in Society, 37,* 161–189.

Rabinowitz, F. E., & Cochran, S. V. (1994). *Man alive: A primer of men's issues.* Pacific Grove, CA: Brooks/Cole.

Radmacher, K., & Azmitia, M. (2006). Are there gendered pathways to intimacy in early adolescents' and emerging adults' friendships? *Journal of Adolescent Research, 21,* 415–448.

Ragins, B. R., & Singh, R. (2007). Making the invisible visible: Fear and disclosure of sexual orientation at work. *Journal of Applied Psychology, 92,* 1103–1118.

Ragsdale, J. D. (1996). Gender, satisfaction level, and the use of relational maintenance strategies in marriage. *Communication Monographs, 63,* 354–369.

Raider, E., Coleman, S., & Gerson, J. (2006). Teaching conflict resolution skills in a workshop. In M. Deutsch, P. T. Coleman, & E. C. Marcus (Eds.), *The handbook of conflict resolution: Theory and practice* (2nd ed., pp. 695–725). Hoboken, NJ: Wiley.

Rakow, L. F. (1992). Don't hate me because I'm beautiful. *Southern Communication Journal, 57,* 132–142.

Ramirez, A., Jr., & Burgoon, J. K. (2004). The effect of interactivity on initial interactions: The influence of information valence and modality and information richness on computer-mediated interaction. *Communication Monographs, 71,* 422–447.

Ramirez, A., & Zhang, S. (2007). When online meets offline: The effect of modality switching on relational communication. *Communication Monographs, 74,* 287–310.

Ramírez, J. M., Bonniot-Cabanac, M.-C., & Cabanac, M. (2005). Can aggression provide pleasure? *European Psychologist, 10*(2), 136–145.

Ramirez-Ponce, A. I. (2005). The influence of social support on the well-being of Latinas living in poverty. *Dissertation Abstracts International, 65,* 3572.

Ramsey, R. P., & Sohi, R. S. (1997). Listening to your customers: The impact of perceived salesperson listening behavior on relationship outcomes. *Journal of the Academy of Marketing Science, 25,* 127–137.

Rancer, A. S., & Avtgis, T. A. (2006). *Argumentative and aggressive* communication*: Theory, research, and application.* Thousand Oaks, CA: Sage.

Rancer, A. S., Kosberg, R. L., & Baukus, R. A. (1992). Beliefs about arguing as predictors of trait argumentativeness: Implications for training in argument and conflict management. *Communication Education, 41,* 375–387.

Randall, N. H., & Delbridge, S. (2006). Perceptions of social distance in an ethically fluid community. *Sociological Spectrum, 25*(1), 103–122.

Raskin, R., & Shaw, R. (1988). Narcissism and the use of personal pronouns. *Journal of Personality, 56,* 393–404.

Rawlins, W. K. (1992). *Friendship matters: Communication, dialectics, and the life course.* New York: Aldine De Gruyter.

Reamer, F. G. (2002). Boundary issues in social work: Managing dual relationships. *Social Work, 48,* 121–133.

Redmond, M. V. (1989). The functions of empathy (decentering) in human relations. *Human Relations, 42,* 593–605.

Redmond, M. V. (1995). Interpersonal communication: Definitions and conceptual approaches. In M. V. Redmond (Ed.), *Interpersonal communication: Readings in theory and research* (pp. 4–27). Fort Worth, TX: Harcourt Brace.

Rehman, U. S., & Holtzworth-Munroe, A. (2007). A cross-cultural examination of the relation of marital communication behavior to marital satisfaction. *Journal of Family Psychology, 21,* 759–763.

Reid, S. A., & Ng, S. H. (1999). Language, power, and intergroup relations. *Journal of Social Issues, 55,* 119–139.

Reid, T. R. (1999). *Confucius lives next door: What living in the East teaches us about living in the West.* New York: Random House.

Reissman, C. K. (1990). *Divorce talk: Women and men make sense of personal relationships.* New Brunswick, NJ: Rutgers University Press.

Resnick, B., Orwig, D., Magaziner, J., & Wynne, C. (2002). The effect of social support on exercise behavior in older adults. *Clinical Nursing Research, 11,* 52–70.

Reyes, A. (2005). Appropriation of African American slang by Asian American youth. *Journal of Sociolinguistics, 9,* 509–532.

Reynolds, D. (2007). Restraining Golem and harnessing Pygmalion in the classroom: A laboratory study of managerial expectations and task design. *Academy of Management Learning & Education, 6,* 475–483.

Rheingold, H. (1988). *They have a word for it.* New York: Tarcher/Putnam.

Riach, K., & Wilson, F. (2007). Don't screw the crew: Exploring the rules of engagement in organizational romance. *British Journal of Management, 18,* 79–92.

Richard, F. D., Bond, C. R., & Stokes-Zoota, J. J. (2003). One hundred years of social psychology quantitatively described. *Review of General Psychology, 7,* 331–363.

Richards, I. A. (1948). Emotive meaning again. *Philosophical Review New York, 57,* 145–157.

Richman, J. (2002, September 16). The news journal of the life scientist. *The Scientist, 16,* 42.

Richman, J. M., & Rosenfeld, L. B. (1987). Stress reduction for hospice workers: A support group model. *Hospice Journal, 3,* 205–221.

Richmond, V., Gorham, J. S., & Furio, B. J. (1987). Affinity-seeking communication in collegiate female-male relationships. *Communication Quarterly, 35,* 334–348.

Richmond, V. P., & McCroskey, J. C. (2000). The impact of supervisor and subordinate immediacy on relational and organizational outcomes. *Communication Monographs, 67,* 85–95.

Richmond, V. P., McCroskey, J. C., & Johnson, A. D. (2003). Development of the Nonverbal Immediacy Scale (NIS): Measures of self- and other-perceived nonverbal immediacy. *Communication Quarterly, 51,* 504–517.

Ricks, G. (1983). *Big business blunders.* New York: Dow Jones-Irwin.

Ridley, C. A., Wilhelm, M. S., & Surra, C. A. (2001). Married couples' conflict responses and marital quality. *Journal of Social and Personal Relationships, 18,* 517–534.

Riggio, R. E., & Friedman, H. S. (1983). Individual differences and cues to deception. *Journal of Personality and Social Psychology, 45,* 899–915.

Rittenour, C. E., Myers, S. A., & Brann, M. (2007). Commitment and emotional closeness in the sibling relationship. *Southern Communication Journal, 72,* 169–183.

Ritts, V., Patterson, M. L., & Tubbs, M. E. (1992). Expectations, impressions, and judgments of physically attractive students: A review. *Review of Educational Research, 62,* 413–426.

Roach, K. D. (1997). Effects of graduate teaching assistant attire on student learning, misbehaviors, and ratings of instruction. *Communication Quarterly, 45,* 125–141.

Robbins, J. E., & Rosenfeld, L. B. (2001). Athletes' perceptions of social support provided by their head coach, assistant coach, and athletic trainer, pre-injury and during rehabilitation. *Journal of Sport Behavior, 24,* 277–297.

Robins, R. W., Mendelsohn, G. A., Connell, J. B., & Kwan, V. S. Y. (2004). Do people agree about the causes of behavior? A social relations analysis of behavior ratings and causal attributions. *Journal of Personality and Social Psychology, 86,* 334–344.

Robinshaw, H. (2007). Acquisition of hearing, listening and speech skills by and during key stage 1. *Early Child Development and Care, 177,* 661–678.

Robinson, W. P., Shepherd, A., & Heywood, J. (1998). Truth, equivocation/concealment, and lies in job applications and doctor-patient communication. *Journal of Language and Social Psychology, 17,* 149–164.

Rochman, G. M., & Diamond, G. M. (2008). From unresolved anger to sadness: Identifying physiological correlates. *Journal of Counseling Psychology, 55,* 96–105.

Rockwell, P., Buller, D. B., & Burgoon, J. K. (1997). The voice of deceit: Refining and expanding vocal cues to deception. *Communication Research Reports, 14,* 451–459.

Roe, D. (2001). Differences in self-disclosure in psychotherapy between American and Israeli patients. *Psychological Reports, 88,* 611–624.

Rogers, L. E. (2001). Relational communication in the context of family. *Journal of Family Communication 1,* 25–35.

Roloff, M. E., Janiszewski, C. A., McGrath, M. A., Burns, C. S., & Manrai, L. A. (1988). Acquiring resources from intimates: When obligation substitutes for persuasion. *Human Communication Research, 14,* 364–396.

Romaine, S. (1999). *Communicating gender.* Mahwah, NJ: Erlbaum.

Rose, A.J., Carlson, W., & Waller, E. M. (2007). Prospective associations of co-rumination with friendship and emotional adjustment: Considering the socioemotional trade-offs of co-rumination. *Developmental Psychology 43,* 1019–1031.

Rosenblith, J. F. (1992). *In the beginning: Development from conception to age two.* Newbury Park, CA: Sage.

Rosenfeld, H. M. (1987). Conversational control functions of nonverbal behavior. In A. W. Siegman & S. Feldstein (Eds.), *Nonverbal behavior and communication* (2nd ed., pp. 563–601). Hillsdale, NJ: Erlbaum.

Rosenfeld, L. B. (1979). Self-disclosure avoidance: Why I am afraid to tell you who I am. *Communication Monographs, 46,* 63–74.

Rosenfeld, L. B. (2000). Overview of the ways privacy, secrecy, and disclosure are balanced in today's society. In S. Petronio (Ed.), *Balancing the secrets of private disclosures* (pp. 3–17). Mahwah, NJ: Erlbaum.

Rosenfeld, L. B., & Bowen, G. L. (1991). Marital disclosure and marital satisfaction: Direct-effect versus interaction-effect models. *Western Journal of Speech Communication, 55,* 69–84.

Rosenfeld, L. B., & Gilbert, J. R. (1989). The measurement of cohesion and its relationship to dimensions of self-disclosure in classroom settings. *Small Group Behavior, 20,* 291–301.

Rosenfeld, L. B., & Kendrick, W. L. (1984). Choosing to be open: Subjective reasons for self-disclosing. *Western Journal of Speech Communication, 48,* 326–343.

Rosenfeld, L. B., & Richman, J. M. (1999). Supportive communication and school outcomes: Part II. Academically at-risk low income high school students. *Communication Education, 48,* 294–307.

Rosenfeld, L. B., Richman, J. M., & Bowen, G. L. (1998). Supportive communication and school outcomes for academically "at-risk" and other low income middle school students. *Communication Education, 47,* 309–325.

Rosenthal, R., & Jacobson, L. (1968). *Pygmalion in the classroom.* New York: Holt, Rinehart & Winston.

Ross, J. B., & McLaughlin, M. M. (Eds.). (1949). *A portable medieval reader.* New York: Viking.

Rowatt, W. C., Cunningham, M. R., & Druen, P. B. (1999). Lying to get a date: The effect of facial physical attractiveness on the willingness to deceive prospective dating partners. *Journal of Social and Personal Relationships, 16,* 209–223.

Ruben, B. D. (1989). The study of cross-cultural competence: Traditions and contemporary issues. *International Journal of Intercultural Relationships, 13,* 229–240.

Rubin, D. L. (1986). "Nobody play by the rules he know": Ethnic interference in classroom questioning events. In Y. Y. Kim (Ed.), *Interethnic communication: Current research* (pp. 158–175). Newbury Park, CA: Sage.

Rubin, L. (1985). *Just friends: The role of friendship in our lives.* New York: Harper & Row.

Rubin, R. B., & Graham, E. E. (1988). Communication correlates of college success: An exploratory investigation. *Communication Education, 37,* 14–27.

Rubin, R. B., Graham, E. E., & Mignerey, J. T. (1990). A longitudinal study of college students' communication competence. *Communication Education, 39,* 1–14.

Rubin, R. B., Perse, E. M., & Barbato, C. A. (1988). Conceptualization and measurement of interpersonal communication motives. *Human Communication Research, 14,* 602–628.

Rubin, Z., Hill, C. T., Peplau, L. A., & Dunkel-Schetter, C. (1980). Self-disclosure in dating couples: Sex roles and the ethic of openness. *Journal of Marriage and the Family, 42,* 305–317.

Rusbult, C. E., Kumashiro, M., Stocker, S. L., Kirchner, J. L., Finkel, E. J., & Coolsen, M. K. (2005). Self processes in interdependent relationships: Partner affirmation and the Michelangelo phenomenon. *Interaction Studies, 6,* 375–391.

Rusbult, C. E., & Van Lange, P. A. M. (1996). Interdependence processes. In E. T. Higgins & A. W. Kruglanski (Eds.), *Social psychology: Handbook of basic principles* (pp. 564–596). New York: Guilford Press.

Rymer, R. (1993). *Genie: An abused child's flight from silence.* New York: HarperCollins.

Sabourin, T. C., & Stamp, G. H. (1995). Communication and the experience of dialectical tensions in family life: An examination of abusive and nonabusive families. *Communication Monographs, 62,* 213–242.

Sacks, O. (1989). *Seeing voices: A journey into the world of the deaf.* Berkeley: University of California Press.

Sadalla, E. (1987). Identity and symbolism in housing. *Environment and Behavior, 19,* 569–587.

Safro, J. (2001). What to do before you interview? *Scholastic Choices, 17*(3), 25–27.

Sagarian, E. (1976, March). The high cost of wearing a label. *Psychology Today, 10,* 25–27.

Sahlstein, E. (2004). Relational maintenance research: A review of reviews. *PsycCRITIQUES, 49*(Suppl.14), np. Available at http://www.apa.org

Salimi, S.-H., Mirzamani, S.-H., & Shahiri-Tabarestani, M. (2005). Association of parental self-esteem and expectations with adolescents' anxiety about career and education. *Psychological Reports, 96,* 569–578.

Samovar, L. A., & Porter, R. E. (2004). *Communication between cultures* (5th ed.). Belmont, CA: Wadsworth.

Samovar, L. A., Porter R. E., & McDaniel, E. R. (2007). *Communication between cultures* (6th ed.*).* Belmont, CA: Wadsworth.

Samp, J. A., Wittenberg, E., & Gillett, D. L. (2003). Presenting and monitoring a gender-defined self on the Internet. *Communication Research Reports, 20,* 1–12.

Samter, W., Burleson, B. R., Kunkel, A. W., & Werking, K. J. (1994, May). *Gender and beliefs about communication in intimate relationships: Moderating effects of type of communication and type of relationship (or, when gender differences make a difference—and when they don't).* Paper presented at the annual meeting of the International Communication Association, Sydney, Australia.

Samter, W., & Cupach, W. R. (1998). Friendly fire: Topical variations in conflict among same- and cross-sex friends. *Communication Studies, 49,* 121–138.

Sanchez, P. (1999, August–September). How to craft successful employee communication in the information age. *Communication World, 16*(7), 9–15.

Sandel, T. L. (2004). Narrated relationships: Mothers-in-law and daughters-in-law justifying conflicts in Taiwan's Chhan-chng. *Research on Language and Social Interaction, 37,* 265–299.

Sanderson, C. A., & Karetsky, K. H. (2002). Intimacy goals and strategies of conflict resolution in dating relationships: A mediational analysis. *Journal of Social and Personal Relationships, 19,* 317–337.

Saohir, M. N., & Chaffee, S. H. (2002). Adolescents' contributions to family communication patterns. *Human Communication Research, 28,* 86–108.

Sarason, I. G., Sarason, B. R., & Pierce, G. R. (1990). Social support: The search for theory. *Journal of Social and Clinical Psychology, 9,* 133–147.

Sargent, J. (2002). Topic avoidance: Is this the way to a more satisfying relationship? *Communication Research Reports, 19,* 175–182.

Savin-Williams, R. C. (2001). *Mom, dad. I'm gay. How families negotiate coming out.* Washington, DC: American Psychological Association.

Scarpero, D. B. (2000). The relationship of organizational communication climates and interpersonal conflict management. *Dissertation Abstracts International, 60,* 4946.

Schachter, S. (1959). *The psychology of affiliation.* Stanford, CA: Stanford University Press.

Schaefer, M. T., & Olson, D. H. (1981). Assessing intimacy: The PAIR Inventory. *Journal of Marital and Family Therapy, 7,* 47–60.

Scharlott, B. W., & Christ, W. G. (1995). Overcoming relationship-initiation barriers: The impact of a computer-dating system on sex role, shyness, and appearance inhibitions. *Computers in Human Behavior, 11,* 191–204.

Schiefenhövel, W. (1997). Universals in interpersonal interactions. In U. C. Segerstråle & P. Molnár (Eds.), *Nonverbal communication: Where nature meets culture* (pp. 61–85). Hillsdale, NJ: Erlbaum.

Schmidt, J. J. (2006). *Social and cultural foundations of counseling and human services: Multiple influences on self-concept development.* Boston: Pearson/Allyn and Bacon.

Scholz, M. (2005, June). A "simple" way to improve adherence. *RN, 68,* 82.

Schrodt, P. (2005). Family communication schemata and the Circumplex Model of family functioning. *Western Journal of Communication, 69,* 359–376.

Schrodt, P., Turman, P. D., & Soliz, J. (2006). Perceived understanding as a mediator of perceived teacher confirmation and students' ratings of instruction. *Communication Education, 55,* 370–388.

Schumacher, J. A., Feldbau-Kohn, S., Slep, A. M. S., & Heyman, R. E. (2001). Risk factors for male-to-female partner physical abuse. *Aggression and Violent Behavior, 6,* 281–352.

Schütz, A. (1999). It was your fault! Self-serving biases in autobiographical accounts of conflicts in married couples. *Journal of Social and Personal Relationships, 16,* 193–208.

Scott, C., & Myers, K. K. (2005). The socialization of emotion: Learning emotion management at the fire station. *Journal of Applied Communication Research, 33,* 67–92.

Scudder, J. N., & Andrews, P. H. (1995). A comparison of two alternative models of powerful speech: The impact of power and gender upon the use of threats. *Communication Research Reports, 12,* 25–33.

Seabrook, J. (1994, June 6). My first flame. *New Yorker,* 70–79.

Sedikides, C., Campbell, W. K., Reeder, G. D., & Elliot, A. J. (1998). The self-serving bias in relational context. *Journal of Personality and Social Psychology, 74,* 378–386.

Sedikides, C., & Skowronski, J. J. (1995). On the sources of self-knowledge: The perceived primacy of self-reflection. *Journal of Social and Clinical Psychology, 14,* 244–270.

Segrin, C. (1993). The effects of nonverbal behavior on outcomes of compliance gaining attempts. *Communication Studies, 44,* 169–187.

Segrin, C., & Fitzpatrick, M. A. (1992). Depression and verbal aggressiveness in different marital couple types. *Communication Studies, 43,* 79–91.

Servaes, J. (1989). Cultural identity and modes of communication. In J. A. Anderson (Ed.), *Communication yearbook 12* (pp. 383–416). Newbury Park, CA: Sage.

Shafer, D. N. (2007). Hearing loss hinders relationships. *ASHA Leader, 12*(9), 5–7.

Shamay, S. G., Tomer, R., & Aharon-Peretz, J. (2002). Deficit in understanding sarcasm in patients with prefrontal lesion is related to impaired empathic ability. *Brain and Cognition, 48,* 558–563.

Sharkey, W. F., Hee, S. P., & Kim, R. K. (2004). Intentional self-embarrassment. *Communication Studies, 55,* 379–399.

Sharlet, J. (2005, May). Soldiers of Christ: Inside America's most powerful megachurch. *Harper's, 310,* 33–54.

Shattuck, R. (1980). *The forbidden experiment: The story of the Wild Boy of Aveyron.* New York: Farrar, Straus & Giroux.

Shaver, P. R., Wu, S., & Schwartz, J. C. (1992). Cross-cultural similarities and differences in emotion and its representation: A prototype approach. In M. S. Clark (Ed.), *Emotion* (pp. 175–212). Newbury Park, CA: Sage.

Shaw, C. L. M. (1997). Personal narrative: Revealing self and reflecting other. *Human Communication Research, 24,* 302–319.

Sheeks, M. S., & Birchmeier, Z. P. (2007). Shyness, sociability, and the use of computer-mediated communication in relationship development. *CyberPsychology & Behavior, 10,* 64–70.

Sherman, M. A., & Haas, A. (1984, June). Man to man, woman to woman. *Psychology Today, 17,* 72–73.

Sherman, S. M., & Dumlao, R. (2008) A cross-cultural comparison of family communication patterns and conflict between young adults and parents. *Journal of Family Communication, 8,* 186–211.

Shimanoff, S. B. (1984). Commonly named emotions in everyday conversations. *Perceptual and Motor Skills, 58,* 514.

Shimanoff, S. B. (1985). Rules governing the verbal expression of emotions between married couples. *Western Journal of Speech Communication, 49,* 149–165.

Shimanoff, S. B. (1988). Degree of emotional expressiveness as a function of face-needs, gender, and interpersonal relationship. *Communication Reports, 1,* 43–53.

Shinagawa, L. H. (1997). *Atlas of American diversity.* Newbury Park, CA: Sage/Altamira.

Shirley, J. A., Powers, W. G., & Sawyer, C. R. (2007). Psychologically abusive relationships and self-disclosure orientations. *Human Communication, 10,* 289–301.

Shook, N. J., Gerrity, D. A., Jurich, J., & Segrist, A. E. (2000). Courtship violence among college students: A comparison of verbally and physically abusive couples. *Journal of Family Violence, 15*(1), 1–22.

Shuler, S. (1998). Emotion 911: Communication and emotion at a county Emergency Communication Center. *Dissertation Abstracts International, 59,* 0664.

Sias, P. M., & Cahill, D. J. (1998). From coworkers to friends: The development of peer friendships in the workplace. *Western Journal of Communication, 62,* 273–299.

Sieberg, E., & Larson, C. (1971). *Dimensions of interpersonal response.* Paper presented at the meeting of the International Communication Association, Phoenix, AZ.

Siegel, S. M., Friedlander, M. L., & Heatherington, L. (1992). Nonverbal relational control in family communication. *Journal of Nonverbal Behavior, 16,* 117–139.

Siegman, A. W., & Snow, S. C. (1997). The outward expression of anger, the inward experience of anger and CVR: The role of vocal expression. *Journal of Behavioral Medicine, 1,* 29–45.

Sillars, A. L., Folwell, A. L., Hill, K. L., Maki, B. K., Hurst, A. P., & Casano, R. A. (1992, November). *Levels of understanding in marital relationships.* Paper presented at the meeting of the Speech Communication Association, Chicago.

Sillars, A., Roberts, L. J., Leonard, K. E., & Dun, T. (2000). Cognition during marital conflict: The relationship of thought and talk. *Journal of Social and Personal Relationships, 17,* 479–502.

Sillars, A. L., Folwell, A. L., Hill, K. L., Maki, B. K., Hurst, A. P., & Casano, R. A. (1992, November). *Levels of understanding in marital relationships.* Paper presented at the meeting of the Speech Communication Association, Chicago.

Sillars, A. L., Pike, G. R., Jones, T. S., & Murphy, M. A. (1984). Communication and understanding in marriage. *Human Communication Research, 10,* 317–350.

Sillars, A. L., Shebellen, W., McIntosh, A., & Pomegranate, M. (1997). Relational characteristics of language: Elaboration and differences in marital conversations. *Western Journal of Communication, 61,* 403–422.

Sillars, A. L., Weisberg, J., Burggraf, C. S., & Wilson, E. A. (1987). Content themes in marital conversations. *Human Communication Research, 13,* 495–528.

Simon, V. A., Kobielski, S, J., & Martin, S. (2008). Conflict beliefs, goals, and behavior in romantic relationships during late adolescence. *Journal of Youth and Adolescence, 37,* 324–335.

Singer, J. K., Miller, L. C., & Murphy, S. (1998). *Sexual harassment and memory: How repetition of behavior and personal experience relate to judgments of sexual harassment.* Paper presented at the annual conference of the International Communication Association, Jerusalem.

Singer, M. (1998). *Perception and identity in intercultural communication.* Yarmouth, ME: Intercultural Press.

Singleton, R. A., Jr., & Vacca, J. (2007). Interpersonal competition in friendships. *Sex Roles, 57,* 617–627.

Sitkin, S. B., Sutcliffe, K. M., & Barrios-Choplin, J. R. (1992). A dual-capacity model of communication media choice in organizations. *Human Communication Research, 18,* 563–598.

Smeltzer, L. R., & Watson, K. W. (1984). Listening: An empirical comparison of discussion length and level of incentive. *Central States Speech Journal, 35,* 166–170.

Smith, L., Heaven, P. C. L., & Ciarrochi, J. (2008). Trait emotional intelligence, conflict communication patterns, and relationship satisfaction. *Personality and Individual Differences, 44,* 1314–1325.

Smith-McLallen, A., Johnson, B. T., Dovidio, J. F., & Pearson, A. R. (2006). Black and white: The role of color bias and implicit race bias. *Social Cognition, 24,* 46–73.

Snodgrass, S. E. (1985). Women's intuition: The effect of subordinate role on interpersonal sensitivity. *Journal of Personality and Social Psychology, 49,* 146–155.

Snyder, M. (1979). Self-monitoring processes. In L. Berkowitz (Ed.), *Advances in experimental social psychology* (Vol. 12, pp. 86–128). New York: Academic Press.

Snyder, M. (1980, March). The many me's of the self-monitor. *Psychology Today, 14,* 33–40, 92.

Snyder, M., & Klein, O. (2005). Construing and constructing others: On the reality and the generality of the behavioral confirmation scenario. *Interaction Studies, 6*(1), 53–67.

Social Security Administration. (2008). *Popular baby names.* Available at: http://www.ssa.gov/OACT/babynames/.

Solomon, D. H., & Knobloch, L. K. (2001). Relationship uncertainty, partner interference, and intimacy within dating relationships. *Journal of Social and Personal Relationships, 8,* 804–820.

Solomon, D. H., & Williams, M. L. M. (1997). Perceptions of social-sexual communication at work: The effects of message, situation, and observer characteristics on judgments of sexual harassment. *Journal of Applied Communication Research, 25,* 197–216.

Sommer, K. L., Williams, K. D., Ciarocco, N. J., & Baumeister, R. F. (2001). When silence speaks louder than words: Explorations into the intrapsychic and interpersonal consequences of social ostracism. *Basic and Applied Social Psychology, 23*(4), 225–243.

Sommer, R. (1969). *Personal space: The behavioral basis of design.* Englewood Cliffs, NJ: Prentice-Hall.

Sommer, R. (2002). Personal space in a digital age. In R. B. Bechtel & A. Churchman (Eds.), *Handbook of environmental psychology* (pp. 647–660). New York: Wiley.

Sopow, E. (2008). The communication climate change at RCMP. *Strategic Communication Management, 12,* 20–23.

Sousa, L. A. (2002). The medium is the message: The costs and benefits of writing, talking aloud, and thinking about life's triumphs and defeats. *Dissertation Abstracts International, 62,* 3397.

Spears, R. (2001). In M. B. Brewer & C. Sedikides (Eds.), *Individual self, relational self, collective self* (pp. 171–198). New York: Psychology Press.

Speicher, H. (1999). Development and validation of intimacy capability and intimacy motivation measures. *Dissertation Abstracts International, 59,* 5172.

Spitzberg, B. H. (1991). An examination of trait measures of interpersonal competence. *Communication Reports, 4,* 22–29.

Spitzberg, B. H. (1994). The dark side of (in)competence. In W. R. Cupach & B. H. Spitzberg (Eds.), *The dark side of interpersonal communication* (pp. 25–50). Hillsdale, NJ: Erlbaum.

Spitzberg, B. H. (2000). What is good communication? *Journal of the Association for Communication Administration, 29,* 103–119.

Sporer, S. L., & Schwandt, B. (2007). Moderators of nonverbal indicators of deception: A meta-analytic synthesis. *Psychology, Public Policy, and Law, 13*(1), 1–34.

Sprecher, S. (1987). The effects of self-disclosure given and received on affection for an intimate partner and stability of the relationship. *Journal of Social and Personal Relationships, 4,* 115–128.

Stafford L., & Canary, D. J. (1991). Maintenance strategies and romantic relationship type, gender, and relational characteristics. *Journal of Social and Personal Relationships, 8,* 217–242.

Stafford, L., & Dainton, M. (1994). The dark side of "normal" family interaction. In B. H. Spitzberg & W. R. Cupach (Eds.), *The dark side of interpersonal communication* (pp. 259–280). Hillsdale, NJ: Erlbaum.

Stafford, L., Dainton, M., & Haas, S. (2000). Measuring routine and strategic relational maintenance. *Communication Monographs, 67,* 306–323.

Stafford, L., & Kline, S. L. (1996). Married women's name choices and sense of self. *Communication Reports, 9,* 85–92.

Stamp, G. H., Vangelisti, A. L., & Daly, J. A. (1992). The creation of defensiveness in social interaction. *Communication Quarterly, 40,* 177–190.

Stanley, J. P. (1977). Paradigmatic woman: The prostitute. In D. L. Shores & C. P. Hines (Eds.), *Papers in language variation* (pp. 303–321). Tuscaloosa, AL: University of Alabama Press.

Stearns, C. A., & Stearns, P. (1986). *Anger: The struggle for emotional control in America's history.* Chicago: University of Chicago Press.

Stebnicki, M. A. (2007). Empathy fatigue: Healing the mind, body, and spirit of professional counselors. *American Journal of Psychiatric Rehabilitation, 10,* 317–338.

Steen, S., & Schwartz, P. (1995). Communication, gender, and power: Homosexual couples as a case study. In M. A. Fitzpatrick & A. L. Vangelisti (Eds.), *Explaining family interactions* (pp. 310–343). Thousand Oaks, CA: Sage.

Steil, L. K. (1996). Listening training: The key to success in today's organizations. In M. Purdy & D. Borisoff (Eds.), *Listening in everyday life: A personal and professional approach* (2nd ed., pp. 213–237). Lanham, MD: University Press of America.

Stephens, C., & Long, N. (2000). Communication with police supervisors and peers as a buffer of work-related traumatic stress. *Journal of Organizational Behavior, 21,* 407–424.

Stern, D. B. (2002). Language and the nonverbal as a unity: Discussion of "Where is the action in the 'talking cure'?" *Contemporary Psychoanalysis, 38,* 515–525.

Sternberg, R. J. (1985). *Beyond I.Q.* New York: Cambridge University Press.

Stets, J. E., & Cast, A. D. (2007). Resources and identity verification from an identity theory perspective. *Sociological Perspectives, 50,* 517–543.

Steves, R. (1996, May–September). Culture shock. *Europe through the Back Door Newsletter, 50,* 20.

Stewart, C. J., & Cash, W. B. (2006). *Interviewing: Principles and practices* (11th ed.). New York: McGraw-Hill.

Stewart, J. (1983). Interpretive listening: An alternative to empathy. *Communication Education, 32,* 379–391.

Stewart, S., Stinnett, H., & Rosenfeld, L.B. (2000). Sex differences in desired characteristics of short-term and long-term relationship partners. *Journal of Personal and Social Relationships, 17,* 843–853.

Stiff, J. B., Dillard, J. P., Somera, L., Kim, H., & Sleight, C. (1988). Empathy, communication, and prosocial behavior. *Communication Monographs, 55,* 198–213.

Stiles, W. B., Walz, N. C., Schroeder, M. A. B., Williams, L. L., & Ickes, W. (1996). Attractiveness and disclosure in initial encounters of mixed-sex dyads. *Journal of Social and Personal Relationships, 13,* 303–312.

Stocker, C. M., & McHale, S. M. (1992). The nature and family correlates of preadolescents' perceptions of their sibling relationships. *Journal of Social and Personal Relationships, 9,* 179–195.

Strachan, H. (2004). Communication. *Research and Theory for Nursing Practice: An International Journal, 18,* 7–10.

Straus, M. A., & Field, C. J. (2003). Psychological aggression by American parents: National data on prevalence, chronicity, and severity. *Journal of Marriage and Family, 65,* 795–808.

Street, R. L., Jr. (2003). Interpersonal communication skills in health care contexts. In B. R. Burleson & J. O. Greene (Eds.), *Handbook of communication and social interaction skills* (pp. 909–933). Mahwah, NJ: Erlbaum.

Stritzke, W. G. K., Nguyen, A., & Durkin, K. (2004). Shyness and computer-mediated communication: A self-presentational theory perspective. *Media Psychology, 6,* 1–22.

Strong, C. M. (2005). The role of exposure to media-idealized male physiques on men's body image. *Dissertation Abstracts International, 65,* 4306.

Sturman, E. D., & Mongrain, M. (2008). The role of personality in defeat: A revised social rank model. *European Journal of Personality, 22,* 55–79.

Sudnow, D. (1972). Temporal parameters of interpersonal observation. In D. Sudnow (Ed.), *Studies in social interaction.* New York: Free Press.

Sugimoto, N. (1991, March). *"Excuse me" and "I'm sorry": Apologetic behaviors of Americans and Japanese.* Paper presented at the Conference on Communication in Japan and the United States, California State University, Fullerton, CA.

Suler, J. R. (2002). Identity management in cyberspace. *Journal of Applied Psychoanalytic Studies, 4,* 455–459.

Sullins, E. S. (1991). Emotional contagion revisited: Effects of social comparison and expressive style on mood convergence. *Personality and Social Psychology Bulletin, 17,* 166–174.

Sullivan, C. F. (1996). Recipients' perceptions of support attempts across various stressful life events. *Communication Research Reports, 13,* 183–190.

Sullivan, P. (2004). Communication differences between male and female team sport athletes. *Communication Reports, 17,* 121–128.

Surinder, K. S., & Cooper, R. B. (2003). Exploring the core concepts of media richness theory: The impact of cue multiplicity and feedback immediacy on decision quality. *Journal* of *Management Information Systems, 20,* 263–299.

Suter, E. A., Bergen, K. M., Daas, K. L., & Durham, W. T (2006). Lesbian couples' management of public-private dialectical contradictions. *Journal of Social* & *Personal Relationships, 23*, 349–365.

Suter, E. A., & Daas, K. L. (2007). Negotiating heteronormativity dialectically: Lesbian couples' display of symbols in culture. *Western Journal of Communication, 71,* 177–195.

Sutter, D. L., & Martin, M. M. (1999). Verbal aggression during disengagement of dating relationships. *Communication Research Reports, 15,* 318–326.

Swain, S. (1989). Covert intimacy in men's friendships: Closeness in men's friendships. In B. J. Risman & P. Schwartz (Eds.), *Gender in intimate relationships: A microstructural approach* (pp. 71–86). Belmont, CA: Wadsworth.

Swami, V., & Furnham, A. (2008). *The psychology of physical attraction.* New York: Routledge/Taylor & Francis.

Swann, W. B., Jr., Rentfrow, P. J., & Guinn, J. S. (2003). Self-verification: The search for coherence. In J. P. Tangney, & M. R. Leary (Eds.), *Handbook of self and identity* (pp. 367–383). New York: Guilford Press.

Swenson, J., & Casmir, F. L. (1998). The impact of culture-sameness, gender, foreign travel, and academic background on the ability to interpret facial expression of emotion in others. *Communication Quarterly, 46,* 214–230.

Sypher, B. D., & Sypher, H. E. (1983). Perceptions of communication ability: Self-monitoring in an organizational setting. *Personality and Social Psychology Bulletin, 9,* 297–304.

Tadinac, M., & Hromatko, I. (2004). Sex differences in mate preferences: Testing some predictions from evolutionary theory. *Review of Psychology, 11,* 45–51.

Tajfel, H., & Turner, J. C. (1992). The social identity theory of intergroup behavior. In W. B. Gudykunst & Y. Y. Kim (Eds.), *Readings on communicating with strangers.* New York: McGraw-Hill.

Tajima, E. A. (2002). Risk factors for violence against children: Comparing homes with and without wife abuse. *Journal of Interpersonal Violence, 17,* 122–149.

Takaku, S., Weiner, B., & Ohbuchi, K (2001). A cross-cultural examination of the effects of apology and perspective-taking on forgiveness. *Journal of Language & Social Psychology, 20*, 144–167.

Talwar, V. (2004). Children's lie-telling in different social situations. *Dissertation Abstracts International, 65,* 71.

Tanarugsachock, V. L. (1994). *The relationship between level of acculturation and descriptions of taboo topics in Chinese immigrant and Chinese-American families-of-origin.* Unpublished master's thesis, University of North Carolina at Chapel Hill.

Tannen, D. (1986). *That's not what I meant! How conversational style makes or breaks your relations with others.* New York: William Morrow.

Tannen, D. (1990). *You just don't understand: Women and men in conversation.* New York: William Morrow.

Tannen, D. (1994). *Talking from 9 to 5: Women and men in the workplace: Language, sex and power.* New York: William Morrow.

Tannen, D. (1996, May 16). Gender gap in cyberspace. *Newsweek,* 52–53.

Tannen, D. (2001). But what do you mean? Women and men in conversation. In J. M. Henslin (Ed.), *Down to earth sociology: Introductory readings* (11th ed., pp. 168–173). New York: Free Press.

Tashiro, T., & Frazier, P. (2003). "I'll never be in a relationship like that again": Personal growth following romantic relationship breakups. *Personal Relationships, 10,* 113–128.

Taylor, A. F., Wiley, A., Kuo, F. E., & Sullivan, W. C. (1998). Growing up in the inner city: Green spaces as places to grow. *Environment and Behavior, 30,* 3–27.

Taylor, D. A., & Altman, I. (1987). Communication in interpersonal relationships: Social penetration processes. In M. E. Roloff & G. R. Miller (Eds.), *Interpersonal processes: New directions in communication research* (pp. 257–277). Newbury Park, CA: Sage.

Taylor, S., & Mette, D. (1971). When similarity breeds contempt. *Journal of Personality and Social Psychology, 20,* 75–81.

Teven, J. J., & Comadena, M. E. (1996). The effects of office aesthetic quality on students' perceptions of teacher credibility and communicator style. *Communication Research Reports, 13,* 101–108.

Tezer, E., & Demir, A. (2001). Conflict behaviors toward same-sex and opposite-sex peers among male and female late adolescents. *Adolescence, 36*(143), 525–533.

Thibaut, J. W., & Kelley, H. H. (1959). *The social psychology of groups.* New York: Wiley.

Thomas, K. W., & Kilmann, R. (1978). Comparison of four instruments measuring conflict behavior. *Psychological Report, 42,* 1139–1145.

Thourlby, W. (1978). *You are what you wear.* New York: New American Library.

Tidwell, L. C., & Walther, J. B. (2002). Computer-mediated communication effects on disclosure, impressions, and interpersonal evaluations: Getting to know one another a bit at a time. *Human Communication Research, 28,* 317–348.

Timmerman, C. E., & Scott, C. R. (2006). Virtually working: Communicative and structural predictors of media use and key outcomes in virtual work teams. *Communication Monographs, 73,* 108–136.

Timmerman, L. M. (2002). Comparing the production of power in language on the basis of sex. In M. Allen, R. W. Preiss, B. M. Gayle, & N. Burrell (Eds.), *Interpersonal communication research: Advances through meta-analysis* (pp. 73–88). Mahwah, NJ: Erlbaum.

Ting-Toomey, S. (1988). Rhetorical sensitivity style in three cultures: France, Japan, and the United States. *Central States Speech Journal, 39,* 28–36.

Ting-Toomey, S. (1991). Intimacy expressions in three cultures: France, Japan, and the United States. *International Journal of Intercultural Relations, 15,* 29–46.

Ting-Toomey, S. (1999). *Communicating across cultures.* New York: Guilford Press.

Ting-Toomey, S., Oetzel, J., & Yee-Jung, K. (2001). Self-construal types and conflict management styles. *Communication Reports, 14,* 87–104.

Todorov, A., Chaiken, S., & Henderson, M. D. (2002). The heuristic-systematic model of social information processing. In J. P. Dillard & M. Pfau (Eds.), *The persuasion handbook: Developments in theory and practice* (pp. 195–211). Thousand Oaks, CA: Sage.

Tolar, T. D., Lederberg, A. R., Gokhale, S., & Tomasello, M. (2008). The development of the ability to recognize the meaning of iconic signs. *Journal of Deaf Studies and Deaf Education, 13*(1), 71–86.

Tolhuizen, J. H. (1989). Communication strategies for intensifying dating relationships: Identification, use and structure. *Journal of Social and Personal Relationships, 6,* 413–434.

Touitou, Y. (1998). Biological clocks: Mechanisms and application. *Proceedings of the International Congress on Chronobiology.* New York: Elsevier Science.

Tracy, L. (1991). *The secret between us: Competition among women.* Boston: Little, Brown.

Tracy, S. J. (2002). When questioning turns to face threat: An interactional sensitivity in 911 call-taking. *Western Journal of Communication, 66,* 129–157.

Tracy, S. J. (2004). Dialectic, contradiction, or double bind? Analyzing and theorizing employee reactions to organizational tension. *Journal of Applied Communication Research, 32,* 119–146.

Trenholm, S., & Rose, T. (1980). The compliant communicator: Teacher perceptions of appropriate classroom behavior. *Western Journal of Speech Communication, 44,* 13–26.

Triandis, H. C. (1975). Culture training, cognitive complexity and interpersonal attitudes. In R. Brislin, S. Bichner, & W. Lonner (Eds.), *Cross-cultural perspectives on learning.* New York: Wiley.

Triandis, H. C. (1990). Cross-cultural studies of individualism and collectivism. In J. Berman (Ed.), Nebraska symposium on motivation (pp. 41–133). Lincoln: University of Nebraska Press.

Triandis, H. C. (1994). *Culture and social behavior.* New York: McGraw-Hill.

Triandis, H. C. (1995). *Individualism and collectivism.* Boulder, CO: Westview.

Tripp, G., Schaughency, E. A., Lanlands, R., & Mouat, K. (2007). Family interactions in children with and without ADHD. *Journal of Child and Family Studies, 16,* 385–400.

Trompenaars, F. (1994). *Riding the waves of culture.* New York: McGraw-Hill/Irwin.

Trosset, C. (1998, September/October). Obstacles to open discussion and critical thinking: The Grinnell College study. *Change Magazine, 30,* 44–49.

Tseung, C. N., & Schott, G. (2004). The quality of sibling relationship during late adolescence: Are there links with other significant relationships? *Psychological Studies, 49,* 20–30.

Tuckett, A. G. (2005). The care encounter: Pondering caring, honest communication and control. *International Journal of Nursing Practice, 11*(2), 77–84.

Turk, D. R., & Monahan, J. L. (1999). "Here I go again": An examination of repetitive behaviors during interpersonal conflicts. *Southern Communication Journal, 64,* 232–244.

Turkle, S. (1996, January). Who am we? *Wired, 4,* 149–152, 194–199.

Turner, E. K. (2008). Learning how to fight: Connections between conflict resolution patterns in marital and sibling relationships. *DAI, 68,* 7680.

Turner, H. H., Dindia, K., & Pearson, J. C. (1995). An investigation of female/male verbal behavior in same-sex and mixed-sex conversations. *Communication Reports, 8,* 86–96.

Turner, R. E., Edgely, C., & Olmstead, G. (1975). Information control in conversation: Honesty is not always the best policy. *Kansas Journal of Sociology, 11,* 69–89.

Tusing, K. J., & Dillard, J. P. (2000). The sounds of dominance: Vocal precursors of perceived dominance during interpersonal influence. *Human Communication Research, 26,* 148–171.

Tuval-Mashiach, R., & Shulman, S. (2006). Resolution of disagreements between romantic partners, among adolescents, and young adults: Qualitative analysis of interaction discourses. *Journal of Research on Adolescence, 16,* 561–588.

Uchino, B. N. (2004). *Social support and physical health: Understanding the health consequences of relationships.* New Haven, CT: Yale University Press.

UCLA Internet Report. (2003). *Surveying the digital future: Year three.* Los Angeles: UCLA Center for Communication Policy. Retrieved from http://www.ccp.ucla.edu

Ulrey, K. L. (2001). Intercultural communication between patients and health care providers: An exploration of intercultural communication effectiveness, cultural sensitivity, stress, and anxiety. *Health Communication, 13,* 449–463.

Underwood, M. K. (2003). *Social aggression among girls.* New York: Guilford Press.

Urberg, K. A., Degirmencioglu, S. M., & Tolson, J. M. (1998). Adolescent friendship selection and termination: The role of similarity. *Journal of Social and Personal Relationships, 15,* 703–710.

U.S. Department of Justice. (2002, February). *OJJDP fact sheet: Highlights of the 2000 National Youth Gang Survey.* Washington, DC: Office of Juvenile Justice and Delinquency Prevention. Available at: http://www.ncjrs.gov/pdffiles1/ojjdp/fs200204.pdf

Valentine, C. A., & Saint Damian, B. (1988). Communicative power: Gender and culture as determinants of the ideal voice. In C. A. Valentine & N. Moar (Eds.), *Women and*

Communicative power: Theory, research, and practice. Washington, DC: National Communication Association.

Valins, S. (1966). Cognitive effects of false heart-rate feedback. *Journal of Personality and Social Psychology, 4,* 400–408.

van der Meulen, M. (2001). Developments in self-concept theory and research: Affect, context, and variability. In H. A. Bosma & E. S. Kunnen (Eds.), *Identity and emotion: Development through self-organization* (pp. 10–38). New York: Cambridge University Press.

Van Gelder, L. (1996). The strange case of the electronic lover. In R. Kling (Ed.), *Computerization and controversy: Value conflicts and social choices* (2nd ed., pp. 533–546). New York: Academic Press.

van Leeuwen, M. L., & Macrae, C. N. (2004). Is beautiful always good? Implicit benefits of facial attractiveness. *Social Cognition, 22,* 637–649.

Van Oudenhoven, J. P., de Raad, B., Askevis-Leherpeux, F., Boski, P., Brunborg, G. S., Carmona, C., Barelds, D., Hill, C. T, Mlacic, B., Motti, F., Rammstedt, B., & Woods, S. (2008). Terms of abuse as expression and reinforcement of cultures. *International Journal of Intercultural Relations, 32,* 174–185.

Van Swol, L. M. (2003). The effects of nonverbal mirroring on perceived persuasiveness, agreement with an imitator, and reciprocity in a small group discussion. *Communication Research, 30,* 461–480.

Vancleave, D. S. (2008). Empathy training for master's level social work students facilitating advanced empathy responding. *DAI*, 68, 4074.

Vangelisti, A. L. (1994). Couples' communication problems: The counselor's perspective. *Journal of Applied Communication Research, 22,* 106–126.

Vangelisti, A. L., & Beck, G. (2007). Intimacy and fear of intimacy. In L. L'Abate (Ed.), *Low-cost approaches to promote physical and mental health: Theory, research, and practice* (pp. 395–414). New York: Springer Science + Business Media.

Vangelisti, A. L., Caughlin, J. P., & Timmerman, L. (2001). Criteria for revealing family secrets. *Communication Monographs, 68,* 1–27.

Vangelisti, A. L., & Crumley, L. P. (1998). Reactions to messages that hurt: The influence of relational contexts. *Communication Monographs, 65,* 173–196.

Vangelisti, A. L., Knapp, M. L., & Daly, J. A. (1990). Conversational narcissism. *Communication Monographs, 57,* 251–274.

VanLear, C. A. (1987). The formation of social relationships: A longitudinal study of social penetration. *Human Communication Research, 13,* 299–322.

VanLear, C. A. (1992). Marital communication across the generations: Learning and rebellion, continuity and change. *Journal of Social and Personal Relationships 9,* 103–123.

Vaughn, D. (1987, July). The long goodbye. *Psychology Today, 21,* 37–42.

Venable, K. V., & Martin, M. M. (1997). Argumentativeness and verbal aggressiveness in dating relationships. *Journal of Social Behavior and Personality, 12,* 955–964.

Veroff, J., Douvan, E., Orbuch, T. L., & Acitelli, L. K. (1998). Happiness in stable marriages: The early years. In T. N. Bradbury (Ed.), *The developmental course of marital dysfunction* (pp. 152–179). New York: Cambridge University Press.

Versalle, A., & McDowell, E. E. (2004–2005). The attitudes of men and women concerning gender differences in grief. *Omega: Journal of Death and Dying, 50,* 53–67.

Versfeld, N. J., & Dreschler, W. A. (2002). The relationship between the intelligibility of time-compressed speech and speech-in-noise in young and elderly listeners. *Journal of the Acoustical Society of America, 111*(1, Pt 1), 401–408.

Vito, D. (1999). Affective self-disclosure, conflict resolution and marital quality. *Dissertation Abstracts International, 60,* 1319.

Vittengl, J. R., & Holt, C. S. (2000). Getting acquainted: The relationship of self-disclosure and social attraction to positive affect. *Journal of Social and Personal Relationships, 17,* 53–66.

Vocate, D. R. (1994). Self-talk and inner speech: Understanding the uniquely human aspects of intrapersonal communication. In D. R. Vocate (Ed.), *Intrapersonal communication: Different voices, different minds* (pp. 3–31). Hillsdale, NJ: Erlbaum.

Vohs, K. D., & Heatherton, T. F. (2004). Ego threats elicits different social comparison process among high and low self-esteem people: Implications for interpersonal perceptions. *Social Cognition, 22,* 168–191.

Von Briesen, P. D. (2007). Pragmatic language skills of adolescents with ADHD. *DAI, 68*(5-B), 3430.

Voss, K., Markiewicz, D., & Doyle, A. B. (1999). Friendship, marriage and self-esteem. *Journal of Social and Personal Relationships, 16,* 103–122.

Vrij, A., & Akehurst, L. (1999). The existence of a black clothing stereotype: The impact of a victim's black clothing on impression formation. *Psychology, Crime and Law, 3*(3), 227–237.

Vrij, A., Akehurst, K., Soukara, S., & Bull, R. (2004). Detecting deceit via analyses of verbal and nonverbal behavior in children and adults. *Human Communication Research, 30,* 8–41.

Vrij, A., Edward, K., Roberts, K. P., & Bull, R. (2000). Detecting deceit via analysis of verbal and nonverbal behavior. *Journal of Nonverbal Behavior; 24,* 239–263.

Vuchinich, S. (1987). Starting and stopping spontaneous family conflicts. *Journal of Marriage and the Family, 49,* 591–601.

Waldron, V. R., & Kelley, D. L (2005). Forgiving communication as a response to relational transgressions. *Journal of Social and Personal Relationships, 22,* 723–742.

Waldvogel, J. (2007). Greetings and closings in workplace email. *Journal of Computer-Mediated Communication, 12,* 456–477.

Wallace, H. M., Exline, J. J., & Baumeister, R. F. (2008). Interpersonal consequences of forgiveness: Does forgiveness deter or encourage repeat offenses? *Journal of Experimental Social Psychology, 44,* 453–460.

Walster, E., Aronson, E., Abrahams, D., & Rottmann, L. (1966). Importance of physical attractiveness in dating behavior. *Journal of Personality and Social Psychology, 4,* 508–516.

Walther, J. B. (1996). Computer-mediated communication: Impersonal, interpersonal, and hyperpersonal interaction. *Communication Research, 23,* 3–43.

Walther, J. B. (2006). Nonverbal dynamics in computer-mediated communication, or :(and the net :('s with you, :) and you :) alone. In V. Manusov & M. L. Patterson (Eds.), *The Sage handbook of nonverbal communication* (pp. 461–479). Thousand Oaks, CA: Sage.

Walther, J. B., & D'Addario, K. P. (2001). The impacts of emoticons on message interpretation in computer-mediated communication. *Social Science Computer Review, 19,* 324–347.

Walther, J. B., Loh, T., & Granka, L. (2005). Let me count the ways: The interchange of verbal and nonverbal cues in computer-mediated and face-to-face affinity. *Journal of Language and Social Psychology, 24,* 36–65.

Waltman, M. S. (2002). Developments in constructivist work in communication studies, psychology, and education: Introduction to the special section on constructivism. *American Communication Journal, 5*(3), 1.

Waring, E. M. (1981). Facilitating marital intimacy through self-disclosure. *American Journal of Family Therapy, 9,* 33–42.

Waring, E. M., & Chelune, G. J. (1983). Marital intimacy and self-disclosure. *Journal of Clinical Psychology, 39,* 183–190.

Warnecke, A. M., Masters, R. D., & Kempter, G. (1992). The roots of nationalism: Nonverbal behavior and xenophobia. *Ethology and Sociobiology, 13*(4), 267–282.

Warren, K., Schoppelrey, S., & Moberg, D. (2005). A model of contagion through competition in the aggressive behaviors of elementary school students. *Journal of Abnormal Child Psychology, 33,* 283–292.

Watkins, L., & Johnston, L. (2000). Screening job applicants: The impact of physical attractiveness and application quality. *International Journal of Selection and Assessment, 8,* 76–84.

Watts, R. E., Peluso, P. R., Lewis, T. F., Anderson, R. N., & Rasmussen, P. R. (2005). Psychological strategies. *Journal of Individual Psychology, 61,* 380–387.

Watts, S. A. (2007). Evaluative feedback: Perspectives on media effects. *Journal of Computer-Mediated Communication, 12.* Retrieved from http://jcmc.indiana.edu/vol12/issue2/watts.html

Watzlawick, P. (1984). *The invented reality: How do we know what we believe we know?* New York: Norton.

Watzlawick, P. (1990). Reality adaptation or adapted "reality"? Constructivism and psychotherapy. In P. Watzlawick (Ed.), *Münchausen's Pigtail: Or psychotherapy and "reality." Essays and lectures.* New York: Norton.

Watzlawick, P. (2005). Self-fulfilling prophecies. In J. O'Brien & P. Kollock (Eds.), *The production of reality* (4th ed.). Thousand Oaks, CA: Sage.

Watzlawick, P., Beavin, J., & Jackson, D. (1967). *Pragmatics of human communication: A study of interactional patterns, pathologies, and paradoxes.* New York: Norton.

Weaver, J. B., & Kirtley, M. D. (1995). Listening styles and empathy. *Southern Communication Journal, 60,* 131–140.

Weger, H., Jr., & Metts, S. (2005). Disconfirming communication and self-verification in marriage: Associations among the demand/withdraw interaction pattern, feeling understood, and marital satisfaction. *Journal of Social and Personal Relationships, 22* , 19–31.

Wei, Y., & Li, Y. (2001). The experimental research on the influence of different empathy training methods on children's sharing behavior. *Psychological Science China, 24,* 557–562.

Weider-Hatfield, D. (1981). A unit in conflict management skills. *Communication Education, 30,* 265–273.

Weigel, D. J. (2008). Mutuality and the communication of commitment in romantic relationships. *Southern Communication Journal, 73,* 24–41.

Weigel, D. J., & Ballard-Reisch, D. S. (1999). Using paired data to test models of relational maintenance and marital quality. *Journal of Social and Personal Relationships, 16,* 175–191.

Weigert, A. J., & Gecas, V. (2003). Self. In N. J. Herman-Kinney & L. T. Reynolds (Eds.), *Handbook of symbolic interactionism* (pp. 267–288). Walnut Creek, CA: AltaMira Press.

Weiss, L., & Lowenthal, M. F. (1975). Life-course perspectives on friendship. In M. F. Lowenthal, M. Thurnher, & D. Chiriboga (Eds.), *Four stages of life: A comparative study of women and men facing transitions* (pp. 48–61). San Francisco: Jossey-Bass.

Welch, I. D. (2003). *The therapeutic relationship: Listening and responding in a multicultural world.* Westport, CT: Praeger Publishers/Greenwood.

Welch, S. A., & Rubin, R. B. (2002). Development of relationship stage measures. *Communication Quarterly, 50,* 24–40.

Wester, S. R., Vogel, D. L., Pressly, P. K., & Heesacker, M. (2002). Sex differences in emotion: A critical review of the literature and implications for counseling psychology. *Counseling Psychologist, 30,* 630–652.

Westmyer, S. A., & DiCioccio, R. L. (1998). Appropriateness and effectiveness of communication channels in competent interpersonal communication. *Journal of Communication, 48,* 27–48.

Wheeler, L., & Kim, Y. (1997). What is beautiful is culturally good: The physical attractiveness stereotype has different content in collectivistic cultures. *Personality and Social Psychology Bulletin, 23,* 795–800.

Whiffen, V. E, Foot, M. L., & Thompson, J. M. (2007). Self-silencing mediates the link between marital conflict and depression. *Journal of Social and Personal Relationships, 24,* 993–1006.

Whitchurch, G., & Dickson, F. C. (1999). Family communication. In M. Sussman, S. Steinmetz, & G. Peterson (Eds.) *Handbook of marriage and the family* (2nd ed., pp. 687–704). New York: Plenum Press.

Whitton, S. W., Waldinger, R. J., Schulz, M. S., Allen, J. P., Crowell, J. A., & Hauser, S. T. (2008). Prospective associations of family-of-origin interactions to adult marital interactions and relationship adjustment. *Journal of Family Psychology, 22,* 274–286.

Whitty, M. T. (2005). The realness of cybercheating: Men's and women's representations of unfaithful Internet relationships. *Social Science Computer Review, 23,* 57–67.

Whorf, B. L. (1956). The relation of habitual thought and behavior to language. In J. B. Carroll (Ed.), *Language, thought, and reality: Selected writings of Benjamin Lee Whorf* (pp. 134–159). Cambridge, MA: MIT Press.

Widlok, T. (2008). Landscape unbounded: Space, place, and orientation in ≠Akhoe Hai//om and beyond. *Language Sciences, 30,* 362–380.

Wiemann, J. M., Takai, J., Ota, H., & Wiemann, M. (1997). A relational model of communication competence. In B. Kovacic (Ed.), *Emerging theories of human communication.* Albany: State University of New York Press.

Wildermuth, S. M., & Vogl-Bauer, S. (2007). We met on the net: Exploring the perceptions of online romantic relationship participants. *Southern Communication Journal, 72,* 211–227.

Wilkins, R., & Gareis, E. (2006). Emotion expression and the locution "I love you": A cross-cultural study. *International Journal of Intercultural Relations, 30,* 51–75.

Williams, K. D., & Dolnik, L. (2001). Revealing the worst first: Stealing thunder as a social influence strategy. In J. P. Forgas & K. D. Williams (Eds.), *Social influence: Direct and indirect processes* (pp. 213–231). Hove, England: Psychology Press.

Willis, F. N., & Hamm, H. K. (1980). The use of interpersonal touch in securing compliance. *Journal of Nonverbal Behavior, 5,* 49–55.

Wilmot, W. W. (1987). *Dyadic communication* (3rd ed.). New York: Random House.

Wilmot, W. W. (1995). *Relational communication* (5th ed.). New York: McGraw-Hill.

Wilmot, W. W., & Hocker, J. L. (2007). *Interpersonal conflict* (7th ed.). New York: McGraw-Hill.

Winer, S., & Majors, R. (1981). A research note on supportive and defensive communication: An empirical study of three verbal interpersonal communication variables. *Communication Quarterly, 29,* 166–172.

Winsor, J. L., Curtis, D. B., & Stephens, R. D. (1997). National preferences in business and communication education: An update. *Journal of the Association for Communication Administration, 3,* 170–179.

Wiseman, R. (2003). *Queen bees and wannabes: Helping your daughter survive cliques, gossip, boyfriends, and other realities of adolescence.* New York: Three Rivers Press.

Witmer, D. F., & Katzman, S. L. (1997). On-line smiles: Does gender make a difference in the use of graphic accents? *Journal of Computer Mediated Communication, 2*(4), np.

Wolf, A. (2000). Emotional expression online: Gender differences in emoticon use. *CyberPsychology & Behavior, 3,* 827–833.

Wolff, F. I., & Marsnik, N. C. (1993). Perceptive listening (2nd ed.). Fort Worth, TX: Harcourt.

Wolfram, W., & Schilling-Estes, N. (2005). *American English: Dialects and variation* (2nd ed.). Malden, MA: Blackwell.

Wolvin, A. D. (1984). Meeting the communication needs of the adult learner. *Communication Education, 33,* 267–271.

Wolvin, A. D., & Coakley, C. (1991). A survey of the status of listening training in some Fortune 500 companies. *Communication Education, 40,* 152–164.

Wolvin, A. D., Coakley, C. G., & Gwynn, C. (1999). *Listening* (6th ed.). Boston: McGraw-Hill.

Won-Doornick, M. J. (1979). On getting to know you: The association between the stage of relationship and reciprocity of self-disclosure. *Journal of Experimental Social Psychology, 15,* 229–241.

Wood, J. T. (2005). *Gendered lives: Communication, gender, and culture* (6th ed.). Belmont, CA: Wadsworth.

Wood, J. T., & Inman, C. C. (1993). In a different mode: Masculine styles of communicating closeness. *Journal of Applied Communication Research, 21,* 279–295.

Wood, V. F., & Bell, P. A. (2008). Predicting interpersonal conflict resolution styles from personality characteristics. *Personality and Individual Differences, 45,* 126–131.

Wood, W., & Eagly, A. H. (2002). A cross-cultural analysis of the behavior of women and men: Implications for the origins of sex differences. *Psychological Bulletin, 128,* 699–727.

Woodward, M. S., Rosenfeld, L. B., & May, S. K. (1996). Sex differences in social support in sororities and fraternities. *Journal of Applied Communication Research, 24,* 260–272.

Woolery, Lisa M. (2007). Gaydar: A social-cognitive analysis. *Journal of Homosexuality, 53*(3), 9–17.

Wortman, C. B., Adosman, P., Herman, E., & Greenberg, R. (1976). Self-disclosure: An attributional perspective. *Journal of Personality and Social Psychology, 33,* 184–191.

Yaveroglu, I. S., & Donthu, N. (2002). Cultural influences on the diffusion of new products. *Journal of International Consumer Marketing, 14,* 49–63.

Wright, C. N., Holloway, A., & Roloff, M. E. (2007). The dark side of self-monitoring: How high self-monitors view their romantic relationships. *Communication Reports, 20,* 101–114.

Yaveroglu, I. S., & Donthu, N. (2002). Cultural influences on the diffusion of new products. *Journal of International Consumer Marketing, 14,* 49–63.

Ybarra, O., Burnstein, E., Winkielman, P., Keller, M.C., Manis, M., Chan, E., & Rodriguez, J. (2008). Mental exercising through simple socializing: Social interaction promotes general cognitive functioning. *Personality and Social Psychology Bulletin, 34*(2) 248–259.

Yee, N., & Bailenson, J. N. (2006, August). Walk a mile in digital shoes: The impact of embodied perspective-taking on the reduction of negative stereotyping in immersive virtual environments. *Proceedings of PRESENCE 2006: The 8th Annual International Workshop on Presence.* Cleveland, OH. Available at: http://www.temple.edu/ispr/prev_conferences/proceedings/2006/confindex.html

Yingling, J. (1994). Constituting friendship in talk and metatalk. *Journal of Social and Personal Relationships, 11,* 411–426.

Yopyk, D. J. A., & Prentice, D. A. (2005). Am I an athlete or a student? Identity salience and stereotype threat in student-athletes. *Basic and Applied Social Psychology, 27,* 329–336.

Young, R. W., & Cates, C. M. (2004). Emotional and directive listening in peer mentoring. *International Journal of Listening, 18,* 21–33.

Young, S. L. (2004). What the ____ is your problem?: Attribution theory and perceived reasons for profanity usage during conflict. *Communication Research Reports, 21,* 338–447.

Young, R. W., & Cates, C. M. (2004). Emotional and directive listening in peer mentoring. *International Journal of Listening, 18,* 21–33.

Yun, K. A. (2002). Similarity and attraction. In M. Allen, N. Burrell, B. M. Eayle, & R. W. Preiss (Eds.), *Interpersonal communication research: Advances through meta-analysis* (pp. 145–168). Mahwah, NJ: Erlbaum.

Zahn, C. J. (1989). The bases for differing evaluations of male and female speech: Evidence from ratings of transcribed conversation. *Communication Monographs, 56,* 59–74.

Zanobini, M., & Usai, M. C. (2002). Domain-specific self-concept and achievement motivation in the transition from primary to low middle school. *Educational Psychology, 22,* 203–217.

Zenmore, S. E., Fiske, S. T., & Kim, H. J. (2000). Gender stereotypes and the dynamics of social interaction. In T. Eckes & H. M. Trautner (Eds.), *The developmental social psychology of gender* (pp. 207–241). Mahwah, NJ: Erlbaum.

Zhang, S., & Stafford, L. (2008). Perceived face threat of honest but hurtful evaluative messages in romantic relationships. *Western Journal of Communication, 72,* 19–39.

Zhang, Y. B., Harwood, J., & Hummert, M. L. (2005). Perceptions of conflict management styles in Chinese intergenerational dyads. *Communication Monographs, 72,* 71–91.

Zimbardo, P. G. (1971). *The psychological power and pathology of imprisonment.* Statement prepared for the U.S. House of Representatives Committee on the Judiciary, Subcommittee No. 3, Robert Kastemeyer, Chairman. Unpublished manuscript, Stanford University.

Zimbardo, P. G. (1977). *Shyness: What it is, what to do about it.* Reading, MA: Addison-Wesley.

Zimbardo, P. G. (2007, March 30). Revisiting the Stanford prison experiment: A lesson in the power of situation. *Chronicle of Higher Education, 53,* B6.

Zimmerman, B. J. (1995). Self-efficacy and educational development. In A. Bandura (Ed.), *Self-efficacy in changing societies* (pp. 202–231). New York: Cambridge University Press.

Zorn, T. E., & Gregory, K. W. (2005). Learning the ropes together: Assimilation and friendship development among first-year male medical students. *Health Communication, 17,* 211–231.

Zuckerman, M., & Driver, R. E. (1989). What sounds beautiful is good: The vocal attractiveness stereotype. *Journal of Nonverbal Behavior, 13,* 67–82.

Zuckerman, M., Miserandino, M., Bernieri, F., Manusov, V., Axtell, R. E., Wiemann, J. M., Knapp, M. L., O'Leary, M. J., & Gallois, C. (1999). Creating impressions and managing interaction. In L. K. Guerrero, J. A. DeVito, & M. L. Hecht (Eds.), *The nonverbal communication reader: Classic and contemporary readings* (2nd ed., pp. 379–422). Prospect Heights, IL: Waveland Press.

Zwingle, E. (1999, August). A world together. *National Geographic Magazine, 196,* 6–33.

Credits

Cartoons

Page 14: © The New Yorker Collection 1995 Bruce Eric Kaplan from cartoonbank.com. All Rights Reserved.

Page 21: © Scott Adams / Dist. by United Feature Syndicate, Inc.

Page 27:© The New Yorker Collection 2007 Larry Hat from cartoonbank.com. All Rights Reserved.

Page 30: © Scott Adams / Dist. by United Feature Syndicate, Inc.

Page 54: © Scott Adams / Dist. by United Feature Syndicate, Inc.

Page 75: © The New Yorker Collection 1991 Edward Frascino from cartoonbank.com. All Rights Reserved.

Page 83: © The New Yorker Collection 1998 Robert Weber from cartoonbank.com. All Rights Reserved.

Page 96: ZITS © ZITS Partnership, King Features Syndicate.

Page 110: ZITS © ZITS Partnership, King Features Syndicate.

Page 115: © The New Yorker Collection 2004 Harry Bliss from cartoonbank.com. All Rights Reserved.

Page 120: © The New Yorker Collection 1999 Edward Koren from cartoonbank.com. All Rights Reserved.

Page 123: © David Waisglass and Gordon Coulthart. FARCUS;® is reprinted with permission from LaughingStock Licensing Inc., Ottawa, Canada. All rights reserved.

Page 130: © The New Yorker Collection 1997 William Steig from cartoonbank.com. All Rights Reserved.

Page 141: © The New Yorker Collection 2003 Eric Lewis from cartoonbank.com. All Rights Reserved.

Page 145: © The New Yorker Collection 2007 Drew Dernavich from cartoonbank.com. All Rights Reserved.

Page 151: © The New Yorker Collection 1987 Lee Lorenz from cartoonbank.com. All Rights Reserved.

Page 161: CATHY © 2004 Cathy Guisewite. Reprinted with permission of UNIVERSAL PRESS SYNDICATE.

Page 177: © Scott Adams / Dist. by United Feature Syndicate, Inc.

Page 186: © 2008 Robert Mankoff from cartoonbank.com. All Rights Reserved.

Page 188: © The New Yorker Collection 2001 William Haefeli from cartoonbank.com. All Rights Reserved.

Page 198: CATHY © 1996 Cathy Guisewite. Reprinted with permission of UNIVERSAL PRESS SYNDICATE.

Page 210: © Aaron Bacall. Reprinted with permission of CartoonStock. All rights reserved.

Page 214: © Marc Tyler Nobleman. www.mtncartoons.com

Page 217: © The New Yorker Collection 1993 Frank Cotham from cartoonbank.com. All Rights Reserved.

Page 232: © Mike Baldwin. Reprinted with permission of Cartoon Stock. All rights reserved.

Page 251: © The New Yorker Collection 1995 Peter Steiner from cartoonbank.com. All Rights Reserved.

Page 253: ZITS © ZITS Partnership, King Features Syndicate.

Page 257: © The New Yorker Collection 1982 George Price from cartoonbank.com. All Rights Reserved.

Page 263: ZITS © ZITS Partnership, King Features Syndicate.

Page 279: © The New Yorker Collection 1993 J.B. Handelsman from cartoonbank.com. All Rights Reserved.

Page 285: SALLY FORTH © King Features Syndicate.

Page 304: © The New Yorker Collection 2007 Leo Cullum from cartoonbank.com. All Rights Reserved.

Page 322: © The New Yorker Collection 2000 John Caldwell from cartoonbank.com. All Rights Reserved.

Page 326: © 2008 Michael Crawford from cartoonbank.com. All Rights Reserved.

Page 333: © The New Yorker Collection 1983 Al Ross from cartoonbank.com. All Rights Reserved.

Page 334: © The New Yorker Collection 2004 Roz Chast from cartoonbank.com. All Rights Reserved.

Page 361: © The New Yorker Collection 1997 Leo Cullum from cartoonbank.com. All Rights Reserved.

Page 363: Calvin and Hobbes © 1993 Bill Waterson. Reprinted with permission of UNIVERSAL PRESS SYNDICATE. All rights reserved.

Page 373: © The New Yorker Collection 2002 Robert Weber from cartoonbank.com. All Rights Reserved.

Page 386: © The New Yorker Collection 1993 Sam Gross from cartoonbank.com. All Rights Reserved.

Page 403: © Scott Adams / Dist. by United Feature Syndicate, Inc.

Photos

Page 3: Digital Vision / Fotosearch

Page 6: O. Louis Mazzatenta / National Geographic Image Collection

Page 8: © Daniel Adler. www.adlerography.com

Page 13: R. Jerome Ferraro / Getty Images
Page 17: Adam Gault / Getty Images
Page 24: © Yevgen Timashov / ShutterStock
Page 35: David Falconer / SuperStock
Page 41: Butch Martin / Getty Images
Page 48: age fotostock / SuperStock
Page 60: Kent Knudson / Index Stock Imagery / JupiterImages
Page 65: © Pete Leonard / zefa / Corbis
Page 68: Bambu Production / Getty Images
Page 71: Ann Brown / SuperStock
Page 76: Digital Vision / Getty Images
Page 78: Image Source / SuperStock
Page 80: Bruce Gardner / Getty Images
Page 86: PhotoAlto / SuperStock
Page 107: Mikael Andersson / Nordic Photos / PhotoLibrary
Page 111: Blend Images / FotoSearch
Page 118: Laurence Dutton / Getty Images
Page 127: © Nice One Productions / Corbis
Page 139: © Ivan Gonzales / epa / Corbis
Page 147: PureStock / JupiterImages
Page 164: © Mikhail Tolstoy / IStock Photo
Page 173: Tanya Constantine / Getty Images
Page 175: Justin Pumfrey / Getty Images
Page 180: Cosmo Codina / Workbook Stock/ JupiterImages
Page 184: Florian Moser / Getty Images
Page 190: Altrendo Images / Getty Images
Page 200: © Elke Van de Velde / Stock This Way / Corbis
Page 207: Comstock Photos / Fotosearch
Page 213: Mark Cass / Brand X Pictures / JupiterImages
Page 218: Antonio Mo / Getty Images
Page 229: PhotoAlto / JupiterImages
Page 243: Karin Dreyer / Getty Images
Page 245: © Milk Photographie / Corbis
Page 252: Thomas J. Abercrombie / National Geographic Image Collection
Page 259: © Masterfile
Page 261: Tim Laman / National Geographic Image Collection
Page 275: Franck Fife / Getty Images
Page 278: David Mendelsohn / Masterfile
Page 283: © Masterfile
Page 291: Ian Murphy / Getty Images
Page 297: Dirk Buwalda
Page 299: Brand X Photography / Veer
Page 308: © Daniel Adler. www.adlerography.com
Page 313: Bruno Morandi / Getty Images
Page 315: Blend Images Photography / Veer
Page 323: © GoGo Images / JupiterImages
Page 329: © Franc Podgoršek / IStock Photo
Page 341: John William Banagan / Getty Images
Page 349: GLG3 / Getty Images
Page 351: Tosca Radigonda / Getty Images
Page 354: Tim Flach / Getty Images
Page 371: Tom Hussey / Workbook Stock/ JupiterImages
Page 385: © Daniel Adler. www.adlerography.com
Page 394: © Norbert Schaefer / Corbis
Page 399: © Paul Barton / Corbis
Page 402: © Dex Image / Corbis
Page 413: © Helen King / Corbis

Author Index

Subject Index